D1609010

CRESTLINE

Encyclopedia of
CHEVROLET TRUCKS

DON BUNN

MBI Publishing Company

First published in 1999 by MBI Publishing Company,
729 Prospect Avenue, PO Box 1, Osceola, WI 54020-0001 USA

MBI Publishing Company books are also available at discounts in bulk
quantity for industrial or sales-promotional use. For details write to
Special Sales Manager at Motorbooks International Wholesalers &
Distributors, 729 Prospect Avenue, PO Box 1, Osceola WI, 54020 USA.

Library of Congress Cataloging-in-Publication Data
Bunn, Don.
    Encyclopedia of Chevrolet trucks / Don Bunn.
        p.   cm.   — (Crestline)
    Includes index.
    ISBN 0-7603-0565-X (alk. paper)
    1. Chevrolet trucks—History. I. Title. II. Series: Crestline series.
TL230.5.C45B86   1999
629.223—dc21   99-31698

On the front cover: The Cameo is arguably the prettiest truck
Chevrolet ever produced, and it is highly prized among collectors.
This stunning 1957 Cameo belongs to Troy Robertson of Huntersville,
North Carolina. *Mike Mueller*

On the back cover: An assortment of Chevrolet trucks, including a
1923 Superior Utility. *AAMA*, 1941 fire truck *Neal A. Van Deusen*,
a 1969 C10 half-ton Fleetside pickup. *AAMA*, and a 1999 C1500
Silverado pickup. *GM Media Archives*

Printed in China

CONTENTS

PREFACE

The reason for writing this book is simple: A book devoted exclusively to the long and distinguished history of Chevrolet trucks, to the best of my knowledge, does not exist. Writing this book has confirmed my feelings. I have learned that many Chevrolet truck devotees care about the truck's history and want this book. I have met some of them, talked to others, took their phone calls, and read their letters. They flooded me with photos and information. Chevrolet guys are loyal. This is the lesson I learned over and over.

The closest book to filling this gap is Motorbook's own *75 Years of Chevrolet* by George H. Dammann, in the Crestline Series. This is an excellent book, but it covers Chevrolet automobiles as well as trucks. In addition, it only covers Chevrolet vehicles through 1986. The reader interested in trucks is generally not very willing to plow through all that automobile stuff to get to the truck information. Since 1986, Chevrolet has introduced two very important new truck series, one in 1988 and another in 1999. It is important to add them to the Chevrolet story. In years past things moved slowly and changes were few and far between, but such is not the case any longer. Improvements and changes are moving at warp speed, so fast that it is a never-ending job to try to keep up.

For many years Chevrolet trucks were closely tied to Chevrolet autos. In the beginning the company built only two models. The smaller one was called a Light Delivery and the larger model was simply called a truck, or Ton Truck. Both models had automobile engines. The Light Delivery was based on Chevrolet's lightest and least costly car, the 490, and it consisted of a chassis cowl only. It was exactly the same as the 490 automobile: engine, transmission, frame, front sheet metal, springs, wheels, and tires. Factory bodies were not available for this model. A factory body was not available on a Light Delivery until 1931. The Sedan Delivery was new in 1929, but this was simply a modified automobile.

The 1-ton was truck-built with a unique frame, axles, wheels, and tires. It was powered by a bigger engine than the 490 had. It was from a larger Chevrolet automobile. Both trucks used front sheet metal, hoods, cowls, fenders, instrument boards, and other parts from automobiles for many years. Both trucks had three-speed transmissions.

The genius here is fairly obvious. The use of the automobile's mechanical components and sheet-metal parts reduced costs and kept prices down. Chevrolet's goal was to build as many cars and trucks as it possibly could; it wanted to be number one in car and truck production. In 1918, the first year of truck production, this was a hugely lofty goal in light of Henry Ford's dominance of the U.S. automobile market. Ford and GM's brilliance were in production and distribution. Don't take this wrong: The product's engineering and quality were also there, but these two attributes were Ford's ticket to the ball game.

Chapter 1

THE EARLY YEARS TO 1929

1908–1918

The history of the Chevrolet Motor Company has much less to do with the man whose name is on the product than it does with the man who founded it: William C. Durant. Billy Durant was a financial genius, entrepreneur, and promoter. Durant founded General Motors Co. on September 16, 1908. He went on a buying spree in 1909 and 1910, snapping up small automakers and suppliers until he had spent all of the company's money. GM's bankers agreed to lend the company $15 million, but only on the condition that Durant leave, because they considered him unfit to manage the affairs of a complex industrial organization. The bankers were determined to reorganize and refocus the company.

Durant started over again when he incorporated the Chevrolet Motor Company on November 3, 1911, with the sole intent of regaining control of General Motors by acquiring a majority of its stock. Louis Chevrolet had anchored a successful racing team that Durant had established when he was involved with Buick. Durant reasoned that he could leverage Chevrolet's favorable reputation to promote his new car. His strategy was to position Chevrolet as a light car, priced just slightly higher than Ford's Model T. With high unit sales, which Durant believed the car could achieve in short order, the company would be very profitable and would be the vehicle by which he could regain control of GM.

The Chevrolet Classic "6" touring car, the car Louis Chevrolet developed for introduction late in 1912, was anything but what Durant wanted. It was a heavy car with a big price of $2,150. Customers could have several Model Ts for the price of one Chevrolet Classic "6" Touring. Therefore, in 1913 a Little "6" selling for only $1,285 was added to the line, and the Classic "6" did not return for the 1914 model year. Louis Chevrolet had his fill of Durant and took off for another auto industry venture, but left the legacy of his name.

The company also introduced two H-series cars as 1914 model year cars: the H-4 Baby Grand, priced at $875, and the H-2 Royal Mail roadster, selling for $750. Both cars were powered by the new 170-ci six-cylinder engine, which remained in production through 1928. These two cars were the first Chevrolets to carry what became the world-famous Chevrolet bow tie. Credit for the bow tie goes to Billy Durant, who suggested it. Meanwhile, Durant was expanding the company's manufacturing and sales facilities with new plants in the East, Midwest, South, West, and Canada, and with factory sales offices at a number of locations.

Chevrolet's successful Model Four-Ninety (490) cars, a touring model and a roadster, made their debut as 1916 model year vehicles. The model number reflects the car's selling price, oddly enough the same price Ford's Model T sold for in 1916. In response, however, Ford immediately reduced the T's price to only $440. In spite of that, the 490s immediately began to sell exceedingly well.

Through clever maneuverings, Billy Durant managed to acquire large amounts of GM stock, and he controlled many more thousands of proxies. By 1916 he had 54.5 percent of GM stock and returned as president. On October 13, 1916, GM was reorganized as a corporation. The company became involved in non-automotive businesses such as refrigeration and auto financing. In 1919, GM bought an interest in the Fisher Body Company (eventually completing a buyout in 1926) and opened the GM Institute in Flint, Michigan, to train automotive engineers and executives.

Chevrolet Motor Company became part of General Motors in 1918. This historical year also saw the debut of the first Chevrolet trucks. Two new truck models appeared this year: the Model 490 Light Delivery and the Model T 1-Ton Truck. There will be more about these trucks in the 1918 section.

Unfortunately, once back in charge, Durant repeated the same mistakes he made the first time. That is, his strategy was to grow the company through acquisitions, which is a legitimate and time-proven method. Durant made too many bad buys, however, which ate up the company's assets. One new and serious mistake was neglecting Chevrolet. His cash cow lost its focus and began to wander from its original path. New Chevrolet models began to grow bigger in size and cost, and sales shrank.

In April 1920, GM stock dropped $14 a share when the nation's economy sank. GM's bankers for the second time saved the company from collapse, but in the process forced Durant out for good. On November 19, 1920, Pierre Du Pont, who was favored by the bankers because the Du Pont Corp. was a major stockholder, took over as president. Du Pont was in favor of dropping the Chevrolet line, but future president and chairman Alfred Sloan talked him into keeping it and redirecting its focus as GM's lowest priced car, to compete just above Ford's Model T price.

Alfred Sloan was known as the professional manager, and he started working on a reorganization plan that continues to affect GM even today. Sloan spent 38 years at GM, 14 as president and 19 as chairman. He became the role model for all future GM executives and for all American businessmen.

1918

As mentioned earlier, this was the year Chevrolet became part of General Motors and the year Chevrolet entered the truck business. Chevrolet built not one but two trucks in 1918, Model 490, which was the Light Delivery rated for a payload of 1,000 pounds (1/2 ton) and the Model T 1-Ton Truck rated for a payload of 2,000 pounds (1 ton). The Light Delivery was built on the 490 auto's chassis while the Ton-Truck was a modification of the chassis from the Model FA passenger car. Four-cylinder engines powered both trucks. The Light Delivery's engine was smaller at 171-ci, compared to the Ton-Truck's 224-ci engine. The Ton-Truck's engine was the same as the car's engine. The only difference was that it was fitted with a Monarch governor that held the truck's speed to 25 miles per hour.

The Ton-Truck chassis sold for $1,125. Chevrolet produced only the truck's chassis, and depended on several outside body manufacturers to produce a variety of bodies supplied and mounted by either the dealer or the customer. A major supplier of commercial body equipment in 1918 was the Martin-Parry Company of Indianapolis,

Indiana. The usual practice by manufacturers of the period was to supply the chassis with cowl, which included the hood, front fenders, short running boards, headlights, and a seat. A front bumper was an option. Customers provided not only the body but also the cab. Cabs generally were of the open "C" type without doors and constructed of wood.

When Chevrolet introduced its first trucks in 1918, the trucks had the same front appearance as the Chevrolet passenger cars of that year. The 490 Light Delivery was derived from the 490 passenger cars, and the Model T 1-Ton Truck was derived from the FA model passenger cars. This practice continued at Chevrolet truck until 1934, when a distinctive, individual front appearance was designed especially for the trucks. Chevrolet built 41 truck chassis in 1916 and 504 in 1917. No details are available as to what type of trucks they were, but an educated guess says they were 490 automobile chassis modified for truck use. They were probably not much different from 1918's 490 Light Delivery chassis.

Chevrolet truck's calendar year sales for 1918 totaled 920 units.

In its first year of truck production Chevrolet offered two models. The lighter of the two was the 490 commercial chassis cowl with a "C" cab and pickup body. Buyers were required to either build, or most likely buy, a cab and body. Chevrolet did not supply a cab or body for a half-ton truck until 1931 (second series only). The 490 commercial chassis cowl was exactly the same as the automobile chassis cowl. The Light Delivery was intended for light loads only. It was powered by a 171-ci four-cylinder engine and had the auto's three-speed transmission. Its 102-inch wheelbase was the same as the automobile. Its list price was $595. *Tom Snivley*

Chevrolet's big truck was the Model T one-ton chassis cowl with a "Covered Flareboard" (a covered pickup). The Model T rode on a 125-inch-wheelbase chassis built for truck service. Chevrolet did not have a 125-inch-wheelbase automobile in 1918. Its engine was a four-cylinder displacing 224 ci and it used a three-speed transmission. Its chassis list price was $1,225. *AAMA*

1919

During World War I trucks were pressed into inter-city transportation of goods starting in 1918. In the interest of national defense, the government was not comfortable with the railroad's monopoly of all inter-city movement of freight. The demand for good roads was so high in 1919 that more than 20 bills were introduced in the 66th Congress. The nation was pushing toward the creation of a national network of highways and a federal highway commission was formed. By 1919 all states had formed highway departments, and that same year the federal government sold 5,336 war surplus trucks.

Two significant developments that promoted inter-city trucking were the nation's rapidly improving road systems and the development of reliable pneumatic tires as standard equipment for medium- and heavy-duty trucks. Goodyear demonstrated the practicality of long hauls by motor trucks when it ran a 5-ton truck from Akron to Chicago, covering 440 miles in 35 1/2 hours.

Trucks began to capitalize on the farm market, an area that was not being served by the railroads. Trucks delivered the goods with low rates and reliable service.

Completely enclosed truck cabs, which contributed to driver comfort, began to make serious inroads against open "C" cabs, particularly in the northern states.

Chevrolet's truck lineup, consisting of the Model 490 Light Delivery and the Model T 1-Ton Truck, continued without change. Chevrolet engineers had purposely designed the T truck to be dependable, simple in design and construction, sturdy, and without undue weight. It also was equipped with worm-drive. Worm-drive is nonexistent today, but in 1919 fully 66 percent of all new trucks were equipped with it. Both Chevrolet truck models came with three-speed selective-type transmissions. Chevrolet was not hesitant to advertise that fact in comparison to Ford's Model T with its planetary-type transmission.

Model 490 Light Delivery was Chevrolet's light truck based on the 490 auto's chassis cowl. Bodies were either built by the buyer or purchased from a truck body firm. This 490 was restored exactly back to original over a period of seven years. Its owner also built the traditional air calliope in the truck's body. The 490 is often displayed at car shows in the Whittier, California, area. Its owner enjoys playing the calliope for car show attendees. The 490's drivetrain consists of the 170.8-ci four-cylinder engine and three-speed transmission. *Daniel Wright*

Chevrolet increased the Model T's price by 17 percent and the Light Delivery's price by 24 percent for 1919. Yet total truck production increased by sevenfold to a total of 9,535 for both models, proof positive that customers approved of these two hard-working trucks.

1920

Chevrolet carried over its entire truck line from 1919 into 1920 without change. The line consisted of the Light Delivery Model 490 built on the 490 automobile's chassis. The Light Delivery rode on a 102-inch-wheelbase chassis and was powered by a 171-ci four developing 26 horsepower. The first Chevrolet 490 truck sold in 1918 for $595, chassis only. Its price increased to $735 in 1919 and increased further to $795 in 1920, still without a body. This little delivery truck was rated for a payload of 1,000 pounds.

The other truck in Chevrolet's line for 1920 was the 125-inch-wheelbase Model T, a 1-ton chassis only rated for a 2,000-pound maximum payload. A 224-ci four-cylinder engine developing 37 horsepower powered the Model T. The Model T chassis sold for a mere $1,460.

An industry trend in 1920 was toward lighter and faster models such as the 1-ton "speed-truck," which became possible due to the development of superior pneumatic tires. Lighter trucks riding on pneumatic tires resulted in higher speeds and therefore better customer appeal.

A few factors contributed to the increase in truck use in the United States. The federal government began to give the states surplus World War I trucks for use in building highways. And a gallon of gasoline sold for 35 cents in 1920.

Despite a poor business climate, Chevrolet truck sales increased 41 percent in 1920 to a total of 9,535 units.

Here is an example of Chevrolet's Light Delivery chassis cowl with windshield, seat, and flatbed. The wheelbase was 102 inches and the 171-ci four-cylinder engine continued without change. The basic chassis cowl's retail price was listed at $795. Chevrolet's truck marketing group as early as the late teens advertised Chevrolet's good looks for the businessman who cared about his company's image in the eyes of his customers. *MBI Publishing Company*

The one-ton Model T was again Chevrolet's big truck in 1920. One of the hallmarks of the Model T was its worm-drive rear axle. The Model T chassis with windshield and seat was advertised for $1,325 FOB Flint, Michigan; with windshield, seat, and express body (pickup) for $1,460 FOB Flint; and the Express body with eight-post curtain top as shown for $1,545 FOB Flint. Chevrolet did not build either of the bodies; they came from several outside body manufacturers. Its engine was the 224-ci valve-in-head four-cylinder, which was mated to a three-speed transmission. *Everett Nebergall*

1921

This was the first year Chevrolet expanded its truck line from two to three models with the addition of the Model G, a 3/4-ton truck rated for a payload of 1,500 pounds. In Chevrolet's terminology, the Model T 1-ton was a Truck, the new Model G 3/4-ton was a Light Truck, and the Model 490 was a Light Delivery Wagon. The Model G was added to fill the gap between a light truck built on a passenger car chassis and Chevrolet's "big" truck. The Model G was built on a 120-inch-wheelbase chassis. The same 224-ci, 37-horsepower four used in the Model T 1-ton powered it. The Model G's front appearance was identical to the 490's. It sold for only $920, completely equipped with a canopy. Chevrolet's truck bodies came from several outside body manufacturers.

At this point in time, the rapid improvements in truck-type pneumatic tires enabled lighter trucks to haul more load at greater speeds than ever before. Pneumatic tires were also becoming an option for heavier trucks, but their high cost was prohibitive to many buyers. In 1920 the price of a 4,000-pound capacity tire ranged from $178.95 to $240. Chevrolet's Model T 1-Ton Truck cost only $1,345 equipped with four pneumatics in 1921.

Two other realities had an impact on the truck market in 1921. First, the post–World War I truck sellers' market ended, forcing a decline in manufacturer's list prices and forcing truck dealers to sharpen their pencils. Chevrolet's Model T truck listed for $1,460 in 1920 and tumbled 8 percent in 1921 to $1,345. The second development was the increased speeds on the nation's quickly improving highways. The Federal Highway Act of 1921 provided for the states and federal government to create a nationwide road system, with Washington paying half the cost on designated Federal Aid roads. The nation had 3.2 million miles of highways, but only 14 percent were surfaced.

Speed governors on trucks of 1-ton capacity and less were being dropped as standard equipment because the superior pneumatic tires permitted maximum speeds through the elimination of vibrations caused by rough roads.

In 1921, Chevrolet set up contracts with several body suppliers to ship their body equipment directly to Chevrolet manufacturing plants for installation. Thus, Chevrolet was able to offer complete vehicles to its dealers.

A postwar recession continued to grip the nation, causing business activity to drop. Chevrolet felt it in its truck sales, which tumbled a painful 57 percent to only 4,145 units sold.

The 490 half-ton Light Delivery chassis cowl continued in 1921. Chevrolet management had contracts with several body suppliers who shipped bodies directly to the Chevrolet plant for installation on Chevrolet-built chassis. The 490 Light Delivery chassis cowl with windshield is shown with a canopy express body from The Hercules Corporation of Evansville, Indiana. The 490 chassis windshield cowl sold for $560. It featured a 102-inch wheelbase, a 171-ci four-cylinder valve-in-head engine, and a three-speed transmission. A new model for 1921 was the Model G, a 3/4-ton chassis windshield cowl on a 120-inch wheelbase. *MBI Publishing Company*

A light truck that found favor with salesmen, professional men, farmers, and small retailers was the 490 Roadster with slide-in pickup box. This low-priced ($625 w/o box) little "convertible" was within the price range of many. It had the same features as the 490 half-ton Light Delivery. *MBI Publishing Company*

1922

Chevrolet's truck line, consisting of 1/2-ton, 3/4-ton, and 1-ton models, continued into 1922 with only minor mechanical improvements. As in the past, bodies were not offered as factory-built units. A delivery body supplied by independent body builders was mounted in the factory and delivered to the customer. It is difficult to find any evidence that Chevrolet mounted bodies in the factory on either the 3/4- or 1-ton chassis.

This was a year of progress for Chevrolet. William S. Knudson became vice president in charge of operations. Also, the company completed the General Motors Building in Detroit.

Chevrolet was proud of the fact that it equipped its 125-inch-wheelbase 1-ton truck with pneumatic tires on all four wheels. Use of these tires eliminated much of the vibration from the road before it reached the truck's chassis and load. Chevrolet wheels were of the "conventional artillery type" built with 12 spokes fashioned from well-seasoned second-growth hickory.

The nation's economy began a strong recovery from the poor business climate that had prevailed for the past two years. As business boomed, truck sales increased. Chevrolet's truck prices also dropped by 19 percent. Truck prices continued to fall while average truck speeds increased. Naturally, a truck's competitive advantage over a horse became quite apparent.

Chevrolet's truck sales for 1922 increased 259 percent over 1921, topping off at 10,732 units.

It was the last year for the 490 Light Delivery Wagon, Model G 3/4-ton, and the Model T one-ton. This 1922 490 Light Delivery chassis windshield cowl has a pickup body. Without the pickup body it sold for $510. The specifications of all three trucks carried over unchanged from 1922. *David Russell*

1923

Alfred P. Sloan, Jr., moved up to the president's office at GM in 1923. Sloan soon proved he was the manager's manager. He put his stamp on GM, and it has stayed in place to the present day.

Chevrolet completely revamped its car and truck lines for 1923, concentrating on one car series and two truck series. The new car was named the Superior Series. Its wheelbase was 1 inch longer, at 103 inches, than the former 490 Series. The new clean design of the Superior's front end was the same design as the new trucks. The higher hood line created a more pleasing and somewhat bigger appearance to Chevrolet's trucks. The Light Delivery, Series B, rode on the car's new 103-inch-wheelbase chassis while the 1-ton, Series D, rode on the old 3/4-ton's 120-inch-wheelbase chassis. Both series shared the car's 171-ci, 35-horsepower four-cylinder engine. The company dropped the former 1-ton series 224-ci four-cylinder engine.

Chevrolet sold the 1-ton Utility Express Truck chassis only for $575 and advertised it as "the lowest-priced quality truck in the world capable of fast heavy-duty service." The operative word here was "quality" because archrival Ford was selling a 1-ton truck chassis for only $380! Chevrolet competed well on the basis of appearance and its selective three-speed transmission, which allowed the driver to "run the motor at the most economical speed under all conditions."

Chevrolet sold the 1/2-ton Commercial Car as either a chassis-only at $425 or as a Light Delivery Wagon, complete with body, for $495. Light Delivery was another term for a canopy.

Chevrolet's management made a determined pitch this year to capture more of the growing commercial fleet business. Commercial fleets consisted of autos, mostly coupes, used by salespeople on

Chevrolet revised its entire auto and truck lines in 1923. Beginning in 1923 models and trade names took on names instead of numbers as previously. Superior's truck line consisted of only two models: the Superior Light Delivery chassis windshield cowl based on the Superior automobile; and the Superior Utility Chassis cowl with a very rare school bus body (shown). The Superior one-ton featured a new 120-inch wheelbase, a 35-horsepower 171-ci four-cylinder engine, and a three-speed transmission. The one-ton truck chassis sold for only $575. *John Kruesels*

Chevrolet's management simplified its truck engine offerings for 1923 by dropping the former 224-ci four-cylinder. Only one engine was available in 1923: the 35-horsepower 171-ci overhead valve four-cylinder. This is a 1923 Chevrolet Superior Utility Express chassis cowl with open cab and stake body. It featured a 120-inch-wheelbase chassis, the 171-ci engine, and a three-speed transmission. *AAMA*

their routes. By 1923, America's rural road system had developed and improved to the point that salespeople could reach by auto most of the country's small towns, many of which had never been served by railroads. Chevrolet sold on the basis of quality, low operating costs, and the car's "excellent appearance." Two models that proved favorites with the public were the Superior Utility coupe and the Roadster (convertible). The coupe's huge trunk allowed the salesperson to carry samples or a light load of product. Many firms mounted a big box for hauling on the car's frame behind the cab.

Chevrolet truck had a very good year, with sales up by 38 percent over 1922, topping off at 14,780 units.

1924

The need for product innovation and improvement was a corporate concern of GM's management team. So it formed a committee in 1923 to develop a private experimental test area that could be utilized by all manufacturing divisions. A parcel of 1,268 acres of land was purchased in Milford, Michigan, about 45 miles from corporate headquarters in Detroit, and work on the test facility began immediately. Opened in midyear 1924, the GM Proving Grounds welcomed its first tenant—the Chevrolet Motor Division.

The truck model lineup was new in 1923 and carried over into 1924 without change, except for series designations. Series F was the Superior Light Delivery 1/2-ton built on an automobile chassis and Series H was the 1-ton truck chassis. The little 171-ci, 35-horsepower four continued to power both trucks.

Chevrolet was rightly pleased with its Superior Series trucks, now in only their second year. Truck buyers voted with their dollars, sending Chevrolet truck sales up 43 percent over 1923. Sales reached 21,157 units, the highest ever truck total. Management credited the sales improvement to the truck's improved design. Outstanding features of the Superior Chevrolets included the new high hood, crowned fenders, a sloping windshield in place of the former vertical style, drum-type headlights, graceful lines, and excellent fit and finish.

Prices dropped $15 for both the Light Delivery chassis and the Light Delivery canopy to $410 and $495, respectively. The 1-ton Superior Utility Express chassis-only dropped $25 to $550.

The two Superior model trucks new for 1923 continued into 1924. They were the half-ton Superior Light Delivery like the one pictured here with a panel body and the one-ton Superior Utility Express chassis windshield cowl. In the early days of the motor truck, the size rating referred to actual payload. In the case of these two trucks, it was 1,000 and 2,000 pounds, respectively. The Light Delivery's chassis was the same as the Superior automobile's chassis—same engine, transmission, wheelbase, tires, and front sheet metal. It had the 35-horsepower 171-ci four-cylinder engine, and its transmission was a three-speed. *AAMA*

Chevrolet's "big" 1924 model year truck was the Superior Utility Express Series D chassis cowl, with a closed cab and stake body. Chevrolet did not build either the cab or body. Both trucks used the same front-end sheet metal. This truck's wheelbase was 120 inches and it was rated for a payload capacity of 2,000 pounds. The Utility Express' drivetrain was the same as that of the Light Delivery: the 25-horsepower 171-ci four-cylinder engine and a three-speed transmission. It did ride on larger wheels and tires, however, with 34 x 41/2 rears verses 30 x 31/2 for the 1/2-ton. *AAMA*

1925

This was a year mostly of change and improvements in Chevrolet's truck line. There were changes in models and improved engineering features. The Superior Light Delivery 1/2-ton and Utility Express 1-ton trucks, Series H, opened the year without change from 1924. The 1925 trucks featured a Fisher Body "all steel" closed cab with ventilating (opening) windshield. The new cab added value to Chevrolet's truck line.

As midyear models, or second series, Chevrolet cars featured an improved engine. It had a redesigned block, connecting rods, and crankshaft. The engine's size remained at 171 ci and the horsepower at 35. In addition, the car's chassis and running gear were substantially upgraded. Chevrolet gave the same upgrades to the two truck chassis. The former cone clutch was replaced by a superior, dry plate disc-type clutch, mated to an improved and stronger three-speed transmission. The second series 1-ton truck was designated Series M.

Front styling for trucks continued to be the same as for passenger cars. The truck's radiator shell, however, was of pressed steel instead of the automobile's cast-aluminum shell.

The 1-ton truck's wheelbase was stretched to 124 inches from the former 120 inches. In spite of all these improvements, the 1-ton's price remained the same as in 1924: $550. The auto-based Light Delivery model's chassis price was increased to $425 from $410.

General Motors Truck Company (GMC) introduced a 1-ton truck, making it the first truck to have four-wheel brakes; Chevrolet would have to wait until 1928 to receive four-wheel brakes.

The year ended with sales increasing by 18 percent, to a total of 24,876 trucks in 1925, as Chevrolet's marketing department continued its strong emphasis on fleet sales for commercial uses.

1926

For the second year in a row Chevrolet automobiles had significant midyear changes. Because Chevrolet's 1/2-ton Commercial Chassis was based on the Superior auto's chassis, and because the 1-ton Utility Express truck chassis shared mechanical components and front sheet-metal styling, changes to automobiles necessarily changed the two truck models.

Mechanical improvements included a belt-driven generator instead of the gear-driven unit. Also, the oil pump was driven by a cam instead of a gear. Braking surface, rear brakes only, increased to 2 1/2 inches from the previous 2 inches. Brakes were still of the mechanical type.

The 1-ton truck chassis was renamed "Series X" at midyear, but changes were very minimal. Wheelbase length remained at 124 inches; tire size changed from 30x3 1/2 to 30x5, front and rear; and the rear spring load capacity changed to 2,000 pounds from 1,750 pounds.

For the first time, a steel cab was made standard equipment for the 1-ton. Interestingly, Chevrolet offered three bodies mounted at the factory for the 1-ton truck only. The new bodies included a stake, a farm box, and a canopy. These bodies were designed by

Because Chevrolet trucks were based on the Superior automobile chassis, the Superior truck models returned again in 1926. The Series K trucks were built early in the year, and Series V later in the model year. Two models made up the Commercial Car line: the 1/2-ton Superior Commercial Chassis that sold for only $395; and the 1-ton Utility Express Chassis selling for $550. Pictured is an original unrestored, 103-inch-wheelbase 1/2-ton Superior K chassis cowl, with a Martin-Parry body. It has removable sliding doors. Its drivetrain is the 35-horsepower 171-ci four-cylinder engine and the three-speed transmission. *Don and Sandy Wester*

The same four-cylinder 171-ci 35 brake horsepower valve-in-head type of engine powered the one-ton Series R/X 1926 Utility Express and the half-ton Commercial Chassis. The engine featured a cast-iron block, a bore and stroke of 3 11/16x4 inches, and a compression ratio of 4.3:1, SAE net horsepower of 21.7, three main bearings, mechanical valve lifters, and a Carter one-barrel carburetor. *John Billingsley*

Chevrolet engineers and produced entirely in the Chevrolet factory. With the availability of complete trucks from the factory, the dealer now only needed to make one sale. The result was a savings in time, effort, and cost, which resulted in greater profits to the dealer and better service to the customer.

Series designations for 1926 Chevrolet trucks were Series V for the 1/2-ton, Series R for the early 1-ton, and Series X for the second series 1-ton.

E. G. "Cannon Ball" Baker drove a fully loaded 2-ton GMC truck from New York to San Francisco in the record-breaking time of five days, 17 hours, and 30 minutes.

This was also the year that GM bought out the Fisher Body Corporation and Ford inaugurated the five-day week.

Chevrolet truck prices showed no change from 1926; the price was $395 for the 1/2-ton Commercial series chassis only and $550 for the Utility Express series, both first and second series, chassis only. The two most popular body types for the Commercial series continued to be a panel with double rear doors and the canopy delivery; screen sides were an option.

This was a record-breaking year for Chevrolet. Sales on the truck side increased a whopping 311 percent, to 77,364 units. The combined car and truck sales for Chevrolet for the first time surpassed the half-million mark, topping off at 646,769 units.

The half-ton and one-ton trucks also shared the same cab interior as pictured here in a one-ton Utility Express. The instrument panel was equipped with an ammeter, oil pressure gauge, speedometer, choke, and headlight knobs. On the floor were the brake, clutch and accelerator pedals, gearshift lever, and emergency brake lever. The seat and back cushions were upholstered in vinyl. *John Billingsley*

1927

Chevrolet's truck line took a big step forward in 1927 when it was announced that its first-ever optional factory-built cabs (built by Fisher Body Co.) would be available for the one-ton Capitol Series LM trucks. The one-ton was built on the 124-inch-wheelbase chassis and was again powered by the 171-ci four-cylinder engine mated to a three-speed transmission. The one-ton chassis cowl, without cab or body, but with four fenders, sold for $495. With a cab and a spare rim, its price jumped to $610; with cab stake body and rim $680; and a one-ton panel with spare rim sold for $755. This is a 1927 Chevrolet one-ton Series LM chassis cab, no body with four fenders. *Mike Larson*

A new style and a new name for Chevrolet automobiles in 1927 also had an impact on the two truck models. The new name was the Capital series, for both cars and trucks. The new style consisted of a new radiator shell, full crown fenders, and bullet-type headlights. Mechanically, nothing much changed. The auto's wheelbase stayed at 103 inches; the 171-ci engine carried over, as did the clutch and all other mechanical components.

Chevrolet continued the practice it began in 1925 of announcing its new models after the model year was under way. The only real differences with the new trucks were the styling changes to the radiator shell, front fenders, and headlights, because these items came from the automobiles. The trucks also adopted from the cars the new rectangular brake and clutch pedal design. The 1927 Chevrolets are easy to identify due to the distinctive dip in their radiator shell.

Chevrolet truck advertising picked up a new theme for 1927: "The world's largest builder of gear shift trucks." This was, of course, a way of getting around Ford and its planetary transmission shifted by foot pedals.

The Capital half-ton chassis' price increased $20 to $395. Chevrolet didn't offer factory-installed bodies for the 1/2-ton series. The 1-ton's chassis price remained at $495. The 1-ton sold for $610 with a cab. Factory bodies mounted on the 1-ton chassis included the panel and stake only. Chevrolet's cab offered "coupe comfort" in a truck. Side glass was lowered and lifted by means of a crank.

A 1927 Chevrolet one-ton Series LM chassis cab with a farm box supplied by an independent body manufacturer. This inexpensive but dependable little truck was well favored by the nation's farmers. The chassis cab without rear fenders sold for only $610 FOB Flint, Michigan. This truck was equipped with small cowl lamps and a full ventilating windshield. Chevrolet advertised this truck as having "Coupe comfort on a truck chassis!" *Gary Benidt*

The windshield was the full ventilating type. Door panels were trimmed with "Fabrikoid," a leather-like substance, for driver warmth and a softer appearance.

The instrument panel was the same as the one used in the automobiles, with two oval clusters. It consisted of a horizontally rotating dial speedometer, a mileage counter and a trip recorder, a manual choke pull, an ammeter, an oil pressure gauge, a light switch, and a three-position ignition switch. This device was called a "coaster switch," and it mechanically locked the steering column. Consequently, when the steering was unlocked, the ignition could be on or off, separately. This unique feature returned for 1928 and then disappeared.

The Hercules Products Company of Evansville, Indiana, introduced a new slip-on body for the Chevrolet roadster or coupe. The pickup-type body easily slid into the trunk and extended approximately 2 feet beyond the body. The trunk lid remained open when in use.

Standard light-duty Chevrolet wheels were discs with 29x4.4-inch tires. For the first time, Chevrolet offered natural wood wheels as an option.

Chevrolet's standard engine for both trucks was the 3 11/16x4-inch bore and stroke four, with a 171-ci displacement. Developed horsepower was 35. The engine was lubricated by a positive pump and splash system. An oil filter was standard equipment, as was an air cleaner.

This year Chevrolet benefited when Ford shut down the assembly lines for six months beginning on May 26 to change production over to the Model A. GM's market share rose from 19 to 43 percent. Chevrolet truck sales increased by 67 percent to a total of 129,099 units. This was the first time Chevrolet truck sales broke the 100,000 barrier.

The engine compartment of the one-ton Series LM truck. The engine is painted gray, which is the correct color for Chevrolet's four-cylinder engines. The generator is located in the bottom left corner. At the top right corner is the vacuum tank, and in the center is the updraft carburetor and intake manifold. This is the 35 brake-horsepower four-cylinder 171-ci engine, which was then in its next to last year. *Gary Benidt*

Chevrolet greatly expanded its one-ton truck series in 1928 by adding an optional cab, a stake body, and a panel body in the LM Series. Here, a 1928 Chevrolet one-ton LM chassis cab with tank body is pictured. The tank was a 300-gallon unit for gas and lubricating oil. Its drivetrain included the 171-ci four-cylinder engine and the three-speed transmission. *John M. Lyon*

1928

The following excerpt, "The Field is Big!" is from the 1928 Graham Brothers new 1/2-ton panel's dealer/salesman booklet. It is very informative concerning the condition of the 1/2-ton delivery truck business.

The total production of commercial vehicles during 1926 was 491,353 and registrations during that year were 2,764,222. Of those totals 78 percent were vehicles of 1-ton capacity or less. Thirteen percent of the totals were trucks of 3/4-ton capacity or less.

Replacement of trucks of larger capacities is often deferred until the vehicles have completed a long term of service. This situation does not prevail to the same extent with Light Delivery equipment due doubtless to the higher annual mileage, lower initial cost, and generally greater importance of good appearance.

Many fleet owners have found that better and more productive service is rendered when larger numbers of smaller trucks are used in place of a few large trucks. Then there are those numerous types of businesses whose requirements are by nature limited to light, fast, and low-cost vehicles. In this category are grocers, launderers, cleaners, jewelers, specialty shops, etc.

These facts present in part the possibilities for selling your new half-ton commercial car. In summing up the situation for the year 1928 three important facts are evident, viz.:

1. The number of competing makes of cars of this type and capacity is not large and of these only two or three offer any real struggle.
2. Between these and ourselves will be divided the sale of possibly 100,000 vehicles of the Light Delivery class during the coming year.
3. No competing manufacturer offers equal quality and appearance within our price.

Don't be surprised by the line in paragraph three that says that several small trucks are more efficient than one large truck for making in-town deliveries. This was considered to be forward thinking in those days. The February 1928 issue of *Power Wagon* magazine contains an article supporting this concept. While it was commonly thought that fewer large trucks were more efficient than numerous small trucks, there were reasons for employing small trucks.

Most retailers in those days were located in a downtown area, as opposed to today's concentration of retail businesses in suburban locations. Heavy traffic, lined up and waiting at loading docks, resulted in lost time making deliveries. Small trucks, on the other hand, could zip up to the front of the store and quickly make smaller deliveries with no wasted time. Additionally, large trucks required two men, and two idle men are more expensive yet.

Another new Chevrolet automobile was introduced in 1928. This introduction was at the beginning of the model year, however, instead of at midyear as in the preceding three years. The new series was named the National Series. The model rode on a 107-inch-wheelbase chassis that measured 4 inches longer than the previous model's. Styling changed only slightly, with a longer body. An important first for Chevrolet was the addition of four-wheel mechanical brakes. All other mechanicals carried over without notable change.

On the truck side, the 1-ton carried over without change except for four-wheel mechanical brakes. The model designations for 1928 were Series LO (early) and LP (late). Four-wheel brakes were new on the LP trucks. The engine's compression ratio increased from 4.3:1 to 4.5:1 at 2,200 rpm. A new four-speed transmission was made standard equipment, replacing the lighter optional four-speed.

Chevrolet reduced prices on the Light Delivery truck in 1928 to $375 for the chassis only, a reduction of $20 from 1927. The half-ton's cab was the same as that of the one-ton. Its wheelbase increased to 107 inches. Its drivetrain consisted of the 35 brake horsepower 171-ci four-cylinder engine and a three-speed transmission. The increase in wheelbase length was in preparation for the six-cylinder engine coming in 1929. Note this pickup's full disc wheels and front bumper. The pickup body is from an aftermarket supplier. *Jim Benjaminson*

The City of Park River, North Dakota, purchased a 1928 Chevrolet one-ton Series LO chassis cowl with four fenders and spare rim and mounted a fire-fighting body for the city's fire department. Without the body this chassis sold for only $495. Note the chains on the rear wheels in the summertime. This truck was built on a 124-inch-wheelbase chassis and featured the 35 brake horsepower 171-ci four-cylinder engine and three-speed transmission. *Jim Benjaminson*

Chevrolet did not offer its own factory-installed bodies for either the 1/2-ton or 1-ton trucks. The National 1/2-ton Series AB was offered only as a chassis, and priced at $375—$20 less than in 1927. In 1928, Chevrolet's National Series was an attempt to be more price competitive with Ford's new Model A models. The Capital 1-ton was offered as chassis only at $495 or chassis cab at $610. Both prices were unchanged from 1927.

A new sedan delivery model was introduced at midyear that was part of the National passenger car series. It had a special Fisher body with a wide rear door.

Chevrolet truck sales jumped 20 percent in 1928, topping off at 154,512 units. This was the first year in Chevrolet history that total car and truck sales topped the one million vehicle mark. At last Mr. Ford was beginning to feel footsteps. Chevrolet sold more total cars and trucks this year than Ford did. In all fairness, however, Ford did not have a full production year. Plus, the start-up on the new Model A was slower than planned. Yet GM's policy of annual model change, now in its fourth year, was beginning to take effect. Mr. Ford had stayed with the Model T for too many years, and many of his customers were looking for more stylish and modern cars.

Another piece of good news for truckers in 1928 was the announcement by the Public Roads Bureau and Department of Agriculture that road construction in 1928 would exceed that of every preceding year. More than 26,000 miles of road construction was scheduled for the year. Of that total, more than 21,000 miles was on the Federal-aid highway system.

These two new 1928 Chevrolet Series LP one-ton tractors were on the job hauling lumber near Minnesota's Itasca State Park (headwaters of the Mississippi River). These trucks were equipped with a new heavy-duty four-speed transmission, which helped a great deal when pulling semi-trailers such as these. This was the last year for the old reliable 171-ci four-cylinder engine. *Bob Bilden*

Without a body, the one-ton 1928 Chevrolet Series LP chassis cowl with cab, four fenders, and spare rim sold for $610. The cab was unchanged from 1927 and featured small cowl lights and a full ventilating windshield. Its four-cylinder valve-in-head engine was unchanged from 1927, but it was in its last year. This beautifully restored truck with a low side body was seen at the 1998 Osceola, Wisconsin, Wheels and Wings Car Show. *MBI Publishing Company*

This 1928 Chevrolet Capitol Express one-ton was purchased new by the owner's father in 1928, and is in original running condition. It is equipped with a very handsome aftermarket canopy express body. Note this truck has an accessory front bumper. Other features included artillery-type wooden wheels, 30x5-inch front and rear tires, 124-inch wheelbase, drop-forged I-beam front axle, semi-floating rear axle, three-speed transmission, 171-ci four-cylinder engine, and mechanical brakes. *W. Robert Diehl*

This 1928 Chevrolet Series LP one-ton truck with a home- or shop-built semi-trailer attached is well loaded with slab wood. This truck saw some very hard service. It was powered by Chevrolet's famous 171-ci four-cylinder engine and was equipped with the standard three-speed transmission. *Bob Bilden*

Chevrolet's 1928 half-ton National Series Commercial chassis cowl was identical to that of the 1928 Chevrolet passenger car's chassis. Without the body, but including fenders and spare rim, the National half-ton chassis cowl sold for $375. Several outside body manufacturers supplied wooden station wagon bodies. The manufacturer of this attractive body is unknown. It is equipped with the optional steel disc wheels. *David Russell*

From their very beginning, Chevrolet trucks have been favored by the nation's fire departments. This 1928 Chevrolet one-ton Series LP chassis cowl with four fenders and spare rim sports a fire-fighting body. Without the body, this 2,000-pound payload-rated unit sold for only $495. Its drivetrain consisted of the 171-ci four-cylinder engine and three-speed transmission. *David Russell*

Chevrolet introduced two new light truck models in midyear 1928—a Roadster pickup and a Sedan Delivery with body by Fisher. Both models were mounted on the National Series passenger car chassis. A 1928 Chevrolet Roadster pickup is pictured with aftermarket pickup box. This pickup's drivetrain consisted of the 171-ci four-cylinder engine and the three-speed transmission. *Jim Benjaminson*

1929

Chevrolet's management thought big in 1929. A brilliant new overhead valve (OHV) six-cylinder engine, the first six in the low-priced field, caused quite a stir in automotive circles. Its cubic inch displacement was 194 from a bore and stroke of 3 5/16x3 3/4; horsepower was 46 at 2,600 rpm. Its compression ratio was 5.02:1. Other quality features included three main bearings and a one-barrel Carter carburetor. Chevrolet advertised it as "A six for the price of a four."

In 1928 all Chevrolet car and truck models were named Nationals; in 1929 their name grew to Internationals. Chevrolet automobile styling changed slightly, with a new more rectangular radiator sporting a Chevrolet bow tie logo at the top of the chrome-plated radiator shell. Other new features included a wider belt molding, one-piece fenders, and bullet-type headlights. These same styling features carried over into the front styling of trucks.

The Sedan Delivery was now in its second year of production. Chevrolet sold 1,004 Sedan Deliveries in 1928, and 9,640 in 1929. The Sedan Delivery was priced at only $595. Chevrolet took advantage of the new six-cylinder-engine–powered Sedan Delivery's superior speed in its advertising. With the fast six a salesman could see more customers per day. The auto-based 1/2-ton Light Delivery chassis sold for $400. This was only $25 more than the four-cylinder–powered 1/2-ton of 1928. A cab was not included with the chassis.

Instead of a 1-ton truck in 1929, management opted to move up to a 131-inch-wheelbase 1 1/2-ton truck—the Utility Series LQ. Four LQ models were offered, with and without cab and with and without larger rear tire equipment. Prices ranged from a low of $545 to a high of $685 with cab and larger rear tires. All models were chassis only; the customer still had to purchase a body from an outside firm or have the dealer handle the transaction. Gross vehicle weight of the 1 1/2-ton truck was 7,000 pounds, an increase of 1,000 pounds. Maximum body length behind the cab was 108 inches. Maximum loading space in a one-unit body was 116 inches.

All truck models this year were equipped with steel disc wheels in place of the former wood spoke type. Standard transmission for 1/2-ton models was the passenger car three-speed. The 1 1/2-ton trucks were equipped with the improved four-speed transmission, which was new in 1928. A front bumper was standard equipment on 1 1/2-ton LQs.

Chevrolet advertised the new six-cylinder-engine–powered Utility 1 1/2-ton truck as having greater speed, 32 percent more power, 50 percent more capacity, 7 inches more wheelbase, and four-wheel brakes (still mechanicals). All of this and priced like a four! Truck buyers looked and then bought. Chevrolet's truck sales increased by 21 percent in 1929 to a total of 187,103. For the second year in a row, Chevrolet's total car and truck sales topped one million units.

Chevrolet advertised its new 1929 six-cylinder engine as "A six for the price of a four." Chevrolet scooped the industry with the introduction of its new six-cylinder engine. Features included overhead valve design, cast-iron pistons, well-designed cylinder water cooling jackets, and non-pressurized lubrication. Its 194-ci developed 46 horsepower at 2,600 rpm. This engine later gained the reputation as "The cast iron wonder" for its excellent durability.

The indirect lighted instrument panel in the new 1929 Utility 1 1/2-ton trucks carried a complete set of instruments and controls, including even spark and throttle. Starter, brake, and clutch pedals were floor mounted, as were the four-speed transmission's shift lever and the emergency brake lever. The cab floor and toe boards were constructed of wood. The new windshield was the ventilating type. The horn button was in the center of the steering wheel.

Chevrolet's one-ton Utility chassis was upgraded to a 1 1/2-ton capacity model and a new front bumper became standard equipment. During the 1929 model year, Chevrolet produced its 500,000th commercial unit and ended the decade of the 1920s with an accumulated truck sales total of 641,482 units. This is a six-cylinder 1 1/2-ton Utility Series LQ with a long pickup body. The new Utility Series rode on a 131-inch-long wheelbase chassis and featured a four-speed transmission and four-wheel brakes. Steel disc wheels were standard equipment. Chevrolet did not supply the body.

Chapter 2

1930 TO 1939

1930

The only styling change of note in the 1930 Chevrolet cars, and therefore in trucks, was a slanting, non-glare windshield. The instrument panel was redesigned and the electrical gas gauge was moved to the instrument panel. The instruments had new circular shapes with dark-colored faces.

Chevrolet's new OHV six-cylinder engine, now in its second year, was given a boost in horsepower to 50, thanks to a revised valve–train with smaller exhaust valves and larger intake valves, and a revised exhaust manifold.

All car and truck model names changed again, this time from International to Universal. The Roadster Delivery, two Sedan Deliveries, and light commercial chassis were Series AD, the same series as passenger cars. The 1 1/2-ton trucks were designated Series LR without cab and Series LS with cab.

The Roadster Delivery was a convertible passenger car with a pickup box added on behind the cab. It used the cowl and doors of the Roadster, but its windshield was 2 inches taller than that used on the car, and its canvas-covered top had a rigid frame that could be lowered. Chevrolet, however, didn't supply the box; the customer was expected to source it for himself.

A second new light-duty model was the Deluxe Delivery truck. It was a luxury version of the Sedan Delivery with carriage lamps just behind the doors. This upscale delivery was intended for use by high-end retail stores for delivering parcels to customers' residences.

A dual rear wheel feature was available for the 1 1/2-ton trucks. Dual wheels raised its gross vehicle weight (GVW) rating to 8,000 pounds compared to 7,000 pounds for single rear wheel models. The six-cylinder engine for 1 1/2-ton trucks was equipped with a four-bladed cooling fan. Other than the fan, the truck engine was the same as that of the automobile.

This was the last year Chevrolet didn't offer factory-built and-mounted truck bodies. Beginning in 1931, there were 11 standard bodies offered.

The Sport Roadster sold for only $515 without a pickup box. The Sedan Delivery was still $595, unchanged from 1929. The Light Delivery chassis decreased $35 from 1929 to $365. Prices of single rear wheel 1 1/2-ton trucks decreased by $10. Dual rear wheel models, which were new in 1930, sold for $545 without cab and $650 with cab. Duals could be added to single rear wheel trucks for only $25.

This first full year of the Great Depression was hard on the auto industry. Sales for Chevrolet trucks declined by 29 percent to only 132,229 units. The automotive industry could expect three more tough years before sales turned up.

The 1930 1 1/2-ton Utility chassis carried over with only minor updates in styling and engineering features. The sensational six-cylinder engine was in its second year and was enthusiastically received by truck operators. The 1 1/2-ton truck rode on a 131-inch-wheelbase chassis; it was available with a cab but not a factory-supplied body. Dual rear wheels were a new factory option. This is a 1930 1 1/2-ton chassis cab with stake body. *Arnold Paradi*

In addition to the 1 1/2-ton Utility Series, Chevrolet also offered a half-ton Roadster Delivery, Sedan Delivery, and a Light Delivery chassis cowl. Chevrolet did not supply the pickup box for the Roadster Delivery, but did manufacture the Sedan Delivery's body (by Fisher Body). Pictured is a 1930 Chevrolet 1 1/2-ton Utility chassis cab with dump body and dual rear wheels. Its drive-train consisted of the new six-cylinder engine and four-speed transmission. Four-wheel brakes were also standard. *MBI Publishing Company*

1931

Chevrolet's truck offerings in 1931 consisted of a Commercial line including a Commercial Chassis, a Light Delivery (closed cab pickup), a Roadster Delivery (convertible cab pickup), a Sedan Delivery, a 1 1/2-Ton Truck, and a Heavy-Duty Truck. Chevy's advertising boasted, "A truck for every business need." The Light Delivery chassis was similar to the passenger car except that it had heavier springs and the fuel tank was mounted under the seat. The 1 1/2-Ton Truck chassis featured a wheelbase of 131 inches and was equipped with single disc wheels; dual rears were an extra cost option. The Heavy-Duty Truck chassis had a wheelbase of 157 inches and was standard with dual rear wheels.

Chevrolet's standard nomenclature at this time designated Commercials for the lightest trucks because these vehicles were built on a car's chassis. A 1931 truck was built on a rugged ladder-type truck frame and had nothing in common with an automobile frame. The Heavy-Duty Truck's wheelbase was longer (157 inches compared to 131 inches) and dual rear wheels were standard equipment in comparison to the standard truck chassis.

Product improvement to the trucks included stronger frames, a heavier front axle with a stronger I-beam, an improved steering knuckle, steering arms, king pins, and thrust bearings. The rear axle was redesigned for dual wheel equipment and to incorporate 16-inch internal brakes (mechanical type). The wheel bearing was larger, as was the hub flange, and all of its related parts were correspondingly larger and stronger. Service brakes for 1931 were changed to the internal expanding type from the former external contracting type, and the brake diameter increased from 12 1/2 to 16 inches. The rear brake diameter increased from 12 to 16 inches. The friction surface of the clutch increased to 95.7 square inches from 65.9 square inches.

Commercial models sported disc wheels with detachable rims and 4.75-19, four-ply tires as standard equipment. The Sedan Delivery was equipped with wire wheels, the same as those on passenger cars. Solid disc wheels on 1 1/2-ton trucks were standard equipment.

The cab for the Commercial Chassis and the 1 1/2-Ton Trucks was redesigned. The roof was a one-piece steel stamping bolted to the framing. It was extremely durable and much stronger than the usual wood and fabric structure. The cab was wider and the seats were also roomier and more comfortable. Considerably wider doors improved entry and exit. A rubber floor mat was standard equipment.

Overload springs, optional at extra cost, could be ordered on trucks carrying heavy loads. A spare tire lock unit was another optional item to prevent theft of the wheel and tire when carried in the fender wells. A full line of front and rear bumpers was optional, as were rear fender guards. A beautiful hinged radiator cap was another option. It was much the same in design as the prior year's ornament. Seat covers could also be ordered; they were made of durable material and fit snugly, but could be easily removed for cleaning.

In 1931, Chevrolet employed a total of 20 engineers between the car and truck divisions. The engineers designed the parts, and then sent them along to the Chevrolet Experimental Laboratories for testing.

The experimental labs were housed in a separate building with 44,400 square feet of floor space. The labs were equipped with the most modern precision machines operated by 107 mechanics, toolmakers, model builders, woodworkers, trimmers, sheet-metal workers, and blacksmiths who could build by hand what would finally be produced in mass quantities by production machines. Dynamometers constantly tested engines for power, torque, fuel consumption, and other performance characteristics. Machines tested frames, axles, and wheels to discover weak points or to prove the strength of the part.

Chevrolet purchased the Martin-Parry Co. of Indianapolis, Indiana, late in 1930, allowing the company to build its own cabs, bodies, and sheet-metal parts. This facility allowed Chevrolet to offer half-ton pickup, panel, and the canopy models such as the one pictured. Its powertrain consisted of the new six-cylinder OHV engine and a three-speed transmission. All 1931 trucks were Independence models, the same as all Chevrolet autos. The Commercial chassis gained 2 inches in wheelbase length, to 109 inches, the same as all autos. *Jim Benjaminson*

Chevrolet's half-ton Commercials shared front sheet-metal styling with 1931 autos. In fact, the Commercial's front sheet metal, chassis, and drivetrain were exactly the same as Chevrolet's autos. This is a front view of the 1931 Commercial canopy. *Jim Benjaminson*

After lab tests were completed, the device was installed on a car or truck and then sent to the GM Proving Ground. The GM Proving Ground comprised 1,125 acres of hills and valleys and every conceivable kind of road condition. Chevrolet vehicles were tested here day and night, in winter and summer. It was here that Chevrolet engineers could study the performance of their designs under extreme road and weather conditions.

The entire Chevrolet line of cars, Commercials, and trucks for 1931 carried the Independence name. The Series AE included passenger cars and Commercials, and the series LT and M were trucks.

The only engine offered across the entire Chevrolet line was the 50-horsepower, six-cylinder, valve-in-head 194-ci six.

The factory supplied bodies for Commercial models only. All 1 1/2-ton trucks were offered as chassis and closed cabs only.

Due to the Depression, Chevrolet truck sales fell for the second year in a row to a total of 105,497 units compared to 132,229 in 1930.

Chevrolet's 1931 1 1/2-ton truck series was named Independence, as were Commercial trucks. Late in 1930 a second wheelbase length, 157 inches, was added to the original 131-inch length. Also late in 1930 dual-rear option became available. Pictured is a 1931 Utility 1 1/2-ton 157-inch wheelbase, Series LT with single steel disc wheels, closed cab, with two fenders, and a spare wheel with platform body. Its drivetrain consisted of the new six-cylinder engine and four-speed transmission.

Chevrolet built many finely styled pickups over the years, but have you ever seen a better one than this 1931 Chevrolet Roadster Pickup? For the first time in 1931 Chevrolet was able to offer exterior paint colors. Prior to 1929 all Chevrolet trucks were painted black. The 1929 and 1930 models were painted "Blue Bell" blue. This Roadster was painted blue with black fenders and running boards with yellow spoke wheels. *David Russell*

From the beginning of Chevrolet truck production and continuing until today, there has been a tradition of fire trucks built on Chevrolet chassis. This 1931 Chevrolet 157-inch-wheelbase single rear-wheel chassis cowl open cab fire truck belonged to the Eagle Lake Lumber Co. of Susanville, California. It had a 100-gallon water tank and a 50 gpm pump. *Bill Hattersley*

1932

The 1932 Chevrolet Commercial line included three distinct types of vehicles: the Light Delivery, the 131-inch-wheelbase truck, and the 157-inch-wheelbase truck. The Light Delivery was rated as a 1/2-ton vehicle. It was built strictly for light duty on a modified passenger car frame with the fuel tank located under the driver seat. Its axles, clutch, steering mechanism, wheels, and transmission were passenger car units. The transmission was the silent synchro-mesh type, but not with free-wheeling. The engine, however, was the same as that used in the heavier trucks. The light commercial truck's radiator shell, fenders, and other related parts had the same appearance as those of the larger trucks.

The 1 1/2-ton 131-inch-wheelbase truck was offered with either single or dual rear wheels. It had a 6-inch deep frame, a four-speed transmission, a 10-inch clutch, and heavy-duty front and rear axles. It had an allowable GVW rating of 7,800 pounds with single rear wheels and 8,200 pounds with dual rears.

The 1 1/2-ton 157-inch-wheelbase truck had the same payload capacity as the shorter truck and used the same major components except that its frame was longer, heavier, and stronger. It was also available with either single or dual rear wheels. This truck was intended to carry bulky loads that required more body capacity.

Chevrolet engineers introduced 95 new features in the 1932 Light Delivery models and 110 new features in the 1932 truck models. A number of the new features were common to Light Deliveries and trucks. A discussion of the most important of the new features follows.

Engineers changed engine mountings from the solid type to front spring cushioned mounting on the truck engine. On the Light Delivery engine, they changed to a front spring cushion and rear rubber cushion mount.

GVW ratings of dual rear wheel trucks increased by redesigning both front and rear springs with thicker leaves, which increased load-carrying capacities front and rear.

The strength of the truck's rear axle increased by 25 percent by changing to a thicker axle housing; its thickness was now 1/4 inch.

For the first time since the company introduced its first OHV six-cylinder engine in 1929, Chevrolet truck engineers improved the engine to make it even better suited for Truck and Light Delivery service. The engine retained the same bore and stroke, but improvements in design allowed it to develop greater horsepower. Peak horsepower of 53 was reached at 2,800 rpms. Maximum torque increased to 131 foot-pounds at 800 rpms from the former 124 foot-pounds. Increased power resulted in better acceleration, as well as improved high-speed performance and the ability to deliver sufficient torque for exceptional pulling power at low speeds.

Jim Benjaminson's fully restored 1932 BB half-ton pickup is outstanding. It stands out with its bright red body, black fenders, running boards, cab roof, and radiator shell, and yellow spoke wheels. Note its driver side outside rear-view mirror, which was a new standard item in 1930, the same year vacuum windshield wipers replaced the hand-operated type. Chevrolet offered an open and a closed cab pickup in 1932. At $440 retail, the closed cab pickup sold for $10 more than the open cab. *Jim Benjaminson*

All Chevrolet car and truck lines were renamed Confederate for 1932. Passenger cars were Series BA, Light Commercials Series BB and Utility 1 1/2-tonners Series N. This is a 1932 Chevrolet Series BB Confederate half-ton pickup. The silent synchromesh three-speed transmission was new in 1932 on half-ton models. The six-cylinder OHV engine's horsepower was raised from 50 to 53 in 1932. Wheelbase continued at 109 inches. *Dale Larrivy*

In addition to the two pickup models, Chevrolet cataloged two closed half-ton Commercials in 1932: the Sedan Delivery and the Panel. All models rode on a 109-inch wheelbase and featured a drivetrain consisting of the 53-horsepower six-cylinder OHV engine and three-speed transmission. At $585 retail the Panel sold for $10 more than the Sedan Delivery. *AAMA*

Chevrolet's biggest 1932 truck was the Confederate Utility 1 1/2-ton dual-rear wheel 157-inch-wheelbase chassis cab pictured with dump body. The front bumper was standard equipment. Its drivetrain included the 53 horsepower six-cylinder OHV engine and a four-speed transmission. Four-wheel brakes were standard equipment. Without the body this truck retailed for $670.

Chevrolet purchased the former Martin-Parry Co. of Indianapolis, Indiana, late in 1930. Martin-Parry Co. was an independent truck bodybuilder, and it produced many of the truck bodies that were mounted on Chevrolet truck chassis. Chevrolet was now able to offer truck buyers bodies of the same high quality as the chassis on which they were mounted. The company carefully controlled body design and manufacturing to ensure perfect balance of chassis strength and rigidity with body strength and load distribution. Chevrolet designed the Commercial bodies to be used in conjunction with the cabs that were built at the Chevrolet assembly plants. Cabs and bodies harmonized in appearance. For 1932, Chevrolet supplied 21 body types and sizes for the three Commercial chassis; 4 for the 109-inch-wheelbase Light Delivery; 11 for the 131-inch-wheelbase 1 1/2-ton chassis, and 6 for the 157-inch 1 1/2-ton truck chassis.

This was by far the toughest year for the auto industry during the Great Depression. Despite the added improvements of an already great truck, Chevrolet's total truck sales dipped below 100,000 units for the first time since 1926, to 61,331 units.

Chevrolet named all 1932 cars and trucks the Confederate models. Passenger cars were the Series BA. Commercials were Series BB, while trucks were Series N.

1933

The 1933 Chevrolet Commercial line, as in the three previous years, included three distinct types of vehicles: the 109-inch-wheelbase Light Delivery, the 131-inch-wheelbase truck, and the 157-inch-wheelbase truck. The Light Delivery was rated as a 1/2-ton vehicle. It was strongly recommended for light-duty work only, and was built on a modified 1932 passenger car chassis. Its axles, clutch, steering mechanism, and wheels were passenger car units.

The engine, however, was the same as that used in the heavier trucks. Its syncro-mesh transmission was also the same as that used in the passenger cars, but without free-wheeling. Available for the first time as an option was the four-speed transmission from the 1 1/2-ton trucks. This was the last year that the Sedan Delivery was part of the 1/2-ton Light Delivery line. The 1/2-ton Light Delivery Roadster pickup was discontinued.

The 1933 Chevrolet passenger car models were renamed Series CA Masters. Half-ton trucks were Series CB Master Commercial models. It's interesting to note that the half-tons retained their former 109-inch wheelbase, while autos increased to 110-inch wheelbases. Light-duty body models included the Sedan Delivery, Panel, and closed cab pickup that is pictured. The six-cylinder OHV engine's size was increased to 206.8-ci and 56 horsepower by increasing its stroke to 4 from 3 3/4 inches. *David Russell*

The 1933 Chevrolet chassis with closed cab and pickup body sold for only $440 retail. Chevrolet produced its one millionth commercial truck in 1933 and ended the year with total sales of 1,044,123 units. The closed cab pickup's powertrain consisted of the new, larger 206.8-ci OHV six-cylinder engine mated to a three-speed synchro transmission. *David Russell*

The truck line received a fresh new look for 1933. This new design consisted of fitting last year's passenger car front end to the trucks, the 1/2-ton and both 1 1/2-ton models. However, the hoods differed from the 1932 cars in that they had louvers for cooling, rather than the more expensive hood ports. The radiator, grille, and headlamps were painted black.

Chevrolet engineers introduced 136 new features on the 1933 Light Delivery. Most were minor in nature, and many were also common to Chevrolet passenger cars. For safety, front and rear brakes were larger with wider and longer linings. The clutch and transmission were beefed up to accommodate the new engine's increased horsepower and torque outputs.

Probably the most significant new feature for 1933 was the improved engine. For the second year, the engine was a special truck engine. Although it was the same size as the passenger car's engine, the truck engine was built specifically for truck use. The engine's stroke was lengthened to 4 inches from 3 3/4 inches, increasing the cubic-inch displacement from 194 to 207. Maximum horsepower increased from 53 to 56, and torque increased from 131 foot-pounds to 146 foot-pounds.

The Chevrolet truck enjoyed a 69 percent rebound in sales, topping off at 103,584 trucks sold. Another 1933 milestone for Chevrolet was the production of its one-millionth truck. Chevrolet ended the year with total truck sales to date of 1,044,123 units.

The 1933 trucks were identified as follows: Series CB Master Commercial Models (1/2-ton) and Master Utility 1 1/2-ton Truck Chassis. These were further broken down to OA and OB for 131-inch-wheelbase models with single or dual rear wheels, respectively, and Series OC and overdrive for the 157-inch-wheelbase models with single or dual rear wheels, respectively.

Chevrolet's 1933 Master Utility 1 1/2-ton truck line consisted of chassis cowl and chassis cab models only, on two wheelbase lengths and with single or dual rear wheels. This is a 1933 Chevrolet Series OD 157-inch-wheelbase dual-rear wheel chassis cab with farm body. Without the body this truck sold at retail for only $625. Its drivetrain consisted of the new 206.8-ci OHV six-cylinder engine and four-speed transmission. *Jan's Motor Service*

This is a 1933 Chevrolet Master Utility chassis with closed cab and a Wide Express body built by its owner, James R. Duclon, of Hales Corners, Wisconsin. Without body this road-ready truck weighed 3,540 pounds. Its drivetrain consists of the new 56-horsepower 206.8-ci OHV six-cylinder engine and a four-speed transmission. *Jim Duclon*

Chevrolet's 109-inch-wheelbase Series CB Master Commercial Models included the half-ton Canopy Express truck like the Strevel's Market truck pictured. Its load space was 72 1/2 inches long, 45 inches wide, and 48 inches high. The height to the top of steel flare boards was 18 1/4 inches. Side and rear curtains were standard equipment. This truck was available with chrome-plated radiator shell, headlights, and tie-bar at small extra cost. Side and rear screens were also optional at extra cost. Power was from the standard Chevrolet 56-horsepower six-cylinder engine mated to a three-speed transmission. *R. Strevel*

1934

The 1934 trucks made the most important step forward since Chevrolet began building trucks. In 1918 when Chevrolet introduced its first trucks, they were light-duty vehicles and had the same front appearance as the passenger cars of the period. Through the years, the truck line expanded in type and capacity, so that passenger car parts began to look out of place on the trucks. Chevrolet corrected this situation in 1934 with styling designed specifically for the trucks. No longer would parts interchange between cars and trucks.

There was one design for both light- and heavy-duty trucks. The entire line displayed a sturdier, more trucklike appearance. The cab, too, was entirely new, larger, and more comfortable. The redesign of the chassis resulted in greater carrying capacities.

Chevrolet's basic truck lineup remained the same as it had been since 1931: the 1/2-ton Delivery truck and the two 1 1/2-ton models on 131- and 157-inch wheelbases. The 1/2-ton, unlike its predecessors, was built on a special frame that was entirely different from, and much heavier and stronger than, the passenger car frame. It had a GVW of 4,400 pounds and a wheelbase of 112 inches. From this point forward all Chevrolet light-duty trucks would be truck-built, not auto-based, except for Sedan Deliveries. The 1934 Sedan Delivery was a modified Series DA Master passenger car. It sold for only $620.

Counting the improvements in bodies, Chevrolet engineers designed 169 new features into the 1934 1 1/2-ton trucks and 179 new features into the 1934 1/2-ton trucks. The most significant features follow.

Starting with the 1 1/2-ton trucks, both models received entirely new frames. They sat higher from the ground, providing more ground clearance—although the body load heights from the ground did not change. The engine was located 3 inches farther forward in the frame, adding 1 3/4 inches to the load space. In both trucks, the kickup over the rear axle was eliminated, providing a continuous flat surface to facilitate body mounting.

I'll bet many enthusiasts share the belief that Chevrolet engineers became involved in developing racing engines in the 1950s and 1960s. Not so. Major improvements in Chevrolet's cylinder head for 1934 came as a direct result of Chevrolet's involvement with racing. Three years prior to this, Chevrolet engineering was asked to design an exceptionally high-powered race-type engine with a very small piston displacement. This demanded valves of larger diameter than could be placed in the available space in a conventional manner. The design the engineers developed paved the way for the 1934 Chevrolet marine head.

Chevrolet's new 1934 light-duty trucks were designated Series DB Master Commercial Models. Body models in the 1/2-ton Commercial Series included the Sedan Delivery (considered part of the passenger car line), pickup, pickup with canopy top, panel, and special panel. This is a 1934 Chevrolet Series DA Sedan Delivery. It rode on a 112-inch wheelbase. Its drivetrain consisted of the 206.8-ci 56-horsepower six-cylinder engine and a three-speed synchro transmission with floor-mounted shift lever. *Jim Benjaminson*

The pickup was everyone's favorite truck—from farmers, businessmen, and tradesmen, to governments and individuals. Chevrolet was on top of the pickup business in 1934 with the Series DB Master 1/2-ton. As pictured, it retailed for only $465 and featured the 206.8-ci six-cylinder engine mated to a three-speed synchro transmission, with a floor-mounted shift lever and four-wheel mechanical brakes as standard equipment. *AAMA*

Chevrolet's 1934 Master Utility 1 1/2-ton truck line consisted of a chassis cowl, chassis cab, 131-inch-wheelbase Panel, and single or dual rear-wheel Stake models. This is a 1934 Chevrolet PB 131-inch-wheelbase dual wheel chassis cab with a hand-crank dump body. It featured the 206.8-ci six-cylinder engine, four-speed transmission, and four-wheel mechanical brakes. Without the body, it sold for $640 with eight-ply tires front and rear. *Fred Widman*

Chevrolet engineers developed an entirely new head based on the lessons learned from their work on the marine engine. One lesson learned was the advantage of high volumetric efficiency, or the ability of the engine to efficiently admit a high volume of gases through the intake valves and expel the spent gases as efficiently through the exhaust valves. They also relocated the spark plugs high in the combustion chamber, very close to the exhaust valves. The plugs now entered at an angle rather than at right angles. This placed the plug in a position where it was always surrounded by a fresh explosive mixture the instant of ignition.

Without increasing the engine's bore or stroke, Chevrolet's redesigned OHV six produced four additional horsepower, bringing it up to 60, and high-end torque increased by 1.5 foot-pounds at 3,000 rpm.

Chevrolet's 1/2-ton 1934 trucks were the Series DB Master Commercial Models; 1 1/2-ton 131-inch-wheelbase trucks were the Master Utility Series PA single wheel; and Series PB was with dual wheels. Series PC and PD identified the 1 1/2-ton 157-inch-wheelbase single and dual rear wheel models, respectively.

The engineers' work paid off in 1934, when the company registered a 58 percent increase in truck sales for a total of 163,819, in an economy slowly recovering from the horrible Depression.

The 1934 Master Utility line was available on two wheelbases: 131 and 157 inches. Other than the Panel body, the only other medium-duty body models were the 9- and 12-foot stakes. This 1934 Chevrolet 157-inch dual-rear-wheel chassis had a closed cab with a 12-foot stake body. With eight-ply tires front and rear, this truck sold for $785 complete. *Arnold Paradis*

1935

Since Chevrolet trucks had been extensively restyled and reengineered for the 1934 model year, they carried over into 1935 without significant change. Chevrolet's entire truck line continued to consist of the 1/2-ton series and two 1 1/2-ton series on two wheelbase-length chassis. For 1935, Chevrolet dropped the term "Delivery," which had been used to describe Chevrolet's lightest truck model. Starting in 1935, the 1/2-ton model and the two 1 1/2-ton models (they differed only in wheelbase lengths, 131 and 157 inches) were referred to as "trucks." Beginning in 1934, the half-ton was built on a truck-type chassis as opposed to its prior slightly modified automobile chassis. A Sedan Delivery, which was a variant of the EC Series Standard passenger line, also continued.

Chevrolet engineers introduced 46 new features in the half-ton trucks and 75 new features in the 1 1/2-ton trucks, most of which were minor. The most important improvements for 1935 dealt with engines and brakes. The engine was now more powerful due to an improved head design and redesigned combustion chambers. Maximum horsepower increased to 68.5 from 60, and maximum gross torque increased to 150 foot-pounds from 146 foot-pounds.

Whenever Chevrolet engineers increased truck performance through additional horsepower and torque, they also improved the truck's ability to stop. Such was the case in 1935, too. They improved the 1/2-ton truck's brakes by changing the brake lining material to one with a higher coefficient of friction, to provide more efficient braking with less pedal pressure. Both front and rear brakes on the 1 1/2-ton trucks were larger in diameter, with thicker and wider linings having a higher friction coefficient. Total lining area increased to 348.6 square inches, an increase of 30 percent.

Late in the model year, the Suburban Carryall body, or Station Wagon, was added to the line of 1/2-ton trucks. This model was the only completely enclosed steel-bodied station wagon built at that time. It was designed to be a dual-purpose vehicle for carrying passengers or for hauling loads of merchandise.

Four seats provided seating for eight passengers. Seat one was for the driver and a passenger. To its right was a small folding seat

that permitted entrance for passengers to the rear seats. The second seat accommodated two and the third seated three.

Chevrolet's Master Commercial 1/2-ton models were designated the EB Series. The 1 1/2-ton Master Utility models were known as the QA, QB, QC, and QD Series for 131-inch-wheelbase models with single rear or dual rear wheels, and the 157-inch-wheelbase models with single rear and dual rear wheels, respectively.

Chevrolet posted only a 7 percent gain in truck sales for 1935 over 1934, with total sales of 175,218.

Chevrolet's 1935 car lines were designated Series EA, ED, and EC Master models. The EA and ED Series rode on a new 113-inch wheelbase, 1 inch longer than 1934's autos. The 1/2-ton Series EB Master Commercial models included a chassis cowl, chassis cab, Pickup, Pickup with canopy top, special Pickup, Panel, Canopy, and special Panel. A Sedan Delivery such as the one pictured was part of the EC standard passenger automobile line. This little delivery rode on a 107-inch-wheelbase chassis.

Chevrolet's Master Utility line for 1935 offered the following body types: Panel, Canopy, 9-foot and 12-foot Stakes, and Pickup. The two wheelbase lengths from 1934 carried over: 131 and 157 inches with either single or dual rear wheels. This is a 1935 Chevrolet 157-inch-wheelbase chassis cowl with fire-fighting body. This pumper belonged to the Beaverton (Oregon) Fire Department. It featured a 500-gallon water tank and a 100-gpm pump. Its drivetrain consisted of the 70-horsepower six-cylinder engine and a four-speed transmission. *Chuck Madderom*

This 1935 Chevrolet Series QD 157-inch-wheelbase chassis with closed cab and 12-foot stake body and dual rears was the biggest truck offered in 1935. It was rated for a maximum GVW of 9,300 pounds. Maximum payload rating was 7,600 pounds. Its drive-train consisted of the 68.5-horsepower 206.8-ci six-cylinder OHV six and the four-speed transmission. With maximum tire equipment, this truck sold for $860. *AAMA*

1936

Chevrolet's 1936 1/2-ton trucks were designated Series FB Master Commercial Models. They rode on a 112-inch-wheelbase chassis, 1 inch less than Chevrolet's Master automobile line. Sometime after the launch of the 1936 trucks, several important changes were made. Both 1/2- and 1 1/2-ton lines received a new modern-style cab. Next, a new commercial called the Coupe Pickup (a standard coupe with a slide-in pickup box) was added to the FC Standard passenger car line. Lastly, the 1 1/2-ton trucks were given full hydraulic brakes. This is a 1935 first series FB 1/2-ton pickup with the "high" cab. *Jim Benjaminson*

Chevrolet began the 1936 model year with trucks only slightly changed from the previous year's models. In midyear the company introduced a second 1936 series with significant changes.

The truck line continued as in the past with a 1/2-ton series and a 1 1/2-ton series on two wheelbase lengths—131 and 157 inches. A Sedan Delivery, which was actually a part of the Series FC Standard passenger car line, was also included in the 1936 truck line. An interesting new "truck" for 1936 and part of the Series FC Standard car line was the Standard Coupe Pickup. It consisted of a pickup box mounted in the rear of the regular 1936 Standard Coupe. It combined utility with passenger car comfort and appearance.

Maximum engine horsepower for all trucks increased from 68.5 to 72 and maximum torque increased from 150 to 155 foot-pounds due to an increase in the compression ratio from 5.6 to 1 to 6.0 to 1. Chevrolet's famous OHV six-cylinder 207-ci engine was unchanged in 1936's second series trucks.

A new chrome-plated, spring steel bumper improved the appearance of the 1 1/2-ton trucks. The former front bumper now acted as a brace for the bumper bars and was redesigned to conform to the new bumper's shape.

The instrument panel on both truck series was entirely new and improved in appearance. The instruments were relocated in a raised portion of the main panel, in front of the driver. Controls were grouped at the center of the main panel, while a glovebox was provided at the right. Instruments consisted of a speedometer at the center, fuel and water temperature gauges combined in one instrument at the left, and the combined ammeter and oil pressure gauge at the right.

Both 1 1/2-ton trucks received a full floating rear axle in 1936. Full floating means that the axle housing carried the truck's entire weight, freeing the shafts simply to turn the rear wheels. The entirely redesigned rear axle was 35 percent stiffer than before.

Second series 1 1/2-ton trucks changed over to all-hydraulic brakes. The emergency brake system continued to be of the mechanical type, working on the rear wheels only through a system of pull rods and cables.

Model designation letters for 1/2-ton trucks were FB. Half-ton body types included a pickup, panel, canopy express (Chevrolet's official term was "single unit express"), and Suburban Carryall.

Serial number plates for all trucks were located on the right-hand side of the dash. Engine serial numbers were stamped on a pad on the right side of the engine, just to the rear of the fuel pump.

The model designation letters for 1 1/2-ton trucks were RA for 131-inch with single rear wheel, RB for 131-inch with dual rear wheels, RC for 157-inch with single rear wheels, and RD for 157-inch with dual rear wheels.

Body types for 131-inch-wheelbase trucks included a panel, stake, canopy express, and pickup. Body types for 157-inch-wheelbase trucks included a stake, platform, and stock rack.

It was a great year for Chevrolet truck sales. The company posted a 22 percent gain over 1935, and sales totaled 213,151.

The new second series cab gave the driver greater comfort and driving ease. Chevrolet called it a coupe-type cab because it was so modern and streamlined. The new cab's height was only 50 11/16 inches compared to 53 3/4 inches for the early cab. Its drivetrain consisted of the 206.8-ci 72-horsepower OHV six-cylinder engine and three-speed synchro transmission. The 72-horsepower engine produced 155 foot-pounds maximum torque at 900 to 1,500 rpm.

This is a rather rare and unusual 1936 Chevrolet 1 1/2-ton Master Utility Series RB 131-inch-wheelbase dual-rear-wheel truck. It has the second series "coupe style" cab. The 206.8-ci 72-horsepower OHV six-cylinder engine powered all 1 1/2-ton trucks. Its transmission was the Chevrolet-built four-speed.

Chevrolet fire trucks were highly favored again in 1936. Pictured is a 1 1/2-ton Series RD 157-inch-wheelbase, dual-rear-wheel chassis, windshield cowl with fire-fighting body. The Roslyn (Washington) Rural Fire Department owned this open cab truck. Its pumper body featured a 350-gallon tank and a 200-gpm pump. *Bill Hattersley*

Chevrolet's 131-inch-wheelbase dual-rear-wheel Series RB chassis with windshield cowl and fire-fighting body. The Grants Pass (Oregon) Fire Department owned this open cab truck. Its pumper body was by Seagrave, and it featured a 500-gallon water tank and a 200-gpm pump. Drivetrains on both fire trucks consisted of the 206.8-ci 72-horsepower six-cylinder and the Chevrolet-built four-speed transmission. *Chuck Madderom*

How about wide white sidewalls on a 1 1/2-ton truck? They actually look pretty good on this 1936 Chevrolet. The fuel tank on Chevrolet 1/2-ton trucks was located at the rear of the frame. The tank on 1 1/2-ton trucks was located under the cab seat. It was filled through a neck extending through the wall of the seat riser. The right side door had to be opened to access the filler neck. All 1 1/2-ton Chevrolet trucks were powered by the 206.8-ci OHV six-cylinder engine and equipped with the Chevrolet-built four-speed transmission. *Leo Stokesberry*

Farmers in 1936 loved the hard working 1 1/2-ton Chevrolet chassis cab with dual rears with a farm body such as the one pictured. New for the 72-horsepower 206.8-ci six-cylinder engine was a 1 1/4-inch Carter downdraft carburetor. The maximum GVW rating of the 1 1/2-ton with dual rears was 9,300 pounds. When equipped with 32x6-inch 10-ply tires and helper springs, the maximum GVW rating topped off at 11,300 pounds. Pete Koropatnicki of Walhalla, North Dakota, owns this truck. *Jim Benjaminson*

Chevrolet designers set out to create the finest appearing truck cab on the road. The new cab featured a single piece all-steel top, in those days referred to as a "turret top." Turret stood for strength and safety. The only wood in the new cab was at the hardwood hinge pillars and a bar across the cowl. All cab interior trim, including the instrument panel, was painted steel with a brown crackled finish. The seat and seatback were upholstered in brown imitation leather. The headliner was made of pressed board painted brown. This is a 1936 Chevrolet 1 1/2-ton Series RB 131-inch-wheelbase dual-wheel chassis cab with platform body.

1937

This was a very important year for Chevrolet's truck program, since there were more improvements and important new models introduced than any other year since 1918.

The backbone of any truck is its engine, since it supplies the power to move the load. Chevrolet's engine took a giant stride in 1937 with the introduction of a new, bigger, and more powerful engine. The new engine was the familiar OHV "stove bolt" six, but displacement grew to 216.5 ci, compression ratio increased to 6.25:1, and horsepower reached 85 at 3,200 rpm.

Chevrolet added two new models to its truck line late in the model year. These new 3/4- and 1-ton trucks precisely filled the gap between the 1/2-ton and 1 1/2-ton trucks. They were built on a 122 1/4-inch wheelbase. Offerings included a chassis cowl, a chassis cab, a pickup, and platform and stake models. Payload ratings were 1,500 and 2,000 pounds, respectively.

The new larger 3.5x3.75 bore and stroke 78-horsepower 216.5-ci OHV engine powered the entire Chevrolet truck line. The clutch and its housing were identical to the 1 1/2-ton truck's transmission. The optional four-speed was identical to the new standard equipment three-speed unit introduced in the 1937 1/2-ton model. For ease of assembly, the three-speed and four-speed were exactly the same length and designed so that either could be installed easily in the drivetrain.

Bodies were available in three types: pickup, stake, and platform. Each was designed to provide for maximum size loads. Inside dimensions of the pickup box measured 87 inches long by 45 3/4 inches wide. Cubic capacity was 32.2 cubic feet, an increase of 13 percent over the 1/2-ton pickup. The stake body was new and sturdy in construction. Its load space was 88 inches long, 32 inches high, and 72 inches wide.

The Master Sedan Delivery and Coupe Pickup, Series GB, rode on a 112 1/4-inch-wheelbase chassis. The front axle was an I-beam, and the rear-axle ratio was 4.11 to 1. The 1/2-ton Commercial Truck series, 112-inch-wheelbase chassis, continued as before except with the new truck styling and a larger engine. The 1 1/2-ton trucks, Series SA, SB, SC, and SD, continued as before except for new styling and the new engine. The four series designated the 131 1/2-inch-wheelbase chassis with single and dual rears, and the 157-inch models with single and dual rears.

Yet in spite of new models, a more powerful engine, and an attractive new design, Chevrolet's truck sales slipped by 14 percent to 184,077.

The new Chevrolet 1937 1/2-ton pickup, like the AAA truck pictured, was powered by an OHV six-cylinder engine, now enlarged to a full 216.5 ci. The new engine produced 78 brake horsepower and 170 foot-pounds torque at 850 to 1,550 rpm. This "Economy Model" pickup made an Around-the-Nation Run in a 10,244.8-mile trip around the rim of the United States. It carried a 1,060-pound load and established a record: Its gasoline mileage averaged 20.74 miles per gallon and cost less than one cent per mile. The American Automobile Association certified the run. *AAMA*

Chevrolet's 1937 1/2-ton pickup rode on a 112-inch-wheelbase chassis. The new 216.5-ci OHV six-cylinder engine featured four main bearings instead of the previous three. The brilliance of the Chevrolet six was its ability to reach maximum torque output at low rpms and retain that output over a broad range of engine speeds. The 1937 Chevrolet trucks shared styling cues once again with Chevrolet autos, which can be seen most clearly in the grille and headlight designs. Series GC 1937 1/2-ton Commercial models consisted of a chassis, chassis cab, Pickup, Panel, Canopy, and Suburban. This 1/2-ton pickup sold for only $475. It has a non-original front bumper, wheels, and tires. *Elliott Kahn*

Chevrolet's 1937 light-duty delivery models included the Sedan Delivery and Coupe Pickup in the GB Master Series (automobile) line and the 1/2-ton Panel in the GC Series (truck) line. This is a 1937 Chevrolet 1/2-ton Panel. It was built on the 112-inch-wheelbase chassis and featured a drivetrain consisting of the new 216.5-ci OHV six-cylinder engine and the three-speed synchro transmission. It carried a maximum GVW rating of 4,400 pounds. The Panel's list price was $575.

Chevrolet engineers created the single unit (single as opposed to the pickup's separate cab and cargo box) 1/2-ton Canopy Express simply by modifying the 1/2-ton Panel body with side openings in the load area, and by removing the full-height rear panel doors. Its drivetrain, wheelbase, and GVW rating were the same as the 1/2-ton Panel. The Canopy Express' list price was $560. Only 1,206 Canopy Express trucks were produced in 1937. This truck still has its original engine and paint and is used as a daily workhorse. *Lou Mac Millan*

Another important addition to Chevrolet's truck line in 1937 was the GC Master 3/4-ton models consisting of a chassis, chassis cab, Pickup, and Stake on a 122 1/4-inch wheelbase. This 1937 Chevrolet 3/4-ton pickup was powered by the new 216.5-ci six-cylinder engine and was equipped with the optional four-speed Chevrolet-built four-speed transmission, standard 15-inch wheels with 7.00x15 tires, and a 4.11: 1 rear axle ratio. Its original list price was $565. Total production was 2,373. *Arnold Paradis*

The only other body model in the new GC Master Series 3/4-ton line was the Stake. This body was built by Chevrolet and mounted to the chassis at the factory. Its drivetrain consisted of the 216.5-ci six-cylinder engine and three-speed synchro transmission. Its list price in 1937 was $600. Total production was only 466. *AAMA*

In 1937, Chevrolet offered a number of special truck bodies like the 1937 1 1/2-ton ambulance pictured, towing a 1940 Wayne-bodied Chevrolet school bus. In the Master Utility 1 1/2-ton Series, Chevrolet offered both a single- rear-wheel chassis on a 131 1/2-inch and a 157-inch-wheelbase chassis. This truck's drivetrain consisted of the 216.5-ci OHV six-cylinder engine and the four-speed Chevrolet-built transmission. *Lou Mac Millan*

When this photo was taken in 1980, the 1937 Chevrolet Series SB 131 1/2-inch-wheelbase chassis cab with fifth wheel equipment was still in service, towing empty trailers. Its owner, Arnold Paradis (pictured), was selling, leasing, or buying the empty trailers. It routinely made the 1,400-mile round trip from Oregon to Los Angeles. The power came from a 216.5-ci OHV six-cylinder engine mated to a four-speed transmission. It was equipped with a non-original two-speed rear axle and air over hydraulic brakes to pull air brake trailers. *Arnold Paradis*

Chevrolet built a total of 97,053 1937 Series SD dual-rear-wheel, 157-inch-wheelbase trucks. The best-selling model at 52,189 units was the chassis cab. Only 5,072 stake trucks like the one pictured were built. Chevrolet built three stake models; the only difference was in their tire equipment. Their list prices ranged from $750 to $835. Their drivetrain included the 216.5-ci OHV six-cylinder engine with the four-speed transmission. *Dick Miller*

This 1937 Chevrolet Series SD 157-inch-wheelbase truck was still in good condition after nearly five years of hard use by Frank LaPlante Farms, Fisher, Minnesota. The truck had rolled up many miles hauling grain, sugar beets, timber products, livestock, and machinery during the hot summers of the late 1930s. A new 1941 Chevrolet Series YS can be seen to its right. This truck was used by LaPlantes for more than 45 years and had several hundred thousand miles on it when last used. Both trucks were Boatswain Blue with black fenders. Both had the 216-ci six-cylinder engine and four-speed transmission. *Bob Bilden*

Chevrolet's chassis cowl models continued to be a favorite with the nation's fire departments. The Series SD 157-inch-wheelbase chassis cowl with dual rears shown was owned by the Sultan (Washington) Fire Department. Howe supplied its open C-cab and body, and it featured a 500-gallon water tank and a 300-gpm pump. Its drivetrain consisted of the 216.5-ci six-cylinder engine and a four-speed Chevrolet-built transmission. *Bill Hattersley*

Chevrolet became a more serious competitor in the tractor-trailer business in 1937 when it introduced the new, powerful 216.5-ci OHV six-cylinder engine. Owners appreciated its output of 78 horsepower and 170 foot-pounds torque. This is a 1937 Chevrolet Series SB 131 1/2-inch-wheelbase dual-rear-wheel chassis cab with fifth wheel equipment and trailer. *Arnold Paradis*

1938

The new 1938 Chevrolet trucks carried over with minor modifications. A different grille design gave the vehicle a new look. Chevrolet once again offered four complete lines of trucks: the 1/2-ton, 3/4-ton, 1-ton, and 1 1/2-ton. The grille on 1938 trucks was composed of thin horizontal bars, as opposed to the vertical bars of the 1937 model.

The front and rear bumpers for 1/2-, 3/4-, and 1-ton trucks had the same appearance and shape as the 1938 passenger car bumpers. All front bumpers were made regular production

Chevrolet's lightest trucks in 1938 were the 112 1/4-inch-wheel-base Master passenger car-based Coupe Pickup and Sedan Delivery. The Series HC Master 1/2-ton 112-inch-wheelbase line consisted of a chassis cowl, chassis cab, Pickup (shown), Panel, Canopy, and Suburban. These trucks carried over as well, but with a revised grille design. The drivetrain continued to consist of the 216.5-ci six-cylinder engine and a three-speed synchro transmission. The list price for this pickup was $592. *Tom Batterson*

A Canopy Express was not available in 1938's 3/4- and 1-ton lines, but could be found in the single-rear-wheel 131 1/2-inch-wheelbase 1 1/2-ton Master Utility line. Its load space was 110 7/8 inches long, 56 3/4 inches wide, and 53 3/16 inches high. It was equipped with a steel, slam-type end-gate that latched automatically when closed. Screen sides were offered at extra cost. The Master Utility line's drivetrain consisted of the 216.5-ci OHV six-cylinder 78-horsepower engine and a four-speed transmission. The list price of the Canopy Express was $852. *AAMA*

equipment. The rear bumpers were also regular production equipment on all 1/2-, 3/4-, and 1-ton body types.

A new windshield wiper motor with knurled control knobs recessed flush with the inside surface of the windshield header for greater safety.

Redesigned seat cushions and backs offered greater durability and comfort. Seat upholstery material was rubberized to retain its original smoothness longer. The driver seat on all panel and canopy bodies was mounted on channels to easily adjust to the driver's needs.

The 3/4-, 1-ton, and 1 1/2-ton transmissions were made much stronger by carbonizing their gears.

An improved 18-gallon fuel tank was used on all 1938 chassis cabs. The tank was mounted directly on top of the frame under the driver seat. The filler neck on all cab types emerged from the end of the riser and extended outside the cab. Engineers also improved the gasoline tank sending unit on all fuel tanks.

Chevrolet's entire 1938 truck line consisted of the coupe pickup, Sedan Delivery; 1/2-ton panel, canopy, pickup, and Carryall Suburban; the 3/4- and 1-ton pickup, panel (new for 1938), and stake; the 1 1/2-ton panel, pickup, canopy, stock rack, stake, tractor with fifth wheel equipment, and 201-inch chassis for school bus, plus chassis cabs for all series.

Chevrolet marketed its first cab-over-engine (COE) trucks in 1938. The Montpelier Company converted the standard Chevrolet 1 1/2-ton trucks. Officially called Chevrolet-Montpelier units, they were offered on three wheelbases, 108, 131 1/2, and 157 inches. The advantages of a COE included extra hauling room, ease of handling in limited space, and conformity with dimension requirements in the laws of numerous states. All advantages resulted from the shorter cab length due to an extremely shortened hood.

Series designations for 1938 were as follows: Master 1/2-ton HC Series; Master 3/4-ton HD Series; Master 1-ton HE Series; Master Utility 1 1/2-ton, 131 1/2-inch wheelbase with single wheel Series TA; the same with dual wheels Series TB; Series TC and TD for 157-inch wheelbase with single or dual rear wheels, respectively.

This was the last tough business year of the Depression. Chevrolet truck sales plunged 32 percent to a total of only 124,852. In spite of that, the company retained its truck sales leadership position.

As roads improved and trucks became more powerful, tractor-trailer combinations continued to grow more popular with the nation's trucking industry. Chevrolet's Master Utility TB Series 131 1/2-inch-wheelbase 1 1/2-ton-chassis cab with auxiliary springs, pictured with fifth wheel equipment, was ideal for this work. Buyers appreciated its low $813 purchase price and more than adequate 78-horsepower 216.5-ci six-cylinder engine with 170 foot-pounds torque. *AAMA*

In 1938, Chevrolet partnered with the Thornton-Tandem Company of Detroit to provide a six-wheel-chassis cab (called a four-rear-wheel drive) directly through Chevrolet dealers. Chevrolet claimed its volume allowed the Chevrolet-Thornton trucks to be priced 35 to 40 percent lower than if the customer had had to have the conversion made on his own. The standard unit yielded a GVW of 26,000 pounds and the optional unit a 30,000-pound GVW. A big two-speed transfer case mounted between the two driving axles provided two driving gears: one for power and one for speed. A 1938 Chevrolet-Thornton tandem dump truck working off-road shown. Its engine was the standard Chevrolet 216.5-ci six-cylinder. *AAMA*

Chevrolet's 1938 Series TD 157-inch-wheelbase dual-rear-wheel chassis cowl was the right-sized truck for many of the nation's fire departments. The Castle Rock (Washington) Fire Department owned this open-cab Chevrolet tanker. It featured a 500-gallon water tank and a 250-gpm pump. Its drivetrain consisted of the 78 brake-horsepower 216.5-ci six-cylinder OHV engine; it was mated to the standard four-speed transmission. *Bill Hattersley*

This 1938 Chevrolet TD Master Utility 157-inch-wheelbase dual wheel 1 1/2-ton-chassis cab with stake body was similar to, but not the exact truck, with which Floyd Wild of Marshall, Minnesota, founded Floyd Wild Trucking with almost 60 years ago. His employees found and restored this truck to honor Floyd for his many years in the industry almost a decade ago (the company has the actual original unrestored truck). This red beauty looks and runs as good as new. *Juli Anne Sanders*

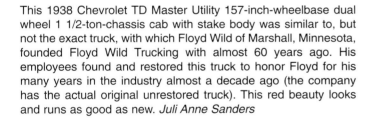

If you look closely, you'll discover that this 1938 Chevrolet fire truck has a custom cab. Notice that its windows are slightly lower than standard. It was owned by the Beekman Fire District of Poughquag, New York, Westchester County. Its body was by Seal and featured a 500-gallon water tank and a 150-gpm pump. A 78-horsepower 216.5-ci six-cylinder OHV engine powered it. *Neal A. Van Deusen*

In 1938, Chevrolet again built 1/2-, 3/4-, 1-, and 1 1/2-ton trucks. Shown here is the 1938 Series HC Master 1/2-ton pickup. Chevrolet sold this little 112-inch-wheelbase pickup for only $562 (Chevrolet called it a "Cab and Box"). The 78-horsepower 216.5-ci OHV six powered it. Standard transmission for 1/2-tons was a three-speed. Its owner continues to use it for daily transportation. *Milton Wright*

This cab-over-engine (COE) was announced in the spring of 1938 and was replaced in the 1939 model year by a Chevrolet-built COE. The Chevrolet-Montpelier COE was offered on three 1 1/2-ton chassis with wheelbase lengths of 108, 131 1/2, and 157 inches. Montpelier converted conventional 1 1/2-ton Chevrolet chassis in its factory. Chevrolet's six-cylinder engine, four-speed transmission, brakes, rear axle, and cab were retained. Tilting the hood forward provided access for servicing and maintenance. *AAMA*

1939

Chevrolet truck division managers saw truck transportation becoming more highly specialized every day. It was evident that different lines of business required specialized trucks that were specifically designed and engineered to meet the demands made upon them.

Chevrolet's many truck lines ranged in rated capacities from 1/2 ton to 1 1/2 tons and in GVWs from 4,400 pounds up to 13,500 pounds. With the many combinations of special equipment, Chevrolet was able to meet almost every conceivable demand of the truck transportation industry.

The 1 1/2-ton trucks were considered to be heavy-duty rigs, and they were, as far as Chevrolet's line was concerned. But these were not heavy-duty rigs compared to other manufacturers' offerings. Chevrolet concentrated on the light- and medium-duty truck business because these were the high-volume truck segments. Heavy-duty truck building was a specialized business, in which every truck was custom built to a customer's requirements.

The appearance of Chevrolet trucks in 1939 would lead one at first to believe they carried over from past years, but in reality the changes were considerable. The general shape and style of the 1939 grille retained the 1938 look, but the cab was all new. The grille was more massive due to far fewer, but wider, horizontal chrome-plated bars. The Chevrolet name was painted in script letters on the grille's wide topmost bar.

The new cab was larger, roomier, and more comfortable. Driver comfort, in fact, was the primary thought in designing the new line. Overall, the cab was 1 1/2 inches longer, 1 1/4 inches wider, and 1 5/16 inches higher. The cab lines were made more attractive, and a single plain convex molding encircled the cab. The most pronounced exterior cab appearance change was the new slanting "V"-type windshield. It was hinged at the top and was fitted with a strap-type crank at the bottom to open for ventilation. Door windows and the rear window increased in size. The new cab had 188 square inches more glass.

A new two-speed rear axle was available as an option on all Chevrolet heavy-duty trucks. Gear ratios were 5.64 and 8.22.

All trucks had a 1 1/2-inch-longer wheelbase in 1939. The wheelbase increased to 113 1/2 inches for 1/2-tons, 123 3/4 inches for 3/4- and 1-tonners, and 133 and 158 1/2 inches for 1 1/2-ton trucks.

In an effort to expand its truck models for a rapidly growing market, Chevrolet introduced a line of heavy-duty COE trucks for 1939. These trucks were designed, engineered, and manufactured in-house; Chevrolet no longer sold the Montpelier conversion. COE models were manufactured in three wheelbase lengths of 107 5/8, 131 1/8, and 156 5/8 inches. Stake and platform trucks were available in each wheelbase. The engine in the COE was the same 216-ci valve-in-head six that was used in all Chevrolet trucks. This engine was equipped with an updraft carburetor that held maximum horsepower to 78 in comparison to 90 for the engine with a downdraft carburetor. The COE was rated at 1 1/2 tons capacity and for a GVW of 11,500 pounds. The GVW increased to 14,000 pounds when equipped with a two-speed rear axle and the bigger authorized tires. It also had the optional vacuum power brake equipment at extra cost, as with all other 1939 heavy-duty trucks. The Chevrolet COE truck gained 28 1/4 inches in load space over the conventional cab trucks.

Chevrolet in conjunction with the Asam Motor Company of Detroit offered 4WD conversions for all heavy-duty trucks including the COE. Asam supplied the transfer case, front axle (ratio of 6.166 to 1), front brakes, and all necessary brackets and shafts, plus the conversion labor.

Series designations for 1939 trucks were as follows: JC, JD, and JE for 1/2-, 3/4-, and 1-ton trucks, respectively; VA, VB, VC, and VD for 1 1/2-ton 133-inch and 158 1/2-inch trucks with single and dual rear wheels, respectively; VE, VF, VG, and BH for 107 5/8-inch and 131 1/8-inch COE trucks with single and dual rear wheels; VJ for 193 5/8-inch school bus chassis; and VM and VN for the 156 5/8-inch-wheelbase COE with single or dual rear wheels.

Chevrolet's truck sales recovered nicely for 1939, posting a 40 percent gain to 175,755.

This wonderful 1939 Chevrolet JC Master 1/2-ton Light Delivery pickup was built in Chevrolet's Buffalo, New York, plant. It spent its working life on a farm in upstate New York until the present owner, Charles J. Stivala of E. Meadow, New York, bought it in 1978, hauled it home, and completely restored it. It has the 216 six-cylinder engine, a three-speed on-the-floor transmission, and 6.00x16-inch tires. Its options include dual wipers, rearview mirrors, front and rear bumpers, deluxe heater, defroster fan with metal blades mounted on the steering column, fog lamps, oak sideboards, and dual taillights. *Charles J. Stivala*

In April of 1939, the Greek Purchasing Commission requested Britain's Export Credit Guarantee Department to guarantee payment for the purchase from GM Ltd. of 150 of the trucks pictured here for use by the Greek Army. The U.S.-built components were to be assembled at GM's plant in Alexandria, Greece. Britain's Export Credit Guarantee Department would not authorize the agreement because their guarantee could only cover equipment assembled in Great Britain or built from British parts. According to British records, it is not recorded whether the full order of 150 trucks was ever completed before the outbreak of the war or not. We know that at least these prototypes were completed. Nine photos like these exist in the Public Record Office at Kew in England. They are described as 1 1/2-ton 4x4s, even though one appears to be a 4x2 judging by its solid front axle. The rolls seen on the front fender are "sand mats" for desert operations. The trucks were left-hand drive. The assumption is that the drivetrain is genuine Chevrolet—the 78-horsepower OHV six-cylinder engine and four-speed transmission. One truck has a gasoline tank on the right side forward of the rear tire; the second truck's tank is under the passenger seat. *Robert P. Gunn*

Chevrolet's lightest trucks in 1939 were again the 112 1/4-inch-wheelbase Series JB Master 85 automobile-based Coupe Pickup, Sedan Delivery, and the wooden-bodied Station Wagon. The regular 1/2-ton 113 1/2-inch-wheelbase Series JC Master light delivery models included the chassis with cowl, chassis cab, Pickup, Panel, Canopy Express, and Suburban. This is a restored 1939 JC 1/2-ton pickup. Its retail price when new was $660.

Chevrolet's 1939 panel line consisted of 1/2-, 3/4-, and 1 1/2-ton models. There was also an auto-based Sedan Delivery. This is a 1939 Chevrolet Series JC 1/2-ton 113 1/2-inch-wheelbase Panel. It featured an all-steel body with a one-piece steel roof. The 1/2-ton Panel combined a large enclosed loading space with the speedy performance delivered by Chevrolet's new 216.5-ci six-cylinder engine. Its three-speed synchro transmission was quick and easy to shift. The 1/2-ton Panel's list price was $658. *AAMA*

The largest Panel in Chevrolet's 1939 truck line was the Master Utility Series VA 133-inch-wheelbase 1 1/2-ton. This heavy-duty truck featured the payload capacity of a 1 1/2-ton in its large cargo space. It had wide rear-opening panel-type doors, a one-piece steel roof, large 6.00x20 six-ply front tires, and 32x6 eight-ply rear tires. It featured a 216.5-ci six-cylinder OHV engine and a four-speed transmission. Its list price was $837. The only other body model in this series was the Canopy Express.

The entire 3/4-ton Series JD Master line consisted of a chassis cowl, chassis cab, Pickup, Panel, and the stake shown here. This series was built on a 123 3/4-inch-wheelbase chassis. Chevrolet built and installed the stake body in its own plants. This was Chevrolet's smallest stake; even so, it was built with the same quality materials and construction techniques as the large stake bodies. The 216.5-ci six-cylinder engine powered the 3/4-ton trucks. A three-speed transmission was standard and a four-speed was an option. The 3/4-ton stake's retail list price was $690. *AAMA*

Designed and built by Chevrolet, the heavy-duty COE was new in 1939. Chevrolet engineers gave it a special front end (axle, bearings, springs, steering, and brakes) to beef it up to carry more of the payload, as its short wheelbase moved the load's weight forward. With its expansion into a wide range of medium-duty models (3/4- and 1-tonners), Chevrolet engineers changed the nomenclature of its biggest trucks to Heavy-Duty Conventional and COE models. The COE was available in two wheelbase lengths: 107 5/8 (shown) and 131 1/8 inches. The COE's drivetrain was the same as all other Heavy-Duty models: a 216.5-ci six-cylinder engine, but with an updraft carburetor and a four-speed transmission. *AAMA*

The smallest of the new 1939 Heavy-Duty Conventional line was the single rear wheel, 133-inch-wheelbase chassis cab with special body. When equipped with standard 32x6 eight-ply tires it had a maximum GVW rating of 7,700 pounds. Its powertrain consisted of the 78-horsepower 216.5-ci (3 1/2-inch bore and 3 3/4-inch stroke) six-cylinder engine developing 170 foot-pounds torque at 850 to 1,550 rpm, and a four-speed transmission. *AAMA*

The largest model of the new 1939 Heavy-Duty Conventional line was the dual rear wheel, 158 1/2-inch-wheelbase Stake model. The Stake body was manufactured in the Chevrolet plant, mounted on the chassis, and shipped complete to the dealer. When equipped with standard tires—6.00x20 six-ply—this truck's maximum GVW rating was 9,500 pounds. Its drivetrain consisted of the 216.5-ci six-cylinder engine and the Chevrolet-built four-speed transmission with provision for power takeoff. *AAMA*

When photographed in June of 1998, this Heavy-Duty Conventional 1939 Chevrolet chassis cab was for sale. It was in quite good condition, considering its age, and it was a worthy candidate for restoring or for putting back to work. It was complete, rust-free (except for surface rust), and in running condition. It does have an aftermarket front bumper, which looks quite good and could probably pass for original by those not well versed in 1939 Chevrolet trucks. *Vintage Power Wagons*

Chapter 3

1940 TO 1949

1940

Appearance changes on 1940 Chevrolet trucks were few and minor. First was the larger nameplate at the top of the grille. It was practically the same design and color as that of 1939, except that it was deeper and took the place of the topmost grille bar. Second, because the new trucks were equipped with sealed-beam headlights, separate parking lamps—the same as the passenger cars had—were mounted on top of the front fenders. Third, 1/2- and 3/4-ton trucks had wider bumpers with the same face bar as that of the passenger cars. This bumper was used on both the front and rear of light trucks. And finally, the trucks were also equipped with larger and flatter passenger car hubcaps.

The most significant cab interior change was a new instrument cluster placed on a curved dashboard, identical to that of the passenger cars. It was set in a wide brown-colored frame.

The 1/2-ton pickup's body was entirely redesigned with an increase in size and strength. Widening the box by nearly 3 inches and lengthening it by 1 inch gained 2 cubic feet of capacity.

All glass on truck bodies was changed to the new safety plate glass that was also used on all passenger cars.

Chevrolet's 1940 model lineup changed only slightly from 1939. Series designations and models were as follows: Series KC 1/2-ton pickup, panel, Suburban, and canopy; New KP Dubl-Duti Package Delivery on the 1/2-ton chassis; Series KD 3/4-ton pickup, panel, platform, and stake; New Series KF 3/4-ton Special, 133-inch-wheelbase panel. Series WA was the 1-ton pickup, panel, canopy, platform, and stake. Series WA was the 1 1/2-ton 133-inch-wheelbase pickup, panel, canopy, platform, and stake. Series WB was the 1 1/2-ton 158 1/2-inch-wheelbase platform, stake, stock rack, and express stake. Series WC was the 193 5/8-inch-wheelbase 1 1/2-ton school bus chassis. Series WD was the 107 5/8-inch-wheelbase 1 1/2-ton COE platform and stake. Series WE was the 131 1/8-inch-wheelbase COE platform, stake, and stock rack. Series WF was the 156 5/8-inch-wheelbase COE chassis and cab only. Note: All series include chassis only and chassis and cab. The exception is Series KP Dubl-Duti, which had only this one body model.

Along with the above trucks, Chevrolet's total commercial offering included the automobile Series KB Master 85 sedan delivery, station wagon and coupe pickup, and Series KH Master Deluxe sedan delivery and coupe pickup. However, the sales of these five vehicles were counted with passenger cars.

Chevrolet had another banner year in 1940, with sales increasing 11 percent to 196,994 trucks.

Chevrolet's automobile-based commercial models for 1940 consisted of the Sedan Delivery, Coupe Pick-Up, and the wooden-bodied Station Wagon. The Coupe Pick-Up was built on the Master 85 passenger car chassis. It was available on the Master Deluxe chassis with Chevrolet's famous Knee-Action at a slight extra cost. The Coupe Pick-Up was the same as a Master 85 Business Coupe with a pickup box added. The rear deck lid was furnished so the owner could easily convert it from a commercial vehicle into a passenger coupe. This 1940 Sedan Delivery was built on the Master 85 and the Master Deluxe passenger car chassis. The Sedan Delivery's rear side windows were blanked out to serve as sign panels, a wide 34 1/4-inch left-hinged door was cut into the rear, and a 47-inch-wide by 71-inch-long cargo carrying platform was installed behind the seats. The load compartment's capacity was approximately 77 cubic feet.

Chevrolet offered three pickups in 1940: The Light-Delivery (1/2-ton), Three-quarter-ton and Heavy-Duty (1-ton). These 1940 Light-Duty pickups were painted the same light green, but one had black fenders and the second was painted one color all over. The cargo box on these light trucks was 78 inches long, 48 1/2 inches wide, and 14 inches high. It rode on a 113 1/2-inch wheelbase. The load floor was constructed of wood, and heavy steel skid strips protected the wood and made it easy to slide cargo in and out. Flare boards were flared out with rolled edges for extra strength. The tailgate (Chevrolet called it an "end gate") was embossed for strength and equipped with anti-rattle chains. The standard Light-Delivery transmission was the three-speed synchro-mesh unit. For 1940, it was improved with silent helical gears throughout, even in reverse. The only engine offered was the 216-ci six-cylinder. The GVWs for the Light-Delivery were either 4,400 or 4,600 pounds, depending on tires—either four-ply or six-ply, respectively. *Roy Carlson*

The heart of Chevrolet's 1940 truck line was its traditional strength—1/2-ton models. Chevrolet called these models its Light Delivery line. The line included a 1/2-ton pickup like the one pictured, a Carry-All Suburban, the Panel, and Canopy Express. The last three trucks were what Chevrolet engineers called "single-unit" trucks. This meant the cab was elongated and extended the entire length of the truck. The genius of these trucks is that they shared a common body. The Carry-All Suburban and Canopy were variants of the base model Panel. The Panel was the biggest-selling model of the three. The Canopy had been the biggest seller in years gone by, but by 1940 its sales had slipped considerably. The Carry-All Suburban was not yet a big seller, but it was profitable for Chevrolet to continue to build these slow-selling models because the Panel was a big seller. The pickup is an excellent example of a two-unit truck. *Barry Weeks*

Chevrolet built two Heavy-Duty truck series again for 1940: Conventional and COE trucks. Standard GVW ratings of the big trucks were limited to 12,000 pounds or 14,000 pounds when equipped with larger tires. This 1940 Chevrolet Conventional tractor was equipped with air-over-hydraulic brakes, the 216-ci six-cylinder engine, four-speed transmission, and two-speed rear axle. This truck continued to be in service up until the mid-sixties. It had just returned from delivering 20,000 pounds of newsprint. *Arnold Paradis*

Exterior appearance changes to the 1940 trucks included a new, larger nameplate at the top of the grille. This plate was practically the same design and color as those of 1939, except its height was increased so that it eliminated the uppermost grille bar. All 1940 trucks were equipped with the new sealed beam headlights and therefore were required to have separate parking lights. The new, streamlined parking lights were mounted on top of the front fenders. This is a 1940 Chevrolet heavy-duty open-cab fire truck. The Milton Freewater (Oregon) Fire Department owned this pumper truck. It was equipped with a 500-gallon water tank and a 500-gpm pump. Its drivetrain consisted of the 216-ci six, four-speed transmission and two-speed rear axle. *Bill Hattersley*

Chevrolet's COE models were now in their second year of production and had been very well received by truck operators. The COE models carried a maximum GVW rating of 12,000 pounds standard and 14,000 pounds with heavier tires. Its standard—and only—drivetrain, consisted of the 216-ci six with four-speed transmission. The two-speed rear axle was an available extra-cost option. The four-speed for heavy-duty trucks was also equipped with a provision for power takeoff. The COE series was offered on three wheelbase lengths: 107 5/8, 131 1/8, and 156 5/8 inches. This is a 1940 Chevrolet heavy-duty 156 5/8-inch-wheelbase COE chassis cab with an aftermarket stake body.

When this 1940 Chevrolet 156 5/8-inch-wheelbase COE platform was photographed in Indiana by the author in the early 1980s, it was in good original condition. Note the parking lights perched on top of the headlights. The red paint on the top grille bar spelling out *Chevrolet* has been lost over the years as well as its original long-arm right and left side rearview mirrors. The chrome-finished bumpers on Chevrolet heavy-duty trucks were standard equipment in 1940. The same 216-ci six-cylinder OHV engine powered all 1940 Chevrolet trucks. It was rated at 85 horsepower and 170 foot-pounds maximum torque.

Helping the war effort along in 1944 was this 1940 Series WB 1 1/2-ton Chevrolet truck, well loaded with pulpwood. Its front bumper is missing and the headlight shown is slightly askew, but otherwise it looks quite sound. The truck had the 158 1/2-inch-wheelbase chassis and heavy-duty aftermarket wheels on the rear. The hypoid ring gear/pinion design introduced with the 1940 models added strength and durability. This information was provided by Bob A. Bilden of Bagley, Minnesota, who later owned and operated the timberland where the 1940 is shown working. Bob began trucking timber in 1953. *Bob A. Bilden*

Chevrolet began producing 1 1/2-ton 4x4 military trucks in 1940, Series G-4100 models with the following bodies: Airfield Crash, Cargo, Cargo w/Winch, Cargo with long wheelbase, Crash, Dump, Dump w/Winch, Oil Service, Panel, and Telephone Maintenance. This is a former 1940 1 1/2-ton Chevrolet military 4x4 converted to a fire truck postwar. The Lomontville (New York) Fire Department owned it. *Neal A. Van Deusen*

Chevrolet's Dubl-Duti Package Delivery unit was new in 1940. Chevrolet engineers designed it as an economical and efficient unit for multiple-stop route work. For example, the driver could work comfortably in its tall cargo area without stooping as he worked his load. Full-height front doors and its low front floor allowed the driver to exit from either side. An exceptionally large windshield and glass side panels gave full vision. Its wheelbase was 113 1/2 inches and its load space was 112 inches at the floor; its width was 65 1/8 inches and its height was 68 inches. The Dubl-Duti's appearance was clean and modern. *AAMA*

Two exterior appearance changes in the 1940 line included the larger nameplate at the top of the grille and sealed beam headlights. The nameplate at the top of the grille was double the height of the previous year. Sealed beam headlights became the new industry standard in 1940. Chevrolet's biggest 1940 model was the Series WB 1 1/2-ton Heavy-Duty dual-rear-wheel-chassis cab with a 158 1/2-inch wheelbase like the one shown with a special body. Its powertrain consisted of the 216.5-ci six-cylinder engine and a four-speed transmission. *AAMA*

1941

Chevrolet engineers set out to create a more massive front appearance for its 1941 trucks. This was accomplished by completely redesigning the truck's entire front end. The hood, hood side louvers, fenders, bumpers, headlights, parking lights, and grille were all new. A 1 1/2-inch increase in wheelbase resulted in larger, more impressive trucks.

The hallmark of the new design was the exceptionally massive two-section grille. The lower grille with its 17 wide grille bars lent a wide, heavy, and massive look to the truck's front end.

The new hood didn't feature a hood ornament, like the trucks of 1940 did. The absence of the shiny hood ornament brought attention naturally to the bright grillwork. New hood louvers with stainless-steel moldings and decorated with a red enamel stripe extended the full length of the louver openings in the hood side panel.

Headlamps were completely new in appearance and location. Much longer and streamlined, they were mounted in shallow wells in the fenders so they blended with the fender lines. New parking

Chevrolet's passenger car–based commercial series for 1941 continued to consist of the four-door Special Deluxe Station Wagon, the Master Deluxe Coupe Pickup, and the Master Deluxe Sedan Delivery. These vehicles received the same restyling as Chevrolet's 1941 passenger cars. The station wagon was more completely transformed than the other two. Chevrolet's 1941 Light Delivery line (1/2-ton series) was built on a 115-inch-wheelbase chassis. All Chevrolet truck wheelbases, except for the two school bus chassis, were increased by 1 1/2 inches. The 1941 Light Delivery line consisted of the pickup, panel, canopy, Carryall Suburban, and chassis cab. This is a Light Delivery 6 1/2-foot pickup.

Chevrolet's 1941 3/4-Ton series consisted of a 125 1/4-inch-wheelbase Pickup, Panel, Stake, and Chassis Cab, and the 3/4-Ton Long Wheelbase Panel (and Canopy Express—134 1/2 inches). Pictured is a 1941 3/4-ton pickup. Its cargo box was 87 inches long by 48 1/2 inches wide and 16 1/4 inches deep. Chevrolet built a 125 1/4-inch heavy-duty version of this pickup as a 3/4-Ton Special. It differed in that it was equipped with 7.00x17 six-ply tires versus the others' 15-inch six-ply tires, and light eight-leaf rear springs versus their seven-leaf springs. All pickup cargo floors were constructed of wood with steel skid strips to facilitate loading and to prolong the life of the body. The maximum GVW rating for the 3/4-ton models was 5,200 pounds, the 3/4-Ton Special was rated at 5,800 pounds, and the 1-ton at 6,700 pounds. *AAMA*

Pictured is a 1941 Chevrolet 125 1/4-inch wheelbase, 3/4-ton stake. A 3/4-Ton Special version of this truck was also offered. Chevrolet supplied the stake body, which its designers had redesigned in 1940, on this truck. Notice the curved front corner of the stake body. The maximum GVW rating of a 3/4-ton was 5,200 pounds. A 3/4-Ton Special stake model was also available; its maximum GVW rating was 5,800 pounds, due to its bigger tires, 7.00x17 six-ply versus 15-inch six ply, and with one additional leaf in the rear springs. The 216-ci six-cylinder engine powered this truck. Engine improvements for 1941 increased its horsepower from 78 to 90 and the maximum torque from 168 foot-pounds to 174 foot-pounds. Its standard transmission was the three-speed. The standard rear-axle rating was 4.55 to 1. *Arnold Paradis*

lamps mounted on top of the headlamps had a more attractive and modern appearance.

Truck bumpers for 1941 no longer echoed those of the passenger cars. Instead they were massive in size, befitting a big truck. All trucks had the same bumper. However, the bumpers on heavy-duty models were thicker for greater protection.

The wheelbase lengths for 1941 trucks had an additional 1 1/2 inches solely for the comfort of the driver. The added length provided more legroom and allowed the seat-back cushion to recline to a more comfortable angle. The addition of cotton to the hair pad of the seat cushion and back added to driver comfort by providing a softer cushion. Also, the springs in the seatback were deeper and their contour was changed to fit the back more comfortably.

A new treadle accelerator replaced the button type used in 1940. An over-center type of cowl vent operating mechanism, similar to that of the passenger cars, was new on all conventional trucks. For 1941, Chevrolet engineers added six studs to the cab floor to provide a positive means of keeping the floor mat in place, preventing it from curling up.

Chevrolet engineers gave heavy-duty truck buyers a real treat with a new RPO engine. The RPO engine had a 3 9/16-inch bore and 3 5/16-inch stroke, giving a 235.5-ci displacement and a compression ratio of 6.62:1. The new engine was essentially the same as the regular one, except for new pistons, rings, and a different crankshaft. To reach the 6.62:1 compression ratio with the longer stroke, the height of the engine block was increased by 1/8 inch. The engine's weight increased only a few pounds. Except for its increased height, the new engine's overall dimensions were the same as that of the regular engine. Using the same exhaust system and engine mountings allowed complete interchangeability between the RPO and the regular engine. The RPO heavy-duty

radiator had to be used with the new engine. Stocking of spare parts was vastly simplified.

Chevrolet engineers did not overlook the regular engine. Its compression ratio increased to 6.5:1. Horsepower increased to 90 from 78, and maximum torque increased from 168 to 174 foot-pounds.

Series designations for 1941 Chevrolet trucks were as follows: Series AJ for the 1/2-ton Dubl-Duti Package Delivery, panel only;

Good design and a pleasing appearance had always been an extremely important consideration for Chevrolet's management because it believed a truck reflected on the owner and his business. The new front-end appearance of Chevrolet's 1941 trucks lifted their design superiority to a whole new level. This design, which remained unchanged through the 1946 model year and into 1947, is considered by many Chevrolet aficionados as the most memorable of all. Engine number 6-3, a 1941 Chevrolet heavy-duty chassis cab with fire-fighting body, was owned by the Castleton Fire Company of Castleton-on-Hudson (New York). Its pumper body was by Sanford and featured a 500-gallon water tank and 400-gpm pump. *Neal A. Van Deusen*

Chevrolet's 1941 Heavy-Duty Conventional line was short and simple. It consisted of two series on 134 1/2- or 160-inch-wheelbase chassis. The 134 1/2-inch chassis is the reason Chevrolet offered the longer Panel, Canopy Express, and Pickup models. Maximum GVWs topped off at 13,500 pounds or 14,000 pounds when equipped with the two-speed rear axle. In order to achieve these maximum GVWs, the truck had to have 6.50x20 six-ply tires in front, 7.50x20 eight-ply dual rears, heavy 10-leaf springs, and auxiliary springs. Chevrolet engineers released a new, more powerful optional engine for all 1941 Heavy-Duty trucks. The new engine had a 3 9/16-inch bore and 3 15/16-inch stroke for a displacement of 235.5 ci. This is a 1941 Chevrolet heavy-duty 160-inch-wheelbase chassis cab with Chevrolet-supplied stake body. *Jan's Motor Service*

The only factory-supplied bodies Chevrolet made available for the 160-inch-wheelbase chassis cabs were the stake and the high rack. The 160-inch heavy-duty-wheelbase chassis cab or chassis cowl, as in this case, accepted bodies up to 12 feet in length. This made them ideally suited for fire fighting. Special frame side-member reinforcing plates were standard equipment on all 160-inch-wheelbase models. The Des Moines (Washington) Fire Department owned this open cab truck. Its body was built by Sanford and featured a 500-gallon water tank and a 100-gpm pump. This truck had formerly been owned by the Corinth (New York) Fire Department. *Bill Hattersley*

This is a 1941 Chevrolet 160-inch-wheelbase chassis cab with fire-fighting equipment. The Port Townsend (Washington) Fire Department owned it. Engine No. 3 was a pumper with body by Cooper. It featured a 500-gallon water tank and a 200-gpm pump. With a two-speed rear axle, this truck carried a GVW rating of 14,000 pounds. The fire chief who ordered this truck equipped it with the new, powerful 235-ci six-cylinder engine. *Bill Hattersley*

Series AK for the 1/2-ton 115-inch-wheelbase pickup, panel, Suburban, and canopy; Series AL for the 3/4-ton 125 1/4-inch-wheelbase pickup, panel, platform, and stake; Series AN for the 3/4-ton Special Commercial wheelbase 134 1/2-inch panel only; Series YR for the 1 1/2-ton 134 1/2-inch-wheelbase pickup, panel, canopy, platform, and stake; Series YS for the 1 1/2-ton 160-inch-wheelbase platform, stake, stock rack, and pickup; Series YT for the 195 1/2-inch-wheelbase school bus chassis; Series YU for the 1 1/2-ton 109 1/2-inch COE platform and stake; Series YV for the 1 1/2-ton 132 5/8-inch-wheelbase COE platform and stake; and Series YW for the 1 1/2-ton 158 1/8-inch-wheelbase COE chassis and cab. Note all series except AJ, AN, and YT also included chassis and chassis cabs.

In addition to these truck series, Chevrolet included in its passenger car lines the following commercial vehicles: Master Deluxe Series AG, the Sedan Delivery, a coupe pickup, and Special Deluxe Series AH, a station wagon only.

With a sales increase of 34 percent over 1940, Chevrolet set a record in truck sales in 1941 at 196,994 units. Passenger car–based commercials were not included in this number.

Chevrolet's other Heavy-Duty truck line for 1941 was the COE Series. Three wheelbase lengths were offered—109 1/8, 132 5/8, and 158 1/8 inches. Like the conventional cab Heavy-Duty Series, the COE Heavy-Duty trucks carried a nominal 1 1/2-ton rating. GVWs of up to 13,500 pounds for a single-speed rear axle and 14,000 pounds for a two-speed rear axle were allowed. Required equipment for these top ratings included 7.00x20 eight-ply front tires, 8.25x20 10-ply dual rear tires, and heavy 10-leaf springs and auxiliary springs. The new, powerful 235-ci six cylinder engine was an option. The only available transmission was the four-speed. This is a 1941 Chevrolet 1 1/2-ton Heavy-Duty COE chassis cab with fire-fighting equipment. The Stanford Township (Illinois) Fire Department owned this truck. Its pumper body was built by Boyer and featured a 500-gallon water tank and 300-gpm pump. *Garry Kadzielawski*

This is a 1941 Chevrolet 1 1/2-ton, 158 1/8-inch-wheelbase COE chassis cab with platform body. The truck's front bumper is painted black and is nearly imperceptible in the photo. The stock bumper was chrome plated. The COE's hood was redesigned for 1941. The top was hinged at the rear, and the upper half of the grille could be easily opened for engine access. Both school bus models, the 160-inch-wheelbase conventional truck and the 158 1/8-inch-wheelbase COE truck, were equipped with fish plates as standard equipment. *David Russell*

Chevrolet offered two 1941 heavy-duty chassis cab models: 134 1/2- and 160-inch wheelbases. This is a 1941 134 1/2-inch-wheelbase heavy-duty chassis cab. The only body models available directly from the factory were the stake/platforms. All 1 1/2-ton trucks were powered by the same 216-ci OHV six-cylinder engine and the four-speed transmission with provision for power takeoff. *AAMA*

America's farming industry accounted for more sales of Chevrolet trucks than any other industry. Pictured is a 1941 Chevrolet heavy-duty conventional 160-inch-wheelbase 1 1/2-ton chassis cab with farm body. Its maximum GVW rating was 13,500 pounds when equipped with the required extra-cost equipment. Its drivetrain consisted of the 216-ci OHV six and the four-speed transmission with power takeoff. *AAMA*

1942

L ong before Pearl Harbor, Chevrolet plants built military trucks, parts for antiaircraft guns, shells, and Pratt & Whitney engines.

Civilian truck production ended in January 1942. It did not resume again until mid-July 1944, and then only on a controlled basis for high-priority civilian use.

Chevrolet trucks for 1942 continued with the same interior and exterior appearance as the 1941 models. The exception was that all truck grilles (besides the COE trucks) were painted instead of chrome plated. Trucks painted white, cream, yellow, or orange had their grilles painted to match. Trucks painted any other color, including black, had grilles painted Turret Gray. Headlight rims were also painted Turret Gray. Engineers made no mechanical improvements of any importance.

Chevrolet began referring to its larger RPO engine as the "Load Master" engine. The smaller engine was called the "Standard Engine." The Load Master could only be ordered in heavy-duty truck models.

For 1942, Chevrolet customers could personalize their new truck with two-tone color combinations at no extra cost. The buyer could specify any two colors from the standard Chevrolet truck color palette. Sedan delivery and coupe pickups were only available in standard passenger car colors. The Dubl-Duti forward-control delivery was only offered in prime.

Chevrolet's model lineup, including bodies, continued without change for 1942. This was the last year the company built the coupe pickup.

Because the federal government ordered truck production halted in January 1942, sales for the short model year amounted to only 70,680 trucks. Yet truck sales exceeded car sales for the first time, and they continued to outpace car sales every year through model year 1945.

Chevrolet's 1942 trucks continued with only one change in appearance and with only a few mechanical specifications. All 1941 models carried over without change in specifications. The single appearance change was brought about because auto manufacturers could no longer use chrome-plated trim items because of the war. All truck grilles were painted. Headlight rims were painted to match the fenders in color and the headlight rims were painted Turret Gray. Body changes included a small change in the way the front fenders were supported from the cowl. Two new simple right-angle brackets were riveted to the cowl. The fender's inner skirt was bolted to these brackets to better support the fender and thus minimize the possibility of fender cracking. New shock absorbers of the type used in Army trucks became the standard offering. They were more durable than the former type and lent a degree of manufacturing expediency since the same unit was used on military and civilian trucks. This is a 1942 Chevrolet Light Delivery 1/2-ton, 115-inch-wheelbase pickup. *D. E. Short*

This automotive-type instrument panel was new in 1940. The rectangle directly in front of the driver houses the speedometer and four gauges—gasoline, oil pressure, water temperature, and voltmeter. The three-speed transmission's shift lever is floor mounted. The glovebox is on the right side; its lock is above the door on the instrument panel. The small handle located at the top of the panel at its center opens the windshield. This pickup is equipped with a genuine Chevrolet heater that is located on the right side of the cowl below the instrument panel (which is out of sight). The seat cushions and backs are upholstered in vinyl, with genuine leather upholstery available as an extra-cost option. With leather, the buyer also got special padding and springing for extra comfort and durability. A cowl vent was standard equipment. Its control handle with a plastic knob can be seen below the ignition keys. *D. E. Short*

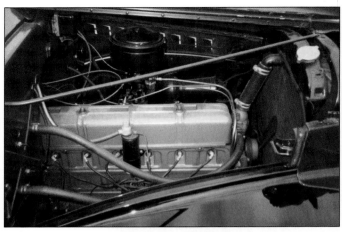

This is Chevrolet's famous 216-ci OHV six-cylinder engine with only 9,000 miles recorded on the odometer. The oil bath air cleaner and carburetor are on the far side of the engine. On the near side you can see the coil, spark plugs, and heater hoses. The radiator cap is on the far right. This engine has not been repainted! Two changes were made in the engines in 1942. Because of the new Load Master engine, the flywheel bolts were increased 1/16 inch in diameter to provide for the extra load on the flywheel from both engines. The second change was making the hole in the starter motor housing smaller. This helped prevent the entry of dirt into the opening. *D. E. Short*

Chevrolet's Heavy-Duty conventional cab models carried over from 1941 without change in two series: the 134 1/2-inch wheelbase and the 160-inch wheelbase. This is a 1942 Chevrolet 1 1/2-ton Heavy-Duty 160-inch-wheelbase chassis cab with farm box. It was rated for a maximum GVW of 13,500 pounds with a single-speed rear axle or 14,000 pounds with a two-speed rear axle. Its standard engine was the 90-horsepower 216-ci OHV six, and the new 235-ci Load Master engine with 93 horsepower was an option. Its transmission was the four-speed with provision for power takeoff. This truck had no chrome at all. *Nollie W. Neill, Jr.*

Chevrolet's complete line of Light Delivery models returned for 1942: The Panel, Carryall Suburban, Pickup, and Canopy Express. Also continued were the automobile-based commercials: The Special Deluxe Station Wagon with wooden body, Master Deluxe Coupe Pickup, and Master Deluxe Sedan Delivery. Pictured is a 1942 Chevrolet 1/2-ton Light Delivery Panel. This truck has a painted bumper in addition to its painted grille, but has chrome headlight rims and hubcaps. Its standard maximum GVW rating was 4,400 pounds with 6.00x16 four-ply tires front and rear. When 6.00x16 six-ply tires were installed front and rear, the truck's maximum GVW rating jumped to 4,600 pounds. Its standard 216-ci engine was rated for 90 horsepower and 174 maximum torque at 1,200 rpm. Its compression ratio was 6.5:1. The new Load Master 235-ci engine was not an option for the Light Delivery trucks. The only transmission available was the three-speed synchro-mesh.

The other 1942 Heavy-Duty conventional cab model was the 134 1/2-inch-wheelbase chassis cab with a fifth wheel. The truck pictured was called Water Tower No. 1 and was owned by the Louisville Fire Department. Its 55-foot tower was a model number 1892 from Hale. Note the partially opened "ventilating" windshield. Because this truck didn't handle heavy loads, only the standard 216-ci OHV six-cylinder engine was necessary to power it. It was equipped with the four-speed transmission with provision for power takeoff. The power takeoff was not necessary for this truck, but it was of considerable importance to the typical pumper fire truck, which powered its pump from the power takeoff. Its rear axle was the two-speed type. *Steve Hagy*

This short 1942 Heavy-Duty 134 1/2-inch-wheelbase chassis cab with pumper body by Van Pelt is a rare truck. It featured a 350-gallon water tank and a 300-gpm pump. Its pump would have been driven off the four-speed transmission's power takeoff. The pump is mounted out front, forward of the grille. The Oakley (California) Fire Department owned truck No. 93. Its maximum GVW rating was 13,500 pounds with a single-speed rear axle. The 90-horsepower, 216-ci OHV six-cylinder engine powered it. The new 93-horsepower 235-ci OHV Load Master engine was an extra-cost option. *Chuck Madderom*

The Heavy-Duty 1 1/2-ton Chevrolet 160-inch-wheelbase chassis cab with fire-fighting body was the most commonly seen Chevrolet chassis used by the nation's fire departments. This chassis was ideal for a 12-foot body such as this truck's pumper body. The Pangborn Field (Washington) Fire Department owned this truck. Its body was by Pybus, and it featured a 500-gallon water tank and a 500-gpm pump. The new Load Master 93-horsepower 235-ci OHV six-cylinder engine powered it. With its two-speed rear axle, it was rated for a maximum GVW of 14,000 pounds. The two-speed rear axle's ratios were 5.64 and 8.22 to 1. It had four-speed transmission with provision for power takeoff. This truck's shipping weight with chassis cab and dual rear wheels was 3,790 pounds. *Bill Hattersley*

For the 1942 model year, Chevrolet offered to paint any truck in a two-tone color combination at no extra charge. The only exceptions were the Sedan Delivery, Coupe Pickup, and Dubl-Duti Package Delivery. This applied to both truck cabs and truck bodies. Chevrolet trucks of this vintage were well adapted to the use of two-color combinations. The standard paint scheme had been to paint the fenders black regardless of cab color, anyway. The two colors had to be from Chevrolet's standard paint colors. The two-tone combinations included in the offer were not limited to one color for the cab and a second for the fenders, however. This is a 1942 Chevrolet Heavy-Duty 1 1/2-ton chassis cab with farm body. This was a standard 160-inch-wheelbase truck with a 216-ci six-cylinder engine, single-speed rear axle, four-speed transmission, and 10-leaf rear springs. *Dick Miller*

1943–1945

The last Chevrolet automobile rolled off the assembly line on January 30, 1942, a little less than two months after the Japanese attacked Pearl Harbor. All Chevrolet assembly plants except the Saginaw Service Manufacturing Plant were converted to the war effort. This plant supplied service parts for the millions of Chevrolet cars and trucks in daily use. The government was very interested in ensuring that all Chevrolet trucks currently in use would be able to stay in service for the duration, because the nation had a lot of work to do before hostilities would cease.

Shortly into the war, Chevrolet efforts were devoted almost exclusively to the production of war materiel —to "Volume for Victory." Chevrolet utilized more than 16 million square feet of floor space in the manufacture of aircraft engines, aluminum forgings, magnesium castings, 90-mm anti-aircraft guns, high-explosive shells, armor-piercing shot, and military vehicles. Chevrolet supplied the military with four-door passenger cars in 1940 and 1942. The cars were rated as "light sedans" and used for transporting personnel. Medium sedans, Packards, were used for transportation of officers. These cars were essentially civilian-type sedans, only slightly modified for military use. Most were mainly for domestic use, although a limited number went overseas. Some Chevrolets went into the Lend-Lease program and ended up in Great Britain. A few 1942 Chevrolet Stylemaster sedans were converted to 15-passenger buses.

Chevrolet Truck supplied 1 1/2-ton 4x2 dual rear wheel panel trucks converted to field ambulances from 1940 to 1942. The Army later switched to all 4x4 trucks for field ambulance service.

In the years 1940, 1941, and 1942, Chevrolet shipped 1/2-ton 4x2 (slightly modified from domestic use) Suburbans, canopies, pickups, and panels, light maintenance and installation, and telephone maintenance trucks. Chevrolet supplied similar but slightly heavier 3/4-ton trucks, too.

Chevrolet also supplied a number of 1 1/2-ton 4x2 stake/platform, canopy, dump, panel delivery, and pickup trucks from 1940 to 1942. Pickup and canopy trucks in 1-ton capacities were also supplied within the same time frame.

Chevrolet supplied an early series of 4x4 trucks from 1940 to 1941 in the following bodies: Airfield Crash, Cargo, Cargo w/Winch, Cargo with long wheelbase, Crash, Dump, Dump w/Winch, Oil Service, Panel Telephone Maintenance, and the same with winch and with earth borer. From 1942 to 1945, Chevrolet supplied the G-7100 Series 1 1/2-ton 4x4 trucks in the following bodies: Airfield, Crash, Bomb Service, Cargo, Cargo w/Winch, Cargo with long wheelbase, Dump, Dump w/Winch, Field lighting, Telephone Maintenance, w/Winch and Earth Borer and Pole Setter, as well as the chassis cab for special bodies. Chevrolet was the Army's mass producer of 1 1/2-ton 4x4 trucks. They were equipped with a civilian cab with front sheet metal and military-style fenders.

The final truck Chevrolet built for military use was a 1 1/2-ton COE stake and platform. This truck had civilian sheet metal with a heavy front bumper and grille guard.

The War Production Board in 1944 authorized Chevrolet the right to build a limited number of heavy-duty trucks for select customers engaged in critical war work, including farmers. This was an effort to inject trucks into a truck-starved, red-hot wartime economy. The trucks were two chassis cab units that differed only in their wheelbase lengths—134 1/2 and 160 inches. Only the special Load Master engine was furnished in both trucks. In styling and all mechanical specifications, these trucks were the same as the 1942 models.

This 1944 Chevrolet truck was eight years old and still capable of hauling sizable loads when this photo was taken during a parade in Bagley, Minnesota, in 1952. It was powered with the 235-ci "Hi-Torque" engine. The rest of its drivetrain consisted of a four-speed transmission and a two-speed rear axle. Behind the 1944 is an Advance-Design tractor trailer rig, heavily laden with a huge load of lumber, followed by a B-Series Dodge rig with another huge load of lumber, which is in turn followed by another Advance-Design Chevrolet with a big load of lumber. The government allowed Chevrolet to sell two models of its heavy-duty chassis cabs in 1944—134 1/2- and 160-inch wheelbases. The truck shown has the long wheelbase. The 235-ci Hi-Torque engine developed 93 horsepower and 192 foot-pounds maximum torque. *Bob Bilden*

This is a yard full of 1943 Chevrolet military trucks. A number of 1/2-ton pickups with U.S. Navy markings can be seen. At the center is a 1 1/2-ton 4x4 chassis cab. This would be Chevrolet's G-7100 Series, built in quantity between 1942 and 1945. The government purchased G-7100s with and without bodies. Their drivetrain was the standard Chevrolet truck engine and four-speed transmission. The chassis cowl in the foreground appears to be waiting for a school bus body. *AAMA*

For 1945, the government authorized Chevrolet to increase its production of heavy-duty trucks to help truck operators meet the nation's demands for essential hauling. Chevrolet again made available the 134 1/2-inch- and 160-inch-wheelbase cab and chassis models to essential and qualified haulers. These trucks were the same models Chevrolet built during 1944. Two 134 1/2-inch models were available: one with a single-speed rear axle and seven leaves in front springs, and the other with a two-speed rear axle and with nine leaves in its front springs. The 160-inch wheelbase was available in five combinations with a single-speed rear axle, two-speed rear axle, and variations of springs and tires. The only engine offered was the 236-ci Load Master heavy-duty.

In 1945, Chevrolet was also authorized to build its 115-inch-wheelbase 1/2-ton pickup for qualified, essential users. This was basically the same pickup the company ceased building early in 1942, except it was a "black out" model, without chrome-plated trim items. Its engine was the 216-ci valve-in-head 90 horsepower six.

The rationing of all new commercial motor vehicles terminated on December 12, 1945, by order of the Office of Defense Transportation (ODT). The director of the ODT said, "A free market will then obtain in the purchase and delivery of commercial motor vehicles: truck sales will be a matter involving buyer and seller except as regulated by agencies other than ODT."

The October 1945 issue of *Power Wagon* magazine stated, "Rationing of commercial motor vehicles was put into effect on March 9, 1942. From that time to July 31, 1945, the ODT released 401,118 trucks, trailers, and bus chassis for civilian use as follows: light trucks, 56,128; medium, 205,293; heavy, 64,943; total, 326,364. . ."

Chevrolet built a total of 201,146 trucks of all types, military and civilians, during World War II. Production by years was as follows: 57,719 in 1943; 65,472 in 1944; and 77,955 in 1945.

By 1944, America's truck plants had produced military trucks in such enormous quantities that the government began slowing down production. The government authorized certain plants to build limited models for civilian use—that is, for civilian jobs deemed necessary to support the war. Chevrolet was authorized to build its two heavy-duty 1 1/2-ton chassis cab models in 134 1/2- and 160-inch wheelbases. This 1944 Chevrolet 1 1/2-ton chassis cab with fire-fighting body is a case in point. Engine No. 3 belonged to the Willisville (Illinois) Fire Department. This truck's original painted grille, hood louvers, and bumper had been traded for chrome-plated pieces. *Dennis J. Maag*

For the second year in a row, the government allowed Chevrolet to build heavy-duty 1 1/2-ton chassis cabs on two wheelbase lengths: 134 1/2 and 160 inches. These trucks were still restricted to businesses engaged in work considered necessary for the war effort. This is a 1945 Chevrolet 1 1/2-ton 160-inch chassis cab with fire-fighting body. The Beavercreek (Oregon) Fire Department owned engine No. 1. Its pumper body was by Howard Cooper and featured a 500-gallon tank and a 250-gpm pump. The government also authorized Chevrolet to build 1/2-ton pickups in 1945. *Bill Hattersley*

1946

Civilian truck production resumed on August 20, 1945. The 1946 models were basically the same as the 1942 models, with the exception of product improvements developed during the war. The 1946 models sported genuine chrome-plated grilles, bumpers, hubcaps, and other trim pieces instead of the wartime "black out" trim. Chevrolet sold its three-millionth truck this model year.

Chevrolet's prewar model line came back with a few changes. The sedan delivery returned, but the coupe pickup didn't. The 1/2-ton line included a pickup, panel, canopy, and two Suburbans, with a rear door and a tailgate. The 3/4-ton line was dropped in favor of a new 1-ton series of pickups, panels, platforms, and stakes. Also new in the 1-ton line were dual rear wheel–equipped platform and stake models.

In the medium- and heavy-duty lines were two school bus chassis on 160- or 195-inch wheelbases. The two medium-duty 1 1/2-ton models, the 134 1/2-inch and 160-inch-wheelbase chassis cabs, dated from 1944. They carried a maximum GVW rating of 11,000 pounds. The heavy-duty 2-ton chassis cab models included the 134 1/2-inch and 160-inch trucks. These trucks carried a maximum GVW rating of 15,000 pounds. Only the 2-ton conventional models and the three COE models could be equipped with a two-speed rear axle. Three other heavy-duty trucks were the two-ton COE chassis cabs rated for GVW of 16,000 pounds.

The 216-ci engine powered the two lightest 1 1/2-ton models (4100 and 4400). The 235-ci engine powered all others.

Chevrolet's (and the truck-building industry's) major problem in 1946 was not reconverting factories, nor was it a lack of customers. The biggest problems were labor unrest and a shortage of materials. Often, labor problems were not directly with the industry's own workers, but were often caused when a supplier—the railroads or others—had a labor problem that stopped the incoming flow of parts. Shortages caused the manufacturers to become creative in finding new sources of supplies and/or substitute materials. The industry built a record 1,300,000 trucks in 1941. The nation had 5,000,000 trucks in operation in 1946. It was estimated that half of them needed to be replaced. The industry forecast 1.5 million trucks for 1946; the actual total was 1,020,000, falling far short of meeting the nation's new truck needs. This 1946 Chevrolet 1/2-ton pickup was one of that number. *David Russell*

Pictured is a 1946 Chevrolet 1/2-ton chassis cab with stake body. Chevrolet did not offer a 1/2-ton stake as a regular production item. It continued after the war to call 1/2-ton models its Light Delivery trucks. These included the 1/2-ton pickup, panel, canopy express, and Carryall-Suburban. The maximum GVW rating for a 1/2-ton was 4,600 pounds. Its standard—and only—engine was the famous Chevrolet 90-horsepower 216-ci six-cylinder. Its transmission was the three-speed synchro-mesh. *Robert J. Creason*

Chevrolet's exclusive dual-purpose Carryall Suburban continued after the war. It would transport up to eight passengers for hotels, schools, clubs, airports, and other organizations. The conversion to transporting a wide variety of cargo was as easy as removing one or two of the rear seats. With both rear seats removed, the Suburban had as much enclosed cargo space as a 1/2-ton panel. The Suburban was available with either panel-type rear doors or with a liftgate/tailgate setup. The Suburban rode on the Light Delivery's standard 115-inch-wheelbase chassis and carried the same maximum GVW rating of 4,600 pounds. The Suburban's interior was well finished, with all seats upholstered in a high-quality, durable vinyl material. This 1946 Chevrolet Carryall Suburban was photographed in Chevrolet's display space at the 1997 North American International Auto Show in Detroit.

Chevrolet had good truck sales in 1946, but did not break a record. The industry was hampered by shortages caused mostly by labor strikes in critical industries such as coal, steel, and railroads. Chevrolet truck sales reached 201,702. With the exception of 1941, when truck and car sales ballooned because of consumers' fears of an imminent war, 1946 was the second best sales year in Chevrolet's history.

Chevrolet's 3/4-ton pickup was built on a 125 1/4-inch-wheelbase chassis and carried a cargo box that was 7 1/4 feet long by 48 1/2 inches wide by 16 1/4 inches deep. Its cargo box floor was constructed of wood covered with steel skid strips to facilitate loading and unloading. The steel sides terminated in wide flare-boards with rolled edges and six steel stake pockets. Chevrolet also offered a 3/4-ton pickup with Heavy-Duty equipment. The 3/4-ton pickup was rated for a maximum GVW rating of 5,800 pounds; the Heavy-Duty 3/4-ton was rated for 6,700 pounds. Standard equipment included the 90-horsepower 216-ci OHV six-cylinder engine, three-speed synchro-mesh transmission (four-speed was optional at extra cost), heavy drop-forged front axle, and disc-type wheels. *Vincent Cahill*

Chevrolet's standard 3/4-ton stake truck has sides only 28 1/4 inches high. It could not be determined that the high rack body seen here on a 3/4-ton chassis cab was a factory offering. High rack bodies were standard equipment for heavy-duty trucks. An owner would have to be careful about what he loaded into this tall body for fear of overloading it. The body's inside dimensions were 87 5/8 inches long by 70 3/4 inches wide. Chevrolet's line of Unit-Design Stake bodies for light- and heavy-duty trucks were built in company-owned factories, so the buyer could buy a complete truck directly from his dealer. This 3/4-ton stake carried a maximum GVW rating of 5,200 pounds. Its standard components included the 90-horsepower 216-ci six-cylinder engine, three-speed synchro-mesh transmission (a four-speed was an extra-cost option), 15-inch six-ply tires, 7-leaf rear springs, and 9 1/8-inch clutch. *AAMA*

Chevrolet's 1946 Heavy-Duty truck line fell into two broad categories: Conventional Models and COE Models. For the first time, Chevrolet began to use Model Series for these trucks. In the Conventional line it included Series 4100 and 4400 1 1/2-ton trucks with maximum GVW ratings of 11,000 pounds and Series 6100 and 6400 2-ton trucks with maximum GVW ratings of 15,000 pounds. The COE Models came in three Series—5100, 5400, and 5700. All three had maximum GVW ratings of 16,000 pounds. The three COE Series had 109-, 132 1/2-, and 158-inch-wheelbase lengths. In the Conventional Models, two wheelbases were offered—134 1/2 and 160 inches. This is a 1946 Chevrolet 1 1/2-ton Series 4400 160-inch-wheelbase stake truck. Its maximum GVW rating was 11,000 pounds. This truck was only available with the 90-horsepower 216-ci six-cylinder engine mated to the four-speed sliding-gear transmission. *Joe Silba*

A 1946 Chevrolet 2-ton Conventional Series 6100 134 1/2-inch-wheelbase chassis cab with wrecker body. The 93-horsepower 235-ci six-cylinder engine was the exclusive powerplant for this Series. It produced 192 foot-pounds maximum torque between 1,000 and 1,900 rpm. A competent driver knew how to maintain his engine's rpm in this maximum torque band through shifting his four-speed transmission up or down, and shifting his two-speed rear axle (when the truck was so equipped) to maximize the engine's torque output. This model carried a maximum GVW rating of 15,000 pounds. The single-speed rear axle had a ratio of 5.43 to 1; the two-speed rear axle's ratios were 5.64 and 8.22 to 1. Dual-rear-wheel standard tire equipment was a 7.50x20 eight-ply and the maximum dual-rear tire equipment was a 8.25x20 12-ply. The optional tire was required equipment for the maximum 15,000-pound GVW rating. *David Russell*

The Goodyear (Arizona) Fire Department owned this 1946 Chevrolet 2-ton Series 6400 160-inch-wheelbase chassis flat-face cowl with fire-fighting body. Its pumper body is by Darley and it featured a 500-gallon water tank and a 250-gpm pump. Chevrolet engineers designed this chassis for a 12-foot body, which was perfect for a fire-fighting body. The pump would have been powered from the truck's four-speed transmission's power takeoff. This truck was equipped with the 93-horsepower 235-ci six-cylinder engine. All heavy-duty trucks from the 4400 Conventional Series up were equipped with frame siderail reinforcing plates. This fire truck was equipped with the 8.25x20 12-ply dual-rear tires in order to have the 15,000 pounds maximum GVW rating. *Greenberg*

Arnold Paradis told me that this 1946 Chevrolet Model 6103 chassis cab with platform body was his last antique truck. The 93-horsepower 235-ci six-cylinder engine originally powered this 134 1/2-inch-wheelbase truck. A 125-horsepower 235-ci six-cylinder engine (one of the last) recently replaced that engine. Arnold built and installed a new platform body before selling the truck in October 1998. This truck has a two-speed rear axle and a four-speed transmission. The men in the photo from left to right: Steve Corbett, Arnold Paradis, and David Paradis. *Arnold Paradis*

Chevrolet's COE Models for 1946 consisted of three Series: 5100, 5400, and 5700. All three Series were 2-ton models carrying a maximum GVW rating of 16,000 pounds. In order to have this maximum GVW rating, they were required to have dual rear wheels with 8.25x20 12-ply tires front and rear. The three wheelbase lengths for the COE Series were 109, 132 1/2, and 158 inches, respectively. All 2-ton trucks, Conventional and COE models, were equipped with governors set for a top speed of 45 miles per hour. The 90-horsepower 235-ci six-cylinder engine powered the COE. It produced 189 foot-pounds maximum torque between 1,000 and 1,900 rpm. This engine's horsepower and torque outputs were less than that of the Conventional cab Series' engine because it was equipped with an updraft carburetor. Its rear axle was rated for 12,500 pounds; a two-speed rear axle was an extra-cost option. The single-speed axle had a ratio of 6.17 to 1; the two-speed rear axle's ratios were 5.64 and 8.22 to 1. All COE Models were equipped with frame siderail reinforcing plates. Three 1946 Chevrolet 2-ton Model 5103 chassis cabs with fifth wheel equipment are shown. *AAMA*

Cargo overloading was a way of life in America at this point in the history of the motor truck. But overall average speeds were quite low. As a prelude to 1947's all-new Advance-Design models, Chevrolet restructured its 1946 truck lineup into medium- and heavy-duty models versus heavy-duty trucks only through 1945. Mediums were powered by the 216-ci OHV six and were rated for a GVW of 11,000 pounds. The heavies were rated for 15,000 pounds GVW and used the bigger 235-ci OHV six. This is a heavy-duty model 6100 chassis cab with fifth wheel equipment and trailer heavily laden with cotton. *AAMA*

Chevrolet's 1946 medium-duty line consisted of models 4100 and 4400. Wheelbase lengths were 134 1/2 and 160 inches, respectively. This is a 1946 4400 chassis cab with platform body. This truck was powered by the 216-ci OHV six and was equipped with the four-speed transmission with provision for power takeoff.

She wasn't very pretty, but she was a runner. Pictured is Mike Pagel's 1946 Chevrolet 1-ton pickup. It was photographed in St. Louis, Missouri, at the American Truck Historical Society's Annual Convention in June of 1984. Mike drove his Chevrolet from Muscatine, Iowa, to the convention. The 1-ton Chevrolet pickup was basically the same as the 134 1/2-inch-wheelbase medium-duty chassis cab except it had a 9-foot pickup box. The famous Chevrolet 216-ci OHV six mated to a four-speed transmission powered it. *Mike Pagel*

1947

Chevrolet led the industry in bringing all-new postwar trucks to market in 1947. The company started production on its new Advance-Design trucks on June 9, 1947. Chevrolet dealers made the first public showings of the new models on Saturday, June 28, 1947.

Marketing took a different approach with the new trucks by dividing the new models into two distinct groups. This was because the new trucks had two completely different sets of sheet-metal appearance parts (hoods, fenders, bumpers, etc.). There was one set for Thriftmaster trucks and a second, larger set for the Loadmaster trucks. A total of 80 chassis and truck models divided into eleven series, or lines, constituted the new offering.

The Thriftmaster group consisted of the 3100, 3600, and 3800 Series trucks, or 1/2-, 3/4-, and 1-ton models, with a GVW range of 4,200 to 8,800 pounds. The Loadmaster group of 1 1/2- and 2-ton models was made up of the 4100, 4400, 6100S, and 6400S Series and the heavier-duty 6100 and 6400 Series trucks, as well as the 4502 and 6702 school bus chassis. Their GVW range was 7,500 to 16,000 pounds.

Both Series looked alike, but were styled slightly differently to reflect the services in which they were engaged. In other words, the light-duty trucks, most often used in urban delivery service, were styled to look smarter and faster than ever before in Chevrolet truck

Chevrolet's Sedan Delivery was almost always the style leader of the truck line. Its styling was that of the current year automobile, which caused it to stand apart from the other trucks. The 1947 Sedan Delivery was not all that well received because it was the only old truck in the Chevrolet truck line. The all-new Advance-Design Chevrolet trucks pushed it into the background. The 1948 Chevrolet Model 1508 116-inch-wheelbase Sedan Delivery pictured is an unusual truck because it hails from South Africa. The 1947 Sedan Delivery featured a revised grille design and hood emblem. Note the lack of body side moldings. Its drivetrain comprised the 216 six and a three-speed manual transmission. *Jim Benjaminson*

Chevrolet's Advance-Design trucks arrived at the dealers in 1947, one model year ahead of arch rivals Ford and Dodge. These trucks were, without a doubt, the most important series in the Division's history. They were responsible for firmly cementing Chevrolet as America's favorite light- and medium-duty truck builder. This is a 1947 Chevrolet 125 1/4-inch-wheelbase Thrift-master Model 3604 3/4-ton pickup. Note the right-side gasoline filler pipe on this pickup's splash panel under the pickup box. Its maximum GVW rating was 5,800 pounds. *AAMA*

Management had always been concerned with style from the very beginning of Chevrolet's trucks in 1918. They felt that style was as important to commercial vehicle buyers as it was to those who purchased an automobile for personal transportation. For commercial buyers trucks represented their business. People tended to judge the character of a business by what they saw in the delivery or service trucks driving up to their home. This is a 1947 Chevrolet 3/4-ton pickup with an aftermarket canopy cover. The entire Chevrolet light-duty Advance-Design line continued to be powered by the famous Chevrolet 216-ci six-cylinder OHV engine. Its horsepower rating was 90 at 3,300 rpm and its torque output was 174 foot-pounds at 1,200 rpm. A three-speed synchro-mesh manual transmission was standard for 1/2- and 3/4-ton trucks and the four-speed was optional. *AAMA*

This is a 1947 Chevrolet Loadmaster 1 1/2-ton Series 4400 model CGN high-rack. This truck had a 161-inch wheelbase and was rated for a maximum GVW of 13,000 pounds. The only engine offered was the 216-ci Thriftmaster. Its horsepower rating was 90 and its torque was 174 foot-pounds. The standard transmission was the Chevrolet-built four-speed, which had provision for power takeoff. Option equipment was limited to a second rear-axle ratio—6.17 to 1 versus the standard of 5.43 to 1. In midseason these numbers were transposed; the 6.17 became standard and the 5.43 was made optional. The idea behind the change was to improve pulling power with a two-speed rear axle, auxiliary rear springs, governor, oil bath air cleaner, and booster brakes. *AAMA*

A tandem-axle model was not a factory offering in 1947. Tandem-axle models were an aftermarket conversion and were seldom seen. Chevrolet's standard six did not produce the horsepower or torque needed to deliver the performance required for this type of service. Chevrolet engineers designed stronger frames for the Advance-Design heavy trucks. Only three standard frames were offered for the Loadmaster group trucks—137 inches, 161 inches, and the 199-inch school bus chassis. They were designed and built so strong and rigid that Chevrolet engineers felt they didn't need to be reinforced with fish plates. They were built with thicker metal and the siderails had much greater depth along their entire lengths. This is a 1947 Chevrolet Series 6400 chassis cab with tandem rear axle and special body. *AAMA*

Chevrolet's heaviest Advance-Design truck was the 2-ton Series 6400 offered as bare chassis, chassis cab, stake/platform, and high rack models. Shown here is a Series 6400 chassis cab with dump body. This series offered only a 161-inch-wheelbase chassis. Its maximum GVW rating was 16,000 pounds. The 93-horse-power Loadmaster 235-ci OHV six powered it. It was governed for 2,800 rpm in high gear. Chevrolet designers gave each of the two groups, the Thriftmaster and the Loadmaster, a distinctive front-end appearance. The following special features created the Loadmaster's more massive appearance: a heavy-duty painted front bumper versus the spring-type chrome bumper of the light-duty models; a slightly higher grille; and a longer hood and front fenders. The cab for both groups was the same. *AAMA*

Chevrolet built two panels in 1947: a 1/2-ton on a 116-inch wheel-base and the Model 3805 1-ton on a 137-inch wheelbase, which is pictured here. Its usable load space length was 151 inches with a capacity of 202 cubic feet. A handy dome light adequately illuminated the load compartment. The rear doors could be locked into an open position to aid in loading and unloading. An auxiliary bucket-type seat was optional. The 216-ci 90-horsepower Thrift-master engine was the only one offered. A four-speed manual transmission was also standard. The largest available tires were the 7.50x17 eight-ply.

Chevrolet's Loadmaster COE trucks for 1947 were made up of Series 5100, 5400, and 5700. Their wheelbase lengths were 110, 134, and 158 inches, respectively. Models included chassis with windshield cowl, chassis cab, 9- or 12-foot stake, platform, and high racks. The cab of the CEO trucks was identical with the conventional trucks except that the rear corner windows were provided as regular equipment, as were assist handles. This is a 1947 Chevrolet Series 5103 110-inch-wheelbase chassis cab COE tractor. This 2-ton was rated for a maximum GVW of 16,000 pounds. Its drivetrain consisted of the 235-ci 90-horsepower six mated to the four-speed transmission. It had a full-floating 13,000-pound rear axle with the optional two-speeds (ratios: 6.13 to 1 and 8.10 to 1). *AAMA*

This fire truck was painted the traditional fire truck red. It is a model 6403S chassis cab with pumper body in the 6400S Series. It was owned by the Summerland (British Columbia) Fire Department. Its body was made by a local firm and contained a 500-gallon water tank and a 250-gpm pump. The pump is located between the bumper and grille. Ladders were stored on a rack above the body. It was powered by the 235-ci six; its transmission was a four-speed. *Frank De Gruchy*

Fire departments required a long wheelbase chassis cab to accommodate a body big enough for a water tank, pump, and hoses. This model 6403S Chevrolet 1 1/2-ton special truck was powered by the 235-ci six mated to a four-speed transmission. The Glendale (Arizona) Fire Protection District owned this truck. It has a body by Howe that contained a 500-gallon water tank and a 500-gpm pump. The attractive curved line that swept down from the cab's roof to join the body characterized Howe bodies. This truck was painted a very attractive two-tone combination, featuring a yellow body and cab, trimmed with a white roof, grille, and front bumper. *Chuck Madderom*

Chevrolet's 1947 Advance-Design trucks arrived at the dealers in June 1947. Chevrolet continued to build and sell 1946 trucks as 1947 models until the new Advance-Design models arrived. This is a 1947 Chevrolet 1/2-ton Light Delivery pickup. This truck was all dressed up with rear fender skirts, designer oak sideboards, and wide white sidewalls. The 90-horsepower Thriftmaster 216-ci six-cylinder engine powered the 115-inch-wheelbase 1947 model. The three-speed synchro-mesh transmission was standard equipment, as was a 9 1/8-inch clutch. *Robert W. Kemp*

One-ton Advance-Design Chevrolet Series 3800 pickups are quite rare. For one thing, they were second series trucks, meaning their production run was short. Secondly, the 1-ton is always a low-production-numbers model as compared to 1/2- and 3/4-ton pickups. The big 1-tonner featured a 9-foot cargo box, 216-ci six-cylinder engine, four-speed transmission (1st was a "granny" gear), and a 5.14:1 rear-axle ratio. *Kathy and Randy Boersig*

history. The heavy truck's styling emphasized its ruggedness and load-lugging ability.

Chevrolet engineers had the advantage of starting with a clean sheet of paper when designing the Advance-Design trucks. Engineers began the new truck development and design process by surveying truck users nationwide. The survey, conducted through personal interviews, gave Chevrolet engineers first-hand knowledge of what users wanted. In turn, the engineers used the survey results to design the new trucks.

The drivers surveyed indicated they first wanted larger, roomier cabs with more comfortable seats and better visibility. The new Chevrolet cabs were 8 inches wider and 7 inches longer, with a larger windshield and windows. A new fully adjustable seat, wide enough for three men to ride comfortably, provided maximum driver comfort.

The well-known, dependable, and proven Thriftmaster engine or the highly regarded Loadmaster engine powered all trucks. These two OHV six-cylinder engines did not change from 1946; the smaller engine's cubic-inch displacement was 216 and the larger's 235 ci.

The Carryall Suburban was regularly painted in a two-tone finish. The lower section of the body received Channel Green paint and the upper portion was painted in a darker paint—Fathom Green. Two wide stripes of cream color decorated the belt molding. Its wheels were painted the darker green.

Chevrolet was the only one of the Big Three (GMC was an exception, of course) to build a canopy model after 1947. Yet the percentage of sales it represented makes one wonder why they even bothered. According to figures from calendar year 1940, Chevrolet's sales of trucks with cabs and cab chassis, including pickups, was 83 percent of production. Half-ton panel trucks followed at 10.7 percent, flat face cowl chassis at .9 percent, 1-ton panels at .8 percent, Carryall Suburbans at .8 percent, 1/2-ton canopies at .3 percent, and 1-ton canopies at .1 percent.

New two-unit models included pickups and stakes, and stakes in light- and heavy-duty series. Pickups were much improved by new cargo bodies with new tailgates, running boards, rear fenders, and bumpers. Stake bodies were only modified to fit the new frames. Stake trucks looked much better on the Advance-Design chassis since they extended less beyond the new cab's width.

A single modern instrument panel with completely restyled and relocated instruments and hand controls was provided for all trucks.

Chevrolet designers grouped the instruments in two large, simply styled, attractive dials that straddled the steering column. A driver could easily read the dials' larger figures through the T-spoke steering wheel. Dials included the battery charge indicator, oil pressure and water temperature indicators, the fuel gauge, the speedometer, the odometer, and the headlamp beam indicator.

Truck sales forged ahead by 29 percent in 1947, to a total of 259,533. Chevrolet built the 20 millionth vehicle in its 35-year history on November 14, 1947.

1948

All 1947 Chevrolet truck models continued into 1948. There was one new light-duty truck model, the 3742, which was a forward-control Delivery Chassis. Excluding the Sedan Delivery, the addition of this new chassis model increased the number of models to 107. The number of wheelbases remained the same, and

lengths were also unchanged. Forester Green, the regular paint color for all 1947 models besides the Carryall Suburban, continued in 1948. The two-tone Fathom Green and Channel Green, the standard colors for the Carryall Suburban, remained unchanged, as did all of the optional colors.

Improvements included a steering column–mounted gearshift lever and a foot-operated parking brake. Removing the hand brake and gearshift levers from the floor area of 1/2- and 3/4-ton trucks made it easier for the driver to enter or leave through the right-hand door. It also freed up additional floor space in panel models for packages or other baggage. In the cab and Carryall Suburban models, there was more foot room for the third passenger.

To completely clear the floor area, Chevrolet engineers relocated the parking brake as well as the gearshift lever. The new foot-operated parking brake had a different location: the far left side of the cab. Plus, it had a quick-set lock.

Chevrolet engineers made five improvements to the truck engines to increase durability. These changes included new precision interchangeable thin-wall babbitt main bearings that had more than double the life of their predecessors. The front, front intermediate, and rear intermediate bearing caps were modified to become more rigid. This reduced bearing deflections and increased bearing life. There were new thin-wall babbitt connecting rod bearings for increased durability. They had been thin before, but became even thinner (to the same thickness as main bearings), which considerably increased bearing life. A heavier, more rigid crankshaft prevented crankshaft distortion and helped the engine run more smoothly. Lastly, new synthetic-rubber valve stem oil seals, developed at Chevrolet, were added. These reduced valve spring surge, and since the cap covers were eliminated, the noise formerly attributed to the rattling of worn valve spring cap covers was a thing of history.

This was the last year for this body style on Model 1508 Sedan Delivery. All Chevrolet cars received their first postwar new styling in 1949. The Sedan Delivery was built on a 116-inch-wheelbase automobile chassis and was rated for a maximum GVW of 4,100 pounds. Its body was styled along the same lines as the 1948 Chevrolet passenger car. The Sedan Delivery was intended for the fast, economical delivery of light loads, generally for home delivery of packages from an upscale retailer. Automobile-type features included Knee-Action front suspension, vacuum power gearshift, a three-speed transmission, rear-axle ratio of 4.11:1, and 6.00-16 4-ply tires. *Bob Waite*

All 1947 Chevrolet truck models continued in 1948. The Advance-Design's exterior appearance continued without change. Forester Green was the "regular" color for all models except the Carryall Suburban, whose regular colors were the two-tone Fathom Green and Channel Green. All other paint colors were options. This is a 1948 Chevrolet Model 3104 Thriftmaster 1/2-ton pickup. It carried a maximum GVW rating of 4,600 pounds on its 116-inch chassis. Its only engine was the 90-horsepower 216-ci six. The three-speed transmission was standard and a four-speed was optional. *AAMA*

Chevrolet's smallest medium-duty Loadmaster truck was this 1 1/2-ton 137-inch-wheelbase Model 4108 platform. Its maximum GVW rating was 12,500 pounds, while its maximum payload was 7,600 pounds. Chevrolet supplied its platform body. The Thriftmaster 216-ci 90-horsepower six-cylinder engine powered this Loadmaster truck. The heavy-duty 235-ci Loadmaster 93-horsepower six was made an option in 1948. A four-speed synchro transmission was the only available transmission. *AAMA*

One other improvement that was made on Loadmaster engines only was changing the camshaft gear from a fiber composition to a more durable aluminum alloy with a bonded steel hub. Heavy-duty truck engines operated under relatively larger loads, and often in lower gear ratios; the camshaft gear made more revolutions per mile and was thus subject to wear.

For 1948, the Chevrolet four-speed transmission was completely new and entirely redesigned. The most important improved feature was its synchro-mesh second, third, and fourth speeds. This transmission was standard for all trucks from a 1-ton capacity and up.

Chevrolet opened its eleventh automobile assembly plant at Van Nuys, California, on February 17, 1948. The plant's one-shift production capacity was 35 passenger cars and 15 trucks per hour. The cumulative number of Chevrolet cars and trucks in operation in 1948 reached an all-time peak of 8,834,811 units, one-fourth of all automobiles in the United States. Chevrolet's retail monthly truck sales of 30,395 set a new record for the month of April.

The automobile industry's average wage rate in 1948 was $1.50 per hour. On May 25, 1948, GM raised that amount with an 11-cent hourly pay boost. The raise was the result of an agreement to adjust wages according to the cost of living.

GM was forced to lay off 200,000 workers on June 11, 1948, due to steel shortages caused by the spring coal strike. Production resumed after a week's suspension. On August 25, GM raised the wages of 265,000 hourly workers by 3 cents an hour, due to another cost-of-living increase. By September 3, 1948, GM's automobile and truck plants in Michigan, except for a few of the fabricating units, shut down and remained closed until September 8, due to a serious shortage of sheet steel. More than 75,000 workers were affected.

Chevrolet raised all truck and commercial vehicle prices in 1947 to between $45 and $90. In spite of shortages and shutdowns during the year, Chevrolet truck sales still increased to 323,648, by 25 percent. Chevrolet led the industry in both car and truck sales.

Buyers of medium- and heavy-duty 1948 conventional cab trucks had a choice of only two wheelbase-length chassis cabs—137 or 161 inches. This is a 6403S 161-inch-wheelbase chassis cab with fire-fighting body. This 1 1/2-ton special, nominal rated truck had a maximum GVW rating of 15,000 pounds. It was powered by the 93-horsepower heavy-duty 235-ci six governed at 2,800 rpm in high gear. It had the new synchro-mesh four-speed transmission with provision for power takeoff. The Greenville (New York) Fire Department owned this truck. It had a 500-gallon water tank and a 300-gpm pump. *Neal A. Van Deusen*

The Model 6103 137-inch-wheelbase chassis cab was the perfect choice for tractor trailer service or dump truck work. This heavy 2-tonner carried a maximum GVW rating of 16,000 pounds, Chevrolet's highest. During the Advance-Design era this was one of Chevrolet's best-selling heavy-duty trucks. Its dual rear wheels could be equipped with large 9.00x20 10-ply tires for extra carrying capacity. A two-speed vacuum-operated optional rear axle allowed this Chevrolet dump to always work at maximum allowable speeds. An optional fresh-air heater, defroster, and ventilator system allowed the driver to be more comfortable and efficient. *AAMA*

This fire truck was built on the 1948 Chevrolet heavy-duty 2-ton 161-inch-wheelbase Model 6403 chassis cab. Engine No. 1, a hose wagon, was owned by the Rock Community (Missouri) Volunteer Fire Association. It was rated for Chevrolet's highest maximum GVW of 16,000 pounds and was equipped with the heavy-duty 235-ci 93-horsepower OHV six, mated to the new synchro-mesh four-speed transmission. It had a Hydrovac power brake, 7,800-pound capacity rear springs, and a heavy-duty frame with six cross-members. *Dennis J. Maag*

The Railroad Express Agency purchased a fleet of these economical Chevrolet Model 4402 flat-face cowls in 1948, onto which it installed its own special package bodies. The 161-inch-wheelbase Model 4409 could accommodate bodies up to 12 feet in length. Notice how this body, which appears to be about 12 feet long including its cab, has almost no overhang behind the rear duals. This chassis was capable of handling GVWs of up to 12,500 pounds. There was a choice of two engines—the 216-ci Thriftmaster or the 235-ci Loadmaster. The four-speed synchro-mesh transmission was standard equipment. Its maximum payload rating was 7,100 pounds. *Richard Doane/Vincent Cahill*

Owner Mike Klepp believes that old cars and trucks should be driven and enjoyed, and that's exactly what he does with his Deluxe 1948 3100 five-window 1/2-ton pickup. It has a non-original 235-ci six and a four-speed granny transmission, deluxe heater-defroster, dual taillights with turn signals, hood ornament, and Fulton sun visor. It runs perfectly and is driven on a regular basis. *Mike Klepp*

1949

Chevrolet's Advance-Design trucks entered a third model year in 1949. There were few improvements. All standard paint colors carried over with no additions or deletions.

Chevrolet fielded 81 models in its complete line for 1949. Due to extremely low demand, all stripped chassis models and the 110-inch-wheelbase COE platform and stake trucks were discontinued.

By applying a different color of paint called Silver Gray to the inner areas of the grille bars, workers were able to give the grille the appearance of having greater depth and more detail, although the grille still had the same five horizontal bars as before. The rounded, outer part of the grille bars was painted the body color. Paint stripes, which had previously decorated the outer grille bars, were removed in 1949.

All 1948 Chevrolet truck models had a nameplate on each side of the hood, which displayed the Chevrolet name and the Thriftmaster or Loadmaster category to identify the capacity group to which the truck belonged. Chevrolet's engineers changed the nameplates to a number system in 1949 to identify the series. The numbers were 3100, 3600, 3800, 4100, and so on.

The instrument panel in the Suburban Carryall model changed color for 1949. The new scheme was a two-tone combination of Wicker Brown and Pecan Brown, the same colors Chevrolet designers used elsewhere in the Suburban. The instrument panel in all other trucks remained the original gray. To improve readability, the instrument cluster and speedometer pointers changed from red to white in all trucks.

Because the frame-mounted gas tank interfered with the installation of certain special bodies, it was relocated to the cab floor, behind the seat. The tank's capacity was 17 1/2 gallons. The filling port remained on the right side of the cab.

Except for the jack and wheel wrench, all tools were discontinued except a tire iron, which continued to be issued with 1-ton and larger trucks.

In August of 1949, a second–forward control chassis, Model 3942, was placed into production. It had a wheelbase of 137 inches and carried a maximum GVW rating of 10,000 pounds.

Chevrolet introduced an all-new Sedan Delivery, Model 1508. The truck was based on Chevrolet's impressive new passenger cars, their first postwar series.

Chevrolet's new cars were well accepted in 1949. Calendar year sales for Chevrolet cars showed a healthy 42 percent increase over 1948. Truck sales, on the other hand, increased only 8 percent, to 350,728. Nevertheless, Chevrolet trucks outsold archrival Ford by the astounding margin of 73 percent. GM reached an all-time peak in total motor vehicle production in 1949. A total volume of 2,678,874 cars, trucks, and buses eclipsed the company's previous record of 2,252,695 units established in 1941. GM had approximately 100 plants in the United States in 1949, while the Chevrolet Division had 13 manufacturing plants and 11 assembly plants.

Chevrolet's truck line for 1949 consisted of only 81 models on nine wheelbases. All stripped chassis models were dropped due to low sales, as was the 110-inch-wheelbase COE platform and stake trucks. For 1949, Chevrolet trucks were no longer called Thriftmaster and Loadmaster but were identified by their series number—3100, 3600, 3800, 4100, and so on. These numbers formed nameplates and were located under the Chevrolet nameplate on each side of the hood. This is a 1949 Chevrolet Model 4104, 1/2-ton 116-inch-wheelbase pickup. Its maximum GVW rating continued at 4,600 pounds. All conventional light-duty body models continued. *AAMA*

Chevrolet's Canopy Express was a very low production numbers model. It was offered in two models: A Model 3107 1949 1/2-ton and a 1-ton Model 3807 version, such as the one pictured. Chevrolet was the last manufacturer to build this body type and the only one to build a Canopy in its new postwar truck series. Chevrolet built three types of what it called single-unit-body trucks. These included the Suburban Carryall, panel, and canopy trucks. The 1/2-ton canopy's maximum GVW rating was 4,600 pounds. *Richard Doane/Vincent Cahill*

The 1/2-ton Model 3116 Suburban Carryall was also not a high volume seller. This high line Suburban had the optional chrome grille bars. Chevrolet's marketing department continued to sell the Suburban as both a dual-purpose passenger carrying-vehicle and a cargo-carrying vehicle. Its roomy interior would accommodate eight passengers with three seats installed—three in the front seat, two in the center, and three in the rear. The Suburban rode on the 1/2-ton's regular 116-inch-wheelbase chassis. Its maximum GVW rating was 4,600 pounds. The two-tone green paint scheme seen on this truck was the Suburban's standard paint treatment. *Bill Wales*

Chevrolet built a truck similar to this truck in two series—a light-duty 3800 Series 1-ton and a heavy-duty Series 4100 1 1/2-ton. Technically, Chevrolet classified only the Sedan Delivery and 1/2-ton conventional models as light-duty trucks. Medium-duty models included all 3/4- and 1-ton conventional cab and forward-control chassis. All other trucks were classified as heavy-duty models, both conventional and COE trucks. The 1-ton 137-inch-wheelbase truck is easily distinguished from its otherwise identical heavy-duty version by its wheels and tires. The heavy-duty model rode on big 20-inch wheels and tires, the 1-ton rode on 18-inch duals. The 3800 Series carried a maximum GVW rating of 8,800 pounds. Its model number was 3809. The Thriftmaster six, mated to a four-speed transmission, powered it.

One of Chevrolet's biggest selling 1949 trucks was the Model 4409 stake. The spacious 12-foot platform of this 161-inch-wheelbase stake truck accommodated long loads weighing up to 7,100 pounds, its maximum payload. Chevrolet offered a choice of two engines, the Loadmaster with 93 horsepower or the Thriftmaster with 90 horsepower. Other options included auxiliary springs, power brakes, and a wide range of tires up to 7.50x20 10-ply rating. *AAMA*

This truck is a 1949 Model 4403 heavy-duty, 161-inch-wheelbase chassis cab with an aftermarket stake/rack body. It was another of Chevrolet's lightest heavy-duty trucks. Its body is 12 feet long and it accommodated long loads with a payload between 4,100 and 7,100 pounds. Its standard 216-ci Thriftmaster engine produced 90 horsepower and 174 foot-pounds torque. The bigger 235-ci Loadmaster engine produced 93 horsepower and 192 foot-pounds torque. A Chevrolet-built four-speed transmission was standard equipment. A two-speed rear axle was an extra-cost option. Standard tires were 6.50x20 six-ply; optional were 7.50x20 10-ply. Hydrovac power brakes were also optional.

Chevrolet's biggest truck, the 161-inch-wheelbase Series 6400S, continued to be popular with the nation's fire departments. Its maximum GVW rating of 15,000 pounds was strong enough to carry a water tank, pump, hoses, and related fire-fighting gear. This is a 1949 Chevrolet 161-inch-wheelbase chassis cab with fire-fighting body. The Leeds (New York) Fire Department owned it. Truck No. 1 had a pumper body by Howe containing a 500-gallon water tank and a 500-gpm pump. This truck had the big 235-ci 93-horsepower Loadmaster six mated to a four-speed transmission and a two-speed rear axle. *Neal A. Van Deusen*

Chevrolet's biggest heavy-duty model for 1949 was Model 6403 with a 161-inch wheelbase. It carried the highest maximum GVW rating of the line—16,000 pounds. This is a 1949 Model 6403 chassis cab with fire-fighting body, owned by the Prosser (Washington) Fire Department. Its body was by Cooper and contained a 500-gallon water tank and a 500-gpm pump. It had the big 235-ci 93-horsepower six and a four-speed transmission. It also was equipped with the optional two-speed rear axle. Hydrovac power brakes were standard on this model. *Bill Hattersley*

Chevrolet's first ever forward-control chassis, the 125 1/4-inch-wheelbase 3/4-ton Model 3742, was introduced in 1948. For 1949, Chevrolet engineers introduced a second forward-control chassis, the 1-ton 137-inch-wheelbase Model 3942. These chassis were designed for users who required a larger load space than was offered in panel trucks. The new forward-control chassis permitted the mounting of bodies with greater cubic content but provided no increase in overall vehicle length. A new three-speed synchro-mesh transmission with steering column gearshift was standard equipment. Frames were extra long for full body support. The engine used in both models was the 216-ci Thriftmaster six. Panel bodies for these chassis were available from many manufacturers. *AAMA*

Chevrolet built two forward-control chassis again in 1949, the Model 3742 125 1/4-inch 3/4-tonner, and the Model 3942 127-inch 1-tonner. Model 3742 had a maximum GVW rating of 7,000 pounds and the Model 3942 was rated for 10,000 pounds. This is a 1949 Chevrolet Model 3942 1-ton forward-control chassis with a Dubl-Duti body. Both models featured the 216-ci Thriftmaster engine with a solenoid-operated starter with push button control. Other features included a full-floating rear axle; special 5:14 to 1 rear axle ratio; and single-acting shock absorbers, front and rear, optional at extra cost. It also featured a heavy-duty front axle with 3,500-pound capacity, a wide choice of tire sizes, dual rear wheels on Model 3942, a foot-operated parking brake, and recirculating ball worm steering gear. Model 3742 had the steering column-mounted shifter for its three-speed synchro-mesh transmission; Model 3942 used the floor-shifted four-speed synchro-mesh transmission. *AAMA*

This is a 1949 Series 4403 Chevrolet 1 1/2-ton chassis cab with lime spreader body. The standard 90-horsepower 216-ci Thriftmaster six powered this truck. Series 4400 models were rated for a maximum GVW rating of 12,500 pounds. Its transmission was the four-speed synchro-mesh. A two-speed rear axle was an option. The heavy-duty 93-horsepower 235-ci six was an extra-cost option. A 6.17:1 rear-axle ratio allowed this big Chevrolet to go into Iowa farm fields and spread a heavy load of agricultural lime. It was equipped with the extra-cost 7.50x20 10-ply-rated tires. *Verne Byers*

This all-original 1949 Chevrolet 4400 conventional 161-inch-wheelbase heavy-duty chassis cab with fire-fighting body has only 4,500 miles logged to date. It has the 216-ci six-cylinder engine and a four-speed transmission. Its pumper body is by Luverne. *Michelle & Jeff Tuma and Jeff Topic*

Chapter 4

1950 TO 1959

1950

Chevrolet engineers knew they had hit a bases-loaded home run with the Advance-Design trucks. Rather than spoil a good thing, they continued the trucks into a fourth year with only minor changes.

Chevrolet's Thriftmaster light-duty 216.5-ci truck engine was more than competitive against Dodge's 218-ci and 230-ci six-cylinder L-head engines, and Ford's 226-ci L-head six and 239 L-head V-8 engines. However, the Loadmaster engine was not quite as competitive against its two major rivals. It competed quite well at the 1 1/2-ton level, but came up a bit short against the other two at the 2-ton level.

Chevrolet engineers introduced an entirely new and more powerful Loadmaster engine in 1950. The new engine was rated at 105 horsepower, versus 93 horsepower for the old engine. The new

engine remained the same size as before (235.5 ci) and had the same compression ratio (6.7 to 1). Horsepower increased to 105 and gross torque to 193 foot-pounds at 2,000 rpm.

Major differences in the 105-horsepower engine and the former engine were centered on increased breathing capacity. Because the Loadmaster engine had a higher output than the Thriftmaster engine, it required larger intake and exhaust passages, since the engine inhaled larger amounts of fuel and air mixture and exhaled greater amounts of exhaust gases. Previously, it had been a compromise for the two engines' manifold to fit both engines. In 1950, however, the 105-horsepower engine demanded a larger manifold of its own.

Front and rear shock absorbers, of the direct double-acting type, were made regular equipment for 1950 on Sedan Delivery and all 1/2- and 3/4-ton trucks.

Model 3106, a Suburban Carryall with panel doors, was added to the 1/2-ton series 3100 in 1950. The panel doors were easier to open when the driver had an armful of packages. Additionally, this new model could be converted into a small bus with a rear exit. The

No change was made in the exterior appearance of Chevrolet trucks for 1950 except for Suburban Carryall paint colors. All regular and optional paint colors were made available for the Suburban models. The regular two-tone paint scheme was eliminated except for fleet use. This is a 1950 Chevrolet 1/2-ton Model 3104 116-inch-wheelbase pickup. Chevrolet advertised more power for the standard 216-ci Thriftmaster engine. It increased by 2 horsepower, to 92 from the former 90. Chevrolet engineers said the increase was not due to any one change but to several incidental engine modifications over several years. Gross torque increased to 176 foot-pounds from 174 foot-pounds. Maximum GVW rating for the 3100 Series 1/2-tonners remained at 4,600 pounds.

Chevrolet's medium-duty Series 4000 models continued without change for 1950. This series was Chevrolet's biggest seller. It was made up of Series 4100 137-inch-wheelbase models and Series 4400 161-inch-wheelbase series offering the following body models: platform, express platform, stake, express stake and high rack, and stock truck. This series was rated for a maximum GVW of 12,500 pounds, a maximum rating that suited the hauling needs of many buyers. The standard engine was the 92-horsepower Thriftmaster six. But to make it more appealing, Chevrolet's largest engine, the new 105-horsepower 235-ci six, was an option. Buyers had the choice of two rear-axle ratios and a two-speed rear axle. Pictured is a 1950 Model 4403 chassis cab with the 161-inch-wheelbase chassis.

rear door frame on the Suburban Carryall was modified, making it possible to install either rear doors or gates. Model 3116, with end gates, was continued. Through model year 1948, the Suburban was officially designated a Carryall Suburban. Beginning in the 1949 model year, the order of the names was reversed to the more familiar Suburban Carryall.

Solid plywood floors in 1/2- and 1-ton panels and canopies became standard construction. A single panel of wood and five skid strips replaced 13 floor boards and 12 skid strips.

The Sedan Delivery, which had been restyled the previous year along the lines of Chevrolet's new 1949 passenger cars, received only a minimum facelift and small mechanical improvements. Its grille sported a restyled hood ornament, just like the cars. The Chevrolet nameplate on the front of the hood was freshened up. Parking lights were revised and a vertical ornamental post was added below each parking light.

GM—Chevrolet in particular—enjoyed a very good year in 1950. The Chevrolet Motor Division posted a record-shattering performance by building 2,015,150 cars and trucks in U.S. plants. Chevrolet was the first manufacturer in history to produce more than 2,000,000 vehicles in a single year. The Chevrolet Motor Division sold 441,281 trucks in the United States during the calendar year, a 26 percent increase over 1949.

In midyear, the Korean War began, and by the end of the year, government controls on the use of critical materials had begun to be felt.

Industrywide, truck production turned up smartly in 1950. Demand for light-duty trucks remained high all year. Light-duty trucks in 1950 were sold principally to farmers; farm prosperity and incomes for the year rose sharply. Heavy-duty trucks also sold very well after being down since 1947. The "scare" buying that followed the outbreak of the Korean War also helped to fuel truck sales.

As had been true for years, Chevrolet was still the truck of choice for many of the nation's fire departments. This is a 1950 Model 4403 chassis cab with a fire-fighting body. The pumper was formerly the Wilmont (Minnesota) Community Fire Truck and had been out of service for a long time when photographed in 1998. Its body manufacturer is unknown, but it does have a water tank, pump, hoses, and other miscellaneous fire-fighting gear. It looks the same today as it did when it was in service. It is powered by the 216-ci Thriftmaster six. Its transmission was the four-speed synchro-mesh.

This is a 1950 Chevrolet Model 6408 platform truck. The truck's chassis wheelbase length is 161 inches. It is equipped with the new 105-horsepower Loadmaster 235-ci six engine and a synchro-mesh four-speed transmission to give maximum power and economy for rugged, heavy-duty operations. This truck has been restored and continues to work hauling its owner's antique tractors to shows. A two-speed rear axle, 9.00x20 10-ply tires, and double-acting shock absorbers were available optional equipment. *Richard Doane*

Chevrolet's biggest truck was also frequently chosen by the nation's fire departments. The St. Mary's (Missouri) Fire Department owned this 1950 Model 6403 chassis cab with a fire-fighting body. Its body is a 1955 model by Central. Engine No. 3 carried a 500-gallon water tank and a 300-gpm pump. This truck has the 161-inch-wheelbase chassis. The new 105-horsepower Loadmaster 235-ci six-cylinder engine powered it. *Dennis J. Maag*

Chevrolet's big Model 6103 chassis cab with fifth wheel equipment was very popular for both city delivery and road tractor service. This is a 1950 Chevrolet Model 6100 tractor pulling a soft-top, single-axle trailer. Notice it has the Deluxe cab, as can be seen from its rear quarter cab windows and chrome-plated grille bars. It also has accessory fog lamps mounted on the front bumper. *Harold Edwards*

The Chevrolet long 161-inch-wheelbase heavy-duty Model 6103 chassis cab was equipped with a hydraulic dump body built to its owner's specifications by one of many reputable body manufacturers across the nation. It was ideal for heavy construction work and highway maintenance. It was equipped with the new 105-horsepower Loadmaster engine, synchro-mesh four-speed transmission, optional two-speed rear axle, and a rugged channel frame. Other optional equipment included 9.00x20 10-ply tires, double-acting shock absorbers, and Deluxe cab equipment. *AAMA*

Chevrolet's heavy-duty conventional cab trucks for 1950 consisted of two Series—4000 and 6000. Chevrolet also built heavy-duty COE Series 5000 trucks. The Series 4000 trucks were rated for a maximum GVW of either 12,000 pounds or 12,500 pounds, and the 6000 Series for a maximum GVW of either 15,000 pounds or 16,000 pounds. This is a 1950 Chevrolet heavy-duty Model 6403 chassis cab with a hydraulic dump body for residential coal delivery. Notice that it has frame reinforcement plates installed in spite of the fact that Chevrolet engineers deemed it unnecessary. Its wheelbase was 161 inches long. Its engine was the new 105-horsepower 235-ci Loadmaster six, which was mated to the Chevrolet-built four-speed synchro-mesh transmission. *AAMA*

An Advance-Design Chevrolet pickup with a highly polished chrome grille is a real standout. This fully restored 1950 1/2-ton pickup is painted Chevrolet's signature dark green. This truly is a 1950 model, for all you sharp-eyed Advance-Design aficionados. Its owner, Terry Klenske, replaced its original doors—which were too far gone to be repaired—with doors from a 1952 pickup. *Terry Klenske*

1951

The 1951 Chevrolet Advance-Design trucks had neither significant exterior appearance changes nor new paint colors. There are a few clues, however, to help you identify their styling. Changes included the addition of new vent wings in the cab and single unit model's side windows. Engineers eliminated the left side cowl ventilator and lowered the position of the rearview mirror on the cowl. As an extra cost option, a chrome-plated grille for heavy-duty conventional trucks was available.

Safety was improved on light- and heavy-duty trucks with the addition of new brakes. Half-ton trucks and the Sedan Delivery were given brand-new brakes, fronts and rears. The brakes provided more effective braking with less effort and better control. New, balanced rear-wheel brakes on heavy-duty trucks were more effective and provided better control and longer life.

For independent operation, parking brakes on the heavy-duty trucks were removed from the rear wheels and applied to the propeller shaft just behind the transmission.

The number of models for 1951 increased to 83, and the number of wheelbases increased to 10. A new, longer-wheelbase series was introduced during the 1950 model year, and the company discontinued all high-rack stake trucks for 1951.

The rear bumper was eliminated as regular equipment on all 1/2- and 3/4-ton chassis models and pickups. The rear bumper was available as an RPO on these models. Several items at the rear end were revised or relocated so that they would not project beyond the body where they might be damaged without the protection of the bumper. These included the taillights, license plate, tailpipe, and tire

The 1951 Chevrolet trucks returned without any appearance changes and without any new paint colors. This is a 1951 Chevrolet Model 4104 116-inch-wheelbase 1/2-ton pickup. It was America's most popular truck. Its maximum GVW rating was increased to 4,800 pounds from the former 4,600 pounds. Standard equipment included the 92-horsepower Thriftmaster 216-ci six-cylinder engine; dual windshield wipers; a three-speed synchro-mesh transmission with its shift lever steering column mounted; 6.00x16 six-ply rated tires; direct double-acting shock absorbers, front and rear; and a foot-operated parking brake. *Wendell Leedy*

Chevrolet's forward control chassis line for 1951 continued to consist of Model 3742, a 3/4-ton on a 125 1/4-inch-wheelbase chassis and Model 3942, a 1-ton on a 137-inch chassis. Dubl-Duti built bodies for both of Chevrolet's two chassis. These door-to-door models featured the 92-horsepower Loadmaster 235-ci engine. They had full-floating rear axles with a 5.14 to 1 ratio to ensure the best acceleration for start-stop operation. A solenoid-operated starter with push-button control was standard on both models. Model 3742 was equipped with a steering-column three-speed transmission for greater convenience, easier handling, and a clear floor area for easy entrance and exit from either side. This is a cutaway display model of the 137-inch-wheelbase Model 3942 1-ton Dubl-Duti package delivery. *AAMA*

Chevrolet built cab-over-engine trucks on three wheelbase length chassis in 1951—110, 134, and 158 inches. Pictured is a 1951 Chevrolet Model 5103 2-ton COE chassis cab. This truck's wheelbase has been shortened to make it a mobile home tractor. Since 1947, Chevrolet used model numbers beginning with a "5" to denote a COE, such as this Model 5103 shown. Notice that this truck has a light-duty truck's spring-type front bumper. This is not correct; it should be the heavy-duty steel channel type. Its Loadmaster "105" engine delivered 100 horsepower, which was 5 horsepower less than a conventional cab because COEs had updraft carburetors. It also had the four-speed synchro-mesh transmission. *William Fox*

carrier. On 1/2- and 3/4-ton pickups, the tailgate could be lowered fully, so that it hung straight down, with the rear bumper eliminated. This was a convenience some pickup operators had requested.

One new extra-cost accessory that was added for 1951 was a portable spotlight. It provided a sealed lamp unit on a 14-foot cord that plugged into the cigarette lighter. It also had a retractable hook and a U-shaped hanger so it could be suspended for various uses.

This was a bittersweet production year for the Chevrolet Truck Division. Overall, the industry set a new high production record, but Chevrolet was not a part of the celebration. Two developments caused Chevrolet's production decline. First, the National Production Authority (NPA) severely restricted the number of light-duty trucks the industry could produce. Since Chevrolet was the leading manufacturer of light-duty trucks, it was adversely impacted. Second, the NPA allowed manufacturers to build all the military trucks they had government contracts for in addition to their quota of civilian models. Unfortunately, Chevrolet was not a government favorite for military truck contracts.

From the third quarter on, the NPA controlled key materials on a percent-of-industry basis. Chevrolet was favored in the medium-duty class, where it historically had been a production leader. In the heavy-duty class, however, it was not a player, so its allotment was zero. In spite of all the bad news, Chevrolet still accounted for approximately one-third of all truck production in 1951.

Chevrolet was favored because of the higher ratio of truck sales to passenger cars in the postwar era. Before World War II, the ratio of deliveries ran approximately one truck to four cars. After 1945, the ratio narrowed to a new low of one truck to every two and one-half cars. After 1949, an increasing share of Chevrolet's total output went to medium-duty trucks rated between 14,401 and 16,000 pounds GVW. Chevrolet's principal strength, however, remained in the light-duty 5,001-pound and less category.

Chevrolet's calendar year truck sales in the United States for 1951 totaled 370,982. This represented a 16 percent decline from 1950, but was still 110,000 units ahead of the second-place producer.

Chevrolet returned to nominal ratings for all truck models in 1951. For example, this 1-ton Model 3803 chassis cab riding on a 137-inch-wheelbase chassis is equipped with a specialized fire-fighting body. The Fire Department of the City of Seattle owned this water vacuum truck. Its maximum GVW rating was 8,800 pounds and maximum payload rating was 4,100 pounds. Its drivetrain consisted of the 216-ci Thriftmaster six and a four-speed synchro transmission. Tires were 7.00x18 eight-ply rated. Hydrovac power brakes were an extra-cost option. This truck was standard with single rear wheels; dual wheels were an extra-cost option. *Bill Hattersley*

Chevrolet's Model 6403S 1 1/2-ton Special 161-inch-wheelbase chassis cab continued to be a favorite truck with the nation's fire departments. It was rated for a maximum GVW of 15,000 pounds. The new 105-horsepower Loadmaster six-cylinder engine powered it. The Chevrolet-built four-speed synchro-mesh transmission put the engine's power at the back wheels. With the optional two-speed rear axle, total speeds doubled. Its long wheelbase was ideally suited for the installation of many types of bodies up to 12 feet in length. The Castleford (Idaho) Mutual Fire Insurance Co. owned this truck. Its 500-gallon pumper body was by ALF. *M. Boatwright*

This was the new in 1951 Chevrolet Model 6503 chassis cab with a 179-inch wheelbase and tanker body. Its maximum GVW rating was also 16,000 pounds. It was designed for bodies up to 16 feet long, with heavy-duty features to handle the really big jobs. Seven sturdy frame cross-members with alligator-jaw attachments supported the load and ensured proper alignment of the frame siderails. This new longer frame supplied up to 81 inches of overhang. Standard mechanical features included new Twin-Action rear brakes, the powerful Loadmaster "105" 105-horsepower six-cylinder engine, a four-speed synchro transmission and rear springs, each of 7,800-pound capacity. *C.S.B. Oil Co. of Portland, Conn.*

Chevrolet's Model 6403 137-inch-wheelbase chassis cab was the ideal truck for dump truck service. With the Loadmaster "105" engine delivering 105 horsepower and high torque over a wide range of usable road speeds, this unit could maintain faster road schedules with maximum loads at top economy. Other standard items that contributed to its outstanding performance included new Twin-Action rear brakes, a heavy-duty frame, a four-speed synchro transmission, and 7.50x20 eight-ply rated rear tires. *AAMA*

The low-priced, economical jack-of-all-trades truck was Chevrolet's 1951 Model 4403 1 1/2-ton 161-inch-wheelbase chassis cab with special bodies up to 12 feet in length. This 1951 Model 4403 chassis cab had a special pickle-hauling body. Its maximum GVW rating was a full 14,000 pounds and maximum payload rating was 8,500 pounds. Its heavy-duty frame and four-speed synchro transmission accommodated either the 216-ci 92-horsepower Thriftmaster engine or the extra powerful Loadmaster "105" 105-horsepower engine. Its new Twin-Action rear brakes provided easier, smoother stops. A two-speed rear axle was an extra-cost option. *AAMA*

Chevrolet's biggest-selling medium-duty 1951 body model was this Model 4409 12-foot stake. Chevrolet truck's market strength at that time was in light- and medium-duty trucks. This 1 1/2-ton truck was built on a 161-inch-wheelbase chassis and carried a maximum GVW rating of 14,000 pounds. Its standard engine was the 216-ci 92-horsepower Thriftmaster six. The powerful Loadmaster "105" engine was available as an option. It had the Chevrolet-built four-speed synchro transmission. A two-speed rear axle was another important option. Chevrolet supplied the stake body. Notice the skinny spare tire attached under at the rear. *Ron Cenowa*

The most compelling reasons for buying a 1951 Chevrolet COE truck included an excellent all-around commanding view of the road and more load space in less vehicle length. Shorter wheelbases made the trucks easier to maneuver and park. Chevrolet built three different wheelbase lengths COE Series models in 1951: 110, 134, and 158 inches. This is a 1951 Chevrolet COE Series 5700 chassis and cab with a platform body. The stake express model, by the way, was a stake-type body with a steel hinged door located in the center of the rear stakes. The heavy-duty 100-horsepower 235-ci six-cylinder Loadmaster engine powered this truck. Its transmission was the standard four-speed synchro unit. Notice the optional grille guard mounted on the front bumper. *Spanky L. Hardy*

Jim McDermott's family owned the Chevrolet-Buick dealership in Gunnison, Colorado, for many years. They used this heavy-duty 2-ton 1951 Series 6503 chassis cab with a famous Holmes W35 twin-boom wrecker body in their business. This big Chevrolet rode on a 179-inch-wheelbase chassis and was rated for a maximum GVW of 16,000 pounds. A 105-horsepower Loadmaster 235-ci six-cylinder engine was standard, as was its four-speed synchro transmission. It also has the optional two-speed rear axle. Jim still owns the truck, but it no longer has the wrecker body mounted. Notice its optional rear corner windows and left side spotlight. *Jim McDermott*

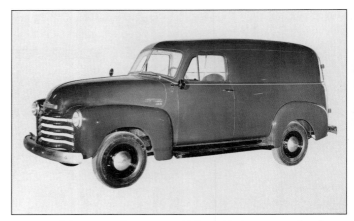

As one might expect from two vehicles with the same wheelbase lengths, the 1/2-ton Panel Model 3105's load space of 6 1/2 feet long was the same as that of the 1/2-ton pickup. Maximum GVW ratings were 4,400 pounds for both trucks. The panel was employed principally as a delivery vehicle to protect expensive commodities from the weather. A Deluxe version was also part of Chevrolet's complete line. This is a 1951 Chevrolet 1/2-ton Model 3105 standard panel. Standard equipment included the 92-horsepower Thriftmaster 216-ci engine; three-speed synchro-mesh transmission with gearshift lever on the steering column; 6.00x16 tires; and bumpers and shock absorbers, front and rear. An advantage of the panel for a delivery truck was the huge area it provided for signage. *Greg Norman*

1952

Chevrolet's truck line dropped to a total of 73 models on 10 wheelbases in 1952. Express platform trucks and express stake and tailgate trucks in both COE and conventional cab series had been discontinued due to low production in midyear 1951.

Truck exterior and interior styling continued mostly unchanged. One new exterior feature was the adoption of push-button door locks in place of turn-handle locks. Because of Korean War materials restrictions, several exterior and interior changes were incorporated on 1952 trucks. For example, deluxe equipment and series nameplates were dropped in midyear 1951. Also dropped were chrome-plated grilles and the optional chrome rear bumpers. On all light- and medium-duty models, gray paint replaced chrome plating on bumpers and hubcaps.

The foot-operated parking brake control replaced the hand-operated lever in 1-ton trucks. The mechanism was the same as that of the 1/2- and 3/4-ton models.

During 1951, a round plastic knob replaced the former diecast T-handle brake release in 1/2- and 3/4-ton trucks. It was also incorporated in 1-ton models for 1952. The knob was the same color as other instrument panel controls, and was modified with the letter "B," painted white for identification.

A positive crankcase ventilation system had been regular equipment on forward-control models. It was made available as an RPO for all Series 5000 and 6000 trucks. A closed valve rocker cover replaced the louvered cover, and a hose connected the air cleaner with the rocker cover. The windstream-suction vent pipe

Chevrolet's truck line for 1952 was reduced from 83 models on 10 wheelbases in 1951 to 73 models on 10 wheelbases. There were no exterior or interior styling changes for 1952. The only clue to tell a 1952 from a 1951 truck is that the 1952 models had the new push-button door handles. As before, only the right side door could be locked with a key. A lock for the left door was offered at extra cost. This is a 1952 Chevrolet Model 4403 chassis cab with special fire-fighting body. This truck had the 161-inch wheelbase and was rated for a maximum GVW of 14,000 pounds. Its engine was the 92-horsepower 216-ci six, but the 105-horsepower 235-ci six was an extra-cost option. The only transmission offered was the Chevrolet-built four-speed synchro. This refueler truck was owned by the San Francisco Fire Department. *Chuck Madderom*

was eliminated and, instead, tubing ran from the ventilator to the intake manifold.

Radiators in all truck series were revised to conserve critical materials. The radiator core height was reduced and air cells were spaced farther apart. In Series 5000 and 6000 trucks, the radiator thickness was reduced by 1/2 inch. For all radiators, a 4-pound pressure cap was adopted to compensate for the reduced radiating surface.

Changes in the Sedan Delivery followed those of the Special series passenger cars. The grille was restyled with five vertical moldings added to the center horizontal bar. Parking lights were wider. The Chevrolet name was relocated from the grille header bar to the hood emblem. The new hood ornament retained the jet aircraft motif.

Car and truck production during 1952 was restricted for the second successive year. The government controlled vital production materials. The NPA limited U.S. manufacturers to 4,342,000 cars and 1,218,293 trucks. This was 14 percent behind the all-time record output of 1951.

Chevrolet produced one out of every four commercial vehicles in the United States in 1952. One of the big keys to the company's success in the truck market, year in and year out, was its supremacy in light-duty models. More than 50 percent, or exactly 171,114 units, of Chevrolet's total 1952 volume were rated at 5,000 pounds and lower GVW.

Chevrolet assembled trucks in 10 plants around the country in 1952. Of the seven million trucks built by Chevrolet up to this time, 40 percent were still registered for operation.

GM overall enjoyed a good financial year in 1952. Total sales were $7.5 billion, a record year. For the first nine months of 1952, defense work sales volume totaled more than a billion dollars—nearly 2 1/2 times the volume for the same period in 1951. Defense work was a bit less profitable than normal business, however.

Chevrolet's truck sales took another heavy hit in 1952 due to government restrictions on truck production. Total calendar year U.S. sales fell 22 percent from 1951, totaling only 290,953 units. Chevrolet continued to be the nation's number one manufacturer of trucks, however, in spite of lower sales.

Chevrolet's 3/4-ton Model 3609 stake rode on a 125 1/2-inch wheelbase and was rated for a maximum GVW rating of 5,800 pounds. Its 7-foot stake body featured a load space 87 5/8-inches by 70 3/4-inches. It could be loaded from either side as well as from the rear. Stake pockets were reinforced with steel to lend strong support to the removable stake sides. Note the heavy load on this commercial stake truck. Series 3600 trucks featured full-floating 5,000-pound rear axles. Its standard ratio was 4.57 to 1; a 5.14 to 1 was optional. The Thriftmaster 216-ci six-cylinder engine produced 92 horsepower and 176 foot-pounds torque. A three-speed synchro transmission was standard, a four-speed was an extra-cost option. *Arnold Paradis*

Chevrolet's Model 3808 1-ton platform rode on a 137-inch wheelbase and was rated for a maximum GVW of 8,800 pounds. The 1952 1-ton pictured has a Napco 4WD conversion. It was still in daily service at a Christmas tree farm in January 1999. It has a two-speed transfer case and the original Chevrolet four-speed transmission. Its original six has been removed and replaced with a new Chevrolet engine—a 366-ci V-8. It is optioned with chrome grille bars and fender-mounted turn signal lights. The big push bumper and festive Christmas wreath mounted on the grille were not standard options. *Joe and Jan Phelan*

Chevrolet's smallest 1952 pickup was Model 3104. It rode on a 116-inch-wheelbase chassis and was rated for a maximum GVW of 4,800 pounds. These versatile little trucks served a wide variety of jobs. Chevrolet engineers built them tough to handle even the hardest tasks. For example, the pickup's cargo box floor was constructed of hardwood planking with flush steel skid strips. It also had an exceptionally sturdy end gate that could be held level to support a long load or dropped to a vertical position to facilitate loading. The 92-horsepower Thriftmaster OHV six-cylinder engine was standard, as was its steering-column-mounted three-speed synchro transmission. The front bumper was standard, the rear was optional, and the wooden sideboards are aftermarket. This is a 1952 Chevrolet 1/2-ton pickup. *Elliott Kahn*

1953

Chevrolet added a 212-inch school bus chassis in mid-season 1952, bringing the total number of truck models to 74 and total number of wheelbases to 11. The new model, the fourth of the school bus line, filled a need for a chassis better adapted to a 54-passenger body.

A highlight of the 1953 Chevrolet trucks was a new range of paint colors. The standard color was Juniper Green with Cream Medium striping. Now buyers had the choice, at no extra cost, of a range of new colors. These included: Ocean Green, Transport Blue, Burgundy Maroon, Coppertone, Autumn Brown, and Shell White with either harmonizing or contrasting striping.

A new Loadmaster engine for 1953 delivered greater maximum power and torque with improved fuel economy. It still displaced 235.5 ci, but with a compression ratio of 7.1 to 1. The new engine was regular equipment on the 2-ton and forward-control model, and available as a regular production option on the 1 1/2-ton models. All other models retained the 216.5-ci, 92-horsepower Thriftmaster engine. Advantages of the improved engine included: greater maximum power, greater maximum torque, a higher compression ratio, chrome-plated top piston rings, valve rotators, exhaust valves with greater strength, stronger connecting rods, a stiffer crankshaft, a stronger crankcase, bypass cooling, an improved ignition system, a larger capacity generator, and easier damp weather starting.

The new engine featured better passing and hill climbing ability, greater durability, and better operating economy. The chrome-plated top piston rings, valve rotators, and hardened exhaust valves extended the period between overhauls and contributed to longer engine life.

Maximum gross horsepower increased from 105 to 108 at 3,600 rpm; maximum gross torque increased from 193 to 200 foot-pounds at 2,000 rpm.

The new cylinder head had a smaller combustion chamber volume and the width of the transfer passage was reduced for a higher compression ratio. Three more head bolts were used to attach the head to the block, increasing its stiffness and promoting better-maintained head gasket durability.

New extra-cost tinted glass shielded the driver from glare and radiant heat, reducing driver fatigue. In fact, the tinted glass filtered out objectionable sun glare and excluded 69 percent of the sun's heat—45 percent more than ordinary safety glass.

The rear bumper, deleted in 1951 due to material shortages, was again available as an RPO for 1/2- and 3/4-ton pickup and chassis models.

A spare tire carrier mounted on the left side of the pickup body was offered as an RPO for 1/2-, 3/4-, and 1-ton pickups. The side mount necessitated dishing a small portion of the rear fender to accommodate the tire.

Because the Sedan Delivery was patterned after Chevrolet cars, the 1953 model was all new, with the same general styling of the two-door Chevrolet automobile.

The NPA's restriction on truck manufacturing ended in February 1953. The effect was that the industry sold approximately 654,000 light-duty trucks in 1953 against 539,000 in 1952, making it the only weight class to show a sharp gain over the two years. Medium-duty trucks dipped to 197,000 from 220,000, and heavy-duty trucks rose to 109,000 from 105,000.

Chevrolet, the annual light-duty leader, benefited by the increase in light-duty trucks, of course. After being down for the past two years due to government controls, Chevrolet's 1953 sales increased by 13 percent, to 327,546. Because of its stunning new 1953 models, Ford closed Chevrolet's lead to only 51,000 trucks. Chevrolet built 3 out of every 10 trucks built in the United States during 1953.

The only appearance change in 1953 was the new series designation plate that replaced the hood nameplate. The most significant change for 1953, however, was the new 235-ci Loadmaster engine. Gross horsepower was increased to 108 and gross torque to 200 lb.ft. This engine was standard equipment for 2-ton trucks and forward-control models, and optional for 1 1/2-ton trucks. All other models retained the unchanged 216-ci Thriftmaster six. The Augusta (Missouri) Community Fire Department owned this 1953 Chevrolet heavy-duty Model 6403 chassis cab with special fire-fighting body. Its pumper body was by Central (a 1954 model body) and contained a 500-gallon water tank and a 500-gpm pump. *Dennis J. Maag*

Chevrolet offered six COE truck models in 1953 in three Series: 5100S and 5100; 5400S and 5400; and 5700S and 5700 on three wheelbase lengths—110, 134, and 158 inches, respectively. The "S" Series trucks carried a maximum GVW rating of 15,000 pounds and the other three Series carried a maximum GVW rating of 16,000 pounds. One engine was available, the heavy-duty Loadmaster 107-horsepower 235-ci six. The only transmission was the four-speed synchro. A two-speed rear axle was an extra-cost option. This is a 1953 Chevrolet Model 5703 COE chassis cab with wrecker body. The wrecker body appears to be the famous Holmes twin-boom unit. *Spanky L. Hardy*

By December 31, 1953, nearly 3 million post–World War II Chevrolet trucks had been produced in 10 U.S. assembly plants. Approximately 32 percent of all trucks registered in the United States bore Chevrolet nameplates. In the closing week of 1953, Chevrolet Division completed its 30-millionth vehicle. Approximately 11 million of these were produced post–World War II.

Chevrolet built the industry's first production sports car, the Corvette, on the last day of the month of June 1953.

Chevrolet constructed its 28th plant in 1953, a 600,000-square-foot facility in Flint, Michigan, to build 25 percent of the division's car frames.

The Model 3104 half-ton pickup continued to be the best selling model in Chevrolet's 1953 Advance-Design truck series. Its useful cargo box featured a wooden floor with flush steel skid strips to facilitate loading. Items slid better on steel than wood. The pickup's box measured 78 inches long by 50 inches wide and 14 inches high to the top of the tailgate. A convenient side step was provided between the rear fender and cab to make loading and unloading over the side easier. Chevrolet's famous OHV 92-horsepower six-cylinder engine was its only available power source. The standard transmission was a three-speed synchro. A four-speed was optional. Model 3104 had a 116-inch wheelbase and a maximum GVW rating of 4,800 pounds. *Mike Anthony*

1954

For the first time since the company introduced Advance-Design trucks, Chevrolet designers created a significantly restyled truck. The 1954's grille, parking lights, and one-piece curved windshield led the all-new look. Chevrolet referred to the new styling as "massive simplicity." That it was. The wide parking lights emphasized width. The three broad horizontal and one vertical grille bars were simple and heavy in appearance. Modern block letters centered on the grille header bar spelled out *Chevrolet*. A massive hood emblem mounted immediately above the grille prominently displayed the famous Chevrolet bow tie trademark.

Cab interior styling changes included a new instrument panel and instruments, windshield garnish molding, a steering wheel and horn button, and new interior colors and trim.

In the regular production Suburban Carryall, cab, and panel models, the seat cushion, backrest, and door panel trim were brown, while the instrument panel, garnish moldings, headlining, and lower door panels were beige. Initially, Chevrolet designers planned a deluxe interior scheme including a unique two-tone color combination for Suburban Carryalls. However, that plan was dropped early on because it was thought production would be limited, due to the extra effort required in assembly. The deluxe Suburban Carryall interior was then changed to an extra-cost RPO item.

Instruments were all new and located directly in front of the driver in two round units. The left unit contained the gauges; the speedometer and odometer were located on the right along with the headlight beam indicator and the directional signal indicator.

The 235-ci engine replaced the 216-ci engine in 1/2-, 3/4-, 1-, and 1 1/2-ton Series trucks. The new engine was painted gray and was identified as Thriftmaster 235 on the valve rocker cover decal. On Series 5000, 6000, and the forward-control models, the decal carried the name Loadmaster 235. All engines featured a full-pressure lubrication system, aluminum pistons, insert-type connecting rod bearings, and more rigid connecting rods and crankshaft. The cylinder blocks, heads, pistons, piston pins, connecting rods, crankshafts, camshafts, and valve springs were interchangeable in all 235-ci engines for 1954.

Maximum gross output for the 1954 Thriftmaster and Loadmaster engines were 112 horsepower, versus 92 in 1953, and 200 foot-pounds torque versus 176 foot-pounds in 1953.

New for 1954 was an optional heavy-duty engine that provided improved performance for heavy-duty operation. It was painted dark green and identified as the Jobmaster 261 by a decal on the valve cover. It was also equipped with a high-lift cam.

Chevrolet's 115-inch-wheelbase 1954 Sedan Delivery had a fresh, new appearance. This passenger car–based delivery's styling was updated annually to keep step with the Chevrolet passenger cars. Its all-steel body was built by Fisher and mounted on a passenger car chassis. Its standard and only engine was the 235-ci Blue Flame, 115-horsepower automobile engine. The new engine and a lower numerical rear-axle ratio gave the 1954 Sedan Delivery greatly improved performance with added fuel economy. Other new mechanical features included a new carburetor with an automatic choke and a 30-inch muffler. Powerglide automatic was an option. *AAMA*

The 1954 Chevrolet Model 3105 1/2-ton panel was built on the same 116-inch-wheelbase chassis as all other 1/2-ton trucks. The Panel was designed for delivery work where load protection from weather and theft was important. Its large rear panel doors opened to 90 or 180 degrees to make loading and unloading quick in order to increase driver productivity. Its load space was finished with sturdy plywood protected with steel skid strips for long life. The new Loadmaster 112-horsepower 235-ci six-cylinder engine was the new standard for light-duty trucks. Its gross maximum torque was an impressive 200 foot-pounds at 2,000 rpm. This panel is the Deluxe model as seen by the chrome trim on the front and rear fenders. *AAMA*

Chevrolet had its first new postwar truck on the market one year before its major competitors, and it stayed with the same models longer. It's a big puzzle why Chevrolet bothered to spend the money for an interim model for 1954 and half of 1955. This is a 1954 Chevrolet Model 3104 1/2-ton pickup. The changes in the new trucks were certainly welcome and added to their value, drivability, and load-moving capabilities. Also, they could be upgraded in appearance with the addition of the new chrome option for Series 3100, 3600, and 3800 trucks. This option included a chrome grille, hubcaps, and front bumper. The Model 3104 1/2-ton pickup's body was enlarged for 1954. It was 1/8 inch longer, the same width but deeper, 17 9/16 versus 16 1/4 inches. Another exciting option for 1954 trucks was a fully automatic four-speed automatic.

With a downdraft carburetor it was rated at 135 horsepower, and with an updraft COE carburetor it was rated at 125 horsepower. Maximum gross torque output was 220 foot-pounds.

A fully automatic four-speed transmission was now available as optional equipment for light- and medium-duty trucks. The truck automatic was a GM Hydra-Matic.

This turned out to be a hard year for the nation's truck producers. Total production was off by almost 200,000 units compared to 1953. The only bright spot in the numbers was that export sales, while not a record, posted a 60,000-unit increase over 1953.

Chevrolet was again number one in sales, but it saw its sales advantage over number two Ford slip. Chevrolet's sales, while 17 percent greater than Ford's, slipped by 11 percent from 1953. Chevrolet was the only member of the Big Three without a modern OHV V-8 engine in 1954. Total Chevrolet truck sales for calendar year 1954 were 292,202.

Chevrolet was gearing up for bigger and better things in the future. Manufacturing capacity was being greatly expanded, with three new plants under construction at the end of the year in Tonawanda, New York, and Flint and Livonia, Michigan.

The two Suburban models differed only in their rear door types. Model 3116 had the tailgate and liftgate station wagon–type rear doors and Model 3106 had the tall panel-type rear doors. The major appeal of the Suburban was its versatility, which allowed it to be converted from a passenger vehicle to a cargo carrier in a few short minutes. As a passenger carrier it could seat up to eight adults in comfort. As a cargo carrier it was rated at the same maximum GVW as other 1/2-ton trucks—4,800 pounds. Suburbans for 1954 were given the same equipment and brown and beige interior for all standard cab trucks. All of the former Suburban deluxe equipment items—interior and exterior—became part of a new RPO package. *AAMA*

The 1954 Chevrolet 3/4-ton pickup was Model 3604. Its wheelbase was 125 1/4 inches and its maximum GVW rating was a hefty 6,900 pounds. Model 3604's cargo box measured 90x50 inches with 17 1/2-inch sides and ends. It, too, used the new 112-horsepower 235-ci six-cylinder Thriftmaster engine. The three-speed synchro-mesh transmission was standard, and the four-speed synchro and automatic were options. Standard tires were 15 inch six-ply rated. Maximum optional tires went up to 7.50x17 eight-ply. The only other available 3/4-ton body models were the 7 1/2-foot platform and stake. *AAMA*

Chevrolet's largest pickup for 1954 was the huge Model 3804 1-ton. It rode on a 137-inch-wheelbase chassis and was rated for a maximum GVW of 7,000 pounds. A dual-rear-wheel option was not offered. Its cargo box measured 108 1/4x50 inches and had 17 9/16-inch sides and ends. Due to its great length, it was equipped with eight stake pockets for installation of optional equipment. It had the same engine as the 3/4-ton pickup and was rated for a payload capacity of 2,900 pounds. This heavy-duty hauler's transmission was the four-speed synchro. A heavy-duty three-speed and the automatic were optional. *AAMA*

Chevrolet offered chassis cab models in 1/2-, 3/4- and 1-ton capacities in 1954. This is a 3/4-ton. The 3/4-ton chassis cab was rated for a maximum GVW of 6,900 pounds. Its wheelbase was 125 1/4 inches, the same as that of the pickup. Its sturdy chassis would accept a wide range of custom bodies. This body has an interesting two-tone paint scheme. This truck was also equipped with the optional Comfortmaster Deluxe cab, as can be seen from its rear quarter windows. Other Deluxe features included: chrome windshield and door window trim reveal moldings; dual horns; right-hand sunshade; driver arm rest; cigar lighter; and harmonizing maroon and gray cab interior trim. *AAMA*

Chevrolet built five 1-ton body models in 1954: pickup, panel, canopy express, platform, and stake. All rode on the 137-inch heavy 1-ton chassis. This panel, like the pickup and canopy express, had a maximum GVW rating of 7,000 pounds. The 1-ton panel was intended for use as a delivery vehicle for heavy and long cargoes. Cargo items as long as 12 1/2 feet could be carried in the truck's 202 cubic feet of space. The distance from the rear door to the back of the driver seat was 9 feet. A long-wearing plywood floor provided total protection for cargo. Steel skid strips made loading and unloading a snap through the two large back doors. The new 112-horsepower, 235-ci Thriftmaster six-cylinder engine was standard. The four-speed synchro transmission was standard; the three-speed HD and the automatic were optional. Deluxe trim equipment was also available. *AAMA*

The driver had a full view of his instruments through the steering wheel. Finger grips on the wheel's horizontal spokes and wheel rim gave a firm, comfortable hold. Housing for the installation of a directional signal control was located below the wheel. The overhanging crown of the instrument panel prevented reflection of the instrument lights onto the windshield. A large glovebox equipped with a combined push-button latch and key lock was located at the far right. A tilt-type ashtray was located immediately to the left of the glovebox and is hidden from view in this photo.

Dual rear wheels were standard equipment on the 1954 Chevrolet Model 3809 1-ton, 137-inch-wheelbase stake truck. A platform version was also available. The body of this stake truck was 9 feet long by 7 feet wide inside the stake racks. Because of its dual rear wheels, the maximum GVW rating of the stake was an impressive 8,800 pounds. The drivetrain consisted of the new 112-horsepower Thriftmaster engine, four-speed synchro transmission, and 10-inch clutch. Options included an 11-inch clutch, HD three-speed transmission, automatic transmission, 7.00x18 eight-ply tires, auxiliary rear springs, Comfortmaster Deluxe Cab equipment, tinted glass, and a left-hand push-button door lock. *AAMA*

Chevrolet's popular, low-priced workhorse for 1954 was the Model 4103 1 1/2-ton chassis cab as pictured with a coal delivery body. This rugged little truck carried a big 14,000-pound maximum GVW rating. Its standard engine (no options) was the 112-horsepower Thriftmaster 235-ci six. Its transmission was the four-speed synchro. A 161-inch-wheelbase version of this model was also available. This truck could be considerably beefed up with the addition of the following heavy-duty equipment: heavy-duty frame, 750x20 10-ply tires, 5.43:1 rear-axle ratio, heavy-duty 4,500-pound capacity front axle and springs, Hydrovac power brakes, and six-leaf auxiliary rear springs. *AAMA*

The new front-end sheet metal on the heavy-duty model was proportionately larger than that for the light-duty trucks. The three horizontal grille bars with a single dividing bar were the dominant design elements. The grille was painted body color. The center bar extended all across the radiator opening and nearly to the outside of the fenders. The Chevrolet name was impressed into the top bar in block letters. The chrome hood emblem was a new design. The bow tie trademark was painted blue, the vertical groves in the center section were filled with red paint. The new, large parking lights fairly well marked the width of the trucks and served well as directional signal lights. The new Chevrolet trucks presented a husky, modern appearance. *AAMA*

Chevrolet's cab-over-engine line for 1954 was short and simple. It consisted of three Series: 5100, 5400, and 5700. Wheelbase lengths were 110, 134, and 158 inches respectively. Within each series was a further breakdown—an "S" Series as well as the standard series. The "S" (1 1/2-ton, Special) models carried a maximum GVW rating of 15,000 pounds versus 16,000 pounds for the standard 2-ton models. A platform and stake model were offered in the 5400 Series. This is a 1954 Chevrolet 2-ton Model 5703 COE chassis cab with special enclosed stake body. The standard engine for all models was the 107-horsepower 235-ci Loadmaster six-cylinder. The 125-horsepower 261-ci Jobmaster six was optional. Only the Chevrolet-built four-speed transmission was available. The Comfortmaster Deluxe Cab was an option. *AAMA*

One of the most popular Chevrolet truck models was the economical, medium-duty 1 1/2-ton Model 4403 chassis cab, pictured here with a custom beverage body. Factory body models for this truck included the 12-foot stake and platform. The new 112-horsepower Loadmaster 235-ci six engine was standard equipment for Series 4000 trucks. The Chevrolet-built four-speed transmission was standard. *AAMA*

The 1954 Chevrolet 2-ton Model 6409 12-foot stake body was one of America's best-selling heavy-duty trucks. It was built on a 161-inch chassis and carried a maximum GVW rating of 16,000 pounds. Chevrolet built three basic models in its 6000 Series: 6100, 6400, and 6500. Wheelbase lengths were 137, 161, and 179 inches, respectively. Both a regular and a special model were offered: the 1 1/2-ton Special with the suffix "S" and the 2-ton. They were rated for maximum GVWs of 15,000 and 16,000 pounds. Both chassis and chassis cab models were offered in each of the three series, but only in the 6100 and 6400 were body models available—9-foot and 12-foot stake and platforms. The 112-horsepower 235-ci Loadmaster engine was standard; the new 135-horsepower 261-ci Jobmaster six-cylinder engine was optional. The four-speed synchro-mesh was the only available transmission. *AAMA*

Chevrolet trucks continued to be the nation's number one choice with fire fighters. This is a 1954 Chevrolet Model 6503 chassis cab with fire-fighting body. It was one of the new, long, 179-inch chassis cabs. The Molalla (Oregon) Rural Fire Protection District No. 73 owned engine No. 83. Its pumper body was built by Cooper and carried a 500-gallon water tank and a 500-gpm pump. The new, optional 135-horsepower 261-ci six-cylinder engine powered this truck. *Bill Hattersley*

The Model 6103 chassis cab, at 137 inches, was Chevrolet's shortest-wheelbase 2-ton heavy-duty 1954 truck. It is pictured here with fifth wheel equipment. The Model 6103 was rated for a maximum GVW of 16,000 pounds. The new 135-horsepower 261-ci six-cylinder engine powered this truck. Its maximum gross torque was 220 foot-pounds. The new engine was painted green and had a decal reading "Jobmaster 261" on its valve cover rocker. This new engine had the same exterior dimensions as the regular production 235-ci Thriftmaster and Loadmaster engines. Its carburetor had a 1/8-inch larger main venturi and throttle body diameters. *AAMA*

John M. Lyon's big 1-ton Series 3804 137-inch-wheelbase pickup looks as good as new. It's an interesting pickup because John uses it to tow a trailer loaded with his 1927 Chevrolet tank truck to truck shows and other events. He does not hesitate to tow the older truck many hundreds of miles to an important event. The original 235-ci Thriftmaster 112-horsepower six-cylinder engine powers the pickup. John has installed a two-speed auxiliary transmission to give him a total of six forward speeds. *John M. Lyon*

Chevrolet's Truck Automatic Transmission was built by GM's Hydra-Matic Division. The automatic for a 1/2-ton pickup was geared to mate with the pickup's rear-axle ratio. For the first time Chevrolet light-duty truck drivers were freed from clutching and shifting manually. The automatic combined a fluid coupling with a planetary gear train hydraulically controlled through a combination of clutches and bands. The fluid coupling cushioned the truck and load from the shock of power shifts. Buyers of an automatic also got push-button starting and an automatic choke in the package, both new items for Chevrolet pickups. On the left through the steering wheel can be seen the engine temperature gauge, voltmeter, and fuel gauge. The hidden oil pressure gauge is located at the five o'clock position. Note that the speedometer registers up to 90 miles per hour and the odometer registers only 88,347.2 miles. *Mike Anthony*

This beautiful two-tone 1954 Model 3104 1/2-ton pickup with Comfortmaster DeLuxe cab equipment has the Hydra-Matic automatic. Other deluxe items included E-Z Eye tinted glass and side-mounted spare tire carrier. The 112-horsepower six-cylinder OHV Thriftmaster engine powered all 1954 light-duty trucks. This pickup's wheelbase length was 116 inches and maximum GVW rating was 4,800 pounds. Chevrolet-approved dealer-installed accessories included a custom built truck radio, cigar lighter, clock, seat covers, windshield washers, directional signals, outside metal sun visor, a high-note horn in addition to the standard horn, heater defroster, inside non-glare rearview mirror, and rail-type grille guard. *Mike Anthony*

1955

The 1955 model year began by carrying the former Advance-Design series forward. It was not until March 25, 1955, that Chevrolet introduced its new truck series.

Chevrolet designers gave the all-new 1955 trucks a capable "load-pulling" look. The new exterior styling featured forward-slanting body and sheet-metal lines, which, when viewed from the side, gave these trucks a look similar to that of a team of draft horses pulling and straining to move a heavy load. To achieve this effect, Chevrolet designers gave all cab and sheet metal a forward slant. The windshield pillar, the upper structure of the cab, the hooded headlights, and the wheel openings formed a forward-slanting profile.

The new line was made up of 75 models on 15 wheelbases, in place of the 74 models on 11 wheelbases of 1954. New models included a 1/2-ton long-wheelbase pickup and the stunning new Cameo Carrier, a 1/2-ton pickup with custom styling and luxury appointments. There were three forward-control models in place of the former two, and the canopy express models were dropped.

New styling cues included a concealed step inside the cab doors that replaced the separate running boards and formed a smooth unbroken line from the front fenders through the cab doors. New series designation plates were located on front fender sides and displayed the series number and the Chevrolet name on a spear-shaped design. Hooded headlights added to the "load pulling" styling theme.

The famous Model 3124 Cameo Carrier pickup featured a deluxe interior, with distinctive appointments and trim. It combined the utility of a pickup with outstanding styling. A unique feature of Model 3124 was the use of fiberglass for the pickup body's outer panel, a technology Chevrolet first used with the 1953 Corvette.

As standard equipment, the Cameo was outfitted with the deluxe cab, a wraparound rear window, a chrome grille, wheel covers, a front bumper, and headlight bezels, as well as a special two-tone exterior of Bombay Ivory with Commercial Red (the only colors available). The inside of the pickup box was also painted red.

Chevrolet designers provided the heavy-duty truck series (4000 series 1 1/2-tons, 5000 series 1 1/2-ton specials, and 6000 series 2-ton models) with proportionately larger front-end sheet metal and a more massive grille design. These trucks also featured the "load pulling" look.

Chevrolet offered four six-cylinder engines for 1955. The standard 235 six-cylinder engine was again furnished in 3000 and 4000 series trucks, and was identified as New Thriftmaster on the rocker cover decal and painted gray. The heavy-duty 235 six was painted green and carried the name New Loadmaster. It featured valve rotators, XCR exhaust valves, and chrome-plated top compression rings for increased durability. This was regular equipment in the 6000 series and was available as optional in Series 4000. A second heavy-duty 235 engine painted gray, and with an updraft

It was almost as if a "pickup revolution" occurred in 1954–1955, because this was the time at which America's pickups moved out of the slow lane and into the fast lane. Dodge and Ford's first OHV V-8 engines came out in 1954, and Chevrolet followed one year later. Pickups reached new heights with the sparkling performance from new engines. Not only that, but in every other way they became more carlike. America's switch to pickups for personal transportation began taking off in earnest. There were many features, some standard and others options, some new in 1955 and others not, which supported the revolution. These included a 12-volt electrical system; tubeless tires; improved cab ventilation systems; a more luxurious, comfortable cab interior; power brakes; power steering; overdrive; automatic transmission; a wraparound windshield; foam rubber seat cushions; full-view rear windows; tinted window glass; electric windshield wipers; two-tone paint schemes; colorful upholstery fabrics; and cab trim. The secret to all this, and the key that unlocked pickups' popularity, was that they now had a distinct, positive appeal to women. This is a 1955 Chevrolet Model 3104 114-inch-wheelbase 1/2-ton pickup. *AAMA*

Chevrolet's new 1955 1/2-ton panel Model 3105 rode on the same 114-inch wheelbase as the 1/2-ton pickup. The modern styling of the panel body featured a concealed cab safety step, integral rear fenders, high-level cab ventilation, and a streamlined roof design. The panel's body was generally wider, lower, longer, and featured more load space than before. Chevrolet also offered an extra handsome Custom Panel for those merchants who delivered packages to upscale retail customers. The standard engine for 1/2-ton trucks was the Thriftmaster 235-ci 123-horsepower six. Optional was the modern new 154-horsepower OHV 265-ci V-8. *AAMA*

Chevrolet scooped the industry with the first-ever pickup designed to appeal to the personal use market. Despite the wide whitewalls and the paint scheme of Bombay Ivory trimmed with Commercial Red, this truck was also capable of doing a hard day's work. The Cameo Carrier was specifically intended to be beautiful and yet retain its traditional utility. At the time Chevrolet said Cameo might just "set an entirely new style trend in the light-duty truck field!" History proves that it was only two years later that Ford offered, as a regular production item, a steel wide-side cargo box named the Styleside pickup. Chevrolet and Dodge followed in 1959 with steel, smooth-side cargo box pickups. Chevrolet's pioneering Cameo Carrier borrowed from Corvette technology. Its wide side box was constructed of reinforced fiberglass. The inside of the cargo box was painted red. The cab interior featured red and beige upholstery and a red floor mat. Full chrome wheel covers were also standard. The standard engine for all 1955 light-duty models was the 235-ci Thriftmaster six. Later in the year, the 265 V-8 became an extra-cost option for all light-duty trucks. *AAMA*

carburetor, powered the forward-control models as before. The 261-ci six-cylinder engine painted yellow and with the name New Jobmaster was continued as optional in the 6000 series because of its serious low-end torque.

Chevrolet's first-ever V-8 engine was put into service in 1955 trucks as standard equipment on the 5000 series. The 265-ci V-8's bore and stroke were 3.75x3.0-inches, the compression ratio was 7.5 to 1, gross horsepower was 145 at 4,000 rpm, and gross torque was 238 foot-pounds at 2,000 rpm. The stroke-to-bore ratio of 0.8 to 1 was among the best in the over-square design of automotive engines then in production. A short stroke meant less piston travel per mile and lower reciprocating loads for smoother operation, which greatly reduced wear on the pistons, rings, and cylinder

bores. The engine was painted yellow with the word *Chevrolet* in black on covers.

The U.S. truck-building industry experienced a major upturn in production during 1955. Total industry output gained 21 percent over 1954 with 1,244,988 units, up from 1,038,046 in 1954. Heavy-duty trucks sold very well. Unfortunately, that was a segment Chevrolet did not participate in until 1956. Light-truck sales reached 657,000 units, up from 560,000 in 1954. Chevrolet captured the number one spot in truck sales again for 1955, selling a total of 343,592 trucks, a 9 percent increase over 1954. This represented good performance, considering the new models didn't go on sale until late in the model year. Chevrolet had 7,500 truck dealers in the United States. On average, each sold 44 trucks; the industry average was 29 trucks per dealer.

A workhorse in Chevrolet's new Task-Force truck line for 1955's second series was the Model 3604 3/4-ton pickup. This truck rode on a 123 1/4-inch wheelbase. Its chassis was completely redesigned and included a new frame, axles, springs, and steering. Chevrolet built two body models in the 3/4-ton series— the pickup and a 7 1/2-foot stake. The husky pickup featured a 50-inch by 7 1/2-foot cargo box. Box and tailgate height was 17 1/2 inches, box sides had flat-tops. Its bed was constructed of wood covered with steel skid strips to facilitate skidding cargo in and out. The 3/4-ton models were rated for a maximum GVW rating of 6,900 pounds. Their engine selection was the same as for 1/2-ton models—235 six and 265 V-8. *AAMA*

Chevrolet's 1955 Suburban Carryall, Models 3106 and 3116, was a variant of the 1/2-ton panel. The two model numbers refer to panel-type rear doors (3106) or station wagon-type rear doors with an independent fold-down end gate and fold-up upper window section (3116). The Suburban also rode on the 114-inch-wheelbase chassis and like all other 1/2-ton 1955 models, it was rated for a maximum GVW of 5,000 pounds. Chevrolet continued to market the Suburban to businesses as a combination personnel and cargo carrier. The Suburban was only secondarily considered a family personal transportation vehicle. Engine options included the standard Thriftmaster 123-horsepower 235-ci six, and the optional 154-horsepower 265-ci V-8. The 1/2-ton truck's transmission options included a three-speed synchro-mesh manual mounted on the steering column, a heavy-duty three-speed, a four-speed synchro-mesh, and a four-speed automatic. *AAMA*

Chevrolet's largest and heaviest-duty pickup in its Task-Force truck line for 1955 was the 1-ton Model 3804. This pickup carried a maximum GVW rating of 7,000 pounds and its payload topped off at 3,100 pounds. It rode on a 135-inch-wheelbase chassis. Its cargo box was 50 inches by 9 feet long and had 37.5 square feet of floor space. The long box dictated the use of eight stake pockets for the installation of racks or canopies; note all eight are in use on this 1-ton pickup. Engine choices included the standard 123-horsepower Thriftmaster 235-ci six and the spirited optional 265-ci Jobmaster V-8. Transmission options included the heavy-duty three-speed manual, four-speed manual, and four-speed Hydra-Matic automatic. *AAMA*

Chevrolet's 1-ton Model 3805 panel truck was hard to beat for usefulness. It was designed to handle the heavy and/or long loads. It was built on the 135-inch-wheelbase chassis and was rated for a maximum GVW of 7,000 pounds with a payload of 2,700 pounds. Its payload rating was less than that of the 1-ton pickup due to the greater weight of its all-steel, fully enclosed body. Its sign panel area on each side measured 16x103 inches. Its cargo area was constructed of wood with steel skid strips to allow cargo to be easily slid in and out. Its engine and transmission options were the same as for the 1-ton pickup. Its push-button rear doors opened 180 degrees for ease of loading. *AAMA*

Another workhorse truck in Chevrolet's new 1955 Task-Force series was the Series 3800 1-ton Model 3803 chassis cab, shown here with a special contractor body installed. Its wheelbase was also 135 inches. This truck was available with either single or dual rear wheels. Its standard engine was the 123-horsepower Thriftmaster 235-ci six. Optional was the new 154-horsepower Taskmaster OHV V-8. A great number of special bodies could be mounted on the versatile Chevrolet 1-ton chassis cab. *AAMA*

Chevrolet's lightest medium-duty Task-Force truck for 1955 was the 1 1/2-ton Model 4108 platform carrying fire-fighting equipment. The Schroon Lake (New York) Fire Department owned this hose truck. Note its spray-directing nozzle located on top of the cab and the fact that its grille's lower bar had been cut, probably for some former piece of special equipment. Its maximum GVW rating was 14,000 pounds. Its standard engine was the 123-horsepower New Thriftmaster 235-ci six, and its standard transmission was the four-speed heavy-duty synchro manual. The heavy-duty engine differed from the standard in that it had premium components such as valve rotators, XCR exhaust valves, and chrome-plated top compression rings for increased durability. It was standard in the 6000 series and optional in Series 4000. *Neal A. Van Deusen*

Chevrolet's new LCF Series 5000 trucks were rated as 2-ton heavy-duty models. They were designed for maneuverability and compactness, and sat higher than the conventional models because the cab was mounted over the engine. The new V-8 engine was used exclusively for Series 5000; a six was not offered. The V-8 engine eliminated the sub-frame, thus lowering the overall height within 7 inches of the conventional 2-ton. The short V-8 engine was mounted in front of the cab as in conventional models, and therefore the hood was shorter and higher than on other trucks. This is a 1955 Chevrolet 2-ton 5400 "short nose." This truck was still working when photographed in 1998. It is powered by the new Taskmaster 265-ci V-8 and has a four-speed transmission with a two-speed auxiliary. *Jim Fromm*

Series 5000 trucks had the same basic cab as the conventional trucks. Cab interiors were finished in beige and black. They had a hump in the center section of the toe panel as well as wheel shrouds at either side to allow for wheel travel. The upper portion of the instrument panel was painted black with a textured paint to minimize light reflections, and it formed an overhanging crown that spanned the entire width of the truck. Instruments were grouped in a single triangular cluster directly in front of the steering wheel: temp, amps, oil, and gas, left to right. The radio was located in the lower center of the dash (not installed here). The radio speaker would be mounted on the header bar above the windshield. This is the instrument panel of the 1955 Chevrolet Series 5400 "short nose." *Jim Fromm*

The Model 6103 2-ton chassis cab with fifth wheel equipment was one of the 2-ton heavy-duty Chevrolet models for 1955. Its standard engine was the New Loadmaster 261-ci six. This one was powered by the optional new Taskmaster 265-ci V-8. The Taskmaster engine turned out 145 gross horsepower and 238 foot-pounds torque at 4,000 rpm. Its standard transmission was the four-speed heavy-duty synchro. Power brakes were standard equipment, standard tires were 7.50x20 eight-ply. The tires on this truck look bigger. A Chevrolet-built planetary reduction heavy-duty two-speed rear axle was an option. Chevrolet engineers built this model with a stiffer frame than the previous model. *Dick Copello*

Another of Chevrolet's heavy-duty 2-ton truck models for 1955 was the big 6403 chassis cab. This truck's maximum GVW rating was 16,000 pounds, or 18,000 pounds with heavy-duty optional equipment. It rode on a 154-inch-wheelbase chassis. A 15,000-pound rear axle was standard, a heavy-duty axle was an option as was a two-speed. This is a 1955 2-ton model 6400 chassis cab with fire-fighting body. This truck was owned by the East Cape County (Missouri) Volunteer Fire Department. Its pumper body was built by Towers and contained a 500-gallon water tank and a 500-gpm pump. The pump was located on the front bumper immediately forward of the grille. Its standard engine was the 123-horsepower New Loadmaster 235-ci six, the optional six was the 140-horsepower New Jobmaster 261-ci six. The new 145-horsepower Taskmaster 265-ci V-8 powered this truck. *Steve Hagy*

The Model 4409 1 1/2-ton medium-duty chassis cab with stake body was one of Chevrolet's bread-and-butter models for 1955. It was rated for a maximum GVW rating of 14,000 pounds. The Model 4409 rode on a 154-inch-wheelbase chassis. Chevrolet built its 12-foot stake body complete. It featured handy swinging side gates for easy loading. Load space was 144 inches by 85 inches inside the stake racks. Its standard engine was the New Thriftmaster 123-horsepower 235-ci six with a four-speed heavy-duty synchro transmission. The 4409 was rated for a maximum payload of 8,400 pounds. The New Thriftmaster six was an option. It was the same engine as the New Thriftmaster, but with premium features for a longer, trouble-free life. *AAMA*

Chevrolet's 1954 style Advance-Design trucks carried over into 1955. Chevrolet printed and distributed sales literature for these trucks. This is a 1955 first-Series Chevrolet Model 3104 pickup. A 1955 first-Series truck can be identified from its front hood emblem due to its white painted background surrounding the bow tie trademark. In addition, the hood side nameplate was restyled. The 1955 nameplate has the four-digit model designation on top with *Chevrolet* in small letters inset into a horizontal bar below. Mechanical specifications remained unchanged. *Kevin Kinney*

Chevrolets were not only the nation's most popular fire truck, they were also the finest styled fire trucks. Pictured is a 1955 first-Series Model 6403 2-ton 161-inch-wheelbase chassis cab with fire-fighting body. Its maximum GVW rating was 16,000 pounds. The 161-inch-wheelbase chassis accepted bodies up to 12 feet in length. The weight of its body and payload totaled 11,100 pounds. The West Athens-Lime Street Fire District No. 1 of West Athens, New York, owned this truck. Its pumper body was by American and contained a 500-gallon water tank and a 500-gpm pump. *Neal A. Van Deusen*

Chevrolet's 2-ton 5000 Series COE models were not quite as high as the COEs of the Advance-Design Series. This cab was only 7 inches higher than that of the conventional cab trucks. Chevrolet engineers didn't even bother to provide the new COEs with grab handles as standard equipment. This is a 1955 Chevrolet 5700 COE with a platform body. Notice the basic difference in styling. The 1955 truck has a shortened conventional hood compared to the earlier truck's almost nonexistent hood. Series 5000 trucks featured a short exterior running board. The driver could walk up into the cab with the aid of the concealed step inside the cab door. *Spanky L. Hardy*

The 1955 Chevrolet Series 6403 chassis cab with dump body was rated as a heavy-duty 2-ton truck. It was available with either a maximum GVW rating of 16,000 pounds or 18,000 pounds. The 18,000-pound GVW was 2,000 pounds heavier than the heaviest standard GVW ever offered by Chevrolet in the past. This truck rode on a 154-inch-wheelbase chassis and was powered by the 235-ci six-cylinder engine. The balance of its drive train consisted of a four-speed transmission and a two-speed rear axle. This photo was taken in 1955. *Verne Byers*

Chevrolet engineers changed the Series 5000 cab-over-engine models more extensively than any other model. These changes were principally in the truck's height and wheelbase. This was made possible by the elimination of the subframe, which was due in turn to the shorter V-8 engine. The lower height resulted in a lowering of the running board height by 2 1/2-inches. Entry and exit to the cab was eased and actually approached that of the conventional cab models. To accommodate the new engine without pushing it into the cab, all Series 5000 wheelbases were increased 2 5/8 inches. The COE's overall length was not increased, however, because Chevrolet engineers reduced the front overhang by a like amount. The COE's front tread was increased by slightly over 2 inches; the rear tread remained unchanged. This is a 1955 Series 5703 2-ton COE chassis cab with fifth wheel equipment. *Arnold Paradis*

This 1955 6500 was originally a fire truck from Stuart, Iowa, and it only had 6,300 miles on it when Verne Byers purchased it. After removing the fire body he completely restored it. The stake body is from a 1949 farm truck he also purchased and restored. Verne retired after 40 years in the construction business and chose this truck to restore because it was like the first truck he purchased for his business. It has the 265 V-8 engine, four-speed transmission, and two-speed rear axle. *Verne Byers*

This gorgeous second series 1955 3100 half-ton pickup was another fine restoration project of Verne Byers. It has the 235-ci six-cylinder engine and three-speed transmission. Note its deluxe touches: sun visor, full wheel covers, white sidewall tires, two-tone paint scheme, and oak side boards. *Verne Byers*

1956

In 1956, Chevrolet entered the heavy-duty end of the truck market with four new 2 1/2-ton Series. These new models included either Low-Cab-Forward (LCF) trucks in the 7000 and 9000 Series, or conventional cab design in the 8000 and 10000 Series—a total of 21 new models.

The basic difference between the 7000 and 8000 series in comparison with the 9000 and 10000 is that the latter two incorporated heavy-duty components, including a heavy-duty engine, five-speed transmission, higher capacity rear axles, and a 13-inch clutch.

In a few short years, Chevrolet progressed from one basic OHV six-cylinder engine in two sizes to a host of six-cylinder and V-8 engines. In the light-duty series, the Thriftmaster 235.5-ci OHV six still reigned as standard equipment. The 265-ci OHV Trademaster V-8 was optional for all models. The six was rated for 140 gross horsepower and the V-8 for 155 horsepower.

For bigger trucks, the Trademaster V-8 returned for its second year as an option for 4000 Series trucks. The Taskmaster, the 265-ci V-8 with premium features (valve rotators, chrome piston rings, positive crankcase ventilation, and optional full-flow oil filter), was standard equipment for the 5000, 7000, and 8000 Series, and optional for the 4000 and 6000 Series. A new V-8 engine, the Loadmaster OHV 322-ci V-8 produced 195 gross horsepower and gross torque of 310 foot-pounds. It was equipped with a two-barrel carburetor. The new V-8 was released for use on the 9000 and 10000 Series 2 1/2-ton trucks. This was a modified Buick "Nailhead" V-8. It produced more horsepower and torque than Chevrolet-built engines and made the 9000 and 10000 models possible until the 348 V-8 was ready. Super Taskmaster and Super Loadmaster engines filled out Chevrolet's V-8 engine lineup for 1956. These two engines, equipped with four-barrel carburetors, were offered as RPOs on the 5-6-7-8000 Series and the 9000, 10000 Series trucks respectively.

This 1956 Model 6102 flat-face cowl is quite an unusual low production Chevrolet truck. Its windshield was not from the factory, but was provided by an aftermarket source. Model 6102 was a 1 1/2-ton special. It was special because it had a maximum GVW rating of 15,000 pounds compared to the 14,000-pound maximum GVW rating of the standard 1 1/2-ton models. It was built on a 130-inch-wheelbase chassis. It was an open cab truck that was used at the San Bernardino, California, airport as a refueler. A local firm made its body. The standard engine for 6000 series trucks, the 235 Thriftmaster Heavy-Duty, powered it. It was rated for 140 horsepower and 210 foot-pounds torque at 2,000 rpm. Its standard transmission was the Chevrolet-built four-speed synchro. *Chuck Madderom*

Full automatic transmissions were offered on all models in Chevrolet's line for 1955, with the exception of Model 4502, a 1 1/2-ton chassis with a flat face cowl. The Hydra-Matic transmission, which was offered last year on 1/2-ton through 1-ton models, was now available on 1 1/2-ton trucks, too. A new Allison automatic was introduced for 2- and 2 1/2-ton trucks. Also, two new five-speed transmissions, one from Spicer and the other from New Process, were available on 2- and 2 1/2-ton models.

Twenty-one heavy-duty models on eight new wheelbases were added to the Chevrolet truck line for 1956. Maximum GVW ratings

One of Chevrolet's best-selling medium-duty trucks in 1956 was the 2-ton model. This is a 1956 2-ton Model 6409 stake truck owned by the U.S. Army. This truck rode on a 154-inch-wheelbase chassis and was rated for a maximum GVW rating of 19,500 pounds. Chevrolet built the 6400 trucks as flat-face cowls, windshield cowls, chassis cab, and complete stake truck. This was a six-cylinder-engine–powered truck, the 235-ci Thriftmaster Heavy-Duty six. *Elliott Kahn*

The introduction of Chevrolet's first V-8 engine with the second series 1955 trucks opened the door for larger and heavier trucks. The V-8 engine improved performance. Owners could do more work and make more trips because the more powerful V-8 allowed for higher overall speeds in traffic and in hilly country. Chevrolet did move into a 2 1/2-ton Series in 1956. These were models numbered 7100, 8100, 9100, and 10100 to 10800. This is a 1956 Chevrolet Model 10400, tandem-axle chassis cab. This truck was rated for a maximum GVW rating of 25,000 pounds and a maximum GCW rating of 48,000 pounds when used as a tractor trailer rig. To power this truck Chevrolet "borrowed" an engine from its sister Buick Division. The Super Loadmaster engine had a cubic inch displacement of 322 and put out 210 horsepower and 320 foot-pounds torque at 2,800 rpm. *Dick Copello*

on the new trucks ranged from 21,000 to 32,000 pounds. The revised and expanded truck line then consisted of 86 models on 23 different wheelbase lengths, including the 65 models on 15 wheelbases carried over from 1955. Also available was Chevrolet engineered and built optional tandem axle equipment for 10000 series trucks. Beginning in 1956 all 3000 series trucks were rated as light-duty models, while the Series 4-5-6000 models were in the medium-duty class. Series 7000, 8000, 9000, and 10000 models made up the heavy-duty class.

Chevrolet management entered the heavy-duty truck market because it was losing market share to Ford, which had been building heavies since 1948. To bring out its heavy-duty series, Chevrolet converted a parts warehouse at Willow Run, Michigan, into a new, 479,000-square-foot truck assembly plant employing 650.

Total industry production for 1956 was down from 1955 by 142,119 units. Chevrolet's production, 619,691 versus 621,417 in 1955, also dropped. But the important thing was that it still led the industry in total trucks built, and its market share increased by 4/10 of 1 percent. Chevrolet built a total of 8,491 heavy trucks in 1956. Not great, but it was a start. Management knew it still had a lot of work to do to be where it wanted to be. The company's timing was right on the mark, because heavy-duty models dominated 1956's truck market. In fact, heavies were the only weight group to show a gain over 1955.

A major impetus for the increase in heavy-duty trucks was the multi-billion-dollar federal highway program (the interstate freeway system) approved by Congress early in 1956. The freeway program was expected to benefit the truck industry for many years in the future.

Chevrolet's light-duty 1956 line made its debut on January 30 and its new heavy-duty line went on sale on February 27.

By the end of 1956 Chevrolet had manufactured over 4 million trucks since the end of World War II, which virtually equaled its production of trucks in its entire prewar history.

Retail truck sales fell 11 percent, to 305,592. Chevrolet comfortably held onto its first place sales position as Ford posted a 17 percent drop in total sales.

Another of Chevrolet's big selling 2-ton line was this Model 6400 chassis cab with fire-fighting body. It rode on a 154-inch-wheelbase chassis and carried a maximum GVW rating of an impressive 19,500 pounds. It is also a six-cylinder-engine–powered truck, as can be seen by the absence of a V-8 plate on its fender side. The Prospect (Ohio) Fire Department owned this truck. Its special pumper body was by Sutphen. It carried a 600-gallon water tank and a 500-gpm pump. The pump is mounted between the special chrome-plated bumper and the grille. Note how the body manufacturer fared the cab and body into one continuous unbroken line. *Steve Hagy*

1957

Chevrolet's truck line for 1957 bore little resemblance to its 1947 line. In 1947, there were two engine options, two transmissions, and GVWs from 4,000 to 16,000 pounds. For 1957, Chevrolet offered a choice of eight engines, eight transmissions (including two automatics), and GVWs up to 32,000 pounds. The 1957 truck line consisted of an all-time company high of 103 models on 22 wheelbases. This represented an increase of 17 models over 1956, and surprisingly enough, a decrease of one in total wheelbase offerings. Much of the model increase was due to the new light-duty 4WD trucks.

Cab and panel models were available with a custom cab option that included additional equipment, trim, and comfort items. These additions included: chrome-plated control knobs, a cigarette lighter, a second sun visor and armrest, a foam rubber seat cushion and backrest, a bright metal-trimmed windshield , and window area reveal moldings. Chrome equipment included: a grille, bumpers, hubcaps, and headlight bezels (Series 3000 cab and panel models only).

Wheelbase lengths of all Series 4000 and 6000 models increased by 2 1/2 inches. The front axle moved forward to permit the use of larger size tires on Series 6000 models. This permitted the use of the maximum 10-22.5 rear tires on the front wheels, for convenient interchangeability. The feature of maximum-size tires for front and rear interchange was also extended to the 9000 and 10000 Series with the release of 11-22.5 tires for the front wheels for all models of these two series, except for school buses and tandem-axle vehicles.

Chevrolet introduced its first-ever optional factory-built 4WD trucks in 1957. All components were factory installed and could be ordered for 1/2- and 3/4-ton pickups, panels, cab chassis, platform trucks, and the Suburban Carryall. The Chevrolet four-speed transmission was standard; it was mated to a two-speed transfer case. A single control lever positioned to the right of the transmission control was used to shift the transfer case from direct drive to underdrive. The underdrive ratio was 1.87 to 1.

Standard engines for light-duty trucks continued without change: the thrifty 235-ci, 140-horsepower Thriftmaster six was standard equipment, and the powerful and rugged 265-ci, 155-horsepower Trademaster V-8 was optional.

A new 283-ci Taskmaster V-8 engine was introduced as standard equipment in Series 5000, 7000, and 8000 and was optional for Series 6000 models. It replaced 1956's 265-ci Taskmaster V-8 engine. It featured a 3.875-inch bore and a compression ratio of 8.0 to 1, up from 7.5 to 1. Gross horsepower was 160 at 4,000 rpm; gross torque was 270 foot-pounds at 2,000 rpm. A higher horsepower 283-ci V-8 engine, named Super Taskmaster, was available as an option on all 5-6-7-8000 models, except the Series 6000 forward-control chassis. This engine featured a four-barrel carburetor and a special intake manifold that had larger inlet ports for increased volumetric efficiency. Dual exhausts were included as standard with this engine.

The Loadmaster 322-ci V-8 was regular equipment for 9000 and 10000 Series trucks. With a two-barrel carburetor and single exhausts, this engine developed 195 gross horsepower at 4,000 rpm and 310 foot-pounds gross torque at 2,200 rpm. A similar engine but with even higher power and better performance was the 322-ci V-8, available for all 9000 and 10000 models as an RPO. It had a

Chevrolet's Sedan Delivery for 1957 took on the same body as the new 1957 Chevrolet Series 1500 2-door station wagon, with rear quarter window areas replaced by solid metal panels. Its front-end design was a carbon copy of the station wagon. The rear door of the Sedan Delivery, as in 1956, was hinged at the top and opened upward, leaving the loading area free of obstruction. Two torsion rods easily held the door up and out of the way. Fourteen-inch wheels were standard for 1957. The driver had a folding, bucket-type seat; a second, passenger seat was an extra-cost option. Engine options included the standard 140-horsepower Blue Flame 235-ci six. The 162-horsepower Turbo-Fire 265-ci V-8 was an option, as was the 185-horsepower two-barrel Turbo-Fire 283-ci V-8, and the 220-horsepower four-barrel Super Turbo-Fire 283-ci V-8. Transmission options included the three-speed, overdrive, and the Powerglide and Turboglide automatics.

The Cameo Carrier pickup was now in its third model year and it was still the style leader. It was more beautiful than ever: Chevrolet designers added two distinctive bright metal moldings that began at the front portion of the rear fender and extended rearward to the taillight. A small chrome metal filler panel at the forward portion contained the Chevrolet trademark, while the word *Cameo,* in script, was located slightly to the rear. The new chrome hubcaps were coupled with an accessory trim ring to provide almost full-width covering for the wheels. The Cameo also received the restyled grille and other styling updates as other light-duty trucks. *AAMA*

four-barrel carburetor and standard dual exhaust system. Gross horsepower was 210 at 4,000 rpm and gross torque was 320 foot-pounds at 2,800 rpm.

On December 4, 1957, Chevrolet produced its 38-millionth vehicle of all time. The Chevrolet Motor Division produced 1,522,536 passenger cars in U.S. plants in 1957, marking the third best year in its history. The division's post–World War II passenger car volume passed the total for all prewar years. In its first 30 years of existence, Chevrolet built 13,459,763 cars. Including 1957, the postwar total was 14,373,763.

Chevrolet retained its leadership as the nation's number one truck producer in the United States. Factory production for the year totaled 351,739 trucks, or 32.4 percent of overall industry truck construction. Chevrolet's retail sales in 1957 totaled 290,960 trucks, or 33.9 percent of the market.

Overall industry truck production in 1957 declined marginally from 1956, to 1,085,932 from 1,104,325. Sales of medium- and heavy-duty trucks slipped, while sales of light-duty trucks gained in relation to 1956. Ford, GMC, Dodge, and Chevrolet held 85 percent of this market.

Chevrolet pickups received a mild styling facelift for 1957, the third year of this very successful series. The grille for light-duty models was first to come in for a restyling; the medium- and heavy-duty trucks retained their former grille design. The new grille featured a central portion that seemed to float in the grille's center. Eight vertical bars held it there. The standard finish for the grille was Arctic Beige paint. The bow tie trademark in the hood emblem was changed from red to black. Hoods on all trucks except the LCF models are easily distinguished by two high wind-splits that run from front to back on each side of the hood.

Chevrolet's pickup lineup for 1957 included 1/2-, 3/4-, and 1-ton models and the Cameo Carrier. Except for the Cameo, they were of the fender-side style. The term Step-Side didn't come into use until a wide, smooth-side style box had become a standard offering. The 1/2-ton pickup's cargo box was 6 1/2 feet long and rode on a 114-inch-wheelbase chassis. The biggest seller was the half-ton Model 3104 pictured with the Custom cab option. The standard engine for all pickups was the 140-horsepower Thriftmaster 235-ci six. Optional was the 155-horsepower Trademaster 265-ci V-8. Transmission options included the standard three-speed manual and optional four-speed Hydra-Matic, overdrive three-speed, three-speed H. D., and four-speed synchro.

Chevrolet designers painted the entire cab interior gray, including the lower portion of the instrument panel. The instrument panel's crown and windshield trim were painted in a textured charcoal paint in order to minimize glare. The new steering wheel and column were also charcoal. The steering wheel was all new for 1957. Its three-spoke design featured a deeply recessed hub for a smart, modern appearance. The horn button displayed the Chevrolet bow tie trademark on a charcoal-painted background.

This is the interior of a Standard cab. The Standard cab's seat was upholstered in vinyl. Note the seat adjustment lever on the left side of the seat. Since 1955 Chevrolet cabs featured a concealed step that allowed the front fenders to blend into the doors to form a smooth unbroken contour from the fender front to the cab's extreme corners. The doors were lengthened to cover the running boards entirely, yet when the doors were opened they became as accessible as on previous models. This view of the steering wheel clearly displays its new "deep dish" design. Notice the gas tank located behind the seat and the jack at its far left.

Fire departments requiring trucks with good load-carrying ability chose the Model 8403 heavy-duty 2 1/2-ton chassis cab with fire-fighting body. The Sheridan (Oregon) Fire Department owned this truck. Engine No. 1 had a pumper body built by Western States, which contained a 750-gallon water tank and a 400-gpm pump. This truck carried a maximum GVW rating of 21,000 pounds. Its engine was the optional Super Taskmaster 175-horsepower 283-ci V-8. It also had the optional five-speed New Process transmission. *Bill Hattersley*

A beautiful 1957 Chevrolet Cameo Carrier pickup leads a parade of new Chevrolet Task-Force trucks. Chevrolet built a total of 103 truck models on 22 wheelbases in 1957, ranging from 1/2-ton to 2 1/2-ton models. For the first time there was standard production of 4WD light-duty trucks. The strength of Chevrolet's truck line was found in its traditional markets—light- and medium-duty models. Chevrolet's engine line ranged in horsepower from 140 to 210. *AAMA*

Chevrolet engineers improved the LCF trucks by making entry and exit easier through lowering the exposed running boards by 4 inches relative to the ground. The fender was unchanged except for the addition of a filler panel that extended the fender contour down to the running board. Assist handles became standard equipment on all LCF models for 1957. The assist handle is hidden behind the rearview mirror in this 1957 LCF 5703 160 5/8-inch-wheelbase chassis cab. When photographed in September 1998 this truck had been just taken out of service. The standard engine for this model was the 160-horsepower Taskmaster 283-ci V-8.

Chevrolet's 1957 model 3204 1/2-ton pickup was still the same basic truck as the 1955 model, the first year of this series. The grille style was slightly changed and so were model number plates and the hood badge. This truck has aftermarket steel-spoke wheels and non-stock tires. The 1/2-ton's standard engine was the Thriftmaster 235-ci OHV six. Transmission choices included the four-speed Hydra-Matic, three-speed overdrive manual, and four-speed manual. The 1/2-ton's GVW rating was 5,000 pounds. *Everett Nebergall*

Chevrolet's best-selling medium-duty 1957 model was the versatile 6403 1 1/2-ton chassis cab. It carried a maximum GVW rating of 15,000 pounds on its 156 1/2-inch-wheelbase chassis. It was powered by the famous 148-horsepower 261-ci six. Optional was the 160-horsepower Taskmaster 283-ci V-8. Its standard transmission was the Chevrolet-built four-speed synchro. The Boothbay Harbor (Maine) Fire Department owned this truck. Its pumper body was by Farrar and contained a 250-gallon water tank and a 400-gpm pump. *Fred Cote*

The nation's fire chiefs looked with favor on the powerful and capable 1957 Chevrolet trucks. Chevrolet offered 62 medium- and heavy-duty models for them to select from. The fire chief of Ashcroft, British Columbia, Canada, chose a Chevrolet Model 8403 heavy-duty conventional chassis cab for his department. It featured a Thibault body with a 750-gallon water tank and a 500-gpm pump. The 160-horsepower 283-ci Taskmaster V-8 mated to a five-speed New Process transmission powered this 21,000-pound GVW truck. *Frank De Gruchy*

1958

Chevrolet's truck line in 1958 consisted of 128 models on 22 wheelbases. Total trucks for 1957 had included 103 models on 22 wheelbases. All vehicles available in 1957 carried over to the new year.

Styling changes on 1958 Chevrolet trucks included an entirely new grille and front sheet metal, dual headlights, new series designation plates, new hood emblems, and a new method of two-toning with seven new colors.

Front fenders of all models were redesigned to house dual headlamps. Dual 5 3/4-inch headlamps improved both high- and low-beam illumination and emphasized the width of the new models. These headlamps were standard equipment on all except forward-control and Step-Van models.

A new 20-inch steering wheel was standard equipment on heavy-duty trucks, while all other series continued with the 18-inch wheel. The 20-inch wheel provided greater leverage to reduce steering effort. It also fulfilled a psychological need by giving operators of the 2 1/2-ton trucks the feel of a "big truck."

Chevrolet management may have been looking over its shoulder at the popular Volkswagen van when it developed the 1958 Step-Van parcel delivery vehicle. This was Chevrolet's first forward-control chassis with an attractive all-steel van-type body. The body was built by the Union City Body Co. and installed by Chevrolet, not the buyer. Other manufacturers' bodies were "factory approved," but it was up to the buyer to purchase the chassis and arrange for the body to be installed.

Chevrolet's 1958 truck engine lineup numbered eight, including an entirely new, larger displacement unit featuring a radical combustion chamber design.

The new, 348-ci V-8 engine was named the Workmaster, and was standard equipment for Series 90 and 100 models. It had an 8.0 to 1 compression ratio; maximum gross horsepower was 230 at 4,400 rpm; and maximum gross torque was 335 foot-pounds at 2,800 rpm. Despite its large displacement, the Workmaster engine was unusually compact, measuring only 1 3/4 inches longer and less than 3 inches wider than the 283-ci V-8. This engine's combustion chamber was actually in the block. That is, the pistons were cut at an angle and served as the combustion chamber. This engine was Chevrolet's most important advancement for 1958.

The U.S. truck industry suffered the same downturn in production as the rest of the nation's economy during the recession of 1958. Annual industry truck production of 871,330 represented a decrease of 20 percent. Chevrolet's total production was off by 20.8 percent, but it still maintained its lead over archrival Ford, whose slippage was 28 percent. This was the first post–World War II year in which total industry production fell below one million units. The truck manufacturing industry's only shining production star for the year was Willys, with an increase of 35 percent.

A very quiet development on the nation's truck scene that had an enormous impact on America's future light-duty truck business, quite possibly forever, was an increase in miscellaneous imported trucks, which consisted for the most part of Volkswagens. They accounted for

Light-duty models in 1958 were named the Apache Series. They consisted of 1/2-, 3/4-, and 1-ton models. They were designated the 31, 32, 36, and 38 models. This is a 1958 Chevrolet Apache Model 3104 1/2-ton pickup. Its cargo box was 6 1/2 feet long and it rode on a 114-inch wheelbase. Its front-end styling changed considerably from the previous year, featuring a new hood, front fenders, grille, quad headlights, parking lights, and series designation plates. The new grille was designed to permit more cooling air to flow past the radiator. It was painted Arctic Beige on all models except the Cameo Carrier and Series 30 models with the Custom Cab option. They had chrome grilles. The other 1/2-ton pickup was Model 3204 that featured an 8-foot cargo box and a 123 1/4-inch-wheelbase chassis. Both models carried a maximum GVW rating of 5,000 pounds.

This is Chevrolet's 1958 3/4-ton pickup Model 3604. It, too, had the 8-foot box and a 123 1/4-inch-wheelbase chassis. It was rated for a maximum GVW of 6,900 pounds. The new front fender crowns extended forward to form hoods over the new dual headlights. The new series designation plates featured a winged spear-type shape containing *Chevrolet* in block letters on a black background as well as the series numbers, 36 in the case of light-duty models. The rear portion of the plate featured the classification's name—Apache for light-duties. The standard engine for this 3/4-ton pickup and all light-duty trucks was the 145-horsepower Thriftmaster 235-ci six. *AAMA*

less than 1 percent of total U.S. truck registrations in 1955, but by 1958 had grown to nearly 4 percent. These vehicles were Volkswagen's small vans, wagons, and pickups. These were vehicles totally foreign to the industry, but they quickly caught on. Chevrolet and other U.S. manufacturers successfully answered their challenge in 1961 by creating a whole new segment in the light-duty truck market.

Chevrolet's sales for the year added up to 247,347 trucks, or 34.1 percent of the market. In July of 1958 there were 3,482,242 Chevrolet trucks operating on U.S. roads, which was a hike of 3.8 percent over the previous year. Chevrolet's share of the nation's trucks on the road as of July 1, 1958, was 34.6 percent.

The first year for a factory-built 4WD Chevrolet light-duty truck was 1957. This is a 1958 Chevrolet 3/4-ton 4WD pickup. Its maximum GVW rating was a husky 7,600 pounds. Its transfer case had a four-position single lever for easy operation—4WD in high or low, neutral, or 2WD. Low range split of 1.86 to 1; high split ratio, 1 to 1. Transmission choices were short and simple— four-speed Hydra-Matic or four-speed manual synchro. Standard features included power takeoff openings for front and rear work applications and heavy-duty front and rear springs. Rzeppa constant-velocity front axle joints reduced front wheel vibration and lessened tire wear. The 4WD was offered in pickups, stakes, panel, Suburban, and cab chassis. Brush truck 394 was owned by the Marystown (Illinois) Volunteer Fire Department. It carried a 250-gallon water tank and a 150-gpm pump. *Dennis J. Maag*

Chevrolet's 1958 1/2-ton panel was Model 3155. The panel shared a body with the Suburban Carryall. Chevrolet engineers called the panel and Suburban-type bodies "single unit bodies." This was unlike a pickup or stake, which were composed of a cab and a separate body mounted behind it. The panel featured a 7-foot body and was available in a Custom model with harmonizing two-tone interior and chrome grille, headlight bezels, hubcaps, and bumpers. It was rated for a maximum GVW of 5,000 pounds. Its engine and transmission options were the same as the 1/2-ton pickup. This is a 1958 Chevrolet Model 3155 1/2-ton standard panel. *AAMA*

Chevrolet's management introduced as a midyear offering the new cab-wide smooth side Fleetside pickups. This new model took the place of the Cameo Carrier that was dropped during the model year. This is a 1958 1/2-ton 8-foot long Fleetside pickup. Fleetside's specifications, engines, GVWs, transmissions, and other items were the same as the conventional fender-side. The overall width of the Fleetside body was an amazing 75 inches. The width between the wheel wells was, of course, the same 50 inches as the other pickup box. *AAMA*

The medium-duty 60 Series Chevrolet trucks in 1958 were part of the Viking nominal classification. This 2-ton 1958 Chevrolet Series 60 Model 6103 chassis cab had a special body for an animal feed company. The truck's wheelbase was 132 1/2 inches. Its maximum GVW rating was a big 19,000 pounds. For more effective braking, air-hydraulic brakes were available on all Series 50 and 60 trucks when equipped with the optional 283-ci engine. The standard engine for the Series 60 was the 150-horsepower, 235 foot-pounds torque at 2,000 rpm Jobmaster 261-ci six. Optional was the 160-horsepower, 270 foot-pounds torque Taskmaster 283-ci V-8. This engine was fitted with a two-barrel carburetor. A four-barrel version of this engine called the Super Taskmaster was also optional. It put out 175 horsepower and 275 foot-pounds torque at 2,400 rpm. *AAMA*

Chevrolet's 2-ton and 2-ton heavy-duty 112 5/8-inch-wheelbase and 124 5/8-inch-wheelbase chassis cab with fifth wheel equipment were very popular with tractor trailer rig operators. This is a 1958 Chevrolet Model 5103H 2-ton heavy-duty 112 5/8-inch-wheelbase chassis cab used for tractor work. Its maximum GCW rating was 32,000 pounds. The optional 175-horsepower Super Taskmaster 283-ci V-8 engine powered it. Its standard engine was the Jobmaster 261-ci six. This engine was standard with dual exhausts. This truck was also equipped with the optional air-over-hydraulic brakes. *AAMA*

Chevrolet's biggest 1958 trucks were the Series 100 models in the Spartan, or heavy-duty, classification. The full air brake option was extended in 1958 to include tandem-axle models. The cast steel-spoke wheels on this truck were standard equipment. The maximum GVW rating of the 2 1/2-ton Model 10503 tandem chassis cab was 25,000 pounds, or 48,000 pounds when used as a tractor trailer. Chevrolet engineers introduced a completely new heavy-duty engine in 1958 for Series 90 and 100 trucks. Called the Workmaster, it had a bore of 4.125 inches and a stroke of 3.25 inches for a total of 348-ci displacement. It had an 8.0-to-1 compression ratio. It developed higher maximum power and torque than any Chevrolet truck engine previously offered. The Chelan County (Washington) Fire Protection District owned this truck. *Bill Hattersley*

This very fine 1958 Chevrolet Apache 31 1/2-ton pickup is all original with only 39,000 miles logged. It has the peppy 283-ci V-8 engine and a four-speed transmission. Most 1/2-tons sold in 1958 had a six-cylinder engine and a three-speed on the column. Danbury Mint used this truck to model its 1958 Apache 31 model. *Walter A. Himmen*

1959

Chevrolet's truck lineup for 1959 was expanded to 139 models on 22 wheelbases. The greatest emphasis was put on styling, chassis, and engine improvements designed to lower operating costs and lengthen vehicle life. The 1959 model line arrived at dealerships on October 16, 1958.

Perhaps the most interesting feature of Chevrolet's 1959 line was the addition of the Sedan Pickup, El Camino. It was designed to satisfy customer demands for a prestige-type light-duty truck, and expanded the total pickup offering to 13. Ford pioneered the Sedan Pickup in 1957 with the Ranchero pickup. An optional heavier-duty powertrain, with a two-barrel 348-ci engine, larger capacity clutch, transmission and rear axle, equipped the 70 and 80 series trucks with increased power and load-carrying ability.

The total of 139 models on 22 different wheelbases constituted the 1959 Chevrolet truck line. All 1958 models were continued except the Cameo Carrier, model 3124, which was discontinued when the Fleetside Pickups were introduced at midyear 1958. Thus, 1959's model lineup included 96 conventional, 22 low-cab-forward, 8 forward-control, 6 tandem-axle, and 5 school bus models. A Sedan Delivery and the new Sedan Pickup rounded out the line.

Series 70 and 80 tractors, when equipped with the new heavy-duty powertrain, featured a higher GCW rating. The new two-barrel 348-ci engine, in combination with the heavy-duty components that made up this drive system, provided approximately 12 percent greater pulling power. As a result, GCW ratings for these trucks increased from 35,000 pounds with the standard powertrain to 38,000 pounds with the heavy-duty drive system.

The six-cylinder engine lineup consisted of two 235-ci Thriftmasters. The 135-horsepower Thriftmaster was standard for the 30 and 40 Series. The Thriftmaster Special, with a down-draft carburetor, was standard for 34, 35, and 37 series forward-control models. The 150 horsepower Jobmaster six was standard for 60 Series trucks.

There were some options and some standards for the V-8s. The 160-horsepower Trademaster 283-ci V-8 was optional for Series 30 and 40. The 160-horsepower Taskmaster 283 V-8 was standard for Series 50 and optional for Series 60. The 175-horsepower Super Taskmaster equipped with a four-barrel carburetor was standard for Series 70 and 80 and optional for Series 50 and 60. The 195-horsepower Loadmaster 322-ci V-8 was standard for the Series 100 school bus.

The 185-horsepower Workmaster Special 348-ci V-8 was optional for Series 70 and 80, except school buses. It was a new engine for 1959, painted gray and identified by a "Workmaster Special" name written on each rocker cover. Its specifications included a bore and stroke of 4.125x3.250 inches, a compression ratio of 7.75 to 1, and a two-barrel carburetor.

The final V-8 engine offering was the 230 horsepower Workmaster with a four-barrel carburetor. It was standard for Series 90 and 100 except for school buses.

The nation's economy bounced back in 1959 from the recession of the previous year. Total industry truck production easily topped one million, at 1,137,401. This was not a record, but certainly a big improvement. An interesting statistic for 1959 was that the average truck wholesale price reached $2,066, the highest ever. The wholesale value of truck production for the year set a new record at $2,350,000,000. The previous record had been set in 1951 at $2,323,859,000. Production of heavy-duty trucks also continued to boom. Chevrolet led the nation as the best-selling truck line in 1959. Sales of 305,837 new trucks made Chevrolet number one in sales with 32.53 percent of the market.

Chevrolet's official designation for its new El Camino was a Sedan Pickup. It was the only really new model in Chevrolet's 1959 truck line. The El Camino and its Sedan Delivery twin made a handsome couple and brought new meaning to light-duty truck styling. Both trucks were, of course, regular production automobiles modified for truck use. The key to their success depended on how clever Chevrolet engineers and designers were in converting them. They managed to retain all the beauty of high-styled autos, but with truck practicality. Chevrolet designers chose horizontal wings at a time when other designers went with vertical wings. Its full-length chrome trimmed side molding suggested speed and fleetness. The chrome trim that outlined the wings and pickup body called attention to the fact that this is a truck. A full-on rear view disguised the fact that it was a truck, since it featured an automobile bumper, taillights, and trim details. The tailgate, however, was very practical. Rotary door locks on either side secured it in a closed position and when opened it was held in the horizontal position by two hinged straps. Inside the cab El Camino featured a luxurious automobile's instrument panel, steering column and wheel, and a full-width bench seat with hinged backs for access to a storage space. The El Camino was rated for a GVW of up to 4,900 pounds. Powertrains included the standard Hi-Thrift 135-horsepower 235-ci six and the two-barrel carburetor Turbo-Fire 185-horsepower 283-ci V-8, and optional Super Turbo-Fire 230-horsepower 283-ci V-8 with a four-barrel carburetor. Transmissions included the three-speed manual, overdrive three-speed, and Powerglide and Turboglide automatics. *Elliott Kahn*

There are two obvious visual styling clues to help distinguish the 1959 pickup from the 1958 model. The more obvious of the two is the hood ornament, which was more massive and wider than before. The second clue is the fender-side series designation plate. The new plate was shaped like a rocket. The "wing" from 1958 was dropped. The pickup was renamed the Stepside. Notice that Stepside was not yet hyphenated. This 1/2-ton Series 31, Model 3104 1959 Stepside carried a maximum GVW rating of 5,000 pounds. Its standard engine was the 135-horsepower Thriftmaster 235-ci six, optional was the 160-horsepower Trademaster 283-ci V-8. Transmission options included the standard three-speed synchro, HD three-speed synchro, four-speed synchro, and four-speed Hydra-Matic. A 1/2-ton Stepside 4WD was also a standard offering.

This 1959 Chevrolet 1/2-ton Model 3103 chassis cab with a utility body was a rarely seen model. The most commonly used light-duty chassis cab was the 1-ton, the 3/4-ton was second, and 1/2-tonners were last. A Custom cab was also highly unusual for a hard-working utility truck. This truck had a Custom cab because it belonged to the West Riverside County (California) Fire Department. It was powered by the standard Thriftmaster 135-horsepower 235-ci six. V-8 powered trucks had a "V" in the hood emblem under the bow tie trademark. The maximum GVW rating of the chassis cab was 5,000 pounds. *Chuck Madderom*

Chevrolet's pickup line for 1959 was made up of the El Camino and 1/2-, 3/4-, and 1-ton conventional models in both Fleetside and Stepside lines. 4WD pickups in all three weight classifications were also available. In addition, 1/2-ton pickups were built on both the 114-inch-wheelbase chassis and the 123 1/4-inch chassis with 6 1/2- and 8-foot bodies, respectively. Short box pickups were Series 31 models and long box pickups were Series 32 models. This is a 1959 Chevrolet 1/2-ton Model 32 8-foot Stepside pickup. The optional 160-horsepower Trademaster 283-ci V-8 powered this truck. *AAMA*

Chevrolet's biggest-selling medium-duty 1955 models were the versatile Series 50 and 60 trucks. A 1959 Series 60 chassis cab with a platform body was the hard-working farm truck of its day. This North Dakota farm truck's working life had not ended as late as 1997, when this photo was taken. Chevrolet offered the Series 60 in five wheelbase lengths—132 1/2, 144 1/2, 156 1/2, 174 1/2, and 196 1/2 inches. Nine- and 12-foot stake bodies were standard offerings. Two versions of Series 50 and 60 models were available: the standard models and "H" models with heavier components and higher GVW ratings. The maximum GVW rating of the 60 was 19,000 pounds. This six-cylinder–powered truck had the 150-horsepower Jobmaster 261-ci standard engine. *Jim Benjaminson*

The Greenwood Delaware Volunteer Fire Department owned this Series 60 truck. Hahn built its pumper body. It had a 1,000-gallon water tank and a 500-gpm pump. The big "V" in the hood ornament indicates it was V-8 powered. Chevrolet offered two V-8s for the Series 60 trucks. They were the 160-horsepower Taskmaster 283-ci with a two-barrel carburetor and the 175-horsepower Super Taskmaster 283-ci with a four-barrel carburetor. *Scott Mattson*

Those pumpers with a large water tank required a husky heavy-duty truck to handle the weight and allow it to move at a fast pace. This is a 1959 Chevrolet heavy-duty Series 80 Model 8503 Spartan chassis cab with a fire-fighting body. The Saltspring Island (British Columbia) Fire Protection District owned this truck. LaFrance built its pumper body. It had a 750-gallon water tank and a 600-gpm pump. This heavyweight had a maximum GVW rating of 22,000 pounds. The optional 185-horsepower Workmaster Special 348-ci V-8 engine powered this truck. This extra-cost engine was equipped with a two-barrel carburetor and dual exhausts. Its mandatory transmission was the Clark 267V five-speed synchro. It also had a 16,000-pound Eaton 16600 two-speed rear axle. *Frank De Gruchy*

Chevrolet's 1959 heavy-duty truck line was made up of Series 70-80-90-100 models. This is a 1959 heavy-duty Spartan 100. The Frontenac (Missouri) Fire Department Engine Co. 2 owned this truck. Its special body was built by Central. It had a 750-gallon water tank and a 500-gpm pump. It was all dressed up with Custom cab chrome grille, headlight bezels, and front bumper. This single-axle 100 had a maximum GVW rating of 25,000 pounds. It had the optional Timken FD-901 9,000-pound front axle and Eaton 17800 18,000-pound two-speed rear axle. The only engine that was offered for this model was the mighty Workmaster 230-horsepower 348-ci V-8. It produced 335 foot-pounds gross torque. The steel cast-spoke wheels were standard equipment. *Dennis J. Maag*

This 1959 Chevrolet Spartan heavy-duty Series 100 tractor is owned by the Carter Trucking Co. of Ninety Six, S.C. The company purchased it new in December 1959 and used it to haul 20-ton loads of brick from 1959 to 1970. It was completely restored by the Carter Trucking Co. It has the big 230-horsepower Workmaster 348 V-8, a five-speed transmission, a two-speed rear axle, and full air brakes. It also has the standard cast-steel spoke wheels. *Nollie Neil*

These big Series 100 Spartan heavy-duty trucks were a favorite with fire departments. This is a 1959 Spartan Series 100 chassis cab with fire-fighting body. The Castleton (New York) Fire Company No. 3 owned it. Its body was by Bean. It had a 750-gallon water tank and a 500-gpm pump. Transmission choices for these big trucks included the Spicer 3152 HD five-speed synchro as standard and the Chevrolet six-speed Powermatic automatic. Its maximum GVW rating was 25,000 pounds. Its only engine choice was the standard 348-ci Workmaster 230-horsepower V-8. *Neal A. Van Deusen*

Chevrolet's Series 40 was its smallest 1959 medium-duty series. The two chassis cab models were the 4103 and 4403, with wheelbases of 132 1/2 and 156 1/2 inches. Maximum GVWs ranged from 10,000 to 14,000 pounds. This is a 1959 Chevrolet Series 40 Viking chassis cab with dump body. Its GVW rating was 11,000 pounds. The standard drivetrain consisted of the 235-ci OHV six with the four-speed synchro transmission. The 283-ci V-8 and four-speed Hydra-Matic automatic were extra-cost options.

Chapter 5

1960 TO 1969

1960

Chevrolet's 1960 trucks represented the division's most radical and all-encompassing change in its history, with a different appearance, new concepts in chassis design, and many refinements to engines and transmissions. In terms of styling, the 1960 models were entirely new. New features included lower overall heights, sheet-metal styling, modern cab design, series designation plates, cab interiors, and grille designs.

Chevrolet engineers' major objective for 1960 was to provide better load-handling ability at higher safe speeds and greater driver comfort. In order to achieve better ride and handling, the chassis design was drastically changed. Independent front suspensions with torsion bars were standard across the entire line, except 4WD and forward-control models. Rear suspensions were also redesigned. Light-duty Series 10 and 20 models featured a two-link coil spring rear suspension. Variable rate leaf springs were standard for

medium- and heavy-duty vehicles. New frames and steering completed the package. Ford light trucks of the 1960s and Dodge light trucks of the 1970s owed a lot to the new ground Chevrolet plowed with its innovative independent front suspensions.

For simplification, model series designations for 1960 were completely revised. New vehicle series numbers began with a letter prefix. For example, series numbers beginning with a "C" prefix indicated a conventional truck; "K" indicated 4WD trucks; "P" forward controls; "L" low cab forwards; "S" school buses; and "M" tandems.

The first numerical digit of the model series designation identified the vehicle's tonnage rating. The second digit denoted the vehicle's wheelbase length. The last two digits of the series number determined the body style. For example, in model number C1434, "C" was a conventional truck, "1" was a 1/2-ton model, "4" was 115-inch wheelbase, and "34" meant a 78-inch Fleetside body. For

These were exciting days at Chevrolet Truck Division. Chevrolet was the nation's number one selling truck and car line. For 1960, the company announced an entirely new truck. Styling of the 1960 models was entirely different, with lower heights, and modern cab design, designation plates, cab interior trim, and grille styles. The 1960 Chevrolet 1/2-ton Fleetside pickup was only in its second model year. The famous Stepside body continued, however. The short box pickup's wheelbase was 115 inches; the long box pickup's wheelbase was 127 inches. The Fleetside was only offered in the 1/2- and 3/4-ton series with 6 1/2- and 8-foot box lengths. The 1-ton Stepside's box was a 9-footer and rode on a 133-inch wheelbase. Chevrolet's innovative light-duty truck's suspension system consisted of independent suspension torsion bars in front and coil springs in the rear. The standard Thriftmaster 235-ci six or the optional Trademaster 283-ci V-8 powered light-duty trucks. *AAMA*

The 1960 Chevrolet all-purpose Suburban Carryall shared front end styling with the new pickup. Buyers were given a choice of panel-type vertical rear doors or a station wagon–type tailgate with the upper window section hinged upward. Chevrolet promoted the Suburban for either a family wagon or for commercial purposes. This is a 1960 Chevrolet Suburban Carryall. Except for its wheels and tires, this truck was totally stock, and in like-new condition when photographed in June 1998. Its strange-appearing two-tone paint scheme was standard in 1960. The Suburban's standard engine was the 235 Thriftmaster six, and the 283-ci Trademaster was optional. These engines delivered 135 and 160 horsepower, respectively. Chevrolet rated the Suburban as an eight-passenger vehicle. A 4WD model was also offered.

model number C4309, "C" was a conventional truck, "4" was a 1-ton model, "3" was a 157-inch wheelbase, and "09" was a 12-foot stake body. This model was a 1 1/2-ton truck, but for 1960 it was reclassified as a light-duty model.

All new cabs and bodies, except for the Step-Vans and tilt-cab models, featured a new floor design that eliminated the concealed inner step, resulting in more usable inside width. Absence of the concealed step permitted greater ease of cab entry and exit, especially on LCF models.

Interior dimensions included 5.1 inches more shoulder room, 5.8 inches more hip room, and 1.3 inches more headroom. The seat itself was 5 inches wider, which contributed to greater comfort.

Suburban models C and K1416 featured a new tail- and lift gate design that permitted the lift gate to be raised independently of the tailgate. The new design was practical in that small packages could be loaded and unloaded by opening only the lift gate.

Greatly increased engine compartment accessibility was afforded light-duty models. The new hood-over-fenders design eliminated conventional fender crowns resulting in a reduction in fender height from the ground.

Chevrolet engineers set out to build trucks with the utmost in handling, ride, and driver comfort ever offered. The only exceptions were the light-duty forward-control and 4WD models.

In 1960, Chevrolet used seven engines and 12 transmissions to move loads ranging from 4,300 to 50,000 pounds.

The engine lineup included four basic powerplants. These were the 235- and 261-ci sixes and the 283- and 348-ci V-8 engines. The 235-ci Thriftmaster was standard for all 1/2-, 3/4-, 1 1/2-ton, and light-duty 2-ton models, except the 3/4- and 1-ton forward controls, which used the Thriftmaster Special (with updraft carburetor). Heavy-duty 2-ton trucks were standard with the 261-ci Jobmaster six. The 348-ci Workmaster Special was available on all lighter 2 1/2-ton units except tandem axle models. The tandems and heavy 2 1/2-ton trucks were powered by the rugged Workmaster 348-ci V-8. For the first time, the optional 283-ci Trademaster V-8 engine was made available for the 4WD series.

Four transmissions were offered in light-duty models: Three-speed, three-speed heavy-duty, four-speed, and Powerglide.

The heaviest trucks had available the following transmissions: Five-speed (Spicer), five-speed close ratio (Spicer), Powermatic, five-speed (Spicer), plus a three-speed auxiliary and Powermatic.

Chevrolet's truck production performance widely outstripped that of the industry. The industry's total was up 5 percent over 1959

Chevrolet's medium-duty Viking models for 1960 consisted of Series C50, C60 (Conventional cabs), L50, and L60 (LCF low-cab-forward). Medium-duty models carried the same general front-end appearance as light-duty models. However, their grilles and front bumpers were unique and their larger-scaled fenders and fender flares accommodated larger wheels and tires, giving these trucks a huskier, heavy-duty appearance. Six-cylinder powered trucks carried the famous Chevrolet bow tie trademark painted red on the front center of the hood and V-8 powered trucks a "V" emblem with the bow tie painted red and located in the same place. This 1960 Chevrolet Series C60 chassis cab has a fire-fighting body. The Union (Missouri) Fire Department owned tanker truck No. 203. Its body was by Howe and it contained a 1,000-gallon water tank and a 275-gpm pump. The standard engine was the 150-horsepower Jobmaster 261-ci six. Optional was the 160-horsepower HD Taskmaster 283-ci V-8. Its transmission was the five-speed New Process model 540C. Maximum GVW rating was 19,500 pounds. *Dennis J. Maag*

while Chevrolet's production was up by 21 percent over 1959. Chevrolet's share of the industry's output was 32.87 percent. Chevrolet's sales increased over 1959 by 6 percent to 326,195 units, giving Chevrolet 34.57 percent of industry sales.

Industry heavy-duty truck production in 1960 fell almost 18 percent; however, light-duty truck production rose by almost 13 percent. This scenario favored Chevrolet, which was the industry's annual light-duty leader. Chevrolet sold seven six-cylinder–powered trucks for every one V-8–powered truck.

Chevrolet's 1960 heavy-duty models were the Spartan line. These included conventional cab Series C70 and C80 trucks, low-cab-forward Series L70 and L80, and tandem axle Series M70. This is a L8103 low-cab-forward 2 1/2-ton chassis cab with fifth wheel equipment. Its wheelbase was 121 inches and it was rated for a maximum GCW rating of 48,000 pounds. The only engine available in this model was the 230-horsepower 348-ci Workmaster V-8. The cast steel-spoke wheels were standard. Ten-stud steel disc wheels (Budds) were optional. Transmission options included the Spicer 3152 five-speed synchro, the Spicer 3152A close-ratio five-speed, and the Chevrolet six-speed Powermatic automatic. Even these big Chevrolets featured independent coil spring front suspensions. *Spanky L. Hardy*

Chevrolet's new 1960 medium-duty Viking Series L60 Low-Cab-Forward trucks offered GVW ratings of up to 19,500 pounds and GCW ratings to 32,000 pounds. The two standard engines Chevrolet had for C60 Series trucks included the 150-horsepower 261-ci six and the 160-horsepower 283-ci V-8. Like all medium- and heavy-duty 1960 trucks, this C60 featured a coil spring independent suspension (5,000 pounds standard rating and optional 7,000 pounds). The Chevrolet four-speed transmission was standard, the New Process 540C five-speed and Chevrolet six-speed Powermatic automatic were optional at extra cost. This truck is on an errand of mercy. The 1965 flood of the Rouge River near Medford, Oregon, took out the bridge to Shady Cove, which was 30 miles upstream from Medford. The L60 shown was loaded to the roof with food and other supplies for Shady Cove. The driver and truck were donated to the rescue. Mr. Paradis, the driver, complained that the Ford visible behind his Chevrolet caused him to have to wait for it at the top of the hills! *Arnold Paradis*

The new line of short Chevrolet tilt cab trucks was introduced in February 1960. It boasted the shortest in class BBC dimension of only 72 inches. Chevrolet's revolutionary torsion bar ride was standard in all models. Its independently suspended front wheels stepped over bumps using the torsion bars to soak up the jolts. This is a 1960 T70 tilt cab chassis cab with fire-fighting body. Its 23,000-pound GVW was moved by the 185-horsepower Workmaster Special 348 V-8 matched up to a Clark 265V five-speed synchro transmission. The Courtenay, British Columbia, Canada, Volunteer Fire Department, owned engine No. 2. Its body was by Thibault and featured a 750-gallon water tank and a 600-gpm pump. *Frank De Gruchy*

1961

The major story of the 1961 Chevrolet trucks was the introduction of the Corvair 95 line, which was designed to compete in the rapid-growing market for light-duty delivery vehicles. This was a market segment that didn't even exist until the late 1950s. It was founded by Volkswagen and consisted of minivans and pickups. Volkswagen was the only player, but the rules changed with a vengeance when Chevrolet kicked off its Corvair line and Ford rolled out its Econoline compact trucks in 1961.

Styling refinements on Chevrolet's other trucks included eight new exterior colors as well as front-end styling changes. New models included three new light-duty forward-control units, three additional 4WD vehicles, two new short-wheelbase forward-control models, and the discontinuance of the Sedan Delivery and Sedan Pickup models, bringing the total lineup to 191 models on 19 wheelbases.

The new Corvair 95 series consisted of the Corvan, a panel delivery, and the Loadside and Rampside pickups. The Corvair 95 design program also included a station wagon, Model R1206, which was not a part of the truck line since it was merchandised as a passenger car.

No changes were made in the GVW ratings of models carried over from 1960, with one exception. The 48,000-pound GVW rating of Series 80 (2 1/2-ton Tilt, Conventional, and LCF tractor-trailer units) models and the 50,000-pound GVW rating of the M70 (straight tandem-axle units) trucks were increased to 51,000 pounds.

The Chevrolet E-80 LCF design used the GMC LCF design, which was not a surprise, since this truck was built in Pontiac, Michigan, at the GMC plant. Chevrolet shared sheet metal with GMC on the conventional and tilt cab trucks, but the LCFs were different. Chevrolet's LCF design was not used on any GMC truck.

Chevrolet management's first concern with the trucks it designed and built was that they would perform, to the complete satisfaction of their owners, the jobs they were designed for. Its second concern was to build the best-designed trucks in the industry. It believed the trucks' appearance contributed greatly to their owners' business success. Obviously, owners who were completely satisfied on both counts would continue to buy Chevrolet trucks year after year.

For 1961, Chevrolet's designers made only minor changes to a two-year-old truck. There are two quick ways to tell a light-duty 1961 model from a 1960. First, the Chevrolet name was prominently displayed in the center of the grille rather than at the bottom. Second, the parking lights on 1961 models featured two sharp spinners that served as bezels for the parking lights.

This was the second and last year for Chevrolet's "double-bubble" hood design. Most people will agree it was probably not Chevrolet's best design effort. One of the foundations for Chevrolet's success over the years was always its superior design. Chevrolet's management considered the styling of its truck line to be every bit as important as its automobile's styling. New hood and grille styling cues for 1961 included the Chevrolet name prominently displayed in the center of the grille. The parking lights located within the hood's "double-bubble" front edge now featured "spinners," which allowed air to enter the engine compartment. Chevrolet's innovative independent torsion bar springing front suspension and its similarly innovative coil-spring rear suspension continued because people appreciated the trucks' comfortable ride. Chevrolet liked to say that its pickup's front wheels "walked" over bumps. All Apache light-duty models from 1960 continued into 1961. The 135-horsepower 235-ci six-cylinder engine remained as standard, and the 160-horsepower 283-ci V-8 engine was optional.

The bread-and-butter Corvair 95 model was the Greenbriar Sports Wagon. The Corvair was new in 1960, at which time only two-door and four-door sedan models were offered. The three truck models were new for 1961: Model R1205 Corvan van or panel, Model R1244 Loadside pickup, and Model R1254 Rampside pickup. The Greenbriar was also new in 1961, but it was a passenger car model, not a truck. The Corvair's bodies and frames were of the "unitized" type. They were combined in a single assembly for high strength, low weight, and lots of load space. Corvair's powertrain was likewise unitized. Its engine, transmission, and rear axle were all one package, neatly fitted between the rear wheels. Corvair's independent suspension consisted of coil springs at all four wheels, which gave excellent handling characteristics unmatched in any other commercial vehicle. Chevrolet kept the Corvair 95 commercial series in the line through 1964; the automobile models continued through the 1969 model year. *AAMA*

Chevrolet's major new light-duty truck introduction was a derivative of the 1960 Corvair compact car. Chevrolet engineers intended for the Corvair 95 truck series to be used for light, bulky-type loads such as in local delivery service. This is a left-side quarter view of the front and rear of a 1961 Corvair 95 Rampside pickup. It is equipped with the Powerglide automatic transmission and non-original wheels. Corvair had a 95-inch wheelbase and a short overall length of less than 15 feet, giving it a short turning radius. A unique innovation of the pickup was its hinged side-loading ramp. It allowed a load to be wheeled up and into the pickup's bed or one could simply walk up and in. Loading height was only 14 inches from the ground at the side opening and 26.5-inches at the rear gate. The rear mounted, air-cooled 80-horsepower 145-ci Turbo-Air six-cylinder engine powered the Corvair 95. An easily removable floor panel in the cargo box gave access to the engine for normal tune-ups and adjustments. A hinged panel below the cargo box and above the rear bumper gave access for routine engine servicing. *James Law*

Corvair's air-cooled 145-ci six-cylinder engine produced 80 gross horsepower at 4,400 rpm and 128 foot-pounds gross torque at 2,300 rpm. It featured two single-barrel carburetors.

With the exception of the new Turbo-Air 6 air-cooled engine for the Corvair 95 series, Chevrolet's engine lineup carried over without change. The 235-ci Thriftmaster and Thriftmaster Special sixes powered light-duty Apache models, and forward-control models with heavy-duty components powered the Series 50 Viking models. For the Series 60 and 60-H models the rugged 261-ci Jobmaster was standard.

The 283-ci Trademaster V-8 was optional for all Apache and Viking models in Series 10 through 50, including 4WDs. There were special heavy-duty components for Series 50 application. For Series 60 and 60-H Vikings the extra-rugged Taskmaster V-8 (with a four-barrel carburetor) was available. At the top of the Chevrolet line, Series 70 and 80 Spartans featured the powerful 348-ci Workmaster Special and Workmaster V-8s as standard equipment.

Truck industry production declined in 1961 because of a general economic slowdown. Total industry shipments slipped by 5.1 percent, to 1,133,804. New truck sales of 918,608 also posted a decline of 2.6 percent. Chevrolet's total production of 342,658 was off by 13 percent, but good enough to lead the industry again. Chevrolet sales topped off at 306,175 for first place in the industry, but down from 326,195 in 1960.

Chevrolet and Ford compact trucks beat back Volkswagen. Volkswagen's sales declined from 31,377 in 1960 to 26,555 in 1961. Chevrolet sold a total of 44,640 Corvair 95s in 1961, including 15,550 wagons, 10,845 pickups, and 18,245 van models. Ford sold a total of 69,977, including 14,564 pickups, 36,913 vans, and 18,500 wagon models. Overall, it was a good showing by both Ford and Chevrolet for their first year. In total, the three companies sold 141,173 total compact trucks. This was the start of an entirely new segment within the truck manufacturing industry—cargo vans and passenger wagons. Wagon (passenger) models from all three companies were tabulated as a passenger car–type vehicle, while the pickups and vans were considered trucks.

This was the year of the six-cylinder engine in the industry and in particular at Chevrolet. Chevrolet sold 86 percent of its trucks equipped with six-cylinder engines. Except for 73 four-cylinder diesels, the rest were V-8 engines. Chevrolet outsold its nearest competitor in six-cylinder engines by nearly 100,000 units.

A careful study of production figures shows that Chevrolet's strength was still its traditional market—that is, light-duty and medium-duty trucks. Chevrolet dominated or showed favorable results in all weight classes through 16,001–19,500 pounds. Those above that the division did not fare well. Chevrolet's management had work to do.

Chevrolet did enter the diesel truck market during 1961, selling 73 four-cylinder diesels and 11 six-cylinder diesels. These 84 diesel trucks were 1962 model year trucks. Its entry into this market was delayed by a GM labor-contract strike. Ford and Dodge also competed in the diesel market in 1961.

Chevrolet's 1961 medium-duty Viking line continued from 1960. The Viking models consisted of the C50 and C60 conventional chassis cab series and L50 and L60 LCF (Low-Cab-Forward) chassis cab series. This is a 1961 C50 conventional cab Viking chassis cab with fire-fighting equipment. The Town of Modoc (Indiana) Fire Department owned it. Its body was by Howe and it contained an 800-gallon water tank and a 500-gpm pump. This truck carried a maximum GVW rating of 16,000 pounds. Its standard engine was the 135-horsepower Thriftmaster 235.5-ci six specially built for extra-duty use. Optional was the 160-horsepower 283-ci V-8. A four-speed Chevrolet-built manual transmission was standard equipment. All Viking trucks featured Chevrolet's innovative independent front suspensions with torsion bars. *Steve Hagy*

The biggest Viking model was the C60 (or L60 LCF). The New Knoxville (Ohio) Washington TWR Fire District owned this 1961 Chevrolet C60 chassis cab with fire-fighting body. It had a body by Howe with a 1,550-gallon water tank and a 500-gpm pump. The C60 was rated for a maximum GVW of 22,000 pounds. Its standard engine was the 150-horsepower Jobmaster 261-ci six; its optional engine was the 160-horsepower HD Taskmaster V-8. This truck had the same independent front suspension and rigid rear axle as the C50 models except with heavier specifications. This truck's cast-steel wheels were standard equipment. A four-barrel carburetor and dual exhausts were options. The Chevrolet-built four-speed manual was the standard transmission, a New Process 540C five-speed was an option, as was the six-speed Powermatic. *Steve Hagy*

Chevrolet built both forward-control chassis only and forward-control Step-Vans in 1961 on 1/2-, 3/4-, and 1-ton models. This is a 1961 3/4-ton P2342 forward-control chassis with a 10-foot body. The maximum GVW rating of this unit was a full 7,000 pounds. The 135-horsepower Thriftmaster Special (with updraft carburetor) 235-ci six powered it. Transmission options included a three-speed, three-speed heavy-duty, four-speed synchro, and four-speed Hydra-Matic. Chevrolet offered six Step-Van models fully equipped and ready for work with all-steel bodies in 8-, 10-, and 12-foot lengths. The three standard wheelbase lengths included 104, 125, and 137 inches. Chevrolet chassis would accommodate bodies from all of the nation's leading body manufacturers. *AAMA*

This is a 1961 Chevrolet LCF L70 heavy-duty 2 1/2-ton chassis cab with platform body. The 348-ci V-8 coupled to the five-speed transmission and a two-speed rear axle powered it. It was also equipped with an air over hydraulic brake system and the big 10.00x20 tires. Series L70 models carried a maximum GVW rating of 23,000 pounds, or 42,000 pounds GCW when used as a tractor trailer. Although they are a little difficult to see in this photo, the two-digit series numerals in the center of the grilles on all medium- and heavy-duty 1961 trucks were a new addition by Chevrolet designers. The grille was painted Cameo White while the lettering was black. *Jim Fromm*

Chevrolet designers designed an all-new instrument panel for the 1960 model trucks. This design carried over and remained basically unchanged until 1967. Pictured is an instrument panel from a 1961 Chevrolet LCF L70 truck. One instrument cluster was developed for Series 10 through 60 trucks and a second for Series 70 and 80 models. This second cluster had provisions for a tachometer and an air brake pressure gauge. A separate instrument panel was provided for flat-face cowl models and another for the Tilt-Cab Series. For the design shown, cluster readability was improved through the use of a nonreflective face cover, and the contrast of light green letters and numerals on a dull charcoal background. Instrument pointers were red-orange. Black plastic control knobs (throttle, choke, and fresh-air ventilator) were conveniently grouped near the driver; they can be seen below the instrument cluster. The ashtray, heater controls, and radio are located in the center of the instrument panel, and the glovebox is on the right. *Jim Fromm*

1962

Chevrolet fielded a lineup of 203 models on 19 wheelbases for 1962, the largest truck lineup in Chevrolet history. Of these, 10 were new medium-duty diesel cab chassis models, and 10 were heavy-duty trucks. New models included 20 new diesel-powered trucks in the 60 and 80 Series, a new school bus chassis in the S60 Series, and six Series C36S models with a special 3/4-ton rating. All models from 1961 carried over with the exception of the entire Series 70, which was canceled. The M70 models (tandem axles) were transferred to the 80 Series. Several changes were made in maximum GVW ratings. Series 60H models were upgraded to 23,000 pounds, and Series K25 models to 7,600 pounds. GVW ratings of the new diesel-powered models were identical to their gas engine counterparts. The GVW rating for Series 60H models was raised to 42,000 pounds.

Expanded powertrains provided the conventional line with a more complete coverage of power options. The company offered four new engines, including two new V-8 gas units of 327 and 409 ci and a four- and a six-cylinder diesel. The 283-ci Taskmaster and 348-ci Workmaster Special engines were dropped. The exhaust systems of all 1962 engines were equipped with extended life mufflers.

The restyled hood lent a totally new appearance to conventional trucks, both from the front and side. It was considerably lower at the front and increased forward visibility to the ground.

Grilles for Series 50 to 80 trucks, except for LCF and tilt-cab models, also featured single headlights, while the tilt-cab grille was carried over with dual headlights.

A sliding rear window unit was available as a dealer-installed accessory for all conventional-line cabs except tilt-cabs. The unit fit into the regular rear window opening, and consisted of a double-channel metal frame carrying left- and right-hand panes of glass.

For extreme off-road operations, two new extra-heavy-duty optional I-beam front suspensions with leaf springs were made available. They were rated at 9,000- and 11,000-pound capacity and were available for only C-E-L-M80 models.

Chevrolet offered seven gasoline engines for 1962. The total included two new models. One was the 327 V-8 available as an option on Series 60 models, and the other was the largest and most powerful engine ever offered by Chevrolet, a 409 V-8 provided as an option on Series 80. The High-Torque 327-ci engine was basically the same as the discontinued 283 Taskmaster V-8, but with internal modifications for an increase in displacement. It featured an 8.0 to 1 compression ratio, 185 gross horsepower at 4,400 rpm, 305 foot-pounds gross torque at 2,000 rpm, and a two-barrel carburetor. A new 13-inch clutch replaced the former 11-inch clutch.

The 409 was patterned after the existing 348-ci engine, but with a larger bore and longer stroke. New items included a new combustion chamber and piston design, larger valves, improved cooling, and induction-hardened exhaust valve seats. The 409 featured a 7.75 to 1 compression ratio, 252 gross horsepower at 4,000 rpm, and 390 foot-pounds gross torque at 2,400 rpm.

The Corvair 95's exterior appearance was generally unchanged for 1962. One change in the Corvair 95's cab interior was that the body panels were painted Fawn Beige. Cameo White was used as an accent color for the steering wheel and hub, instrument panel front face, and the ashtray. The glovebox door was painted silver, as was the instrument cluster bezel. Multi-color stripes in the vinyl seat fabric allowed Chevrolet designers to key the interior colors to any exterior color. Corvair 95 models were also available with an interior Custom Equipment option including seat trim, fawn and white steering wheel, white front door panel inserts, and red or fawn vinyl armrest top. This is a 1962 Chevrolet R1254 Corvair 95 Rampside pickup. Its engine was again the 145-ci air-cooled six, producing 80 horsepower. Standard transmission was the three-speed manual synchro; a four-speed synchro and a two-speed Powerglide were options. Corvair 95 pickups were rated as 1/2-ton trucks with payload ratings up to 1,850 pounds.

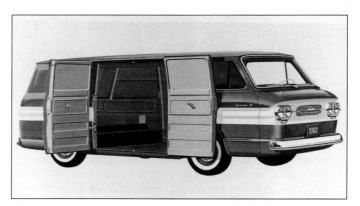

The Corvan rode on a trim 95-inch-wheelbase chassis, yet offered more cargo space than conventional 1/2-ton trucks. Its low 16 1/4-inch floor height ensured easy loading. Note the step-up in the rear of the cargo space to accommodate its rear-mounted engine. Loads traveled safely and easily on Corvan's four-wheel independent suspension system. Corvair 95 model continued to feature dual headlights, even though the balance of Chevrolet's light-duty truck line switched to single headlights in 1962. The Corvan rode on tubeless 7.00-14/4PR tires. The whitewalls shown were optional, as were six-ply rated tires, blackwall or whitewall. Note the attractive two-tone paint scheme with the white painted band encircling the middle portion of the Corvan's body. Loading was convenient and easy through spacious double side doors. A 1962 R1205 Corvan is shown. *AAMA*

The 235-, 283-, and 261-ci engines carried over without change. The 261-ci six, formerly used as standard equipment on Series 60, now was optional for Series 10-50, except for forward-control models. The 1961 Taskmaster and Workmaster Special engines were discontinued.

Also new for 1962 was a new engine identification system. The engine names, as such, were discontinued. All engines were now known as "High-Torque" and were distinguished only by the number corresponding to their displacement. In the case of the 235-ci engines, both the downdraft and updraft carburetor versions were known as "High-Torque 235." Each was counted separately in the engine lineup, however.

Chevrolet engineers released two GM-built diesels for 1962 Chevrolet trucks. Both were proven designs with many years of service and many satisfied customers. Both diesels were the two-stroke cycle type using a blower that gave them the ability to produce more horsepower per cubic inch of displacement, higher horsepower to weight, and higher horsepower to size.

An extremely high ratio of parts interchangeability existed between the two engines. For example, the exhaust valve–operating mechanism, valves, springs, pistons, rings, cylinder liners, injectors, and fuel pumps were common.

The Model 4-53 engine was standard for series D60, D60S, and D60H. Features included four cylinders, 3.875x4.5 inch bore

and stroke, 212.3-ci displacement, a 17 to 1 compression ratio, 130 gross horsepower at 2,800 rpm, and 271 foot-pounds gross torque at 1,500 rpm.

The Model 6V-53 engine was standard for series E-U80. Features included six cylinders ("V"), same bore and stroke as above, 318.4-ci displacement, a 17 to 1 compression ratio, 195 gross horsepower at 2,800 rpm, and 423 foot-pounds gross torque at 1,500 rpm.

An interesting statistic regarding Chevrolet's entry into the diesel market was that diesel trucks represented about 3.5 percent of all trucks produced in 1962. Two-thirds of all truck engines sold in 1962 were six-cylinder models. This was true for gas and diesels. Seventy-eight percent of the gas engines Chevrolet installed were six-cylinder engines compared to only 22 percent V-8s.

Diesel engine usage was only 2.5 percent of total truck production in 1962. Interestingly, Chevrolet, Dodge, and Ford built a total of 800 diesel trucks in 1961; the combined total for 1962 went way up to 4,700 trucks, an almost sixfold increase. Chevrolet built 84 diesel trucks in 1961 and 1,777 in 1962.

In total, the truck industry's production was up by 11 percent over 1961, with 1,254,220 units compared to 1,127,505. Chevrolet's production of 396,918 was up 12 percent over 1961's 342,658. This was more than enough to retain the industry leadership. Chevrolet built a total of 19,788 1962 Corvair vans and pickups.

Chevrolet continued to consider its Series C40 trucks part of its light-duty models. For 1962, Chevrolet did change from Series names back to identifying individual trucks by numbers only. Previously the 1962 Chevrolet chassis cab model C1403 would have been part of the Apache Series. A new-design series nameplate located high on the cowl sides displayed the series number, "40." The C40 was available only as a chassis cab with maximum GVW ratings up to 14,000 pounds and maximum payload ratings of 8,400 pounds. They were capable of handling a wide variety of special bodies up to 12 feet long on wheelbases ranging up to 157 inches. This 1962 Chevrolet C40 chassis cab with fire-fighting body was owned by the Delta (British Columbia, Canada) Fire Department and was used for rescue work. Three engines were available for this model: the 235 six, the new 261 six, and the 283 V-8. *Bill Hattersley*

Chevrolet's bread-and-butter medium-duty 1962 truck was the C50 model, pictured with a farm grain box. This one looked a bit old and tired when photographed in September 1998, but it was still on the job. Note the aluminum scoop shovel hanging on the side of its box. Chevrolet trucks represented an outstanding value at a low initial purchase cost and the lowest possible operating costs. Farm trucks typically did not log many miles per year, but they did work hard and overloading was a way of life. The maximum GVW rating of the C50 ranged from 14,000 to 16,000 pounds. Its single-speed Chevrolet-built rear axle had a 6.60:1 ratio and was rated for 13,000 pounds. An optional 15,000-pound capacity two-speed axle was extra cost. Engine choices included the 135-horsepower 235 six, 150-horsepower 261 six, and 160-horsepower 283 V-8. The only available transmission was the Chevrolet-built four-speed.

Chevrolet's top-of-the-line medium-duty truck in 1962 was the C60. This is a very rare C60 open cab fire truck, owned by the Galt (California) Fire District. The fact that it was a California truck explains its open cab. For the first time in its history Chevrolet began to make available a diesel-powered D60 chassis cab in 1962. This pumper had a body by Van Pelt that contained a 750-gallon water tank and a 500-gpm pump. This model had a maximum GVW rating of 19,500 pounds. Its standard engine was the 150-horsepower 261 six and its optional engine was the new 185-horsepower high-torque 327 V-8, equipped with a two-barrel carburetor. The clutch for this model was also increased from 11 to 13 inches. *Chuck Madderom*

At the other side of Chevrolet's medium-duty line were the LCF L50 and L60 Series. All told, Chevrolet built 50 gasoline-powered conventional-cab models in its Series 50 and 60 and 18 LCFs. This truck was built using the same cab as the C Series, called a Comfort-King cab, except it was mounted higher and featured a shorter hood for additional maneuverability and a better view of the road. The LCF Series was identical to the C-Series in terms of wheelbase lengths, GVW ratings, engine, transmission, axle, and spring options. The North Palos (Illinois) Fire Protection District owned this 1962 Chevrolet L60 medium-duty chassis cab with fire-fighting body. Engine No. 804's body was built by the fire department. The new 185-horsepower 327 V-8 powered this truck. Cast spoke wheels were an option. *Chuck Madderom*

Chevrolet's famous and popular Tilt-Cab Series was in its third model year. It was found in both medium- and heavy-duty lines. This is a 1962 Chevrolet T60 medium-duty chassis tilt cab with fire-fighting equipment. This truck was owned by the New Bremen (Ohio) German Township Fire Department. Its body was by American and contained a 750-gallon water tank and a 750-gpm pump. Chevrolet offered two new 17,000-pound single and two-speed vacuum shift rear axles to replace the 16,000-pound unit previously used. Also new was a two-speed 17,000 pound Eaton axle. On tilt-cab models clutch and brake pedals were floor-mounted, reducing pedal pressure by 40 percent. The new 185-horsepower 327 V-8 powered this truck. Its maximum GVW rating was 19,500 pounds. Alternators were available at extra cost with gasoline engines. *Steve Hagy*

This was the first year for the famous long-lived Chevrolet 1/2-ton P-10 Step-Van 7. The "7" referred to its body length. It was a specialized door-to-door delivery truck with 211 cubic feet of load space astride an easy-handling 102-inch wheelbase. This is a 1962 Chevrolet Step-Van 7 model P1345. The Union City Body Co. of Union City, Indiana, built the Step-Van's body. In the background is a P2545 Step-Van of the rounded-body type. Chevrolet also built a line of forward-control chassis only on which the customer could have the body of his choice mounted. *AAMA*

Chevrolet's new heavy-duty entrant for 1962 was the LCF E80-Series. This was the first Chevrolet heavy-duty truck model that was a re-rebadged GMC model. It used the GMC truck's DB7000 cab and B4000 sheet metal. The only difference was that the E80 had exterior ornamentation, with a Chevrolet bow tie emblem added at the center of the hood front, a series nameplate placed lower on the cowl, and a diesel nameplate placed below the series nameplate. Its interior was identical to L80 models—that is, the conventional cab LCF model—except that the full-width bench seat was replaced with two tilt-cab driver seats. Its maximum GVW rating was 25,000 pounds when used as a tractor trailer. Early in the model year, Chevrolet offered only the two-cycle GM-built 4-53 diesel, which developed 130 horsepower and 271 foot-pounds torque. The only diesel offered in the E80-Series was the GM-built two-cycle V-6 318-ci, which produced 195 brake horsepower and 423 foot-pounds torque. *AAMA*

Chevrolet also offered its 72-inch BBC tilt-cab truck as a heavy-duty gasoline or diesel model. This is a 1962 Chevrolet T80 heavy-duty gasoline powered tilt-cab tractor. Chevrolet also built the same truck as a model U80 with a diesel. The tilting mechanism for 1962 tilt-cabs incorporated a new torsion bar adjustment feature for optimum cab counterbalancing. The basic design of the mechanism wasn't changed. The new version simply improved the tilting action. The standard engine for the T80 was the 220-horsepower 348 V-8; the optional engine was the new 252-horsepower 409 V-8. This was the largest and most powerful engine ever offered by Chevrolet. The 409 was a larger version of the 348 with a larger bore and longer stroke. Its maximum GVW rating was 25,000 pounds, and when used as a tractor trailer rig its maximum GCW rating was 51,000 pounds. *AAMA*

In the middle of Chevrolet's 1962 medium-duty Jobmaster Truck line was its hard-working C60 Conventional Series. This is a 1962 Chevrolet C6503 chassis cab with panel body by Fruehauf. This truck was powered by the optional high-torque 327 V-8, the 150-horsepower 261 six was standard. It featured Chevrolet's innovative coil spring independent front suspension and a Chevrolet four-speed transmission and two-speed rear axle. This truck worked for five long years in stop-and-go service without mechanical repairs in spite of serious and routine overloading. It was rated for a maximum GVW of 19,500 pounds. Chevrolet also offered LCF and Tilt-Cab 60 Series models. The Chevrolet disc wheels shown were standard equipment; Budd discs and steel cast spokes were options. *Arnold Paradis*

This was the first year for Chevrolet's E80 Series diesel-powered LCF trucks. It was a GMC "B" Series LCF truck with a Chevrolet emblem. GMC "B" Series models were built between 1960 and 1965. The LCF design saved space with a 90-inch BBC (bumper to back of cab) dimension. This series was designed specifically for tractor use or for installation of bodies up to 13 feet. Maximum GVW ratings up to 25,000 pounds and GCW ratings up to 51,000 pounds were permissible. Its only engine was the 195-horsepower GM 6V-53 diesel, producing 423 foot-pounds torque. Its transmission was a Spicer five-speed turning a two-speed 18,500-pound rear axle. This is a 1962 Chevrolet U80 chassis cab with platform body. *Dick Copello*

1963

Chevrolet's 1963 truck program included many new and improved features to make these superb trucks even more reliable and hard working. Coil spring independent front suspensions for light-duty trucks, and I-beam axles with variable-rate leaf springs for medium- and heavy-duty trucks, offered outstanding durability, along with good riding qualities. Increased carrying capacity was featured for Series 10 and 20 models, with new two-stage coil rear springs and optional cantilever leaf-type auxiliary springs.

Chevrolet's new light-duty front suspension design was used with very few changes until 1987 (1991 if one counts the Suburban/Crew Cabs). One of the major reasons the torsion bars were dropped was because they required a heavy frame with extra bracing and thus reduced payload capacities.

Chevrolet's truck lineup for 1963 consisted of 178 models on 19 wheelbases—a decrease of 25 models from the 1962 lineup. The medium-duty category was the area of greatest change with the deletion of all Series 40 trucks and the rerating of all Series 50 vehicles to 1 1/2- from 2-ton.

The front fenders, running boards, and bumper width on the conventional cab Series 50-80 were decreased by 7.2 inches, which greatly improved maneuverability. The new I-beam front suspensions of these series also reduced front tread width, which further contributed to better maneuverability.

For the most part, Chevrolet frames for 1963 were extensively revised in all weight categories. Frames were completely redesigned to eliminate the earlier independent front suspension systems, except for

Chevrolet's Corvair 95 Rampside pickup continued into its third year. The Rampside concept was exclusive to Corvair. It took much of the work out of loading and unloading. Two easily operated handles released the rugged double-walled ramp door, which formed a loading platform almost 4 feet wide, allowing heavy loads to be rolled into the cargo box without lifting. The floor was only 16 1/4 inches off the ground. A conventional tailgate was also furnished for loading at the rear. The Rampside's cargo area equaled 80 cubic feet of space. The versatile Corvan was also continued for 1963. The Corvair 95's 145-ci six-cylinder 80-horsepower air-cooled engine continued unchanged. Notice the standard cab interior of this 1963 Chevrolet Corvair 95 pickup. The manual transmission had a multi-curved shift lever. The automatic transmission's control lever was dash mounted.

light-duty models. Gauge thickness of frame side rails were changed to better suit the truck's job requirements for greater reliability.

In the light-duty category, where ride qualities were of significant importance, a coil spring independent front suspension was provided on Series C10, C20, and C30 models, replacing the former torsion bars.

Ride quality was not significantly affected by changing from torsion bars to coil springs. With the absence of the torsion bar rear-mounted cross-member and other related components, however, vehicle ground clearance was increased. Maintenance, too, was practically eliminated, since the new coil springs never had to be adjusted. Series C10 and C20 models were also given new two-stage coil springs and new cantilever leaf-type auxiliary springs rear suspensions. Series C30 models with 10,000 pound GVW ratings were given new main and auxiliary spring setups.

In the medium- and heavy-duty category, new variable-rate front springs and I-beam front axles replaced the previous independent front suspensions. Chevrolet engineers released five separate axle assemblies with rated capacities of 4,000, 5,000, 7,000, 9,000, and 11,000 pounds covering the entire line of medium- and heavy-duties.

This was a historically significant year for Chevrolet trucks in relation to the six-cylinder engine lineup. Highlights of the program included a new family of four- and six-cylinder inline engines of 153, 230, and 292-ci displacements. The new 230 engine replaced the 235-ci six and the 292 replaced the former 261-ci six. The 235 and 261 six-cylinder engine's roots went all the way back to 1929.

All three engines were of OHV type, with a bore of 3 7/8 inches. Strokes differed, with 3 1/4 inches for the 152- and 230-ci engines and 4 1/8 inches for the 292-ci engine.

The 230 engine was almost 2 inches shorter and 3 inches lower in overall height than the 235, while the 292 was shorter by a like amount, and approximately 1/4 inch lower.

The 153-ci four-cylinder engine was basically two-thirds of the 230-ci engine, with identical features. So all components such as pistons, connecting rods, and valvetrains were the same for both engines. Crankshafts, camshafts, blocks, heads, oil pans, manifolds, and rocker covers were tailored to the four-cylinder engine.

The truck industry set a new record production high of 1,426,828 in 1963. That meant 1963's volume was 18 percent ahead of 1962. Of the total, 1,316,265 trucks and buses were sold to the domestic market and the balance was exported.

Competition at the heaviest end of the truck market was becoming more intense. Heavy-duty truck sales boomed in 1962 and continued in 1963. Chevrolet's heavy-duty volume had begun to grow in 1960. In 1963, Chevrolet shipped 242 trucks in the 26,001–33,000 pound class versus zero in 1962. In the over 33,000 pound segment, Chevrolet's shipments increased to 1,078 from 925. In 1959, Chevrolet shipped no trucks rated at over 19,500 pounds; in 1963 it shipped 15,000.

Competition also increased dramatically in 1963 in the diesel truck business. This was historically a stronghold of the independent heavy-duty truck manufacturers. Ford, Dodge, Chevrolet, and GMC each now had strong diesel models with which to compete in this segment.

In 1963, Ford doubled its market share of diesels from 4.1 percent in 1962 to 8.8 percent. Chevrolet's share grew to 3.9 percent from 3.8 percent in 1962; Dodge's percentages for 1962 and 1963 were

The restyled grille was new on light-duty 1963 Chevrolet trucks, as seen on this three-quarter-ton K2534 4WD Fleetside pickup with fire-fighting equipment. This brush fire truck from Fire Station No. 78 was owned by the Greenwood (Delaware) Fire Department. It had a 250-gallon water tank and a 300-gpm pump. On 1/2- and 3/4-ton models, a ladder-type channel section riveted frame replaced the former X-type. The frame's siderails were basically parallel with 34-inch spacing for easier mounting of special bodies. This truck carried a maximum GVW rating of 7,600 pounds. Engine choices included the standard, 140-horsepower 230 six, the optional 165-horsepower 292 six, and the powerful 175-horsepower 283 V-8. A single-lever control operated the transfer case. The shift lever had four positions: 2WD direct, 4WD direct, neutral, and 4WD underdrive (1.94 gear reduction). A rugged three-speed synchromesh transmission was standard. A heavy-duty four-speed transmission with power takeoff opening was optional. *Scott Mattson*

Chevrolet's medium-duty truck models changed from the previous independent front suspension to the conventional tough ladder-type frames with a solid I-beam front axle. In medium-duty series the straight-channel section frames had increased side rail gauge thickness in most models for greater strength. This is a 1963 Chevrolet C60 2-ton chassis cab with fire-fighting body. The Atwood (Kansas) Fire Department owned engine No. 1. Its body was by Boardman and contained a 750-gallon water tank and a 500-gpm pump. Cast spoke wheels were optional. Chevrolet-built steel disc wheels were standard, a Budd disc wheel was an option. The appearance of these trucks carried over without noticeable change. The one exception was their narrower front fenders, running boards, and bumper width. The overall width was decreased by 7.2 inches due to the use of an I-beam front axle in place of the former independent front suspension. Series 60 trucks retained the same rear axle lineup as used in 1962. The Chevrolet-built 15,000-pound single-speed rear axle was base equipment, and a Chevrolet 17,000-pound single-speed axle was an upgrade. Chevrolet 15,000- and 17,000-pound two-speed axles and an Eaton electric shift 17,000-pound two-speed axle were options. The 165-horsepower 292 six was the standard engine, and the 185-horsepower 327 V-8 was optional. *Dennis J. Maag*

exactly the same as Chevrolet's. Total diesel-powered trucks increased by 28.6 percent over 1962 and reached a new high of 56,402 units.

Chevrolet's production rose 12 percent over 1962 to a new high of 483,119 units. Chevrolet retained its title of industry leader again for 1963. Its share of the industry was its largest ever at 33.01 percent, up from 31.65 percent in 1962. Sales reached 425,406 or 34.2 percent of the market, its highest total ever.

In gasoline engines, Chevrolet was the industry's leader in six-cylinder output, with 378,059 trucks, equal to 78.6 per-

cent of total output. This, however, was below the 82 percent and 86 percent of production of sixes in 1962 and 1961, respectively. Production of V-8 engines rose to 102,419 or 40 percent from 1962.

Chevrolet sold only 483 four-cylinder gasoline engines in 1963, but expected this total to climb dramatically in 1964 with the introduction of its new line of compact trucks. The four was new in 1962 when it was first installed in the new Chevy II compact cars.

Chevrolet built three series of its tilt-cab truck in 1963: T60, 60-H, and 80. Pictured is a heavy-duty Series T80 tilt-cab chassis cab with van body. The Tilt's ultra-short cab—only 6 feet from bumper to back of cab—gave exceptional compactness and maneuverability. Its engine accessibility was also unsurpassed by any other model. The maximum GVW rating of the T80 was 25,000 pounds. When used as a tractor trailer, its maximum GCW rating was 51,000 pounds. This truck was powered by Chevrolet's largest gasoline engine, the optional High-Torque 252-horsepower 409 V-8. Its gross torque was 390 foot-pounds at 2,400 rpm. Transmission choices included two five-speed Spicers and the Chevrolet-built Powermatic automatic. *AAMA*

The Series D80's cab and sheet metal durability was vastly improved with new flexible hood mounting and shackle-type rear body-mounting systems. The new system used a slip-fit attachment of the central hood panel to the cowl and spring-loaded latch-type locks for the left- and right-hand hood panels. The new rear body-mounting system permitted the chassis to move both torsionally and laterally without imparting these movements to the cab and sheet metal. This 1963 E80 chassis cab with fifth wheel carried a maximum GVW rating of 25,000 pounds, and a 51,000-pound GCW rating when used as a tractor. Its only engine offering was the 6V-53 GM-built diesel. *AAMA*

1964

Chevrolet's conventional line was given a fresh, new appearance for 1964. The major change was replacing the former wrap-around windshield with a more modern curved windshield. In addition to the new modern look, the new windshield facilitated entry and exit, since it didn't obstruct the door opening like the previous windshield, and also increased cab torsional strength. Other highlights included new grilles, hubcaps, and series designation plates. On the interior, the entire instrument panel and cluster, door interior panels, and seat trims were completely restyled.

This was the last year for the Corvair 95 Series; it was replaced in midyear with the new front engine Chevy Vans. Corvairs were given an increase in engine power for their last year. A 164-ci unit replaced the original 145-ci engine. The increase in size was a result of increasing the stroke from 2.60 to 2.94 inches. Power increased from 80 to 96 gross horsepower. An optional high-performance, 110-horsepower engine was also made available for 1964 Corvairs.

Chevrolet's truck program for 1964 was expanded to 193 models from 184, while wheelbase count rose to 21 from 19. The new models included the El Caminos, three low-cab-forward diesel tandems, and four forward-control vans.

Also new for 1964 were four forward-control vans designated the Step-Van Kings. They were offered in 1/2- and 3/4-ton capacities on either 125- or 137-inch wheelbases. They featured a new square-front, high-cube, fiberglass-insulated panel body in lengths

of 10 and 12 feet, with 72 inches inside height. These new body lengths provided a cubic foot capacity of 375 and 480, respectively. Two optional body lengths of 10 1/2 and 12 1/2 feet and an optional interior body height of 76 inches expanded total body choices to eight different bodies. Straight sides permitted better stacking of cargo and increased load space. Step-Vans now came in 21 body sizes, including the previous round-front models.

The three new tandem axle models were powered by the 6V-53 Detroit Diesel engine. The new models—designated as the W80 Series—were of the low-cab-forward body design with a conventional Eaton-Hendrickson tandem rear suspension that rated at 30,000-pound capacity. Front-end sheet-metal styling was identical to the carryover Series E80 trucks.

The 292 six-cylinder engine featured a higher lift camshaft for improved volumetric efficiency and greater engine power. Horsepower increased from 165 to 170. A new stainless-steel exhaust manifold heat valve in the 154, 230, and 292 six-cylinder engines cut down carburetor icing and improved fuel vaporization.

Chevrolet introduced in its 1964 line a diesel-powered tandem series in wheelbase lengths of 145, 163, and 181 inches. Power came from the 195 horsepower GM 6V-53 diesel engine because it offered greater operating economy in dump, mixer, and other heavy-duty service requiring dual-drive axles. Rear suspension, rated at 30,000 pounds, was a Hendrickson bogie with Eaton axles. Front I-beam axle was rated at 7,000 pounds. Heavier front and rear axles were options.

Suburban Carryalls, 1/2-ton panels, and long-wheelbase 1/2- and 3/4-ton pickups featured a new two-piece driveline. The two propeller shafts were supported by a center bearing and were coupled

After four years without an El Camino pickup, Chevrolet introduced an all-new 1964 El Camino. This was a dual-purpose vehicle that combined passenger-car styling, ride, comfort, and performance with the genuine economic utility of a light-duty truck. It was built on the mid-sized Chevelle's 115-inch wheelbase and had 38.5 cubic feet of cargo space in its cargo box. It was rated for a payload capacity of 1,200 pounds. Chevrolet offered four models: two Standard six-cylinder series and two Custom V-8 series. Engines included the 194-ci 120-horsepower six or a 283-ci 195-horsepower V-8. Chevrolet truck's marketing group targeted El Camino to fill the needs of sportsmen, suburbanites, salesmen, farmers, businessmen, and construction foremen. Its bucket seats and four-speed floor shift were available sporty options. Full coil suspension made for an easy, soft ride. Despite the truck's decrease in overall length compared to earlier models, the cargo box actually *increased* in size, to 78 1/2 inches long and 59 3/4 inches wide.

This 1964 eight-door Chevrolet Corvair 95 Greenbriar Sports wagon is a very rare vehicle. It has two double doors on each side, single front doors and two rear doors. This was a standard factory offering, but was very seldom seen. This was the last year for the Corvair 95 commercial trucks—pickup, with and without ramp, and Corvan. The Greenbriar wagon continued through 1965 and autos through 1969. The Corvair 95 engine featured a higher 164-ci displacement. Horsepower was subsequently increased from 80 to 95. A 110-horsepower version was an option. Also new was an air inlet grille shut-off door that ensured more-effective front compartment heating. *Gary Benidt*

The new Chevy Van came out in December 1963. Ford's conventionally designed Econoline vans had been outselling Chevrolet's air-cooled, rear-engine, automobilelike vans. Chevrolet management didn't relish losing market share to its chief competitor in any single segment of the light-duty truck market. Its new forward-control Chevy Van (no pickup was offered) was built on a conventional chassis with front-mounted engines. The accepted van design at the time was a flat front with the engine wholly contained in a "dog house" located between the front seats. The standard engine in the Chevy Van was an economical four-cylinder, 90-horsepower 153. The optional engine was the 120 horsepower, 194 six. Transmission choices included a standard three-speed manual and optional two-speed Powerglide automatic. Note the wide-opening double side doors for easy opening. Rear doors with windows were also provided. *AAMA*

For fleet operators, Chevrolet offered a total of 193 truck models in the 1964 model year. New Step Van models widened the selection. The Step Van line offered four new forward-control models in 1/2- and 3/4-ton capacities on either 125- or 137-inch wheelbases. They featured a new square-front, high-cube, fiberglass-insulated, panel bodies in lengths of 10 or 12 feet with 72-inch inside height. This is a square-front body 1964 Chevrolet Model P2535 Step-Van. Step-Van King's bodies featured all-steel construction, welded and bolted for maximum strength. Steel panels lined the body interior, providing a smooth surface that was both durable and practical. Corrugated steel was used for the cargo floor. Easy entry and exit were afforded with sliding side doors of double-wall construction. Double rear doors of 38-inch width were standard, 60-inch and 74-inch wide rear doors were options. *AAMA*

to a shorter transmission extension housing. The new design was expected to reduce whipping action, vibration, and noise.

In December 1963, Chevrolet announced the addition of the new Chevy Van. Unlike the Corvan that it replaced, the forward-control van rode on a conventional chassis with a front-mounted gasoline engine. Its 90-inch wheelbase afforded a high degree of maneuverability in city delivery work.

Standard engine for the Chevy Van was the economical inline 153 four rated at 90 horsepower. Transmission choices included a standard three-speed manual and optional Powerglide automatic. A limited-slip differential was offered as an option with the six-cylinder engine.

The truck-building industry set another high output record in 1964 and topped 1.5 million units (1,540,453) for the first time ever. Truck production increased by 5.3 percent over 1963. Diesel-powered trucks, on the other hand, increased by 14.7 percent—to 64,711 from 56,402, setting an all-time high. V-8 engine installations in trucks increased by 100,000 units over 1963, yet six-cylinder engines took 55 percent of the market versus 37 percent for the V-8. In spite of the company's best efforts, Chevrolet's percent of diesel engine installations dropped in 1964 to 1.8 percent from 3.9 percent in 1963.

The industry performed exceedingly well in the lightest trucks—6,000 pounds or less. Chevrolet gained a 2.5 percent increase in this category by selling 41,000 more of these lighter-weight trucks. This increase may well have been due to its hot-selling new Chevy Van models.

Chevrolet's total 1964 production was 523,790, an increase of 8 percent over 1963. Chevrolet easily held onto first place, increasing its market share to 33.56 percent from 33.01 percent the year before.

Although Chevrolet truck building halted for more than a month due to a United Automobile Workers strike, an all-time production record was set in 1964. Strike losses amounted to nearly 50,000 trucks, yet the division reached a new record high.

Chevrolet truck retail sales fell just short of the half-million mark in 1964 with 496,480 trucks sold. This was a healthy 13 percent increase over the previous record set in 1963 when 440,912 Chevrolet trucks were sold.

Chevrolet also built a line of forward-control chassis in 1964. Many body manufacturers mounted their special bodies on these. The Maple Ridge (British Columbia, Canada) Volunteer Fire Department owned this 1964 Chevrolet forward-control chassis with a special fire-fighting body by Haney Iron Works. The fire department used it for fire safety education. The 140-horsepower 230 six-cylinder engine powered this P-20 forward-control chassis. *Bill Hattersley*

Chevrolet's top-of-the-line pickup in 1964 was the stunning model C1534 C10 1/2-ton Custom Fleetside. This handsome pickup was offered with either a 6 1/2-foot Fleetside cargo box or the 8-foot box pictured. All Series 10 and 20 Chevrolet pickups offered as standard equipment a tough ladder-type frame and independent coil-spring suspensions in front and two-stage coil spring in the rear. Two cab trim levels were offered: Standard and Custom cab. Custom cab features included a full-depth foam bench seat upholstered in colorful and handsome fabrics, a driver armrest, a right door lock, chrome-trimmed control knobs, a cigarette lighter, a passenger side sunshade, a horn ring, white trim on doors, and a trim plate on glovebox. Exterior Custom features included a chrome bumper, grille, windshield trim and hub caps, and full-length chrome body side moldings. The 1/2-ton's maximum GVW rating was 5,000 pounds. Engine choices included the 230 and 292 sixes and the 283 V-8, mated to either three- or four-speed manuals or a two-speed Powerglide. *AAMA*

Chevrolet's light-duty models took on a new, modern look for 1964 chiefly due to the fact that Chevrolet engineers gave a slope to the front pillars on cabs for easier entrance and exit. The old "dog-leg" style, which dated back to the mid-fifties, had at long last passed. To provide more driving comfort, reduced maintenance, and longer vehicle life, Chevrolet engineers added the following features for 1964: self-adjusting brakes, reduced transmission hump, longer front-suspension lube intervals of up to 6,000 miles on light-duty trucks, and longer-life exhaust systems. This is a 1964 Chevrolet C10 8-foot Stepside pickup, model C1504. The body had a capacity of nearly 50 cubic feet. The C1504 had a maximum GVW rating of 5,000 pounds. The Chevrolet 1/2-ton pickup line also included a 4WD version of the Stepside pickup. The C10's standard engine was the 140-horsepower 230 six; the extra-cost 170-horsepower 292 six and 175-horsepower 283 V-8 engines were optional. The three-speed manual transmission was standard, a four-speed manual and a two-speed Powerglide automatic were options. *AAMA*

Chevrolet offered a 1-ton chassis cab with a 9-foot stake. The stake body rode on a rugged 133-inch-wheelbase chassis. The dual rear wheel 1-ton was rated for a maximum GVW of 10,000 pounds. Steel-lined stake pockets supported its long-lasting hardwood racks. Chevrolet also offered a 7-foot stake body mounted on a 3/4-ton chassis. Engine options included the standard 140-horsepower 230 six and optional 170-horsepower 292 six and the powerful 175-horsepower 283 short-stroke V-8. This is a 1964 Chevrolet C30 1-ton Standard cab chassis cab with 9-foot stake. Note the Standard cab's painted front bumper and grille. *AAMA*

Chevrolet built two panel models in 1964: the C10 model C1405 1/2-ton with 7 1/2-foot body length and the 1-ton C3605 with a 10-foot body. The 1/2-ton's payload capacity was 1,300 pounds and the 1-ton's payload capacity was 3,300 pounds. This is a 1964 Chevrolet C10 model C1405 panel. It was the Custom model, as is evident by its chromed grille, bumper, windshield trim, and hubcaps. The narrow band white sidewalls were a factory option. Loads rode easily and undamaged due to Chevrolet's coil-spring independent front suspension. Engine choices included the 230 and 292 sixes and the 283 V-8. As in all 1/2-ton C10 models, transmission choices included either a standard or wide-ratio three-speed manual, four-speed manual, and two-speed Powerglide automatic. Suburbans and long-wheelbase 1/2-ton and 3/4-ton pickups featured a new two-piece driveline designed to reduce whipping action, vibration, and noise. *AAMA*

Chevrolet's bread-and-butter medium-duty model with either conventional or LCF cab C50 Series chassis cabs with 9-foot or 12-foot stakes continued to be the low-cost leader. This series was unsurpassed for economical hauling in trucks up to 20,000 pounds GVW. Buyers could choose from four chassis cab models with wheelbases from 133 to 175 inches. This is a 1964 conventional Chevrolet Model C5309 C50 12-foot stake. Its maximum payload rating was 13,950 pounds. The stake body featured heavy platform planking, steel-reinforced for extra durability. Stakes had heavy steel cargo skid strips, a smooth steel rub rail all around, and steel-lined stake pockets. Hardwood racks were finely finished with hardware recessed to leave the interior snag-free. The optional 175-horsepower 283 V-8 engine mated to a standard four-speed transmission powered this truck. *AAMA*

Firefighters all across the nation purchased 4WD trucks for brush firefighting. Chevrolet did not make a 4WD 1-ton in 1964. This is a very rare 1964 C30 chassis cab converted to 4WD by an unknown company. It was owned by the Manchester (Mississippi) Fire Department and has a fire truck body also by an unknown manufacturer. It had a 300-gallon water tank and a 200-gpm pump. This 4WD 1-ton is a very tough and aggressive-looking 4WD conversion, sitting high on big wheels and tires. Its engine was the high-torque 170-horsepower 292 six. *Fred Cote*

Chevrolet built a full range of medium- and heavy-duty LCF models in 1964—L50-60-60H-80. This is a 1964 L-60H chassis cab with fifth wheel. When used as a tractor trailer, this truck carried a maximum GCW rating of 42,000 pounds. New for 1964 was the 220-horsepower 348 V-8 as a special engine limited to upper medium-duty trucks. LCF truck's length from bumper to back of cab was 12 inches less than conventional cab models to give more load space with the same wheelbase, or less overall length for the same size body or trailer. It gave tighter turning for easier handling as well as better driver visibility because of the higher, forward driving position. When used as a tractor, it eased parking and docking problems. LCFs were available in two cab trim levels—Standard and Custom. The Custom model featured a full-depth foam seat cushion upholstered in attractive fabrics, a driver armrest, right and left door locks, a passenger sunshade, a cigar lighter, extra insulation, and full cab undercoating. This truck was powered by the 348 V-8. It had a close-ratio five-speed transmission and a two-speed rear axle. *AAMA*

Chevrolet built its biggest 1964 model two ways: Series M80 with gas engines and Series W80 with diesel power. Pictured is a 1964 Chevrolet W80 heavy-duty tandem axle ready-mix truck. It was offered in three wheelbase lengths—145, 163, and 181 inches. It was rated for a maximum GVW of 36,000 pounds. These big new diesel-powered tandem models featured space-saving LCF cabs, reducing wheelbase and overall length 1 foot from CA sizes. A 30,000-pound bogie was standard and a new 34,000-pound was optional at extra cost, both with special diesel gearing and powered by the big 6V-53 diesel with 423 foot-pounds gross torque at 1,500 rpm. Chevrolet referred to this engine as a "Chevy-GM" diesel. Tandem bogies came from Eaton-Hendrickson. The big Eaton axles were geared specifically for the type of power employed. The 30,000-pound capacity bogie had leaf springs of 17,250 pound capacity each. The 34,000-pound bogie was furnished with 19,500-pound springs. Standard transmission was a five-speed; a four-speed auxiliary was optional. Standard wheels were steel cast spokes; Budd discs were an option. *AAMA*

Sometimes it takes a fleet to get the job done. This is a fleet of the various Chevrolet trucks it took to move the old Federal Building in Medford, Oregon, to its new quarters. Note there is also a Chevrolet panel parked at the curb around the corner. The first truck in line is a 1964 Chevrolet C-30 1-ton chassis cab with panel body. With dual rears it was rated for a maximum GVW of 10,000 pounds. The standard engine for C-30s was the 140-horsepower 230 six; optional engines included the 170-horsepower 292 six and the 175-horsepower 283 V-8. The standard transmission for a 1-ton was the four-speed synchro and optional was the three-speed synchro. The only body models that were offered in this series were 8- and 9-foot stakes. *Arnold Paradis*

A 1964 Chevrolet 93-inch BBC LCF L60H chassis cab with a Miller Equipment body. A non-original 350 V-8 powered this truck. Its transmission was a five-speed synchro and its rear axle was a two-speed rated at 17,500 pounds. Chevrolet's 1964 V-8 truck engine lineup included the snappy 283 for Series 50, a 327 V-8 for Series 60, and for extra torque there was the mighty Special 348 V-8 with a two-barrel carburetor. The 1964 LCF medium-duty models were available as either Series L50 or L60. Six-cylinder engine options included the 230 for Series L50 and the big 292 six for Series L60 trucks. *Spanky L. Hardy*

Chevrolet's workhorse medium-duty Conventional model in 1964 was the C60. It carried a maximum GVW rating of 21,000 pounds. C60s were available with one of five gas engines and one diesel engine. This 1964 C60 tractor was originally powered by the 348 V-8, the largest available engine for medium-duty trucks in 1964. The 348 was replaced at 180,000 miles with a 409 big block. This tractor had a five-speed transmission and a two-speed rear axle. Drivers routinely ran this truck at 70 miles per hour, turning 4,000 rpm. A hailstorm had removed the North American decal on front of the trailer. When this photo was taken, the truck was delivering costumes and stage props to the Oregon Shakespeare Festival at Ashland, Oregon. The owners had received permission to back the trailer up the narrow sidewalk to load at the theater. Four actresses showed up to help Arnold Paradis (far left) and his driver Bob Claason (far right). *Arnold Paradis*

1965

Chevrolet's 1965 Workpower truck line featured 324 models on 24 wheelbases. This represented an increase of 128 over 1964. Of the total, 145 were diesel powered. The diesel lineup was extended to a total of six, including three new four-cycle types and one three-cylinder two-cycle.

The 1965 Chevrolet gas-powered truck line comprised 179 models in 106 series, including four El Caminos. The 1965 engine lineup for conventional line gasoline models remained unchanged from 1964 except for an increased power option on Series 60 models. There was also the interim addition of a 327 engine for Series C20 and 30 models, and the 230 six replaced the 194 six in G10 (Chevy Van) models as the optional engine. A new optional 348 V-8 four-barrel carburetor engine for Series 60 models provided an increase of 35 horsepower over the two-barrel version offered in 1964 and discontinued for 1965. The new 327 V-8 engine option, an interim for C20 and 30 models, provided increased power for sustained highway speeds, with reserve power for mountain grades required for campers.

Diesel engines were offered in all nominal weight categories including, for the first time, the 1 1/2-ton (Series D50), up through the 2 1/2-ton category. GVW ratings for the new diesels were generally the same as those of comparable gasoline models.

Chevrolet's gasoline engine line consisted of eight basic types in 13 configurations. There was the four-cylinder 90-gross-horsepower 153 L-4; the six-cylinder 120-gross-horsepower 194 L-6; the six-cylinder 230 L-6 in three versions—a 120-net-horsepower version for CK 10, 20, and 30 models, with a 115-net-horsepower version optional for Chevy Vans; the 230 six-cylinder L-6 with economy carburetor and 100 net horsepower, optional for C10; and finally the 292 six-cylinder with 170 gross horsepower for Series 60 trucks.

For V-8s, there was the 283 V-8 195-gross-horsepower version for El Caminos; the 283 V-8 with 175 gross horsepower optional for CK 10, 20, and 30; the 327 V-8 two-barrel 185 gross horsepower for 3/4- and 1-tons; the 327 V-8 with a four-barrel optional for El Caminos; the 348 V-8 220 gross horsepower for Series 80; and the 409 252 gross horsepower optional for Series 80.

This was the first year in truck-building history when total truck output began to receive media attention. In 1964 total U.S. production broke 1.5 million units for the first time; in 1965 production exceeded 1.75 million, topping off at 1,785,109, and limited to that

The Chevelle based El Camino was now in its second year. Its appearance changed for 1965 with the addition of a new grille design, front fenders, and hood. By anyone's standard, the new El Camino was America's finest styled truck. It was as luxurious as an expensive passenger car, yet could handle a payload up to 1,200 pounds. Big coil springs gave it beautiful handling and ride. On the inside it had every option known to passenger cars. The cab interior came in two levels—Standard and Custom. The standard scheme offered a full-width bench seat. In the Custom, interior bucket seats with center console were an extra-cost option. But the Custom interior provided luxurious upholstery, deep-pile carpeting, deluxe steering wheel, electric clock, glovebox light, and other features. The truck had power brakes, steering, and windows; air conditioning; and whatever else the customer wanted or needed for his personal comfort and enjoyment. Six-cylinder engines included the small 140-horsepower 194 Hi-Thrift and the 140-horsepower Turbo-Thrift 230. The 195-horsepower Turbo-Fire 283 was the base V-8 engine. For the first time the Turbo-Fire 327 V-8 was the high-performance engine in the customer's choice of either 250 or 300 horsepower. *AAMA*

Chevrolet's Corvair 95 series of commercial trucks did not return for 1965. The Chevy Van, new last year, replaced the rear-engine Corvair 95 models. The first Chevy Vans, Series G10s, were only available as 1/2-ton models with a maximum GVW rating of 5,000 pounds (equal to C10 pickups) and a maximum payload rating of 2,200 pounds. For 1965, Chevy Vans offered up to 10 side and rear windows at extra cost. Glass options included the following choices: rear doors only (2); right side doors (2); rear doors and right side door (4); ten windows (eight are shown; missing are two small triangular windows between the front door and first side door); and four right side windows, with or without rear door glass. The Chevy Van was given a more powerful six-cylinder optional engine for 1965, the 140-horsepower 230 six. The 90-horsepower 153 four remained as the standard engine. Standard transmission was the three-speed manual handily mounted on the steering column; optional was the two-speed Powerglide automatic. *AAMA*

number only because of capacity limitations and supplier problems. Some writers called 1965 "The Year of the Truck" in recognition of this new milestone. It was the fourth consecutive year that truck output increased over the preceding year.

For the first time in history, light-duty trucks (6,000 pounds and less) reached a million units. While pickups sold strongly, it was the exploding growth in the compact segment, principally vans, which made this record possible.

Another encouraging sign was that output and sales of new trucks increased across the board, from compacts to off-road diesel trucks. For the first time in history, heavy-duty trucks topped 100,000 units, totaling 114,571 versus 93,772 in 1964. This part of the market had traditionally been owned by the independents, but Chevrolet, Dodge, Ford, and GMC began to become significant players.

Chevrolet had a very good year. Of the six largest producers, it accounted for 567,473 sales in 1965—or 37 percent of the 1,528,859 total U.S. sales. This was 17 percent above its previous high of 483,853, registered in 1964. The Big Four—Chevrolet, Dodge, Ford and GMC—accounted for 84 percent of the total. Chevrolet's total production for 1965 was 619,691—an 18 percent increase over the 523,790 built in 1964.

Six-cylinder gas-engine–powered trucks accounted for 57.4 percent of the trucks built by GM, Ford, Dodge, IH, and Jeep. Chevrolet led in six-cylinder production, even though its number of six-cylinder installations dropped by 5 percent from 1964.

Chevrolet doubled its 1964 diesel engine installation total in 1965, reaching 2,400 units compared to 1,200.

Chevrolet engineers created a dream truck, or "futuristic freighter" (these were the days when concept cars were routinely called "dream" cars) in 1965. Named the Turbo Titan II, it was a test bed for Chevrolet's latest gas turbine Turbo Titan engine. Dodge and Ford also tested gas turbine engines in trucks at this time. Chevrolet's entry, pulling a 40-foot trailer, was bigger, bolder, and very impressive. Its fiberglass and steel cab tilted forward at the touch of a button to reveal the engine.

Another interesting Chevrolet truck that was developed in association with GM's Research Laboratories in 1965 was the articulated Sidewinder. It was a 3/4-ton-rated military vehicle developed with an eye toward future production (which never happened.) Its articulated configuration made possible the use of huge diameter tires, 14.00x20, which afforded increased mobility over soft ground and in water.

The 4,400-pound vehicle had a top speed of 60 miles per hour. Its engine was from a light commercial vehicle, which was mated to a two-speed automatic transmission with a torque converter. Final drive was from a two-speed transfer case, driven to front and rear axles by short driveshafts.

In 1965, GM was the first U.S. company of any type ever to earn two billion dollars or more in a single year. The record net income of $2,125,606,440 resulted from record sales of $20,733,982,295. Sales and income were up 22 percent over 1964.

GM's passenger car sales for 1965 hit a new high of 4,653,821, compared with 3,970,280 in 1964. GM's market share hit 53.1 percent, compared to 52.1 percent in 1964. The corporation's total truck and bus sales posted a record—698,045 units.

The only visual change to the appearance of 1965 Chevrolet light-duty models was relocating the model number nameplate higher up on the cowl. This is a 1965 Model C1534 Chevrolet C-10 Custom cab Fleetside pickup—America's favorite pickup. Americans fell in love with camping and traveling vacations, as much of the new federal freeway system was in operation. Chevrolet built two series of 1/2-ton pickups: the short 6 1/2-foot cargo box on a 115-inch-wheelbase chassis and the 8-foot cargo box on a 127-inch-wheelbase chassis. The 1/2-ton's maximum GVW rating was 5,000 pounds. The three available engine included the standard 230 six, the optional 292 six, and the 283 V-8. *AAMA*

Chevrolet's dual-purpose pickup for 1965 was the C10 Stepside. Many times this truck was purchased for commercial work because of its rock-bottom price, but many others purchased it for personal use. Some bought it for price reasons, but more bought it because it was unique and reflected their personalities. This truck was easily personalized with custom wheels, fancy tires, special paint schemes, and a host of dealer and or after-market accessories. A 1/2-ton Stepside 4WD was highly favored by the personal use buyer. The Stepside's cargo box floor was constructed of wood with metal skid strips to easily slide cargo in and out. The front of the cargo box was accessible from over the side by using the handy "side-step." The engine lineup for this truck included the 230 and 292 sixes and the 283 V-8. *AAMA*

Chevrolet's other bread-and-butter 1/2-ton pickup was the C10 short box Fleetside Standard cab. A new overdrive transmission (Option M10) was released for Series C10 trucks to give them even greater economy through increased fuel mileage. It consisted of a 0.7-to-1 ratio planetary gear unit integrated with the Chevrolet three-speed transmission. The overdrive unit could be manually locked out by the driver through a hand control, or by fully depressing the accelerator pedal. It could be used only in combination with the 4.11-to-1 ratio rear axle and with all available engines—230 six, 292 six, and 283 V-8. The overdrive couldn't be used with the Positraction rear axle. The maximum GVW rating of this model was 5,000 pounds. *AAMA*

In the mid-sixties Chevrolet's competition for its Suburban Carryall was slim and getting slimmer. Dodge built its truck-built Town Wagon people or cargo mover. International built a four-door truck-built people or cargo mover. These competitors would soon vacate because of the expanding van-type wagon market and sport utility market. Chevrolet soon owned this specialized market and began to expand the product with first three and later four doors. The 4WD Suburban had been around for several years and was slowly growing in popularity. Chevrolet claimed a maximum passenger capacity for the two-door Suburban of eight on three seats. With only two seats installed, it could easily seat five people and carry luggage; with three seats there was almost no room for luggage. Pictured is a 1965 Chevrolet Suburban Carryall Model K1406. Buyers had the choice of panel-type rear doors as shown, or station wagon doors with a hinged tailgate and hinged upper section. A three-speed manual transmission was standard. Options included the Powerglide automatic, overdrive, a wide-ratio three-speed, and a four-speed. Available engines included the 230 and 292 sixes and 283 V-8. *AAMA*

Chevrolet's 4WD K-Series trucks for 1965 included 1/2- and 3/4-ton Stepside and Fleetside pickups, 1/2-ton Panel and Suburban Carryall, and 1/2- and 3/4-ton chassis cabs. This is a 1965 Chevrolet K10 1/2-ton Stepside pickup. Note its left-side outboard-mounted spare tire. Chevrolet's 4WD chassis featured parallel frame construction with extra strength and rigidity and with additional cross-members for rugged off-road work. Unlike the 2WD models, the 4WD trucks had high-capacity leaf springs at all four wheels designed for rough, tough 4WD work. Both the Standard cab and Custom cabs were offered with the 4WD trucks. Chevrolet's K-Series featured a simple single lever to operate the transfer case. Its lever had four positions: two-wheel direct, four-wheel direct, neutral, and 4WD underdrive (1.94 gear reduction). The standard engine for all 4WD trucks was the 140-horsepower 230 six. The optional six was the 170-horsepower 292 six and the optional V-8 was the 175-horsepower 283. *AAMA*

Chevrolet built a line of forward-control chassis on which the buyers could have a body of choice mounted. Chassis were available with wheelbase lengths of 102, 104, 125, 137, 157, and 175 inches to fit special bodies ranging from 7 to 16 feet. Chevrolet built three series of Step-Vans: the traditional model with rounded body lines, the compact 1/2-ton Step-Van 7, and the bigger Step-Van King series. The regular series differed from the King series in its body's cubic space. The Step-Van King bodies featured straight lines to make maximum use of available space. It was also taller, which gave the operator 72 inches of height for his convenience and for added cubic capacity. All Step-Van and forward-control chassis featured rugged ladder-type frames and tough coil or leaf spring suspension to ensure long-lasting, low-cost performance. Six-cylinder engines powered all but the Step-Van 7 and the 102-inch chassis, which were equipped with Chevrolet's 153 four. *AAMA*

By the mid-sixties the panel truck was another truck body style that had been around for a long time and was rapidly disappearing. Dodge still built its Town Panel model, but that was about the extent of Chevrolet's panel competition. Van-type panels (vans with rear doors only and no body side windows) and small forward-control delivery vans were taking the place of the traditional van. Chevrolet was not only still in the business, but actually built two models—a 1/2-ton and a 1-ton. Chevrolet only offered 4WD in the 115-inch-wheelbase 1/2-ton panel. The Custom C-10 1/2-ton panel pictured here typified the traditional high-style panel truck that was most favored by upscale retailers for delivering packages to retail customers. The panels had durable wooden floors with recessed steel skid strips. It had telescoping door checks and high, wide rear doors. As with all other Chevrolet light-duty trucks, the panels were powered by the standard 230 six; the 292 six and 283 V-8 were options. *AAMA*

Chevrolet's 1965 medium-duties consisted of two broad categories—gasoline- and diesel-powered models. Gasoline-powered medium-duty trucks included Series C and L50-60 conventional cab and LCFs; Series T50 and 60 Tilt-Cabs; Series C and L60H (heavy) conventional cabs and LCFs; and Series T60H Tilt-Cabs. Chevrolet's biggest seller continued to be the C50 conventional cab Series. Chassis cab models with up to 20,000 pounds maximum GVW were offered, as were 9- and 12-foot stake body models. These versatile medium-duty trucks were offered in wheelbases ranging from 133 to 175 inches. Standard power was the 140-horsepower 230 six; the 170-horsepower 292 six was an option, as was the 175-horsepower 283 V-8. The standard transmission was the four-speed. The Compton (California) Fire Department owned this 1965 C50 chassis cab with firefighting body. *Chuck Madderom*

Chevrolet's middle medium-duty truck for 1965 was the Series C60. It carried a maximum GVW rating of 21,000 pounds. The heaviest medium-duty model, the C60-H, carried a maximum GVW rating of 24,000 pounds. The Allen (Texas) Fire Department owned this 1965 Chevrolet C60-H chassis cab with firefighting body. This pumper with body by Central carried a 500-gallon water tank and a 500-gpm pump. Standard power for this model was the 170-horsepower 292 six; options included the 185-horsepower 327 V-8 and the 220-horsepower 348 V-8. Transmission options included four- and five-speed manuals and a six-speed Powermatic automatic. *Hansen*

Chevrolet's Tilt-Cab diesels were offered in medium- and heavy-duty weight classes from 15,000 pounds GVW and up. There were 50-60-60H-80 Series diesel models. This is a 1965 Chevrolet 72-inch BBC tilt-cab heavy-duty diesel U80 Series tractor. This model carried a maximum GCW rating when used as a tractor of 51,000 pounds. It was powered by the Chevy-GM 6V-53N two-cycle 318-ci diesel. It put out 195 gross horsepower and gross torque of 447 foot-pounds. A four-cycle Torq-Flow DH-478 diesel boasted 170 horsepower and 310 foot-pounds gross torque. Full air brakes were standard on U80s when equipped with the complete extra cost, extra-heavy-duty equipment package. The standard transmission for this model was a five-speed manual; an eight-speed manual and a six-speed Powermatic were options. Steel cast spoke wheels were standard and Budd discs were an option. *AAMA*

Chevrolet built gasoline-powered heavy-duty 80 trucks in its conventional cab Series C80, LCF Series L80, and the Tilt-Cab Series T80. Chevrolet also built diesel-powered heavy-duty trucks in the following series: 105-inch BBC conventional cab Series Q80; 93-inch BBC LCF Series A80 and E80; 72-inch BBC Tilt-Cab Series N80 and U80 and tandem models in the LCF (the GMC-type) W80 Series and the Conventional cab V80 Series. This is a 1965 Chevrolet heavy-duty C80 chassis cab with platform body. This was a gasoline-powered model. Its standard engine was the 220-horsepower 348 V-8 and optional was the 252-horsepower 409 V-8. If this had been a diesel-powered model, it would be a Series Q60 model and would have been powered by the Chevrolet Torq-Flow four-cycle 170-horsepower, 310 foot-pounds-torque DH-478 engine. There wasn't an optional engine for this truck. This truck's ten-bolt Budd-type disc wheels were optional. A five-speed manual transmission was standard equipment. *AAMA*

Chevrolet built heavy-duty tandems in two Series in 1965 with either gasoline or diesel power. This is a 1965 M80 tandem axle gasoline-powered chassis cab with a dump body. Chevrolet also built a tandem axle Series 60 with a trailing axle. These were the M60, V60, and S60 models. The M was gasoline-engine–powered, the V was powered by the four-cycle Torq-Flow D478 and DH478 diesel engines, and the X was powered the Chevy-GM-Detroit 4-53N four-cylinder two-cycle diesel. The maximum GVW rating of these trucks was 30,000 pounds. They were equipped with a Chevrolet-Hendrickson bogie. Either the standard 220-horsepower 348-ci V-8 or the optional 252-horsepower 409-ci V-8 powered the M80 shown. Series V80 tandems were powered by the 170-horsepower, 310-foot-pounds-torque Torq-Flow DH-478 diesel; and the W80 was powered by the 195 horsepower, 447-foot-pounds-torque two-cycle Chevy-GM-Detroit 6V-53N diesel. The maximum GVW rating of the M80 was 36,000 pounds. The V80 was rated at 43,000 pounds and the W80 at 34,000 pounds. All three used an Eaton-Hendrickson Bogie. *AAMA*

Chevrolet's complete 1965 LCF line consisted of Series L50, L60, and L80. This is a 1965 L80 chassis cab with a famous twin-boom Holmes 600 wrecker body. This biggest L-Series was rated for a maximum GVW of 32,000 pounds. A 252-horsepower big block 409-ci V-8 powered it. This was the last year for this engine. It was replaced by the new truck-built 366-ci V-8 in 1966. This truck also has the five-speed transmission and a two-speed 23,000-pound rear axle. In addition it has air brakes, power steering, and big back glass. *Spanky L. Hardy*

Chevrolet offered its 93-inch BBC LCF chassis cab models with either a single axle or tandem rear axles. However, it was only powered by diesel engines. This 1965 Chevrolet single-axle 93-inch BBC LCF chassis cab has fifth wheel equipment. This truck was offered in three Series A60, A80, and E80. A60 was rated for a maximum GCW rating of 42,000 pounds and was powered by the 150-horsepower, 275-foot-pounds-torque, four-cycle Torq-Flow D-478 diesel. A80 was rated for a maximum GCW rating of 45,000 pounds and was powered by the 170-horsepower, 310-foot-pounds-torque four-cycle Torq-Flow DH-478 engine. E80 was rated for a maximum GCW rating of 51,000 pounds and was powered by the 195 horsepower, 447-foot-pounds-torque two-cycle Chevy-GM 6V-53N diesel. These specs are for single-axle models. This truck was engineered and manufactured by the GMC Division. They were identical except for nameplates. Only the E80 was available with the optional six-speed Powermatic automatic. This was the last year for this LCF Series, which was replaced in 1966 by a new, modern 92-inch BBC LCF Series. *AAMA*

Chevrolet's biggest 1965 LCF was the L80 model L8203 chassis cab pictured with a fifth wheel. It was rated for a maximum GCW of 51,000 pounds when used as a tractor. The optional 252-horsepower 409 V-8 engine powered this truck. It had the close-ratio five-speed transmission. A two-speed rear axle was mandatory with this transmission. The two-speed was a 23,000-pound Eaton axle. It was equipped with every accessory available from Chevrolet. Note the covered gas tanks, sanders, rear fenders, and white sidewall tires. The LCF's short 93-inch BBC dimension gave it increased compactness and maneuverability. Its length from BBC was 12 inches less than conventional models. *Arnold Paradis*

The 1965 C60 chassis cab with a Doyle 8-foot lime spreader body fell right into the real strength of Chevrolet's medium-duty line. Light-duty models and medium-duty models in the 15,000 to 21,000 pound GVW ratings were Chevrolet's traditional strong suits. For years Chevrolet mass-produced these dependable, economical, high-value trucks for all businesses from coast to coast. The tough, standard 170-horsepower 292 six-cylinder engine powered this well-worn truck. It had Chevrolet's own four-speed transmission, a two-speed rear axle, hydraulic brakes and no power steering. It was available on five wheelbase length chassis: 133, 145, 157, 175, and 197 inches. There was a length to fit 98 percent of customer demand. Two other optional engines delivered greater power and performance: the 185-horsepower 327 and the 220-horsepower 348 V-8s. Other transmissions included two five-speeds and the six-speed automatic. *Jim Fromm*

This E8203 chassis cab with fifth wheel, 133-inch wheelbase was Chevrolet's biggest single-axle 1965 LCF model. The only engine offered was the 195-horsepower, 447-foot-pounds-torque two-cycle Detroit Diesel 6V-53N diesel engine. It was rated for a maximum GCW rating of 51,000 pounds when used as a tractor. Its transmission was the standard five-speed close ratio. It also had a 23,000-pound, two-speed rear axle, and standard full-air brakes. The steel cast wheels were standard equipment; Budd ten-stud disc wheels were an option. Other transmissions included an eight-speed manual and a six-speed Powermatic automatic. The rig shown was conducting a test of triples in October 1967. This photo was taken on the summit of Sexton Mountain north of Grant's Pass. *Arnold Paradis*

Chevrolet built its heavy-duty 80 models in both gasoline and diesel series. This is a 1965 C80 Conventional. The truck-built 252-horsepower 409 V-8 engine powered this truck. It was equipped with a five-speed transmission with a short fourth and a two-speed rear axle. When this photo was taken, the truck was being used to move safety deposit boxes into the remodeled U.S. National Bank in Medford, Oregon. Note the Kentucky moving van trailer and the ten-stud Budd disc wheels on the tractor. This truck had a maximum GCW rating of 51,000 pounds when used as a tractor. *Arnold Paradis*

Chevrolet's A60-A80-E80 93-inch BBC LCF diesel-powered trucks were in their last model year. Maximum GVW ratings ranged from 24,000 to 27,000 pounds and maximum GCW ratings when used as a tractor ranged from 42,000 to 51,000 pounds. Model numbers designated the respective truck's engine type. A60s were the Torq-Flow D-478, A80s the Torq-Flow DH-478, and E80 the Chevrolet-GM-Detroit 6V-53N. The last is the famous Detroit 318-ci engine pulling 447 foot-pounds gross torque. This is a 1965 Chevrolet E80 tractor with trailer. This photo is from an unknown country in South America. It was standard with cast spoke wheels and air brakes. *Dick Copello*

Chevrolet offered the 93-inch BBC LCF diesel truck in five series. There was the single-axle medium-duty A60/A60-H and the single-axle heavy-duty A80 and E80. The only difference between the A80 and the E80 was that the A80 was powered by the Chevrolet-GM four-cycle Torq-flow DH-478 diesel engine, while the Chevrolet-GM Detroit Diesel two-cycle 6V-53N powered the E80. The other two Series were tandem-axle models V80 and W80, again powered by the two diesel engines listed above. These are 1965 Chevrolet heavy-duty Series E80 LCF tractors. They were powered by the two-cycle Chevrolet-GM Detroit Diesel 6V-53N diesel engine, which produced 447 foot-pounds torque. They carried a maximum GCW rating of 51,000 pounds when used as a tractor trailer. They are shown moving the old Medford, Oregon, City Hall to its new quarters. *Arnold Paradis*

1966

Chevrolet's Workpower truck line for 1966 consisted of 366 models, a total of 260 models on 21 wheelbases with regular line models in the 10 through 80 Series. All 260 carried over from 1965.

The company left styling of the conventional Series 10 through 80 trucks generally unchanged. Exterior colors, seat upholstery trim, model plates, and standard equipment items such as seat belts constituted the new features.

The engine lineup for Chevrolet's trucks for 1966 consisted of 15. There were nine gasoline and six diesels. The six diesel engines from 1965 carried over unchanged for Series 50, 60, and 80 trucks. The most significant change consisted of replacing the 348 and 409 gas engines with two new 366 V-8 engines. Chevrolet engineers replaced the 153 four-cylinder engine, which had been standard on the 1/2-ton Step-Vans, with the 194 six-cylinder. Also, the 327 220-horsepower V-8 engine, introduced in midyear 1965 for Series C20 and 30 models, became available for Series C10 in midyear 1966.

The 366 was based on Chevrolet's new Mark IV design. This engine replaced the 349-409 Mark I, or "W" engines. The 348-409s were excellent truck engines, but left a bit to be desired on the race track. Since high-performance cars were so popular during these years, Chevrolet redesigned the entire big block family. It was quite similar to the famous 396 car engine, except that it had smaller valves, a taller block to accommodate a four-ring piston, and a smaller bore.

Two completely new 366-ci engines joined the gas engine lineup. The basic unit was built for medium-duty service, and a heavy-duty version with increased power and maximum durability was built for heavy service. The medium-duty engine was optional for Series 60 models; the heavy-duty engine was also optional for Series 60 models and was base equipment for Series 80. The medium-duty engine did not have certain premium quality components that were required for durability in heavy-duty operations.

Both engines had the same performance figures: Maximum gross horsepower was 220 at 4,400 rpm and maximum gross torque was 345 foot-pounds at 2,400 rpm.

A new, smoother operating and more powerful 250 six-cylinder engine replaced the 230-ci six. Its maximum output was increased by 10 horsepower and 15 foot-pounds' torque. The larger displacement was reached by increasing stroke to 3.53 from 3.25 inches.

Chevrolet truck's management vaulted the division into the serious heavy-duty truck business for 1966. Of the total of 366 models offered by Chevrolet that year, 101 consisted of the new, high-tonnage Series 70,000 and 80,000 models. Coming out with this impressive lineup of heavy-duty trucks showed the company's major commitment to the heavy-duty truck market.

The entirely new 70,000 and 80,000 models were the short conventional cab type. This cab was aerodynamically configured with a tapered front end and shallow windshield rake.

This was another one of those, "end of the series years," which always meant the new trucks were fundamentally unchanged because resources were earmarked for the following year's new models. The 1966 C10 Fleetside 1/2-ton pickup was, as usual, Chevrolet's best-selling model. It was a 2WD model but a 4WD was also offered in both 1/2- and 3/4-ton Series. 2WD pickups featured coil springs at all four wheels, plus independent front suspension, which gave exceptional riding ease and durability. The C10 carried a maximum GVW rating of 5,000 pounds. Its standard engine was the 250 six; optional engines included the 292 six plus the 283 and 327 V-8s. The standard transmission was the three-speed on the column and options included the three-speed overdrive, three-speed wide-ratio, four-speed, and the two-speed Powerglide automatic. For the first time Chevrolet offered the three-speed Turbo Hydra-Matic, but only for 3/4- and 1-ton models.

Chevrolet's other pickup type was the practical Step-Side series, available in either 2WD or 4WD configurations. This is a 1966 C10 1/2-ton Step-Side. Chevrolet also offered Step-Side pickups in 3/4- and 1-ton series C/K 20, 30. The 1/2-ton Step-Sides were available with 6 1/2- or 8-foot bodies. The 3/4-ton models had only the 8-foot body, and the 1-ton models the 9-foot body. The C/K30 1-ton model chassis had leaf-spring rear suspension and a maximum GVW rating of 7,800 pounds. Half- and 3/4-ton C10-20 trucks featured coil springs at all four wheels. Only the front axles were independent, however. The Step-Side's cargo box floors were constructed of select wood planking with recessed steel skid strips. The engine and transmission choices available for this truck were the same as for the Fleetside 1/2-ton pickup. The C10 Step-Side's maximum GVW rating was 5,000 pounds.

Chevrolet offered two new gasoline engines for Series 70,000 and 80,000 trucks. First was the GMC truck 401-ci V-6 with a two-barrel carburetor. As an option for 80,000 models only was the GMC Truck 478 V-6 engine with a two-barrel carburetor.

The 194 six-cylinder engine rated at 120 gross horsepower replaced the 153 four-cylinder engine on the Chevy Van.

The El Camino came in for a new front appearance in 1966 with a new grille, restyled hood, new front bumper, and restyled fenders. The grille carried a central mounted emblem carrying the name "El Camino." The model retained its dual headlights, and combination parking and directional signal lights remained located in the front bumper. Custom models featured a chrome hood ornament. All basic body panels below the beltline were restyled except for the tailgate's outer panel.

The 1966 calendar year was a bit of a disappointment for the industry, with the year's total production falling 20,000 trucks short of the previous year. However, Chevrolet again was the leading producer, accounting for 621,417, or 35.2 percent, of the total.

The trend in 1966 was away from six cylinders and toward the larger, higher-powered V-8 engines. Six-cylinder-engine–powered trucks dropped to 53.6 percent of the total compared to 57.4 percent in 1965. Chevrolet's installation of six-cylinder engines dropped 7 percent. Chevrolet installed almost 50,000 more V-8s in 1966 than 1965. Even with the additional diesel truck models Chevrolet introduced in 1966, total diesel sales dropped by 100 units to 2,300.

The best news for Chevrolet in 1966 was the company's posting an industry record 588,320 truck sales in the United States, 2.5 percent above 1965 totals.

That year the GMC truck plant in Pontiac, Michigan, assembled 39,624 Chevrolet trucks. The GM Assembly Division plant in Fremont, California, contributed another 95,374.

Chevrolet offered two cab trim levels for 1966: Standard cab and Custom cab. This is the Standard cab interior of a 1966 C10 Fleetside pickup. The Standard cab featured a full-width bench seat; no bucket seat option was offered. The bench seat was the foam-type for greater driving comfort, and it was upholstered in easy-to-clean black vinyl. The Custom cab featured a driver armrest, right and left door locks, chrome-trimmed control knobs, a cigarette lighter, passenger's sunshade, horn ring, white trim on doors, and a trim plate for the glovebox door. It had an optional radio. Safety items added as standard equipment in 1966 included seat belts, a windshield washer, and two-speed electric wipers. *Chris Lublin*

This high-line 1966 Chevrolet K20 3/4-ton 4WD Custom cab Fleetside pickup was fully restored when spotted in 1998. It has been mildly customized as seen by its non-original wheels and tires. This truck carried a maximum GVW rating of 7,600 pounds. The optional 175-horsepower 283 V-8 engine mated to the rugged four-speed transmission power it. Its standard engine was the economical 150-horsepower 250 six, the 170-horsepower 292 six was an option. Unlike their coil spring–equipped 2WD brothers, 4WD Chevrolet pickups featured a chassis with leaf springs on all four wheels and solid axles front and back. Extra capacity 8-leaf rear springs (standard was 6-leaves) was available on K20 trucks. A power-takeoff could be attached to the opening provided at the rear of the transfer case. The four-speed main transmission also had a power-takeoff opening on its left side. Manual front locks were available for all 4WD models. *Merlin H. Mausolf*

Chevrolet's popular new Chevy Van was in its third model year, basically unchanged. It was still only offered in the 1/2-ton G10 Series. This van was intended for delivery service and would carry over a ton of cargo in a 211-cubic-foot load compartment. For the first time a Chevrolet Sportvan people mover version was offered. It was the 10-window van version that was new in 1965, with two bench seats installed behind the front buckets, and trimmed out for passenger service. A broad range of special equipment racks, shelves, and bins was offered for the Chevy Van. Owners were able to individualize the load space to suit individual job requirements. The standard engine was upgraded to the 120-horsepower 194 six from the previous year's four-cylinder, the high-torque 140-horsepower 250 six was the extra-cost option. The three-speed manual transmission with steering column shift lever was standard equipment; the two-speed Powerglide automatic was an option *AAMA*

Chevrolet's truck line for 1966 totaled 260 regular line models. The largest concentration of models was in the medium-duty category (Series 50, 60, 60S), which totaled 127 trucks. The next largest was the heavy-duty category, with a total of 72 trucks (Series 60H and 80). And 61 units made up the light-duty category (Series 10, 20, 30, 30S). The best-selling medium-duty truck was the conventional cab C50. The front bumper of this truck should be painted to be correct. It was chrome plated during its restoration. Series 50's standard engine was the 150-horsepower 250 six. Options included the 170-horsepower 292 six and the 175-horsepower 283-ci V-8. This truck is powered by the 292 six. Its standard transmission was the Chevrolet-built four-speed; the New Process four-speed was the only option. A two-speed rear axle was an option. *Ed Martineau*

Chevrolet offered a full line of forward-control chassis, Step-Van, and Step-Van King models for 1966. The line consisted of P10-20-30 and 50 Series. The P50 was rated for a maximum GVW rating of 20,000 pounds and accommodated bodies up to 16 1/2 feet on a 175-inch wheelbase. This is a 1966 Chevrolet Model P1335 Step-Van 7 in the P10 Series. It rode on easy riding independent front suspension, coil springs front and rear. The rear coil springs were the two-stage type. Step-Van 7 had a 7-foot body length, with either 65- or 69-inch heights. The standard engine was the 120-horsepower 194 six; the 140-horsepower 230 six was an option. Step-Van 7's maximum GVW rating was 5,400 pounds. *AAMA*

The hard worker of Chevrolet's 1966 medium-duty line was the conventional cab C60 Series. A 60 Series was also included in the L or LCF Series and the T or Tilt-Cab Series. As with the three 50 Series trucks, all specifications are the same for all three Series 60 models—C, L, and T. Their maximum GVW rating was a big 24,000 pounds, and 42,000 pounds when used as a tractor. Their standard engine was the 292 six; optional was the powerful 220-horsepower 366 V-8. This was the first year for this famous Chevrolet truck engine. This engine was not used in any Chevrolet auto. It continued to power Chevrolet medium-duty trucks through the 1998 model year. Standard transmission was the Chevrolet-built four-speed; various manufacturers' four- and five-speed transmission were options. A six-speed automatic was offered only for the C60 trucks. Pictured is a 1966 Chevrolet C60 chassis cab with lineman's body. *AAMA*

Chevrolet's dependable Series C80 trucks were immensely popular with fire departments. This is a 1966 Chevrolet C80 chassis cab with firefighting body. Engine No. 322 was a dependable C80 owned by the Wendell (Idaho) Rural Fire Department. Its pumper body was by Alf and it contained a 750-gallon water tank and a 500-gpm pump. The only engine offered for Series 80 C, L, and T trucks was the new 220-horsepower 366 V-8. A five-speed transmission was standard; a close-ratio five-speed was an option. The six-speed automatic was offered only on the C80 and T80 Series. Note this truck's ten-stud disc wheels. *Bill Hattersley*

Chevrolet built three series of Tilt-Cabs in 1966—T50, T60, and T80. This is a 1966 Chevrolet heavy-duty T80 tilt-cab chassis cab with firefighting body. The Prospect Heights (Illinois) Fire Department owned it. Engine 9R's body was built by Howe. It contained a 1,000-gallon water tank and a 1,000-gpm pump. It's interesting to note that before Prospect Heights purchased it from them, this truck had been owned by the Long Grove (Illinois) Fire Department. Tilt-cabs featured a 72-inch BBC dimension that made them highly maneuverable and able to snake through heavy traffic. Only one engine was released for this Series: the new 220-horsepower 366 V-8. The standard engine was a five-speed with normal ratios; optional was a Spicer five-speed with close ratios and the six-speed automatic. Both disc wheels and steel cast spokes were offered. A diesel version of the Series T80 trucks was also offered for 1966. *Garry E. Kadzielawski*

The only big change in Chevrolet trucks for 1966 was the release of the heavy-duty short 92-inch BBC conventional cab LCF chassis cabs. These trucks replaced the former E80/W80 LCF chassis cabs. They were offered in four Series: HM70000, HM80000, JM70000, and JM80000. The first two were single-axle models, the last two had tandem axles. The new JM80000 were the biggest trucks ever built by Chevrolet. (Actually, they were engineered and built by GMC and rebadged for Chevrolet.) The maximum GVW rating of the single-axle models was 32,000 pounds and the maximum GVW rating for the tandem-axle models was 48,000 pounds. These numbers were the same for the diesel powered series. The Montpelier (Idaho) Fire Department owned this 1966 Chevrolet model HM70000 chassis cab with firefighting body. Its pumper body was built by Alf and it contained a 1,000-gallon water tank and a 500-gpm pump. The only engine released for this model was the big 237-horsepower GMC 401 V-6. It put out an awesome 372 foot-pounds of torque at 1,600 rpm. No optional engine was available. Its standard transmission was a New Process five-speed; three other five-speeds were options. *M. Boatwright*

This beautifully restored and maintained Chevrolet 1966 C10 1/2-ton Fleetside pickup appears to be stock and it is. It's unusual in that a woman owns it. Jan Phelan shows it at car and truck shows and attends other old truck events. Its 220-horsepower 327 V-8 engine is stock, its five-speed transmission isn't. Even though it has the upscale Custom Cab, it doesn't have power brakes, power steering, or air conditioning (this was the first year for factory air conditioning), and it has the original, 4.11 rear axle ratio. Chevrolet's coil-spring independent front suspension and two-stage coil-spring rear suspension provided the industry's smoothest ride, which was one big reason women drivers chose Chevrolet. *Jan Phelan*

Chevrolet's 1966 medium-duty conventional cab line included the C50, C60, M80 tandem, and C80 Series trucks with maximum GVW rating up to 32,000 pounds. This is a 1966 Chevrolet C60 chassis cab with wrecker body. Chevrolet introduced the new high-torque 366 V-8 gasoline engine in 1966. It had 220 horsepower and 345 foot-pounds torque to move big loads in less time. The two big gasoline six-cylinder engines from GMC were in the line, but Chevrolet engineers did not make them available in the conventional cab line. The series was backed by the standard Spicer five-speed, close-ratio five-speed, or the Allison fully automatic transmission. A two-speed rear axle with up to 23,000-pound capacity was available. *Steve Bowman*

Chevrolet's conventional cab C-Series truck line for 1966 included the M80 tandem model. There were two tandem models available in 1966: trailing-axle tandems and dual-drive tandems with maximum GVW ratings of 30,000 pounds and 45,000 pounds, respectively. This is a 1966 Chevrolet M80 dual-drive tandem-axle chassis cab with dump body. The standard and only engine available for this truck was the 220-horsepower 366 V-8. This truck was equipped with a Spicer five-speed main transmission and a four-speed auxiliary transmission. The Allison six-speed automatic transmission was an extra-cost option. Its dual-drive rear-axle equipment was made up of a Hendrickson suspension and 34,000-pound Eaton axles with a 7.17 ratio. *Verne L. Byers*

Chevrolet built two heavy-duty 72-inch tilt-cab series in 1966: Series 70000 and 80000 gasoline models and 70000 diesel models. Pictured is a 1966 Series TM70000 gasoline tilt-cab tractor. Both single and tandem rear axles were offered. Single-rear-axle models used the prefix "TM" and tandem axle models "WM." Chevrolet offered nine TM70000 models in six sizes. Maximum GVW ratings topped off at 32,000 pounds, and 60,000 pounds GCW when used as a tractor. Only one engine was offered—the GMC 237-horsepower 401 V-6, producing 372 foot-pounds torque. Transmission options included the standard NP 541GL five-speed and optional NP 541D five-speed CR (close ratio), Spicer 5652 five-speed, and Spicer 5752C five-speed CR. Full air brakes were standard equipment on some models. *AAMA*

Chevrolet's medium- to heavy-duty truck series consisted of the C50-C60-C80; L50-L60-L80, and T50-T60-T80. C series were conventional cab models; L series were LCFs; and T series were tilt cabs. Plus M80 Series were conventional cab tandems with either a trailing-axle or dual-drive bogies. The 50 series trucks' maximum GVW ratings ranged from 10,000 to 20,000 pounds; 60 series from 15,000 to 24,000 pounds; and 80 series from 18,500 to 32,000 pounds. All major features and specifications were basically the same for C, L, and T series. Engine options included 250 six, 292 six, 283 V-8, and 366 V-8. These models were the bread and butter of Chevrolet's medium- and heavy-duty trucks. They offered excellent values, dependability, and long life. This is a 1966 L-series chassis cab with wrecker body. *Dick Copello*

Chevrolet's 1966 diesel tilt-cab Series 70000 was made up of two models: TG and TJ 70000. They differed only in that the 478 Torqu-flow V-6 diesel powered the TGs and the TJs were powered by the 637 Torq-Flow D637 and DH637 V-8 diesels. All three engines were the four-cycle-type. Pictured is a 1966 tilt cab TJ 70000 tractor with trailer. The DH637 V-8 produced 220 gross horsepower and 458 foot-pounds gross torque. The TJ was rated for a maximum GVW of 32,000 pounds and maximum GCW rating, when used as a tractor, of 65,000 pounds. It was equipped with the Clark five-speed close ratio transmission and standard air brakes. *Dick Copello*

New trucks in 1966 were the 92 3/4-inch, BBC Conventional Cab Series 70000 diesel models and 70000 and 80000 gasoline models. This is a 1966 Chevrolet Series JV70000 tandem-axle chassis cab with tank body. This was, of course, a truck designed and built by GMC but wearing a Chevrolet nameplate. The GM 6V-53N diesel engine powered the JV70000 models. They had standard full-air brakes. GVWs up to 45,000 pounds and a GCW rating of 60,000 pounds were permissible. The JV700000 had an Eaton-Hendrickson bogie and a Clark 385V five-speed transmission. *Dick Copello*

Chevrolet's marketing group used the following saying to describe the 1966 El Camino, "Likes to Work, Loves to Play." A rather catchy phrase, and one that nails the essence of the dual-purpose El Camino. The truck shown had the new-for-1966 396 V-8 engine, which was offered in two configurations: 325-horsepower Turbo-Jet and 360-horsepower Turbo-Jet with a Muncie four-speed transmission. The El Camino was the perfect vehicle for those who couldn't decide between a truck and a musclecar. Mike Smith of Los Angeles owns this one. *Bob Bray*

1967

Chevrolet's light-duty workhorse trucks turned into show horses in 1967. Lower and more stylish, the new pickups were almost as good looking as passenger cars. Some truck aficionados believed the new pickups presented the finest styling of any light-duty trucks ever. Under the glamour of their exteriors, Chevrolet trucks continued the decades-long tradition of toughness, economy, and longevity.

An all-new cab for conventional medium-duty trucks (40, 50, and 60 Series) was only 96 inches BBC (bumper to back of cab). This new dimension plus a shorter wheelbase (with no change in cab-axle dimension) gave excellent maneuverability. Drivers had a better view of the road over the truck's short sloping hood. This design replaced both the former conventional cab and the LCF designs.

In the heavy-duty range, Chevrolet offered two distinct types of trucks. First was the 72-inch tilt cab 70 and 80 Series with either gasoline or diesel power. GVW ratings for single-axle models ranged from 18,500 to 32,000 pounds. GVW ratings for tandem-axle models ranged from 36,000 to 48,000 pounds and GCW ratings ranged up to 65,000 pounds. Gasoline engines included the 401 and 478 V-6s. Diesel engine options included the two-cycle Detroit Diesel-built 6V-53N and the D637 and DH637 Toro-Flow V-8, four-cycle diesels built by GM.

The other heavy-duty models were the 92-inch BBC Series 70 and 80 conventional cab trucks. Note that this conventional cab series was not the same as the Series 40, 50, and 60 medium-duty conventional cab models. Instead, they were the trucks first introduced in 1966 and built for Chevrolet by GMC in Pontiac, Michigan. They were originally numbered the 70,000 and 80,000 Series. Only minor changes in appearance were made for 1967.

Other advances in the 4WD series, K10 1/2-ton pickups and K20 3/4-ton pickups, included power steering and the availability of the 327-ci, 220 horsepower V-8 engine as an option. Another important engineering change was the use of tapered leaf springs in the suspension, requiring fewer leaves and improving ride quality.

The 4WD models featured a convenient single-lever shift control that permitted easy shifting between 2WD and 4WD. Shift positions included 4WD low gear, neutral, 4WD high gear, and 2WD high gear.

Chevrolet's 1967 pickups were completely restyled with lean, angular lines that gave the trucks a long, low appearance. Nearly every styling or engineering change that was made aimed to make the trucks more attractive to the person who bought a truck for recreational and personal transportation.

The new Custom Sport Truck (CST) option extended to 4WD trucks for those primarily interested in recreational use. Chevrolet engineers put most of their efforts toward developing work trucks, but the CST interior proved that Chevrolet was serious about moving toward luxury pickups.

Two standard engines for light-duty trucks were the 250 six and the 283 V-8; optional were the 292 six and the 327 V-8.

Suburbans (which lost the Carryall part of their names) and panels came in for the most important changes since 1935. They were available on the long pickup's 127-inch frame in 1/2- and 3/4-ton capacities, with or without 4WD. The longer wheelbase allowed for a longer body and seating for nine, with luggage

All new for 1967 was the Chevy Van 108, with a 108-inch wheelbase and a whopping 256 cubic feet of load space. Chevrolet engineers made it longer and tougher for the big jobs. The original Chevy Van 90 with 209 cubic feet of cargo area was continued. Both models offered the new grille and bumper. The longer van was rated for either 1/2- or 3/4-ton capacities; the 90 Series was only rated as a 1/2-ton. Note the additional body length that can be seen between the front passenger door and the side doors on this 1967 Sportvan 108. The Sportvan utilized GM's Unitized body-frame construction. It was capable of hauling up to 2,000 pounds of payload. Also new for 1967 was the choice of a six-cylinder or V-8 engine power. The standard six was the economical 140-horsepower 230; optional was the 155-horsepower 250. The standard V-8 was the spirited 175-horsepower 283. *AAMA*

Chevrolet's Step-Van 7 (7-foot body) was highly maneuverable, yet had adequate interior space for four persons when converted into a travel coach. It was fully self-contained with cooking, sleeping, and sanitary facilities for comfortable living away from home, yet did not require as big an investment as the larger camper alternatives. Because of its shorter dimensions, it was easier to maneuver in traffic or campgrounds and required less parking area. The 140-horsepower 230 six was standard and the 155-horsepower 250 six was an option. Transmission choices included three- or four-speed manuals and two-speed Powerglide or three-speed Turbo Hydra-Matic. *AAMA*

For the larger family or for the family who wanted more travel space, the 1967 Chevrolet P-20 Step-Van King with 12-foot body could be converted to accommodate six persons in comfort. It offered full sleeping, cooking, and sanitary facilities. This van came with a standard 155-horsepower 250 six or with an optional 170-horsepower 292 six. Chevrolet promoted the Step-Van King as a vehicle with which the customer could make his own camper conversion by adding carpet, cabinets, tables, beds, etc. Transmission choices included three- or four-speed manuals and two- or three-speed automatics. *AAMA*

Chevrolet continued to offer its very successful 72-inch Tilt-Cab Series 70 and 80 in 1967. Gasoline- and diesel-powered series were offered. The gasoline-powered series was available with either single or tandem rear axles, while the diesel series was offered only with a single rear axle. Gasoline engines included the two rugged V-6s. The standard engine for Series 70 and 80 trucks was the 401 V-6 with a two-barrel carburetor and 237 horsepower. The optional engine for Series 80 was the powerful 478 V-6 with gross horsepower of 254. Diesel engines for the Series 70 trucks included the two-cycle 318 V-6 with 447 foot-pounds gross torque and the four-cycle Toro-Flow inflow 637 six in two power outputs—450 and 458 foot-pounds torque. This is a 1967 Chevrolet Series 70 gasoline-powered tilt chassis cab with fire-fighting body. The Lodi (California) Fire Department owned this city service ladder fire truck. *Chuck Madderom*

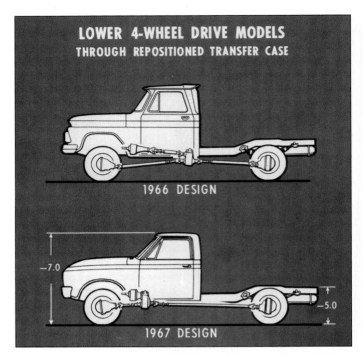

Chevrolet engineers reduced 4WD models' overall height by 7 inches and chassis height by 5 inches compared to the 1966 models. They accomplished this by repositioning the transfer case forward to just behind the transmission, eliminating one propeller shaft assembly and reducing sheet-metal clearance above the front wheels. In addition to the engines available for 4WD models in 1966, the 220-horsepower 327 V-8 was made an option. For the first time, power steering was an option. Tapered leaf springs with two or three leaves, depending on capacity ratings, were offered for all 4WD trucks. *AAMA*

Chevrolet's new conventional cab medium-duty models for 1967 gave the buyer a 9-inch shorter BBC and an 8-inch shorter wheelbase than 1966 trucks. The new truck's cab was also 6.2 inches lower in overall height. The shorter wheelbase gave better weight distribution by moving more weight toward the front axle. However, cab to axle (CA) dimensions remained the same to accommodate the same size bodies or fifth wheel settings as before. Unlike in 1966, the new conventional cab series included only Series 40-50-60. The Zell (Missouri) Volunteer Fire Department owned this C50 chassis cab tanker. It carried a maximum GVW rating of 22,000 pounds. Its standard engine was the 170-horsepower 292 six; the 185-horsepower 327 V-8 and 220-horsepower 366 V-8 were options. Its standard transmission was the Chevrolet four-speed. *Dennis J. Maag*

space behind the third seat. A second passenger door was added on the right side for easier access to the second and third seats. For this reason, these models are commonly called the "three door" Suburbans.

Chevy Vans and Sportvans (passenger vans) came in for major revisions in 1967, too. In addition to the original 90-inch wheelbase, a 108-inch wheelbase for bigger loads was added. Model availability was expanded to include both 1/2 - and 3/4-ton Series 10 and 20.

Engine options included the 230 six for both series as standard. The 250 six was optional for both, and for the first time a V-8 engine was an option. The High Torque, lively and spirited 175-horsepower 283 V-8 was an option for all Chevy Vans and Sportvans. A three-speed manual transmission was standard and the Powerglide automatic was the only option. Tapered leaf springs were adopted on the Chevy Van and Sportvan.

Truck industry production in 1967 declined for the second year in a row. All weight classifications posted lower results for the first time in seven years. The 1967 total of 1,539,500 units was down 11.1 percent from 1966's 1,731,200 and even further below 1965's record of 1,751,800. The biggest decline was in medium-duty models, 10,001 to 19,500 pound (classes 3, 4, and 5). They were off 29 percent—109,900 versus 154,300.

Light-duty trucks, 10,000 pounds and under (classes 1 and 2), dropped 10 percent—to 1,189,600 from 1,317,200. Light-duty trucks did, however, manage to exceed one million, a milestone first reached in 1963.

Chevrolet's production of V-8 trucks in 1967 climbed to 49 percent of its total, compared with 40 percent in 1966.

Chevrolet again led the industry in truck production in 1967, but its total of 549,663 units was 12 percent below its 1966 record of 621,417.

Total industry diesel truck output fell off 13 percent in 1967 along with the general downtrend. Chevrolet's diesel production was level with 1965's total of 2,300.

Chevrolet competed strongly in classes 1, 2, 4, and 5 and did quite well in class 6, but showed poorly in classes 7 and 8. Class 3's industry total was only 4,645 trucks, shared between Divco and IH. GMC competed well in the higher weight classes and poorer in the lowest classes.

GM produced its 100 millionth vehicle in the United States on April 21, 1967. The milestone car was a regular size Chevrolet assembled in Janesville, Wisconsin.

Chevrolet's heavy-duty 1967 series were the Series 70 and 80 Conventional cab models. These heavy-duty models, built by GMC, carried over unchanged. Except for their cabs and frame differences due to set back front axles, they were essentially the same trucks as the Series 70 and 80 Tilt-Cabs. The gasoline-powered Conventional Series 70 and 80 trucks' cab featured a three-man bench seat, while the diesel models had only a single driver seat. A matching passenger seat was an option. These trucks also featured a big truck-type instrument panel. As expected in a heavy truck, it featured a complete and orderly easy-to-read layout of gauges and controls for clarity. A 1967 Chevrolet Conventional Series 70 chassis cab with a firefighting body is shown here. This Conventional Series 70 chassis cab with firefighting body had a 1,000-gallon water tank and a 750-gpm pump. It was owned by the Kalida (Ohio) Volunteer Fire Department. Note its chrome grille and headlight bezels. *Steve Hagy*

Chevrolet offered its 1967 Conventional Series 70 and 80 trucks with gasoline or diesel power. Gas engines were the rugged, truck-built 401 and 478 V-6s. Diesel engines included the two-cycle 6V-53N Detroit Diesel producing gross horsepower of 195 and gross torque of 447 foot-pounds and the D637 and DH637 GM Toro-Flow diesels. They produced 195 and 220 gross horsepower and gross torque of 450 and 458 foot-pounds, respectively. These trucks had the very short BBC dimension of only 92 3/4-inches. Single- and tandem-axle models were offered. Maximum GVW ratings of 32,000 pounds with single axles and up to 48,000 pounds with tandem axles were offered. GCW ratings when used as a tractor trailer maxed out at 65,000 pounds. This is a 1967 Chevrolet Conventional Cab Series HM70 chassis cab with firefighting body. The Perryville (Missouri) Fire Department owned truck No. 4. Its body by Towers had a 750-gallon tank and 750-gpm pump. *Dennis J. Maag*

Many consider the strikingly new, lower, sleeker, trimmer 1967 pickups to be the best-looking trucks Chevrolet ever built. The restyled Fleetside pickup cargo box was restyled to complement the cab's new style. Tailgates had a central mechanical latch for a one-hand operation. Cabs were lower and narrower, but interior dimensions remained virtually unchanged. Seat height was lowered for easier entry and for a more comfortable driving position. The graceful inner slanting upper cab section helped protect window glass from mud splash and gravel blasting. Slimmer pillars and larger glass area increased driver visibility. *AAMA*

A common task for 1967 Chevrolet pickups was carrying a slide-on pickup camper. This was one of America's favorite ways to vacation. "See the U.S.A. in your Chevrolet!" Dinah Shore would sing every week on television. This is a 1967 3/4-ton C20 pickup truck with a 10-foot camper body. The chassis design retained coils, springs, and independent front suspension for excellent ride and handling. A chrome "Custom Camper" emblem was supplied free with this model. In addition to suspension and performance items, a long list of comfort, convenience, and appearance options was available to tailor the truck to the owner's individual taste and budget. *AAMA*

Chevrolet's famous and popular CST option was another new innovation. The CST option was offered on 1967 Chevrolet's light-duty cab models. CST features included a fully carpeted interior including the fuel tank, bucket seats, and luxury trim. Other CST equipment included a chrome front bumper; chrome metal frames for clutch, brake, and accelerator pedals; chrome-trimmed instrument knobs and horn button; right-hand padded sunshade; and underbody coating. In the top photo, the padded fold-down combination armrest and seat back is in its up position for third passenger use. In the bottom photo, it's shown in use as an armrest. The swing-up padded middle seat also served as a cover for a convenient concealed storage compartment. *AAMA*

Chevrolet's other pickup style was the Stepside. This is a 1967 C10 Stepside short box pickup. Chevrolet also offered 8-foot Stepside 1/2-ton and 3/4-ton pickups, and a big 9-foot 1-ton Stepside with a maximum GVW rating of 7,800 pounds. The Stepside body differed from the Fleetside in that it was completely contained between the rear fenders to provide an entirely unobstructed load area. Its floor was built of durable select wood with recessed steel skid strips. A pair of wedge-type anti-rattle latches kept the tailgate securely closed. Rubber-covered support chains held the tailgate in the open position to handle long loads. Stepsides were offered with either 2WD or 4WD.

Chevrolet sold many light-duty chassis cabs on which the buyer would mount a special body built by an outside body company. Most of the chassis cab sales came from 3/4- and 1-ton models. The 1967 Chevrolet 1/2-ton chassis cab with utility body pictured here is a rare exception. In almost all cases these trucks were for commercial use and therefore were ordered as base models. The maximum GVW rating of the C10 was 5,000 pounds. Engine availability for C10 Series trucks included the 155-horsepower 250 six and the 170-horsepower 292 six. The standard V-8 engine was the 175-horsepower 283 V-8, and the 220-horsepower 327 V-8 was optional. Available transmissions included the base three-speed manual, three-speed with overdrive, four-speed manual, Powerglide, and Turbo Hydra-Matic.

A light, easy-on, easy-off shell-type camper was extremely popular in 1967 because of its broad applications and low cost. It provided two persons with sleeping quarters and other living accommodations. New features of the 1967 pickup that made it attractive for this type of service included the CST package with bucket seats, console, and other luxury items. Other available passenger car-type options providing comfort and driving ease included a lively V-8 engine, automatic transmission, power steering, and power brakes. *AAMA*

Chevrolet was the only one of the Big Three light-duty truck manufacturers to offer a Panel Delivery model in 1967. This unusual truck featured sleek, functional styling, and its wheelbase length and other dimensions were the same as other Chevrolet light-duty trucks. It was built as either a 1/2- or 3/4-ton model on a single 127-inch wheelbase with a 9-foot panel body. The standard individual driver seat was adjustable fore and aft, and the adjustable backrest could be locked in position. The seat back was covered in metal to protect against load damage. A forward-tilting passenger seat was an option. *AAMA*

This 1967 Chevrolet C-20 Fleetside Custom workhorse pickup is owned by Scott Diaz of Los Angeles, who continues to use it as an everyday driver. The optional 220-horsepower 327 V-8 engine, along with the Turbo 400 automatic transmission, powers the truck. It has the optional air conditioning and the standard, small rear window. In 1968, the government made large back windows mandatory equipment in all pickups. The maximum GVW rating for the C-20 pickups ranged from 5,500 to 7,500 pounds. The 283 V-8 was standard equipment for a C-20 with the 7,500 pound GVW rating. *Bob Bray*

Workhorse trucks are what Chevrolet is all about, except for the show horse El Camino. Of course it could work, and did. But most buyers bought it for its eye appeal, comfort, and performance. Work with an El Camino was fun. As you can see from this view of a 1967 El Camino, its cargo box was designed and built for loads. Rear air-booster type shock absorbers were standard equipment. They could be adjusted by varying air pressure to meet load and road conditions. Engine options ranged from mild to wild. Standard was a 140-horsepower Turbo-Thrift 230 six; the 155-horsepower 250 six was an option. V-8 engines included the 195-horsepower 283, 275-horsepower 327, 325-horsepower 327, and 325- and 350-horsepower 396s. Transmission options started with the three-speed and optional HD three-speed, four-speed, Powerglide, and Turbo-Hydra-Matic.

Chevrolet's heavy-duty tilt-cab truck lineup remained the same in 1967 as in 1966, except for a slight change in model numbers. Gasoline Series were 70 and 80 and diesel Series was 70 only. This is a 1967 Chevrolet diesel 70 Series single-axle tractor. Its power came from a 6V-53N Detroit Diesel engine. This rugged two-stroke with a Roots-type blower produced 195 gross horsepower and 447 foot-pounds gross torque at 1,400 rpm. The maximum GVW rating with this engine was 32,000 pounds with a GCW rating of 60,000 pounds. Its transmission was a five-speed with close ratios. *AAMA*

In 1967, Chevrolet's 93-inch BBC single- and tandem-axle model short-conventional cab models continued in two series: gas and diesel powered. Two standard gas engines included the 237 gross-horsepower 401 and the 254 gross-horsepower 478 V-6s. The diesel engine lineup consisted of the Detroit Diesel 6V-53N and the D637 and DH637 GM Toro-Flow Diesels. Tandem model GVWs ranged from 45,000 to 48,000 pounds and GCW ratings from 45,000 to 65,000 pounds. The higher ratings in both cases were with the 254 gross-horsepower gas-powered engine. Pictured is a 1967 Chevrolet HM80 gas-powered single-axle chassis cab with dump body. It has the Coleman 4WD conversion. *Dick Copello*

1968

Styling of Chevrolet's 1968 "Job Tamer" truck line carried over without change, except for one completely new truck, a few engine changes, and several new transmission options.

Three-quarter and 1-ton Step-Vans received a completely redesigned chassis in three wheelbase lengths of 125, 133, and 157 inches to accommodate 10-, 12- and, for the first time, 14-foot bodies. Also for the first time, the Step-Van line featured an independent front suspension that resulted in a better ride and easier handling. The elongated hood made outside engine servicing convenient for the mechanic. For the first time, too, Step-Vans offered V-8 power from either the new 307, standard in light-duty truck for 1968, and the optional 327, 240-horsepower engine.

Chevrolet engineers introduced their largest and most powerful gasoline engine ever: the 427, 260-gross horsepower, 405 foot-pounds gross torque V-8. It was optional with a four-barrel carburetor in the light/heavy 60 Series. The 427 was developed from the 366 V-8 but with a larger 4.25-inch bore and modified cylinder block and heads.

A new 307 V-8 engine was standard in the light-duty series. It had the same bore as the discontinued 283, but its stroke was lengthened to 3.25. It also had new pistons, block, heads, connecting rods, and larger crankshaft journals and bearings.

Chevrolet, along with all other truck manufacturers, came under the new 1968 National Traffic Agency Standards that set the norm for truck safety. Standards included a standard transmission sequence and windshield defroster. All 1968 pickups had extra-large cab rear windows, wheel nuts, and seat belts. They also had lamp and reflective surfaces and devices, rearview mirrors, and fuel tank mountings. All trucks had to have blunted dials and knobs. Anything that would shine in the driver's eyes was not permitted.

Chevrolet's Custom Campers (CC) for 1968 consisted of factory-installed equipment to make C/K pickups and chassis cabs more suitable for camper service. In addition to a CC nameplate, the following equipment was included in the CC package: A front stabilizer bar, heavier rear springs and auxiliary springs, heavy-duty shock absorbers, and larger tires.

A new auto industry phenomenon came about forcefully in 1968 and has remained an issue to this day. This was the market share that was being taken by imported cars. The import car market was up to 10.5 percent in 1968, which was more than enough to capture the attention of executives of the Big Three. That was the bad news. The good news was that industry truck production reached almost two million (1,950,713), beating the previous all-time industry record of 1,785,109 set in 1965. For the first time in the history of the automotive industry, trucks became a major force as the automobile's star began to wane. Some called 1968 "The Year of the Truck" in recognition of its climb into a leadership role within the industry.

Sales of commercial vehicles meant more than merely sales units. The truck's role in the U.S. economy was to move goods to consumers, to factories, to distributors, and to retailers. This related to the health and growth of the nation's economy. And a healthy economy creates more and better jobs, which in turn raises families' living standards.

This was when light-duty trucks began to make a solid impact in the personal lives and leisure activities of Americans. Many thousands of Americans took advantage of the rapidly expanding Federal Interstate Highway System. Many were in automobiles, of course. But many thousand more used new pickups to carry or pull a camper. The pickup's styling had become more attractive and had received the approval of women.

Chevrolet's 1968 4WD light-duty truck line consisted of 1/2- and 3/4-ton models: Fleetside and Stepside pickups, chassis cabs, Suburbans, and Panels. For the first time, it included a 1/2- or 3/4-ton Custom Camper 4WD model. Items in the Custom Camper package included a special "Custom Camper" nameplate, heavy-duty rear springs, heavy-duty rear shocks, and a wide choice of 16, 16.5, and 17-inch tires specially selected for heavy loads. This is a 1968 Chevrolet 3/4-ton 4WD Fleetside pickup. The new standard V-8 engine for light-duty trucks in 1968 was the 200-horsepower 307. The 327 V-8 was an option. Six-cylinder engine offerings included the 250 and 292. One styling change for 1968 was the addition of front and rear fender-mounted side marker reflectors. The CST option was offered on 4WD trucks. *AAMA*

This is a top-of-the-line 3/4-ton 1968 Chevrolet Camper Special with an El Dorado slide-on camper body. 2WD Custom Camper equipment included heavy-duty springs and shock absorbers, high capacity tires, and front stabilizers. One characteristic that made a Chevrolet pickup ideal for camper service was the remarkable way it combined truck toughness with a smooth ride. The 3/4-ton pickup was rated for a maximum GVW rating of 7,500 pounds. Providing the muscle were three V-8 engines. The new 200-horsepower 307, the 240-horsepower 327, and the new for 1968 325-horsepower 396. The first two engines burned regular fuel but the 396, with a 10.25:1 compression ratio, required premium. *AAMA*

A second significant industry milestone was the fact that more than one million V-8 engines were installed in trucks in 1968. V-8s outsold sixes for the first time in 1967.

The use of the pickup for personal transportation had been gathering steam for several years. In 1968 pickups made significant inroads into auto sales.

The record 1,950,713 trucks built in the United States in 1968 meant that a two million production year was near. The previous high had been 1,785,109, built in 1965. The record set in 1968 was up 23 percent over 1967's total of 1,585,481.

The industry set a production record for light-duty trucks in 1968. The 6,000-pound-and-less category accounted for 1,136,059 trucks, up 26 percent from 1967's 899,996, and 7.4 percent above the previous high of 1,058,211 set in 1965.

The 385,803 trucks produced in the 6,001- to 10,000-pound GVW category were ahead 33.1 percent over the 289,835 shipped in 1967, and 30 percent ahead of the 296,957 in 1966, the previous record. A great deal of the increase in the 6,001-pound plus category was attributed to the increase in sales of bigger vans and pickups for recreational vehicles.

Output of the V-8 engine passed the million mark (1,082,721) for the first time. An interesting point about this record is that the demand for V-8s was strong at the lowest end of the GVW scale and at the top of the GVW scale at the same time. Truck buyers believed the higher horsepower output of the V-8 engine as compared to the six-cylinder engine allowed them to pull bigger payloads at higher average road speeds. Chevrolet's V-8 engines accounted for 60.4 percent of the company's total output in 1968 compared to 38.6 percent for sixes.

Trucks powered by diesel engines climbed to 93,819 in 1968 from 84,025 in 1967. Chevrolet's diesel engine sales, on the other hand, decreased markedly, from 2,297 in 1967 to 1,030 in 1968.

Chevrolet's truck production of 680,599 for 1968 set another record, and kept Chevrolet at its number one ranking in the industry for another year.

Chevrolet's truck sales of 626,858 for 1968 outsold the rest of the industry. However, archrival Ford sold only 1,964 trucks fewer than Chevrolet.

Chevrolet's 1-ton chassis cab was an excellent choice for carrying a large camper, but its installation was permanent and restricted the truck's utility value. Nevertheless the rig shown here with an Open Road camper was a popular choice for many. When the camper was permanently attached to the chassis it made both into one solid, integral unit with a low center of gravity. It was an easy and safe-handling package. A Chevrolet 1-ton would carry a bigger camper—up to 14 feet long. It also offered the advantage of plenty of headroom, gear storage space, and a full-height side entrance. The 1-ton was rated for a maximum GVW of 10,000 pounds. The new high-performance 325-horsepower 396-ci V-8 was an option. *AAMA*

Chevrolet's 1968 three-door Suburban Carryall was again in a class by itself. Its closest competitors were car-type station wagons. The Suburban had it all over station wagons, because it would seat more people in comfort and safety, carry more cargo, and pull more weight. The Suburban was the king of trailer-towing vehicles. It also offered the 4WD option in two models—C10 and C20—1/2- and 3/4-tons. Two rear door options included the tailgate/liftgate combination and the panel-type double doors. The Suburban's engine choices for 1968 included the new 307 V-8 and the high-performance 396 V-8. It was made to order for heavy hauls at freeway speeds. There was a choice of manual and automatic transmissions as well. *AAMA*

Chevrolet's Suburban-based Panel Delivery returned for 1968. It, too, received the new and larger V-8 engines featured in other Chevrolet light-duty trucks. The 307 V-8 had the same bore as the discontinued 283 model, but its stroke was lengthened to 3.25 inches. It also had new pistons, cylinder case, heads, and connecting rods and larger crank journals and bearings. A new paint treatment for all light-duty trucks tended to give the grille a new, more massive appearance. Its sloping hood provided a superior line-of-sight vision to the road. Side marker lights, a new federal safety standard item, were standard equipment. The Panel was offered in both 1/2- and 3/4-ton models. Its 9-foot body held 207 cubic feet of cargo. *AAMA*

Chevrolet's Sportvan conversions were ideal for small groups and short trips. A wide choice of conversions was available for both the Sportvan 90 and Sportvan 108. Not only did these units offer a modest-budget answer to close-to-the-road camping, but they also doubled as a second car. This is a conversion for the Chevy Van 108. McNamee Coach Co. manufactured this model. New this year was a steering column mounted four-speed manual transmission and the 307 standard 200-horsepower V-8. Other upgrades included 8.00x16.5 tires as optional equipment on 3/4-ton models and a 25-gallon fuel tank. Side reflectors were required by the federal safety standards act. *AAMA*

The 1968 Chevrolet Sportvan was also offered in two sizes on 90- and 108-inch wheelbases. It was ideal for large families or groups of up to eight adults. Optional center and rear seats were removable to accommodate cargo or for wheel-chair patients or camper equipment. The Sportvan 90 had more than nine feet of space behind the front seat, and the 108 was 18 inches longer in both wheelbase and interior length. The 230 and 250 sixes and the new 307 V-8 engines were available, as well as three- and four-speed manual transmissions mounted on the steering column and an automatic. This is a 1968 Chevrolet Sportvan 108. *AAMA*

The Chevy Van for 1968 was available in two sizes on 90- and 108-inch wheelbases. It offered efficient cargo-hauling capacity with full load protection from weather and pilferage. One-piece front and side panels, galvanized rocker panels and wheelhousings, and zinc-rich underbody primer contributed to corrosion resistance. The two wheelbases provided optimum weight distribution in relation to body length. Note that the additional length was inserted immediately behind the driver/passenger doors. Capacity was 209 cubic feet for the 90 and 256 for the 108. Two six-cylinder engines, the 230 and 250, and the new 307 V-8 were offered. An automatic transmission was an option. A Chevy Van 108 is shown in the foreground and a Chevy Van 90 in the background. *AAMA*

A complete chassis and front-end redesign for the 3/4- and 1-ton 1968 Chevrolet Step-Van made it an ideal vehicle for converting to a travel coach. A new independent front suspension greatly improved driving and riding qualities. The extended front provided easy accessibility for routine servicing from outside without disturbing passengers. Power steering was available for the first time, as were V-8 engines in the 3/4- and 1-ton Step-Vans. Standard V-8 was the new 200-horsepower 307 V-8; the 240-horsepower 327 V-8 was optional. The 1/2-ton Step-Van 7 continued with its old design. The Detroit Diesel 3-53N, 94-horsepower diesel was dropped for 1968 and replaced by the 3-53 diesel with 82 horsepower. *AAMA*

Chevrolet's conventional chassis cab models were designed to accommodate separate bodies up to 13 1/2 feet long. Chassis cab models with GVW ratings up to 14,000 pounds and on four wheelbases up to 157 inches were offered. They had 34-inch frame rail widths to accommodate bodies. Inside the cab either a standard three-man bench seat or individual bucket seats plus a console-type center seat for a third person were provided. The console seat had a padded cushion, which could be raised to utilize storage space underneath, and a padded backrest that could be folded down to provide an armrest for driver and passenger. This long wheelbase C30 dual rear wheel Crash Rescue truck operated at the Tucson, Arizona, airport. *Chuck Kadzielawski*

Chevrolet's medium-duty truck line for 1968 offered either gasoline or diesel engines. Diesel engines for Series 50 and 60 trucks consisted of the two-cycle Detroit Diesel 4-53N 212-ci, with 130 horsepower and 278 foot-pounds torque at 1,800 rpm. It was equipped with a Rootes-type blower for free and easy breathing. The other diesel offering was the four-cycle DH478 Toro-Flow with 478-ci, 170 horsepower and 310 foot-pounds torque at 2,000 rpm. The 4-53N was the only diesel offered on the Series 60 trucks. Gasoline engines for the Series 60 included the standard 292 six and standard 327 V-8, options included the 366 and 427 V-8s. This is a 1968 Chevrolet Series 60 chassis cab with fire-fighting body. It was operated by the New Egypt Volunteer Fire Department of Plumstead Township, New Jersey. Engine No. 2 had a 750-gallon tank body. *Scott Mattson*

Chevrolet's medium-duty "Job Tamer" trucks for 1968 consisted of Series 40-50-60 and tandem models in Series 50 and 60. Pictured here is the lightest medium-duty truck, the C40 stake. Nylon tires were standard equipment. New side marker reflectors required by new safety standards were also standard. A new option was a dual master cylinder brake system on single-axle mediums. This little 1 1/2-ton stake was rated for a maximum GVW of 18,000 pounds. Standard engines were the 155-horsepower 250 six and 180-horsepower 307 V-8; optional was the 170-horsepower 292 six. *AAMA*

Chevrolet's Series 50 medium-duty trucks, such as this 1968 C50 van, were offered with either gas or diesel engines. Chevrolet offered two trim levels in medium-duty cabs: standard and custom. The standard cab offered a full-width bench seat upholstered in durable, easy-to-clean vinyl. The functional instrument panel featured a cluster assembly finished in textured charcoal to provide a contrasting background for the gauges. A padded overhanging crown also contributed to good instrument readability. Standard equipment included seat belts, a driver's sun visor, a dome light, a left-hand outside mirror, two-speed electric windshield wipers, a windshield washer, a hazard warning switch, and a rubber floor mat. Series 50's maximum GVW rating was 22,000 pounds. Standard gasoline engines included the 292 six and 327 V-8; the 366 V-8 was the only option. *AAMA*

Chevrolet continued to offer its 72-inch BBC Tilt Cab Series 40-80 with either gas or diesel power in 1968. Pictured is a 1968 T50 tilt chassis cab with farm box. This gas-powered truck was still in service when photographed in September 1998. Series T50 was rated for a maximum GVW of 22,000 pounds. Standard engines were the 170-horsepower 292 six and the 185-horsepower 327 V-8. The 235-horsepower 366 V-8 was an option. Chevrolet's tilt-cab truck's popularity stemmed from three characteristics: its extra-short design with setback front axle providing ideal weight distribution, its excellent maneuverability, and its exceptionally good maintenance accessibility. The cab tilted forward on counterbalanced hinges for easy operation.

The nation's fire departments made use of nearly every type of truck, including light-duty models. The Cumberland Volunteer Fire Company of Maurice River Township, New Jersey, operated this 1968 Chevy Van 108 as its Emergency/Command Unit. It was a basic van with a custom interior outfitted for the job. Several outside firms specialized in designing and manufacturing special equipment for vans including cabinets, bins, baskets, racks, and load compartment partitions for nearly every application. Chevrolet built its G-Series vans in two weight ratings: 1/2- and 3/4-ton models with maximum GVW ratings up to 6,200 pounds. Three engines fit every need; the 140-horsepower 230 and 155-horsepower 250 sixes and the 200-horsepower 307 V-8. Transmission options included three- and four-speed manuals and the Powerglide. *Scott Mattson*

Chevrolet's short 96-inch conventional trucks were offered with single rear axles, dual-drive or trailing axle tandems in a wide variety of wheelbases to provide the right weight distribution requirements for both tractor and truck applications. They were available with gas or diesel engines and a broad selection of other components—transmissions, front and rear axles, springs, clutches, and other features. This is a 1968 Chevrolet Conventional Cab Series 60 medium-duty single-axle tractor. The maximum GCW rating of this tractor was a remarkable 60,000 pounds. It was available with the most powerful gasoline engine ever offered by Chevrolet for its truck line, the 260-horsepower 427 V-8. The largest diesel engine that was offered for this truck was the two-cycle 4-53N Detroit Diesel. It developed 130 gross horsepower and 278 foot-pounds gross torque at 1,800 rpm. *AAMA*

1969

The rapid shift to light-duty trucks for recreation and personal transportation influenced many of the changes and improvements in Chevrolet's light-duty truck line. Appearance changes were few. The basic cab and body styles remained the same except for a new grille, whose style created a more massive front appearance.

Increasing pressure from camper owners for more power to carry heavier loads at higher sustained highway speeds resulted in more powerful V-8 engine offerings. A new 255-horsepower 350 engine replaced the discontinued 240-horsepower 327 V-8. To meet maximum power requirements, a 310-horsepower four-barrel 396 V-8 was available. The two-barrel version of this engine was dropped, however. Engine options for 4WD trucks were the same as for 2WDs, except the 396 V-8 was not offered.

Chevrolet engineers specified power steering as an option for 2WD pickups in 1968, and also made it available for 4WD pickups in 1969. Other refinements for 1969 Chevrolet trucks included: automatic chokes on all engines; two stage multi-leaf rear springs; a foot-operated parking brake; wide base tires on 3/4- and 1-ton series; access holes in headlight doors for easy lamp adjustment; and a new steering shaft that isolated road noise. Optional front identification and clearance lights had a new inverted bowl lens design, making them visible from any direction. Side marker lamps replaced standard reflectors. Side visibility problems with high-bulky side mirrors were eliminated with a standard below-eye-line type that had no upper arm supports. The mirrors also generated less wind noise and were adjustable for close-in maneuvering.

Improvements in the Chevy Van and Sportsvan made them ideal for low-cost recreational travel. This was especially true when they were equipped with camper conversions, including an optional three-speed transmission for use with all engines and airconditioning. It was a high-capacity unit, integrated with the body. It incorporated a roof-mounted condenser and ceiling duct with adjustable outlets front and rear. The optional 200-horsepower 307 V-8 engine provided top freeway performance for work or play.

A midyear introduction, possibly one of the most important new products in Chevrolet history, was the all-new Blazer. First, Jeep; second, Scout; third, Bronco; and now Blazer. Chevrolet engineers had a "better idea." The first three went the smaller vehicle route, while Chevrolet gambled on making its first Sport Utility Vehicle (SUV) the same basic size as its standard full-size pickup, albeit with a shorter wheelbase and body.

The Blazer actually started as a concept to offer a "mini" pickup. Chevrolet toyed with the idea of a light-duty 1/2-ton truck with a 6-foot integral bed. The concept was reportedly shown to various Chevrolet dealers, who were not too impressed with it. Somebody took the cab roof off, added 4WD, a back seat, and thus, the Blazer was born.

The Blazer had two standard engines. They were the smaller 155-horsepower 250 six and the 200-horsepower 307 V-8. An optional engine was the 255-horsepower 350-ci V-8.

The Blazer's wheelbase was only 104 inches, while the overall length was 177.5 inches. Front overhang was 33.3 inches, while the rear was 40.2 inches. These dimensions translated into an approach angle of 35.2 degrees and departure of 25 degrees.

Single and tandem rear axles were offered for all trucks—medium- and heavy-duty models. This included both the trailing-axle type and dual-drive type. Series 50 tandems were equipped with a Chevrolet forward driving axle and a sturdy tubular trailing axle. This bogie assembly, rated at 28,000 pounds, had a hypoid ring gear and pinion with a 7.20 ratio. A two-speed drive axle was also available.

The gasoline engine lineup for medium- and heavy-duty trucks was as follows: 250 and 292 sixes; 350 (new for 1969), 366, and 427 V-8s; 401 and 478 V-6s. There were diesel engines in the lineup, including two-cycle Detroit Diesels, the 4-54N and 6V-53N, and the four-cycle Toro-Flow DH478.

The other medium- and heavy-duty Chevrolet truck line for 1969 was the 72-inch BBC dimension Series 50, 60, 70, and 80 tilt cabs. The only appearance change was that the Chevrolet bow tie trademark was deleted from the front of the cab.

The industry's only high-style and high-performance pickup, the El Camino, continued with moderate appearance changes. The El Camino was again based on the flashy Chevelle two-door passenger car. The SS 396 option was new for 1969.

Late 1969 saw the introduction of the Titan 90, a large line-haul aluminum cab-over based on the GMC Astro-95.

Truck production set another record in 1969 with 1,919,100 units built compared to 1,896,100 in 1968. It was an increase of only 1 percent, but an increase just the same. Chevrolet's production increased, too, but not by much—684,400 as against 680,599 in 1968. Yet it was still good enough for first place in the industry. Chevrolet actually lost sales in the 6,000 pound and less category, which is hard to understand in light of its exceptionally strong product offerings. In class two, 6,001 to 10,000 pounds, however, Chevrolet performed well by building 7,700 additional trucks.

For the industry, two-thirds of all trucks built in 1969 were equipped with V-8 engines. Chevrolet's percentage was 69, or just slightly higher than the industry average—472,528 V-8 installations versus 410,178 in 1968. Chevrolet sold more diesels in 1969 than in 1968—1,214 versus 1,030. This was a pathetic performance. Chevrolet dealers sold 693,448 new trucks in 1969, an 8 percent gain over the previous record 643,990 of 1968.

Chevrolet light-duty trucks were boldly restyled for 1969 with a more massive front-end appearance highlighted with a higher hood line and a silver-anodized aluminum grille. The former model's sloping hood may have improved the driver's view of the road, but the 1969's higher hood line gave these trucks a bigger, bolder, more rugged appearance. Other improvements included new brighter interiors, a foot-operated parking brake, tighter door sealing, automatic chokes on all engines, and revised cab and sheet-metal mountings for a quieter ride. A new option was a four-barrel 350 255-horsepower V-8. Pictured is a 1969 Chevrolet C10 1/2-ton Fleetside pickup. *AAMA*

Chevrolet's Stepside pickups were rugged, efficient, and hard working. They shared the new front-end styling with Fleetside models. Step running boards on either side between cab and rear fenders greatly facilitated side loading. The wide, flat flareboards on the cargo body's sides added to the body's strength. These bodies were contained between the rear wheels. Inside box width was a full 50 inches to accept standard 4-foot-wide building materials. Floors were of wood with steel skid strips to slide cargo in and out. This is a 1969 Chevrolet K10 Stepside pickup. The standard six for this model was the 155-horsepower 250; the 170-horsepower 292 six was optional. The standard V-8 was the 200-horsepower 307; the new, powerful 255-horsepower 350 V-8 was an option.

For 1969 Chevy Van continued its proved versatility, economy, maneuverability, and easy driver-compartment accessibility that has made it popular with fleets, tradesmen, and retail businesses. This is a 1969 Chevy Van 90 with windows all around. A three-speed automatic transmission was available for the first time as an option with all engines. Below-Eye-Line, low-mounted outside mirrors for unobstructed side vision and reduced wind noise, were a new option. Chevrolet offered this van as either a 1/2- or 3/4-ton model. Maximum GVW ratings were 5,000 pounds and 6,200 pounds, respectively. Engine options included the 230 and 250 sixes and the 307 V-8. The 200-horsepower V-8 engine was the engine of choice for owners hauling loads over the nation's freeway system. With the high-performance V-8s, the Chevy Van could carry a full load and maintain maximum speeds even in hilly terrain. *AAMA*

No, this is not a factory-built crew cab. It's a custom-built one-off. The rear doors, actually front doors, do look a bit odd. It was probably less costly for the converter than redoing the top portion of the door, cutting new glass, and so on. Other than that it is quite an attractive truck. Because there was a market for crew cab pickups, Chevrolet later built a factory-assembled crew cab. This truck was photographed in North Dakota in 1991. *Jim Benjaminson*

Chevrolet's 1-ton C30 chassis cab was a versatile all-purpose truck. There was no end to the special bodies it could accommodate. The nation's fire departments alone accounted for many special body installations on the four standard wheelbase lengths: 115, 127, 133, and 157 inches to accommodate bodies up to 13 feet long. 4WD units could handle bodies from 6 to 8 feet long. Maximum GVW ratings ranged as high as 14,000 pounds. This 1969 Chevrolet C30 1-ton chassis cab with special utility body was owned by the Winters (California) Fire Department. *Bill Hattersley*

This was the first year Chevrolet offered an all aluminum-bodied Step-Van. Steel bodies were also available. The aluminum body was identical in all basic aspects to the regular steel Step-Vans. The aluminum model dramatically increased the allowable payload rating. Not only that, but body corrosion became a thing of the past. The aluminum Step-Van was not painted except as an option. Step-Vans were offered on three wheelbase lengths: 125, 133, and 157 inches—in two series, P20 and P30. New for 1969 were two-stage rear springs with rubber eye bushings for an improved ride, reduced weight, and better durability. Wide base tires, previously an option, were made standard. They afforded a better ride, handling and traction, and lower vehicle height. Diesel power was offered in the 1-ton category. Pictured is a 1969 P20 aluminum Step-Van King. *AAMA*

Chevrolet was serious about its Tilt Cab business in 1969. The Series consisted of models 50–80 on eight wheelbases, with gas and diesel engines and maximum GVW ratings ranging from 15,000 pounds to 32,000 pounds and GCW ratings up to 65,000 pounds. Chevrolet's high-efficiency tilt-cab models featured a short 72-inch BBC dimension. Its setback front axle shifted the load forward for better weight distribution, excellent maneuverability, and exceptional maintenance accessibility. Engine choices began with an inline 292 six, then progressed to three V-8s—350, 366, and 427 ci. Two heavy-duty sixes topped out the gasoline engine lineup—401 and 478 V-6s. One diesel engine was the Detroit Diesel two-cycle 6V-53N, which produced 447 foot-pounds torque and was the strongest engine offered. This is a 1969 diesel-powered TE60 tilt-cab chassis cab with firefighting body. The Griffith (Indiana) Fire Department owned this Alfco-bodied rig. It featured a 1,000 gallon tank and a 1,250-gpm pump. *Chuck Madderom*

Chevrolet offered two conventional cab series for 1969. One was the 96-inch BBC Conventional Cab Series 40-50-60. These trucks shared a cab with the light-duty models, but with a shorter hood. The 93-inch BBC bigger Series 70-80 trucks were also called Conventional Cab trucks, but were different from the lighter Conventional Series. Series 70-80 were GMC trucks, engineered and manufactured by GMC, but with Chevrolet nameplates. The Mehlville (Missouri) Fire Protection District owned rescue No. 1, a C50 Conventional chassis cab. Its body was by McCabe-Power. It had a maximum GVW rating of 24,000 pounds and was powered by the 200-horsepower 366 V-8 engine. Note its high-style chrome grille and headlight surrounds. *Dennis J. Maag*

The top-of-the-line model in the 96-inch BBC Conventional Series was the Model 60. This 1969 chassis cab with firefighting body was owned by the New Melle (Missouri) Community Volunteer Fire Department. Engine No. 1's body was by Towers and it featured a 500-gallon water tank and a 500-gpm pump. Its pump was mounted between the bumper and grille. Cast spoke wheels on C60 were standard equipment. The maximum GVW rating of a C60 was 32,000 pounds. Its standard engine was the 200-horsepower 366 V-8; the 225-horsepower 427 V-8 was an option. This model was not offered with diesel power; however, the two lighter models were. *Dennis J. Maag*

Chevrolet's heaviest 96-inch Conventional Cab truck was the Series 60 tandem. This is a 1969 Series 60 tandem chassis cab with dump body. Engine changes for increased power in the 1969 heavy-duty truck line included a 366 V-8 as standard equipment in models formerly using a 327 V-8 as their base powerplant. The optional engine was the 225-horsepower 427 V-8. The Series 60 tandem carried a maximum GVW rating of 45,000 pounds. For 1969, this truck had an optional emergency air brake system incorporating spring-loaded chambers for parking and automatic emergency braking if the air supply failed. Series 60 tandems had an Eaton dual-drive axle arrangement in a 30,000-pound Hendrickson bogie assembly. For extra-heavy-duty operations, a 34,000-pound bogie was available. A four-speed auxiliary transmission could be ordered, when close gear splitting was required. *AAMA*

First came Jeep's CJ in 1945, then International's Scout in 1961, followed by Ford's Bronco in 1966. Where was the light-duty truck sales leader's SUV? Finally, in 1969 Chevrolet answered, but it took a different tack. Those that came before were small, spartan, and light. IH and Ford's utility vehicles were totally different vehicles from the other light-duty trucks in their line. Chevrolet engineers borrowed heavily from the company's 1/2-ton 4WD pickup to create its SUV. The Blazer's front sheet metal, interior, and chassis, including its 4WD system, were borrowed from its K10 pickups. So the Blazer was different because it was wider and longer and looked like another model of its light-duty truck line. Engines, transmissions, transfer case, front suspension, and other mechanicals also came from the K10 pickup. This is a preproduction prototype of a 1969 Blazer. Note its tiny wheels and tires. *AAM*

Chevrolet's innovative Longhorn pickup was new for 1969. It was the first pickup engineered specifically for camping. It was built to deliver extra support and better balance on its 133-inch-wheelbase chassis to enable it to carry larger loads than ordinary pickups. Its big, 8 1/2-foot box was the industry's longest for a 3/4-ton pickup. It was designed to carry camper bodies up to 12 feet long. The long campers had the spaciousness and convenience the serious camper demanded. Rugged two-stage rear leaf springs easily handled the long, heavy camper bodies for sure and steady going on- and off-road. Chevrolet engineers made available five engines, up to 310 horsepower, and five different transmissions, as well as a long list of camper-designed options and accessories. *Tom Brownell*

Chevrolet's biggest conventional in the C-Series was the 96-inch BBC Series ME-60 dual-drive tandem. Shown here is a 1969 Series ME-60 tandem. The 260-horsepower 427 V-8 powered this truck. This was the optional engine. The standard engine was the 235-horsepower 366 V-8. Chevrolet did not offer a diesel engine for this model. A five-speed main transmission was standard equipment. A 10-speed was optional, as was an automatic. This truck has a five-speed main and the optional four-speed auxiliary. The owner took this photo in September 1970. *Verne L. Byers*

Chapter 6

1970 TO 1979

1970

Chevrolet began its move into the heavy-duty truck business in 1955 with its first V-8-powered models. For 1970, Chevrolet made an impressive heavy-duty model introduction with the extra-heavyweight, top-of-the-line Series 90 tilt cab tractors. These were the largest trucks ever offered, and the largest that would ever *be* offered by Chevrolet. The aluminum cab Titan 90 boasted a 54-inch BBC. Sleeper versions with 74- and 86-inch BBCs were available.

In addition to the Titan 90 Series, the 90 Series steel conventional cab heavy-duty models made their debut. The long conventional 90 featured a fiberglass-reinforced plastic hood and fenders that tilted forward from the front bumper. A 90 short conventional model with steel fenders and butterfly-type hood was also new. Series 90 conventional trucks came in 22 basic models with horsepower to 335 and GCWs to 76,800 pounds.

Power options for the 90 Series included Detroit Diesel and Cummins engines. These were the "big bore" diesels favored by over-the-road (OTR) operators. A full range of transmissions, front and rear axles, clutches, and other components allowed the purchaser to specify his truck to fit the job.

The addition of these big OTR rigs made Chevrolet truly a "full line" truck marketer. Notice it was a marketer, not a manufacturer. The new big trucks were built for Chevrolet by GMC at GMC's plant in Pontiac, Michigan. Chevrolet's 90 Series was "badge engineered" GMCs. Chevrolet's total 1970 truck line ranged from the 4,400-pound

GVW Blazer to the 50,500-pound GVW or 76,800-pound GCW Series 90. Chevrolet's line contained a total of 578 models on 47 wheelbases and included virtually every type of truck in use.

Beginning in mid-October 1969, Chevrolet began marketing its 70, 80, and 90 Series trucks under a separate heavy-duty selling agreement that was offered only to dealers who met special qualifications. These qualifications included physical facilities, trained heavy-duty mechanics, a parts stock, and trained sales personnel. The dealers selected for this new program also sold all other Chevrolet trucks.

GMC's Astro-95 was the same truck as Chevrolet's Titan 90. Both trucks were assembled at GMC's Pontiac, Michigan, plant. They featured an ultra-modern comfortable interior with wraparound instrumentation. The steering wheel tilted to several positions. Sleep versions had full insulation and accommodated 24-, 32-, or 36-inch bunks. The Astro-95/Titan 90 twins were 1970's most modern, innovative, and unique cab-over tractors. This was possibly because the famous automotive designer Larry Shinoda designed them.

The balance of Chevrolet's 1970 truck line from lights to heavies carried over without appearance changes. However, they had a number of engineering improvements, refinements, and new extra-cost options to make them better suited to perform their intended jobs, to last longer and operate more economically. These included air-inflatable shock absorbers on models with coil springs in the light-duty line and the addition of a 2WD version to the 4WD Blazer introduced late in 1969.

Chevrolet's 1970 pickups and other light-duty trucks carried over without noticeable change. This is a 1970 C10 Custom Fleetside pickup. Chevrolet offered four cab trim levels in 1970: Standard, Custom, CST with bench seat, and CST with bucket seats and console. Chevrolet continued to lead the industry with its attractive, colorful, and comfortable interiors and world-famous soft but controlled ride. In 4WDs Chevrolet continued to offer only 1/2- and 3/4-ton pickups, chassis cabs, Suburbans, and Panels, and the new Blazer. Engine choices for all 2WD pickups included the standard 250 six and 307 V-8; the optional engines were the 292 six and the 350 and 400 V-8s. The 396 V-8 from 1969 was dropped and replaced with the 400 V-8. The 4WD pickup's engine lineup differed from above only in that the 400 V-8 was not offered. *AAMA*

Chevrolet's top-of-the-line pickup for 1970 was the CST Fleetside with bucket seats and console and two-tone paint. The CST option included the following items: chrome front bumper, CST nameplate on front fenders, full-width vinyl seats (bucket seats were an option), bright frames for clutch, brake, and accelerator pedals, extra insulation, carpeting, and cargo light. This pickup has a two-tone paint combination of white over red. These were Chevrolet's signature colors for 1970.

Chevrolet's truck sales took a beating in 1970 from a 67-day shutdown of GM by the UAW, beginning in mid-September. The strike hurt both GMC and Chevrolet and, of course, impacted the entire industry. Truck production at Chevrolet in 1970 amounted to 490,886, down 28.2 percent from 1969's record 683,694. The total count in 1970 was the lowest at Chevrolet since 1963. Perhaps what hurt worst of all was losing the coveted number one production position to Ford. Ford, however, actually built fewer trucks in 1970 than in 1969—625,900 versus 640,500.

Trucks with V-8 engines accounted for 371,308, or 76 percent, of Chevrolet's total output. Chevrolet's 1979 diesel engine installations totaled 1,299 versus 1,214 in 1969. Chevrolet dealers

In 1970, the young and adventurous chose Chevrolet's sporty 4WD, 115-inch-wheelbase short box Stepside pickup. This is a 1970 Chevrolet K10 Custom Stepside pickup. Its sporty wheels and tires are aftermarket items. Chevrolet's Custom model was its middle model for 1970, between the CST at the top and the Standard cab model at the bottom. Two popular engines for this truck were the hot 255-horsepower 350 V-8 and the hotter 310-horsepower 400 (402) V-8. A 127-inch-wheelbase 1/2-ton with an 8-foot box and a 3/4-ton model of the same description plus a 133-inch-wheelbase 1-ton with a 9-foot box filled out the Stepside offering.

The hot-selling Blazer was only in its second year in 1970. It's interesting to note that the early Blazers offered seating arrangements for one to five people. The base Blazer included only the driver seat. A passenger seat was optional, as was the rear bench seat. A new fiberglass reinforced hardtop for 1970 was easily bolted on and was easily removed. The top also featured a lockable lift gate. A 2WD Blazer was a new offering for 1970, but very few buyers chose it over the 4WD. For both the 2WD and 4WD models, the standard engines were the 250 six and the 307 V-8; the optional engine was the powerful 350 V-8.

Chevrolet introduced its fully redesigned Chevy Van in the spring of 1970 as a 1971 model. Chevrolet engineers wanted to design a van that would provide its commercial customers with a greatly increased load space and a third more payload capacity. They accomplished this by moving the engine forward out of the cargo area and by giving the van a short hood instead of the straight front of its former van. By lifting the hood, one could reveal the engine, battery, and radiator for easy service. Chevrolet boasted that 26 service points could be checked under the extended hood. The new Chevy Van was offered in three series: G10 1/2-, G20 3/4-, and G30 1-ton. GVWs ranged from 4,000 pounds to 7,600 pounds. A new wide-opening sliding right side door was easy to operate with one hand. Its front suspension was Chevrolet's patented easy riding independent-type with deep coil springs. Engine options included the standard 155-horsepower 250 six; the standard V-8 was the 200-horsepower 307; and for the first time in a van a high-performance V-8, the 255-horsepower 350 V-8, was an option. This is a 1971 Chevy Van 1/2-ton G10. *AAMA*

Chevrolet's 1970 medium-duty truck line consisted of the 96-inch BBC Conventional Series 40-50-60 and the 72-inch BBC Tilt Series 50-60. This is a 1970 Series C60 tractor trailer. Except for the tandem-axle Series M60 truck, the Series 60 single-axle tractor was the biggest conventional cab medium-duty. However, when in use as a tractor, the single-axle tractor's maximum GCW rating of 60,000 pounds was the same as that of the tandem-axle tractor. Its maximum GVW rating when used as a straight truck was 32,000 pounds. The largest V-8 engine in Chevrolet's truck line, the optional 260-horsepower 427 V-8, powered this tractor. It was also equipped with a New Process five-speed transmission. Diesel engines were an option for the Tilt Cab Series but not for the Conventional Cab Series. *AAMA*

sold 562,231 trucks in calendar year 1970, 19 percent below 1969's 693,448.

Two significant engine changes in light-duty trucks for 1970 included dropping the 396 V-8 and adding the new 400 V-8. This change was true for 1/2-, 3/4-, and 1-ton 2WD models. The 400 was the 396 Mark 4 big block with a slight increase in bore. Its actual displacement was not 400, but 402. In 2WD light-duties, the 250 six and 307 V-8 engines were standard. Optional engines included the 292 six and the 350 and 400 V-8s. For 4WD models including Blazer and Suburban the engine lineup was the same except that the 350 V-8 was the largest engine offered.

The 1970 El Camino SS 396 option was the only light-duty model powered by the 396 V-8. The new 400-ci V-8 was also an option for the El Camino.

Chevrolet's heavy-duty Conventional Series 70-80-90 continued in 1970. All three sizes in the series could be ordered with either a long nose or a short nose. This 1970 Chevrolet short-nose Series 70 chassis cab tanker body was made by Alexis and was equipped with a 750-gallon tank and a 1,000-gpm front-mounted pump. The Elburn (Illinois) and Countryside Fire Protection District owned engine No. 306. This series were re-rebadged GMC models. They were engineered by GMC engineers and assembled in GMC plants. This truck was powered by the standard Detroit Diesel 6V-53N diesel and was equipped with a five-speed Spicer transmission and the standard two-speed Eaton rear axle. It was rated for a maximum GVW of 32,000 pounds. A steel butterfly-type hood was standard equipment on Series 70 trucks. *Garry Kadzielawsk*

There was nothing else like the 350-horsepower 1970 El Camino SS 396 (Super Sport). Features of the SS 396 included a special raised hood, front disc brakes, sport wheels, special-duty springs, stabilizers, and shocks, front and rear. It sported an SS 396 badge located in the center of the grille and on each front fender side. The cab interior featured Strato bucket seats, deep-pile carpeting, center console, floor-mounted shift, and special instruments including oil pressure and ammeter gauges and tach. *John Gunnell*

The 260-horsepower 427 V-8 engine mated to a five-speed transmission and a two-speed rear axle powered this 1970 Chevrolet conventional cab C60 chassis cab with a 10-foot dump body. The standard engine for this model was the 235-horsepower 366-ci V-8. In addition, it had air brakes and 10.00x20 tires. Jim Fromm, its owner, reports, "It would haul 10 ton loads of rock without trying." The heavy-duty C60 model was rated for a maximum GVW rating of 32,000 pounds and a GCW of 60,000 pounds. Chevrolet's Standard cab was quite deluxe. It featured seat belts, padded sunshades, a dome light, two-speed windshield wipers, and a choice of six cab interior colors. Custom Appearance and Comfort and Convenience packages were optional. Included in this package were Soft-Ray tinted glass, Bostrom seats, air conditioning, a push-button radio, and various mirrors. *Jim Fromm*

GMC designed, engineered, and built this new heavy-duty Chevrolet truck, the Titan 90. It was Chevrolet's version of GMC's Astro 95. The largest engine ever used in a Chevrolet truck, the 851-ci Detroit Diesel 12V71 engine, which developed 390 SAE net horsepower at 2,100 rpm, powered it. Its SAE net torque was 1,078 foot-pounds at 1,200 rpm. The Titan 90 rode on a 150-inch wheelbase with a CA dimension of 124 inches. It carried a standard GVW rating of 48,500 pounds and maximum of 50,500 pounds. Its maximum GCW rating was 76,800 pounds. Standard equipment included a 12,000-pound front axle, 38,000-pound Hendrickson rear bogie, and a Fuller three-speed transmission. Chevrolet marketed its 70, 80, and 90 Series trucks under a separate heavy-duty selling agreement that was offered to dealers that met special qualifications for service facilities, trained heavy-duty truck mechanics, parts stocks, and the like. With the new Titan 90 Series in its lineup, Chevrolet became a "full line" truck marketer. This top-of-the-line over-the-road tractor was designed to appeal to fleet buyers and individual owner-operators. *AAMA*

Compared with its previous heavy-duty truck line, the new Chevrolet Titan 90 was an extra-heavy-duty truck and was Chevrolet's top-of-the-line model. This truck was, like all other Chevrolet heavy-duty models, engineered, designed, and built by GMC and marketed through Chevrolet's select group of dealers who had committed to a heavy-duty selling agreement. These dealers had to meet special qualifications for service facilities, trained heavy-duty mechanics, parts stocks and the like. Arnold Paradis, along with others, formed the I-5 Freightline in 1970. They purchased 60 Chevrolet trucks for delivery service. They also purchased C60 Series tractors with full air brakes, 350 V-8s and five-speed transmissions, as well as a fleet of Titan 90 tractors equipped with the biggest Cummins offered, the 335 horsepower, 10-speed Fuller transmissions and single-speed single rear axles. *Arnold Paradis*

The 115-inch-wheelbase short-box CST/10 pickup was Chevrolet's most popular personal use truck. CST's high-line cab had all the custom comfort and appearance trim features desired by personal use buyers. CST options included optional bucket seats with console; full instrumentation; standard bright frames for clutch, brake, and accelerator pedals; extra insulation; carpeting; and a cargo light. The preferred drivetrain was the 255-horsepower 350 V-8 engine and Turbo Hydra-Matic automatic transmission. The 310-horsepower 400 V-8 (402) was an option. *John Gunnell*

1971

In 1971, Chevrolet Division became the first automaker to break the three million mark in combined car and truck sales. The actual count was 2,307,051 autos and 695,264 trucks, for a total of 3,002,315 sales. This was a historic achievement, but maybe for a reason not readily apparent. A quick bit of arithmetic reveals that trucks accounted for 23 percent of total sales. The hidden story is that while Chevrolet's truck sales in 1971 were a record, car sales did not set a record. Chevrolet's car sales record of 2,416,419 was set six years earlier in 1965. The numbers also don't reveal that truck sales had been on the march for several years. Chevrolet's combined record sales were possible only because trucks led the way.

In 1971, Chevrolet, as well as the rest of the Big Three, had in

place most of the products that would eventually move truck sales ahead of car sales. The only exceptions were the hot-selling small domestic pickups and minivans.

Chevrolet's truck production in 1971 increased to 739,478 from 490,886 in 1970, which had been crippled by the strike. This production figure beat out the old record of 683,694 set in 1969.

The V-8 was the most popular Chevrolet truck engine, with sales of 599,207. Other buyers opted for the L-6—128,660. A total of 345 buyers (heavy-duty trucks only) chose the V-6. Chevrolet sold 2,146 diesel-powered trucks. And for the first time since 1928, Chevrolet installed four-cylinder engines in 9,120 Vega Panels.

The popularity of the GMC V-6 had slipped. The 366 and

Chevrolet's 1971 El Camino was a delightful combination of beauty and strength in a luxurious pickup. It was no secret that the El Camino was more car than truck, and most buyers purchased them for personal transportation. But they could work and they did. The El Camino had a double-wall pickup box. This 1/2-ton rated pickup could handle payloads up to 1,000 pounds. It was also a serious tow vehicle. With up to 425 horsepower available in the SS model from the Turbo-Jet 454 V-8, the El Camino had the horses to pull horses. El Camino featured a new grille and front appearance for 1971. The biggest change was seen in the single headlights. Chevrolet designers also moved the parking lights out to the leading edge of the front fenders. The top-of-the-line model for 1971 was the SS 454, and an SS badge appeared in the middle of the grille and on each front fender. Engine choices began with the standard 250 six and 307 V-8, optional engines included the 350, 400, and 454 V-8s (365- and 425-horsepower versions of the 454).

Chevrolet pickups had new styling highlighted by an alluring egg crate-type grille design. The new grille gave the pickups a more massive frontal look. But Chevrolet's big news for 1971 was its industry-leading move into disc brakes. Chevrolet was the first to make front disc brakes standard in the light-duty truck field. New 15x6 front wheels with a stronger disc and rim replaced the 15x5 wheels on 1/2-ton models. To keep pace with the move to lower lead fuel requirements, Chevrolet engineers reduced engine compression ratios to a range of 8.0 to 8.5. Fuel requirements ranged from 89 to 91 octane ratings. Other engine modifications included piston head changes and revised distributor settings. This is a 1971 Chevrolet C10 Fleetside pickup. *AAMA*

Chevrolet made seven basic paint colors permanent offerings to make it easier for fleets to stay with one color. An option for 1971 pickups was a white two-tone side panel as seen on this 1971 Chevrolet C10 Fleetside pickup. Chevrolet's front disc brakes were standard on all light-duty trucks. A power booster was standard on all trucks with a GVW of 5,000 pounds and over. A combination indicator switch, delay valve, and pressure proportioning valve were part of the system. The delay valve teamed front disc brake application with rear brakes for balanced braking. The new top-of-the-line pickup for 1971 was the Cheyenne model with such luxuries as carpeting, deluxe vinyl trim, headlining, chrome bumpers, special insulation, and other luxury items. *Monty Montgomery*

Chevrolet offered three trim levels in its 1971 pickup line. This is a 1971 Chevrolet C10 Fleetside Custom Deluxe pickup. Custom Deluxe models featured bright metal windshield and rear window moldings and bright window vent frames. On the inside was a full-width foam bench seat in fabric and vinyl. Color choices included black, blue, parchment, and olive. On the floor was a vinyl-coated color-keyed floor mat. Other items included a cigar lighter, dual horns, special insulation, and a door-operated dome light switch. The Cheyenne package consisted of these items plus Cheyenne nameplates; chrome front bumper; cargo compartment light; and on Fleetside models, bright lower body side moldings, fuel filler cap, and tailgate trim. *Monty Montgomery.*

Chevrolet's 4WD system was unique in the industry in that its system created an exceedingly low silhouette while maintaining the needed ground clearance for effective off-road driving. Chevrolet's 4WD was available on 14 pickup and chassis cab models. It could also be ordered on all Suburbans and was standard on 4WD Blazer. Chevrolet continued to build only 1/2- and 3/4-ton 4WD trucks, unlike its major competitors, who also offered 1-ton 4WD trucks. Standard engines for 4WD pickups were the 250 six and 307 V-8. Optional engines were the 292 six and 350 V-8. This engine lineup was also true for 2WD trucks; however, the massive 400 V-8 was an option for 2WD trucks only. When photographed in September 1998, this 1971 Chevrolet K10 Fleetside truck looked new and was used for daily transportation. *Gary Otto*

427 V-8s had as much power and were less costly to build. The V-6 was also handicapped by a well-deserved reputation of being a gas hog.

The truck industry's production passed the two million mark, at 2,053,100. More than half of the total, 1,196,600, were class-one trucks—6,000 pounds or less GVW. It's interesting to note that Chevrolet built more passenger cars in 1971 than the industry, in total, built trucks. Few believed in 1971 that the day was coming when trucks would outsell cars.

Chevrolet made the history books in 1971 by being the first to make front disc brakes standard equipment on all light-duty trucks. To go along with the new disc brakes, 15x6 front wheels with a stronger disc and rim replaced the 15x5 wheels formerly used on 1/2-ton models.

Chevrolet offered three cab interior comfort packages for 1971. First was the base Custom that offered only the basics—a vinyl bench seat and a spattering of chrome trim on doors and instrument panel trim. The next step up was the Custom Deluxe, which featured a combination of fabric and vinyl upholstery, and a few more amenities such as a cigar lighter and dual horns. The best—and new for 1971—was the Cheyenne. It featured deluxe trim on the seat, carpet, headliner, and door panels. Bucket seats and a console were available.

Two other new models were the second generation Chevy Van and Sportvan. They were larger, impressively styled, thoroughly modern vehicles. They also featured an optional sliding door for easier parking, docking, and loading. The Series included 1/2-, 3/4-, and 1-ton models.

In the medium-duty line, Chevrolet made the Allison AT 540 automatic transmission available on C40 to C80 series single-axle trucks with V-8 engines (10,000 to 27,500 pound GVW range).

Because of the success of the new Chevy Van, Chevrolet's conventional panel models were discontinued. A full line of optional modular cabinets, bins, shelving, security screens, racks, and other special equipment were offered with the 1971 Chevy Van. They were designed to meet the needs of utilities, plumbers, painters, appliance repair services, fleet maintenance units, general delivery services, and others requiring fitted interiors for tools, supplies, and other equipment. There was virtually no limit to the ways an owner could adapt Chevy Van interiors to special uses. The new van was in its first full year of production and already proved to be a big winner with commercial customers. Chevy Vans were offered in three series with GVWs as high as 8,000 pounds and payload capacities up to 296 cubic feet and 4,040 pounds. *AAMA*

To keep pace with the changing scene of the 1970s, Chevrolet offered its customers a whole new concept in light-duty commercial vehicles passenger trucks. Chevrolet's marketing folks were well aware that for some time more and more people were buying trucks for passenger use, or "passenger trucks," as Chevrolet liked to call them. GM's Styling department created nine different and highly colorful decal patterns for its dealers to sell to the growing number of personal-use truck buyers. Decals available included the Blazer "Feathers" design (top) and the Suburban "Flame" (bottom). The checked running-light covers of the Blazer were designed to add an extra decorative touch and to protect the lights from stones when not in use. Other available decal designs were named the Eagle, Sandman, Rippler, Hawk, Spirals, and 1776. Decals were constructed of permanent-adhesive vinyl. They could be dealer installed in less than four hours. The average cost was less than $65 plus installation labor. The program was kicked off with publicity in automotive enthusiast magazines featuring similarly decorated, customized Chevrolet trucks. Chevrolet was aware that many former owners of hard-to-insure musclecars had turned to the light-duty truck market for the answer to their needs. The decals helped to distinguish their trucks from their plainer cousins. *AAMA*

Chevrolet's Step-Van 7 was redesigned with a longer front-opening hood for quick and convenient servicing. It was built on a trim 102-inch wheelbase, which allowed it to get around quickly and easily in heavy city traffic. Chevrolet built the Step-Van 7 two ways: with a 7- or an 8-foot body, and with a choice of a 65-inch or a 69-inch interior height. The operator had from 211 to 258 cubic feet of capacity to carry up to 1,490 pounds of payload. The Step-Van 7 had sliding side doors and wide-opening rear doors to make loading a snap. Drivers appreciated its smooth-riding coil spring suspension front and rear. This is a 1971 Chevrolet P10 Step-Van 7. Its standard and only engine was the lively 250 six. The three-speed manual transmission was standard; a four-speed manual and Powerglide and Turbo Hydra-Matic automatics were optional.

Chevrolet's 1971 medium-duty Conventional line consisted of Series 40-50-60. This 1971 Chevrolet C60 chassis cab with fire-fighting body was operated by the Pierce County (Gig Harbor, Washington) Fire District. Engine No. 5's pumper body contained a 1,300-gallon water tank and a 300-gpm pump. The single, rear-axle Series 60 trucks carried a maximum GVW rating of 32,000 pounds. The standard 235-horsepower 366 V-8 engine powered this truck. Its transmission was the standard Chevrolet-built CH-465 four-speed with a two-speed Chevrolet-built CH-17000 rear axle. The 366 engine was specifically engineered for rugged, long-lasting truck service. This engine was not offered for passenger car service. *Bill Hattersley*

Chevrolet's Step-Van King was the forward-control truck designated for the big jobs. It was like a warehouse on wheels. Maximum GVWs ranged from 6,500 to 14,000 pounds. Bodies from 10 to 14 1/2 feet were available. This is a 1971 Chevrolet Step-Van King Model P30 with a 14 1/2-foot body converted to firefighting duty. The Union (Missouri) Fire Protection District for rescue work operated rescue Unit No. 236. Note its heavy-duty grille guard. Its vast interior was filled with specialized equipment. The Step-Van was an easy-riding truck due to its work-proved girder-coil–type independent front suspension and two-stage rear leaf springs. This truck was equipped with the optional 250-horsepower 350 V-8 engine and optional Turbo Hydra-Matic automatic transmission. *Dennis J. Maag*

The largest single delivery of Chevrolet Titan 90 heavy-duty diesel tractors took place in 1971, when 26 FH-9153 Titan 90s were purchased by the Gateway Transportation Co. of LaCrosse, Wisconsin, one of the nation's largest motor common carriers. Gateway purchased the trucks from Braeger Chevrolet, Inc., in Milwaukee, Wisconsin. Gateway primarily serviced the Midwest and South, and operated these units out of its Atlanta, Georgia, terminal. They had a GCW rating of 76,800 pounds. The BBC measurement of the standard cab was only 54 inches. A 74-inch BBC sleeper cab was available with a 24-inch wide bunk, and an 86-inch BBC with 32- or 36-inch bunks was the largest available. Titan 90's cab tilted a full 90 degrees with a hydraulic tilt mechanism and could be stopped at any position from zero degrees to full tilt. Only diesel engines powered Titan 90; either Detroit Diesel or Cummins supplied standard diesels. Cummins' inline six model NTC-335, with 335 horsepower and 926 foot-pounds gross torque, was the biggest diesel engine offered for 1971. *AAMA*

In its medium-duty lines, Chevrolet offered for the first time the Allison AT 540 automatic transmission. It was offered on Series 40-50-60 single-axle trucks with V-8 engines. Other new features of the 1971 medium-duty line included high-intensity headlamps, anti-theft door locks, and markings on the brake drum for safe turndown depth. This is a 1971 Chevrolet T50 Tilt Cab medium-duty chassis cab with panel body. The Tilt Cab Series consisted of models 50-60 in the medium-duty line and models 70-80-90 in the heavy-duty line. The T50 was rated for a maximum GVW of 26,000 pounds. Its standard engines were the 170-horsepower 292 six and the 215-horsepower 350 V-8; the 235-horsepower 366 V-8 was optional. Chevrolet's Tilt Cab Series was very popular with firms involved in city delivery work because of its outstanding maneuverability in traffic. Its extremely short 72-inch BBC dimension and setback front axle gave it excellent weight distribution. *AAMA*

This is a 1971 Chevrolet conventional cab Series M60 tandem axle chassis cab with lime spreader body. The standard 200-horsepower 366 V-8 engine powered it. The 230-horsepower 427 V-8 was an option. It was also equipped with a five-speed main transmission (Chevrolet offered five-speed transmissions from New Process, Clark, and Spicer and a six-speed automatic from Allison) and a Spicer 6041 four-speed auxiliary. This truck was equipped with Hendrickson tandem suspension and air brakes. Chevrolet offered Eaton rear axles with 30,000- and 34,000-pound capacities. They had a built-in interaxle differential to eliminate wheel fight and helped provide improved tire life. A driver-operated differential lockout supplied equal power to each axle for traction whenever needed. *Jim Fromm*

Chevrolet continued to build the 3/4-ton Longhorn pickup through the 1972 model year for the serious pickup camper. The Longhorn's 8 1/2-foot cargo box took camper bodies up to 12 feet long. Chevrolet engineers designed the Longhorn with extra strength and support to carry long campers and heavy loads. Notice a vertical line in the Fleetside cargo box on this truck, immediately to the rear of the cab. This is the extra 6 inches the Longhorn's box was stretched. Buyers normally specified one of the two biggest V-8 engines: either the 250-horsepower 350 or the 300-horsepower 400 V-8. The transmission of choice was typically the trouble-free three-speed Turbo Hydra-Matic. The 3/4-ton C20 Longhorn could be optioned for a maximum GVW rating of 7,500 pounds. The Longhorn's front suspension was Chevrolet's famous independent coil spring setup. Rear suspension was standard with coil springs but heavy-duty leaf springs were an extra-cost option. *Tom Brownell*

In 1971, Chevrolet built short conventional, 93-inch BBC models, and long conventional, 115-inch BBC models. This is a 1971 JV70 tandem chassis cab with a special roofer's body. The entire hood and front fender assemblies were constructed of lightweight reinforced fiberglass. The entire assembly tilted forward to expose the engine, radiator, and front-end components. A butterfly-type steel hood was standard on Series 70 and 80 models and optional on the big Series 90 short Conventionals. Their side hood panels swung up and out of the way for routine maintenance. By removing eight bolts a fender could be taken off for complete engine access. *Dick Copello*

What is most interesting about this 1971 Chevrolet ME60 tandem was that it looked almost as good as new, and it was still in use when spotted and photographed in the fall of 1998. It has a large farm grain box. It is equipped with a Clark five-speed main, Spicer four-speed auxiliary, air brakes, the 260 gross horsepower, 405 foot-pounds gross torque 427 V-8, the optional 11,000-pound front axle, and the optional 34,000-pound single-speed Eaton tandem. *Calvin Gray Farms*

1972

Engineers revised the engine lineup for light-duty 1972 Chevrolet trucks. The 250 six and 307 V-8 engines were standard equipment for all light-duty models including 4WD trucks. The 400 V-8 was optional for 1/2-ton 2WD models only. For all other light-duty trucks, optional engines were the 292 six and 350 V-8. The 400 V-8 was optional for 2WD Suburbans. Besides that, the Suburban's engine options paralleled that of the pickups.

The most important change in the medium-duty truck line was the optional three-speed automatic transmission for straight trucks. It was limited to models equipped with V-8 engines up to 366, with GVWs not exceeding 19,500 pounds. This transmission was named the AT 475 Easimatic. In reality it was a heavy-duty version of the Hydra-Matic Turbo 400. It was used for many years in the larger motor home chassis and medium-duty trucks.

The Titan 90 tandem-axle tractor added the Detroit Diesel 12V71, the largest engine ever offered in a Chevrolet truck. Horsepower outputs of 390, 434, or 475 filled the specialized needs of long-haul carriers pulling high gross loads. Base GVW was 48,500 pounds and 50,500 pounds when equipped with the optional 16,000-pound front axle and larger tires. Maximum GCW was 76,800 pounds.

The Fuller 13-speed transmission, a 12,000-pound front axle, and 38,000-pound Hendrickson rear boogie were standard equipment for the Titan 90.

History repeated itself in 1972. Remember when Volkswagen began to make inroads into the U.S. truck market in the late 1950s with its unique and very functional line of imported mini-vans and wagons? Ford and Chevrolet entered that market in 1961 and pushed VW's products back into the Atlantic Ocean. In 1965 imported trucks totaled fewer than 16,000 units. In 1971, their total reached an impressive 96,000 units, mostly Japanese-built mini-pickups. Ford and Chevrolet responded in the only way they could in a short time frame: they imported Japanese mini-pickups with their own nameplates affixed and sold them through their own dealer network. Chevrolet's LUV (Light Utility Vehicle) was built in Japan by GM's partner Isuzu Motors Ltd. of Tokyo. This small truck went on sale starting in late March 1972 at Chevrolet dealers. Initially it was sold only in the coastal areas of the United States where demand for these trucks was the strongest. LUV featured a roomy, comfortable cab, a four-cylinder engine, torsion bar independent front suspension, heavy frame, dual headlights, and bright grille trim. It had a maximum payload rating of 1,100 pounds, plus driver and passenger. This is a 1972 Chevrolet LUV 1/2-ton mini-pickup. It would be 10 more years before Chevrolet would begin to sell a mini-pickup engineered and assembled in the United States. *AAMA*

Because this was the last year for this style of truck, no major revisions were made in styling or engineering. Cab interiors were improved with molded plastic door trim panels. In effect, Chevrolet trucks were built with a body within a body. Chevrolet marketing called it a "Truck-and-a-half." To help preserve these trucks, Chevrolet painted them with baked acrylic enamel exterior paints in 15 color options. Both the cab and box were double walled. For long life Chevrolet included a fully aluminized exhaust system. The 292 inline six was discontinued as an option for 1/2-tons and the 3/4-ton Suburban. Pictured is a 1972 Chevrolet Series C10 Fleetside Cheyenne Super pickup. The four interior and exterior trim levels for 1972 Chevrolet pickups included Custom, Custom Deluxe, Cheyenne, and the top-of-the-line Cheyenne Super. *AAMA*

A longer 163-inch-wheelbase model was added to the Series 50 and 60 tilt-cab lineup.

In 1972, Chevrolet had a truck dealer network from coast to coast selling and servicing cars and trucks. Chevrolet had also signed on 120 specialized dealers who sold and serviced heavy-duty trucks.

America's love affair with the truck was in high gear in 1972. As early as February 1972, truck sales were racing 40 percent ahead of 1971. In its February 28, 1972, issue, *Time* magazine predicted the industry would build 2,200,000 trucks in 1972. The actual total for the calendar year was 2,446,807, an increase of 19 percent over 1971. The article further reported that the fastest growing segment of the business was pickups, which retailed for $2,800 to $4,300. *Time* magazine characterized pickups as recreational vehicles used for hauling campers and towing snowmobiles and/or dune buggies.

Another interesting statistic was that the Big Three produced 60 percent of the heavy-duty trucks sold in 1971 and the rest were built by the independents. This is a remarkable achievement in light of the fact that the Big Three only began building heavy-duty trucks in earnest in 1960.

Chevrolet benefited from the boom in light-duty trucks for personal transportation. Retail sales soared to 774,871, up from 643,668 in 1971. Chevrolet's management was confident that the company's first million Chevrolet truck sales year could happen as early as 1973. Chevrolet achieved this sales year record by selling from dealer's stocks, since production during 1972 fell short of sales. Strikes and the startup delays on the redesigned 1973 light-duty line caused the production shortfall.

Chevrolet's truck production for 1972 topped off at 770,741, which finished in second place to Ford, which built 25,000 more trucks than Chevrolet. Industrywide truck production in calendar year 1972 boomed to its second annual record in a row. The following five corporations combined to produce 97 percent of all trucks in 1972: General Motors, Ford, Chrysler, International, and American Motors.

Engine installations also hit highs. For the first time V-8 gas engine installations nudged the two million mark. Chevrolet's diesel engine installations increased from 2 percent of industry in 1971 to 2.7 percent of industry in 1972.

During the year, Chevrolet began importing the small LUV (Light Utility Vehicle) pickup from its Japanese partner Isuzu and sold 39,000 during the 1972 calendar year. Datsun imported the first of these small trucks in 1959. Toyota later joined Datsun, and by 1971 their combined sales total was in excess of 90,000 units. Chevrolet, Ford, and Mazda joined the hunt in 1972.

Detroit's marketing groups identified three types of buyers for these miniature trucks. First there were those who needed them for some practical business purpose: light delivery, hauling tools and equipment, and so on. Next there were those buyers looking for everyday transportation, which was even a bigger group. Some of these everyday trucks were fitted with camper shells or camper units. The third group consisted of those making these small trucks the "in" vehicle. They may not have served any practical function but were fashionable because they were able to express a distinct personality in a way that no other vehicle could quite capture.

Chevrolet's Stepside pickup continued to be offered in 14 models in three series—1/2-, 3/4-, and 1-ton models and choice of 2WD or 4WD. Engine options ranged all the way from the little 250 six to the stump-pulling 210 (net)-horsepower 400 V-8. Last year's 400 was rated for 300 gross horsepower and 240 net horsepower. The industry changed to these more realistic net horsepower numbers. Stepside pickups were the fair-haired boy with many truck aficionados who enjoyed personalizing them to suit their tastes. The 1972 C10 Stepside pickup pictured was just such a truck. It was lowered 3 1/2 inches in the front and 3 inches in the rear. Its hood was louvered and its tailgate was filled and louvered. An early Falcon rear bumper replaced the original and the taillights were lowered to fit the bumper. Its owner drove it daily in all types of weather. This photo was taken on June 4, 1981. *Ray Beagan*

Rural fire departments frequently bought 4WD pickups to serve as brush firefighters. The Greenville (New York) Fire District owned this 1972 Chevrolet K20 Fleetside Truck No. 1. Its special equipment was by Bean and included a 300-gallon water tank. Chevrolet's 4WD pickups offered excellent performance both on- and off-road. Power steering was an option; power brakes were standard equipment. The K20 4WD 3/4-ton pickup was rated for a maximum GVW of 7,500 pounds. Standard engines included the little 110-horsepower 250 six and the more powerful 135-horsepower 307 V-8. Optional engines included the 125-horsepower 292 six and the 210-horsepower 400 V-8. Transmission choices included the three- and four-speed manuals and the Turbo Hydra-Matic automatic. *Neal A. Van Deusen*

Chevrolet's small SUV, now in its fourth year, continued into 1972 without noticeable change. The Blazer's top-of-the-line model for 1972 was the CST K10 model. The 104-inch-wheelbase K10 8-cylinder (307) 4WD Blazer carried a manufacturer's suggested retail price of $3,258.25. The CST option number Z84 cost $355. It included the following equipment: vinyl bucket seats; console; RH sunshade and armrest; a cigar lighter; nameplates; special insulation; undercoating; chromed bumpers, control knobs; pedal trim; bright windshield, body side, tailgate, taillight, and back-up light moldings; bright fuel filler cap; side marker reflectors; and transfer case shift levers. It also included door and body trim panels with bright upper retainers, spare tire cover, and front color-keyed carpeting. The 350 V-8 cost $43 and the Turbo Hydra-Matic $236.

Chevrolet's other vans were the passenger-carrying models. Five-passenger seating was standard on all Sportvans. This included two front bucket seats and a rear bench seat. An additional three-passenger rear bench seat was available on 3/4- and 1-ton models. A third rear bench seat was available on 125-inch-wheelbase 1-ton models to increase seating capacity to 12. This is Chevrolet's first-class luxury passenger van, the Beauville Sportvan. It featured deep-pile carpeting and other soft trim, keyed to any of four interior colors—blue, green, parchment, or saddle—and a full-length headliner. The Sportvan's engine options were the same as for Chevy Van. *AAMA*

Chevrolet's new G-Series Chevy Van was only in its second full model year. It returned without styling change and few engineering improvements. Rear-axle capacities were increased to 3,100 pounds on the 1/2-ton and to 5,500 pounds on the 3/4-ton. All three Series G10-20-30 Chevy Vans could be ordered with either a 110- or 125-inch wheelbase. GVW ratings ranged from 4,500 to 8,300 pounds. Like all Chevrolet light-duty trucks, Chevy Vans featured independent front suspension. Driver's appreciated Chevy Van's soft, even, and controlled ride and its responsive handling. Chevy Vans featured standard, durable, fade-resistant, single-piston floating caliper disc brakes. Power brakes were standard on all but Series G10 models, where it was optional. *AAMA*

Most everyone believes that the 1967 to 1972 model year Chevrolet pickups were the finest-appearing trucks the division ever built. Most collectors and observers also agree that the 1971 and 1972 are the finest of the fine. If one truck can be singled out as the choicest of all, it is the 1972 Chevrolet Cheyenne Super, Series C10 pickup. The only item missing from this C10 is a two-tone paint scheme. Other than that, this truck has every option Chevrolet offered in 1972. It has been totally restored. It has the desirable 350 V-8 and Turbo Hydra-Matic automatic, air conditioning, power steering, and brakes.

Changes for Chevrolet's forward-control chassis line, motor-home chassis, and Step-Vans included engine improvements: stellite-faced exhaust valves in the 350 V-8s used in the 3/4- and 1-ton models, and exhaust valve rotators added to the 307 V-8. Other improvements included tough acrylic enamel exterior paint that resisted chipping, dirt pickup, and chemical spotting. A new tailpipe design for the 350 V-8 reduced engine noise. Improved water pump sealing, as well as higher capacity base front springs on the 1-ton Step-Van, rounded out the improvements for 1972. This is a 1972 Chevrolet P-10 Step-Van 7 with a short 102-inch wheelbase. Step-Vans continued to be built with either aluminum or steel bodies. The only engine for the P-10 models was the 250 six. *AAMA*

The most important news in Chevrolet's 1972 medium-duty truck line was the optional three-speed, Chevrolet-built automatic transmission, the AT475, for straight trucks. It was limited to models equipped with V-8 engines up to 366-ci, with GVWs not exceeding 19,500 pounds, or C40 and C50 models. This 1972 Chevrolet C60 chassis cab with firefighting body was owned by the Accord (New York) Fire District. Its body was built by American and included a 1,000-gallon water tank and a 750-gpm pump. The 230-horsepower 427 V-8 powered this truck. Its transmission was the Allison AT540. It carried a maximum GVW rating of 31,500 pounds. Like the light-duty Chevrolet trucks, medium-duty trucks also featured a special bathtub-type fender liner to help fight rust. *Neal A. Van Deusen*

Chevrolet's 1972 steel Tilt Cab Series included the 50 and 60 models. This is a 1972 Chevrolet T60 chassis cab with firefighting body. The Maple Bay (British Columbia, Canada) Fire District owned engine No. 32. Thibault built its body, and it featured a 1,000-gallon water tank and a 600-gpm pump. The high-torque 230-horsepower 427 V-8 engine powered this truck. A 163-inch-wheelbase model was added to 1972's 50 and 60 Series tilt-cab line. Chevrolet's short 72-inch tilt-cab design with its setback front axle was favored by fire departments, because its maneuverability and short turning diameters made it easy to snake through traffic. *FDG*

Camping was a popular activity with American families in 1972, and Chevrolet aggressively pursued this business. Chevrolet had many offerings, including pickups with Camper Special equipment for slide-on campers; regular pickups with shell campers; camping trailers towed by pickups, Suburbans, El Caminos, Blazers, Chevy Vans, and even the Vega Panel Express. There were full-sized family travel trailers towed by various trucks; Chevy Van conversions; Chevy Van Mini-motor-home conversions; Chevrolet motor-home chassis with bodies by others; and chassis-mounted campers. This is a 1972 C30 chassis cab with camper. The C30's standard dual rear wheels gave this unit unusually good stability. These units were self-contained with range, refrigerator, toilet, shower, and other features. A typical chassis cab and camper sold for between $6,300 and $9,300. Most often, the popular 175-horsepower 350 V-8 with an automatic transmission powered them.

Chevrolet's stunning 1972 El Camino continued the long-running tradition of building the industry's finest dual-purpose carlike pickup. Up front, the El Camino was a luxurious passenger car; out back it was a cargo box that featured double-wall construction and a tailgate the owner could open with one hand. Also the El Camino was as adept at pulling a load as it was carrying a load. An El Camino SS model was offered in 1972. Its available engines ranged up to a 454 V-8. The 454 V-8 could be ordered with a four-speed manual or smooth Turbo Hydra-Matic transmissions. Appearance items for the SS included 15x7-inch sport wheels with white letter bias belted ply F60x15 tires, a Cowl Induction hood with hood pins, center console, Strato-bucket seats, tachometer, and other special instruments. Air Booster rear shocks were standard equipment.

155

Many Chevrolet pickup collectors believe the 1972 Fleetside Cheyenne Super C20 pickup (pictured) is the best looking and most desirable truck Chevrolet ever built. What makes this pickup even more interesting is the fact that it looks nearly as good from the back as it does from the front. This particular truck is unique, too, because it is all original and is in surprisingly good shape. The owner does plan to give it a frame-off restoration. It is powered by the largest engine Chevrolet offered in 1972, the 210-horsepower 400 V-8, and is equipped with Chevrolet's durable three-speed Turbo Hydra-Matic. *Phyllis and Merlin Mausolf*

The biggest-selling medium- and heavy-duty series in Chevrolet's line were the Conventional Series C40-50-60, single-axle models, and ME60 tandem axle. This was the last year for these trucks. They were replaced with a new series in 1973. The optional 230-horsepower 427 V-8 engine powered this ME60 tandem-axle tractor with refrigerated trailer for hauling produce. The ME60 carried a maximum GCW rating of 60,000 pounds. Tandem-axle equipment included rugged 30,000- and 34,000-pound Eaton axles and Hendrickson suspension. This truck listed for $10,679 without options, the 427 V-8 added $220.60. *Dick Copello*

1973

This was another pivotal year for Chevrolet trucks. Chevrolet engineers completely redesigned and reengineered the C/K pickups, Blazer, Suburban, and medium-duty (C50, 60 and 65s) trucks. Those that carried over either without changes or with only minor styling updates included the Vega Panel, El Camino, Chevy Van, Step-Vans, Tilts, short and long conventionals, and the Titan.

Chevrolet's former light-duty truck line (1967 to 1972) had just completed a phenomenally successful six-year run. But the best was yet to come. Between 1967 and 1973 pickups metamorphosed. The former compact truck that served two purposes—daily transportation and light hauling of almost anything—had grown heavy, big, and comfortable. Interiors changed from Spartan to sumptuous with fancy fabric upholstery, carpeting, padded doors, and interior roof panels. Air conditioning was one sensible addition. Because of the pickup's new weight and size, power steering and brakes became necessities.

The reasons behind all the change and improvements, including increased size, of America's new-found favorite vehicle was due above all to the national freeway system. It successfully tied America together from coast to coast and border to border with safe, high-speed, divided highways. Secondly, Americans discovered they could take advantage of the new freeway system and enjoy safe and comfortable traveling or camping, most often by pulling a trailer or carrying a camper on the family pickup.

In November 1973 Chevrolet announced that the 1/2-ton Fleetside pickup was the largest-selling body style of any GM passenger car or truck series. GM gave much of the credit for the success of the 1/2-ton pickup to women and urban dwellers who had come to appreciate its versatility and found it to be attractive as a second vehicle for many families. Chevrolet's total sales of 1/2-ton Fleetside pickups for the year exceeded 300,000.

Chevrolet's LUV mini pickup was new in March of 1972. Chevrolet's marketing team found that it made some mistakes with it in the early days. Marketing looked on it as an economy vehicle and reasoned therefore that it should be sold as bare-bones transportation. This turned out to be a mistake, as bare-bones products rarely do well in the U.S. market. When dressed up with dealer-installed flashy options, the LUV began to do well. Chevrolet designed a luxury cab interior option, the Mikado, but this would not be ready until 1974.

In 1973, Chevrolet sold about 39,000 LUVs, compared with 21,098 in 1972.

Recreational Vehicles (RVs) continued to be big business in 1973. Chevrolet offered a total of four motor-home chassis. Two new units made their debut in 1973: A 158 1/2-inch-wheelbase chassis and a big 178-inch chassis with a GVW of 14,000 pounds. Chevrolet was deeply involved in the lucrative RV market with Camper Special pickup packages, towing packages, and the options and amenities campers wanted. Pickup campers were the second most popular types of RVs, bested only by travel trailers. In 1973 there were 1.7 million travel trailers on the road and 1.1 million pickup campers. Motor homes had only 6 percent of the market at 240,000 units.

Chevrolet engineers labored hard to develop the trucks buyers told them they wanted. The fresh new Chevrolet trucks once again made a splash. Engineers concentrated on many things, such as appearance, both interior and exterior. They also worked on a smooth but safe ride, a wide, three-person cab, power for every purpose, and a wraparound instrument panel with full instrumentation—no warning lights.

The standard Chevrolet six was the 250 model; the 292 six was optional. The standard V-8 was the 307. An optional V-8 included

Chevrolet's pickup line was new for 1973—reengineered and restyled. Chevrolet engineers' major areas of concern with the new light-duty trucks was providing a comfortable ride in a new wide, luxurious cab; attractive exterior styling to suit the demands of fleet buyers and individuals; a stronger and deeper frame; durability; and a host of optional equipment. The top-of-the-line pickup model was the C-10 1/2-ton Fleetside Cheyenne Super. Four series were offered: Custom, Custom Deluxe, Cheyenne, and Cheyenne Super. The simulated wood-grain insert on fenders and cab was also carried over into the interior with wood-grain trim on the new instrument panel. *AAMA*

Also new for 1973 was the most powerful engine ever in a Chevrolet 2WD pickup, the 240 net-horsepower 454 V-8. Net torque was a brawny 355 foot-pounds at 2,800 rpm. It was recommended for applications involving unusually heavy loads such as carrying a camper or towing a heavy trailer. The 454 was optional on C10, C20, and C30 trucks only, not on 4WDs. The 1973 C10 Cheyenne Fleetside pickup pictured was equipped with the optional 454 and Turbo Hydra-Matic automatic. This truck has clocked 113,000 miles and is used for daily transportation. It has a 3.07 rear axle and base vinyl upholstery. *Mike Larson*

Fleetside pickups were by far the most popular, but many buyers still preferred the traditional Stepside style. This is a 1973 117.5-inch-wheelbase K10 4WD Stepside with a 6 1/2-foot cargo box. This pickup's name was derived from its convenient side steps in front of the rear fenders. The cargo box has a floor made of kiln-dried southern pine supported by heavy steel cross sills. Chevrolet's 4WDs were designed to provide an extremely low silhouette, yet maintain the necessary ground clearance for off-road driving. Two standard engines were available: the 250 six and 350 V-8. *Jim McDermott*

Also new was a six-man 3 + 3 crew-cab with four doors and seating for six. It could be ordered directly from a Chevrolet dealer. Previously those buyers in need of a six-passenger pickup had to buy a standard cab model and have it custom modified by an outside firm. Its two full-width foam-cushioned seats accommodated six in comfort. The new 3 + 3 was available in both Series 20 and 30, either as Fleetside pickup or chassis cab models. Dual rear wheels were also available on Fleetside pickups. This is a 1973 C20 crew cab Fleetside pickup. *AAMA*

The 1973 Suburban received the same new body, instrument panel, and wide front seat. This was the first Suburban with four side doors. When equipped with double rear doors, it became a six-door Suburban. Also new was a station wagonlike tailgate with a manually retractable window. An electric window was an option. This was the first year for the Cheyenne Super luxury model pictured here. The Suburban was offered in three trim levels—Custom, Custom Deluxe, and Cheyenne Super. The two-tone paint scheme was called a Special Two-Tone. This meant white paint between chrome upper and lower side moldings. The "Estate" model was similar but used a wood-grain exterior in place of the white paint and included an "Estate" nameplate. *AAMA*

the 350. But the biggest and most powerful V-8 that was ever offered in a Chevy 2WD pickup was the 454. The 454, a stroked 427 V-8, replaced the 400 (402). The biggest V-8 available for 4WD trucks was the impressive 350 V-8. 4WD models were available only in the K10 and K20 series.

Also new for 1973 was the big 3+3 six-passenger four-door crew cab. The 3+3 was offered only in Series C20 and C30. Dual rear wheels were also available on Fleetside conventional cab 1-ton pickups.

New for 1973 Chevrolet Fleetside pickups were a choice of four luxurious cabs. The Custom interior was the base model; the

Custom Deluxe was the first step up; the Cheyenne interior was next up the line; and at the top of the line was the Cheyenne Super. There were four levels of exterior trim to accompany each of the four interior trim levels.

Chevrolet truck output for the entire calendar year totaled a record 1,013,860 trucks versus the previous year's high of 770,773. Chevrolet set an industry milestone on December 19, 1973, by

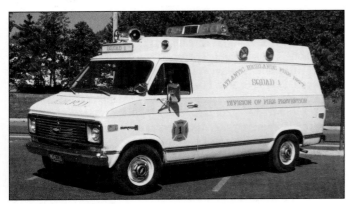

Chevy Van was all new in 1971, so unlike the conventional Chevrolet light-duty trucks, it didn't change in 1973. This 1973 G10 1/2-ton van had been converted to service as a fire prevention vehicle for the Atlantic Highlands (New Jersey) Fire Department. Chevy Vans were routinely converted to increase their height and cubic capacity for any number of commercial purposes. Note the raised roof on this fire truck. Chevy Vans were equipped with a sliding right-side cargo door, which required only 4 1/2 inches of clearance to open. The wheelbase on the 1/2-ton Chevy Van was 110 inches and GVW rating was 5,100 pounds. Standard engines were the 250 six and 307 V-8. The 350 V-8 was an option. *Scott Mattson*

New for 1973 was the Step-Van with extended hood design for quick and easy service. The front-opening hood provided improved engine accessibility. The trim 102-inch-wheelbase design of the Step-Van 7 (7-foot body) allowed it to maneuver in and around heavy city traffic. The Step-Van 7 was short in length, but long on quality. Other features included sliding side doors and extensive rustproofing. A new interior height of almost 69 inches allowed the driver to comfortably work his load. The 7-foot body offered 225 cubic feet of load space; the 8-foot body a generous 258 cubic feet. The Step-Van's standard engine was the 150 six; it could be mated to a three-speed manual transmission or a smooth automatic. *AAMA*

Chevrolet's Blazer also came in for a complete redo, acquiring the same new good looks of the pickup and Suburban. Chevrolet continued to offer both 2WD and 4WD versions. This was the last year for part-time 4WD. When equipped with 4WD, the Blazer offered plenty of ground clearance, 7 inches, but still retained a pleasingly low silhouette. The standard engine was the 250 six with either 2WD or 4WD; the 350 V-8 was optional, equipped with either a two- or four-barrel carburetor. Transmission options included three- and four-speed manuals and the Turbo Hydra-Matic. This is a 1973 Cheyenne Blazer. *AAMA*

Chevrolet engineers moved the front axle forward to provide a long wheelbase for the 1973 chassis cab and stake models. Their redesigned chassis and frame offered a stronger, stable foundation for special bodies or the platform, which is pictured. Chassis cab 2WD models were built in 10, 20, and 30 Series and 4WD models in 10 and 20 Series only. With dual wheels, GVWs ranged up to 10,000 pounds. Combination two-stage and auxiliary rear springs were available on C30 models to handle big loads or rough roads. Heavy-duty rear shock absorbers were also available. Chevrolet's entire light-duty engine line was offered on C30 trucks: 250 and 292 sixes and 307, 350, and 454 V-8s.

breaking the one million truck mark with one year's production. It erased the old calendar year record of 795,987 set by Ford in 1972.

Retail sales for the year topped off at 1,055,273. This broke the previous calendar year industry truck sales record of 909,577 for a single make set by Ford in 1972.

Combined car and truck production of 3,347,995 at the Chevrolet Division shattered by 7.7 percent the old record of 3,107,178 set in 1965. It was 8.8 percent ahead of 1972's combined assembly record of 3,070,545.

These records are even more amazing in light of the Arab oil embargo, which cut back on gasoline production in favor of home heating oil and caused gas rationing. Because of this, sales of large cars took a heavy hit in the fourth quarter.

GM's worldwide factory sales of cars and trucks totaled 8,684,000 units, compared with the previous high of 7,791,000 units sold in 1972. GM's 1973 worldwide sales of $35.8 billion set a new record for the corporation. Profits, however, were off slightly—to 6.7 percent versus 7.1 percent in 1972.

The truck industry enjoyed a tremendous year that pushed sales to 3.1 million units. Going into the year, the industry only projected total sales of 2.8 million.

According to U. S. Department of Commerce figures, fully 63 percent of all trucks in operation in 1972 were pickups. The largest single use of trucks in 1972, according to the same report, was for personal transportation. The report didn't say so, but we can safely assume the lion's share of this number were pickups.

Chevrolet produced a total of 1,013,784 truck engines in calendar year 1973. This number breaks down as follows: 3,270 fours

(Vega Panel Express), 96,373 sixes, 909,548 V-8s, and 4,593 diesels. It is interesting to note that Ford actually built almost exactly 8,000 more sixes than Chevrolet, but Chevrolet built almost 90,000 more V-8s. It's also interesting to note that only six years before, in 1967, Chevrolet built more truck sixes than V-8s, by 280,000 to 267,000.

The Rock Community Fire District of Arnold, Missouri, employed this 1973 tilt-cab tanker truck. Chevrolet offered the tilt cab in two Series: 60 and 65. This Series 65 tanker was powered by the optional high torque 427 V-8; the 366 V-8 was standard. Maximum GVW rating for Series TE65 was 32,500 pounds. Standard transmission was the four-speed New Process 435L and the AT540 Allison automatic was optional. The cast spoke wheels were standard equipment along with air brakes. *Dennis J. Maag*

Chevrolet's conventional cab medium-duty trucks were also all new for 1973. An alligator-type hood provided access for routine maintenance, inspection, or servicing of the engine and other underhood components. A tilting fiberglass hood was also available. The entire hood, fenders, and front end were one unit and tilted to allow complete access to the engine. Use of the fiberglass hood reduced weight and increased the payload by an equal amount. For driver safety, the cab roof was of the double-wall type, consisting of an inner and outer panel, welded together to form a strong, durable assembly. This is a 1973 Series 65 conventional tandem ME65 with dump body. Maximum GVW of this rig was 43,000 pounds. Standard engine was the 366 V-8; the 427 V-8 was an option. No diesel was offered. *AAMA*

Chevrolet's conventional medium-duty trucks were offered in three Series: 50-60-65. This is a 1973 C60 chassis cab with a 300-gallon Semo tank body belonging to the Goldman, Missouri, fire department. This truck was right in the middle of Chevrolet's medium-duty conventional line and was rated for a maximum GVW of 24,000 pounds. It has the alligator-type hood and ventilated steel-disc wheels. The standard engine was the 305 GMC-built V-6, which was rated for an SAE net horsepower of 148 at 4,000 rpm and SAE net torque of 238 foot-pounds at 1,600 rpm. The 379 V-6 was the optional engine. It was also a GMC engine and was designed specifically for heavy-duty truck service. It produced SAE net horsepower of 170 at 3,600 rpm and SAE net torque of 266 foot-pounds at 1,600 rpm. *Dennis J. Maag*

This 1973 Chevrolet tandem C65 fire truck model number ME65 is equipped with an American tank with a 750-gallon capacity. The truck belongs to the Tillson, New York, fire department. It is fitted with an alligator hood, a front-mounted water pump, steel-spoke wheels, and air brakes. The 230 SAE net-horsepower V-8 produced 360 foot-pounds SAE net torque power for this C65. Tandem suspension was the Hendrickson driving and braking forces were transmitted through torque rods and equalizing beams. Eaton rear axles allowed a maximum GVW rating of 34,000 pounds. *Neal A. Van Deusen*

Chevrolet's conventional Series 70-80 trucks carried over with minimal changes. This Series 80 short conventional gas tractor featured a trim 93-inch BBC dimension for increased maneuverability in city operation, and it had the ability to carry extra long loads and still stay within maximum length requirements. A butterfly-type side opening hood swung up and out of the way for easy access to the engine, oil filter, oil dipstick, radiator cap, and other service points. Gas engine options included the 432 V-6 and the 478 V-6. Both engines were designed for heavy-duty truck operation and had large bores and short strokes. High torque was available over a broad range of speeds. SAE net-horsepower ratings were 190 and 192 at 3,200 rpm and SAE net torque ratings were 336 and 371 foot-pounds, respectively. Only one diesel engine was offered, the famous Detroit Diesel "318." *AAMA*

Chevrolet's long, conventional diesel tractors also carried over with minimal changes. This Series 90 long conventional diesel tractor was only available with diesel power. The buyer could specify one of five Detroit Diesel engines or one of six Cummins' engines. It carried a maximum GCW rating of 76,800 pounds or, as a tandem, 50,500 pounds. Full air brakes were standard equipment. It was a Class 8 truck. Its tilting hood and front fender assemblies were constructed of lightweight, strong fiberglass-reinforced plastic. This assembly tilted forward to expose the entire engine. A butterfly-type hood was available on Series 90 short Conventionals. *AAMA*

Chevrolet's top-of-the-line heavy-duty Class 8 Titan 90 aluminum tilt-cab was now in its fourth model year. It continued without change. This truck was also powered only by diesel engines. Cummins supplied five models with SAE net-horsepower ranging up to 319 and SAE net torque climbing up to 890 foot-pounds. Also listed as standard were six Detroit Diesel models ranging in SAE net horsepower up to 390 and SAE net torque ratings up to a mighty 1,078 foot-pounds. A 1979 Chevrolet Titan 90 single-axle day cab tractor shown. The 238-horsepower Detroit Diesel 6-71 powered this tractor. It has a 10-speed Road Ranger transmission and air assist steering. *Bill Wasner*

Chevrolet's 1973 Series 90 Short Conventional's tilting hood and front fender assemblies were constructed of lightweight, fiberglass-reinforced plastic. For servicing, the entire assembly tilted forward as a unit to expose the engine, radiator, and front-end components. A butterfly-type steel hood was standard on Series 70 and 80 models and optional on Series 90 Short Conventionals. Hood panels swung up and out of the way for servicing. The single axle's maximum GVW was 33,500 pounds, and its maximum GCW was 76,800 pounds. The tandem-axle model's maximum GVWs ranged from 45,500 to 50,500 pounds and maximum GCW was 76,800 pounds. Diesel engines from Detroit Diesel and Cummins were the only power sources. *Dick Copello*

The Central Minnesota farmer owner of this 1973 Chevrolet Series 90 Conventional tandem chassis cab with grain body was still using it in 1998, when this photo was taken. Its powertrain consisted of the Detroit Diesel 8V-71N engine along with a Fuller RT09513 three-speed main. Chevrolet engineer's specified five Detroit Diesel and five Cummins engines. Engine horsepower outputs ranged from 201 to 325 and from 552 to 939 foot-pounds net torque. This truck had a single-speed 38,000-pound capacity tandem rear axle.

1974

Chevrolet had completely restyled its entire light-duty truck line in 1973 including pickups, Blazers, and Suburbans. The medium-duty C50, C60, C65, and M65 Series were also restyled and reengineered that year, because they shared a cab with light-duty conventional trucks. Therefore, there were no significant styling changes for the light-duty and medium-duty trucks in 1974.

Chevrolet did, however, change to full-time 4WD for its entire line. Full-time 4WD was only available on V-8 Blazers in 1973. The full-time 4WD system provided continuous power to all wheels at all times, with an additional differential within the transfer case, compensating for the difference in revolutions between the front and rear wheels. The third differential could be locked out when encountering heavy, off-road terrain. Full-time 4WD was made possible by the Chrysler-owned New Process Gear Co.'s transfer case.

The only new model from Chevrolet for 1974 was a Cutaway Van for use as a motor home chassis. The LUV pickup, Vega Panel Express, El Camino, Chevy Vans, Chevy Sportvans, Step-Vans, conventional mediums, medium- and heavy-duty tilt cabs, Titan Series, and the heavy-duty long- and short-nose conventionals were carried over.

In spite of the fuel crisis that hit the last quarter of 1973, the 4WD market did not collapse, as some predicted. As a matter of fact, 4WD sales for 1974 increased over the year before. This was interesting, since the 4WD vehicle was recognized as a gas guzzler at a time when fuel economy was foremost on people's minds.

Sales of 4WDs were so strong that suppliers of certain key components had difficulty keeping up with the demand. In fact, 4WD sales in the United States had tripled since 1969. Many owners used their 4WD trucks for pleasure, off-roading, and vacationing.

The fuel crisis had some influence on industrywide sales of engines in 1974. The V-8 engine lost a share of the market, falling from 83 percent in 1973 to 79 percent in 1974. Commercial buyers may have influenced more of this crossover than buyers of

trucks for personal transportation. Six-cylinder engines picked up 3 of the percentage points lost by V-8s, and diesels picked up the other 1 percent.

The El Camino was given a new, fresh appearance for 1974, due to the Chevrolet automobile on which it was based. As was true for 1973, only V-8 power was offered for El Camino. However, a new V-8 was added: the Turbo-Fire 400 with either a two-barrel or

Chevrolet's best-selling pickup was the C10 Fleetside. Because this was only the second year for this series, its styling was unchanged. When this 1974 Fleetside Cheyenne Super pickup was photographed in October 1998, it still looked good as new, even though it was being used for daily transportation. It was equipped with the 350 V-8 with a two-barrel carburetor mated to the optional Turbo Hydra-Matic. A four-barrel 350 and a four-barrel 454 were options. The Cheyenne Super's interior was the lap of luxury, featuring a fabric-covered bench seat with a full-depth foam cushion almost 7 inches thick. A full-gauge instrument panel was set in a simulated wood-grained panel trimmed with chrome.

a four-barrel carburetor. The new 400 was a small block–based engine in order to reduce weight and size.

This was the last year for the GMC V-6 engine in the larger trucks, and the last year for the larger gas and diesel steel tilt cabs. However, gas-powered medium-duty steel tilt cabs were still offered.

Chevrolet truck production and sales in 1974 were not affected as much as the car division, but they lost ground nevertheless. Production was at 867,913, compared to 1,013,860 in 1973.

Retail sales fell from 1,055,273 in 1973 to 885,362 in 1974. Despite this, it was Chevrolet's second best truck sales year.

Chevrolet car sales, on the other hand, fell to their lowest level since 1970. Only 1,903,857 cars were built in 1974. This was an 18.3 percent drop from 1973's 2,334,113. Factors affecting car sales included the energy crisis and a two-month strike at GM's Lordstown, Ohio, plant, the only plant building the subcompact Vega. Other work disruptions and steep price increases held car sales down.

Chevrolet's second-best-selling pickup in 1974 was the C10 Fleetside with the 6 1/2-foot cargo box. This truck is Washington (Missouri) Fire Department Foam Supply Unit No. 156. To keep its cost down, the fire department purchased the base, no-frills Custom model. The 250, 100-horsepower six mated to the three-speed manual transmission power it. Standard cab trim included vinyl seat upholstery and a black rubber floor mat. Its silver plastic grille insert, chrome door handles, chrome Custom nameplate, white-painted front bumper, and hub caps are standard equipment for the Custom model. *Dennis Maag*

Chevrolet's four-door six-passenger 3 + 3 crew cab pickup was a new model. This 1974 C30 "Big Dooley" Cheyenne was still in daily use when photographed in July 1998. It is equipped with the 8-foot Fleetside cargo box covered with an aftermarket topper. Two full-width foam-cushioned seats seated six comfortably. This model was also available with Camper Special Equipment. The standard engine for this truck was the 250-ci, 100-horsepower six, but mostly these big pickups were powered by the 230-horsepower 454 V-8 producing 350 foot-pounds SAE net torque. With dual rear wheels, this huge pickup was a favorite with owners towing heavily laden trailers.

Chevrolet offered a full range of forward-control chassis and Step-Vans in Series P10, P20, and P30. Forward-control chassis featured 102-, 125-, 133-, and 157-inch-wheelbase lengths on which buyers could mount custom van bodies in 9-, 10-, 12-, and 14-foot lengths. Chevrolet also offered a complete line of Step-Vans on the same four wheelbase lengths with factory-supplied bodies ranging in length from 7 to 14 1/2-feet. The 1974 102-inch-wheelbase Chevrolet P10 Step-Van 7 with aluminum body pictured was also available with an 8-foot body. The only engine offered was the 250 six. A three-speed manual transmission was standard and a four-speed manual and a Turbo Hydra-Matic were options. GVWs ranged from a low of 4,900 pounds for the P10 Series to 14,000 pounds for the P30 Series. *AAMA*

The St. Clair, Missouri, Fire Department operated this 1974 Custom C30 chassis cab, equipped with a Steelweld utility body. The 1-ton chassis cab was rated for a maximum GVW of 10,000 pounds. This 131 1/2 inch-wheelbase truck is equipped with the optional 120-horsepower 292 six. Its SAE net torque is 215 foot-pounds at 2,000 rpm. Two transmissions were offered: the standard four-speed manual and the optional Turbo Hydra-Matic. All conventional cab Chevrolet trucks came standard with power flow-through ventilation. When the ignition was turned on, the heater fan automatically brought in outside air, which exhausted through outlet valves at the bottom of each side door. The same system also provided for pressure relief when closing the doors with all windows rolled up. *Dennis J. Maag*

Chevrolet's forward-control chassis could be fitted with special van bodies to meet the buyer's needs. Several major body manufacturers were approved by Chevrolet to assist forward-control customers. The New Melle (Missouri) Fire Protection District chose a 1974 Chevrolet P20 forward-control chassis onto which the Boyertown Auto Body Works, of Boyertown, Pennsylvania, mounted this Fire Rescue body. Maximum GVW rating was 8,000 pounds. Standard engine was the 250 six. The 292 six was an option, as was the 350 V-8. Power disc/drum brakes were standard equipment, as was manual steering. Power steering was an option. *Dennis J. Maag*

The lighter of Chevrolet's three steel tilt-cab trucks was this 1974 T60 750-gallon tank fire truck owned by the Nevada Division of Forestry at Spring Creek. It is a former U.S. Marine Corps truck. Chevrolet built this setback front-axle beauty in a broad range of wheelbase lengths: 97, 109, 133, 145, 163, and 175 inches. It was enough to suit almost any vocational application. The standard engine was the 350 V-8. The powerful 366 V-8 was an option. Maximum GVW rating for the T60 was a big 25,000 pounds. The cab tilted forward a full 55 degrees to expose the engine and front components. There was plenty of room for a mechanic to stand between the frame and front tire to work on the engine. *Garry E. Kadzielawski*

The middle series medium-duty Chevrolet for 1974 was the C60 pictured with a 400-gallon pumper fire body. This series was now in only its second year. It's interesting to note that its life would eventually total 17 years. Its standard engine was the 292 six; the 350 and 366 V-8s were options. Maximum GVW was 24,000 pounds. Series 60 wheelbases included nine selections ranging from 125 to 218 inches. Chevrolet and its dealers encouraged buyers to select from a wide selection of off-road and/or heavy-duty components as well as custom equipment of all types to suit the buyer's job. *Dennis J. Maag*

Chevrolet built three Series of steel tilt-cab trucks in 1974: T60-65-80. This 1974 T65 chassis cab with pumper body by American had a maximum GVW rating of 32,500 pounds. The Boles Fire Prevention District of Labadic, Missouri, owned the truck. The standard engine for the T65 was the 366 V-8. The truck pictured here is equipped with the 427 V-8. Transmission choices included four-speed and five-speed manuals from New Process, an Allison automatic, and Clark models 282 and 285. The tilt cab was big and roomy but only had seating for two. However, a one- or two-passenger auxiliary seat was an option. *Dennis J. Maag*

Chevrolet built its conventional series medium-duty trucks in four series: C50, C60, C65, and tandem C65. GVWs ranged from 18,500 to 43,000 pounds and GCWs when used as a tractor ranged from 45,000 to 60,000 pounds. This is a 1974 Chevrolet C50 fire truck from the Washington, Missouri, Fire Department. The standard engine for this truck was the 250 six, and the 292 six was optional. The 50 series was offered in wheelbases ranging from 125 to 167 inches for a wide range of applications. These trucks shared a cab with the new pickups. *Dennis J. Maag*

Chevrolet's biggest single-rear-axle conventional medium-duty truck for 1974 was the C65. This Three Rivers District No. 2 Fire Rescue truck from Palmer, Massachusetts, had a custom body by Providence. Note its heavy-duty custom extended front bumper with front-mounted pump. The cast spoke wheels were standard for Series 65. Air brakes were an available option. The standard engine for this truck was the 366 V-8; the 427 V-8 was an option. Maximum GVW rating was 31,500 pounds. This truck has the top-of-the-line Custom Deluxe cab appointments. Its wide bench seat was comfortable for three big men. *Fred Cote*

Chevrolet's two Class 8 models were the Titan 90 and the Conventional cab Series 90, which is pictured. Both trucks were powered only by diesel engines. The buyer of this Series 90 tandem tractor had a choice of five two-cycle Detroit Diesels and five Cummins diesels. The biggest engine in the line was the Cummins NTC350, boasting 325 horsepower and 939 foot-pounds torque. Both short and long hood Conventional models were offered; pictured is the short Conventional. The hood and front fender assemblies of all 90 Series models tilted for easy engine servicing. A butterfly-type steel hood was also available on Series 90 short Conventionals only. Hood panels swung up and out of the way for routine maintenance. *AAMA*

Chevrolet's other conventional heavy-duty truck line was Series 70-80-90. Chevrolet segregated the "light" Series 70-80 models from the Class 8 Series 90 heavy-duty. This is a 1974 Series 70 single-axle tractor. The Model HV70 single-axle tractor was rated for a GCW rating of 55,000 pounds. The only diesel engine offered for this model was the Detroit Diesel 6V-53N, the famous "318." Its displacement was 318-ci, from which it produced SAE net horsepower of 190 at 2,800 rpm and SAE net torque of 414 foot-pounds at 1,800 rpm. No gas engines were available for the HV70. All Chevrolet heavy-duty trucks were rebadged as GMCs, built in GMC plants, and engineered by GMC's engineering department. *AAMA*

This farmer-owned 1974 Chevrolet ME65 tandem twin-screw chassis cab with grain body was hard at work in September 1998, when photographed at the Gibbon, Minnesota, Farmer's Elevator. It is powered by a 427 V-8 and has a five-speed transmission and a four-speed auxiliary. The cab and body had been recently repainted, and it looked as if it were new. The owner said it still works as well as did when it was new. These big farm trucks are typically not driven many miles per year, usually during a short harvest season, and then back into the shed until next year.

Chevrolet's top-of-the-line pickup was the C-10 Cheyenne Super Fleetside. This truck was used for daily transportation by its trucker owner, who specified his personal truck for comfortable cruising: the 145-horsepower two-barrel 350 V-8 (a 160-horsepower four-barrel 350 was also available), Turbo Hydra-Matic, with power steering, power brakes, and air conditioning. Creature comfort cab features included a fabric upholstered 7-inch-thick foam-cushioned bench seat; door trim panels in simulated wood-grain and storage pockets; nylon carpeting; insulated headliner; and insulation under the seat, floor, cowl, hood, and on the cab's back panel for quiet luxury. *Verne L. Byers*

The biggest 1974 Chevrolet Conventional Series truck was the ME65 tandem. The optional 230-horsepower 427 V-8 teamed with the five-speed ALLISON MT650G automatic powered this big black beauty. The standard engine for this model was the 200-horsepower 366 V-8. Standard air brakes were required with the automatic. The maximum GVW of the tandem was 43,000 pounds; maximum GCW was 60,000 pounds. The tandem setup consisted of a Hendrickson suspension and Eaton tandem rear axles with capacities of either 30,000 or 34,000 pounds. A driver-operated differential lockout supplied equal power to front and rear axles. Buyers had a choice of hoods: either all-steel alligator-type or an optional fiberglass where hood, fenders, and front end tilted open as a single unit to allow complete access to engine and front-end components. *Verne L. Byers*

Chevrolet's regular school bus chassis were offered in four wheelbases—189 1/2, 165 1/2, 267 1/4, and 327 1/4 inches—to accommodate bodies with capacities from 48 to 66 students. A few of the well-known school bus body makers who supplied bodies included Blue Bird, Wayne, Superior Coach, Carpenter Body Works, Ward Body Works, and Perley A. Thomas Car Works. Available engines for school bus chassis included both gas and diesels. The gas engine line included the 292 in-line six and 379 V-6. Available V-8s included the 305, 350, and heavy-duty 366. The only diesel was the 478 V-6. Manual transmission choices included a standard four-speed (five-speed on diesel models) and five-speeds, both regular and close-ratio. Automatics included the three-speed AT475 and four-speed AT540. This is a 1974 Chevrolet school bus chassis cowl with body by Blue Bird.

The Suburban was a suburban woman's best friend. The marketing group's strategy for selling Suburbans was as a truck-built station wagon. This was the classic case of a no contest. Suburban would outhaul and outpull any station wagon. The Suburban was the only wagon with 4WD. Like an ordinary wagon, the Suburban offered a wagon-type tailgate with a retractable window. After cranking down the glass, the tailgate could be lowered. An electrically operated rear window was an option. C20 Suburban was capable of towing up to 14,000 pounds GCW when equipped with the 230 net-horsepower 454 engine and with either the Turbo Hydra-Matic or four-speed manual transmission. Seating capacity was up to nine adults, all facing forward (some wagons at that time had a rear-facing back seat). The second seat folded and the third seat was removable for cargo hauling. *AAMA*

Chevrolet's big Series 70 steel tilt cabs were available with either single or tandem axles. The WV70 tandem-axle model pictured here carried a maximum GVW of 44,500 pounds and maximum GCW of 60,000 pounds. This truck was powered only by Detroit Diesel's famous "318" 6V-53N two-cycle diesel. It produced 190 horsepower at 2,800 rpm and 414 foot-pounds torque at 1,800 rpm. A five-speed synchro manual transmission was standard, and Allison automatics were optional in four- and five-speed versions. The cast spoke wheels were standard equipment; ten-stud disc wheels were optional. Full air brakes were also standard. *AAMA*

Mini-motor homes were big business in 1974. This was a time when camping was most popular. Chevrolet competed in the motor-homes segment in addition to van camper conversions, trailering, pickup campers, and motor home chassis. Chevrolet's Mini-motor home chassis was new in 1974. It was a chassis engineered and built for easy economical conversion into a Mini-motor home. The wheelbase was 146 inches and GVW was up to 8,400 pounds with the standard 350 V-8. An 8,900-pound rating was also offered with dual rear wheels and other heavy-duty equipment. Motor-home bodies were added by various outside suppliers. *Harold Chevrolet*

This is a 1974 Chevrolet Series 90 Long Conventional tandem chassis cab with dump body. This model carried a maximum GVW of 50,500 pounds and GCW of 76,800 pounds. An important advantage of Chevrolet's 115-inch BBC Series 90 Long Conventional diesel was that it had ample room for a Detroit Diesel 8V-71 or a Cummins NTC-350 diesel engine. The entire engine was forward of the firewall, resulting in outstanding accessibility, and eliminating the doghouse provided more room inside the cab. *Dick Copello*

1975

Chevrolet's 1975 trucks, now in their third model year, came in for a few timely modifications and improvements. But before getting into the details, a few words about the numbers game the industry played with the EPA in 1975. The cutoff between a "light" truck and a "heavy" truck was set at 6,000 pounds GVW. A truck whose GVW rating fell below this figure was required to be equipped with a catalytic converter and in turn burn unleaded fuel. Consequently, manufacturers built light-duty trucks with enough heavy-duty components to raise their GVWs just above the magic number of 6,000 pounds.

The EPA's 1975 emissions classifications put most Series 10 models in the light-duty emission vehicle group (up to 6,001 pounds GVW), thus requiring them to have catalytic converters. Heavy-duty Series 10 and all 20 and 30 Series fell into the heavy-duty emissions category and were not required to have a catalytic converter or run on unleaded gasoline.

The 350 was no longer the largest V-8 engine offered on 4WDs in 1975. A new, optional 400-ci V-8 with a four-barrel car-

buretor was available, providing greater power for 4WD vehicles.

Also new for 4WD vehicles was an improved and modified suspension, to provide much better ride qualities. Springs and shock absorbers were reworked for an improved ride in short-wheelbase vehicles such as the Blazer.

In addition to the new 400-ci V-8, the more efficient 250-ci six-cylinder engine was vastly redesigned with an integral cylinder head and inlet manifold. It was made available for light-duty trucks. The 250 six and the 292 six were made available when equipped with optional airconditioning on 2WD and 4WD models. Previously, airconditioning was offered on these models only with V-8 engines.

One exterior change of note was the grille. An all-new, more massively scaled grille was installed on all light trucks.

For the first time the Blazer's hardtop was no longer an option. Instead it was offered as standard equipment, along with a standard roll bar. The open Blazer models were still available with or without the soft top.

A high efficiency ignition system was base equipment on all 1975 Series 10-20-30 truck engines to give a virtually maintenance-free ignition system, improved starting, and improved ignition performance at all engine speeds.

Fleetside pickups featured a new quick-release tailgate that enabled the owner to quickly and easily remove and reinstall the tailgate. This was an ideal arrangement for owners who carried slide-in camper bodies on their pickups.

The Sportvan's interior was extensively redone for 1975. A key change was the addition of the more comfortable high-back seats in the front for both driver and passenger.

Engineers placed larger tires with 15-inch wheels on the vans in 1975. This change was the result of a move to larger 11.86x1.28-inch front brakes. One of the benefits of the change was a higher GVW rating for the vans.

Chevrolet added two new van models, both with 146-inch wheelbases. Available as cutaways, a wide range of bodies from independent converters could be installed on them.

The El Camino luxury pickup received exterior restyling for 1975. It had a new appearance both from the front and the rear. Four models ranging from the base El Camino to the SS, Conquista, and Classic offered something for all buyers. Engine options ranged from the standard 250 six to three V-8s—350, 400, and 454.

A new light-duty truck engine small block 400 was available for 1975. Big blocks were considered too expensive and heavy for auto and light-truck use. Engineers attempted to design an engine that would perform better in pickups and large cars than the small block, but would be more economical to produce than the big block. The small block 400 was the result. It was basically a 350 with a larger bore and stroke. Due to a lack of clearance between the connecting rods and the sides of the block, the rods on the 400 were not as strong as those found in the 350. The cylinder bores had been opened up to the point that there was no room for coolant passages between the cylinders, and the head bolts were awfully close to the cylinder bores as well. These changes compromised the 400, which in turn restricted it to low-performance applications. The 400 performed reasonably well in service, but it suffered from high oil consumption due to uneven cylinder wall temperature, and distortions caused by the head bolts when they were torqued down.

Chevrolet's entire broad truck line continued without change from 1974. In addition to the popular light-duty models, Chevrolet built the conventional cab medium-duty models, the medium- and heavy-duty tilt cabs, long- and short-nose heavy-duty conventionals, and the massive heavy-duty Titan 90 Series.

Chevrolet's imported mini-truck the LUV was now in its fourth model year. GM began importing this little truck from its Japanese partner Isuzu as a means to compete with Datsun's, Toyota's, and Mazda's imported mini-trucks, which began to take a big bite out of the light-duty truck market. In 1975, LUV offered the upscale Mikado luxury model option. It included full-width seats upholstered in deluxe fabrics, matching door insert, carpeted floor and door kick panels, leatherlike covered three-spoke steering wheel and gearshift knob, deluxe dome lamps, ashtray lamp, and dual-note horn. Its standard interior was a vinyl bench seat with Spartan trim. Its 6-foot cargo box could handle a 1,460-pound load. This was a tough, hard-working truck. Its four-cylinder 111-ci engine put out 75 horsepower and 88 foot-pounds torque. Its transmission was a four-speed, full-synchronized type. *AAMA*

Chevrolet's handsome new pickups for 1975 featured an all-new grille style and a new top-of-the-line Silverado model. This is a 1975 C10 Silverado Fleetside. The new model lineup began with Custom Deluxe, which replaced the original base or Custom model. The next step up was the Scottsdale, which replaced the former Custom Deluxe nameplate. Cheyenne was the third trim level. It continued unchanged from 1974, and then Silverado took the place of the former top name Cheyenne Super. Basically, the seat construction, instrumentation, and other interior trim items in each of the four levels continued without change. Exterior trim details including two-tone paint schemes carried over without change also. Engine lineup changes included a new 400-ci V-8 for K10 and K20 4WD trucks. The 250-ci six was dropped from all models except from the C10 and K10 1/2-tons. *AAMA*

Chevrolet's other pickup style was the Stepside with its patented narrow cargo box with attached rear fenders and "step" running board between the cab and rear fender. Chevrolet offered the Stepside in Series C/10, 20, 30, and K 10, 20 4WD trucks. This is a 1975 Custom Deluxe K20 Stepside fire truck with the Waterloo, Illinois, rural fire department. Unit number 281 (they called it a Mud Buggy) carried a 250-gallon water tank, and a PTO-powered 250-gpm pump. Engine options for the K20 pickup included the 292 six, 350 V-8, and new for 1975 400 V-8. Maximum GVW rating for the K20 was 8,400 pounds. K20 trucks were standard with full-time 4WD. Full-time 4WD was new in 1973. *Dennis J. Maag*

Chassis cabs in two- and four-door models were an important segment of the business, for the most part in C/K20 and C30 models. Chevrolet provided a wide selection of wheelbases and GVWs up to 10,000 pounds with dual rear wheels. This is a 1975 Custom Deluxe K20 chassis cab with a utility body modified by the Goodland, Kansas, Fire Department as its spill control and rescue support unit. Lockouts have been installed on this truck. Unlike some competitors, Chevrolet's 4WD trucks featured a low silhouette, high ground clearance, and a short step getting in and out. Chevrolet's 4WD trucks featured strong multi-leaf front and rear springs. Some exposed sections of brake lines were wrapped with steel wire for protection against flying stones and gravel. *Dennis J. Maag*

Chevrolet's bread and butter medium-duty line ranged in GVW ratings from 13,500 pounds in the C50 series to 42,820 pounds in the ME-65 tandem series. Engine options ranged from the 292 six to the 427 V-8. The 350 was the standard eight-cylinder engine.

A new exterior brightwork package for mediums offered windshield molding, bright grille, and chrome bumper. Three trim levels with a variety of options graced the interiors of the 50-60-65 Series.

Total industry truck production took a heavy hit in 1975, declining 16 percent from 1974. Total industry truck production of 2,272,160 was down by almost 500,000 units from 1974. Chevrolet's production, at 777,863, was down from 867,913 in 1974. Even at that, Chevrolet was still number one in production.

Heavy-duty truck production and sales took even a heavier hit. Diesel truck shipments plunged 39 percent to only 102,508 from 167,395 in 1974.

It's interesting to note that the 6,000- to 10,000-pound class set a new record of 962,987 units. This obviously came about because truck buyers opted out of the lighter trucks with catalytic converters and unleaded fuel requirements.

Chevrolet's van sales increased immensely and helped to offset the decline in pickup sales. Total truck sales at Chevrolet were 858,430. Other trucks posting an increase during the model year included the LUV, with sales of 46,303 versus 33,643 in 1974; and Blazer, with 50,976 versus 47,227 in 1974.

This long-wheelbase 1975 Chevrolet C30 with a rollback body was still running strong in October 1998. Its maximum GVW was 10,000 pounds. Engine availability included a 292 six and the 350 and 454 V-8s. At this time, truck engines were divided into two groups. The first group comprised the engines with light-duty emissions for models of 6,000 pounds GVW and below. The second group comprised the engines with heavy-duty emissions for models of 6,001 pounds GVW and above. The 454 in this truck fell into both groups. The light-duty 454 was rated for 215 SAE net horsepower at 4,000 rpm and SAE net torque of 350 foot-pounds at 2,400 rpm. The heavy-duty 454, on the other hand, was rated for SAE net horsepower of 245 at 4,000 rpm and SAE net torque of 355 foot-pounds at 3,000 rpm. Light-duty engines were equipped with a catalytic converter and required unleaded gasoline. Heavy-duty engines burned leaded gasoline and did not have a catalytic converter.

Chevrolet's Suburban was in a class by its self. No other manufacturer built anything close. Many families found it was the perfect wagon for their lifestyle. With three seats in place Suburban would transport nine passengers in comfort and safety with a cargo area behind the third seat. As a tow vehicle, it was rated for a GCW of up to 14,000 pounds. Suburbans were offered in C/K 10 and 20 models. Its largest engine option in C10/20 versions was the powerful 454 V-8 with a four-barrel carburetor. In the K10 and 20 models the 400 V-8 with a four-barrel carburetor was the largest engine. For the economy minded, the C10 was available with the 250 six. *AAMA*

Chevrolet's forward-control chassis and Step-Van lines continued without major change. The forward-control line consisted of chassis on three wheelbases and three weight classifications. Chevrolet built the chassis only and the customer could choose from the industry's leading manufacturers of special bodies. The Step-Van line was made up of three wheelbase lengths and three Series—P10, P20, and P30. GVW ratings ranged from 6,200 to 14,000 pounds. Standard power was the 292 six; the 350-4 V-8 was standard for V-8 models. The 454-4 V-8 was available for P30 Step-Vans. This is a 1975 133-inch-wheelbase Chevrolet dual rear wheel P30 Step-Van. *AAMA*

The Waterloo (Illinois) Fire Department's Emergency Management Agency chose this 1975 P30 157-inch Step-Van for their Emergency Operations Center. Chevrolet built this van with either a steel or aluminum body. Its GVW rating was 14,000 pounds. Chevrolet supplied the bare truck only. Specially equipped Step-Vans performed all kinds of special duties, but buyers were responsible for having the special equipment installed. The big 454-4 V-8 engine powered this Step-Van. Two transmission options included a four-speed manual or the Turbo Hydra-Matic automatic. *Dennis J. Maag*

Chevrolet's LUV continued in 1975 without change. This popular little pickup was economical to buy and operate. The versatile LUV featured a 6-foot cargo box and easily carried 1,460 pounds of payload. Like the big pickups, LUV was built tough. Its efficient overhead cam, 75-horsepower four could handle loads at highway speeds while sipping gasoline. The popular luxury blue fabric Mikado option continued along with the standard vinyl-trimmed interior. Standard equipment and features included a four-speed manual transmission, power brakes, power flow-through ventilation, all-steel cab, and a tough ladder-type frame. A sample of available options and accessories included a rear step bumper, a rear chrome bumper, factory air conditioning, an AM or AM/FM radio, a sliding rear window, front bumper guards, mud flaps, a right-hand exterior mirror, and chromed wheel covers. *AAMA*

Chevrolet's popular medium-duty conventional trucks continued in four series: 50-60-65- and Series 65 tandems. Chevrolet built a model with traditional Chevrolet quality and value for every farm and/or business task. GVW's ranged from a low of 18,500 to 43,180 pounds, and GCW ratings up to 60,000 pounds. This is a 1975 CE65 with tanker body. Chevrolet's medium-duty trucks' engine offerings included gas models only. The standard engine for the C65 Series was the 200 SAE net horsepower at 4,000 rpm 366 V-8 that produced SAE net torque of 305 foot-pounds at 2,800 rpm. The optional engine was the 220-horsepower, 360-foot-pounds torque 427 V-8. *AAMA*

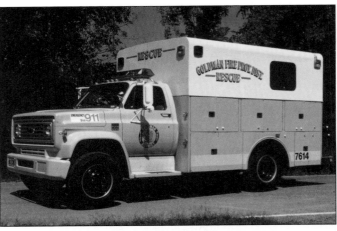

Chevrolet offered three trim levels in conventional medium-duty trucks. This Custom Deluxe interior was the base level. The next level up was the Cheyenne interior, and the top-of-the-line interior was the luxurious Scottsdale. It included fabric seat upholstery over a thick foam rubber cushion for the full-width seat, simulated wood-grained trim on door panels, a cigarette lighter, full undercoating, and floor insulation. The Custom Deluxe interior featured vinyl upholstery on the bench seat. Chevrolet designers allowed good legroom and adequate clearance between the steering wheel and seatback. The wraparound instrument panel provided a cockpit-type instrument cluster to reduce eye movements when reading gauges. Its flat-black panel finish was non-reflective. *AAMA*

Chevrolet's short 97 1/2-inch BBC conventional trucks continued as a favorite with the nation's businessmen and farmers. This truck is a 1975 Chevrolet C60 with a Semo Rescue body in service with the Gold (Missouri) Fire Protection District. This body was mounted in 1993. Prior to that, it carried a Semo tank body. Chevrolet offered this model on nine wheelbase length chassis— 125, 137, 149, 167, 173, 179, 189, 203, and 218 inches. Two standard engines were available, the 130-horsepower 292 six and the standard 160-horsepower 350 V-8. The 200-horsepower 366 V-8 was an option. Maximum GVW rating was 24,000 pounds. *Dennis J. Maag*

Except for the tandem-axle ME65, the CE65 Series 1975 tanker truck was Chevrolet's biggest conventional medium-duty truck. This 1500-gallon water tank with a 250-gpm pump tanker served with the High Ridge, Missouri, Fire Department. Maximum GVW rating of the CE65 was 31,620 pounds. The standard engine for this truck was the 200-horsepower 366 V-8, and the 220-horsepower 427 V-8 was optional. The chrome bumper and grille were factory options. The cast steel spoke wheels were standard equipment for the CE65 Series. *Dennis J. Maag*

Chevrolet's popular medium-duty steel tilt cabs continued in 1975 basically unchanged. These short 72-inch cab mediums were a particular favorite with fire departments because of their maneuverability in city traffic and on rural roads. The Raymond Community Fire Protection District of Harvel, Illinois, owned this 1975 TE65 tilt tanker. This husky truck was rated for a maximum GVW of 29,000 pounds. Its standard engine was the 200-horsepower 366 V-8, and the optional engine was the 220-horsepower 427 V-8. The Tilt's cab has plenty of room for three men with available seating. Only the driver seat was adjustable. *Dennis J. Maag*

Chevrolet's other conventional cab series was the 70-80 heavy-duty models. These husky brutes handled loads up to 44,860 pounds GVW or 60,000 pounds GCW. These trucks featured a true heavy-duty cab with a non-glare easy-to-read instrument panel with five big white-on-black round instruments located directly in front of the driver. A tilt steering column could be easily adjusted to the driver's height and reach. A chair-height, full-width bench seat was standard on all Series 80s. A single driver seat was standard for Series 70. This is a 1975 Chevrolet Series 80 chassis cab with a packer body. The only engine available was the 220-horsepower 427 gas engine. This engine was engineered and built for demanding heavy-duty service. Premium components included a forged-steel crankshaft, sodium-cooled exhaust valves, and positive exhaust valve rotators, which helped minimize deposits and prolong valve life. *AAMA*

Chevrolet's top-of-the-line truck was still the monster Titan 90. This truck was engineered and designed from the wheels up as a heavy-duty truck. The only engines offered were diesels. There were six models from Detroit Diesel and three from Cummins. The most powerful diesel engine offered was the 12V-71N Detroit Diesel producing 390 horsepower and 1,078 foot-pounds torque. Titan-Aire suspension was available to smooth the ride and reduce cargo damage by offering a smooth, firm ride and easy servicing. This axle setup was rated at 34,000-pound capacity. Air bellows carried the load, while a leveling valve automatically maintained vehicle height under varying weights. Heavy torque bars helped control roll and sway and functioned as springs to reduce road shock. Titan 90s GCW maximum rating was 76,800 pounds. *AAMA*

Chevrolet's 1975 medium- and heavy-duty Conventional line consisted of Series 50-60-65 and ME65 tandem. This is a 1975 Chevrolet ME65 tandem chassis cab with dump body. The optional 220-horsepower 427 V-8 engine powered this truck. The 200-horsepower 366 V-8 was the standard engine. The New Process-542CL was the standard five-speed transmission. Chevrolet offered as options four other five-speed transmissions from New Process, Clark, and Spicer. The Allison-MT650G five-speed automatic was also an extra-cost option. This truck was painted Skyline Blue, which was a new color for 1975. Buyers could choose from 13 standard solid colors, regular two-tones, or new-for-1975 shaded two-tone schemes. Chevrolet's standard paint was acrylic enamel. This big heavy-duty dump truck was rated for a maximum GVW of 43,180 pounds. *Verne L. Byers*

Chevrolet's smallest delivery truck was in its fifth model year. The Vega Panel Express was a version of the subcompact Vega auto, based on the Kammback wagon with the rear side windows blanked out. The economical-to-operate Vega Panel had 68 cubic feet of cargo space and a 5 1/2-foot load length by 3 1/2-feet wide between the wheel housings. A choice of two four-cylinder overhead cam aluminum engines was offered: the standard 78-horsepower single-barrel carburetor and the optional 87 horsepower with a two-barrel. Only the driver seat was standard equipment, a second seat was an option. *John Gunnell*

The 1975 Chevrolet El Camino continued with only minor styling updates. This dual-purpose little truck found favor with ranchers, businessmen, contractors, professional people, salespeople, and others. It rode and drove like a car, but had the practicality of a small pickup. The El Camino could haul or tow a load. The El Camino's standard engines for 1975 were the 250 L6 and Turbo-Fire 350 V-8 with a two-barrel. Optional engines included the Turbo-Fire 350 V-8 with a four-barrel, a Turbo-Fire 400 V-8 with four-barrel, and top-of-the-line Turbo-Jet 454 V-8. A three-speed manual transmission was offered for the three smallest engines and a Turbo Hydra-Matic was available for all engines. *Stovebolt Engine Company*

Farmers played a major role in Chevrolet truck's success since their very beginning in 1918, and continue to be a big market to this day. This is a 1975 Series TE65 steel tilt-cab chassis with grain body and tag axle. Without the tag axle it carried a maximum GVW of 29,000 pounds. Its drivetrain consisted of the optional 220-horsepower 427 V-8, five-speed New Process-542CL manual transmission and a 17,000-pound Chevrolet two-speed rear axle. One particular advantage of the setback front axle of the tilt cab was its short BBC and tight turn angles, which was of particular advantage in congested urban areas. It seems this truck is somewhat out of place on the farm, but on the other hand, these short, heavy-haulers were fun to drive.

1976

Series 5 LUV pickups were new for 1976. A front-end appearance included a redesigned bumper with parking lights built in. The standard LUV's interior featured all-vinyl seat and door trim stitched in a new pattern for a snappy look. Interior colors were saddle or blue, depending on exterior color. Also new were a shoulder belt and a redesigned speedometer dial, which displayed both miles and kilometers per hour. The luxury Mikado model featured cheerful plaid fabric upholstery offered in blue, saddle, and red. Smart-looking knit vinyl fabrics were also available in saddle or blue with Mikado interior. For the first time, a three-speed automatic transmission was available. It was the Turbo Hydra-Matic model THM-200, designed and manufactured by GM. A T-handle selector was pedestal-mounted on the floor. Chevrolet boasted that the new LUV gave the best mileage of any truck the consumer could buy in America, with a manual transmission, 23 miles per gallon, city and 33 miles per gallon, highway. *AAMA*

Chevrolet's truck lines remained virtually unchanged for 1976. Chevrolet took additional anti-corrosion measures in the body structures of trucks, especially in the inner areas of panels, fenders, and doors for more durability.

One change of note with the Blazer was the new body design, which featured an integral steel roof and full doors for the front compartment, resulting in increased structural rigidity. Chevrolet engineers added what amounted to a pickup cab around the passenger-driver compartment, but with the back wall cut away. The roll bar was integrally built into this unit. The new Blazer's cab roof featured double wall construction with integral drip gutters.

Optional chrome deluxe bumpers featuring rubber-type impact strips became available for front and rear bumpers of Fleetside pickups, Suburbans, and Blazers. Instrument clusters were revised to include features such as a kilometer scale on the speedometer of all models. A voltmeter replaced the ammeter in the optional gauge package on conventional cab, van, and 4WD models. Full-time 4WD was available in 1976 only with the automatic transmission, regardless of the engine used.

Chevrolet's entire truck line carried over in 1976. This included everything from the imported LUV mini pickup to the mighty Titan aluminum cab road tractor.

The only new vehicle was a recreational version of the Blazer—the Blazer Chalet. This was a first for Chevrolet—a total recreational vehicle package offered fully built and ready to roll. Production of the Chalet began April 19, 1976, at the Chevrolet Truck Plant in Flint.

Chevrolet also introduced the CHEV 76 (Chevy Heavy Efficiency Vehicle), which included fuel-saving features such as Dragfoiler (on Titan 90), steel radial tires, more efficient gearing, and light-weight suspensions, frame rails, and fuel tanks.

The 4WD market boomed in 1976. Chevrolet was a leader in all segments of the 4WD market, including Sport Utilities, pickups, and cab chassis units. Suburban sales began to take off as full-size passenger cars were downsized; about 25 percent of Suburban sales were 4WDs. Suburban sales were running 53 percent ahead of the previous year as of July 1976. The 4WD trucks increased from less than 50 percent of sales five years ago, to 62 percent in July 1976. The market forecast for the entire year was set at 65 percent.

Early in the year, Chevrolet brought out a new model called the Big Ten 1/2-ton pickup. It was Chevrolet's C10 model 1/2-ton, built so it wouldn't require a catalytic converter. The Big-10 was simply a C10 assembled on an optional F44 heavy-duty chassis. The F44 option resulted in a C10 with an over-6,000 pound GVW. The standard engine was the 250 six. Optional engines included the 350 V-8 with either a two-barrel or a four-barrel car-buretor, and the 454, four-barrel V-8.

The EPA issued a list of fuel mileage comparison figures for a variety of trucks and passenger cars, both foreign and domestic. Chevrolet took three places in the top ten. An LUV was number one with 26 miles per gallon, another LUV came in third with 24 miles per gallon, and an El Camino came in seventh place with 20 miles per gallon.

Total truck industry shipments jumped 31.1 percent in 1976 to 2,979,049, only 641 units short of the 1973 record of 2,979,690. Light-duty trucks and heavy-duty trucks were the vol-ume heroes; medium-duty trucks showed no growth over 1975.

Chevrolet's production of 1,044,600, was 34 percent ahead of 1975, comfortably in first place. Record production of Blaz-ers, vans, and Suburbans led Chevrolet's production surge. Total sales of trucks by Chevrolet reached a record 1,045,169, compared to 796,412 in 1975. The old model-year sales record was 1,009,564, set in 1973. LUVs and medium- and heavy-duty models were the only trucks showing a decline in 1976 from 1975.

America's finest and still the best-selling pickup was Chevrolet's C-10 Silverado Fleetside. The Fleetside pickup was offered in five basic series on three wheelbases totaling eleven models. Two cargo boxes included a 6 1/2-foot short box or an 8-foot long box. Double-wall-type construction was used in both its cab and box. Chevrolet's massive girder beam coil spring front suspension on 2WD models delivered best-in-class ride and drive. Available engine options included the 250 six and 350-2, 350-4, and 454-4 V-8s. Net horsepower outputs ranged from 105 for the 250 six to an amazing 245 for the 454-4. *AAMA*

Chevrolet's Stepside pickup was a favorite hauler with the sporty crowd, for the beach, a hill climb, or the off-road cycle course. Chevrolet capitalized on this phenomenon by offering a new Step-side trim package as pictured on this 1976 C10 short box. The package consisted of special striping, chromed front and rear bumpers, Rally wheels, white-lettered tires, Scottsdale trim includ-ing a Custom vinyl bench seat and choice of four solid exterior col-ors: blue, orange, red, and black. The GVW rating was up to 6,200 pounds. Special Stepsides with full-time 4WD were also available. Engine choices included those normally used for 1/2-ton trucks: the 250-1 six and 350-2, 350-4, and 454-4 V-8s. *AAMA*

The standard C10 Stepside pickup continued to be popular with those owners who used their pickup for personal transportation. This basic style dates back to the 1930s, and with every passing year, its sales and popularity waned. Its practicality was a ques-tion mark with many pickup buyers because of its narrow cargo box, and many didn't care about fussing with two chains when opening or closing the tailgate. The Fleetside was modern, it offered additional cubic feet of available load space, was priced the same, and featured an easy-to-operate one-hand tailgate that could be easily removed for accepting a slide-on pickup camper. This is a 1976 C10 short-box Silverado. *AAMA*

This is the biggest pickup Chevrolet built in 1976: a C30, 3 + 3 crew cab Silverado Fleetside "Big Dooley." It was in truth operating as a crew cab. Note the construction scene in the background and the driver and crew wearing hard hats. This same pickup was also very popular with the slide-on camper and trailer towing crowd. A family of six could be seated in comfort. The Big Dooley could haul a massive slide-on camper or tow a luxury camper. The maximum GVW rating of the C30 with dual rears was a hefty 10,000 pounds. With an available 454-4 V-8 engine, the Chevrolet was more than capable of performing any task assigned. *AAMA*

Chevrolet's other C30 crew cab was the single rear wheel model. A 1-ton 4WD model was not yet available from Chevrolet. Chevrolet also built a "Bonus Cab." This was a four-door, three-passenger model with nearly 56 cubic feet of lockable inside load space. Its advantages included the large cargo capacity, the convenience of four-door loading and unloading from both sides, and cargo access from the driver seat. The bonus cab was offered in both Series 20 and Series 30 models. You might say it was Chevrolet's bigger answer to Dodge's new Club Cab pickup. Chevrolet also offered the crew cabs as a chassis cab model. *AAMA*

"Super Wagon" is the term by which Chevrolet characterized the 1976 Suburban. Chevrolet knew that its Suburban competed against station wagons because no other manufacturer offered a similar vehicle. It could be said that a Suburban was a station wagon built on a truck chassis. The Suburban was, however, bigger, stronger, and longer than every other vehicle. In addition, it was also unique because it was the only 4WD station wagon built in America. 4WD Suburbans had not yet caught on in the 1970s like they would in the 1980s and 1990s. Even so, there were a number of buyers who really needed a tough 4WD vehicle. The Suburban was offered in three trim levels: Custom Deluxe, Scottsdale, and Silverado. *AAMA*

Chevrolet's other SUV was the popular K10 Blazer. The Blazer had a new special suspension in 1976. It was engineered to provide a softer ride than previously, yet retain the same off-road capability. For 1976, all Blazers had a steel half-top with a built-in roll bar. It was an integral part of the roof construction. The sturdy roll bar had a flat shape, which provided more interior space than conventional tubular roll bars. A new removable fiberglass-reinforced plastic top enclosed the rear seating or cargo area. All K-model Blazers with Turbo Hydra-Matic transmission had full-time 4WD. On K-model Blazers with three-speed or four-speed manual transmissions, a two-speed transfer case was standard equipment along with part-time 4WD. These models were equipped with front lockouts. This is a 1976 K-5 Blazer hardtop. *AAMA*

In May 1976 a new Chevrolet Blazer convertible went into production. Chevrolet management had identified a new market: the demise of passenger-car convertibles opened a new market for a "soft top." Blazer's convertible top was either white or black vinyl-coated fabric. It could be ordered as a model the same as the hardtop version. The top folded back into a boot. A structural foam header helped seal the top to the steel cab roof panel. The top featured steel hardware with aluminum side rails and large plastic side windows. The Blazer sales increased by 38 percent over the year before. List price of the convertible with 4WD was $5,069.60 for a six-cylinder, and $5,264.60 for the V-8. The 2WD was $982 less. *AAMA*

The popular Step-Van series continued into 1976 with minor changes. This is a 1976 P20 Step-Van King with a 12-foot aluminum body and dual rear wheels. Aluminum bodies meant additional payload-carrying capacity and long life. Side sliding doors were nearly 3 feet wide for easy driver entry and exit even when loaded with packages. Step-Van King P20 models were offered in three wheelbase lengths: 125, 133, and 157 inches. Maximum GVW ratings of P20s ranged from 6,800 to 8,000 pounds. Standard engines were the 292 six and the 350-4 V-8. Chevrolet also continued to offer a full line of forward-control chassis in addition to the Step-Van Series. *AAMA*

Chevrolet's Hi-Cube vans held up to 570 cubic feet of cargo. Pictured here is a 1976 dual rear wheel Chevrolet 12-foot aluminum body Hi-Cube van. Chevrolet built these practical vans on G30 Series chassis with either a 125-inch or a 146-inch wheelbase. They were ideal vehicles for carrying high, wide loads. Factory-installed options included a sliding partition between the driver seat and load compartment, twin-hinged wider rear doors, and a roll-up overhead rear door. Chevrolet also built an RV Cutaway Van on two wheelbases. Standard equipment included power front disc/rear drum brakes. The RV Cutaway Van had standard power steering. Available engines included the 292 six and 350-4 and 400-4 V-8s. *AAMA*

Chevrolet again offered its best-selling medium-duty conventional trucks in four series: C50-60-65 and Tandem C65. They were built in a huge plant in Pontiac, Michigan, with 38 acres under one roof. Its chassis assembly line was a full quarter-mile long. Every day, one truck was taken to undergo a thorough 2 1/2-hour quality-control inspection. This is a 1976 Chevrolet CE60 with van body. The C60 Series was Chevrolet's best-selling medium-duty truck by a wide margin. This truck was rated for a maximum GVW of 24,000 pounds and a maximum GCW of 45,000 pounds when used as a tractor trailer. Standard engines were the 292 six and the 350 V-8. The 366 V-8 was an option. *AAMA*

The biggest truck in Chevrolet's conventional cab medium-duty line was the ME65 tandem. This model was rated for a maximum GVW of 44,860 pounds. In actuality, this model was a heavy-duty Class 8 truck; it slipped into Class 8 because of its tandem axles. Chevrolet used Eaton tandem axles with a Hendrickson suspension in capacities of 30,000 and 34,000 pounds. Driving and braking forces were transmitted through torque rods and equalizing beams. Springs served only to cushion the load, which was divided equally between the axles. A driver-operated differential lockout supplied equal power to each axle for added traction as needed. The standard engine for ME65 tandem was the 366 V-8; the 427 V-8 was optional. *AAMA*

Chevrolet's other medium-duty trucks were the Steel Tilt 60-65 Series. The Rosewood Heights, Illinois, Fire District 62 owned this 1976 Chevrolet TE65 tilt chassis cab with fire engine body. The 750-gallon tank body was by Tower. Its 31,620-pound maximum GVW rating easily handled the load. The tilt cab was standard with two bucket seats but a third seat was available. The tilt cab's setback front axle allowed higher weight distribution to the front axle—as much as a thousand pounds more than conventional cabs. Its short 72-inch BBC permitted longer truck bodies or semitrailers within a given overall length. The optional 220-horsepower 427 V-8 powered this truck. *Steve Hagy*

Chevrolet's other conventional series was the midrange heavy-duty Conventional Series 70, 80. This is a 1976 Series 70 tractor with flatbed trailer. Chevrolet engineers added a second standard diesel engine for 1976. It was the Caterpillar model 3208-V-8, featuring 636-ci displacement. It was offered in two power levels: 164 horsepower and 390 foot-pounds torque or with 199 horsepower and 473 foot-pounds. The added power came from a change in injectors and injection pump. As before, the only gas engine was the 220-horsepower 427 V-8. This truck was powered by the 427 V-8. It was rated for a maximum GCW of 50,500 pounds. *AAMA*

A single-axle Titan 90 was a standard offering. In fact, Chevrolet catalogued four single-axle models and all four were rated for a maximum GVW of 32,940 pounds and/or 80,000 pounds maximum GCW for tractor trailer service. This 1976 Chevrolet Titan 90 tandem-axle chassis cab with trailer was powered by the popular Cummins NTC-350 diesel. Its transmission was the 13-speed Fuller Road Ranger. Single-speed tandem rear axles were from Rockwell-Standard rated at 44,000 pounds. *Dick Copello*

1977

Chevrolet's new Bison heavy-duty long-nose tractor took to the highways in 1977. The Bison was designed to appeal to owner-operators, and to take the latest high horsepower diesels, such as the new Detroit 92 series. These bigger engines required radiators that the 90 series conventionals could not house. This was not a problem, however, with the Titan 90s.

It was, like all Chevrolet heavy trucks, a rebadged GMC (GMC's General). The M/N Series featured a conventional cab. It was offered in two BBC lengths of 108 and 116 inches. The 108-inch model was designated the N Series and the 116-inch, the M Series. Maximum GCWs ranged up to 80,000 pounds and GVWs up to 55,080 pounds. The 108-inch BBC model was mainly intended for pure truck applications as dumpers and mixers. The 116-inch BBC was designed to be an over-the-highway tractor.

Ten Detroit Diesel engines and five from Cummins were offered. Caterpillar engines were to be added later.

The Bison cab was welded aluminum with steel doors. Extensive noise reduction materials insulated the cab for quiet and comfort.

The Series 30 1-ton 4WD models were the most interesting and most needed new introduction in light-duty trucks for 1977. Until this year, 4WD trucks were only available in Series 10 and 20, 1/2- and 3/4-ton categories.

There were several pieces of equipment, new and existing, released for the new 1-ton 4WD models. Some included a 4,500-pound-capacity front axle, a 7,500-pound rear axle, power steering, and both four-speed and automatic transmissions. As far as engines were concerned, the 292 six was standard and 350 and 400 V-8 engines were options. There were single or dual rear wheels and part-time or full-time 4WD, depending on the transmission choice and disc-drum brakes.

A Caravan option and a Nomad option were also new for 1977. These were based on the Chevrolet Van models. The Caravan was intended to be a personal use vehicle for the younger generation that wanted to customize the interior with floor to ceiling carpeting, water beds, black light, stereo, and graphics. The Nomad was a multi-use travel/RV vehicle, capable of towing motorcycles, snowmobiles, or bikes, while carrying five passengers in comfort. Some interior space was reserved for cargo inside.

Light-duty standard cab Chevrolet trucks received a new grille style with only five rows of openings versus the former eight rows. It was still painted silver and displayed the Chevrolet bow tie. The paint trim color for the central areas of the head lamp bezels changed from silver to dark gray.

A number of cab interior upgrades resulted in a more comfortable and better appearing cab. New driver convenience options included power door locks and power windows. Another new option was an inside hood latch release for all C/K models.

Model choices included the conventional cab chassis, conventional cab Fleetside pickup, the crew cab chassis, and the crew cab Fleetside pickup. The 454 V-8 was optional for C10, 20, and 30 trucks, but not for K models.

The 1977 Chevrolet LUV came in for a number of interesting improvements. First, the automatic transmission was made an option, and it even sported a neat T-handle selector lever. The suspension was redesigned from the tires up for a smoother ride. New D78-14 B bias-belted passenger car tires mounted on 1-inch wider wheels resulted in improved handling. Front disc brakes added to the little truck's safety by greatly decreasing its stopping distance. Two interior packages included the standard and the optional Mikado package. It consisted of colorful plaid fabric seat upholstery and interior door panels of the same fabric. Factory air-conditioning was a welcome option.

Chevrolet's pickups continued to be available in four levels of interior trim: Custom Deluxe, Scottsdale, Cheyenne, and top-of-the-line Silverado. The Silverado level gave Chevrolet pickup buyers the most luxurious interior. It included a full-gauge instrumentation set in a simulated chestnut wood-grain panel, full door panels with bright trim, color-keyed carpeting on the lower section, full cowl side trim panels, and Silverado instrument panel nameplate. Exterior trim included bright chrome upper and lower body side and tailgate moldings, wheel opening moldings, full tailgate appliqué, bright cab back panel appliqué molding, and Silverado nameplates. The Griffith (Indiana) Fire Department owned this 1977 C30 Silverado Chevrolet fire truck with a 250-gallon water tank. *Dennis J. Maag.*

At long last, Chevrolet announced its first 1-ton K30 pickup. Now Chevrolet's 4WD offerings spanned its whole light-truck lineup: pickups, chassis cabs, Blazer, and Suburban. Chevrolet heavily promoted its full-time 4WD system. Full-time was made possible by an inter-axle differential built into the transfer case. It compensated for variations in speed between the front and rear axles, while constantly delivering power to both. What is interesting is that full-time was available only on trucks equipped with an automatic transmission. Chevrolet offered a part-time or conventional system as standard on 4WD pickups, Suburbans, and Blazers when equipped with three- or four-speed manual transmissions. *AAMA*

The light-duty truck industry faced two serious problems in 1977. The number one problem was fuel economy. Before the last quarter of 1973, light-truck fuel economy had never been an issue. Owners never expected high fuel mileage before the arrival of the energy crisis. High mileage would have been acceptable, of course, but it wasn't realistic. During 1974 and 1975, there was serious concern that the world fuel supply was just about gone. By 1977 those fears had subsided, yet truck owners stayed more aware of fuel economy. Now Chevrolet truck engineers faced two problems. One, how to increase fuel mileage and two, how to meet stiffer emissions standards.

In 1977, Chevrolet engineers faced the challenge of meeting an average fuel consumption of 18.7 miles per gallon for the 1979 model year for all trucks to 6,000 pound GVW rating. In 1977, the fleet delivered about 17 miles per gallon on average. The difference between 17 and 18.7, a full 10 percent, was formidable. The changes in exhaust emission regulations for 1979 made the fuel economy job all the tougher. To make it even more difficult, the exhaust rules would apply to all light trucks up to 8,500 pounds GVW in 1979.

The truck industry took a larger share of the combined new car and truck market in 1977 than ever before. Total truck sales accounted for 24.5 percent of new vehicle sales, compared to just 15.4 percent 10 years before in 1967. Both light and heavy trucks performed well in 1977. Yet lights took 89.2 percent of total truck sales.

Chevrolet's model year sales rose to 1,188,449 from 1,045,169 in 1976. However, Ford just barely beat Chevrolet for the sales lead in the calendar year 1977. Chevrolet's truck production was a record 1,122,769 units, topping the previous year's 996,318 units by 12.7 percent.

Chevrolet introduced this truck series in 1973, and in 1977 it took on its third different front-end appearance. Chevrolet's 1975 and 1976 grille was made up of eight vertical rows of rectangular shapes. Chevrolet designers made only a slight change to five vertical rows of slightly larger rectangular shapes. For all three grille styles since 1973, the common threads were rectangular shapes and a big bold Chevrolet bow tie emblem mounted in the center. This is a 1977 Chevrolet C30 3+3 six-passenger crew cab Silverado Fleetside pickup. A Bonus Cab option was also available. The Bonus Cab was a four-door model with seating for three and nearly 56 cubic feet of lockable load space inside the cab. The standard engine was the 292 six; the 350-4 and 454-4 V-8s were options. *AAMA*

Chevrolet offered 2WD and 4WD K5 Blazers. Pictured here is a 1977 K5 4WD Blazer. As was true for pickups, the Blazer was equipped with full-time 4WD on vehicles with automatic transmissions, and with conventional part-time 4WD for trucks equipped with a manual transmission. The Blazer was famous for its low 20.6-inch entry height and 7.0-inches of ground clearance. The Blazer Chalet, a self-contained camper unit featuring a fiberglass-reinforced plastic body over a permanently mounted steel frame, was also offered. The camper top popped up when parked to give more than 6 feet of headroom. *AAMA*

During the camper era, Chevrolet enjoyed one very important advantage over its competition. No one offered a vehicle to compete with the Suburban. The Suburban could seat up to nine and could move up to 14,500 pounds of trailer, cargo, and passengers. Chevrolet was very competitive in the towing market. For example, a whole series of factory options were offered to customize a Suburban to suit an owner's personal driving needs. Equipment items included a front-mounted spare tire carrier, high-rise front bumper guard, engine oil cooler, transmission oil cooler, CB radios, grille guards, a wide selection of mirrors, and weight-distributing trailer hitch platforms. For brute force, Chevrolet offered its 454-4 V-8 engine in Suburbans. This is a 1977 Chevrolet C10 Suburban. *AAMA*

Chevy Vans were versatile enough for work or recreation uses. A buyer could have a Chevy Van personalized to suit his or her own taste. Imaginative paint schemes on the outside and luxurious interiors with thick carpeting, paneled walls, stereo sound systems, and more features were available. Chevy Vans lent themselves to a wide variety of RV conversions by outside converters. Vocational uses of Chevy Vans included fire vehicles, ambulances, school buses, and many others. Chevy Vans were also favored by America's businessmen and tradesmen. Buyers could choose from two wheelbase lengths—110 and 125 inches. There were three series: G10, G20, and G30 with GVWs ranging from 4,800 to 8,400 pounds. This is a 1977 Chevrolet G20 commercial van. The buyer could choose from windows all round or windows only in the front. *AAMA*

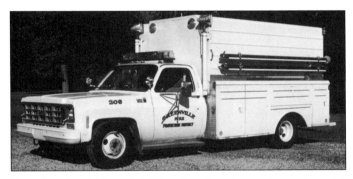

The other 1977 Chevrolet 1-ton chassis cab was the C30 model, pictured here with a special fire department utility body. The Greenville (Illinois) Fire Protection District owned unit 208. The dual rear wheel 1-ton 159.5-inch C30 had a maximum GVW rating of 10,000 pounds. Its standard engine was the 292 six; optional engines included the 350-4 and 454-4 V-8s. Front suspension was independent coil springs. The rear axle had a 7,500-pound capacity and 4.10 standard ratio. Disc/drum power brakes were standard equipment, but manual steering was standard, although power steering was an option. A four-speed manual was standard, and the Turbo Hydra-Matic was an option. *Dennis J. Maag*

Chevrolet's steel Tilt Cab Series carried over without styling changes. It was still famous for its compact 72-inch BBC and wide-track setback front axle. Its cab was roomy and comfortable and tilted a full 55 degrees for convenient engine service. There was plenty of room for a mechanic to stand between the frame and front tire when working on the engine. Tilts were still offered in two series: TE60 and TE65 with 25,160 and 32,760 pound GVW ratings. This 1977 TE65 fire truck was from the Township of Georgian Bay Fire Department of Port Severn, Canada. The optional 220-horsepower 427 V-8 engine powered it. This tanker had a capacity of 1,050 Imperial gallons and a 500-gpm pump. *Dennis J. Maag*

Chevrolet's two- and four-door chassis cabs accepted special bodies for special jobs. This is a 1977 Chevrolet K30 1-ton chassis cab with a special fire truck body. It has a Pierce rescue body, and was also equipped with a 300-gallon water tank and a 250-gpm pump. With dual rear wheels, this truck carried a maximum GVW rating of 10,000 pounds. The Dunklin (Missouri) Fire Protection District owned rescue Unit 118. The biggest V-8 engine available for K30 trucks was the 175-horsepower 400-4. *Dennis J. Maag*

Chevrolet continued to offer the Chevy Big 10 model pictured here on a C10 Fleetside with aftermarket grille bars. The Big 10 was rated for a GVW of 6,050 pounds. The Big 10 also offered the choice of using regular or no-lead gasoline. These GVW ratings compared to the conventional C10's ratings of 4,900 to 5,600 pounds. Big 10's front-suspension capacity was 300 pounds heavier than standard, and its rear-spring capacity was 450 pounds heavier. Big 10 was also equipped with larger tires and was standard with power brakes, unlike the manual brakes for the C10 pickups.

Chevrolet's medium-duty conventional line consisted of Series 50-60-D60-65 and tandem 65 models. The new D60 was diesel powered, and it was the first conventional medium diesel in this series. It was designed and recommended for high idle stop-and-go conditions as in city pick-up and delivery work. Its engine was the Detroit Diesel 4-53, one of a family of two-cycle diesels that provided a power stroke on every piston downstroke. It featured unit fuel injectors, wet-type cylinder liners, hardened valve seats, and precision construction for dependability and long component life. The 4-53 was an inline 212-ci 4 producing net horsepower of 136 and maximum torque of 282 foot-pounds. Pictured here is a 1977 Chevrolet CD 60 chassis cab with van body. *AAMA*

Farmers purchased thousands of the economical, reliable Chevrolet medium-duty conventional trucks such as the C60 pictured here, topping off a large load of shelled corn during the 1998 harvest season. This husky truck was rated for a maximum GVW of 24,000 pounds. Pulling these big loads was the optional 350 V-8. Chevrolet's mediums were offered in three cab trim levels. The Custom Deluxe was the standard cab and biggest seller; the Scottsdale offered additional equipment including simulated wood-trim door panels, a cigarette lighter, color-keyed floor mats, floor insulation, and full undercoating, and the seat back tilted forward for access to in-cab stowage space. The top-of-the-line Cheyenne interior added an instrument panel pad, door trim panels with pockets, a headliner, a door-operated dome light switch, and cowl insulation.

The largest conventional cab medium-duty was the C65. The California Division of Forestry at Colfax owned this 1977 C65 chassis cab. It had a Master Body with a 300-gallon water tank and 500-gpm pump. With hydraulic brakes, the C65 carried a maximum GVW of 30,500 pounds; with air brakes its maximum GVW was 32,760 pounds, which placed it only 241 pounds less than a Class 8 truck. Its standard engine was the 200-horsepower 366 V-8, and the optional engine was the 220-horsepower 427 V-8. Both of these engines were engineered for severe service and featured forged-steel crankshafts, four-bolt mains, heavy bearing support bulkheads and heavy-duty components throughout. The 427 had an 8-quart oil sump. *Garry E. Kadzielawski*

Chevrolet continued to build its forward-control chassis series consisting of P10, P20, and P30 models in 1977. Chevrolet built only a chassis, and the customer was responsible for purchasing a body. These bodies were designed and built by several manufacturers. Some body builders included the J.B.E. Olson Corp., Boyertown Auto Body Works, Union City Body Co., Penn Versatile Van, and Airstream Inc. Maximum GVW ratings for these chassis ranged from 6,200 to 14,000 pounds. Chevrolet also continued to build a series of motor-home chassis. Chevrolet's Step-Van King Series was a complete unit with body mounted by Chevrolet. Engine choices included the 292 six and the 350-4 and 454-4 V-8s. This is a 1977 Step-Van CP30 with dual rear wheels. *AAMA*

Chevrolet's short 93-inch BBC Series 70-80-90 continued for 1977. It's interesting that Chevrolet offered the 70 Series trucks only with diesel engines, 80 Series only with a gas engine, and 90 Series only with diesel engines. This is an 80 tandem tractor equipped with the 427 V-8. The entire diesel engine consisted of seven two-cycle-design Detroit Diesel engines, three Cummins engines, and two Caterpillar diesels. Maximum GVWs ranged from 33,200 to 34,800 pounds for single-axle units. They ran from 45,840 to 50,580 pounds for tandem-axle units. Interestingly, maximum GCW ratings for both single- and tandem-axle tractor trailers topped off at 80,000 pounds. *AAMA*

Chevrolet added two new models to its Chevy Van line for 1977: Nomad, a three-fourths passenger/one-fourth cargo van; and the Caravan, a customized model for the growing hot-rod van market. This G10 1/2-ton Nomad was built on the 125-inch-wheelbase chassis. GVW ratings up to 5,600 pounds were available with the G10 and up to 8,400 pounds with the G30. Engine choices included the 250 six and 305-2 and 350-4 V-8s. A sliding side door was standard equipment on all Chevy Vans. Standard on all six and V-8 engines was Chevrolet's High-Energy Ignition system, which delivered a hotter spark than conventional systems. It helped provide quick starting because its solid-state design eliminated ignition points and condenser and extended the time between recommended tune-ups. *AAMA*

Believe it or not, this is a Chevrolet fire truck. Its chassis and engine are pure Chevrolet, and its body is by Alf Spartan. It could be construed that it has a Tilt Series chassis, judging by its set-back front axle, possibly a TE65 powered by the 427 V-8 engine. It appears to have a five- or six-man cab. It was owned by the El Monte, California, Fire Department. It was equipped with a 1,000-gallon water tank and a 500-gpm pump. *Chuck Madderom*

New for 1977 was the heavy-duty Bison, Chevrolet's version of GMC's General. The Bison was a long-hood version of the Titan 90. All of GM's medium- and heavy-duty trucks were engineered, designed, and built by GMC. These trucks differed only in the nameplate affixed to the truck's exterior. The Bison was an upscale heavy-duty truck targeted at the owner operator. It offered an upscale instrument panel with a full complement of gauges and controls located within easy reach in a wraparound design. Its adjustable steering column could be adjusted to any one of four positions for driver comfort. Buyers could select from a full menu of diesel engines, axles, transmissions, auxiliaries, and other components to exactly meet the buyer's requirements. Chevrolet built the Bison only as a Series CN90. Maximum GVW rating was 44,860 pounds—80,000 pounds GCW when used as a tractor. This is a 1977 Bison CN90 car hauler. *Elliott Kahn*

Chevrolet's biggest model, the Titan 90, was one of its shortest lines. It was available with either single or tandem axles, and in both cases with the buyer's choice of four wheelbase lengths. The Titan 90's BBC dimension for the basic day cab model was only 54 inches. Full-width sleeper versions were available in three sizes: 24, 32, and 36 inches by 88 inches long. They were fully insulated, acoustically and thermally, for comfort. Air conditioning was an option. To keep weight down, Titan's cab was almost entirely of aluminum construction. Aluminum front wheels, fuel tanks, and other parts helped keep the truck's weight down and payload weights up. Standard diesel engine options included six models from Detroit Diesel, four models from Cummins, and one from Caterpillar. The Canadian Broadcasting Corporation (CBC) owned this 1977 Chevrolet Titan 90 with tandem axles and an integral sleeper. CBC used it as a mobile production facility. This photo was taken in April 1994 in Halifax, Nova Scotia, Canada. *Mac Mackay*

Paradis Transfer operated a fleet of these huge Chevrolet Titan 90 tractors from 1970 through 1980. Paradis owned the trailers, but Coca-Cola paid to have them painted in Coke colors in exchange for exclusive use. The 105-foot-long triples on this 1977 Titan 90 grossed out at 105,000 pounds. This truck was on an 85-mile haul from Medford, Oregon, to Klamath Falls, Oregon. It had to cross the Cascade Mountain range with a 5,280-foot summit, which meant 16 miles of 6 percent grade. The tractor could maintain a speed of 22 miles per hour up the grade. The drivetrain on this rig included the 435-horsepower Detroit Diesel and a 13-speed Fuller transmission. Detroit Diesel's new 92 V-Series featured free-breathing cylinder heads with larger valves; a new, stronger crankshaft; and a more efficient turbocharger. *Arnold Paradis*

Chevrolet offered four single-axle Titan 90s in 1977 and eight tandem axles. Maximum GVW ranged from 34,080 pounds for all the single-axle models to 50,580 pounds for all tandem models. Titan 90s were powered only by diesel engines from Detroit Diesel, Cummins, and Caterpillar. Eleven standard diesel engines made up the diesel line. Most buyers opted for Cummins engines. Drivers loved this big Chevrolet. Its cab was designed for driver comfort and convenience. And it was easy to service and maintain. *Dick Copello*

The big, bold, beautiful Bison joined Titan 90 in 1977 as Chevrolet's second premium heavy-duty over-the-road tractor. The Bison's cab was constructed of lightweight aluminum. Its hood was constructed of lightweight fiberglass. Aluminum wheels were also offered. Like the Titan 90, the Bison was only diesel-powered from these engine manufacturers—Detroit Diesel and Cummins. Maximum GCWs for all models was 80,000 pounds. Maximum GVWs ranged from 33,860 to 44,860 pounds. Custom cab interiors were available, as were sleepers. *Dick Copello*

1978

The diesel-powered C10 pickup was 1978's big news. The light-duty diesel was only available on 2WD two-door Fleetside and Stepside models. The diesel, called a GM diesel, was adapted from the 350 gas engine by GM's Oldsmobile Division. It was expected to cut fuel consumption by 20 to 25 percent compared with a similar gasoline engine and produce exhaust emissions low enough to meet federal standards without a catalytic converter.

The diesel was rated at 120 horsepower at 3,600 rpm with a torque rating of 220 foot-pounds at 1,800 rpm. It was a naturally aspirated four-cycle engine with a compression ratio of 22 to 1. Its combustion chamber included a pre-chamber where fuel ignition began before spreading to the piston area. It also included glow plugs that continued to stay activated until the engine reached normal operating temperatures. The diesel-powered pickups sold well the first year or two because buyers did not yet know what a dog the diesel was.

Pickup appearance changes included black inserts in bright metal moldings, and new bright moldings at the rear of the hood. Interior upgrades included a instrument panel appliqué and instrument cluster face plate, plus door trim for Cheyenne and Silverado models, seat trim, and custom-look steering wheels. There was new galvanized steel for the radiator grille lower filler panel and door glass run channels, side outer panels, and tailgates of Fleetside pickups.

Chevrolet continued to offer 4WD in K10, K20, and K30 Series as well as in the Blazer, Suburban, and chassis cab. When equipped with available automatic transmission, full-time 4WD was standard; when equipped with a manual transmission, conventional 4WD was available. The Blazer was also offered with 2WD.

Chevrolet light-duty engine lineup, in addition to the diesel, remained the 250 and 292 sixes, and 305, 350, 400, and 454 V-8s. Transmissions included three- and four-speed manuals and the three-speed automatic.

Appearance changes on Chevy Vans and Sportvans (G-Series) included a new front-end treatment that created a stronger family resemblance to light-duty pickups. Their new grilles, headlights, parking lights, and bumpers mirrored that of the pickups. Base models featured round headlights and silver-painted components, while the top-end Beauville passenger vans featured the new grille with outline moldings, bright metal headlamp bezels, and rectangular headlights.

A new instrument panel with a removable extension that fit over the engine housing contained an ash tray, lighter, cup holders, and package tray freshened up the Van interiors.

The 1978 Blazer was given a lowered rear floor area that was the same level as the front compartment floor. This provided increased legroom for rear-seat passengers. Also, an optional removable folding rear seat was available for Blazers.

El Camino was completely new for 1978. It was nearly a foot shorter than the 1977 model. However, the El Camino's cargo-carrying capacity was unchanged. A new 200 V-6 engine was standard; a 231 V-6 was an option, as were the 305 and 350 V-8s. It was available in three versions: the base model, a Super Sport model, and a two-tone painted high-styled model, the Conquista.

In the heavy-duty end of its truck line, Chevrolet opened the model year carrying over the H and J Series long- and short-hood conventionals. Late in November 1977, Chevrolet's latest conventional truck, the Bruin, made its debut. The short conventional truck featured styling similar, but not identical, to the Bison introduced in 1977. The Bruin's cab offered the driver added comfort and efficiency. Its windshield was increased for greater visibility.

The Bruin was the same as GMC's Brigadier. It replaced the H/J 90 series, but to confuse matters, the Bruin hood was an option

The LUV's major competitors in 1978 were Ford (Courier), Datsun, and Toyota. The LUV's retail list price was consistently $300 less than the competitors. Chevrolet liked to sell it as a "bona fide 1/2-ton pickup," because its payload was an honest 1,510 pounds. The LUV was manufactured by Isuzu in Japan. Chevrolet promoted it as "The compact pickup tough enough to be a Chevy." These little pickups were surprisingly tough and proved to be quite able to do a full day's work. For model year 1977, a new LUV Stepside became available. This cargo box looked like a miniature version of the full-size Stepside. A chassis cab was ordered and the LUV Stepside package was installed on the West Coast. *AAMA*

Pickup styling for 1978 carried over without change. This is a 1978 Chevrolet C10 Fleetside Silverado pickup. The Silverado was the top of the line. The Custom Deluxe was base, Scottsdale was next, and Cheyenne was third. The wheelbase continued to be 117.5-inches for the 6 1/2-foot box and 131.5 inches for the 8-foot box. Chevrolet's gas engine line consisted of the 250 and 292 sixes, and 305-2, 350-4, 400-4, and 454-4 V-8s. Chevrolet pickups were available in six basic series: C/K10, C/K20, and C/K30. The Fleetside and Stepside Sport pickup models also carried over into 1978. *AAMA*

Chevrolet introduced the GM 5.7-liter V-8 diesel engine in C10 1/2-ton, 2WD Fleetside, and Stepside pickups. The diesel was expected to produce fuel savings of as much as 20 to 25 percent, compared to gasoline engines. The four-cycle diesel developed 120 net horsepower at 3,600 rpm. Other features included a pre-combustion chamber cylinder head for a quieter running engine, with less exhaust smoke than an engine with open chamber design; a rotary fuel injection pump; and an electric glow plug cold start system. The diesel engine package also included 4,000-watt heavy-duty Freedom batteries, engine block heater, power brakes, power steering, automatic transmission, dual exhaust, engine oil cooler, 63-amp Delcotron alternator, and cowl and floor insulation. This is a 1978 C10 diesel-powered Fleetside pickup. *AAMA*

Chevrolet's Big 10 pickup returned for 1978. It was engineered to carry big loads on regular gas. The Big 10 was the heavy-duty 1/2-ton equipped to handle bigger and tougher jobs than a regular 1/2-ton. It was offered in GVWs of 6,050 or 6,200 pounds. The Big 10 ran on either lead-free or regular gasoline in all states except California, and had a payload capacity over 1 full ton. The major differences between the Big 10 and a regular 1/2-ton were its heavy-duty independent front suspension with 3,400-pound capacity, heavy-duty front coil springs, heavy-duty rear leaf springs, heavy-duty front disc/rear drum brake system with vacuum power assist, and larger L78-15B tires. Available engines included the 250 six or 350-4, and 454-4 V-8s for 6,050-pound models, and a selection of 350-4 or 454-4 V-8s on 6,200-pound models. Body models included Fleetside or Stepside pickups on either 6 1/2-foot or 8-foot cargo boxes.

on the 70 and 80 series. The Bruin's steel cab was the same used on the H/J series; only the hood and interior differed. The steel butterfly hood continued to be offered on the 90 series Bruin when equipped with the 6-71 Detroit Diesel engine.

The Bruin had a 92 3/4 inch BBC length, and a front end constructed of molded fiberglass. The Bruin's hood tilted 90 degrees for greater engine accessibility. The new front-end design permitted 1,400 square inches of radiator cooling capacity for expanded engine offerings, including the Cummins NTC 350.

It was obvious that Chevrolet's heavy-duty truck names suggested massiveness: Bruin, Bison, and Titan. In marketing the Bison, a 1978 Chevrolet ad said, "The magnificent beast is not a burden."

In the spring of 1978, Chevrolet introduced the Series 8 LUV. The Series 8 was actually two trucks. The new Series 8 included a long-wheelbase model with an extended cargo box, as well as the standard short-wheelbase, short-bed version. The longer model was built on a 117.9-inch wheelbase with a 90.1-inch cargo box.

The U.S. truck market grew 11.8 percent in 1978 to a record 4,110,335 trucks, domestic and imported. The previous record of 3,675,436 had been set in 1977. Trucks thus took a record 26.6 percent share of total new vehicle sales in 1977, an increase of 8.6 percent. This was up from 24.5 percent share in 1977.

All these numbers are magnificent except for one thing: Ford outsold Chevrolet by a healthy margin. Based on model year numbers, Ford was at 1,362,278 versus 1,317,466 for Chevrolet. On a calendar year basis Chevrolet sold 1,340,259 trucks, a new record. Ford beat Chevrolet for the sales crown based on Ford's better performance in medium- and heavy-duty trucks, 94,130 to 44,482.

The 1-ton Fleetside "Big Dooley" was one of Chevrolet's special models. The Big Dooley featured dual rear wheels for the capacity to haul large loads, as well as capacity for towing large fifth-wheel trailers. It had Chevrolet's highest light-duty GVW rating of 10,000 pounds. This truck was offered in 1-ton C30 or K30 Series with the 8-foot Fleetside. In the K30 Series, the engine lineup consisted of the standard 292 six and optional 350-4 and 400-4 V-8s. The C30 Series biggest engine was the 454-4 V-8. 4WD models front suspension featured a hypoid driving axle and leaf springs, unlike the independent coil springs of the C30 Series. *AAMA*

The 1978 Blazer was as tough and rugged as ever and offered more conveniences. New features included an available fold-up rear seat, a recessed floor behind the front seat for more rear seat legroom, power windows and door locks, a new and smaller diameter steering wheel, and increased corrosion protection. It also featured new high-back bucket seats, standard for driver and optional for the passenger side, for traveling comfort. This is a 1978 Custom Deluxe Blazer. Engine choices remained unchanged. As with all 4WD Chevrolets, the largest available V-8 for Blazer was the 400-4. The Cheyenne Blazer Convertible was retained for 1978. *AAMA*

Chevrolet's "Superwagon," better known as the Suburban, came in for only minor tweaking. The exterior featured a black insert color for bright metal moldings, a bright molding on the hood rear edge, an optional wheel opening molding package, and choice of optional Rally or Styled steel wheels. Interior refinements included a new instrument panel faceplate and pad appliqué, newly styled soft vinyl steering wheel and horn button, and new seat and door trim for the top-of-the-line Silverado. All other major specifications and engine availability remained unchanged. Pictured here is a 1978 Chevrolet C20 Silverado Suburban. *AAMA*

The crew cab C30 1-ton chassis cab was popular with fire departments, because it was capable of transporting six firemen, and it had a special firefighting body on a chassis engineered for a maximum GVW rating of 10,000 pounds. This truck happens to be 2WD model, but Chevrolet also built a 4WD Crew Cab. The wheelbase of this unique 1-tonner was 164.5 inches, long enough to accept an 8-foot body. The Union, Missouri, Fire Department owned this truck. Its body was by Pierce. The powerful 240-horsepower 454-4 V-8 engine powered this truck. *Dennis J. Maag*

Chevrolet's Sportvan had a stylish front design that included a new grille, outline moldings, and combination headlight-parking light bezels. The van's styling was now more in line with that of the pickup than had been the practice previously. The available Beauville trim level featured single rectangular headlamps. The instrument panel and engine cover were also new. The instrument panel design had a removable extension that fit over the engine housing cover and contained an ash tray, a beverage holder, a parcel tray space, an optional cigarette lighter, and storage compartment with door. There was also a new 16-inch diameter steering wheel and seat and door panel trim for the Beauville. This 1978 Beauville Sportvan was powered by the 350-4 V-8. Its transmission was the optional automatic. *AAMA*

Chevrolet's Hi-Cube Vans featured the Chevy Van cab chassis plus a higher wider van-type rear body. Built on wheelbases of 125 and 146 inches, Hi-Cube Vans offered a selection of bodies with load space ranging from 384 cubic feet to 570 cubic feet. This is a 1978 125-inch-wheelbase Hi-Cube Van with 385 cubic feet of load space. The standard engine for 125-inch-wheelbase models was the 292 six, while the 350-4 V-8 was required on the 146-inch-wheelbase models. Rear-axle capacity was 5,700, 6,200, or 7,500 pounds, depending on the model. A 10-foot body length, 82.5 inches or 95 inches in width, was available for the 125-inch-wheelbase van. GVWs up to 8,900 pounds were possible with dual rear wheels. *AAMA*

Chevrolet's largest Step-Van King for 1978 was the P30 dual-rear-wheel chassis with a 14 1/2-foot body. This model was available with a steel or aluminum body. The maximum GVW for this model was 14,000 pounds. The standard engine was the 292 six and the 350-4 and 454-4 V-8s were options. With this model, four-wheel disc brakes were standard equipment. Sliding side doors were standard. Lightweight, tough aluminum construction consisted of heavy-gauge aluminum paneling riveted to a rigid aluminum body framework. Aluminum construction saved up to 886 pounds of weight, which went directly into additional payload. *AAMA*

Chevrolet's conventional cab medium-duty models for 1978 consisted of Series 50-60-D60 (diesel), 65-D65 (diesel), ME60 (tandem), and ME65 (tandem). Outwardly, these trucks appeared the same. But for 1978, Chevrolet engineers improved them significantly. First, the diesel engine line was tripled. It was actually the same basic block, but now with three power outputs. The three Detroit Diesels were designated model numbers 4-53, 4-53T(55), and 4-53T(60). The 55 and 60 suffixes indicated 55mm and 60mm injectors. With a diesel engine, by putting more fuel in, you get more power out. Power outputs increased from 125 net horsepower and 265 net foot-pounds torque to 146 and 160 net horsepower and 350 and 385 foot-pounds torque, respectively. Thus the 4-53T(60) engine produced more torque by 25 foot-pounds than the largest V-8, the 427. Also new for 1978 was a lightweight tilt hood option, which allowed easy access to the entire engine for service and repairs. A torsion bar spring assembly operated it. This is a 1978 Chevrolet CD60 diesel-powered medium-duty stake truck. *AAMA*

Chevrolet's CE65 Series medium-duty truck was very husky. When equipped with air brakes, it was rated for a GVW of 33,200 pounds. The heavy-duty Class 8 classification begins with trucks having a GVW rating of 33,001 pounds. The CD65 (diesel powered) was rated for 33,200 pounds GVW and the two tandem models, ME60 and ME65, had GVW ratings of 41,000 pounds— and 42,000 pounds with hydraulic brakes. It rated 50,000 pounds with air brakes. Pictured here is a 1978 CE65 chassis cab with a contractor body. This truck has the chrome grille and front bumper option. It was still in service and looked good as new when photographed in October 1998.

New for 1978 was a factory-installed tag axle for ME60 Series available in 185-, 195-, and 209-inch-wheelbase lengths with a GVW range from 34,000 to 41,000 pounds. Hydraulic brakes and a Hendrickson U-340 suspension were standard. The advantage over twin screw tandems included less tire scuff and initial cost. Another new item for 1978 was what Chevrolet called a "Trac Pac" brake system. It provided hydraulic brake tractors with air controls for pulling air-brake semi trailers. The New Baden, Illinois, Fire Department owned this 1978 Chevrolet CE65 medium-duty chassis cab with firefighting equipment. This pumper had a Grumman body with a 750-gallon water tank and a 300-gpm pump. *Dennis J. Maag*

Chevrolet's steel Tilt Cab Series continued without appearance change. This popular short 72-inch BBC with setback front axle was now in its 18th season. Chevrolet built it in two series: TE60 and TE65. This is a 1978 tilt-cab TE65 chassis cab with fire truck equipment. The Springfield Township Fire Department of Michigan City, Indiana, owned tanker No. 7. It was equipped with an S & S tank body with a 1,800-gallon capacity. It is not unusual that fire trucks have bodies newer than their chassis' age. Frequently, departments obtain equipment from other departments or from governmental agencies. This truck was standard with the 366 V-8; the 427 V-8 was optional. This husky truck was rated for a maximum GVW of 32,600 pounds. *Garry E. Kadzielawski*

Chevrolet restyled its short conventional 90 series truck, giving it a family resemblance to the heavy-duty Bison. Chevrolet named it the Bruin. It featured a multi-piece molded fiberglass front end for ease of maintenance and weight reduction. The hood tilted 90 degrees for better engine accessibility. The Bruin's cab had been redesigned for added driver comfort and convenience, and the windshield's size was increased. This truck was a true heavy-duty Class 8 engineered and designed for heavy service, from the tires up. Cab designers repositioned the seats for more driver head, shoulder and hip room, and more clearance between the seat and steering column. Pedal locations for the accelerator, brake, and clutch were also changed for added convenience. The entire line consisted of 70, 80, and 90 Series in single- and tandem-axle configurations. *AAMA*

From a front view, it's very difficult to tell that this is the best looking 1978 truck. It handled, rode, and drove like a passenger car. Its wheelbase was extended from 116 to 117 inches to help it ride smoother. Its cargo area had 38 cubic feet of space and an allowable carrying capacity of 800 pounds. The luxurious cab offered all the comfort and convenience options of a fine automobile to add to the owner's enjoyment. Three available 1978 models included the El Camino (pictured), El Camino Super Sport, and El Camino Conquista. Engine options included the standard 3.3-liter V-6 and a choice of two powerful V-8s: the 305 with two-barrel carburetor and the 350 four-barrel. A three-speed manual was standard with the 3.3-liter V-6 and an automatic was available. Either a four-speed manual or an automatic was offered for the V-8s. This 1978 El Camino had 305 V-8 power.

Chevrolet's G-Series Hi-Cube Commercial Cutaway Vans were available in two models: 125- and 146-inch-wheelbase lengths. Maximum GVWs reached 8,400 pounds with single rear wheels and 10,000 pounds with dual rears. The Cutaway featured the 292 L-six as the standard engine on the 125-inch model and the 350 four-barrel standard on the 146-inch wheelbase. The short wheelbase could handle bodies up to 10 feet in length and the long wheelbase, bodies up to 12 feet. Hi-Cube Vans were selected for a wide variety of vocational applications due in most part to their outstanding ability to haul huge loads.

The ME65 tandem was Chevrolet's biggest Conventional medium-duty truck. With air brakes, it carried a maximum GVW of 50,000 pounds. It has been converted to AWD by an unknown source. Tanker truck No. 25 belonged to the Eaton (Indiana) Volunteer Fire Department. The fire chief ordered this Chevrolet with chrome grille and bumper to go with the stainless-steel tank. This truck was powered by the optional 220-horsepower 427 V-8 engine, which was mated to a 13-speed Fuller RT613 transmission. The standard engine was the 366 V-8, a diesel option was not offered. *Dick Copello*

An outstanding feature of the Bison was its comfortable cab interior. The cab was roomy, with plenty of hip, leg, and shoulder room. The standard cab was comfortable and color-coordinated. It was upholstered in easy-cleaning vinyl and well insulated to absorb sound. A premium custom cab with colorful fabrics was an extra-cost option. The Bison's vast, spring-assisted, fiberglass hood opened wide for quick and convenient servicing of a choice of 26 diesel engines from either Detroit Diesel or Cummins. Chevrolet engineers provided components from the industry's most respected manufacturers, such as Spicer clutches, axles from Rockwell and Eaton, and transmissions from Fuller, Spicer, and Allison. This is a 1978 Bison chassis cab. *Dick Copello*

1979

Chevrolet's truck line remained constant for 1979. Everything from the LUV to the heaviest truck Chevrolet built, the Titan, returned. Engineers were more concerned with meeting federally mandated reduced emissions and improved economy, so they focused on powertrain changes, improvements to carburetors, installation of catalytic converters on all vehicles up to 8,500 pound GVW, and improved aerodynamics.

The front hood area on conventional cab light-duty trucks was revised to provide better airflow. Engineers raised the area on the front of the hood, and a rubber seal was installed between the hood panel and radiator support. This change was made to effect a small improvement in fuel mileage. Trucks under 6,000 pound GVW received an air dam hidden underneath the front bumper. The air dam directed air into the grille opening. In addition, the lightest trucks received an underhood gasket for sealing air from flowing under the hood. The 4WD trucks did not have to meet as strict

mileage requirements for 1979. Thus, they did not get the gasket and air dam, although all Chevrolets had the new hood.

The chromed headlight bezels were enlarged to enclose the parking lamps as well as the headlights. The chrome strip under the grille was also enlarged to conceal the air intake slots directly under the grille opening. The grille was painted a new dark gray, which when combined with the other changes, gave the 1979 Chevrolets a fresh front appearance.

Power steering was made standard on all 4WD trucks, from K10 through K30 models, including the Blazer and Suburban. The K30 came standard with front locking hubs on part-time 4WD. All Chevrolet light-duty trucks except the K30 pickups were equipped with catalytic converters and burned unleaded gas.

The fuel filler cap on all Chevrolet trucks, even the Stepside model, was now hidden behind a swing-open door. The new door cleaned up the truck's appearance, but the change was actually made to comply with new vapor recovery laws in California. The swing door also offered protection in case of a rollover accident. With a door and recessed cap, the likelihood of the cap coming off was lessened.

In 1978 there were no corporate fuel economy requirements for light-duty trucks. But for 1979, the sales-weighted fleet average for vehicles up to 6,000 pounds GVW was 17.2 miles per gallon for 2WDs. Unleaded fuel and catalytic converters were required.

Chevrolet engineers hoped to meet these standards by more extensive use of the 250 six along with new carburetors—Mod-Quad,

Varajet, and Dualjet. The 250 six was also improved internally in an effort to meet emissions standards.

Chevrolet's LUV pickup was the first mini pickup to offer 4WD as an option. The Series 9 4WD was offered only in the 102.4-inch wheelbase with a 6-foot pickup bed. Styling was the same as the conventional LUV; both models featured a new grille for 1979. Front suspension of the 4WD LUV featured a fully independent front axle with torsion bar suspensions.

The El Camino was largely unchanged for 1979, except for minor restyling at both ends. It sported a restyled grille and slight

The 4WD LUV was new for 1979. The LUV 4x4 had a four-speed, fully synchronized manual transmission with a choice of Hi and Lo 4WD positions. The transfer case was combined with the transmission in a single unit. Manual locking hubs were an additional standard feature. The LUV 4x4 offered 7.5 inches of ground clearance, even though its overall height was only 1 1/2 inches higher than the 2WD. The LUV 4x4's suspension was of the independent type, utilizing upper and lower control arms, ball-type joints, and torsion bars. Rear suspension featured semielliptic, rubber-bushed, leaf-type springs, and direct, double-acting shock absorbers. Other features included 14x5 1/2-inch styled wheels and white lettered F70x14B bias-belted all-terrain tires. The LUV's engine was a OHC 111-ci four-cylinder producing 80 horsepower at 4800 rpm and 95 foot-pounds torque at 3000 rpm. *AAMA*

Chevrolet's El Camino had the style, comfort, and luxury of a fine passenger car, plus the ability to haul up to 800 pounds. The El Camino offered 35.5 cubic feet of cargo space. It was available in four series. Pictured here is the base model, El Camino, which boasted a 3.3-liter V-6 engine, frameless door glass, and thin pillars. The El Camino Conquista had a special paint and molding treatment. The basic body color appeared on the roof, upper portion of pickup box, lower body sides, and on the tailgate. The third model was the El Camino Super Sport, which came with a large front air dam, matching sport mirrors, special black paint treatment around grille openings, and decal stripes. The El Camino Royal Knight version consisted of a hood decal and side striping color-keyed to the body color. *AAMA*

Light-duty conventional models received a revised front appearance. For better fuel economy, radial tires became standard equipment. New front air dams also improved fuel economy. Pickups featured extensive powertrain changes designed to reduce emissions and improve economy and drivability. New carburetor, cylinder head, and dual exhaust manifolds reduced emissions and improved performance of the 4.1-liter L-6 engine. Other standard engine options for the 1/2-ton C10 pickup included the 5.0- and 5.7-liter V-8s. This is a 1979 top-of-the-line C10 Fleetside Silverado pickup. *AAMA*

Chevrolet's K20 Fleetside with tough 4WD capability was well suited for getting into hard-to-get-to areas. Chevrolet offered either full-time 4WD or conventional on-demand 4WD to adapt the model specifically to the customer's job. Full-time 4WD was standard with trucks with an automatic transmission, and part-time 4WD was standard with a manual transmission. This 1979 Chevrolet K20 Custom Deluxe Fleetside fire truck was owned by the Aspen Mountain Fire Department of Aspen, Colorado. Unit 33 carried a 200-gallon water tank and a 200-gpm pump. Maximum GVW for this pickup was 8,400 pounds. Engine options included the 5.7- and 6.6-liter V-8 engines. *Dennis J. Maag*

rear end changes. A new small block 267-ci V-8 filled the performance gap between the V-6s and the four-barrel 305 V-8.

Chevy Van and Sportvan were relatively unchanged for 1979. Engines ranged from the 250 six up to the optional 400 V-8. Improved acoustic insulation was added to the passenger vans above the headliner. A higher quality, thicker dash mat was installed in all models for better acoustic control.

The 350 diesel carried over into its second year, but now with a new glow plug, which lowered the warm-up time to just six seconds. It was still not available in 4WD trucks, however, due to lack of production. And it was still only available teamed up with an automatic transmission.

Versatile chassis cabs could be custom outfitted to answer the customer's need. This chassis cab K30 with a special firefighter's body could go off-road or in snow, sand, or mud with ease. The Elwood (Illinois) Fire Protection District owned it. Rescue Unit 618 had a 250-gallon water tank and a 250-gpm pump. The 1-ton K30 was rated for a GVW of 10,000 pounds when equipped with dual rear wheels. The standard engine for this truck was the 4.8-liter L-6; the 5.7- and 6.6-liter V-8 were options. This truck was equipped with the Scottsdale level cab interior trim. It appears to have a front-mounted winch. One unusual feature is that the stock Chevrolet front bumper has been mounted in front of the winch extension. *Dennis J. Maag*

Chevrolet's roomy and durable Superwagon had major revisions in its powertrain components, including the use of catalytic converters and other emission equipment. The standard 4.1-liter L-6 engine had a staged carburetor for good low- and high-speed drivability; the 5.0-liter engine option had Dualjet carburetor, with exhaust gas recirculation and cold engine driving improvements. The 5.7- and 6.6-liter V-8s had carburetors with hot air choke. Body and front-end sheet metal had improved corrosion treatment. 4WD models had standard power steering, and all models had front hood area modifications for styling and less wind resistance. This is the 1979 Chevrolet C10 top-of-the-line Silverado Suburban. High-back bucket seats were available with Silverado trim. The driver seat was adjustable fore and aft to permit the most comfortable driving position. *AAMA*

Chevrolet's truck production in calendar year 1979 totaled 1,015,345, 97 percent of which were light-duty models, Chevrolet's forte. Production was down by 17 percent from the 1,216,050 built in calendar 1978. The decrease was due primarily to the sudden and dramatic downturn early in the year when buyers became aware of fuel economy once again. OPEC (the Organization of Petroleum Exporting Countries) caused a shortage of crude oil supply resulting in long gas lines in many areas of the country.

Chevrolet's medium-duty models, on the other hand, performed well. When combined with GMC's production they gave GM the medium-duty sales leadership over Ford and IH. Chevrolet's strength in the medium-duty field resulted from the fact that each of the division's 5,000-plus car/light-truck dealers also handled medium-duty trucks. This gave Chevrolet the largest potential dealer network in the medium-duty field.

However, Chevrolet had only about 150 dealers selling heavy-duty trucks in 1979, resulting in total Class 7 and 8 sales of 3,674, a drop of 5 percent from the 3,848 sold in 1978.

A downturn in the overall heavy-duty market in the last half of the year was responsible for Chevrolet's decline. GM corporate announced in late 1979 that Chevrolet would cease selling Class 7 and 8 trucks effective October 1980. Heavy trucks accounted for only 1 percent of total Chevrolet truck sales in 1979. Chevrolet planned to continue selling medium-duty trucks. Chevrolet's Class 6 (medium-duty) trucks were designed and built by the GMC Division.

An interesting anomaly of the year's truck production was that for the first time total 4WD sales topped one million—pickups and SUV. This was about a tenfold increase over total production in the 1970 model year. Chevrolet sold 33,843 4WD LUV pickups, about 30 percent of total LUV sales.

The Blazer was improved with engine refinements, additional corrosion treatment, and engineering changes. The standard 4.1-liter engine had a new two-barrel carburetor that provided excellent power in low and high ranges. The optional 5.2-liter V-8 had a Dualjet carburetor, new exhaust gas recirculation, and vacuum spark systems, all designed to improve performance. Catalytic converters were now on all models for improved emission controls, and power steering was standard on all 4WD models. Hood and grille styling changes improved aerodynamics and in turn fuel economy. This is a top-of-the-line 4WD 1979 Blazer Cheyenne. Its standard engine was the 4.1-liter six; the 5.0-, 5.7-, and 6.6-liter V-8s were options. *AAMA*

Chevrolet's Beauville Sportvan for 1979 emphasized engineering. All engines were refined and had catalytic converters and other emissions devices. The standard 4.1-liter L-6 engine had improved carburetion, and the optional 5.0-, 5.7-, and 6.6-liter V-8s had changes in carburetion and emission control design. Body and sheet-metal corrosion resistance was improved. Glass-belted radial tires were standard on all 1/2-ton models for better gas mileage. Refinements were made to the heater, and front disc brakes lining-wear sensors were made standard. Custom and Beauville Sportvans, Nomad, and Chevy Van with available Beauville interiors had new and improved acoustic insulation. The Sportvan also featured new, thicker front floor and rear wheel-housing insulators. All van models had higher quality thicker dash mats for improved acoustic insulation. The color of the grille was changed to dark gray. Pictured here is a 1979 Chevrolet G10 1/2-ton Beauville Sportvan. *AAMA*

Commercial Cutaway Vans continued to be big business for Chevrolet. The 146-inch-wheelbase 8,900-pound GVW model had standard dual rear wheels. The Commercial Cutaway Vans featured the 5.7-liter V-8 as standard with the 6.6-liter V-8 optional. Businessmen considered them an excellent value because they handled heavy payloads for a moderate investment and were economical to operate. This is a 1979 Chevrolet G30 Commercial Cutaway Van. Hydraulic power brakes and power steering were standard. Base transmission was a three-speed manual and an automatic was available.

Chevrolet continued to supply a full line of forward-control chassis. Special van bodies were designed and built by several manufacturers approved by Chevrolet. Builders included J.B.E. Olson Body Co., Boyertown Auto Body Works, Penn Versatile Van, and Airstream Inc. Chevrolet also offered a complete series of walk-in vans with chassis and body shipped complete from the factory. Chevrolet's Step-Van King was a tough and roomy delivery truck with choice of steel or aluminum bodies. They were built on wheelbases of 125, 133, and 157 inches in Series P20 and P30. This is a 1979 P30 Step-Van King with 14-foot aluminum body. Available GVWs up to 14,000 pounds were available. Standard engine was the 4.8-liter L-6; the 5.7- and 7.4-liter V-8 were options. *AAMA*

Series nomenclature for 1979 Chevrolet medium-duty trucks changed to three basic series—C50, C60, and C70. The Clark County Fire Department of Laughlin, Nevada, owned this 1979 Chevrolet C60 fire truck. Its fire equipment body is by American LaFrance, and it contained a 1,000-gallon water tank and a 750-gpm pump. This truck had a GVW rating of 24,000 pounds. The standard engine was the 4.8-liter six, the standard V-8 was the 5.7-liter, and the optional V-8 was the 6.0-liter. Diesel engine options included the 4-53T(55) and the 4-53T(60). The low-power 4-53T version was dropped. *Garry E. Kadzielawski*

This C70 medium-duty chassis cab with fire equipment body would have formerly been a Series M65 model. With hydraulic brakes, it had a maximum GVW of 30,500 pounds. With air brakes, its GVW was 31,700 pounds. The standard engine was the 6.0-liter V-8; optional were the 7.0-liter and the 7.4-liter V-8s. The 7.4-liter was new for 1979. Both diesels were also optional. SAE net torque for the 366, 427, and 454 V-8 engines were 305, 360, and 380 foot-pounds, respectively. The same numbers for the two diesels were 362 and 382, respectively. The Burley, Indiana Fire Department owned this C70. Its body was by Alf and had a 1,000-gallon water tank and a 750-gpm pump. *Bill Hattersley*

Medium-duty trucks for 1979 featured a new gas-powered 7.4-liter V-8. The addition brought the choice to seven: two diesel and five gas. The new V-8 had an 8:1 compression ratio and generated 245 horsepower at 4,000 rpm. It ran on all grades of gasoline from regular to premium, leaded and unleaded. The engine offered 25 more horsepower than was available in the 1978 line. The mediums also featured a new auto-type fuse block, which allowed easy fuse removal and eliminated the majority of in-line fuses. The new engine was available only in the C70 line, the top of the medium-duty series. *AAMA*

Chevrolet completely redesigned its heavy-duty J80 and J90 conventional series for 1979, and named them the Bruins. Its new tilting hood and fender assemblies were constructed of strong, lightweight SMC fiberglass. Both single- and tandem-axle models were offered. A wide selection of Detroit Diesel, Cummins, and Caterpillar engines were available. The single gasoline engine was the 427 V-8, a carryover from the previous models. It was only released, however, for Series J80 models. The Bruin was designed around the driver. It featured as standard the National Cush-N-Aire adjustable chair-high driver seat in the J90 Series. Also, a tilt steering wheel was standard equipment. The ergonomically designed instrument panel had an easy-to-reach, easy-to-read arrangement of controls and gauges. Pictured here is a 1979 Bruin J90 heavy-duty tandem-axle tractor trailer. *AAMA*

For 1979 model series nomenclature had been changed. The H70, J70, H80, and J80 trucks all became J80 Series trucks; H90 and J90 trucks became J90 Series trucks. The Chesterfield (Missouri) Fire Protection District owned this 1979 Bruin with the standard Series J80 (previous) style chassis cab. This model featured the standard side-opening hood. It could be ordered on the J90 with the Detroit Diesel 671-N engine. As is evident from the photo, a tilt hood wouldn't have worked for this truck. Maximum GVW for J80 models was a big 43,000 pounds. Its standard engine was the 427 V-8. The Detroit Diesel 6V-53N and Caterpillar 3208 diesels were options. *Dennis J. Maag*

Chevrolet changed the series model identification for the 1979 steel tilt cabs. TE60 Series trucks became the Series W60, and Series TE65 trucks became Series W70 trucks. This well-worn 1979 W60 chassis cab with an electrical contractor body continued to work as late as the fall of 1998. It is shown here at a job site. The medium-duty W60 was rated for a GVW rating of 25,160 pounds. Its standard engine was the 350 V-8; the optional engine was the 366 V-8. Chevrolet did not offer a diesel engine option for tilt cabs.

Chevrolet's top-of-the-line heavy-duty Class 8 Titan 90 aluminum tilt cab was in its tenth model year. This truck was only powered by diesel engines. Cummins supplied six models with displacements ranging up to 1150. Also listed as standard were 18 two-cycle Detroit Diesel engines with displacements ranging up to 736, and two Caterpillar diesels with a displacement of 893. The Titan 90's standard models included single and tandem rear axles and day cab or integral sleeper cabs. This 1979 single-axle Titan 90 day cab tractor has the standard grille. Chevrolet did offer a new oversized stainless-steel grille for 1979 with larger radiators to handle the biggest diesels. It was part of a premium package for the Titan 90 to make it more appealing to owner-operators. The new grille was styled like that of the Bison Conventional, and it bolted to the front of the cab. *AAMA*

Chevrolet's big long-nose heavy-duty Bison Series continued into 1979 without change. GM engineers designed Bison for easy service and maintenance. It offered GVWs up to 44,860 pounds and GCW ratings up to 80,000 pounds. Chevrolet offered a broad lineup of engines, suspensions, frames, front and rear axles, brakes, and other components, to make Bison an ideal vehicle for fleets and owner operators. The Freeman (Washington) Fire District 8 owned this 1979 Chevrolet Bison tandem chassis cab with firefighting body. Outstanding cab features included attractive and comfortable color-coordinated vinyl trim saddle upholstery. It also featured a contour-molded, padded headliner with optional roof-mounted radio. The Bison offered an ergonomically designed instrument panel with tachometer, temperature, and air cleaner gauge located in front of the driver for easy reading. It also had a four-way adjustable steering column; wide choice of the industry's leading driver seats and matching passenger seats; extensive cab soundproofing; and large, deluxe sleeper cabs with separate heating and air-conditioning controls. *Bill Hattersley*

Chevrolet's smallest pickup, the imported LUV, was now in its eighth model year. LUV's Series 9 models included 102.4- and 117.9-inch-wheelbase 2WD pickups, the 102.4-inch-wheelbase 4WD pickup, and chassis cabs. The OHC four-cylinder 80-horsepower engine was the only engine offered. Pickup cargo boxes measured either 6 or 7 1/2 feet in length. They were rated as 1/2-ton models because payload capacities for the 2WD models were 1,125 for the regular box, 1,635 pounds for the long box, and 1,165 pounds for the 4WD model. The four-cylinder engine powered this LUV. It also was equipped with the optional automatic transmission. *Verne L. Byers*

The Bruin's appearance did not change for 1979. Chevrolet engineers designed the Bruin as a rugged linehauler. Its cab was designed with the driver in mind. The Bruin's hood tilted forward a full 90 degrees for easy servicing. Both single- and tandem-axle models were available. A wide selection of Detroit Diesel, Cummins, and Caterpillar engines, manual and automatic transmissions, wheelbases and front and rear axles allowed the buyer to specify his Bruin to perfectly match his job requirements. This is a 1979 Chevrolet Bruin J90 tandem-axle chassis cab with dump body. This truck was equipped with a 3208 636-ci Caterpillar engine with a 13-speed transmission. It was rated for a maximum GVW of 44,860 pounds. *Verne L. Byers*

The Titan was another heavy-duty diesel-power-only truck from Chevrolet featuring diesel engines from the nation's leading manufacturers: Detroit Diesel, Caterpillar, and Cummins. Cummins' NTC 350 855 six was Titan's best-selling engine, especially popular in 80,000-pound GCW applications. All four Titan 90 Series had an 80,000-pound GCW rating. GVW ratings when used as a straight truck ranged from a low of 33,860 pounds to a high of 44,860 pounds. This is a 1979 Titan tandem chassis with sleeper cab and fifth-wheel equipment and standard grille. Series nomenclature was changed for 1979. The F90 (single axle) trucks and D90 (tandem axle) trucks were all identified as D90 Series trucks. The full name Titan/90 had been changed to simply Titan. This was the next to last year for Titan. *Dick Copello*

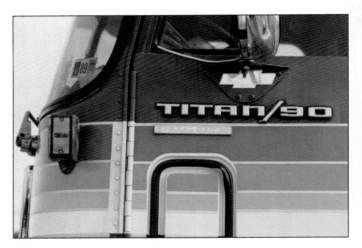

The Titan SS (Special Series), an optional factory-installed Appearance and Convenience Package, gave a custom look without high cost. The basic package included a Custom Deluxe interior consisting of a four-spoke leather-wrapped sport steering wheel, a chrome gear shift lever, a cigar lighter, an AM/FM stereo, and a stereo tape and CB. Other features included air conditioning and ammeter, power windows, chrome West Coast mirrors, dual air horns with snow-shield horn guards, an exterior sunshade, Perlux lamps in the bumper, and an 88-inch sleeper cab with 36-inch-wide innerspring mattress. The buyer could also select a special paint package and wheel package as pictured. The nameplate below the "Titan/90" nameplate reads: "Special Series." *Dick Copello*

Chapter 7

1980 TO 1989

1980

If calendar year 1979 was a tough year for the truck industry, 1980 was an absolute disaster. It was a disaster not only for the truck industry, but for the auto industry as well. In 1980 truck manufacturers sold 51 percent fewer vehicles than they did in 1979. Another interesting change for 1980 was that the six-cylinder engine doubled its share of the market. Six-cylinder engine usage in 1979 was 17 percent; it doubled to 35 percent in 1980. V-8 engines fell from to 60 percent in 1980 from 82 percent in 1979. Four-speed manual transmission usage increased to 28 percent in 1980 from 1979's 16 percent.

A combination of the country's second energy crisis and tightening engine emissions standards was almost more than engineers could handle. Their challenge was to keep trucks tough and able to fill their purpose: to move loads in the shortest possible time at the lowest possible cost. The other side of the coin was the difficulty of meeting tightening emissions requirements. Both of these design demands hindered efforts to increase fuel economy.

Government and consumers dictated the demand—energy efficient, non-polluting, yet rugged trucks. From the consumers' point of view, if trucks couldn't fulfill these expectations, they simply wouldn't purchase them.

For 1980, Chevrolet engineers concentrated on detail refinements to improve efficiency and overall value of its light-duty trucks. All new Chevrolet pickups and vans featured new radial tires, new grilles, exterior paint colors, radio options, and revised instrument panels. A front air dam was added to the Blazer, Suburban, and all pickups to increase aerodynamics and, consequently, mileage. Full-time 4WD was phased out in favor of the more efficient part-time, or on-demand, 4WD system.

A torque converter clutch system was now available for use with automatics on most trucks of less than 8,500 pounds GVW. The clutch engaged automatically at about 30 miles per hour to lock all elements of the converter.

Driveline changes made in the interest of increasing fuel mileage included making the new 229 V-6 standard on the El Camino. The largest engine available in 1979, the 350 four-barrel, was dropped.

For other Chevrolet pickups, the 400 and 454 V-8 engines were either discontinued or restricted to vehicles over 8,500 pounds.

Chevrolet's most popular 1980 pickup was the Fleetside. This is an 8-foot cargo box C20 Fleetside Silverado. Its grille received a mild styling upgrade with eleven rows versus the five rows of 1979's grille design. The bold bow tie emblem was carried over unchanged. It wouldn't be a Chevrolet without a bow tie! Chevrolet pickups for 1980 featured energy-saving engineering, including a new thermostatically controlled fan and a dual exhaust system. Radial tires were standard equipment on all C/K 10 and 20 models up to 8,500 pounds GVW. The standard engine for the C20 pickup was the 4.1-liter L6; the 5.7-liter V-8 served as an option. *AAMA*

Chevrolet's top-of-the-line model was the Fleetside Silverado, a C20 with 8-foot box. An energy-saving feature of these pickups was a new air deflector located behind and below the front bumper. The standard engine was the 4.1-liter L6, but most often the C20 was equipped with the optional 5.7-liter V-8. The standard transmission was a three-speed manual; a four-speed manual and an automatic were options. Its Rally wheels featuring the Chevrolet bow tie on the hubs were also an option. The Fleetside Silverado was equipped with a full tailgate insert. *AAMA*

Other engineering changes to improve fuel efficiency included new axle ratios, intake and exhaust manifolds, and the use of thermostatically controlled fans on most models.

Engineers also made improvements to medium-duty trucks to increase fuel economy. The biggest change was the expanded

The El Camino for 1980 featured fuel-economy engineering. Included was a new standard lightweight 3.8-liter engine with an energy-efficient torque converter clutch system, thermostatically controlled fan and a new exhaust system. New styling highlights included a new grille and larger bezels surrounding headlamps and parking lamps. The popular Royal Knight package was again available on Super Sport models. The 1/2-ton rated, 117.1-inch-wheelbase El Camino was a personal truck but was very capable of hauling a significant payload. *AAMA*

The Blazer featured the same restyled front appearance as pickups. This model featured the new optional chrome grille and rectangular headlights. An Argent Silver grille with round headlamps was standard. The Blazer also featured the one-piece air dam. This top-of-the-line model was equipped with the special optional 4x4 Rally wheels and front bumper guards. Like the pickups, the Blazer featured improved fuel economy with the new exhaust system, thermostatically controlled fan, and energy-efficient torque converter clutch system. 4WD models had only part-time transfer cases with manual locking hubs. Radial tires were standard. Engine choices included the 4.1-liter L6, 5.0-liter, and 5.7-liter V-8s. *AAMA*

diesel engine offerings for the medium-duty (mid-range) trucks. The most important new engine was the Detroit Diesel Allison 8.2-liter turbocharged "Fuel Pincher" diesel. Two other fuel efficient diesels added for 1980 were the Cummins VT-225 9.1 liter and the Caterpillar 3208, 10.4 liter. It is not definitely known if any of the Cummins VT-225 engines were ever installed in these trucks. It's possible a few installations were made, but this engine had reliability problems and was not looked upon with much favor.

Midrange diesels accounted for only 9.6 percent of the market in 1978. It was projected that they would take fully 50 percent of the market by 1985. The new "Fuel-Pincher" diesels were purposely designed for the market to displace gas engines. They were about the same physical size as the 366 gasser; the 366 weighed about 850 pounds versus 1,100 pounds for the diesel. The Fuel-Pincher was designed for quiet operation. The diesel's fuel economy was double that of the gas engines and its service lifetime was significantly longer. Detroit Diesel engineers claimed the extra cost of the diesel could be paid back in two years.

Chevrolet's entire truck line carried over into 1980 with the changes mentioned above. Every model from the mini LUV to the giant Titan returned. The truck with the greatest changes for 1980 was the downsized El Camino.

This was the last year for Chevrolet's heavy-duty truck line. This was also the last year for medium-duty steel cab tilts. A gradual phase-out of the heavy-duty dealer network went on during the year, and by October the job was done. Most of the former 150 Chevrolet heavy-duty dealers switched to GMC.

This was also the first year for the Kodiak. It more or less replaced the Bruin, and used the standard light- and medium-duty truck cab but with a fiberglass hood. The cab sat farther forward and higher than other medium-duty trucks, so it could mount the Cat 3209 diesel or the Detroit turbo 8.2-liter diesel engines. The 3208 had been an option in the Bruin.

Chevrolet's Big 10 pickup was a heavy-duty 1/2-tonner equipped to haul over a ton of payload. A heavier frame plus heavy-duty suspension, brake system, and tires gave it GVW ranges of 6,050 to 6,200 pounds. This compares to GVW ranges of 4,900 to 5,600 pounds for the conventional C 10 pickups. Unlike the C 10 pickup, the Big 10's standard engine was the 5.0-liter V-8; the 5.7-liter V-8 was an option. Radial tires provided long wear and low rolling resistance. This is a 6 1/2-foot Stepside cargo box. The 4.1-liter six was made available on Big 10 models and C/K20 series up to 7,500 pounds. *AAMA*

In the entire 1980 calendar year, Chevrolet sold only 2,053 heavy trucks. Its medium-duty sales for 1980 totaled 30,108, down from 41,373 the year before. To be fair, the industry was down due to an economic recession. Chevrolet's future "big-truck" activities (classes 4 through 6) would be sold through the 5,700 dealers franchised to handle Chevrolet cars and light trucks.

Either way one looks at it, by calendar year or by model year, Chevrolet's 1980 results were disappointing. Calendar year sales totaled 756,491 versus 1,104,616 in 1979. Model year sales totaled 828,021 versus 1,205,497 in 1979. Chevrolet came in second place in sales ranking to number one Ford. All models across the board declined in about the same percentages except for the LUV, which was off by only about 5 percent. The buyer's number one interest in 1980 was fuel economy at a time when gas was selling for a buck a gallon.

Chevrolet's Beauville Sportvan could seat up to 12 and hold plenty of cargo. High-back front bucket seats with choice of attractive fabrics were standard. The "people moving" Sportvans from Chevrolet were offered in 1/2-, 3/4-, and 1-ton series (G10, G20, and G30). G10 and G20 models were available on both a 110-inch or 125-inch wheelbase, and G30 on the 125-inch wheelbase only. The Sportvan's easy opening and extra-wide side door offered easy access for passengers and ease of loading luggage, packages, or cargo. Standard engine was the 4.1-liter six for G10 and G20 and the 5.7-liter V-8 for G30. Engine options included the 5.0-, 5.7-, and 6.6-liter V-8s. Standard transmission with all engines was the three-speed manual, but most vans were ordered with the automatic. *AAMA*

Chevrolet's 1980 1-ton K20 chassis cabs provided a tough 4WD chassis on which to mount any number of custom-designed specialized bodies, such as a wrecker pictured. Big Dooley dual rear wheels were an option. GVWs ranged from 9,200 to 10,000 pounds. The standard engine was the 4.8-liter L-6. The 5.7- and 6.6-liter V-8s were available as options for severe duty applications. A four-speed manual transmission was standard, and an automatic was optional. Transfer case was the New Process NP 205. K30 chassis cab wheelbase lengths included 131.5, 135.5, and 159.5 inches. *AAMA*

Chevy Vans featured energy-saving engineering. Included were a new torque converter clutch system, thermostatically controlled fan, and a dual exhaust system. Other changes included additional corrosion-resistant materials and a new grille. Front and rear seats were redesigned for comfort and roominess, and there was a new standard combination lap-shoulder belt. The Chevy Van was offered in three ratings: G10, G20, and G30. This is a G20 3/4-ton. The standard engine for G10 and G20 was the 4.1-liter six and the 5.7-liter V-8 for G30. Optional engines included the 5.0-, 5.7-, and 6.6-liter V-8s. A three-speed manual transmission was standard, and an automatic was optional. *AAMA*

Chevrolet's conventional 4WD system made these trucks dependable on the job or on the trail. Standard features of Chevrolet four-wheelers included power steering, manual-locking hubs, a front stabilizer bar, and power front disc/rear drum brakes. It also included multi-leaf springs front and rear, drop-center frame design for low cab floor height, a two-piece drive shaft for rugged simplicity and a one-piece front air deflector on 1/2- and 3/4-tons. This is a 1980 1/2-ton 4WD Stepside Sport with factory-installed Sport Package on a 6 1/2-foot box. The Sport Package consisted of two-tone paint, sport striping, chromed grille, rectangular headlights, body colored bumpers with black impact strips, color-keyed carpeting, extra-thick floor insulation, and Chevy Sport graphics. *AAMA*

This 1980 C10 Suburban Silverado could seat up to nine passengers. With the available third seat installed, there was still 35 cubic feet of cargo area at the rear. The third seat could be easily removed by releasing cam-type latches and sliding the seat off the front anchors. The Silverado trim was Chevrolet's top-of-the-line interior and exterior. Seats were upholstered in soft velour fabrics. On the floor was color-keyed cut-pile carpeting. Other deluxe interior appointments included a visor-mounted mirror on the passenger side, bright brushed instrument cluster frame, and needle-type full-gauge instrumentation. Standard engine for C10 and C20 Suburbans was the 5.7-liter V-8. The 7.4-liter V-8 was optional for the heavy-duty C20 and the 6.6-liter was optional for the K20. *AAMA*

Roomy Chevrolet P-Series Step-Van Kings were built tough. There were designed for service ranging from parcel delivery trucks to rescue vehicles and TV mobile units, to name a few. P20 chassis and P20 Step-Vans came in wheelbases of 125, 133, and 157 inches with body lengths of 10, 12, and 14 feet. Cargo bodies were constructed of either steel or aluminum. The short-wheelbase P10 Step-Van had a 102-inch wheelbase with 7- or 8-foot steel bodies or an 8-foot aluminum body. The standard engine for P10, P20, and P30 was the 4.8-liter six; the 5.7-liter V-8 was optional for P-20 and P-30 models. This is a 1980 P-30 Step-Van King with 12-foot body. *AAMA*

Chevrolet's conventional cab medium-duty trucks for 1980 featured an all-new Detroit Diesel 8.2-liter diesel engine, the "Fuel-Pincher," which offered fuel economy savings of up to 100 percent over comparably powered gasoline engines. Two versions were available: turbocharged 192 net horsepower and naturally aspirated 153 net horsepower. In addition, the naturally aspirated 3208 Caterpillar diesel in four power versions was offered. Also new for the medium-duty line was an economical 10-speed lightweight transmission that did not require air to shift. Pictured here is a 1980 C50 conventional chassis cab with aircraft fueler body. *AAMA*

Pictured here are Chevrolet's two medium-duty 1980 trucks, the husky Kodiak in the foreground, and the Conventional cab behind. The Kodiak was equipped with a Caterpillar four-cycle diesel engine, available with 160, 175, or 210 horsepower. The diesel was new to Chevrolet's medium-duty line, but had been available in heavy-duty models. The standard medium-duty Chevrolet offered an all-new 8.2-liter engine from Detroit Diesel. Chevrolet began installing these new engines in February 1980. *AAMA*

Chevrolet's Bison was the "Magnificent Beast" of its heavy-duty line. It was a tough, high-performance heavy-duty truck well liked by drivers. The Bison was offered in two models: a 108-inch BBC, for construction and off-road use, and a 116-inch BBC for highway use. The Bison's cab was constructed of lightweight aluminum. Its fenders and hood were of lightweight fiberglass. Bison's hood tilted forward a full 90 degrees. Engine choices ran the gamut of diesels: choice of 16 from Detroit Diesel, 5 from Cummins, and 1 Caterpillar. A diesel to suit every application and owner preference. Bison's maximum GVW rating ranged from 33,860 to 44,860 pounds, and GCW of 80,000 pounds. *AAMA*

Chevrolet's Bruin for 1980 offered a full line of diesel power, featuring a new turbocharged V6-53T engine from Detroit Diesel in J80 models, along with other Detroit Diesel, Caterpillar, and Cummins diesel engines. The new diesel provided fuel economy, higher horsepower, and better heat rejection, at only a minimal price increase over the 1979 V6-54N diesel. The 427 V-8 was still available as standard power on the J80 Series. The J80 had the traditional butterfly hood and the J90 had a fiberglass tilt hood that swung outward 90 degrees for excellent engine accessibility. Bruin models could be equipped for up to 80,000 pounds GCW. This is a 1980 J90 Bruin. *AAMA*

This was Chevrolet's last year as a marketer of heavy-duty trucks. Chevrolet's medium-duty and heavy-duty trucks were built by GMC. The Chevrolet Titan, the flagship of Chevrolet's fleet, featured a major cost and weight reduction program for 1980. Included were a new transmission shift tower, a stamped front frame cap, cable clutch controls, a redesigned lower cab pivot bracket, new engine mounts, an aluminum clutch housing, an aluminum transmission trail support, tapered leaf springs, and a redesigned passenger seat support. These changes reduced weight by almost 349 pounds. Chevrolet engineers took out 40 additional pounds by making cab doors of sheet-molded compound plastic. The Titan's new "SS" grille offered better styling and appearance. Titan's diesel-only engine options included 11 models from Detroit Diesel, 2 from Caterpillar and 7 from Cummins. Transmission options included four from Fuller, two from Spicer, and two from Allison. *AAMA*

Chevrolet's Cutaway Van chassis model CG31303 with a 125-inch wheelbase was often used for small school bus applications using bus bodies by independent suppliers. With dual rear wheels, maximum GVWs up to 10,000 pounds were possible. Small school buses, such as the one pictured, were a fast-growing part of the Cutaway Van chassis business. The nation's public schools added more and more new special needs services such as "Head Start," and other programs for children with special needs. The standard drivetrain for this small bus consisted of the 350 V-8 engine and either a three-speed manual or an automatic. *Iten Chevrolet*

Chevrolet offered three Step-Van Series in 1980: P10, P20, and P30. The P10's maximum GVW was 6,200l pounds. The P20's maximum GVW was 8,000 pounds and P30's maximum GVW was 14,000 pounds. Chevrolet did not build the Step-Van's bodies. The Union City Body Co. made them and mounted them on Chevrolet's forward-control chassis. The complete truck was then shipped to the selling dealer who delivered it to the customer. Chevrolet also sold the chassis only, for the mounting of any number of other quality bodies. Engine options included the standard 115-horsepower 4.8-liter six cylinder engine, the 165-horsepower 5.7-liter V-8, and the 180-horsepower 6.6-liter V-8. Transmission options included three- and four-speed manuals and an automatic. This is a 1980 Chevrolet P30 Step-Van King 14-foot steel body. The Nappanee, Indiana, Fire Department owned rescue 80. *Dennis J. Maag*

The Bison's cab was constructed of aluminum, but the big, rugged, long conventional Bison had a heart of steel. This beautiful giant was available only with diesel power: Detroit, Cummins, and Caterpillar, a total of 22 standard diesels from all three manufacturers. Standard transmission offerings included Fuller and Spicer manuals with up to 15 speeds and Allison four- and five-speed automatics, and a four-speed Spicer auxiliary. Pictured here is a last of the breed, 1980 Bison Series N9F064 tandem-axle chassis cab with sleeper and fifth wheel equipment. Is there an available option not seen on #1 "Super Sport?" Note that the headlights are not stock. *Dick Copello*

A straight 1980 Bison powered by a Detroit Diesel 8V-71N was in its last year of production. This tanker/pumper Truck No. 151 was beautiful in yellow and trimmed with bright metal. The Oxford, Maryland, Fire Department owned it. Welch in Wisconsin built its body. The only missing items are a pair of tall chrome exhaust pipes. As a straight truck the Bison's maximum GVW was 43,860 pounds. Bison offered two basic models: a 108-inch BBC targeted for construction and off-road use, and a 116-inch BBC intended for over-the-road tractor trailer service. *Dick Copello*

1981

In 1971 the pump price of premium gasoline was 36 cents per gallon. Ten years later 94-octane premium unleaded sold as high as $1.50 per gallon. Gas in 1981 was in abundant supply, however.

In the third quarter of 1980 GM lost $567 million, Ford lost $595 million, Chrysler lost $490 million, and AMC lost $85 million. That added up to a third quarter total loss for the auto industry of $1.7 billion!

Business was tough going into the 1981 model year. All truck manufacturers for 1981 highlighted improved fuel economy, reduced weight, and better aerodynamics for their new models. Chevrolet was no exception. The manufacturers said pretty much the same things the year before, and the year before that, but in 1981 there was some concrete evidence. Fuel economy was up,

wind resistance was down, and the trucks actually dropped a few pounds of weight. Chevrolet, like the others, was serious about getting back to selling trucks.

Chevrolet used the words light and lean to describe its 1981 2WD and 4WD light-duty fleet. Its trucks were more extensively overhauled than in any year since 1973. Chevrolet engineers aerodynamically designed the sheet metal from the cowl forward. Without sacrificing size or cargo-carrying capacity, the 1981 light-duty trucks were reduced in weight by 115 to 309 pounds. On top of this, engineers added a new computer-controlled 5.0-liter engine, a new "all-time" transfer case (on demand) system, automatic locking hubs, and low-drag disc brakes, all to improve mileage.

Chevrolet's LUV was completely restyled for 1981. The success of this truck proved it was right on target. It was even more right beginning in 1981, due to its up-to-date appearance. It sleek aerodynamic look made it more like an American truck than an imported truck. The LUV's new cab provided more interior room than the previous model, as well as more legroom and shoulder room. Also new was a distinctive dash and instrumentation, rich new upholstery and trim, a new glovebox with lock, and side window defoggers. The LUV had a 7 1/2-foot cargo box and an impressive payload capacity of 1,680 pounds. The 1.8-liter four with cast-aluminum head and cast-iron block burned unleaded gasoline. This is a 1981 LUV 4WD pickup. The LUV's standard interior was all vinyl. The upscale Mikado interior was available in choice of two color schemes—blue or red. *AAMA*

Chevrolet offered this Custom Deluxe C10 Fleetside as a "Special Economy Truck" (SET). SETs on long and short wheelbases were real fuel economy champs. They were available with either a new high-compression 5.0-liter V-8, or 4.1-liter L-6 engine, and with new aerodynamically front sheet metal and a four-speed overdrive manual transmission. The SET short wheelbase model was offered with L-6 engine only. It was rated for 21 miles per gallon city and 30 highway, and 24 combined. The high-compression V-8 engine was available in either long or short wheelbase pickups rated for 20 miles per gallon city, 28 highway, and 23 combined. These mileage figures were based on the use of a manual transmission. At this period in time, just after the nation's second energy crisis, car and truck owners' major focus was on economy. Before the first energy crises in 1973, gasoline sold for 30 cents per gallon. In 1981, gas sold for over a buck a gallon. *AAMA*

Light-duty trucks featured a fresh new grille design and stacked rectangular headlights, aerodynamically designed front sheet metal plus engine and drivetrain refinements designed to enhance fuel economy without sacrificing utility. This is a 1981 C10 Fleetside pickup with optional Silverado trim package. Available engines included a 4.1-liter L-6 as standard, and the 5.0-liter V-8 with either two-barrel or four-barrel carburetors, and electronic spark control. Both gasoline and diesel versions of the 5.7-liter V-8 were also offered. Chevrolet engineers took weight off pickups ranging from 121 to 307 pounds. This truck was about 140 pounds lighter than a comparable 1980 model pickup. *AAMA*

Chevrolet's Suburban had the same new front styling as all other light-duty models. The only other styling changes included new paint schemes and new side molding treatments. This is a top-of-the-line 1981 C10 Suburban Silverado. Three Suburban trim levels were available: The standard Custom Deluxe, optional Scottsdale, and Silverado. The standard front seat was a full-width bench. The Silverado Suburban could be ordered with sporty high-back custom bucket seats. A new center console had a lockable storage compartment, plus a cover that could be folded rearward for use as a snack tray. The Suburban's engine lineup was chosen with gas mileage in mind. C10's engines included the 5.0- and 5.7-liter V-8s. C20 models, on the other hand, were powered for towing—standard 5.7-liter and optional 7.4-liter V-8. The only engine offered for K10 and K20 was the 5.7-liter V-8. *AAMA*

Chevrolet's 1981 Nomad was a modified Series G20, 125-inch-wheelbase van, with a luxurious Beauville interior in the passenger area, and an insulated plywood load space in back. It featured passenger seating for five with high-back bucket seats up front and a removable bench-type seat behind. Swing-out windows in the sliding side door and opposite panel were standard. Other special features of Nomad included special sport-striping, sliding side door extender line, styled wheels, deluxe front-end styling with chrome-trimmed grille and grille air intakes painted black, chrome trim tail light bezels, and five special paint color combinations. The engine lineup for G20 vans included the standard 4.1-liter six and 5.0- and 5.7-liter V-8s. Standard transmission was the three-speed manual; optional was an automatic. *AAMA*

Chevrolet built P20 and P30 Series forward-control chassis on three wheelbases in 1981: 125, 133, and 157 inches. The 1/2-ton P10 was no longer offered. Step-Van series also continued for 1981 without style changes. These ever-popular vans were still available with both steel or aluminum bodies on 125-, 133-, and 157-inch wheelbases in Series P20 and P30. The small P10 1/2-ton Step-Vans were dropped. The short wheelbase C10 Step-van with 7- or 8-foot steel or aluminum bodies were last built in 1979. Payload ratings ranged from a low of 1,315 to 8,682 pounds. GVW ratings ranged from 6,800 to 10,000 pounds. Engine availability included the 4.8-liter six and 5.7-liter V-8. *AAMA*

The 5.0-liter V-8 engine saved gas due to a 9.2:1 high-compression ratio that combined a four-barrel carburetor with Chevrolet's ESC (electronic spark control). The ESC unit adjusted distributor timing continually, igniting the fuel mixture at just the right instant for varying engine load and gas octane conditions. The engine produced 20 percent more power while delivering the same fuel economy as last year's 5-liter V-8 with a two-barrel carburetor. The combination of high compression with ESC to protect against pre-ignition significantly boosted horsepower without the need for high-octane premium fuel.

The new 4WD system, which was lighter and featured automatic locking hubs, was available on 1/2- and 3/4-ton pickups, Blazers, and Suburbans. Shifting into 4WD was possible at speeds up to 20 miles per hour, and the truck was returned to 2WD by stopping, disengaging the transfer case, and driving in reverse about 10 feet. The weight loss was said to improve gas mileage by 1 mile per gallon in GM's 1981 truck fleet average.

A new instrument panel featured international symbols, keyed switches, a combination console/drink holder for the Blazer, and some new trim and upholstery options added to Chevrolet pickups traditional practical comfort.

The Chevrolet LUV was in reality an Isuzu P'UP pickup. Under a different name, it was extensively restyled for 1981 with a slippery new body and a new grille, wraparound front bumper, new doors, and curved rear window glass. In the cab, there was more legroom and shoulder room, and a new instrument panel, seats, and steering column completed the package.

Isuzu offered the P'UP with either gas or diesel power. Chevrolet announced late in 1980 that beginning in May 1981 with the new Series 11 LUV, the 136.6-ci diesel engine would also

be offered for 2WD and 4WD models. The EPA rated the diesel 32 miles per gallon city, and 44 highway for the 2WD. The 4WD was rated 28 miles per gallon city and 35 miles per gallon highway by the EPA.

Chevrolet's 1981 Step-Van models featured extensive improvements in suspensions, interiors, and bodies. Heavy-duty front and rear shocks, plus a heavy-duty front stabilizer bar, became standard. Other equipment made standard included tinted windshields, power steering, wide-angle rearview mirrors, and an extra cargo lamp. Additional cargo capacity became available by adding 6 1/2 inches to the length and 4 inches to the height of bodies. Body choices included aluminum or steel construction.

GM formed a new Worldwide Truck and Bus Group in 1981, which was responsible for all truck and bus operations worldwide. GMC's role was to coordinate design and production of GM's GVW Class 6 through 8 trucks and buses. GMC also continued as the corporation's manufacturer of all medium- and heavy-duty trucks, including those marketed by Chevrolet. GMC's U.S. plants ran at less than 50 percent capacity in 1981.

Retail sales of Chevrolet's medium-duty trucks in 1981 fell 36 percent below those of 1980, to 20,638 from 32,161. This was due in most part to the deepening U.S. economic slump.

Although Chevrolet ended Class 7 and 8 distribution, it nevertheless sold 1,228 heavy-duty units in 1981. However, these heavy-duty models were Class 6 (medium-duties) optioned with tandem axles and heavier components.

Chevrolet's truck sales came in second place again to Ford in 1981. Chevrolet's 675,628 retail sales were off 11 percent from 1980's total of 756,491. Chevrolet's management had forecast sales of one million units.

Chevrolet offered both 2WD and 4WD chassis cab models in four wheelbases to accept bodies from 7 to 13 feet long. A new C30 heavy-duty chassis cab had a 10,500-pound GVW rating and included optional heavy-duty suspension components and dual rear wheels. This is a 1981 Chevrolet K30 1-ton 4WD chassis cab with firefighting body. The Keokuk, Iowa, Fire Department owned attack 1. It was equipped with a 1982 model Smeal body with a 300-gallon water tank and a 250-gpm pump. Chevrolet's 4WDs featured automatic locking front hubs. K10 and K20 models had a new lightweight aluminum transfer case with synchro gears that allowed the driver to shift from 2WD to 4WD at speeds under 24 miles per hour. The console was floor-mounted with lighted indicator. In 2WD the transfer case and front axle shaft didn't turn to reduce wear and contribute to fuel economy. *Dennis J. Maag*

Chevrolet reengineered its trucks for 1981, but kept the features that had proved their value. The trucks were substantially improved to keep pace with the demands of the 1980s. Outstanding features such as their rugged steel frames, double-wall construction in inner and outer steel walls in doors, front fenders, the cab rear panel, the hood, the Fleetside pickup box side panels, and the tailgate were all retained, as was the big roomy cab. The 5.0-liter V-8 was improved with a four-barrel carburetor and Electric Spark Control. It was available on selected 10 series trucks. It had a substantial 9.2:1 compression ratio and offered very good acceleration and horsepower for an engine of its size. The dependable 4.1-liter six was improved with a recalibrated carburetor and a redesigned camshaft for smooth idling and driving. The Palm Desert, California, Volunteer Fire Company owned this 1981 Chevrolet C30 chassis cab with a firefighting body. The lettering low on the body says "Purchased with donations from the people of Palm Desert." *Chuck Madderom*

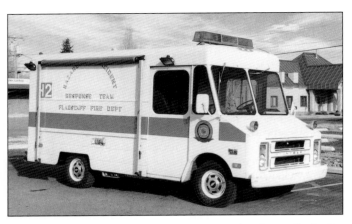

The Step-Van was frequently put to use by the nation's fire departments. The Hazardous Accident Response Team of the Flagstaff, Arizona, Fire Department specially converted this 1981 P20 Step-Van truck for service. For 1981, Chevrolet engineers increased its standard cargo capacity by adding 6 inches in length and 6 inches in height to the body. Heavy-duty shocks and a heavy-duty front stabilizer bar were made standard to improve the suspension. For driver convenience, a new tinted windshield glass, power steering, exterior wide-angle mirrors, and an extra cargo lamp were made standard equipment. The standard engine for the P20 was the 4.8-liter L-6, and the 5.7-liter V-8 was optional. *Greenberg*

Chevrolet engineers knew many operators performed much of their own service work, so they made a great effort to make servicing as easy as possible. A big part of the solution was to make three hood designs available. The standard steel alligator hood opened wide and long to provide easy access to engine and components from either side or the front. Note how the hood has a deep skirt on both sides so when opened, the technician could more easily reach all underhood areas. A tilt hood was an option. This one-piece counterbalanced unit incorporated the hood and front fender in one light fiberglass unit that could be tilted forward easily by one person. The third hood was the fiberglass tilt hood with the Kodiak option. When Caterpillar 3208 or Cummins VT-225 diesel engines were ordered on a C60 or C70 model, the Kodiak option was required. This hood on a 1981 Chevrolet C60 consisted of the massive grille and front fenders. It was about 7 inches higher than the conventional cab for a high view of the road. The Outagamie County Airport in Greenville, Wisconsin, owned unit 52. Pierce built its body, and it included a 500-gallon water tank and a 500-gpm pump. Its 4WD conversion was by Marmon-Herrington. *Dennis J. Maag*

Chevrolet presented two medium-duty trucks for 1981. The Conventional Series continued without change. The medium Kodiak was a new model. The Kodiak was basically the same truck as the conventional cab series, but when a C60 or C70 model was ordered with the Caterpillar 3208 engine, a higher hood was required. The Kodiak's hood, grille, and front bumper design appeared to be completely different from the conventional cab series, but such was not the case. Tandem models were offered in both C60 and C70 Series. In addition to the Cat 3208 and Cummins VT-225 diesel engines, the Detroit Diesel 8.2-liter diesel, in two horsepower versions, was made an option for various C60 and C70 trucks. This 1981 Chevrolet C60 chassis cab with dump body had a GVW of 24,500 pounds. This truck had a five-speed transmission, a two-speed rear axle, and a 5-yard box. It weighed 10,000 pounds empty. *Nollie W. Neill, Jr.*

Chevrolet's biggest single-axle Conventional medium-duty was the C70. This is a chassis cab with firefighting body. The El Dorado Hills, California, Fire Department owned Engine 285. It had a Beck body with a 500-gallon water tank and a 500-gpm pump. The maximum GVW rating of the C70 was 33,200 pounds. The standard engine for this model was the 6.0-liter V-8; the 7.0-liter V-8 was an option. Both Detroit Diesel engines, the four 3208 Caterpillar diesels, and the Cummins VT-225 diesel were options. If it had been powered by any of the Caterpillar engines or the Cummins engine, it would have had the higher, optional Kodiak hood, grille, and front fenders. *Garry E. Kadzielawski*

Chevrolet exited the heavy-duty truck business in 1980, but continued to be a builder and marketer of medium-duty trucks. Chevrolet showed only one medium-duty line in 1981. It was called the Conventional Series 50-60-70, and Series 60-70 tandems. From an appearance standpoint, the 1981 mediums retained the same look as 1980 models. The Kodiak option consisted of a massive grille and fiberglass tilt hood. This option was required because of the need for a larger, taller radiator to provide adequate cooling. The Kodiak's cab rode about 7 inches higher than the conventional cab. Paturel Seafoods, Shediac, New Brunswick, Canada, owned this 1981 Chevrolet C60 Kodiak tandem chassis cab with sleeper and van body. It hauled fish or lobsters from remote ports to packing plants. *Mac Mackay*

The Chevrolet Blazer was the right truck to take off-roading, over the roughest terrain. The 4WD Blazer offered new automatic locking front hubs as standard. Also new for 1981 were quad front shocks as an option for the buyer who took his Blazer off-road. It could also be ordered as a 2WD model. Optional cruise control had a "resume speed" feature and was available on all engines with an automatic transmission. Rectangular halogen-type headlamps were a new option offered on trucks with the deluxe front appearance option. New 4WD system featured automatic locking front hubs. When shifted from freewheeling 2WD to 4WD, the hubs automatically locked up, eliminating the need to get out to set them. To revert to 2WD, the driver simply stopped, shifted into 2H, backed up slowly about 10 feet, and then went on his way. The economical 115-horsepower 250-ci L6 engine powered this Blazer.

Chevrolet's workhorse school bus series was the B60 Chassis. The B60 came in six wheelbases—149, 189, 218, 235, 254 plus an extended 274-inch. These chassis accommodated a wide range of bus bodies from various manufacturers with capacities up to 72 passengers. For 1981, the cowl was redesigned without the vent to help eliminate a source of water leaks into the body. This B60 72-passenger school bus was powered by the 8.2-liter Detroit Diesel Allison Fuel Pincher naturally aspirated diesel, producing 165 gross horsepower. A turbocharged 205-horsepower version was available for B60. Chevrolet's school bus chassis met or exceeded all NEA-recommended minimum standards for school buses. A four-speed manual transmission was standard equipment, and an automatic was an option.

In an era of downsizing, economy, and high mileage, the El Camino toned down its former reputation of power and performance. El Camino's engine lineup for 1981 started with tiny 3.8-liter V-6, bumped up to the slightly larger 4.4-liter V-8, and topped off with the big-for-the-times 5.0-liter V-8. Horsepower ratings were 110, 115, and 145, respectively. However, the El Camino didn't give up anything in terms of beauty and driving pleasure. This is a base 1981 Chevrolet El Camino. Other 1981 models included Royal Knight, Super Sport, and Conquista. The Conquista amounted to a special two-tone paint scheme, decal on the tailgate, and a dash nameplate. El Camino's rugged cargo bed would hold up to 35.5 cubic feet of cargo and a maximum GVW of 1,250 pounds.

The Hi-Cube Van was one of Chevrolet's hardest-working trucks. It was built in two series: 125- and 146-inch wheelbases, with maximum GVW ratings of 8,600 and 10,000 pounds. The 146-inch-wheelbase series was standard with dual rear wheels; the 125-inch series was available with either single or dual rears. The only engine offered for Hi-Cube Vans was the 5.7-liter V-8. Transmissions included a three-speed manual and an automatic. Hi-Cube Van's bodies were offered in either steel or aluminum. The longest body offered on the 125-inch-wheelbase series was a 10-footer; the longest body on the 146-inch chassis series was a 12-footer. This is a 1981 Chevrolet 146-inch-wheelbase Hi-Cube Van with 12-foot body.

Chevrolet's G30-RV Cutaway Van was the same basic vehicle as the commercial Hi-Cube Van. The difference was in their bodies. The G30-RV Cutaway Van Series was also offered on 125- and 146-inch wheelbases. Maximum GVW ratings were 8,900 and 10,500 pounds, respectively. Dual rear wheels were standard equipment on the 146-inch-wheelbase series. The only available drivetrain was the 5.7-liter V-8 with an automatic. Power steering and brakes were standard.

Chevrolet's biggest gas-powered 1981 truck was the C70 Conventional Series. Pictured here is a 1981 C70 chassis cab with dump body (a heavy-duty Schwartz hydraulic hoist). The standard 6.0-liter gas V-8 engine mounted to a five-speed main transmission powers it. It also has a 22,000-pound two-speed Eaton-22221 rear axle. Its maximum GVW rating is 33,200 pounds. This truck was recently cleaned and fixed up by its owner, and as of 1999, was still employed in his trucking business. *Bill Wasner*

1982

For the first time since 1979, there was a bit of cheer in the truck industry. Chevrolet led the way with its new S-10 compact pickups, the first of the new small domestic trucks. The S-10 went on sale in the fall of 1981, a full six months before Ford's Ranger and Dodge's Rampage hit the streets. These trucks led the upsurge in light-duty truck sales. Chevrolet sold 152,956 S-10s to Ford's 76,684 Rangers.

Chevrolet's total model year sales jumped 9 percent to 758,387, putting Chevrolet back in first place in sales for the first time since 1976. Full-size pickups trailed model year 1981, but showed an improvement. Only Dodge and GMC sold more full-size pickups in 1982 than in 1981.

A small truck used to refer to a Japanese mini-truck. But that all changed in March 1982, when sales of American small trucks surpassed the imports. The American trucks didn't drive the imports into the ocean, however, as some in the industry had predicted.

During their first year, S-10/S-15, Ranger and Rampage sold an impressive 359,177 compact trucks, giving the U.S. manufacturers 47 percent of the market.

In July of 1982, GM received an order from the Army for 53,000 4WD light-duty vehicles. The opening order was worth $689 million, and the contract could go as high as $1.3 billion, if the Army exercised options to double the order.

The contract covered Chevrolet Blazers and 4WD pickups, slightly modified for military use, for delivery beginning in 1983. All would be powered by the 6.2-liter diesel engine. The Army's plan was to make 95 percent of its truck fleet diesel by 1987.

Chevrolet's calendar year sales of 808,085 units were up 20 percent from 675,628 in 1981. This increase over 1981 was good enough to beat Ford out of first place. Medium-duty sales topped off at 31,032 units. This total was down from 1981's 33,668, but reflected some stabilization in the commercial medium-duty market.

GM strengthened its medium-duty school bus chassis in 1982 by adding the Allison AT-545 automatic transmission as an option with the Detroit Diesel 8.2-liter Fuel Pincher engine, and two new GM-built rear axles, a single-speed and a two-speed. Also new for the school bus line was a full 27,500-pound GVW chassis unit. This allowed for the use of the Fuel Pincher engine with the 72-passenger, 274-inch-wheelbase model.

Other new medium-duty features included improved exhaust routing on the right side for better transmission and power take-off option clearance. Roof marker lights became standard equipment. A new two-tone vinyl bench seat and three interior trim levels were offered. New exterior colors and two-tone combinations were also available.

Chevrolet unveiled an all-new 6.2-liter (379.4-ci) diesel engine designed from a clean sheet of paper. It was designed for light-truck service in city delivery, for stop and go work with considerable idle time, for light and moderate-weight trailering, or extended highway driving. It was available on all pickups, 2WD and 4WD (K10 only), chassis cabs, Blazers, Suburbans, Step-Vans, forward-control chassis, and motor-home chassis models. The new 6.2 diesel opened the door for the Army truck contract; it was the only diesel available in any U. S. built light-duty truck.

The 1/2-ton pickups, Blazers and Suburbans, were mostly unchanged for 1982. The standard engine was the 4.1-liter (250) six; the 5.0-liter (305) V-8 was an option (with ESC, electronic spark control), as was the 5.7-liter (350), and 7.4 liter (454) V-8s. Chevrolet added corrosion protection to the brake lines, hydraulic power steering lines, and the rear step bumper in 1982. For 4WD models, automatic locking hubs were standard, as was synchronized gearing in the NP205 transfer case. The heavier pickups, C/K 20 and C/K 30, had added heavy-duty 32mm shock absorbers, a new height-sensing brake system, 16-inch wheels instead of 16 1/2, and a 63-amp generator and roof marker lights.

The LUV imported mini-truck carried over basically unchanged from 1981. The 2.2-liter Isuzu diesel introduced in midyear 1981 carried over, too. The Series 11 LUVs featured a five-speed (2WD) and a four-speed (4WD) manual transmission as standard equipment with the diesel. The diesel models offered power steering as an option.

Chevrolet's 1982 S-10 pickup featured double-wall construction of its tailgate, hood, front fenders, and doors. Extensive use of zinc-metal and galvanized steel was used for corrosion protection. The new pickup came in short- and long-box models in four trim levels: base (pictured), Durango, Tahoe, and Sport. The S-10's engine choices included the standard 1.9-liter four and the 2.8-liter V-6. Later in the model year, a five-speed manual with overdrive was available on S-10s with the V-6 engine. The S-10 pickups immediately began to be identified with the term "compacts." The S-10 was only offered as a Fleetside model. The entire industry was pushing hard for the end of the Stepside-type because its assembly costs were high and demand continued to fall. *AAMA*

Coming around the steeply banked curve of GM's Proving Grounds is a C10 pickup (left), and on the inside lane, the new S-10 pickup. It was bigger than the imported LUV mini-pickup, but smaller than the 1/2-ton full-size pickup. The new S-10 was available in two wheelbase lengths (108 and 118 inches) and two payload ratings (1,000 and 1,500 pounds). It had four trim levels, and two gasoline engines—the base four-cylinder, 1.9-liter, 82-horsepower or optional V-6, 2.8-liter, 110 horsepower, the latter of which was the only V-6 in the small truck market. The base engine with a four-speed manual overdrive had an EPA rating of 28 city and 39 highway, while the same engine coupled with the optional three-speed automatic transmission was rated at 25 and 34. *AAMA*

This 1982 S-10 Sport carrying a short Fleetside cargo box was an attractive little truck. Lower body side moldings, two-tone paint, chrome bumpers, and stylized wheels were some of the Sport model's upscale features. The S-10's styling presented a fresh aerodynamic appearance that set it apart from other small trucks. The base price of a 1982 S-10 pickup was only $6,269.58; a Durango model's price was pegged at $9,763.24. Its front suspension included independent A-arms and coil springs. Rear suspension featured a solid axle and leaf springs. The S-10's cab could accommodate three persons, with 53 inches of shoulder room, 39 inches of headroom, and 42.5 inches of legroom. It shared the big pickup's smooth ride characteristics. A bench seat was standard equipment, but bucket seats were an option. *AAMA*

Chevrolet's new S-10 was an economical choice for many personal, commercial, and recreational uses. This is a 1982 Chevrolet S-10 long 118-inch-wheelbase chassis cab with a commercial body. Payload capacity was 1,425 pounds. Chassis cab S-10s were not big business for Chevrolet, but a number of commercial users found them more than adequate. A lower initial purchase price and small operating costs were very attractive attributes. The long wheelbase chassis was particularly well suited for special bodies. Chevrolet produced and sold the body shown. It was 92.3 inches long, 40.4 inches deep, and 64 inches wide. A large variety of special equipment items such as ladder racks, factory rustproofing, and fleet decals were also available. Its riveted aluminum utility body was durable, lightweight, and versatile. *AAMA*

Chevrolet's full-size 1/2-ton pickup carried over without change. Pictured here is a top-of-the-line 1982 C10 Fleetside Silverado. Its standard engine was the 4.1-liter L6, with the electronic spark control–equipped 5.0-liter V-8 as an option. The 5.0-liter was upgraded with a four-barrel carburetor for better performance with about the same fuel economy. The 5.7- and 7.4-liter V-8s were options. Chevrolet added corrosion protection to the brake lines, hydraulic power steering lines, and the rear step bumper this year. *AAMA*

This was the last year for Chevrolet's LUV pickup. The whole idea behind the S-10 was to fight off the imported mini-pickups, captive and non-captive models. For 1982, Voyager, Inc. announced a new fiberglass topper. It had a high roofline, which extended 8 inches above the cab. Light was allowed to enter the pickup bed through the skylight, recessed safety tempered-glass sliding side windows, and full-view rear door. It was offered in two colors: Creamy Tan and the standard Polar White. The LUV was also available with the new 2.2-liter diesel engine; it was a midyear introduction. It boasted a hefty net torque output of 93 foot-pounds at 2,200 rpm and a Quick-On system, which meant the engine was ready to start in just 3 1/2 seconds or less. A new five-speed manual transmission was standard on 2WD LUV diesel models. The LUV diesel 2WD pickups were rated for a fantastic 44 miles per gallon highway and 32 miles per gallon city. Driving range for the 2WD long-wheelbase pickup with the new 19.1-gallon tank was 611 miles. The 4WD was rated for 35 miles per gallon highway and 28 city. *AAMA*

Chevrolet offered a new Step-Van Series to meet the growing demand for vocational trucks in the lower medium-duty GVW range. Chevrolet's Step-Van Series stepped it up a notch. Formerly, forward-control chassis and Step-Vans were built in Series P10-20-30. Now they were offered in Series P20-30-40. Wheelbase lengths ranged from 137 to 209 inches to handle all types of delivery requirements. These heavier chassis featured an I-beam front axle to help improve drivability. Aluminum walk-in bodies from Grumman Olson and Union City Body Co. offered load space lengths from 12 1/2 to 20 feet. This is the slightly restyled 1982 Chevrolet Step-Van with aluminum body and dual rear wheels. Note its new grille and higher roofline. *AAMA*

Chevrolet's high and wide G30 Hi-Cube Van continued without appearance change for 1982. This economical van was designed for carrying more, but still had the advantages of a tough Chevy Van. Hi-Cubes were built on wheelbases of 125 and 146 inches. They offered a selection of bodies with load space ranging from 406 to 570 cubic feet. Bodies constructed of either steel or aluminum were standard offerings. Maximum GVW rating was 10,000 pounds with dual rear wheels. The 5.7-liter V-8 was the only engine offered. A three-speed manual transmission was standard, and the automatic was optional. *AAMA*

Chevrolet's upper range of light-duty trucks (C/K20-30) had added 32mm shock absorbers on K30s, a new height-sensing brake system on C/K30s, 16-inch wheels instead of 16 1/2-inch on C/K20 and C30, and a 63-amp generator and roof marker lamps on K30. This is a 1982 Chevrolet K20 Fleetside pickup with firefighting equipment. The Greenville (Illinois) Fire Protection District owned brush truck 217. Its body was by Towers and featured a 200-gallon water tank and a 250-gpm pump. The GVW rating of the K20 was 6,600 pounds. The only gas engine offered was the 5.7-liter (350-ci) V-8. The new diesel was the only option. Its transmission offerings included a three- and four-speed manual and the automatic. This truck was equipped with a front bumper–mounted electric winch. *Garry E. Kadzielawski*

Chevrolet's Blazer basically continued in 1982 without appearance changes. Pictured here is a 1982 Chevrolet K5 Blazer. The Blazer did have the new 6.2-liter (379-ci) diesel V-8. Both 2WD and 4WD versions returned. Gasoline power choices included the 4.1-liter straight six, the 5.0-liter (305-ci) V-8 with electronic spark control, and a 5.7-liter (350-ci) V-8. A four-speed manual or three-speed automatic transmission was standard, depending on engine. The Blazer seated four in comfort with generous legroom all around. The rear cargo area was wide and fairly long, and would hold a good deal of luggage or camping gear even with the removable back seat in place. The full-size Blazer suffered in gas mileage because it was a heavy vehicle. *AAMA*

Chevrolet announced an all-new diesel engine for 1982 available in 2WD and 4WD pickups, Suburbans, chassis cabs, and 4WD Blazers. The 6.2-liter (379-ci) V-8 diesel was the biggest news ever in diesel-powered Chevrolet trucks. Chevrolet now offered the industry's widest variety of light-duty trucks powered by a diesel engine. This engine was totally new and made in America and designed specifically for light-duty truck service to move loads up to 13,500 pounds. It was rated for 31 miles per gallon highway and 23 miles per gallon city in a 2WD pickup equipped with a manual overdrive transmission. The same ratings for a 4WD pickup with a manual overdrive transmission were 29 miles per gallon and 22 miles per gallon. The Greenville (Illinois) Fire Protection District owned this 1982 K30 pickup with firefighting body. Brush truck number 217 was equipped with a Towers fire equipment body and a 200-gallon water tank with a 250-gpm pump. Note its front-mounted electric winch. *Dennis J. Maag*

Chevrolet made available 2WD and 4WD chassis cab models in four wheelbases able to accept bodies from 7 to 13 feet long. A new 1982 C30 heavy-duty chassis cab had a 10,500-pound GVW rating. It included optional heavy-duty suspension components and dual rear wheels. The Valparaiso, Indiana, Fire Department owned this 1982 K30 chassis cab with firefighting body. Squad 1's GVW rating was 10,000 pounds. Note the winch behind the opening in the center of the front bumper. The standard engine for this truck was the 4.8-liter L6; the 5.7-liter V-8 gas and 6.2-liter diesel V-8 engines were options. The standard transmission was a four-speed manual and the automatic was optional. *Garry E. Kadzielawski*

Conventional medium-duty models for 1982 features included improved exhaust routing on right side for improved transmission and power takeoff clearance. Shock-mounted roof marker lights were standard. For school buses a new 29,000-pound GVW rating was offered with a full 9,000-pound front axle and new 20,000-pound single and two-speed rear axle. Optional heavy-duty 15x5-inch front brakes and 15x7-inch rear brakes were offered. This 1982 Chevrolet C60 chassis cab has a firefighting body by Alexis. The Blue Mound (Illinois) Fire Protection District owned engine No. 36. It carried a 750-gallon water tank and a 1,500-gpm pump. *Dennis J. Maag*

Chevrolet built a full-line of medium-duty conventional cabs for 1982 consisting of single-axle Series C50-60-70, and tandems in Series C60-70. In medium-duty trucks, fuel-efficient midrange diesel engines, the Detroit Diesel 8.2-liter and the Caterpillar 3208, were again available, along with three gasoline engines. For the 1982 Chevrolet school bus chassis, the Allison AT-545 automatic transmission was offered as an option with the turbocharged Fuel Pincher engine. Two new GM-built rear axles, a single speed and two speed, were available for C60 and C70 Series mediums and school bus chassis. The 15,000-pound capacity single-speed and two-speed rear axles for medium-duty Conventionals and school bus chassis had been redesigned for 1982 to include expanded ratios for diesel engines. This is a 1982 Chevrolet C70 chassis cab with a firefighting body. The Benton County (Washington) Fire Protection District No. 1 owned this big 4WD conversion, Truck No. 6581. It carried a 350-gallon water tank and a 500-gpm pump. Note its heavy-duty mechanically powered front-mounted winch. *Bill Hattersley*

The second energy crisis of 1979 continued to have an impact on the industry, which manifested itself in downsized autos with smaller, more fuel-efficient engines. Families and others, however, continued to have need for a full-size passenger vehicle. For many, the answer was a passenger van or conversion van. Chevrolet's van continued to soldier on with minimal annual changes. The company had its hands full downsizing autos and developing a domestic mini-pickup. The 1982 Chevrolet G20 full-size conversion van was the choice of families for traveling in comfort along with adequate room for traveling gear, or towing. This van was available with the 165 net horsepower, 350-ci V-8 engine and automatic transmission—just the way most owners preferred for interstate cruising. Buyers could choose seating arrangements and other options to suit their lifestyle.

1983

With the introduction of domestic-built compact pickups in 1982, Japanese brands suffered a serious decline in market share, as did the captive brands imported by GM and Ford. In 1981, the imports, both captive and non-captive, accounted for 88 percent of compact pickup sales, with 766,628 units. In 1982, the compact pickup market almost doubled, but the imports' share plunged to only 53 percent. The industry looked for improved compact pickup sales in 1983, expecting to reach 900,000 units.

Chevrolet declared that 1983 was "T-Time," referring to the new model designations of the 4WD version of the S-10 pickup. For 1983, Chevrolet introduced a 4WD pickup, a downsized, S-10-based Blazer, and an extended cab S-10. T-10s were offered in three wheelbase lengths, giving buyers the widest possible options. The standard wheelbase for the S/T-10 was 108 inches, with a cargo bed just over 6 feet long. For those who required a long-bed pickup, the wheelbase stretched 9 inches and the bed 16 inches.

The extended cab version's wheelbase extended to 122.9 inches. This version gave buyers a pair of jump seats behind the two front reclining buckets. Rear seating space was limited, and better suited for children than adults, except for short distances. The extended cab trucks with 122.9 inch-wheelbase length provided one of the smoothest truck rides on the road.

The highlight of Chevrolet's new offerings for 1983 was the 100-inch-wheelbase T-Blazer. It gave riders a spacious interior without compromising fuel economy or cargo space. T-Blazers (4WD pickups, too) boasted a luxurious ride on a new independent front suspension system with torsion bars in front and a live, solid axle in the rear. Both 2WD and 4WD versions rounded out the T-Blazer's offerings.

For the first time, buyers could get a diesel engine in a G20-30 Series Chevy Van. With diesel power, the G20 Chevy Van was advertised to get a 40 percent better EPA estimated mileage rating than the same van with a gasoline V-8 engine.

Chevrolet managed an impressive 22 percent sales increase in calendar year 1983, to 934,587 from 1982's 808,805 sales. Still, Chevrolet came in second to Ford for the year.

The nation's economy recovered strength in 1983. Employment increased, as did consumer confidence, and gasoline prices stabilized.

Chevrolet won the 1983 model year sales crown with 917,240 trucks sold, to Ford's 896,587. Chevrolet's six-month head start in compact pickups, plus a fire sale of leftover 1981 and 1982 model LUV import compact pickups, received the credit for its win in the model year race. Chevrolet outsold Ford in the light-duty truck segment due to strong sales of the S-10 Blazer, LUV, Suburban, and El Camino. Ford led in full-size pickup sales, however.

Chevrolet's engine output by type for 1983 tells an interesting story. The six-cylinder engine's count was up by more than 100,000 units; this increase was attributable to the installation of V-6s in S-10 trucks. The gasoline V-8 engine's count was off by 376 units, but only because almost 67,000 V-8 diesels replaced similar numbers of gas V-8s. Four-cylinder engine usage was down slightly because the LUV was closed out and most S-10 buyers opted for the V-6 rather than the standard four.

The strong economy brought commercial buyers back into the market and drove Chevrolet medium-duty sales to a gain over those of 1982, 15,351 to 14,691. Combined medium-duty sales from Chevrolet and GMC put GM in second place in this market to leader IH.

The S-10 pickup, in its second year, returned without styling changes. This is a 1983 Chevrolet S-10 short-box Tahoe. The wheelbase length for the short-box pickup was 108.2 inches. After only one year, the S-10 high-mileage pickup had become the hottest selling new truck in Chevrolet's history. Helping to make the S-10 a top seller was its powerful optional V-6 engine, a new 5,000-pound maximum towing capacity when equipped with special towing equipment, and its market-proven appealing appearance and comfortable interior. A Sport Interior featuring comfortable high-back bucket fabric seats and a center console was an available option. The S-10 was engineered for the installation of special bodies and offered as a chassis cab with GVWs up to 4,600 pounds. When equipped with the 1.9-liter L4 and four-speed manual transmission 2WD, the S-10 was rated for an estimated 39 miles per gallon highway, and 27 miles per gallon by the EPA. *AAMA*

Chevrolet blasted the competition with both barrels—the new 4WD Maxi-Cab S-10. The new Maxi-Cab featured a 122.9-inch wheelbase and a 14.6-inch cab extension. The Maxi-Cab was equipped with the S-10's 73.1-inch short box only. It offered jump seats behind the stock buckets to carry an extra pair of passengers or 18.8 cubic feet of extra cargo space within its safe and dry confines. Two unique advantages of the Maxi-Cab were its longer seat travel, which provided more legroom, and comfortable reclining seats. The S-10 for 1983 also offered a new 4WD system called Insta-Trac. The driver could shift from 2WD to 4WD high and back at any speed without stopping. The 4WD S-10 also featured a new independent front suspension with torsion bars for better traction. *AAMA*

Chevrolet's bread-and-butter light-duty pickup for almost three decades was available again in 1983 in 2WD and 4WD, long and short box, and three trim levels. There was a wide choice of L6 or V-8 gasoline engines, or the 6.2-liter V-8 workhorse diesel in GVW ranges from 4,900 to 10,000 pounds. Chevrolet estimated that of approximately 18.5 million Chevrolet pickups built since the Fleetside first appeared in 1955 (the Cameo Carrier), about 11 million were still on the road in 1983. This is a top-of-the-line C10 Fleetside Silverado pickup. The new models were basically unchanged except for a revised grille design. The grille's horizontal center bar was painted body color. Wheelbase length for the 1/2-ton pickup remained at 117.5 inches. Standard engine for C/K10 pickups was the 4.1-liter L6. *AAMA*

Chevrolet's Suburban (they loved to call it the Superwagon because the station wagon was its only competition) continued without change except for the restyled grille. With the new 6.2-liter diesel option, the Suburban moved up to 13,500 pounds GCW, including passengers, cargo, equipment, and trailer (15,500 pounds on C20 gasoline engine–powered models). Chevrolet rated the 2WD C10 diesel Suburban for 30 miles per gallon highway. Chevrolet pushed the diesel in all of its light-duty trucks as a means to increase its average overall fleet fuel mileage. This is a 1983 Chevrolet K20 Suburban with Scottsdale trim. *AAMA*

RV sales recovered along with the economy, resulting in a 40 percent increase in sales over 1982 of all five RV categories: travel trailers, camper trailers, truck campers, motor homes, and multi-use van conversions. Class A motor homes rose by 160 percent, which was a big boost to Chevrolet. Chevrolet built almost its entire six-wheel forward-control motorhome chassis at a Detroit factory. Workers built 30 an hour, working nine-hour shifts and two of every three Saturdays to keep up with the demand.

Two major new product introductions from Chevrolet in 1983 were the S-10 2WD Blazer and 4WD T-10 Blazer. Both vehicles were two-door models. Pictured here is a 1983 Chevrolet T-10 Blazer. Based on list prices for basic models, the 4WD sold for $1,534 more than the 2WD. The 2WD Blazer accounted for about 25 percent of total sales. Interestingly, the 2WD sat only 2 inches lower than the 4WD. The S-10 Blazer was intimately related to the S-10 pickup. The basic chassis from the firewall forward was the S-pickup, including its popular styling. The Blazer differed from the pickup in almost every way behind the firewall. Its wheelbase at only 100.5 inches was much shorter than that of the short wheelbase S-10. Mechanically, Blazer was the same as the pickup. It offered two engines: a 122 inline four and the 173 V-6. *AAMA*

Chevrolet's ultimate off-roader was the full-size 4WD Blazer. It continued to be the only SUV to offer an optional 6.2-liter diesel in addition to standard gasoline engines. The Blazer featured additional corrosion protection for 1983, standard automatic-locking front hubs and an optional Quad-Shock off-road handling package. The Blazer could be upgraded for comfort with the optional Silverado interior, which featured high-back front bucket seats with center console. The full-size Blazer was also offered in 2WD. Many owners purchased Blazers for an on-highway tow vehicle and felt no need for the 4WD option. Pictured here is a 1983 K5 Blazer. *AAMA*

Chevrolet continued to capitalize on its new 6.2-liter diesel by making it available in Chevy Van and Sportvans, earning GM the distinction of building the industry's first and only diesel-powered vans. This engine was engineered as a real diesel rather than a "dieselized" gas engine as the 1978 350 V-8 was. The 350 proved to be a major mistake, but to GM's credit, it dropped it for a better engine. The 6.2-liter diesel performed well, more like a gasoline V-8 but with higher mile per gallon readings. The diesel delivered its 130 horsepower through a "new-for-vans" four-speed automatic overdrive transmission with a lockup torque converter. Chevrolet claimed fuel mileage increases of between 25 and 50 percent over a V-8 gas engine. The standard engine for vans was the 250 six; the 305 V-8 was an option. Also new for 1983 was a floor-mounted shifter for manual transmissions. This is a 1983 Chevrolet Beauville diesel. *AAMA*

Chevrolet carried over its G-Series Hi-Cube Vans with a restyled grille similar in appearance with the other light-duty truck models. This is a 1983 G30 Hi-Cube Van with 146-inch wheelbase and dual rear wheels. Hi-Cube Vans also featured the new 6.2-liter diesel and the four-speed automatic overdrive transmission. Other new features included a steering column angle approximating that used in the pickups. There was a floor-mounted manual transmission shift lever; a tilt steering column was offered with manual transmissions. A new anti-chip coating along the lower body protected the paint. An inside hood release was also new. The sliding side door was improved for easier and more dependable operation. A full line of gasoline-powered engines were also available. *AAMA*

Crew cab chassis cab units were favored by the nation's fire departments because of their ability to transport up to six. The Cairo, Illinois, Auxiliary Fire Department owned this 1983 Chevrolet K30 crew cab chassis cab fire truck with utility body. 4WD models were important to emergency vehicles for their ability to get through regardless of the road conditions. The new 6.2-liter diesel engine was also released for crew cabs. The maximum payload rating for this heavy-duty 1-ton 164.5-inch wheelbase was 4,837 pounds. Its standard gas engine was a 4.8-liter L6; the 5.7-liter V-8 was an available option. *Dennis J. Maag*

Chevrolet offered a C30 heavy-duty chassis cab in 1983. More 1-ton chassis cabs were sold every year than either the 1/2-tons or 3/4-tons, whether 2WD or 4WD. The New Orleans, Louisiana, Fire Department owned this 1983 Chevrolet C30 chassis cab with a firefighting body. It has a hose tender body; hoses can be seen on the big reel. This truck was rated for a maximum GVW of 10,500 pounds and was equipped with optional heavy-duty suspension components and dual rear wheels. It could have been equipped with the new 6.2-liter diesel or either of two gas engines: the 4.8-liter L6 or the 5.7-liter V-8. *Hansen*

Chevrolet didn't build a heavy-duty 1-ton chassis cab in the K30 Series, as was offered in the C30 Series. The K30 chassis cab was rated for a GVW of 10,000 pounds. The Bullhead City, Arizona, Fire Department owned this 1983 Chevrolet K30 chassis cab with firefighting body. Squad 3 was equipped with a 250-gallon water tank and a 250-gpm pump. The K30 would accept bodies from 7 to 13 feet long. This truck could have been equipped with the new 6.2-liter diesel engine as an option. Its standard engine was the 4.8-liter L6 and optional was the 5.7-liter gas V-8. 4WD capability was important to an Arizona fire truck for off-road work in the desert. *Chuck Madderom*

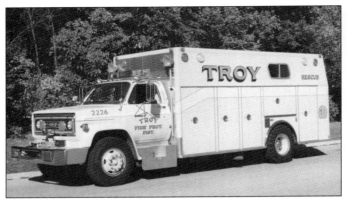

Medium-duty Chevrolet trucks were widely accepted for a broad range of vocations because they offered solid value. Chevrolet built truck and tractor models with a wide selection of wheelbases, GVW ratings, with fuel-efficient diesel or gas engines, drivetrains, and chassis components in Series 50-60-70. Rugged single- and tandem-axle Kodiak truck and tractor models were powered by Caterpillar diesel engines with up to 619 foot-pounds torque for impressive pulling muscle. Chevrolet offered driveline and chassis equipment, including manual or automatics to fill a wide variety of vocational applications. In 1983 new 3-inch-wide rear leaf springs were standard on all single-axle models. Single-axle 70 Series featured standard front and rear disc brakes. Pictured here is a single-axle Chevrolet C60 chassis cab with firefighting body. The Troy Fire Protection District of Shorewood, Illinois, owned it. Rescue 2226 had a special body built by Marion. *Garry E. Kadzielawski*

In 1983, Chevrolet's El Camino rode on a 117.1-inch wheelbase and its standard engine was again a 110-horsepower 229 V-6. The optional powerful V-8 was the 165-horsepower 305. For the first time ever, a diesel V-8 was an option. Its hallmark continued to be its beauty and luxury. The El Camino's list of optional creature comfort and convenience items rivaled that of expensive passenger cars. Three trim levels included Base, Super Sport, and Conquista. This is a 1983 base El Camino pickup. Standard equipment items included an automatic transmission, power steering, and air adjustable rear shocks.

Chevrolet's biggest 1983 pickup was a brute, the K30 Fleetside Big Dooley Crew Cab. Typically, this model was employed as a tugboat pulling huge trailers. It was no slouch either when it came to carrying a load, since its payload capacity ranged all the way up to 4,692 pounds. The motive power for Big Dooley came from the monster 5.7-liter V-8 engine. A four-speed manual was standard and the three-speed automatic was optional. New Process' model 205 two-speed transfer case was the only offering. This same truck was also offered as a Bonus Cab. Bonus Cab meant it had a three-man bench seat up front, and the space behind the seat was for indoor cargo storage. *Iten Chevrolet*

America's businesspeople chose Chevrolet medium-duty trucks for their heavy-duty payloads without heavy-duty prices. This is a 1983 C70 tractor with the Kodiak option. As a tractor, the C70 carried a maximum GCW rating of 60,000 pounds. The owner had shaved off all name badges from his truck, but this is a Chevrolet. The Kodiak lightweight fiberglass tilt hood with its massive grille was required with the Cat 3208 diesel. The cab rode about 7 inches higher than the conventional cab for a better view of the road. The Cat 3208 was offered in nine power ratings ranging from 160 to 250 horsepower. Allison automatic transmissions and a host of manuals were available.

This is a rare 1983 medium-duty Kodiak Crew Cab shown with firefighting body. The need for a crew cab by a fire department is obvious. The Marissa (Illinois) Fire Protection District owned engine No. 353. Its tank/pumper body was by Towers, and it featured a 1,000-gallon tank and a 500-gpm pump. This C70 was rated for a maximum GVW of 33,200 pounds. It was powered, of course, by a Caterpillar 3208 diesel. Nine power ratings ranging from 160 to 250 horsepower were standard. Six of these models were naturally aspirated and the top three had turbos. The Kodiak cab was required with all of these engines. *Dennis J. Maag*

In 1983, the industry was still a bit shell shocked because of the second energy crisis of 1979–1980. There was a concerted effort to go with smaller more fuel-efficient engines. The 1983 K10 Silverado short-box pickup pictured here was one such vehicle. The little 305 V-8 engine powered it. It had a four-speed manual transmission. Its performance was at best adequate. This truck looked good and was still in daily service when photographed in 1999. Its retail price in 1983 was approximately $13,500, reasonably equipped.

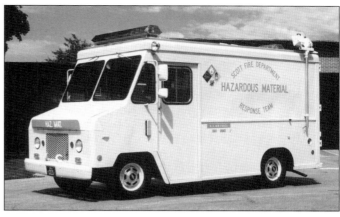

Forward-control vans are not often thought of as fire trucks. But because of their high cube cargo capacity, they were ideal for certain specialized fire department tasks. This is a 1983 Chevrolet P20 chassis with van body used by the Scott Air Force Base (Illinois) Fire Department for its Hazardous Materials Response Team. Its drivetrain consisted of the 350 V-8 engine and a three-speed automatic transmission. Its maximum GVW rating was 8,000 pounds. *Dennis J. Maag*

Chevrolet's C70 medium-duty chassis cab was rated for a maximum GVW of 33,200 pounds, more than enough to handle this big tank body. The DeSoto (Missouri) Rural Fire Protection District owned engine No. 7. Semo built its tank body. It was powered by the 10.4-liter (636-ci) turbocharged Caterpillar 3208 diesel producing 250 horsepower. Its transmission was a Fuller 10-speed. *Dennis J. Maag*

1984

Chevrolet's 1984 trucks came in for some minor refinements to a well-accepted lineup of light- and medium-duty trucks.

The S-10 2WD and extended cab models received an optional 2.2-liter diesel engine from Chevrolet's Japanese partner, Isuzu. The little diesel put out 62 horsepower and 96 foot-pounds torque with natural aspiration. The new oil burner was small, but long on quality. It had been proven for a number of years in Isuzu mini-trucks. The overhead-valve four-cylinder diesel was mated to a five-speed manual transmission and was rated for mid-30s city and mid-40s highway fuel mileage.

S-10 chassis refinements included softer rate front springs and a new sport suspension. The optional street handling package included wide 65-series white-letter radial tires on fancy wheels, a special quick-ratio power steering gear, larger shock absorbers, and a bigger swaybar. The 4WD S-trucks featured Bilstein single-tube gas-pressure shock absorbers that delivered better and more consistent suspension control. The gas shocks were not available for the S-10 handling package. This package vastly improved cornering stability.

Other new S-10 features included improved rear brakes, a retuned torque converter to take better advantage of gas engine power outputs, and a new hydraulic clutch for the manual transmissions.

The few improvements to full-size pickups included an improved fuel/water separator unit for the 6.2-liter diesel and a new light to signal when it was time to change the filter. There was a smart switch for the cruise control system with a one-touch mile per hour rate increase or decrease. There were semi-metallic linings on the front disc brakes. The full-size Blazer lost its 2WD option, but the S-Blazer continued untouched. The 1/2- and 3/4-ton Suburbans continued with either 2WD or 4WD. Chevy Vans received hinged side doors with a 4-foot-square opening available with or without windows. The El Caminos got sports optional cloth buckets along with a freestanding floor console for the shifter. The engine options for El Caminos remained unchanged—the 229 V-6, 305 V-8, and the 350 V-8 diesel.

Chevrolet's engine selection for medium-duty trucks included two diesels and four gassers. Gasoline engines included the 4.8-liter six, 5.7-liter, 6.0-liter, and 7.0 liter V-8s. The diesels included the 8.2-liter Detroit Diesel Fuel Pincher with or without a turbocharger and the naturally aspirated Caterpillar 3208 V-8s, which produced up to 190 horsepower while three turbocharged 3208 engines put out up to 222 horsepower.

The medium-duty line included the C50, C60, and C70 series with GVWs ranging from a single-axle C50 at 16,000 pounds to a tandem C70 at 50,000 pounds, and a 60,000-pound GCWR as a tractor. The medium-duty line also included a forward-control P60 chassis that could be equipped with a walk-in van body with up to 957 cubic feet of cargo space.

After the first of the year, Chevrolet introduced a new Isuzu-built low cab-forward tilt-cab model called the Chevrolet Tiltmaster. GMC sold a similar model called the Forward. Both trucks were sold through about 250 Chevrolet and GMC truck dealerships.

The truck industry for the first time in several years finally hit its stride, selling 3.98 million trucks in the model year (Oct. 1, 1983, through Sept. 30, 1984). This was the best year since 1979, and well over 1983's 2.9 million units. Light-duty sales of 3.7 million, up from 2.7 million in 1983, were the key to success. Huge sales of new compact vans from Chrysler and compact pickups, both foreign and domestic, helped fuel the increase. Model year

Visually the 1984 El Camino showed very little change for the new year. The diesel engine option, which was new in 1983, carried over. It's interesting to note that the El Camino's diesel was the original 105-horsepower 5.7-liter gasoline V-8 based 350, not the newer 6.2-liter diesel engineered for truck service. This was a dramatic change from the high-performance big block engines El Camino had featured in the past. Its standard engine was the 110-horsepower 229-ci V-6. The optional gas engine was the peppy 155-horsepower 305 V-8 (5.0-liter). The El Camino's wheelbase was 117.1 inches. The base model for 1984 was the El Camino; two upscale models were the Conquista and Super Sport. The diesel option provided about an additional four miles per gallon. The base price of a El Camino Super Sport was approximately $8,500.

Last year, a new S-10/T-10 Blazer and an extended cab pickup were new. For this reason, Chevrolet declined to announce major introductions for 1984. This 1984 S-10 short-box pickup towing a boat bigger than itself meets an S-10 long-box pickup hauling a healthy load. The standard powerplant for all S-10 trucks was the anemic 2.0 liter 83-horsepower four-cylinder engine borrowed from Chevrolet's J-car. New this year was a normally aspirated 2.2-liter diesel in 2WD and Maxi-Cabs, but it was even weaker at 62 horsepower, torque produced was only 96 foot-pounds This was the Isuzu-built engine used in the 1982 LUV. Chevrolet did sell a number of LUVs in 1983 to clear its inventory of leftover product. The star of S-10's line was the 2.8-liter V-6, which produced an honest, hard-working 110 horsepower. It received its start in GM's X-cars. All S-10 trucks could be ordered with a 5,000-pound trailering package. *AAMA*

sales at Chevrolet reached 1,108,340 units. But even at that, Chevrolet fell about 42,000 units short of Ford. Truck sales of 4,092,000 units for calendar year 1984 virtually tied 1978's all-time record. Only 15 percent of truck sales in 1984 were imports, but imports still took up 24 percent of the car market.

In anticipation of an all-new 1987 model full-size pickup, GM's Truck and Bus Group set in motion construction of a "factory of the future" facility in Fort Wayne, Indiana. It also consolidated medium- and heavy-duty truck production at Pontiac, Michigan, to free a plant there to build the new generation pickup.

Chevrolet's 1984 medium-duty truck sales climbed 30 percent, to 19,911, from 15,351 in 1983. Chevrolet sold 400 plus of the new Tiltmaster low cab–forward city-delivery–type trucks imported from Isuzu.

Chevrolet sold 62,843 P-model RV chassis versus 51,800 in 1983. These were built at the Piquette Street plant in Detroit.

Chevrolet's S-10 Maxi-Cab was new in 1983 and instantly became a best seller. It was only offered with the 73-inch cargo box on a 122.9-inch wheelbase. The cab was 14 1/2 inches longer than the standard cab. The extra space was convenient for hauling those items an owner did not want to place in the open pickup box. A 4WD version of the Maxi-Cab was standard. Chassis refinements for the S-Series included softer rate front springs and a new sport suspension. This optional handling package included wide 65-series white-letter radial tires on styled wheels, a special quick-ratio power steering, and Bilstein single-tube gas-pressure shocks. This package substantially improved the cornering stability of the S-series. The full-size C10 pickup carried over with only minor trim and detail changes shared by the rest of the full-size line. Pictured here is a 1984 Chevrolet S-10 Maxi-Cab pickup shown in the foreground and a C10 top-of-the-line Silverado pickup above. *AAMA*

Chevrolet's 1984 full-size pickups were available with either 2WD or 4WD in 1/2-, 3/4-, and 1-ton sizes. Corrosion protection included new two-sided galvanized steel interior door panels. Also new were semi-metallic front brake linings on all 1/2- and 3/4-ton models and non-asbestos rear brake linings on most models. There were 22 diesel models, all with 6.2-liter V-8 diesel power. The 5.7-liter diesel engine was limited to the El Camino. Available gasoline engines included the 4.1- and 4.8-liter L6s, and 5.0-, 5.7-, and 7.4-liter V-8s. Model availability included Fleetside, Stepside, crew cab, Bonus Cab, and chassis cab with short or long box in a number of appearance packages. This is a 1984 C10 2WD Fleetside. *AAMA*

Chevrolet's popular S-10 4WD Blazer featured an improved ride and handling achieved by use of optional new, single-tube gas pressure shock absorbers from Germany's Bilstein. 4WD S-10 Blazers and pickups did not get the new 2.2-liter four-cylinder diesel engine. In 1984, Chevrolet trucks accounted for some 40 percent of total Chevrolet sales. The rear brake piston size on the S-trucks was decreased to cure the premature brake lockup tendency that occurred on S-10s when the brakes were applied with great force. The automatic transmission received a retuned torque converter to take better advantage of gas engine power outputs. A new hydraulic-operated clutch vastly improved shifting ease with the manual transmissions. *AAMA*

Full-size light-duty trucks received a new smart switch for the electronic speed-control system and semi-metallic linings on the front disc brakes. The multifunction smart switch was available with one-touch, one-mile-per-hour rate increase or decrease. The stalk-mounted switch housed the turn signals, windshield washer and wiper, optional variable-speed wiper, headlamp dimmer, and cruise control. GVW on this husky 1984 Chevrolet C30 1-ton chassis cab with wrecker body was 10,500 pounds when equipped with dual rear wheels as pictured. The standard engine for the C30 was the 4.8-liter L6 and the 5.7-liter V-8 was optional, as was the 6.2-liter diesel.

Not all fire trucks belong to governmental units. Some, such as this K30 fire truck, were owned by private companies to protect owned facilities. The Olin Corporation of East Alton, Illinois, owned this truck. Pumper 1 had a body by Pierce containing a 400-gallon water tank and a 250-gpm pump. Its cab had the base Custom Deluxe trim level. This 1-ton truck had a maximum GVW of 11,000 pounds. Its base engine was the 4.8-liter 115-horsepower L-6. The available V-8 was the 5.7-liter. The 6.2-liter diesel was not an option for this model. *Dennis J. Maag*

This was the first year Chevrolet offered the Isuzu-built Tiltmaster, a low cab-forward tilt model. It was offered in four wheelbases of 142, 165, 181, and 197 inches, and had GVW ratings of 27,500 and 29,700 pounds. Its standard inline six-cylinder turbocharged diesel had a net horsepower rating of 165. No gas engines were available. The Tiltmaster's front axle was located farther back than on conventional cab trucks, thereby providing greater maneuverability, and more-efficient weight distribution. The tilt cab improved accessibility for service and maintenance. Isuzu Motors Ltd., GM's Japanese partner, built it. *Ron Cenowa*

Chevrolet's 1984 medium-duty truck line comprised Series C50-60-70. Series C50 and C60 trucks were 4x2 models only; Series C70 offered both 4x2 and 6x4 models. Kodiak models were found in Series C60-C70, and C70 tandems. Single-axle GVWs ranged from a low of 13,800 pounds for C50 to 32,800 pounds for C70. Tandem-axle maximum GVW rating was 50,000 pounds. The Snohomish (Washington) Fire Protection District owned this 1984 Chevrolet medium-duty C70 chassis cab with firefighting body. Its body was by FMC. It contained a 1,000-gallon water tank and a 750-gpm pump. With this big tank, it needed the C70's GVW rating of 27,500 pounds. A 210-horsepower 6.6-liter gas engine powered it. *Bill Hattersley*

Medium-duty trucks were available with a broad selection of diesel and gas engines. Diesels included Caterpillar 3208 with 11 different horsepower ratings up to 222 at 2,600 rpm and Detroit Diesel Fuel Pincher V-8s for C60 and C70 trucks, offered in naturally aspirated and turbocharged versions up to 193 net horsepower. For dump truck applications in the construction industry, the tandem-axle Series C70 Kodiak was standard with a Caterpillar 3208 V-8. Four gasoline engines also powered medium-duty trucks. In the C50 and C60 Series, the 5.7-liter V-8 was standard, but a 4.8-liter inline six could be specified. A 6.0-liter V-8 was the standard gasoline engine in the C70 Series, while for the real hard work, there was a 7.0-liter V-8. This is a 1984 Chevrolet C70 medium-duty chassis cab with firefighting body. The Nappanee, Indiana, "Nappanee Smokey Stovers" owned it. Its body was by Alf. It contained a 1,000-gallon water tank and a 750-gpm pump. *Dennis J. Maag*

To reduce driver fatigue and wear on driveline components, many medium-duty trucks were equipped with Allison automatics. Manuals could be ordered, of course, in a range of five-speed transmissions in combination with a four-speed auxiliary. A 13-speed Fuller transmission was offered on Series C70 trucks. The medium-duty line offered a total of 33 wheelbases and a variety of wheels, tires, and hoods completed the line. GVW ratings ranged up to 18,500 pounds for Series C50; to 24,000 pounds for Series C60; and to 35,000 pounds for Series C70. The tandem-axle C70 was rated up to 50,000 pounds and up to 60,000 pounds as a tractor trailer. The Bliss, Indiana, Fire District owned this 1984 Chevrolet medium-duty C60 chassis cab with firefighting body. It carried a 400-gallon water tank. This big Chevrolet was a 4WD conversion and was equipped with a heavy-duty grille guard for off-road duty. *M. Boatwright*

Chevrolet offered four gasoline engines for its 1984 medium-duty trucks and two diesels with a dozen different power ratings. The medium-duty lineup included a forward-control commercial chassis (P60), which could be equipped with a walk-in van body with up to 957 cubic feet of cargo space. Forward-control chassis were also available for transit bus applications in 167-, 189-, and 203-inch wheelbases. They featured a Detroit Diesel engine, four-speed automatic transmission, heavy-duty radiator, generator, and full air brakes. The Wakarusa, Indiana, Volunteer Fire Department owned this 1984 Chevrolet P-60 forward-control chassis with a walk-in body outfitted for fire/rescue service. *Dennis J. Maag*

During this period in Chevrolet truck's history, the emphasis was on downsizing, aerodynamics, and improving fuel economy. Chevrolet engineers had been hard at work on these issues and had launched the successful S-10 pickups and most recently the red-hot S-10 Blazer. But Chevrolet was still very much in business with its full-size pickups and SUVs. The full-size Blazer continued without change; the 2WD Blazer configuration was dropped at the end of the 1983 model year. The Blazer's standard engine was the 160-horsepower 305 V-8. Optional engines included the 350 V-8 gas engine and the 130-horsepower 379 V-8 diesel. Chevrolet dealers sold 46,919 K10 Blazers in calendar year 1984. This 1984 K10 full-size Blazer was owned by a sheriff's department and was used to pull a boat for the water patrol division.

The Chevrolet C10 Fleetside short-box pickup has stood the test of time. It was now in its eleventh model year, and was still a favorite with the public whether for work or play. Its clean, sharp lines were distinctive and approaching classic proportions. The C10's cab interior with Silverado trim was plush. Standard seating was a full-size bench seat upholstered in custom fabric or vinyl upholstery. There was plenty of stretch-out room for tall people and the seat was comfortable for extended trips. The instrument panel contained a full complement of gauges in a well-organized fashion. A well-equipped C10 Fleetside Silverado, such as the one pictured, retailed for about $13,500, not including freight, tax, or license. The standard engine for C10 pickups was the 4.1-liter L6. Optional engines included the 5.0-liter V-8, 5.7-liter V-8, and 6.2-liter diesel V-8.

Chevrolet's C30 Crew Cab was a favorite with landscapers and lawn care contractors. These businesses transported crews, hauled supplies, and towed equipment to job sites. This 1984 Chevrolet C30 2WD Crew Cab with dump body was rated for a maximum GVW of 10,000 pounds. Its standard powerplant was the 5.7-liter V-8. Chevrolet's biggest, the 7.4-liter V-8, was an option, as was the 6.2-liter diesel V-8. The four-speed manual transmission was standard, and the three-speed automatic was optional.

Steel and aluminum Step-Van models were offered in 1984 in Series P20 and P30. P20s carried a maximum GVW of 8,000 pounds and the P30 up to 14,000 pounds. This is a 1984 P30 12.5-foot Grumman aluminum body Step-Van. The City of Seattle Fire Department owned Hazardous Materials Emergency Response Unit 77. Two engine options were available for this unit: 5.7-liter gas V-8 and 6.2-liter diesel V-8. A four-speed manual was standard and a three-speed automatic transmission was an option. *Bill Hattersley*

A rarely seen model was a C70 medium-duty crew cab with the Kodiak option. This truck belonged to a construction company working on the tracks at a railroad crossing. Chevrolet offered mediums in a range of wheelbases from 125 to 254 inches. The chances that Chevrolet offered a wheelbase to match the customer's needs based on body length were very good. Caterpillar 3208 diesel engine-powered C70 models required the Kodiak option, a lightweight fiberglass tilt hood with a massive grille, to house the huge radiator required by the 3208. The maximum GVW of the C70 was 33,200 pounds. Cat offered nine power ratings for its 3208 ranging from 160 to 250 horsepower.

The biggest truck in Chevrolet's 1984 line was the Tandem C70 Kodiak, pictured here with a tank body. The Long Lake, Illinois, Volunteer Fire Department owned this one. Its tank body was by Semo. The Tandem C70 was rated for a maximum GVW of 50,000 pounds. This truck was powered by the turbocharged Cat 3208 250-horsepower diesel and it was mated to an Allison MT653DRG automatic transmission. It had the optional Rockwell single-speed SQ100 38,000-pound rear axle and an optional 12,000-pound front axle. Chevrolet offered three cab interior trim levels: standard Custom Deluxe and optional Scottsdale and Silverado. *Dennis J. Maag*

1985

Chevrolet's medium-duty 1985 line was considerably more comprehensive than it was in 1981, the first model year after GM dropped out of the heavy-duty truck market. In 1981, mediums consisted of the conventional cab and the high cab Kodiak. Conventionals featured a steel, alligator-type hood and front fenders. They were mostly powered by gas engines: the 292 six or 366 and 427 V-8s. But the Detroit Diesel Fuel Pincher 8.2-liter diesels were optional. The Kodiak used the same cab but with a fiberglass tiltcab and front fenders. Engineers introduced two fiberglass hoods on the medium trucks. One was styled exactly like the steel hood, and was used on trucks with gas or 8.2L diesels. The other was the tall hood used on the Kodiak. This hood had four square headlights; the other had two round headlights.

Chevrolet added the medium-duty forward-control P-Series delivery with GVW ratings from 16,000 to 20,000 pounds in 1984 and the W-Series medium-duty tilt cabs imported from Isuzu in 1984.

GMC Truck and Coach Operations had full responsibility for the design, engineering, and manufacturing of medium-duty trucks. Likewise, Chevrolet had the same responsibility for light-duty trucks. In 1985, GMC and Chevrolet sent letters to dealers to separate those interested in medium-duties from those who weren't. About 50 percent expressed interest in the franchise. In order to remain medium-duty dealers, those who opted to stay had to commit to certain vehicle stocking levels and certain sales and service training and parts and tool requirements. Out of a total of 2,400 GMC and 5,200 Chevrolet dealers, only about 2,150 in total for both brands were expected to stay on as authorized dealers under the new program. Non-authorized dealers would be able to sell medium-duties, but would have to buy them from an authorized dealer.

Isuzu Truck of America was also setting up its own dealers for its medium-duty cab NPR models. Thus, the same truck could be purchased with one of three nameplates.

The biggest product news from Chevrolet in 1985 was the new

Chevrolet's 1985 S-10 Maxi-Cab pickup had room for four and a whole lot more. It was the value leader in Chevrolet's line. Rear jump seats behind available front bucket seats added to its people-carrying capacity of the S-10 pickup. Two new seat trims were available for 1985—a new custom fabric, or a vinyl with fabric trim combination. Chevrolet beefed up its basic four-cylinder engine for 1985, which was standard equipment on the S-truck line. The new 2.5-liter base engine featured throttle-body injection, which boosted rated horsepower to 92 at 4,400 rpm and torque to 134 foot-pounds at 2,800 rpm, a 9-horsepower and 26 foot-pounds boost compared to the standard 2.0-liter engine. *AAMA*

Chevrolet was the only manufacturer of a sporty, personal car–based pickup. The El Camino carried over into 1985 without significant styling updates. It was still based on Chevrolet's popular Chevelle. As with other Chevrolet trucks for 1985, the El Camino's new standard engine was the 4.3-liter V-6. The El Camino's engine was a fuel-injected version and cranked out 150 horsepower. It rode on a 117-inch-wheelbase chassis and was rated for a maximum GVW of 4,791 pounds. Rear-axle ratios included the 2.41, 2.56, 3.08, and 3.73. Model lineup included the El Camino, Super Sport, and Conquista. The Super Sport featured an aero-style nose cap like the Monte Carlo SS. A non-functional power blister hood, dummy side pipes, and pickup bed rails were options. An optional engine was the 150-horsepower V-8. This is a 1985 Chevrolet El Camino Conquista. *AAMA*

It was a challenge for a manufacturer to compete in the small truck 4WD market in 1985. There were no fewer than 10 major manufacturers chasing the available sales. The term Sport Truck had come into vogue by this time to replace the original mini-truck moniker. The Sport Truck segment included not only U.S. producers, but also the well-entrenched import brands. The U.S. full-size 4WD truck producers had that market to themselves, but not so with the Sport Trucks. Fortunately, Chevrolet's S-10 (technically T-10 for 4WD) entry competed very favorably in this segment. The good news for Chevrolet in 1985 was again the new, more powerful standard four-cylinder engine offering. The new engine incorporated a lightweight block, head, and crankshaft castings. It sported an aluminum intake manifold and featured an exhaust header fabricated from stainless steel. Best of all, the carburetor was dumped in favor of electronic fuel injection. Other changes in the 4WD trucks included low-pressure, gas-filled shocks as standard and a dash light that indicated optimum rpm for economy upshifting. This is a 1985 Chevrolet S-10 short-box standard cab pickup. *AAMA*

Astro van. It was positioned against Chrysler's Caravan/Voyager twins. The Astro was a truck-based van, whereas the Chrysler van was based on a car. The Astro looked like a downsized Chevy Van, and featured a front engine with rearwheel drive. The Astro was the tallest and heaviest of the minivans.

In commercial form, the Astro featured a 1,700-pound payload capacity and a 5,000-pound towing rating. For passenger use, the Astro was available with seating for four, seven, or eight people. It could also be loaded up with about every option known to large

Chevrolet's full-size C10 pickups received the restyled grille treatment for a bold new look. Its wider, horizontal grille bar was painted body color. A new standard engine, the 4.3-liter V-6, provided additional power for 1985. Driver comfort and convenience were Chevrolet engineers' top-priority considerations in the 1985 model lineup with bench seat angles increased for riding comfort, and a new, larger fuse block, which allowed easier accessibility to fuses and plugs. In its full-size pickup line, Chevrolet continued to offer only the standard three-man cab, unlike its S-10 Series Maxi-Cab model. This 1/2-ton pickup rode on a 117 1/2-inch or 131 1/2-inch-wheelbase chassis, depending on its cargo box length. Pictured here is a 1985 C10 long-box 1/2-ton Silverado pickup.

Chevrolet cars. The Astro's standard engine was the 2.5-liter four; the 4.3-liter V-6 was optional.

The standard Chevrolet light-duty line looked pretty much the same as in 1984. Under the hood, however, there were some interesting changes. First, Chevrolet beefed up the S-10's basic four-cylinder engine. The new 2.5-liter base engine featured throttle-body fuel injection, which boosted horsepower to 92 at 4,400 rpm and torque to 134 foot-pounds at 2,800 rpm. This was a 9 horsepower and 26 foot-pound boost compared to the former 2.0-liter engine. This "new" 2.5L engine was the former Pontiac "Iron Duke," a modernized version of the Chevrolet Nova 153-ci four. The earlier S-10 four-cylinder, the 2.0L, was the Chevrolet Cavalier engine.

Full-size pickups also got a new engine. The 4.3-liter Vortec V-6 replaced the 4.1-liter inline six as the standard powerplant. It featured swirl-port combustion chambers for improved mixing of fuel and air. It was a carbureted engine with 150 horsepower at 4,000 rpm and 225 foot-pounds of torque at 2,400 rpm. This engine was essentially the 350 V-8 with two cylinders cut off. The 292 six remained as the optional engine for medium-duty C50s. The 350 V-8 was standard for both C50 and C60 trucks.

The light-duty segment's sales led the industry to a calendar year record of 4,680,458 units to beat 1984's total sales of 4,092,803. The new record beat the old 1978 industry record of 4,110,335 by nearly 14 percent.

Chevrolet sold 1,278,383 light-duties, up from 1,091,928 in 1984. Chevrolet beat Ford for only the second time in nine years to become the industry's best-selling brand.

Chevrolet's total sales of light- and medium-duty trucks totaled 1,300,130; well over 1984's total of 1,111,839.

By introducing its new Astro van late in 1984 before Ford could launch its new Aerostar, Chevrolet pulled into first place ahead of Ford for the calendar year. Chevrolet also dominated the compact sportutility market in 1985 with its red-hot S-10 Blazer sales and was further helped along by the popularity of the 2WD version, a model Ford didn't have.

Chevrolet claimed that the S-10 Blazer was the number-one selling SUV ever, and it was even better in 1985! Features included the new electronic fuel-injected 2.5-liter, four-cylinder engine, and low-pressure gas shock absorbers for improved ride characteristics. Increased corrosion protection, and new paint and trim options made the Chevrolet S-10 Blazer even more exciting. A new upshift light was added to the instrument panel to indicate when the manual transmission should be shifted to maintain optimum engine speed, vehicle road speed, and good fuel economy. Chevrolet continued to offer both the 2WD and 4WD S-10 Blazers. *AAMA*

Major revisions in Chevrolet's full-size pickups and SUVs for 1985 were few and far between. Gradual refinements and carefully planned upgrading was the name of the game. This 4WD Chevrolet full-size K5 Blazer was given the new four-barrel carburetor–equipped, 150-horsepower 262-ci V-6 engine. This new six replaced the venerable inline six that had been around for many years. The 6.2-liter diesel was improved; its rated SAE net horsepower was upped to 150 at 3,600 rpm with 250 foot-pounds torque at 2,000 rpm. The big Blazer rode on a 106 1/2-inch wheelbase. The Blazer was rated for a maximum GVW of 6,000 pounds. As a tow vehicle, for which it was well suited, Blazer was rated for a GCW of 11,000 pounds. *AAMA*

Chevrolet's biggest people/cargo hauler Suburban was in a class of its own. The Suburban had more power, more passenger room, and more payload than any car-type wagon. In addition, the Suburban was offered in both 2WD and 4WD versions in either C/K10 and 20 Series. With its optional second and third seats, the Suburban accommodated up to nine persons in comfort, and still had a generous 35 cubic feet of cargo space. The Suburban was also Chevrolet's top tow vehicle. When equipped with the optional 7.4-liter V-8 gas engine and a heavy-duty trailering package, it could move up to 15,000 pounds, a feat no car-type wagon could duplicate. This is a 1985 Chevrolet C10 Silverado Suburban. The 7.4-liter V-8 pumped out 230 horsepower and 260 foot-pounds torque. Right behind it was the other optional powerful engine, the new 6.2-liter V-8 diesel with 150 horsepower and 260 foot-pounds torque. *AAMA*

The genius of Chevrolet's new 1985 Astro Van was its trucklike characteristics such as its "torquey" engine (almost 100 foot-pounds more than the second-place van), 5,000-pound maximum towing capacity, and panel rear doors. A van is a truck, and by definition a work vehicle. Pulling and load capacities are critical factors for the consumer to consider when buying a truck. In 1985, the hottest segment of the light truck market was the mini-van market, a segment that didn't even really exist until 1984, when Chrysler brought out its new minivans. Chevrolet's minivan standard engine was the new 2.4-liter four. It produced more torque than either of its two major competitors. Its optional V-6 engine was where Astro shined brightest. It produced 225 foot-pounds torque at 2,400 rpm. Its nearest rival's optional engine produced only 150 foot-pounds torque at 2,600 rpm. A 1985 Chevrolet Astro Van without side windows was designed for commercial and van conversion applications. *AAMA*

Chevrolet's Astro Van delivered impressive spaciousness and payload capacity that set it apart from other small vans. Astro offered commercial customers versatility with cargo volume of 151.1 cubic feet, a choice of three optional payload capacities that were not affected by the addition of optional equipment, and convenient ease of access unsurpassed by any other small van. Each rear panel door swung wide open, and the sliding side door was designed for one-hand operation. The Astro's unitized body was robot welded from a number of large metal stampings to ensure better panel fit and reduced areas where rust and corrosion could start. The Astro's front suspension consisted of coil springs and upper and lower A-arms. Its rear suspension was a live axle with plastic leaf springs (like those used on the Corvette). *AAMA*

Chevrolet's versatile new Astro Van was designed and engineered for both commercial and passenger carrying applications. This is a 1985 Chevrolet Astro passenger van. The Astro was Chevrolet's first all-new van design in 20 years. Its interior design was such that it could seat four, seven, or up to eight passengers, or carry more than 150 cubic feet of cargo—features that set it apart from other small vans. The Astro could also be optioned with just about every item available on Chevrolet's top-of-the-line passenger cars. With the base four-cylinder engine and four-speed manual transmission, the Astro was rated at 22 miles per gallon city and 26 highway. With the powerful V-6 engine and four-speed automatic transmission, fuel economy slipped to 18 city and 24 highway. *AAMA*

Chevrolet's tough, go-anywhere K30 1-ton chassis cab was favored by many fire departments. The Channahon (Illinois) Fire Protection District owned this 1985 K30 Chevrolet chassis cab with brush truck body. Its firefighting body was by Pierce. It carried a 400-gallon water tank and a 250-gpm pump. The K30 1-ton chassis cab with dual rear wheels was rated for a maximum GVW rating of 11,000 pounds. Payload ratings ranged up to a maximum of 6,215 pounds. For the 11,000-pound GVW rating, K30 chassis cab models required the C7E Option package, which included dual exhaust, 12-inch clutch, 3,750-pound capacity rear springs, engine frame cross-member reinforcements, LT215/85R16/D (8 ply) tires, and cab roof marker lamps. *Dennis J. Maag*

Chevrolet's medium-duty conventional line offered 33 wheelbases and a variety of wheels, tires, hoods, axles, transmissions, and engines—gas and diesel. Wheelbases ran from 125 to 254 inches. GVWs ranged up to 18,500 pounds for C50, to 24,000 pounds for C60, and to 35,000 pounds for C70. The tandem-axle C70 straight truck was rated up to 50,000 pounds, and the tractor version could pull up to 60,000 pounds GCW. The Brazoria County (Texas) Fire Protection Unit owned this 1985 Chevrolet C70 chassis cab with firefighting body. Boardman built its body. It contained a 750-gallon water tank and a 750-gpm pump. Its engine was the 7.0-liter gas V-8 and carried a maximum GVW of 35,000 pounds. *Dennis J. Maag*

The SUV was a new addition to the Army's fleet. These trucks had 24-volt electrical systems, military blackout lights, and heavier frames and axles. The Blazer version was powered by the 6.2-liter diesel mated to the Turbo Hydra-Matic. They also had 3/4-ton axles. The pickup was a 1-ton with the same drivetrain and New Process transfer case, a Dana 60 front axle, a 10.5-inch GM rear axle, and troop seats in the bed. These hard-working, dependable Chevrolet military haulers were phased out by the all-new Hummers, which were powered by the same GM 6.2-liter diesel, by the way.

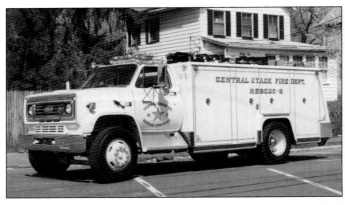

Chevrolet's Conventional cab medium-duty line consisted of Series C50-60-70 with single rear axles and Series C70 tandem axle. The balance of the medium-duty line consisted of the P40 walk-in van and the W70 tilt cab. The Central Engine Company of Central Nyack, New York, Fire Department owned this 1985 Chevrolet conventional cab C60 chassis cab with firefighting body. Rescue 2's body was by Salisbury. The GVW rating of this truck was 25,400 pounds. The 7.0-liter gas V-8 powered this truck. Broad choices of Caterpillar and Detroit Diesel engines were also offered. *Fred Cote*

Chevrolet's Kodiak was a version of the C60 and C70 models. When equipped with the largest standard diesel engines, the tilt-cab Kodiak's taller, one-piece, fiberglass hood and front fenders were required. Kodiaks made Chevrolet's medium-duty trucks take on a unique appearance. Many owners preferred its strong, aggressive look. The Clark County Fire Department in Las Vegas operated this Hazardous Materials Unit 24. Its special body was built by Marks Air. *Garry E. Kadzielawski*

Chevrolet announced in 1984 that the U.S. Army had contracted to buy approximately 53,000 Chevrolet full-size Blazers and pickups—23,500 Blazers and 29,500 pickups. They were to be powered by the 6.2-liter diesel V-8. The Army desired to have diesel-powered light-duty trucks because the heavy-duty trucks in its fleet and other vehicles were either diesel powered or would be in the near future. It saved money to have only one type of fuel to inventory. The Army's diesels would differ in size and origin, but the fuel would be the same. Training and servicing were also less complicated. Chevrolet was the only source of diesel-powered light-duty trucks. The Army's contract called for completion and delivery by the end of 1986. These trucks would basically be "civilian" trucks, except for the obvious differences required by the Army, which included a special electrical system, grille guards, special paint, and tow hooks. The Army's designation for these trucks was M1009. They replaced the late-seventies Dodge gas-powered pickups.

This was a historically significant year for Chevrolet trucks because it was the first year the famous 4.3-liter V-6 was the standard engine. It was fitted with a normal carburetor and produced 150 horsepower at 4,000 rpm and 225 foot-pounds torque at 2,400 rpm. The engine was essentially the old reliable small block 350 V-8 with two cylinders shaved off. The base transmission behind the new V-6 was a four-speed manual. A four-speed overdrive automatic was optional. The new V-6 replaced the venerable inline six (various versions, but always a six) that had powered Chevrolet trucks since 1929. Through the years, the 4.3-liter V-6 has played a larger and larger role in Chevrolet trucks—minivans, mini-pickups, full-size pickups, and vans. It made its debut in 1985 for use in Chevrolet's new Astro van line. Engineers needed a short block engine to package in Astro's short hood and it was quite important that this engine delivered a sparkling performance to compete well in the minivan market. A 1985 C10 Fleetside Silverado is pictured in the foreground, and a 1985 K10 Stepside in the background. Both were powered by the new 4.3-liter V-6. *John Gunnell*

The 1985 Chevrolet pickups carried over from 1984 without any startling changes in appearance. A new grille and headlight styling treatment freshened up their front appearance, and some exterior trim revisions added to an updated look. All paint colors and two-tone paint schemes carried over. The 379-ci V-8 diesel was upgraded for 1985 with one big improvement. Its rated SAE net horsepower was increased to 150 horsepower at 3,600 rpm with 250 foot-pounds of torque. The clutch on manual transmission models was now hydraulically operated through a slave cylinder for more precision and smoothness than the old system. Chevrolet's Crew/Bonus cab pickup continued as the biggest model in the line. This is a 1985 Crew Cab powered by the upgraded diesel V-8 engine with single rear wheels. The Big Dooley was optional.

Chevrolet medium-duty 1985 trucks offered two diesel engines—Detroit Diesel 8.2-liter V-8 and Caterpillar 3208 six. The Cat 3208 required the use of the Kodiak option lightweight fiberglass tilt hood and massive grille to house a larger radiator for additional cooling. The Cat 3208 was offered in eight power ranges from 160 to 250 horsepower. The Granbury, Texas, Fire Department owned this 1985 Chevrolet C70 Kodiak tractor with tank trailer. Its 4,000-gallon tanker was by Heil. C70 carried a maximum GCW rating of 60,000 pounds when used as a tractor. *Hansen*

Chevrolet offered medium-duty truck buyers three ways to go: C50, C60, and C70. The C50 models were gas-only, the C60 and C70 were either gas or diesel powered by Detroit Diesel or a Caterpillar. The Cat 3208 engine required the use of the optional Kodiak lightweight fiberglass tilt hood. A Chevrolet Tiltmaster tilt cab with a 5.7-liter turbocharged Isuzu engine was also offered. This is a 1985 Chevrolet C70 chassis cab with a tanker body. It was powered by the Cat 3208 diesel and equipped with a 13-speed Fuller Road Ranger transmission. The maximum GVW rating for C70 was 33,200 pounds.

This 1985 Chevrolet C10 Fleetside pickup is equipped with a four-barrel 4.3-liter V-6 and the Turbo 700 four-speed overdrive automatic. The 700 was a light-duty transmission used in 1/2-ton trucks, Camaros, and Corvettes. It was the forerunner of the 4L60 and 4L60E transmissions. The Turbo 400 was an option. These pickups proved their reliability and dependability to the Southern California Gas Company for more than 10 years while working for the fleet maintenance department. They had an excellent balance of power and economy. *Bob Bray*

1986

Chevrolet engineers hit a home run when they designed the Astro Van in 1985. They built their minivan on a front engine, rear drive, truck platform instead of a car platform like industry leader Chrysler did. There were a number of intelligent reasons for making it truck based. One reason was substantial towing and cargo capacity because of Astro's rear drive configuration. Payloads ranged up to 1,700 pounds and towing capacity up to 5,000 pounds when equipped with the 145-horsepower optional LB4 4.3-liter V-6 Vortec engine. The standard engine was the 92-horsepower LN8 2.5-liter four. The Vortec V-6 was equipped with throttle-body fuel injection, but the 2.5-liter Tech IV was equipped with electronically controlled fuel injection. This 1986 Astro Van passenger model boasted of available seating for up to eight. *AAMA*

This was a big, big year for trucks. First of all, Chevrolet sold a total of 1,247,594 new trucks in 1986, compared to its previous record of 1,300,130 in 1985. This was a drop of only 4 percent with a truck that had been around for years and was in its last full sales year. The new GMT400 trucks would go on sale in 1987 as 1988 models. The Chevrolet Suburban was voted "National Car of Texas" by *Texas Monthly* magazine. Chevrolet sold 61,226 Suburbans in 1985, up 4 percent.

Light-duty truck sales (Classes 1 to 3) reached an all-time high of 4.8 million units versus 4.7 million in 1985. Chevrolet estimated that 600,000 buyers purchased a truck instead of a car in 1986. Chevrolet management was convinced that the company's new 1987 GMT400 full-size pickups would cause many buyers to purchase this full-size truck instead of compact pickups.

GM announced in 1986 that it had entered into a deal with Volvo to jointly develop, produce, and sell Class 8 trucks. GM merged its Class 8 truck operations with Volvo-White Truck Corp. and formed the Volvo GM Heavy Truck Corporation. Volvo owned 65 percent and GM owned 35 percent of the corporation. The deal was implemented in October 1986; it was expected that in two years Volvo GM would build a single line of Class 8 trucks.

GM planned to move its medium-duty truck manufacturing activity to Janesville, Wisconsin, in June 1989. This plant would build both GMC and Chevrolet mediums. The idea was to reduce costs to better compete with the flood of imported medium-duty trucks, including its own trucks imported from Isuzu. Overall, the total industry imported 24,696 medium-duty trucks in 1986, 16.3 percent of all medium-duties.

Chevrolet's medium-duty truck sales fell by 16 percent in 1985, from 21,647 the previous year to 18,157. GM's Truck and Bus Group was busy developing a new line of medium-duty GMC and Chevrolet trucks to be built at Janesville, Wisconsin, for sale late in the 1980s.

In 1986, GM added Class 3 and Class 6 forward-control Isuzu Motor Co. trucks to those already in the line—the Chevrolet Tiltmaster and GMC Forward models. In order to be more competitive against other imported mediums, GM made a deal with Isuzu Truck of America to combine importing and distribution activities of the three brands (they differed only in their nameplates). The move saved several hundred dollars per truck in distribution costs.

In 1986, Chevy dealers sold 507 W4 (Class 4) and 601 W7 (Class 7) Tiltmaster models compared to GMC's 1,292 W4 and 1,666 W7 Forwards. Isuzu sold 4,954 NPRs, a version of the W4.

Chevrolet's 443,051 full-size pickups made it the top-selling nameplate at GM. Because this was the last year for Chevrolet's full-size pickup line, all models carried over without change.

The compact S-10 pickups, on the other hand, did receive a few changes. For example, the optional 2.8-liter V-6 was changed from carburetion to fuel injection and its horsepower rose to 125. Other new items were a Delcotron generator, a high-tech instrument panel that relocated the controls and instruments, a new package tray, and trim plates.

Chevrolet's full truck lineup continued without change in 1986. Its broad line ranged from the diminutive El Camino to a medium-duty diesel with a GVW rating of 35,000 pounds and a GCW rating of 60,000 pounds when used as a tractor. Chevrolet's traditional strength had always been in the light-duty range, and that was where it was in 1986, the last year before it made major changes in its full-size pickup line.

Because Astro Van was a truck-based vehicle, it was ideally suited for all types of commercial applications. Astro's generous 189.9 cubic feet of cargo space and cargo length of 116.6 inches (with passenger seat removed), or 88.9 inches to the back of seats, made it an intelligent choice for delivery service. Its 1,700-pound maximum payload rating made it an attractive alternative to a full-size van for any number of trades—plumbers, carpenters, carpet installers, and the like. Skilled workers typically used their van as a storeroom for their heavy tools and equipment, and then piled on other items required for specific jobs. The Astro's rear panel doors opened a full 57.0 inches and a sliding side door easily opened 34.5 inches wide and 44.5 inches high. *AAMA*

Chevrolet was vitally interested in making the Astro Van a major player in the van conversion market. This 1986 Chevrolet Astro "RS" was an interesting concept vehicle designed to demonstrate the versatility of Astro for van converters. The Astro did catch on with converters and quickly became the industry's favorite minivan with the van conversion industry. The Astro RS featured special exterior decor and a handling package consisting of a sport suspension, gas shocks, low-profile tires, and a rear stabilizer bar. It had a high-output V-6 Vortec engine with 170 horsepower, compared with 145 horsepower on the standard Vortec V-6 engine. *AAMA*

The 1986 Chevy Van line consisted of three models on two wheelbases. On the 110-inch short-wheelbase chassis, Chevrolet offered the G10 and G20 1/2- and 3/4-ton models. On the 125-inch-wheelbase chassis, G10, G20, and G30 models were offered. Chevrolet engineers designed the full-size van using "Unitized Construction." The vans had a body and frame that was integrated into a single unit, as opposed to the body-on-frame concept used, for example, in the construction of pickups. Chevy Van's floor panels were welded to heavy-gauge steel side rails, cross sills, and outriggers. This construction technique allowed Chevy Vans to be rated for maximum GVWs up to 8,600 pounds for the 1-ton G30 models. Engine options ranged from the 145-horsepower standard 4.3-liter V-6 to the 145-horsepower 6.2-liter V-8 diesel. The 160-horsepower 5.0-liter and 165-horsepower 5.7-liter V-8 gas engines were options. *AAMA*

Chevrolet's versatile 1986 Sportvan was an interesting and unusual vehicle. The 125-inch-wheelbase G30 1-ton Beauville Deluxe Package van could be equipped to do just about anything. It could seat up to 12 passengers with luggage and/or tow up to 13,500 pounds of van, passengers, cargo, and trailer. The 125-inch-wheelbase model had 256 cubic feet of usable space when all the rear bench seats were removed. Buyers had a choice of side doors: a standard sliding door, or 60/40 hinged doors at no extra cost. Panel doors in the back opened a full 180 degrees. A unique travel bed option featured a center bench seat that folded flat to form a sleeping area. *AAMA*

Chevrolet's 1986 S-10 pickup was again one of America's best-selling compact pickups. The standard cab 1986 Chevrolet S-10 4WD pickup pictured here was one of the most popular. The standard cab was purposely designed to provide adequate leg, head, hip, and shoulder room. Many buyers selected it strictly for work, but many others wanted it for fun and personal transportation. S-10 4WD pickups featured Insta-Trac. This patented 4WD system let the driver shift from 2WD to 4WD high and back at any speed. An available Off-Road Package was an extra-cost option. S-10's standard engine was the 92-horsepower 2.5-liter Tech IV. An electronically fuel injected 2.8-liter V-6 was optional at extra cost. The S-10's transmission lineup included a four-speed manual, five-speed manual, and four-speed automatic. Base price for a 1986 2WD S-10 standard cab pickup was $5,990. *AAMA*

Chevrolet's handsome, practical, and tough 1986 S-10 Blazer was America's favorite sport utility vehicle. The Blazer also offered the new optional 2.8-liter V-6 engine with throttle-body electronic fuel injection. Its horsepower was up to 125 at 4,800 rpm. The standard 2.5-liter four-cylinder engine had been improved with lighter weight pistons that produced lower reciprocating forces and cooler operation. Also new for 1986 were an optional factory-installed rear-mounted spare tire carrier and an instrument cluster with a high-tech appearance. The 4WD Blazer also had Chevrolet's nifty Insta-Trac that let the driver shift from 2WD to 4WD high and back again without stopping. The Blazer's short 100.5-inch wheelbase made it highly maneuverable and fun to drive. Its base list price was only $8,881. *AAMA*

Chevrolet's full-size 2WD pickups for 1986 included 26 models in 1/2-, 3/4-, and 1-ton series. This is a 1986 Chevrolet C10 Fleetside Custom Deluxe longbox. Cab types included the standard and Crew Cab/Bonus Cab twins. The Bonus Cab had only one bench seat, the area usually taken up by the second was for inside cargo. The 2WD Stepside cargo box was also offered in 1/2-, 3/4-, and 1-ton models. Three cab trim packages included the standard Custom Deluxe, the midrange Scottsdale, and the top-of-the-line Silverado. The standard engine for this C10 pickup was the LB1 4.3-liter 155-horsepower V-6. Optional was the LE9 (B) 5.0-liter 160-horsepower V-8. Also optional was the LH6 6.2-liter 130-horsepower V-8 diesel. Transmission options included the three-speed manual as standard and optional four-speed manual, four-speed manual with overdrive, three-speed automatic, and four-speed automatic. Base price of the C10 pickup was $7,904. *AAMA*

Chevrolet didn't change its full-size 4WD trucks. It stayed with its proven models with only minor styling and mechanical improvements. Chevrolet's 4WD pickups were offered in 1/2-, 3/4-, and 1-ton versions—K10, K20, and K30. The base engine for K-trucks was the 4.3-liter Vortec, 90-degree V-6 with swirl ports. It was the most powerful standard engine ever offered in a Chevrolet pickup. Now in its second year, it pumped out 144 horsepower and 230 foot-pounds of torque. Optional engines included the 5.0-liter V-8, 5.7-liter V-8, and the 7.4-liter V-8, plus the 148-horsepower 6.2-liter diesel V-8, especially designed for truck use. New engineering improvements in the full-size pickup included a five-ribbed, polyvee generator accessory belt and an electric booster fan for extra cooling when needed for the 7.4-liter V-8 engine. This is a 1986 Chevrolet K10 Fleetside pickup with aftermarket wheels. The 1986 K10 Fleetside pickup's list price without freight, taxes, or license was $15,798.

Chevrolet's full-size SUV was America's favorite truck of its type. It carried over essentially unchanged except for minor technical and cosmetic upgrades. The K10 Blazer was available with a 5.0-liter V-8 or a 6.2-liter diesel V-8. With the 5.0-liter engine, the buyer could select either a four-speed manual or an automatic transmission. With the diesel and the 5.7-liter gas engine only, the automatic was available. The New Process two-speed transfer case was standard equipment for K10 models and automatic locking hubs were an available extra-cost option. With this option drivers could shift into 4WD high at speeds up to 25 miles per hour—without leaving the cab. Its maximum GVW rating was 6,100 pounds with gas engine and 6,250 pounds with the diesel. *AAMA*

Chevrolet's huge 1986 Suburban was still in a class of its own. The Suburban, America's Superwagon, celebrated its 50th birthday in 1986. A Trailer Special Package was an important part of the Suburban's presence. Trailering Special Packages required a four-speed automatic transmission with overdrive and big engines—350 four-barrel V-8 was standard, and the 454 four-barrel was optional or the 6.2-liter diesel V-8. The Suburban for 1986 featured refinements, rather than complete technological and appearance improvements. The top GVW rating was 8,600 pounds for the 3/4-ton 2WD and 4WD series. The maximum GCW rating for the 3/4-ton with the 454 four-barrel V-8 was 15,500 pounds. Maximum payload was a whopping 3,799 pounds when properly equipped. Pictured here is a 1986 C10 Suburban Silverado. *AAMA*

Chevrolet's 4WD light-duty truck's mechanical foundation was based on an age-old design, ruggedly built on solid front and rear axles with semielliptical leaf springs. The front single-stage leaf springs were controlled by optional front dual shocks. Multistage leaves were used on the rear suspension with single shocks, but they were staggered for superior axle control. This 1986 Chevrolet K20 chassis cab with brush firefighting equipment was a prime example of toughness. Fire and Rescue truck No. 4 was owned by the Rawlins County, Kansas Fire Department. It featured a 250-gallon water tank and a 300-gpm pump. Note its heavy-duty steel grille guard and optional steel spoke wheels. Its powertrain was made up of the 165-horsepower 5.7-liter V-8 joined to the four-speed automatic overdrive transmission. *Dennis J. Maag*

A good percentage of the 4WD full-size pickups Chevrolet sold in 1986 were destined for duty as personal transportation and recreational vehicles. This was not so with the 1986 K30 heavy-duty 1-ton 4WD dually pickup. It was all business, rugged and hard working. Clark County (Washington) Fire Protection District No. 1 owned this brush firefighter. Its body was built by Pacific, and it featured a 300-gallon water tank and a 100-gpm pump. Note its eye-catching 10-stud chrome wheels, utility-type body, and high-mounted hose reel. Because of its dual rears, this 1-ton K30 carried a maximum GVW of 10,000 pounds and was rated for a maximum payload rating of 5,790 pounds. An LE8 7.4-liter 240-horsepower V-8 engine powered it. A full-floating 7,500-pound capacity rear axle was required equipment with the 454. It was equipped with a four-speed manual transmission and the New Process 205 two-speed transfer case. *Bill Hattersley*

This 1986 Chevrolet C30 chassis cab with firefighting body is so big, it almost looks like a medium-duty. It is a C30 1-ton chassis cab with rescue body built on a 159 1/2-inch-wheelbase chassis. The Brazoria, Texas, Fire Department owns it. Its body is by Wes-tex and features a 250-gallon water tank and a 250-gpm pump. This model carried a maximum GVW rating of 10,500 pounds. Its powertrain consists of the 240-horsepower 7.4-liter V-8 engine and a four-speed manual transmission. *Dennis J. Maag*

Chevrolet's only new truck for 1986 was the W4S042 (W4) Tilt-master. It boasted a 67.9-inch BBC dimension. Its four-cylinder powerplant was a 3.9-liter 4BD1-T turbo diesel rated for 116 SAE horsepower at 3,000 rpm. W4's short LCF design offered a 36.7-foot turning circle. Its great maneuverability made it perfectly suitable for working in congested streets and alleys doing city delivery work. Premium features included an exhaust brake, a cooling fan clutch that automatically disengaged when not needed, power steering, a built-in oil cooler, and a five-speed direct drive transmission. The truck on the right is a W7 Chevrolet Tiltmaster LCF. This model was in its third year and had been extensively upgraded. New features included a front stabilizer bar and tapered leaf springs. The cab interior had more shoulder and headroom than before, plus a handy storage shelf up front, and a larger windshield. W7 was rated for a maximum GVW of 27,500 pounds. *AAMA*

Chevrolet's 1986 medium-duty trucks were available in Series C50, C60, and C70. C50 Conventionals were gas-powered single-axle models only. They offered wheelbases from 125 to 167 inches for a wide range of applications. Maximum GVWs ranged from 16,000 to 18,500 pounds and maximum GCW ratings from 30,000 to 32,000 pounds. The C60 Conventionals featured gas and diesel engines from either Detroit Diesel or the Caterpillar 3208 Series; the Kodiak cab option was required with the Caterpillar 3208 engine. This 1986 Chevrolet C60 conventional chassis cab with firefighting body has been converted by an unknown source to 4WD. The Castlewood, Colorado, Fire Department owned engine No. 36. Its body was by KME and featured a 1,000-gallon water tank and a 750-gpm pump. *Dennis J. Maag*

The biggest Chevrolet medium-duty conventional cab series was the C70. It had a single rear axle, but a tandem axle was an option. Wheelbases for the series ranged from 125 to an extra-long 254 inches. Gas engines were standard, but both Detroit Diesel "Fuel Pincher" and the Caterpillar 3208 were available. The Caterpillar engine required the use of the optional Kodiak cab. The single-axle C70 models had a GVW range from 23,160 to 33,400 pounds. The rugged tandems carried a 50,000-pound maximum GVW rating and a maximum GCW rating all the way up to 60,000 pounds. This is a 1986 Chevrolet C70 conventional medium-duty chassis cab with a fire department rescue squad body. Its body was by Knapheide. *Dennis J. Maag*

Chevrolet's C70 medium-duty Conventional series trucks, when powered by the Caterpillar 3208 diesel engine, were required to use the optional Kodiak hood option. This is a 1986 Chevrolet crew cab C70 Kodiak chassis cab with firefighting body. This engine required a bigger radiator for better cooling than could be provided in the standard cab. The Marissa (Illinois) Fire Protection District owned engine No. 353. Its pumper body was by Towers and featured a 1,000-gallon water tank and a 500-gpm pump. Note the pump, controls, and gauges located between the bumper and grille. Chevrolet's medium-duty wide-track front axle provided impressive maneuverability, with turning angles as tight as 42 degrees and turning diameters as small as 44.5 feet. *Dennis J. Maag*

The C10 Silverado pickup was generally not chosen for pickup camper duty. This truck belonged to an elderly couple who enjoyed many a happy mile seeing the USA in their Chevrolet. Camper owners generally opted for the stronger C20 models for this service, but as you can see, this was not the biggest camper body. With Silverado trim and snappy two-tone paint, this was one attractive unit. It was powered by the largest V-8 engine Chevrolet offered for 1/2-ton pickups in 1986, the 160-horse-power 5.0-liter. Its four-speed overdrive automatic performed flawlessly on the interstate. When properly equipped, the C10 would handle a 2,558-pound payload. *Iten Chevrolet*

America's favorite full-size SUV returned for 1986 with the same minor changes as the balance of Chevrolet's full-size trucks. It was again only available as a 4WD. The Blazer was a versatile truck. It was the perfect choice for those into heavy hauling. When equipped with the heavy-duty trailering package, the Blazer could tow up to 11,000 pounds. The Blazer offered two two-tone paint schemes for 1986: With the one shown, the second color was applied down the middle portions of the side between the upper and lower moldings and striping. The K10 gas-powered Blazer was rated for a maximum GVW rating of 6,100 pounds, and the diesel was rated for a maximum 6,250 pounds. *Iten Chevrolet*

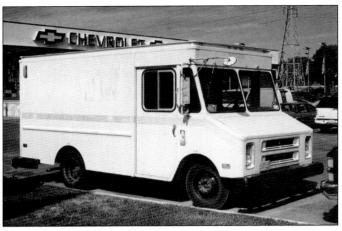

Chevrolet's forward-control Step-Van delivery trucks were America's most popular trucks in this category. For the 13 years prior to 1986, no one sold more Step-Van-type vehicles than Chevrolet. The complete Step-Van line for 1986 consisted of Series P20 and P30. The G30 Hi-Cube Van had replaced the former P10 Series. This is a 1986 Chevrolet P30 dual rear wheel Step-Van with a maximum GVW rating of 14,000 pounds. The standard engine for this model was the 115-horsepower 4.8-liter inline six cylinder; the 185-horsepower 5.7-liter V-8 and the 148-horsepower 6.2-liter diesel V-8 were options. A four-speed manual transmission was standard and a three-speed automatic was optional. *Harold Chevrolet*

The ideal truck for a company with a big, tough workload was the 1986 Chevrolet Crew Cab K30/C7E heavy-duty, 1-ton chassis cab with custom body. This brute carried a maximum payload rating of 3 tons—5,970 pounds on its 164.5-inch wheelbase. Power steering, power brakes, a two-speed transfer case, and locking hubs were standard equipment. The Crew Cab had plenty of room inside for six big men and four doors for easy entry and exit. The mighty 7.4-liter V-8 was the powerplant of choice. The proven, dependable four-speed manual was standard for Crew Cab. *Harold Chevrolet*

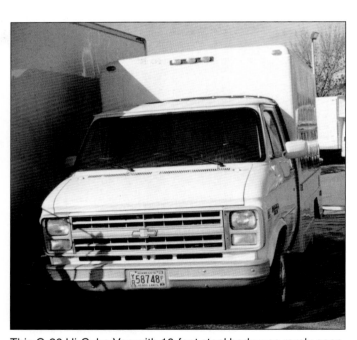

This G-30 Hi-Cube Van with 10-foot steel body was rarely seen. Most buyers preferred the higher capacity model with dual rears than this narrow body, single-wheel rig. Its 10-foot body rode on the 125-inch wheelbase. It was standard with a walk-through between the cab and load area. An available screen could be added if desired. Depending on spring and rear-axle capacities ordered, 7,400- to 8,600-pound GVWs were possible. Buyers could choose from three engines: 115-horsepower 4.8-liter L-six, 185-horsepower 5.7-liter V-8, and 148-horsepower 6.2-liter V-8 diesel. The only transmission offered with the G-30 series was the three-speed automatic with a column-mounted shift lever. *Iten Chevrolet*

Many small- and medium-size operators favored these economical, powerful, and dependable C70 tandem dump trucks. A drivetrain consisting of the Cat 3208 diesel engine, Fuller Road Ranger transmission, and Rockwell or Eaton tandem axles rated for 34,000 to 38,000 pounds was as good as it could get. The Cat 3208 diesel engine required the optional Kodiak lightweight tilt fiberglass hood to house its huge radiator. The naturally aspirated Cat 3208 was available in seven power ratings; it was also available in four turbo-charged ratings. Cat engines were highly respected throughout the entire industry.

1987

This was another barnburner year for industrywide truck sales, with the total coming a mere 52,200 units short of 5,000,000. Total light-duty sales reached a new record of 4,668,132 trucks. Unfortunately, Chevrolet slipped to 1,504,684 from 1,647,631 in 1986. It was the second year in a row that sales had declined.

Chevrolet marketing executives looked forward to 1988 and the new GMT400 C/K trucks. They held hopes that the new pickups would put them back into first place in truck sales. Three plants would produce the new trucks: Fort Wayne, Indiana; Pontiac (East), Michigan; and Oshawa, Ontario, Canada.

It was estimated that a half-million buyers switched annually from cars to light trucks, specifically to compact vans and SUVs. Light trucks had captured 16 percent of the market in 1968 and took 30 percent in 1987. Those in the know predicted that light trucks would take 40 percent of the market in the year 2000. They were too conservative: In 1998, the actual percentage was just short of 50 percent.

GM's Detroit Diesel Allison Division was sold to the Penske Corporation, which renamed it the Detroit Diesel Corporation. Penske owns 60 percent of the stock. The Allison Division remained with GM.

Medium-duty truck sales (Classes 4–7) posted a 4 percent gain in 1987, to 157,179 from 151,414 in 1986. Most of the gain was in the Class 4 segment that was added again in 1987, after being absent for several years. Chevrolet's 1987 medium-duty sales totaled 18,136, essentially the same as 1986's 18,157, but fewer than the 21,647 mediums built in 1985. In 1987, Chevrolet sold 1,110 forward-control Isuzu-built trucks under the Tiltmaster nameplate.

GMC stopped building Class 8 trucks late in 1987, turning that responsibility over to Volvo GM Heavy Truck Corp. The new company produced big trucks under the new name White GMC.

GM Truck Group finalized plans for an all-new line of medium-duty trucks for the 1990 model year. Due to labor strife at GM's Pontiac, Michigan, truck facility, the company planned to move all medium-duty truck production (GMC and Chevrolet) to Janesville, Wisconsin.

A study conducted in 1988 by Maritz Marketing Research showed that women accounted for 750,000 truck purchases in 1987. Women generally preferred the type of truck useful for passenger carrying as opposed to commodity hauling. For example, they purchased far fewer full-sized pickups, the type of light truck most commonly used for cargo hauling. Women mostly purchased vans, both full-size and minivans; compact pickups and SUVs—mostly compacts, but also full-size SUVs.

Chevrolet introduced its new pickup in midyear 1987 as a 1988 model, which will be discussed in the 1988 section. The old truck was built through the end of July. The official introduction date for the new pickup was April 23, 1987. It is interesting to note that GM referred to the new pickup as a GM truck, with a Chevrolet and a GMC version selling through two distinct dealer bases. GM's code name for the new truck program during its development phase was GMT400.

The major change in Chevrolet's light trucks for 1987 was the addition of throttle-body fuel injection to all full-size trucks under 10,000 pounds GVW. Carbureted 454 and 292 engines were still found in some P chassis and chassis cabs, however. Compact trucks across the board already had throttle-body fuel injection.

A whole host of other improvements were made to compact- and full-size trucks, vans, and SUVs. These changes included mechanical improvements, new options, and more comfortable interiors, all designed with the intent of making them better able to perform the jobs they were designed to fill.

The other vehicle in Chevrolet's 1987 minivan offering was the Astro Van. The Astro Van was a big reason car buyers purchased a truck instead of a car. It was a much better buy for the same or less money. It delivered performance. Also, it would fit into any standard garage, it had seating capacity greater than even a full-size station wagon, it had a smooth ride and a long list of creature comfort options. For 1987, Chevrolet increased the Astro Van's towing capacity to 6,000 pounds. This was the largest towing capacity available in any compact van (except for GMC). Five-passenger seating was standard, and with a third optional seat total capacity increased to eight. A new model for 1987 was the LT, or Luxury Touring. After chalking up two years of sales experience, Chevrolet's marketers discovered the M-van (Astro) sales were skewed strongly to the passenger side. A full 77 percent of total sales went to the passenger model and or a van conversion. Originally it was estimated that sales would split down the middle between cargo and passenger vans. *AAMA*

Chevrolet's small cargo and conversion vans were called Astros. The passenger van was called Astro Van. This is a 1987 Chevrolet Astro commercial. It was now entering its third model year. The Astro was a truck-built van with a front engine and rear drive layout. It had the industry's highest GVW rating of 5,600 pounds. At 3,070 pounds, it weighed the most. It had the industry's highest trailer towing capacity of 6,000 pounds and the highest cargo capacity of 151.6 cubic feet. The Astro had the widest body by 4 inches, which contributed to its greater capacity. Of most interest to many buyers, especially commercial users, was its lead in available power. Its 4.3-liter Vortec V-6 with EFI (engine code LB4) cranked out 150 SAE net horsepower at 4,000 rpm and 230 foot-pounds torque at 2,400 rpm. *Ron Cenowa*

Chevrolet's S-10 pickups returned in 1987 with only minor improvements and one new 4WD package. As before, it was available in both 2WD and 4WD configurations in standard and Maxi-Cab series, and both 6-foot short-bed and 7 1/2-foot long-bed models. The standard 92-horsepower 2.5-liter Tech IV engine with Electronic Fuel Injection (EFI) featured new high-flow cylinder head ports for enhanced efficiency and performance. An updated, lighter, and more powerful 85-amp Delcotron generator now supplied electric power. A high-tech new serpentine, single-belt accessory drive replaced the conventional multiple V-belt arrangement of the past. This is a 1987 Chevrolet S-10 Maxi-Cab pickup. Base price for a standard cab 1987 S-10 was about $6,595. *AAMA*

Chevrolet's 4WD S-10 pickups featured Insta-Trac off-road capability with a simple shift that switched from 2WD to 4WD high and back again at any speed. Engine options for 4WD S-10s included the 92-horsepower standard 2.5-liter Tech IV with EFI and the 125-horsepower 2.8-liter V-6 with EFI. The four-speed manual transmission was standard; a five-speed with overdrive was optional, as were the three- and four-speed automatics. S-10's standard seat was a vinyl bench; a fabric bench and bucket seats were options. Four cab interior trim levels included the Base, Durango, Tahoe, and Sport. Each of the four levels was more luxurious than the last. *AAMA*

For the full-size vans, the proper terminology was Chevy Van for the workhorse commercial/conversion van, and Sportvan for the passenger van. Most conversion vans eventually wound up as people movers. The factory delivered a plain commercial van to one of a number of factory-authorized converters who then transformed it into an upscale passenger mover. This is a 1987 Chevrolet Beauville Sportvan. Beauville had top-of-the-line interior/exterior trim levels. Chevrolet built both van types in three series: G10, G20, and G30 or 1/2-, 3/4- and 1-ton nominal ratings. The two wheelbases were: 110 inches for Series G10 and G20, and 125 inches for Series G10, G20, and G30. Power options for the Sportvan included the base 4.3-liter V-6 and optional 5.0 and 5.7-liter V-8 gas engines and the 6.2-liter diesel V-8. Transmission options included three- and four-speed manuals and automatics. *AAMA*

The full-size Blazer, formerly known as the K-Blazer, was now the V-Blazer. Chevrolet's full-size Blazer had been around since 1969. It was a well-established all-purpose vehicle that served individuals and families well. It was versatile and comfortable, and as at home running to the store for groceries as it was playing off-road or pulling a boat or trailer on the nation's freeway system. It was a tough, rugged, and highly functional truck. One of its strongest features was its roomy interior—plenty for driver, passengers, and a load of luggage. The Blazer's big change for 1987 was in its engine lineup. The 170-horsepower 5.0-liter EFI V-8 was the base engine and the 210-horsepower 5.7-liter EFI V-8 was available. The 130-horsepower 6.2-liter diesel was another option. Actually, the diesel was considered a separate series. *AAMA*

Chevrolet owned the super-sized SUV market again in 1987. Chevrolet's "Superwagon" was a versatile multiple use vehicle—passenger carrier, cargo mover, and unrivaled tow vehicle. The Suburban was well established because Chevrolet had been building it for satisfied customers for over half of a century. It was offered in both 2WD and 4WD models. For 1987, Chevrolet dropped the former C/K model designators for new R/V designators for 2WD and 4WDs, respectively. The gas engine line consisted of the 305, 350, and 454 V-8s with horsepower ratings of 170, 210, and 230, respectively. The 6.2-liter diesel was rated for 148 horsepower. A 1987 Chevrolet V10 Suburban is shown here pulling a boat and trailer out of a Goodyear Tire dealer's shop.

As with the Suburban, Chevrolet dropped the C/K designations and replaced them with the new R/V designations (2WD and 4WD, respectively). Chevrolet's bread and butter light-duty trucks continued to be its full-size pickups. They were built in 2WD or 4WD configurations, 1/2-, 3/4-, and 1-ton Series, Stepside or Fleetside, long wheelbase and short wheelbase to meet the needs of every buyer. This is a 1987 Chevrolet C10 1/2-ton 2WD short-box Stepside. The big news for 1987 was that all V-6 and V-8 gasoline engines incorporated the use of throttle-body fuel injection (TBI) system that replaced the carburetor and allowed higher compression ratios and greater horsepower. Computer controls incorporated in the TBI system improved drivability and performance. *AAMA*

Chevrolet built a total of 20 rugged 4WD models in 1987. The 4WD trucks were redesignated V-models for 1987, and were available in 1/2-, 3/4-, and 1-ton series. Buyers could choose Fleetside or Stepside cargo boxes and Crew Cab/Bonus Cab options for V30 Series. In 1987, nearly 67 percent of light trucks were bought for personal use or what was sometimes called "lifestyle choices." Additionally, research showed that only 11 percent of main family vehicles in 1987 were pickups, but the second, third, or fourth family vehicle in 40 percent of households was a pickup. This 1987 Chevrolet V30 Fleetside pickup with firefighting equipment was not one of those. This was a tough 4WD with an important job to do. The Pacific (Missouri) Fire Protection District owned this brush truck. *Dennis J. Maag*

Chassis cab versions of trucks smaller than a 1-ton are quite rare. This is a V20 4WD 3/4-ton chassis cab with a firefighting body. Many 1-ton chassis cabs for a multitude of uses are sold each year. The St. Clair (Missouri) Fire Protection District owned truck No. 321. This brush truck has a body by Steelweld that featured a 250-gallon water tank and a 250-gpm pump. It is unusual for a body manufacturer to build a standard-type pickup cargo box. Another unusual feature is the grille guard that is made of round pipes, which continue back to protect the truck's hood and windshield. The firefighters in St. Clair evidently had to contend with some serious brush. Chevrolet's V20 was rated for a maximum GVW of 6,600 pounds. The big 210-horsepower 5.7-liter V-8 engine powered it. Its transmission was the four-speed manual. *Dennis J. Maag*

Chevrolet's biggest 1987 pickup was Series R30/V30 1-ton Fleetside with dual rear wheels. The maximum GVW rating of this truck was 10,000 pounds. It could move up to 18,000 pounds' worth of trailer, truck, equipment, cargo, and people when equipped with the required optional equipment. Its standard engine was the 210-horsepower 5.7-liter V-8. Optional was the 230-horsepower 7.4-liter V-8; it also had 385 foot-pounds torque. The standard transmission for the V30 Big Dooley pickup was the four-speed manual; the three-speed automatic was the only option. A diesel engine was also available. The two-tone paint design shown on this pickup was special for the Big Dooley only. *AAMA*

Chevrolet's 1-ton chassis cab models were well liked by a whole range of users including the nation's firefighters. This is a 1987 Chevrolet 1-ton chassis cab with a firefighting body. Chevrolet offered this truck in two series: R/V 2WD and 4WD. The Guadalupe, Arizona, Fire Department owned truck No. 241, a fire-rescue rig. Its body was by Pierce and featured a 300-gallon water tank and a 250-gpm pump. This truck carried a maximum GVW rating of 10,500 pounds. Its engine was the 5.7-liter V-8 and its transmission was the four-speed manual. *Greenberg*

Chevrolet moved away from its familiar C/K designations for light-duty 2WD and 4WD trucks, and adopted R/V as the new designators. The reason for the change at this time was to prevent confusion when the entirely new pickups were introduced one model year later. The new truck line would consist only of pickups at the outset. The new Crew Cab, full-size Blazer, and Suburban followed several years later. When introduced, the new pickups reverted to the former C/K designations and the three other models continued to use R/V. Pictured here is a 1987 Chevrolet 6.2-liter diesel-powered V-20 3/4-ton Silverado pickup driving off into history. It was about to be replaced with the new 1988 truck. *AAMA*

For many years, much of America's business was carried by Chevrolet's popular, capable Chevy Vans. Chevrolet offered three basic series: G10, G20, and G30 with maximum GVW ratings of 4,900, 6,600, and 8,600 pounds, respectively. Buyers could further choose between 110-inch and 125-inch wheelbases. The short wheelbase featured 207 cubic feet of load space, and the long wheelbase 260 cubic feet. The Chevy Van was standard with a sliding side door; 60/40 swing-out side doors were available as a no-extra-cost option. Power choices included the base 4.3-liter V-6 and 5.0 and 5.7-liter V-8s plus the 6.2-liter diesel V-8. Transmission choices included a three-speed manual, four-speed manual, three-speed automatic, and a four-speed automatic with overdrive. This is a 1987 commercial Chevy Van G20 125-inch wheelbase. *Harold Chevrolet*

Buyers had their choice of three engines in 1987 Chevrolet C70 medium-duty trucks: 7.0-liter 220-horsepower V-8, Detroit Diesel 8.2-liter V-8 diesel in six power ranges from 145 to 230 horsepower, and the Caterpillar 3208 in seven power ratings ranging from 200 to 250 horsepower. The larger Kodiak hood was required with the Cat 3208 diesels; it was optional with the Detroit Diesel. The Cat engine required additional cooling from a larger radiator than the standard hood would accommodate. The Cat 3208 powered these trucks. They also were specified with the 13-speed Fuller Road Ranger transmission.

Chevrolet's four-door pickup/chassis cab could be ordered as either a Crew Cab or Bonus Cab. The difference in the two was that the Bonus Cab only had one seat. The area normally occupied by the second seat became cargo space. A lawn service company typically ordered the Crew Cab. The 5.7-liter V-8 engine powered this R20 Crew Cab. Its transmission was the three-speed automatic. R20 carried a maximum GVW rating of 8,600 pounds.

America's cities and municipalities found excellent values in Chevrolet's full-size pickups and chassis cabs in Custom Deluxe trim. The city of Franklin, Minnesota, owned this 1987 C30 chassis cab with platform body. The R30 1-ton had a maximum GVW rating of 10,000 pounds. Its standard engine was the 5.7-liter V-8; optional engines were the 7.4-liter gas V-8 and the 6.2-liter diesel V-8. The city bought the standard engine to go with the standard four-speed manual transmission. The cab interior had a full-width vinyl-covered bench seat.

1988

The truck industry turned in another banner year in 1988, the fourth record year in a row. Light-duty models led the way as they had for several years, because 600,000 buyers per year continued to trade in cars for trucks.

Record truck sales for 1988 sent the industry total to the lofty high of 5,209,267, marking the first time the five million barrier was broken. Trucks accounted for one in three vehicle sales in the United States. Full-sized pickups took over the sales lead from compact pickups for the first time in three years. Currency exchange rates hit the Japanese-built trucks hard, an event that led pickup buyers to see better values in American-built full-size models. During the 1980s, compact pickup sales grew steadily while market share of the full-size pickups declined. Full-sized pickups dropped from 52 percent of the industry light truck sales in 1980 to 26 percent in 1987. The reversal began in the first six months of 1988. Compact pickups' market share dropped from 30 percent to 26 percent in July 1988. In the first half of 1987, compact pickups outsold full-size pickups by 119,217 units; during the same period of 1988, compact pickups trailed full-sized pickups by 49,356.

GM signed a contract with Caterpillar in February 1988 to begin buying Cat's new 3116 diesel engine for GM's all-new line of 1990 model medium-duty trucks. The new line of trucks was expected to begin production in GM's Janesville, Wisconsin, plant at the end of 1989. Cat at the time supplied its 3208 engine for the GMC Top Kick and Chevrolet's Kodiak series, the heavy end of GM's medium-duty line. Many of these models were registered as heavy-duty models.

The real story in Chevrolet trucks for 1988 was the new C/K model pickups. Actually introduced in midyear 1987, the model wasn't actually sold until July 1988 as 1988 trucks and were new from the frame rails up. These trucks represented a $2.6 billion investment by GM. They were billed as the country's first all-new full-size pickups in a quarter-century.

The new trucks were longer, lower, and more aerodynamic than the series they replaced. The old series continued to be available in chassis cab and crew cab configurations. The old chassis continued to be used for full-size Blazer and Suburban models, too.

Some fleet users didn't quite know what to make of the new truck at first. They felt it looked quite a bit smaller than the old one, but when they started buying them, they noticed that the cabs were actually roomier and the bed was the same size. They drove very well, and when drivers adjusted to them, they made the competitor's trucks look dated.

The new 4WD had independent front axles with torsion bars in place of the former truck's solid front axle. The use of torsion bars made it possible to lower the height of the pickups by 3 1/2 inches. They were also the first full-size Chevrolet pickups available with an optional extended cab.

The standard and optional engine lineups remained unchanged. All engines had been revised with the addition of throttle body fuel injection. This change affected the whole truck line.

Chevrolet turned up the heat a few notches in 1988 with the midyear introduction of the 4.3-liter Vortec V-6 engine. The standard engine continued to be the 2.4-liter L4, and the 2.8-liter V-6 was optional. Every 1988 engine was equipped with EFI. The five-speed manual transmission with overdrive was standard equipment and the four-speed automatic with overdrive was optional. No one was more excited to see the 4.3-liter V-6 become available in S-10 pickups than the off-road crowd. The optional Back Country off-road appearance package was new in 1987 and available in 1988. This 1988 Chevrolet 4WD S-10 Maxi-Cab pickup sports the Back Country appearance package. The package consisted of a front grille guard with driving lamps, a light bridge with off-road lamps, tubular rear bumper, switches in the instrument panel for off-road driving lamps, black-chrome accent on wheels, headlight and taillight bezels and grille, and striping around wheel openings and front of hood. Other required equipment for the Back Country package included power steering, a 1,500-pound payload package, an off-road chassis equipment package and a 2.8-liter V-6 engine. *AAMA*

Chevrolet's hot-selling Astro Van was now in its fourth model year and was selling quite well. Chevrolet expanded the Astro to three models in 1988: the CS (Custom Sport), CL (Custom Luxury), and LT (Luxury Touring) interior/exterior trim packages. These three new models were significant because the Astro's most important niche was the passenger van market. Chevrolet management reasoned that the more carlike the Astro was, the more crossovers from cars it would capture. Astro passenger vans accounted for 75 percent of sales. The Astro Van featured a soft but controlled ride, the biggest engine in any small van, seating for up to eight adults, and the highest optional towing capacity at 6,000 pounds. The Astro's 4.3-liter Vortec V-6 pumped out 150 horsepower and 230 foot-pounds torque at 2,400 rpm. *AAMA*

A full-size, extended-cab Silverado pickup with 4WD, automatic transmission, and most options retailed for about $100 less than $20,000.

In January, GM cut prices on about 60 percent of its trucks by an average of $200 to match Ford. Ford trucks outsold Chevrolet trucks in 1987, and for the first time in a non-strike year since 1959, Ford division sold more cars and trucks than Chevrolet— about 100,000 more cars and 200,000 more trucks. The price reductions, which ranged up to $400, included many of the new full-size pickup models. Chevrolet's price-cutting was aimed at overtaking Ford in full-size pickup sales.

The second part of Chevrolet's strategy for overtaking Ford was splitting its advertising budget for the 1988 model year evenly between cars and trucks. Trucks did not yet account for half of Chevrolet's sales. In the 1987 model year the advertising budget was divided 57 percent for cars and 43 percent for trucks. Of the truck ad budget, 60 percent was used to advertise full-size pickups.

In April 1988, Chevrolet notched up the pickup war with Ford by increasing production. Ford answered by adding $200 million to its truck advertising budget. Chevrolet's added production came about with the addition of a second shift at its Pontiac East assembly plant—where the new pickups were built.

This was a good year for RV sales because of a sound national economy and stable gas prices. The average price for regular unleaded was 92.9 cents per gallon. Chevrolet had averaged sales of 100,000-plus motorhome chassis for the past three years. Chevrolet's RV lineup included a cutaway van chassis; a Sportvan with an optional 7.4-liter V-8; the Suburban; full-size pickups; and the compact Astro, which became a favorite with van converters.

Chevrolet's 1988 Maxi-Cab S-10 4WD pickup rode on a 122.9-inch wheelbase. The Maxi-Cab had 18.4 cubic feet of in-cab cargo space behind the standard bench seat. The same space could be used for passengers by ordering optional front bucket seats and rear jump seats. The S-10's Maxi-Cab option was extremely popular because people fell in love with its utility. The Maxi-Cab's cargo box was 6 feet in length. Outstanding features of S-10's 4WD system included the Insta-Trac 4WD system that provided "shift-on-the-fly" capability, standard independent front suspension, rubber-bushed upper and lower control arms with torsion bar springs, enhanced riding comfort, and a generous 6.25-inch front/7.25-inch rear ground clearance. Power teams included the 2.5-liter L4, 2.8-liter V-6, and 4.3-liter V-6 engines and five-speed manual transmission with overdrive or four-speed automatic with overdrive. *AAMA*

Chevrolet continued to build both 2WD and 4WD S-10 Blazers in 1988. This is a 1988 4WD S-10 Blazer with the optional High Country package. America's most popular 4WD SUV was an even more desirable vehicle in 1988, due to the addition of the powerful 4.3-liter Vortec V-6 engine as an option. The S-10's Insta-Trac 4WD system made four-wheeling easy for even the beginner. All that was required was to shift into 4WD mode. The driver could shift from 2WD to 4WD high and back again at any speed. A convenient console display indicated the driving mode with every shift. The 2.8-liter V-6 engine and power steering were standard for the 4WD model. High Country equipment included reclining front seatbacks, deep-tinted glass, center storage console, Midnight Black/Nevada Gold custom two-tone paint, graduated-color body side decals, black chrome grille, black chrome headlight trim, taillamp trim, door handles, nameplates, color-keyed front and rear bumpers, and special gold-tone aluminum wheels. *AAMA*

Chevrolet's huge Suburban continued to be the industry's only "Superwagon" and "King of the Road." The Suburban was so much a luxury station wagon that its truck roots were often overlooked. It was available in 2WD and 4WD configurations, with panel rear doors or station wagon–type rear tailgate, in luxurious Scottsdale or even more upscale Silverado trim, as a 1/2-ton or 3/4-ton, but always with four doors and with loads of interior space. The Suburban boasted a maximum GCW rating of 16,000 pounds. Power brakes and power steering were always standard equipment. The Suburban offered only big engines: 210-horsepower 5.7-liter V-8, 230-horsepower 7.4-liter V-8, and 148-horsepower 6.2-liter diesel V-8. Only automatic transmissions were offered—either a three-speed or a four-speed with overdrive. This Suburban Outdoorsman contained the following equipment: panel rear doors, a rear tire carrier (with cover) mounted on left door, a ladder mounted on right door to rear top cargo roof rack, and front brush guard with driving/fog lights. Also included were running boards, front reclining bucket seats and armrests, a center console, and special interior wood trim. *AAMA*

Chevrolet's full-size Blazer continued on top of the list of full-size SUVs. It delivered the combination of size, ride, and performance people wanted. Chevrolet introduced an all-new full-size pickup for 1988, but both the Blazer and Suburban had to wait a few more years before getting the new pickup's design and mechanical improvements. Like its big brother, the Blazer's model nomenclature was the new R/V prefixes replacing the old familiar C/K labels. This change was made for the 1987 model year. The R was for 2WD and V for 4WD. For added fuel economy, Chevrolet had gone to all overdrive transmissions: four-speed overdrive manual and four-speed overdrive automatic. The standard engine was the 5.7-liter V-8; the 6.2-liter diesel V-8 was an option. New features for 1988 included a fixed mast antenna, a trip odometer, and an improved pulse windshield wiper control. *AAMA*

Chevrolet's new full-size pickup was its first since 1973. The former model served GM well for 15 years. The new state-of-the-art pickup cost the company $1.3 billion. The GMT 400 (the new truck's code name) project took five years to complete, but was worth every penny. Profit margins per truck were wide and sales were high. The GMT 400 was a "ground-up" redesign. Notice the code name uses the all-inclusive prefix of GMT for General Motors Truck. It was not only a Chevrolet truck, it was also a GMC truck. Chevrolet Division had corporate responsibility for light-duty truck engineering and manufacturing; GMC had the same responsibilities for medium-duty trucks. Chevrolet engineers adopted the fully automatic 4WD engagement system called Insta-Trac, which they had been using for several years in the S-10 trucks. This 1/2-ton standard cab 1988 Chevrolet pickup was one of the first seen; it was photographed early in June 1987.

Chevrolet sold 18,084 medium- and heavy-duty trucks in 1988, nearly even with 1987's 18,173. Chevrolet's medium-duty market share dropped to 10.8 percent in 1988 from 1987's 11.5 percent.

Chevrolet and GMC's combined sales of medium-duty trucks (Tiltmaster and Forward brands, respectively) built by Isuzu Motors totaled 4,456 units in 1988 compared to 4,156 in 1987.

Chevrolet sold 1,336,407 trucks in 1988, compared to only 1,173,675 in 1987. Chevrolet came in second to Ford, but cut the margin significantly from the previous year—from 226,000 units in 1987 down to only 106,000 units in 1988.

The bulk of Chevrolet's sales increase in 1988 came from the first full-year availability of its GMT400 full-size pickups, plus increased sales of S-10 compact pickups, and S-Blazer compact SUVs.

To the credit of domestic makes, imported truck volumes dropped a huge 25 percent. Domestic compact truck sales gained almost 7 percent in 1988.

GMT 400 pickup spelled technology. Designers used the wind tunnel to get the smooth lines and rounded corners of its new cab just right for a "slippery" body shape. Reduced wind drag increased fuel efficiency. The 4.3-liter Vortec V-6 was the standard engine for all 1/2- and 3/4-ton trucks, 2WD, and 4WD. By improving the computer control of the throttle-body fuel-injection system, the addition of roller valve rockers, and a single-belt accessory drive, the 4.3-liter V-6's horsepower was boosted by five and picked up an additional 10 foot-pounds torque. Horsepower and performance of the 5.0- and 5.7-liter V-8s were substantially improved as a direct result of applying Vortec V-6 technology to them. The new engines had 175 and 210 horsepower, respectively, with torque outputs of 270 and 300 foot-pounds for the 5.0 and 5.7 engines, respectively. This is a new 1988 Chevrolet full-size 3/4-ton Extended Cab pickup. *AAMA*

The Chevrolet pickups engine lineup for 1988 was short and simple. The 4.3-liter Vortec V-6 was the base engine for all 1/2- and 3/4-ton 2WD and 4WD models. The 5.0- and 5.7-liter V-8s were options for those trucks. For 1-ton 2WD and 4WD models, the 5.7-liter V-8 was standard and the 7.4-liter big block was optional. The 6.2-liter V-8 diesel was available for all 1/2-, 3/4-, and 1-ton 2WD and 4WD models. The diesel was rated for 150 horsepower and 255 foot-pounds torque at 2,400 rpm. Manual transmissions included two four-speeds and a five-speed overdrive. Two automatics included a three-speed and a four-speed overdrive. The only transfer case used for all 4WD models was the New Process 241. A new independent front suspension system for 4WD trucks was similar to, but much stronger than, the system used in the S-10 series trucks. Pictured here is a 1988 Chevrolet 1/2-ton standard cab pickup. *AAMA*

Chevrolet's new Sportside pickup replaced the ages-old Stepside pickup. During the development phase of the GMT 400, this truck was first called the "Texas Two Step." The name didn't stick, however, because of resistance from the marketing folks. The Sportside differed from the old Stepside in one significant way; it was only offered in a short-bed version of the 1/2-ton standard cab C/K trucks. The Sportside featured 6 1/2-foot plastic side panels with steps in the front and back of the fenders. They were integral parts of the fender supported by steel hangers. The front panel, inner side panels, and tailgate used two-sided galvanized steel. When equipped with the 5.7-liter V-8 and a five-speed manual transmission the Sportside was a rocket. It had the look and feel of a genuine hot rod. Somehow it just didn't look like your average work truck. The graphics on its rear fender announce to the whole world that this is a 4WD truck; a 2WD Sportside was also offered. The Sportside was selected the "1988 Four Wheeler of the Year by *Four Wheeler* magazine on the basis of its overall performance. *AAMA*

Chevrolet's C/K3500 1-ton 131.5-inch-wheelbase pickup and chassis cab was a tough, hard-working truck. This is a 1988 Chevrolet 1-ton chassis cab with firefighting equipment. With single rear wheels, the 1-ton's maximum GVW rating was 8,600 pounds. What is interesting, however, is that when equipped with dual rear wheels, the three-speed automatic, a 4.56:1 rear-axle ratio, and the 7.4-liter V-8 engine, its GCW rating was a lofty 19,000 pounds. The same truck with a diesel engine carried a GCW rating of only 13,500 pounds. The Riverside County, California, Fire Department owned Squad No. S 36. Its utility-type body was by Harbor. Chevrolet only offered three engines for 3500 models: 5.7- and 7.4-liter gas V-8s, and the 6.2-liter diesel. The only transmission options for the 1-ton trucks included the four-speed manual (with low ratio first gear) and three-speed automatic. *Chuck Madderom*

Chevrolet's full-size Sportvan was in its 17th model year. Yet it was still one of the industry's leading vans in terms of sales, quality, function, and drivability. Three interior/exterior trim levels were available—Sportvan, Bonaventure, and Beauville. This is a top-of-the-line 1988 Chevrolet Beauville van. Three Sportvan models were available—G10/G20/G30, on two wheelbases—110 and 125 inches. New for 1988 was the 7.4-liter engine option. With this engine, the Sportvan was rated for a maximum GCW rating of 16,000 pounds, including vehicle, trailer, passengers, equipment, and cargo. The diesel engine option was also available. A sliding right-side door was standard and the 60/40 swing-out doors were optional at no extra cost. Maximum passenger capacity with the long wheelbase Sportvan was 12. *AAMA*

Chevrolet's 1988 medium-duty lineup consisted of C50-C60-C70 Conventionals. The C70 Conventionals were available as single or tandem-axle models. The Brazoria, Texas, Fire Department owned this 1988 Chevrolet C70 chassis cab with firefighting body. Tanker No. 404's body was by Freeport Welding. It contained a 1,000-gallon water tank and a 250-gpm pump. This truck was offered on 11 wheelbase lengths ranging from 125 to 254 inches. Gas and diesel engines were offered. This truck was powered by the 220-horsepower 7.0-liter V-8 (427). The standard alligator hood opened wide to provide clearance for the mechanic to reach components from either side or the front. Available transmissions included four and five-speed manuals from GM, Clark, Spicer, and New Process, Fuller Road Ranger 10- and 13-speeds, and the Fuller six-speed was new in 1987. Automatics included the Allison AT-545 four-speed, Allison MT-643 four-speed, and MT-653 five-speed. *Dennis J. Maag*

Tandems were only available in the C70 Conventional series. The Wakarusa, Indiana, Fire Department owned this 1988 Chevrolet C70 tandem chassis cab with fire fighting body. Its tank body was by Marion, and it featured a 2,500-gallon water tank and a 250-gpm pump. The 6.0-liter V-8 was the standard gas engine and the 7.0-liter was an option. This truck was equipped with the optional lightweight fiberglass tilt hood, counterbalanced for easy operation. The Eaton DS341 tandem axle, rated at 34,000 pounds, was standard. The Rockwell 34,000-pound SL 100 and Rockwell 40,000-pound SQ 100 tandems were also available. The tandems; maximum GVW rating was 50,000 pounds. Maximum GCW rating was 60,000 pounds. *Dennis J. Maag*

The large Kodiak hood was required with the 10.4-liter Caterpillar 3208 diesel. The standard 3208 was naturally aspirated; six turbocharged versions were also available. This is a 1988 Chevrolet medium-duty chassis cab with special body equipment. The Parsippany, New Jersey, Fire Department owned this heavy-duty rescue and recovery unit. Its body was by Swab. The lettering on its hood wind deflector reads "Ain't No Mountain High Enough." This truck had a maximum GVW rating of 33,200 pounds. Chevrolet single-rear-axle trucks featured Eaton spiral-bevel gearing. Single-speed rear axles were standard; two-speed rear axles were available on Series C60 and C70. The Kodiak was equipped with standard disc brakes front and rear; full air brakes were extra. *Scott Mattson*

1989

Calendar year 1989 turned out great for Chevrolet, but was not the best year for the industry. Total light-duty truck sales registered about 200,000 fewer sales than in 1988. Nevertheless, this was the second best in history. Chevrolet's total of 1,309,837 was fewer than 30,000 units behind its 1988 totals. It was good news for Detroit because the domestic car market had been losing ground to imported cars for the past several years. Every U.S. built light truck sold was one fewer sale of an imported car. GMC was the only maker to sell more light-duty trucks in 1989 than in 1988. Chevrolet's sterling performance enabled it to gain ground on Ford, cutting the margin between the two to only 92,000 units.

Chevrolet's total had the help of the Geo Tracker SUV that was new late in 1988 and sold briskly in 1989. Also, the first sales of the new Lumina APV minivan took place in 1989. Finally, this was the first year for a Chevrolet extended cab full-size pickup with the short cargo box.

The light truck industry continued to expand by attracting record numbers of women buyers. About 936,000 light trucks were sold to women in 1988, representing 19 percent of total light truck sales. The number included 327,000 minivans and 214,000 compact SUVs. Contrast this with the 1970s, when only 2 percent of light truck buyers were women! In overall terms, women accounted for only about 5 percent of the full-size pickup market in 1989.

The other factor helping light-duty truck sales was the "crossover factor." These were buyers who abandoned autos in favor of light trucks—pickups, SUVs, and vans. Nearly one million buyers, about 23 percent of them, got out of cars and into trucks as their primary vehicle.

Chevrolet beefed up its strength in the lower end of the medium-duty segment with the new LoPro option package for 1989. It was added to the 60-Series conventional cab line and was offered at GVWs of 14,840 and 16,000 pounds. Equipped with the 6-liter V-8 gas engine and either an Eaton five-speed manual or Allison four-speed automatic transmission, the LoPro was aimed at specialty applications such as ambulances, wreckers, and delivery trucks.

GM's all-new GMT530-series medium-duty trucks were introduced in August 1989 as 1990 models. A new 160,000-square-foot addition to the plant in Janesville, Wisconsin, was completed earlier in the year, bringing the total plant space to one million square feet for medium-duty truck production.

Total sales of medium-duty trucks fell from 1988's total of 334,451 to 311,916. Chevrolet sold 15,930 mediums in 1989 versus 17,811 in 1988. For the first time in many years, Chevrolet did not produce a heavy-duty truck. In reality, Chevrolet was only in the medium-duty truck business. Yet when its largest medium was equipped with tandem rear axles, its GVW rating pushed it into the heavy-duty category. Chevrolet sold 273 heavy-duty units in 1988.

Chevrolet's advertising focused on its superiority over Ford. The truck ads demonstrated what Chevrolet pickups could do. In one TV ad, a Chevrolet C/K full-sized pickup scaled a rock pile with a Ford and a Chevrolet on its back. The camera then pulled back and showed the entire trailer being pulled by a C/K truck.

Chevrolet's Geo Tracker SUV went into production in fall 1989 at the GM/Suzuki Motor Co.'s joint Canadian plant. This plant's production was shipped to the United States to replace

This was another excellent year for Chevrolet trucks and vans. Sales dropped a bit from 1988, but 1.3 million Chevrolet trucks found buyers. Astro and Astro Vans continued to be popular vehicles. Pictured here is a 1989 Astro Van. Passenger models had a rear wheel anti-lock (RWAL) braking system as standard. RWAL prevented rear wheel skid under varying road and load factors. A sport suspension package was a midyear 1989 offer and included special tires, gas pressure shocks, front and rear stabilizer bars, and rally or aluminum wheels. The Astro Van's standard engine was the 150-horsepower high-performance 4.3-liter Vortec V-6. The Astro Van would seat up to eight adults, more than any other minivan. With the second and third seats removed, the Astro Van provided a maximum cargo space of 151.8 cubic feet. The Astro Van featured panel rear doors and a sliding side door, which made passenger entry and cargo loading a snap. *AAMA*

S-10 pickups came in second behind the Ranger in 1989. But the popular S-10 Series trucks still continued to be one of America's favorites. This is the 1989 Chevrolet conventional cab short-box EL S-10 2WD pickup. The EL, Economy Leader, was a very popular model. Its low price was due to dressing down the 2WD regular cab S-10 with the 6-foot box. A few options were available, such as air conditioning and an AM radio. For the buyers not so much interested in economy, Chevrolet also offered the up-level Durango, and the optional top-level Tahoe. The standard S-10 engine was the 125-horsepower 2.8-liter V-6 with EFI. Optional was the 160-horsepower 4.3-liter V-6 engine with EFI. Payload capacity was 1,000 pounds. Power steering and brakes were standard equipment as was a five-speed manual transmission with overdrive. A four-speed automatic was an option. *AAMA*

Chevrolet's S-10 Maxi-Cab with the Vortec 4.3-liter V-6 engine was a very capable tow vehicle for trailers weighing up to 6,000 pounds. The Maxi-Cab's 13.7 cubic feet of secure inside storage was another reason this smart small truck was highly popular. Chevrolet's 4.3-liter V-6 produced 160 horsepower at a low 4,000 rpm and 230 foot-pounds torque at only 2,400 rpm. It had impressive power and delivered over 21 miles per gallon. This was better mileage than that given by the standard 2.8-liter V-6. Another prominent selling point of the Maxi-Cab was its comfortable bucket seats and handy center console. The dash had full instrumentation, including an optional tachometer. The Maxi-Cab had auxiliary seats that folded down from the sides of the cab behind the bucket seats. The extended cab S-10 pickup had a 122.9-inch-wheelbase chassis. A well-optioned S10 Maxi-Cab with the 4.3 V-8 and a four-speed automatic overdrive transmission listed for approximately $13,255. *AAMA*

The 1989 Chevrolet S-10 Blazer was an interesting alternative to the S-10 pickup. In appearance they were the same to the back of the doors. Many drivers preferred the enclosed four-seat configuration of the S-10 Blazer to a pickup. The Blazer was a comfortable, enclosed, capable four-wheeler. The Blazer also had the high-performance Vortec 4.3-liter V-6 engine. Its 117.9-inch-wheelbase length proved to be highly maneuverable on and off-road. The Blazer also had a 6,000-pound towing maximum, the same 1,000-pound payload capacity, and generous amounts of inside storage space behind the front seats. A five-speed manual was standard, but most buyers paid the extra cost for the optional four-speed automatic. The RWAL system provided better straight-line braking in emergency stops. It was available with 2WD, too. This 1989 S-10 4WD Chevrolet Blazer listed for approximately $16,500. *AAMA*

Chevrolet gained ground on Ford in truck sales for 1989, shortening the gap. This was in large part due to the new C/K pickups. In its first full calendar year, Chevrolet's large pickups posted an increase over 1988 and Ford didn't. This was not surprising, since GMC's sales also increased and it had the only new pickups in the industry. Buyers liked the aerodynamic styling and updated mechanicals. Chevrolet's timing was good. Eight years before, only one truck was sold for every four cars. In 1989, that ratio had doubled to two trucks for every four cars. The new pickups were offered in three trim levels: Cheyenne, Scottsdale, and Silverado, which was the top-of-the-line model. Chevrolet's new Extended Cab option was a major factor in the new pickup's success. Pictured here is a 1989 Chevrolet K1500 standard cab long-box pickup. *AAMA*

Chevrolet built two 1-ton models in 1988 and 1989. These were the 1-ton standard cab and Extended-Cab pickups, and chassis cabs and one-ton Crew/Bonus cab pickups and chassis cabs. The full-size Blazer, Suburban, and Crew/Bonus Cab models did not change to the new GMT 400 style until 1993. This 1-ton Extended Cab mounted on an extended wheelbase was rated for a maximum GVW of 10,000 pounds. The standard engine for this truck was the L19 7.4-liter V-8. It was rated for 230 horsepower at 3,600 rpm and 385 foot-pounds torque at 1,600 rpm. The LL4 6.2-liter V-8 diesel engine was also standard. With either engine, the standard transmission was a four-speed manual. Standard tire equipment was the LT245/75R-16E. *Elliott Kahn*

imports from Japan, which were subjected to a 25 percent import-truck tariff. Canada, which had no such tariff, imported its Trackers from Japan.

It's interesting to note that in the first year of the decade, total truck industry production in 1980 was a paltry 1,638,259 units. In 1989, the end of the decade total production was almost 2 1/2 times greater—4,061,950 units. Between 1982 and 1989 car production increased by only one-third.

Another interesting figure spanning a decade is the CAFE (Corporate Average Fuel Economy) rate for the industry in total. For 1978, the first year of CAFEs, it was 19.9 miles per gallon; in 1989 it rose to 28.3 miles per gallon. Both averages exceeded the standard.

The last interesting statistic to look at is the changing mix of car sales in the United States. For the period 1975–1979, U.S. makes sold 42.3 million cars versus 9.5 million for the imports. However, in the period 1985–89, U.S. makes sold 38.1 million cars versus 15.2 million imported cars. In other words, U.S. makes lost 10 percent of their volume and imported makes gained by 60 percent!

Chevrolet built two 1-ton models in 1988 and 1989. These were the 1-ton standard cab and Extended-Cab pickups, and chassis cabs and one-ton Crew/Bonus cab pickups and chassis cabs. The full-size Blazer, Suburban, and Crew/Bonus Cab models did not change to the new GMT 400 style until 1993. This 1-ton Extended Cab mounted on an extended wheelbase was rated for a maximum GVW of 10,000 pounds. The standard engine for this truck was the L19 7.4-liter V-8. It was rated for 230 horsepower at 3,600 rpm and 385 foot-pounds torque at 1,600 rpm. The LL4 6.2-liter V-8 diesel engine was also standard. With either engine, the standard transmission was a four-speed manual. Standard tire equipment was the LT245/75R-16E. *Elliott Kahn*

This truck is an excellent example of Chevrolet's former R-style Crew/Bonus Cab Big Dooley R3500 pickup with an 8-foot cargo box. When equipped with two bench seats, it was a Crew Cab. When equipped with only one bench seat and 55.8 cubic feet of lockable rear cargo space, it was called a Bonus Cab. The R3500 pickup was rated for a maximum GVW rating of 10,000 pounds. Chevrolet's 1989 pickups were available in three trim levels: Cheyenne, Scottsdale, and Silverado. The engine choices for this truck included the 7.4-liter gas V-8 and the 6.2-liter diesel V-8. A four-speed manual transmission was standard for either engine. *AAMA*

Chevrolet's Suburban continued to use the R/V series designations because Suburban, too, continued to be based on the 1987-type truck. The Suburban had a great sales year; its figures were second only to the new C/K pickups. The Suburban's grille was updated for 1989 with new headlamp bezels and body-side trim. Chevrolet engineers added more two-sided galvanized steel in the rear doors, rocker panels, end gate, body, and front-end sheet-metal components. The Suburban's ride comfort was improved through new rear springs and front and rear shock absorbers. The versatile Suburban's strong points included cargo carrying, trailering, and people moving. When properly equipped, the Suburban could move up to 16,000 pounds, including vehicle, trailer, people, cargo, and equipment. Buyers could choose between rear panel doors and optional wagon-type rear tailgate with available power window and between 2WD or 4WD capabilities in either 1/2- or 3/4-ton ratings. Engine options for 1500 models included the 5.7-liter gas V-8 and the 5.2-liter diesel. Engine options for 2500 models included the 5.7-liter and 7.4-liter gas V-8s and the 6.2-liter diesel V-8.

Chevrolet's full-size Blazer sport 4x4 celebrated its 20th anniversary in 1989. The Blazer, like the Suburban, continued to be built on the 1987-type truck. It did, however, have the same new grille, headlight bezels, and body-side molding as the Suburban. Chevrolet engineers designed the Blazer with a rugged 4WD system (a 2WD Blazer was not available), big engines, and high road clearance to be as at home on the highway as on the trail. The Blazer was rated for a maximum payload rating of 1,708 pounds, including passengers, equipment, and cargo. It featured two standard engines: the 5.7-liter EFI V-8 and the 6.2-liter diesel V-8. Both models had standard power brakes and power steering. Buyers could choose between two trim-packages—the standard Scottsdale and top-of-the-line Silverado. Full-sized, full power Suburban and Blazer models increased in popularity when the big front engine rear-wheel-drive autos disappeared. *AAMA*

Chevrolet's Suburban was the king of big, but the Sportvan was the passenger-carrying king. The largest Sportvan (a 125-inch wheelbase G30 Series) had optional seating for up to 12. Or, with the second and third seats removed, the Sportvan had 260 cubic feet of cargo capacity. The 230-horsepower 7.4-liter big block V-8 became an optional engine in midyear 1989 for heavy-duty G30 Sportvans. Buyers had a choice of a sliding side door or hinged doors for the same price. Chevrolet's Sportvan lineup consisted of three series: G10, G20, and G30 on two wheelbases—110 and 125 inches. The Sportvan's long list of appearance and convenience extra-cost options rivaled that of expensive automobiles. Chevrolet's mid-price-level Bonaventure series was dropped; only the entry-level and high-priced series continued. This is a 1989 Chevrolet top-of-the-line Beauville Sportvan. *AAMA*

Chevrolet's Hi-Cube Van and Cutaway Van chassis business was an important segment in 1989. These work or play vehicles provided significant sales units to Chevrolet's important specialty forward-control chassis and Step-Van models. Chevrolet supplied a Cutaway Van chassis that included the entire front section back to the B-pillar, and a flat galvanized steel floor panel extension that had been hot-dipped to prevent corrosion. The two wheelbase lengths provided were 125 and 146 inches long. Single or dual rear-wheel options, and gasoline or diesel V-8 power were other options. Maximum GVW ratings ranged from a low of 7,400 pounds all the way up to 10,000 pounds with duals. Chevrolet shipped these chassis units to various outside companies who mounted specialized cargo bodies or camper bodies. The standard engine was the 5.7-liter gas V-8. For diesel power and operating economy diesel, Hi-Cube Van models came with the "trucks only" 6.2-liter V-8 diesel. Transmissions included a four-speed manual and three-speed automatic. *AAMA*

Chevrolet was also a principal player in the large motor-home chassis business. For 1989, Chevrolet manufactured chassis ranging from 10,500 to the new 16,000-pound-GVW-rated unit pictured. The chassis featured a new reinforced shock bracket, a ring gear size to upgrade the load carrying capability of the rear axle, heavy-duty single-stage rear leaf springs and shock absorbers for better ride and handling, and a heavy-duty suspension. Chevrolet motor-home chassis were available in various wheelbase lengths: 137, 158.8, 178, and 208 inches and could accommodate bodies as much as 33 feet long. The 7.4-liter V-8 was the standard gasoline engine, and the 6.2-liter V-8 diesel engine was an option. *AAMA*

Chevrolet's Tiltmaster series trucks for 1989 included the little Class 4 W4 with a maximum GVW of 11,000 pounds diesel-powered chassis cab, and the W5 with a 16,000-pound GVW rating. There was also the W6 with a 22,000-pound rating; the Class 7, rated for maximum GVWs ranging from 27,500 pounds with a single-speed rear axle, to 29,700 pounds with a two-speed rear axle; and the W7HV for hauling large loads, which boasted a maximum GVW rating of 32,900 pounds. This is a 1989 Chevrolet W7 Tiltmaster chassis cab with platform body. The Tiltmaster's LCF design offered smaller turning diameters compared to a Conventional cab medium-duty—as much as 18 feet less. This was a big boost to handling ease in crowded urban areas. It was powered by a 353-ci direct injected, six-cylinder, turbocharged diesel engine producing 165 net horsepower at 3,000 rpm. It was standard with an exhaust brake, a large 14-inch diameter clutch, a five-speed manual transmission, high back reclining driver seat, and tilt/telescope steering wheel. It was imported from Isuzu. *AAMA*

In preparation for the introduction of the new medium-duty truck line in the fall of 1989, Chevrolet's marketing began a new dependability advertising campaign. A year's worth of research on the medium-duty truck market conducted by Chevrolet/GMC showed owners' number one concern was dependability. Downtime for repairs represented a loss of profits. Owners judged trucks by personal experience, advice from other truck owners, and specialized publications to find out which trucks were dependable. This research spurred Chevrolet to run ads touting its trucks' dependability. Chevrolet trucks had always been considered dependable by the nation's fire departments. The Riverside County, California, Fire Department owned this 1989 Chevrolet C70 conventional medium-duty chassis cab with a firefighting body. Engine No. 23 had a pumper body by KME that featured a 1,000-gallon water tank and a 500-gpm pump. The firm responsible for the 4WD conversion is not known. *Chuck Madderom*

Chevrolet's conventional cab 1989 medium-duty line consisted of Series C50-C60-C70. C70 Conventionals were available as single- or tandem-axle units. The Golden Valley, Arizona, Fire Department owned this 1989 Chevrolet C70 tandem-axle chassis cab with a tanker body. Its tanker body was by Demo and featured a 3,000-gallon water tank and a 500-gpm pump. This very handsome heavy-duty Chevrolet featured a white cab, stainless-steel body, chrome front bumper, and aluminum wheels. Firefighters insisted on buying the best-looking rigs. The Kodiak-type large hood shown was required when the Caterpillar 3208 diesel engine was specified. It was also optional with the 8.2-liter Detroit Diesel V-8. Many owners preferred the big, bold look of the Kodiak option to the standard hood and grille. The tandem featured a standard Eaton DS341 tandem axle rated at 34,000 pounds. Rockwell 34,000-pound SL 100 and Rockwell 40,000-pound SQ 100 tandems were also available. The tandem was rated for a maximum GVW of 50,000 pounds and a maximum GCW rating of 60,000 pounds. *Chuck Madderom*

Chevrolet introduced a LoPro conventional cab medium-duty in 1989. It was available in GVWs of 14,840 and 16,000 pounds. LoPro provided excellent maneuverability for congested city driving and a low frame height for ease of loading—as low as 27.8 inches. It offered a two-step entry configuration to lower driver fatigue after a long day's work. LoPro was powered by the 6.0-liter V-8 gas engine and featured an Eaton 15,000-pound capacity single- or optional two-speed rear axle and GM's four-speed or Eaton five-speed manual or Allison four-speed automatic transmission. The LoPro was available in nine wheelbases, from 125 to 218 inches. This is a 1989 Chevrolet C60 LoPro chassis cab. *AAMA*

Fire Chiefs liked their trucks "all dressed up" like this well-dressed 1989 Chevrolet C70 chassis cab with firefighting body. Note its flashy chrome grille, front bumper, windshield moldings, rearview mirror brackets, and the bright aluminum trim on the body, below the cab door and behind the front bumper. The Mid County (Maryland) Fire Protection District owned this truck. Its pumper body had a 1,000-gallon water tank and a 500-gpm pump. The 240-horsepower 427-ci V-8 engine powered it. *Dennis J. Maag*

Commercial light-duty trucks were an important segment of Chevrolet's business in 1989 as they had been for years. The most often-selected model for any number of specialized applications was the C/K3500 Series. This is a 1989 Chevrolet C3500 chassis cab with body by an independent manufacturer. Most often commercial trucks were pretty basic models, usually specified with big engines, manual transmissions, and vinyl interiors. For example, the engines available for C/K3500 trucks included the 190-horsepower 5.7-liter V-8, the 230-horsepower 7.4-liter V-8, and the 143-horsepower 6.2-liter diesel V-8. Power steering was standard, standard brakes were Chevrolet's Dual/Hy-Power hydraulics. Standard transmission was a four-speed. *Iten Chevrolet*

This was the last year for the school bus series. Chevrolet's two school bus series were short and simple. The B-Series was the conventional type with chassis and cowl. They were offered with either hydraulic brakes or air brakes, and with either gas or diesel power. GVW ratings were 21,000 pounds when fitted with hydraulic brakes, and 24,000 pounds with air brakes. The only wheelbase length offered was 189 inches. Gas power was from the 350 V-8 and diesel from the Detroit Diesel 8.2-liter. The S-Series school bus chassis was a forward control. It was only available in a 170-inch wheelbase and a maximum GVW rating of 30,000 pound for all models. Chevrolet offered hydraulic or air brake models and gas or diesel power. The gas engine was the 366-ci V-8, and the diesel was the Detroit 8.2-liter. This is a 1989 Chevrolet B-Series school bus chassis cowl with bus body and diesel power. *Iten Chevrolet*

S-10's 4x4 Baja model was new for 1989. Baja was a rugged off-road appearance package, which was available for any 4WD S-10 pickup. The Baja package was all appearance; there were no performance upgrades in drivetrain or chassis. It included special paint (red with black) and graphics, front grille guard with driving lamps, black tubular rear bumper, cargo net in place of tailgate, switches in instrument panel for driving lamps, and black chrome accent on headlight and taillight bezels and grille. At the same time, a new special package for 2WD S-10s called the Cameo appearance package was offered. It was only for appearance, inside the cab and out, and was offered in three color options—red, white, or black paint.

Pictured here is a popular, basic, no-frills Conventional cab Chevrolet C20 3/4-ton pickup for general hauling and transportation. This pickup was much favored by commercial customers and governmental bodies as well. The Water Department of the City of Bloomington, Minnesota, used this truck. The standard engine for 3/4-ton trucks was the economical 4.3-liter V-6; this engine was standard also in the C6P 3/4-ton pickup, a heavy-duty 3/4-ton model. The C6P was rated for a maximum GVW of 8,900 pounds versus the 8,600-pound GVW of the standard 3/4-ton pickup. The city specified the manual five-speed overdrive transmission for its trucks. When equipped with either the 4.10 or 4.11 rear axle ratio, the 4.3-liter V-6 powered truck's maximum GCW rating was a big 10,500 pounds. *City of Bloomington*

The 1989 Chevrolet R3500 cab and chassis with a Royal-covered service body belonged to the Southern California Gas Company. It was equipped with a LO5 5.7-liter V-8 engine, Turbo 400 three-speed automatic transmission, and Cheyenne level trim. This truck carried the equipment to service and calibrate large industrial gas meters and regulators. It is also equipped with the heavy-duty 11,000-pound GVW package and air-assisted front springs. *Bob Bray*

Chapter 8

1990 TO 1999

1990

Chevrolet introduced a whole bundle of interesting new light-truck models for 1990. Beginning in October the Lumina APV front-wheel-drive composite body minivans went on sale in both passenger and cargo versions. Passenger minivans are counted as trucks, by the way. The passenger version would seat up to seven people and the commercial version only two.

In order to breathe new life into the Astro vans, the company released an extended body length and an all-wheel-drive version. It featured 10 cubic feet more cargo capacity due to the 10-inch extension behind the rear wheels.

The new for 1990 high-output version of the 4.3-liter V-6 was a midyear introduction. Its extra power came from a low-restriction intake and exhaust system and a high-lift camshaft.

Chevrolet also unveiled a new extended-length Sportvan model seating up to 15 persons. It was available only on the G30 1-ton series and featured the 5.7-liter V-8 with a heavy-duty-rated three-speed automatic transmission.

S-10 compact pickups received a five-speed manual transmission for use with the Vortec 4.3L V-6, engine improvements, fixed GVW ratings and more standard equipment. The 1989 models with the 4.3-liter were limited to the four-speed automatic.

The first new full-size pickup model was the 454-SS high-performance, limited edition (10,000 in 1990) C1500 2WD regular cab with a short box. Standard were the 7.4-liter V-8 and the Turbo 400 three-speed automatic transmission, performance handling package, and 3.73 rear-axle ratio.

The second new pickup was the C/K Work Truck "WT." Chevrolet's first full-size price leader pickup line, it was a low-option regular cab model. As its name implies, it was intended for commercial/fleet work. It was available only in standard Cheyenne trim, but featured a new grille, filler panel, and charcoal-painted bumper.

Early in 1990 Chevrolet began building the new four-door Blazer in 2WD or 4WD as a 1991 model, in anticipation of Ford's 1991 four-door Explorer SUV. The Oldsmobile Bravada was a variant of the four-door Blazer. All new Blazers featured the 4.3L Vortec V-6 engine improved with the 220-Series TBI (throttle body fuel injection). The Hydra-Matic 5LM60 four-speed manual transmission and ABS were standard equipment. The four-door Blazer's base price was $14,300.

Other than these new models, no major changes took place. Chevrolet's goal remained the same: build quality, great performing trucks.

Production of Chevrolet's new conventional cab medium-duty GMT530 Kodiak trucks got off to a slow start in August 1989 at GM's Janesville, Wisconsin, assembly plant. These were Chevrolet's first all-new medium-duty trucks in 25 years. Kodiaks came in 50, 60, and 70 series and were available as trucks or tractors, in single- and tandem-axle models. GVWs ranged from 16,850 to 53,220 pounds and they featured GCW ratings up to 74,000 pounds.

Engines included 6.0L and 7.0L gas engines and the Cat 3116 diesel, a 6.6L turbocharged, intercooled in-line six. After 1990, neither the Cat 3208 nor the Detroit Diesel 8.2L would meet new

In a move to maintain its minivan market share, Chevrolet engineers added all-wheel-drive and an extended-length model, adding 10 inches of length behind the rear wheels and 19 cubic feet of space. All-wheel-drive was available on regular-length Astros in October 1989 when the new models were introduced and on the extended-length models in January. This is a 1990 Astro RS with a sport-handling package. The Astro continued to be available in three trim levels for 1990, but standard equipment was increased significantly. The Astro CS trim included a restyled instrument panel with a larger glovebox, tinted glass on all windows, carpeting on wheelhouse and floor, intermittent wipers, halogen headlamps, and other miscellaneous items. The Astro CL package was upgraded with a custom steering wheel, air dam, and fog lights, swing-out rear- and side-door glass, color-keyed floor mats, auxiliary lighting package, wide body-side moldings, deluxe grille, painted bumpers with end caps, rally wheels, and visor vanity mirror. The top-of-the-line Astro LT touring models added deep tinted glass to all windows and velour fabric trim. *AAMA*

diesel-emission standards. The 350 V-8 and 292 six were no longer offered in medium-duty trucks. The 292 was replaced by a new heavy-duty 4.3L V-6. It had lower compression pistons, valve rotators, a roller timing chain, and a high flow exhaust. It was offered in the P-20 chassis and 3/4-ton pickups with the 8,600 pound GVW package (RPO C6P).

Chevrolet increased its market share of medium-duty trucks by 4 percent over 1989 with the new models (Kodiaks), despite a lower sales total of 16,572. Due to the slowdown in the nation's economy and political problems in the Persian Gulf, the medium-duty truck business dropped off with the rest of the car and truck industry.

Industry medium-duty sales dropped by 6.5 percent, to 156,032. Nevertheless, Chevrolet's medium-duty market share rose to 10.6 percent from 9.6 percent in 1989.

In 1990 U. S. truck production fell by less than 6 percent to 4,805,084, down from 5,100,195 in 1989. The continuing growth in demand for minivans and SUVs as passenger vehicles allowed truck production to hold up better than that of passenger cars.

Chevrolet's total sales fell to 1,240,062 in 1990 from 1,340,666 in 1989, an 8 percent dip in sales that was right on with the industry's overall sales decline.

Chevrolet's 1990 Lumina APV (All-Purpose Vehicle) was introduced early in 1989 as a 1990 model. The Lumina is interesting because it was constructed using the largest exterior body panels ever made of plastic. In the assembly plant, robots were used to apply adhesives to the Lumina's cagelike steel space frame rather than the traditional mechanical fasteners attaching the plastic components. All exterior panels were made of sheet-molding compound except for its front fender and fascias, which were polyurea; there was a total of 270 pounds of plastics per van. Chevrolet marketed the Lumina in both passenger and cargo versions. The cargo version was geared to light- delivery service. The FWD (front-wheel-drive) van could seat up to seven persons in the passenger version and two in the cargo version. A 3.1-liter V-6 and three-speed automatic transmission was the only powertrain offered. The Lumina provided 54.8 cubic feet of cargo space with the front and center seats and 104.6 cubic feet without the center seat. It had a fully independent MacPherson front suspension, trailing twist-axle rear suspension, power front disc/rear drum brakes, power steering, and a long list of other standard items such as flush mounted, wraparound tinted glass; halogen headlamps; and a 20-gallon fuel tank. Pictured are the 1990 Lumina APV passenger van and cargo van. *AAMA*

Chevrolet's S-10 pickup received a new Getrag-designed, Hydra-Matic-built five-speed manual transmission, the "Hydra-Matic 290." It was available with the 4.3-liter V-6 for the first time. The 1989 models with the 4.3-liter were limited to the four-speed automatic. The 2.5-liter four-cylinder engine in the S-10 pickups was improved with such changes as new oil system plugs, plastic crankcase ventilation hoses, plastic evaporation emission pipes, closed-bottom charcoal canister, and one-piece welded crankshaft pulley and hub. The optional 2.8-liter V-6 and five-speed manual transmissions were only available on 2WD models. New payload ratings for S-10 pickups ranged from 1,375 to 1,973 pounds. Again, there were four trim levels. The S-10 EL/S-15 Special price leader models included tinted glass on all windows, front stabilizer bar, halogen headlamps, and cigarette lighter. This is a 1990 Chevrolet S-10 Special price leader pickup. *AAMA*

Chevrolet's popular S-10 Blazers were available in either 2WD or 4WD configurations and in three trim levels: Standard and two luxury-levels—Tahoe and Sport. The Tahoe trim included black body-side moldings with bright trim, plus bright wheel trim rings (4WD only). Inside Tahoe features included reclining front bucket seats with buyer's choice of vinyl or fabric, plus color-coordinated carpeting. The Sport trim for the 4WD Blazer included cast-aluminum wheels, color-keyed front and rear bumpers with black rub strips, black chrome grille, headlamp bezels, and black wheel-opening and body-side moldings. On the inside the Sport featured reclining bucket seats with lockable center console. Other features were fabric upholstery, or optional leather, chrome "Sport" nameplate on stowage box door, and Sport steering wheel with a leather look. S-10 Blazer's standard transmission with the 4.3-liter Vortec V-6 was the new-for-1990 Getrag-licensed five-speed manual, which offered easy shifting and quiet operation. Pictured is a 1990 S-10 Blazer 4WD Sport. *AAMA*

Why did it take so long to build what the people wanted? Twenty-one years after the first Chevy Blazer was sold, the four-door S-10 Blazer was launched. The Blazer was a midyear introduction, but regarded as a 1991 model year vehicle. The rumor is that Chevrolet's management heard that Ford was about to introduce its four-door Explorer as a 1991 model year vehicle, so it quickly rushed the four-door Blazer along. The fact is that Jeep had already been building a four-door SUV for 18 years and doing quite well with it. Chevrolet's four-door Suburban had been around for some time, too. The four-door S-10 Blazer was offered in either 2WD or 4WD. It rode on a 107-inch-wheelbase chassis, 6.5-inches longer than two-door models, and provided 74 cubic feet of cargo space. Its full-size rear seat had 15 inches of additional hip room. A four-wheel anti-lock brake system was standard. *AAMA*

The hot new model for 1990 was Chevrolet's 7.5-liter–powered 454 SS 2WD pickup. The 7.4-liter engine was General Motors' most powerful. This short wheelbase 1/2-ton hauler was a midyear model. The high-performance, 2WD Silverado pickup was equipped with a three-speed automatic and a 3.73 rear axle. This hot handler was a fantastic trailer puller for a race car or off-road vehicle, which made it a sensation among sport truck buyers. This black and beautiful Chevrolet was a head-turning rig. Chevrolet limited production by only building 10,000 454 SS pickups in 1990. The sport truck-minded buyer couldn't find a sharper model or beat the performance of the 454 SS pickup. Standard features included air conditioning, tilt steering wheel, sport appearance package, power door locks, power windows, high-back bucket seats with console, AM/FM stereo radio with equalizer, sliding rear window, electronic speed control, and auxiliary lighting. *AAMA*

The C/K 1500 WT (Work Truck) was the first price leader in Chevrolet's full-sized pickup line. It was a low-option regular cab model. The W/T1500 was offered only in standard Cheyenne trim, but it featured a new grille, filler panel, and charcoal-painted bumper. It was offered in either 2WD or 4WD versions and had a maximum 5,600 pound GVW rating, with a payload rating at 1,870 pounds. This was a no-frills, no-nonsense, hard-working truck. It was created specifically for the economy-minded full-size pickup buyer. W/T1500 had fewer amenities than standard C/Ks, plus limited options. It was only available in Quicksilver Metallic, Smoke Blue, Flame Red, and Summit White, and only with an 8-foot box. The standard 1/2-ton model had a 4.3-liter Vortec V-6 with EFI and Getrag-licensed five-speed manual transmission with overdrive. *AAMA*

The Extended Cab pickup was a new model in Chevrolet's full-size pickup line as of 1988. Two Extended-Cab models made up Chevrolet's offering. The 8-foot cargo box version was the original offering and the short-bed was new the previous year. These two trucks quickly became the mainstays in terms of sales and profit they returned to the company. Many owners preferred the short-bed model because it was the best of both worlds. First, it offered seating for up to six and or inside storage protected from the weather; and secondly, its wheelbase length was not so long as to present a problem with parking and maneuverability. The cab extension only added 24 inches to the length of a regular cab pickup and added 40.5 cubic feet of storage or seating for three facing forward. The Extended-Cab short-bed pickup was offered in both 1/2- and 3/4-ton versions. This is a 1990 Chevrolet Extended-Cab 2500 3/4-ton short-bed pickup. *AAMA*

To simplify dealer ordering and plant production loading schedules, Chevrolet forced dealers to order all extra accessories through equipment packages. As an incentive, it gave special package pricing for each vehicle and greatly increased the number of packages. Prior to 1990 there were about three equipment packages per line. For 1990 the number of packages increased to eight per vehicle. Under the new program, no option could be ordered without using some kind of factory ordering package. The program was well accepted by dealers because of the discounts. GM made many items that had been options standard equipment, dropped other low-volume options, and combined the rest into the special packages. This 1990 Chevrolet full-size Sportside pickup replaced the previous Stepside model. The sporty Sportside was well accepted. Its appearance was a big improvement over the old-fashioned Stepside while it still retained much of the Stepside's classic flair. Sportside pickups were always short-box 1/2-ton models, but could have either 2WD or 4WD. Sportside models lent themselves to any number of interesting appearance packages and Sport Handling Packages, either 2WD or 4WDs. *AAMA*

The 1990 Suburbans with Scottsdale trim added heavy-duty shock absorbers in the 2WD and 4WD 1500 series, a pulse windshield-wiper system, a heavy-duty battery, front tow hooks on 4WD models, electronically tuned AM radio, a 37-gallon fuel tank, and a headlamp warning buzzer. The Silverado Suburbans added a deluxe front appearance package, deluxe moldings, auxiliary lighting package, and color-keyed front and rear floor mats. The Suburban's wheelbase was 129.5 inches. Maximum seating was nine adults, maximum payload was 3,788 pounds (2WD) and 3,520 pounds (4WD), and maximum GCW rating for towing was 16,000 pounds. Standard engines for Suburbans were the 5.7-liter V-8 and the 6.2-liter diesel V-8. The 7.4-liter V-8 was optional only for the R2500 Series. Standard transmissions were rather confusing. For diesel models, no manual was offered. Standard transmission for 1/2-ton diesel models was the four-speed automatic with overdrive; for 3/4-ton models it was the three-speed automatic. For gas-powered Suburbans, the four-speed automatic overdrive was standard for the half-ton 2WD. The four-speed manual was standard for the 3/4-ton 2WD, 1/2-ton 4WD, and 3/4-ton 4WD. *AAMA*

The full-size 1990 Blazer received rear-wheel anti-lock brakes, an electronic speedometer, more two-sided galvanized steel, and more standard equipment. A floor-mounted four-speed manual transmission was standard on the Blazer with the 5.7-liter V-8 engine, and a four-speed automatic was optional. More buyers purchased the optional automatic than opted for the manual. Diesel models were limited to the automatic. The Scottsdale trim package added a pulse windshield-wiper system, heavy-duty battery, front tow hooks, power-operated tailgate window, and headlamp warning buzzer. The Silverado added a deluxe front appearance package, deluxe moldings, and auxiliary lighting equipment. The Blazer's wheelbase was 106.5 inches; maximum cargo space was 106.5 cubic feet; payload was 1,570 pounds; and maximum GCW rating for towing was 12,000 pounds. The Blazer was only offered as a 4WD. *AAMA*

The new all-wheel-drive Astro differed from the 2WD Astro in that it had a stub frame, single-speed transfer case, front stabilizer bar, front propshaft with constant velocity joints, and specific exhaust manifolds for frame clearance. The new high-output (H.O.) version of the 4.3-liter V-6 was unavailable in the all-wheel-drive Astro. The new-for-1990 H.O. version of the 4.3-liter got its extra power from a low-restriction intake and exhaust system and a high-lift camshaft. The engine featured a high-stall torque converter, performance shift calibrations for the automatic transmission, and dual sport exhausts. The H.O. 4.3 was rated for 175 horsepower versus 150 for the standard 4.3-liter. Torque at 230 foot-pounds was unchanged. This is a 1990 2WD regular-body Astro commercial van. The standard engine for this little hauler was the 2.5-liter L4 engine with EFI; the 4.3-liter V-6 was optional, as was the H.O. 4.3-liter. Only the four-speed automatic transmission with overdrive was offered.

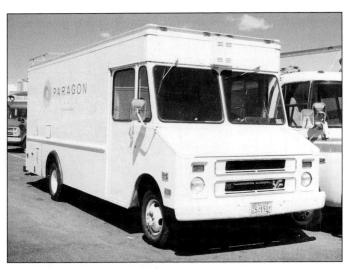

Chevrolet's 1990 P30 Step-Van series was offered in both steel and aluminum bodies. Due to their lower weight, the aluminum-bodied Step-Vans were offered in lengths up to 18 feet versus a maximum 14-foot, 6-inch body for the steel vans. This P30 14-foot, 6-inch aluminum-bodied model P31442 had a cubic capacity of 781 cubic feet. The Step-Van's maximum GVW ratings ranged all the way up to 14,100 pounds. A heavy-duty I-beam front axle with leaf springs was offered with 10,000 through 14,100 pound GVWs. Standard front suspension was independent with coil springs. Engine options began with the standard 4.3-liter V-6 and continued with the 5.7-liter and 7.4-liter gas V-8s and the 6.2-liter V-8 diesel. A four-speed manual transmission was standard, and the three-speed automatic was the only option. *Iten Chevrolet*

Chevrolet offered its popular Hi-Cube Van with steel and aluminum van bodies. This 1990 Chevrolet G30 10-foot steel bodied Hi-Cube Van had the standard 125-inch wheelbase with single rears; duals were an option. With the correct springs, rear-axle capacity and tires, the maximum GVW rating of the single-rear-wheel model ranged from 7,400 to 8,600 pounds. Its high-cube body could carry up to 564 cubic feet of cargo. The cargo area's height from floor to roof was 76 inches. The load space was accessible from the driver seat. The 190-horsepower 5.7-liter V-8 was standard equipment, as was the 155-horsepower 6.2-liter diesel V-8 also. The 230-horsepower 7.4-liter V-8 was an option. Other standard equipment included power steering and brakes, an easy-riding independent front suspension with coil springs, and a three-speed automatic transmission. *Iten Chevrolet*

Chevrolet's new Kodiak medium-duty trucks were the first new Chevrolet medium trucks in 25 years. The Kodiak was offered in series 50, 60, and 70. All series were Conventional models in single- or tandem-axle (70 series only) models. Maximum GVW ratings ranged from 16,850 to 53,220 pounds, and GCW ratings up to 74,000 pounds. The line had nine wheelbase lengths available, ranging from 132 to 261 inches. The BBC dimension was 104 inches. The new cab featured streamlined aerodynamics with a tilting fiberglass hood and front fender assembly with rounded corners, angled windshield, and flush-mounted windows. The entire cab except the roof was made of two-side zinc-coated, galvanized steel for improved corrosion protection. This cab had more interior space than the cab it replaced. Kodiak offered standard SL and optional SLE trim levels. Power included gasoline and diesel engines. The gas engine line from 1989—350, 366, and 427 V-8s—continued. A new Caterpillar 3116 diesel, a 6.6-liter turbocharged, intercooled, inline six was offered for 60 and 70 models. All models carried only a Kodiak nameplate, no series number plate. This chassis cab, with the standard 366-ci gas engine, and without taxes had a retail price of about $23,000. *Elliott Kahn*

The Caterpillar 3116 diesel engine featured horsepower ratings of 165, 185, 215, and 250 and maximum torque up to 650 foot-pounds. This engine was exclusive to GM for the medium-duty highway-truck market segment. A five-speed manual Fuller transmission was standard on all models. Other five- and six-speeds as well as 10-speed and three-speed manual transmissions and four- and five-speed Allison automatic transmissions were offered. A power takeoff provision was available for powering specialized equipment. All 2WD models had a tapered-leaf front suspension as standard equipment. An optional 14,000-pound front axle used a multi-leaf suspension. Power steering was standard on all models. Notice this truck has the steel cast spoke wheels and the optional hood access panels. Evidently this truck was to be equipped with some piece of equipment that would be positioned in front of the hood to prevent it from tilting open. *Elliott Kahn*

Chevrolet offered five types of bumpers, including rugged channel bumpers, shown in front of this truck's front-mounted power winch, and bumpers with solid or flexible end caps. GM formed a special truck unit within its parts organization to ensure complete and immediate availability of replacement parts for these new trucks and to take care of special vehicle orders by vocational users. This is a 1990 Chevrolet Kodiak series 70 tandem chassis cab with dump body Cat diesel power. A 34,000-pound rear suspension was standard on 70 series tandem models. Other suspensions could carry up to 44,000 pounds. The Kodiak's new frame design featured straight, flat, full-depth side rails, an integral front frame extension options and increased GVW ratings. It was designed for easy body and equipment mountings. Batteries were boxed and frame-mounted under the side cab steps, close to the engine starter for improved cranking. This 1990 C70 tandem 6x4 chassis cab was standard with air brakes and power steering and retailed for about $41,500 (without taxes) with a diesel. *AAMA*

Two school bus series were included in the 1990 medium-duty line. The B-Series school bus chassis with cowl was available in two models. The first model had hydraulic brakes, power steering, and either a gas or diesel engine. It was built on a 189-inch-wheelbase chassis and was rated for a maximum 21,000 pounds GVW. The second model had air brakes, power steering, and a diesel engine only. It was rated for a maximum GVW of 24,000 pounds. The S-Series was a forward-control chassis only. It, too, was offered with gas or diesel power and with hydraulic brakes and power steering. Its wheelbase was 170 inches, and it was rated for a maximum GVW of 30,000 pounds. A second model was equipped with air brakes, power steering, and diesel power. This is a 1990 Chevrolet B-Series school bus chassis cowl with school bus body by Blue Bird. *Iten Chevrolet*

A Chevrolet Extended-Cab chassis cab was not often seen employed in commercial use. This truck is a 1990 C2500 Extended-Cab chassis cab with the short 141.5-inch wheelbase (standard for the Extended-Cab short-box pickup) with a short Animal Control body. A quick peek into the cab's extension shows it was used for storing supplies and equipment, not passengers. Because this is a government truck, it is a basic, no-frills Cheyenne model. The 3/4-ton Commercial Series carried a maximum GVW rating of 8,600 pounds. The city specified the 150-horsepower 4.3-liter V-6 engine and the five-speed overdrive manual transmission. *City of Bloomington*

Chevrolet built basic, hard-working commercial pickups as well as classy, high style pickups purchased for personal transportation. The City of Bloomington, Minnesota, purchased a small fleet of basic Chevrolet C2500 trucks and was well satisfied with their performance. The city purchased trucks with standard paint colors and identified them through the use of easily applied decals. This pickup carried a maximum GVW rating of 7,200 pounds. The city specified pickups with a drivetrain consisting of the 160-horsepower 4.3-liter V-6 engine and the five-speed overdrive manual transmission. Other standard features included independent front suspension with coil springs, rear-wheel ABS, power steering, and power front disc/rear drum brakes. *City of Bloomington*

Chevrolet's R/V (R, 2WD and V, 4WD) commercial chassis models for 1990 consisted of Crew/Bonus Cab pickups and chassis cabs. R/V designations replaced the former C/K in that interim period between when the new pickup model was launched in 1988 and when the Suburban/Blazer and Crew Cabs were upgraded with the new body. This is a 1990 Chevrolet V3500 Crew Cab chassis cab with dump body. Its extra-long 164.5-inch wheelbase chassis accepted bodies up to 8 feet. Maximum payload capacity was 10,000 pounds and maximum payload was 5,760 pounds. Engine options included the 5.7-liter and 7.4-liter gas engines and 6.2-liter diesel V-8. *Harold Chevrolet*

The new-for-1990 C1500 454 SS model in Onyx Black with luxury-level Silverado trim was available in November 1989. This truck is a 1990 C1500 454 SS. It has the Turbo 400 three-speed automatic transmission, which was available only in the 1990 454 SS. It also has the standard Silverado red velour bucket seats, console, and air conditioning. *Bob Bray*

1991

Production of Chevrolet's HD3500 began in October 1990. This truck was targeted as a direct competitor of the Ford F-Super-Duty, which had been the only player in the Class 4 market since late 1987. The Chevrolet C3500 HD had a 15,000-pound GVW rating. The 3500 HD provided a higher GVW, a lower frame height, bigger brakes, a huskier frame, larger tires and wheels, and a larger radiator than the regular C/K series trucks. GM projected sales of 10,000 to 11,000 units during the first year of sales. Initial sales of the HD3500 models featured an automatic transmission and gas engine only. A manual transmission was scheduled for availability beginning in April 1991, and a turbodiesel was expected the following October.

The Kodiak's gas engines, the new Mark V 366, 427, and 454, came in for engineering refinements, including better oil sealing and new valve covers. The horsepower of the Cat 3116 diesel engine was boosted to 170 horsepower from 165 horsepower.

Also new this year was the Hydra-Matic 4L80E transmission. This was a four-speed overdrive automatic, which replaced the venerable Turbo 400. It was used in all light-duty trucks heavier than 8,600 pounds GVW, including the 3500 HD.

A new raised-roof option for the construction and utility industries was also new.

GM recorded the biggest loss in its entire history in 1991. The loss was $4.5 billion on $123.1 billion versus $124.7 billion in 1990. Chevrolet sold 1,077,115 trucks in 1991, down from 1,259,474 in 1990. Medium-duty trucks took a heavy hit, dropping by 35 percent to only 10,574 from 16,572 in 1990. Medium- and heavy-duty trucks fared poorly industrywide in 1991, due to a very weak economy. Neither Chevrolet nor GMC recorded a heavy-duty (Class 8) truck sale this year.

Chevrolet and Ford dueled hot and heavy during the year for the honor of having the "best selling truck in America." Chevrolet had not had that honor since 1977. At the end of April, Chevrolet had a slim 3,725-unit sales lead over Ford's F series for the model year. Chevrolet's advantages over Ford included better availability of manual transmissions and more short-box extended-cab pickups. In this category alone, Chevrolet had sold 6,313 more through April 30 than it had for the same period in 1990. Chevrolet expected another advantage from a new extended-cab Sportside C/K model that was just beginning to arrive at dealerships.

Full-size pickup sales have always been critical to the Big Three. They have been responsible for huge profit dollars, about $4,000 per unit. Ford's pickup dated back to 1980, and it was restyled in 1987. Chevrolet's pickup dated back only to 1988, its first in 17 years. Since then, Chevrolet had narrowed the gap with Ford, but couldn't make it to the winner's circle.

The NHTSA ruled that light-duty trucks, SUVs, and vans sold after September 1, 1993, would be required to meet roof-crush standard in order to protect passengers in rollover accidents. The new regulation came about due to the large number of buyers that were switching from cars to trucks.

Chevrolet's extended-body Astro cargo was new in 1990. It had 19 cubic feet more cargo capacity with the 10-inch extension added behind the rear wheels. All the additional space was strictly for cargo. The extended-body Astro's cargo space totaled 200.1 cubic feet (these figures are with the passenger seat removed). The new H.O. 4.3-liter V-6 engine, which was introduced midway through the 1990 model year, was the most powerful engine in any 1991 minivan. The extended-body Astro was available in both 2WD and AWD configurations. The AWD had a full-time split-torque system for better traction on slick or icy roads. Astro's AWD system directed the most power to the wheels with the best traction. The maximum GVW rating for 2WD models was 5,400 pounds; for AWD models it was 5,850 pounds. The only transmission was the four-speed automatic with overdrive and the only engine was the 4.3-liter. *Harold Chevrolet*

The 1991 AWD extended-body Astro Van's nameplate, located on the driver and passenger doors, has the suffix "Ext" behind the word Astro and the words "All-Wheel-Drive" written in smaller letters above Astro-Ext. The word Astro was in white, while the other words were in red. The additional length of the extended-body models was added immediately behind the rear wheels. The extra length was used exclusively for additional cargo space. The only engine offered for the Astro passenger models was the 150-horsepower 4.3-liter V-6. The H.O. 170-horsepower 4.3-liter V-6 was limited to the AWD models. The maximum GVW rating of the passenger Astro was 6,100 pounds. Its maximum GCW rating was 6,000 pounds. Its transmission was the four-speed automatic with overdrive. Maximum seating with optional third seat was eight. *Harold Chevrolet*

Chevrolet's Lumina APV was a vehicle for sporty family transportation and a genuine cargo-hauler when in its commercial trim. With the maximum optional seats installed, the Lumina comfortably seated seven adults. The Lumina's lightweight modular seats featured quick releases to allow two-, five-, or seven-place seating. Chevrolet plowed new ground with Lumina's rustproof, lightweight plastic body skins. Chevrolet engineers took the work out of driving the Lumina with a 3.1-liter V-6 engine with EFI mated to a three-speed automatic transmission, a fun-to-drive Sport suspension, and power steering and brakes. The Lumina was offered in two trim levels: Standard and up level CL (Custom Luxury). CL's interior included fabric seats and door panel trim, air conditioning, an auxiliary lighting group, and a Comfortilt steering wheel. *AAMA*

Certainly this 1991 Chevrolet Lumina APV Cargo Van was the most dramatic-looking delivery/commercial vehicle in America. It displayed an "APV" nameplate forward on the hinged doors. The Lumina APV Cargo was more than a pretty face; it was rated for a respectable 1,357 pounds maximum payload and a maximum GVW rating of 4,886 pounds. Business owners were attracted to the APV's rust-free fiberglass-reinforced composite body panels, something no other van could match. The Cargo Van version of the APV used the same 120-horsepower 3.1-liter V-6 engine with EFI and a three-speed automatic transmission that the passenger van did. The sum total of these features made it easy for owners to hire drivers. Lumina APV rode on a 109.8-inch wheelbase. Its cargo capacity was 115.4 cubic feet with the front seats installed. APV's standard interior included two bucket seats; interior trim color was gray. *AAMA*

Chevrolet's full-size passenger vans were the Sportvans; the cargo versions of the same vehicle were called Chevy Vans. This is a 1991 Chevrolet G20 Sportvan with the optional Beauville trim. The Sportvan line consisted of G10, G20, and G30 gas, and G20 and G30 diesel models. Sportvans could be equipped to carry 5, 8, 12, or 15 (G30 Extended-Body only) passengers. Chevrolet built its Extended-Body model in its own unique way. The others simply tacked an extension onto their longest regular body. Chevrolet, on the other hand, did it right. Chevrolet engineers called for single-stampings for their Extended-Body model, plus an extended wheelbase for a better ride and load distribution characteristics. This Sportvan is not an Extended-Body model. The only engine provided for the G30 was the 195-horsepower 5.7-liter V-8. There was also a G30 diesel model. The heavy-duty G30 model offered the 230-horsepower 7.4-liter as an option. The only transmission available for any Sportvan was the four-speed automatic with overdrive. Power brakes and steering were standard. *AAMA*

This was the second model year for Chevrolet's Geo Tracker. One may wonder whether this is a truck. That is questionable, but the fact that it is a 4WD vehicle is clear. Technically, it is an SUV. The Tracker and its Suzuki twin were built at CAMI Automotive, Inc. in Canada. For 1991, the Geo Tracker added a new entry-level 2WD convertible to the line. The Geo Tracker LSi was the same vehicle, but with 4WD. It sold for about $13,600. It rode on an 86.6-inch wheelbase and featured an L4 80-horsepower engine and five-speed manual transmission. It weighed 2,238 pounds. The Tracker delivered good mileage of up to 27 miles per gallon. *Harold Chevrolet*

Chevrolet's S-10 compact Baja model for 1991. Technically, the Baja was an extra-cost off-road appearance package. Chevrolet offered it in three color choices—Midnight Black, Apple Red, and Frost White. The Baja's interior sported high-back bucket seats upholstered in fabric, with reclining seatbacks in Maxi-Cab 4WD models. The Baja package included a light bar with off-road lamps (it was not a true roll bar); front grille guard with driving lamps; a tubular rear bumper; LT235/75R-15 all-terrain T/A white-lettered tires; brushed aluminum wheels; black grille with black headlight and taillight bezels and special "Baja" graphics. Optional equipment included a cargo-net endgate and a special pickup-box–mounted spare-tire carrier. Required options for the Baja package included the luxury-level Tahoe interior trim, an under-body shield package, and a suspension package. A Maxi-Cab S-10 short-box model Baja was also offered. *AAMA*

Chevrolet's ever popular two-door S-10 Blazer found itself sharing center stage with the new four-door S-10 Blazer. The public said yes to both vehicles. Two-door models continued to do very well in spite of the good start four-door Blazers got off to. It didn't take long for both vehicles to find their particular market niches. The two-door S-10 Blazer's wheelbase length was a compact 100.5 inches. A short wheelbase doesn't lend itself to the most comfortable highway ride. Short is more in off-roading, which wasn't what these trucks were purchased for. Chevrolet offered three trim levels for both vehicles: Standard, Tahoe, and Sport. The two-door Blazer seated four in front buckets and a rear folding bench. A 2WD model was a regular production option. The powerful 160-horsepower 4.3-liter V-6 was the only engine option. Buyers could choose from either a five-speed manual transmission with overdrive or a four-speed automatic with overdrive. *AAMA*

The rise in popularity of four-door SUVs was a "good news, bad news" story. The good news was that the government had placed a 25 percent import duty on foreign pickups and two-door sport utilities, the big sellers. Four-door SUVs were defined as passenger cars instead of trucks, and therefore were exempt from the 25 percent duty. The Japanese soon after started to export four-door SUVs, principally the Mitsubishi Montero and Isuzu Trooper II (Jeep also had a four-door Cherokee). It was good news for the importers that these vehicles sold well, but bad for domestic manufacturers who didn't have a four-door SUV. It didn't take long to react, which resulted in the four-door S-10 Blazer and Ford's Explorer. The four-door S-10 Blazer was built on a 107-inch wheelbase and offered 25 percent more cargo space (74 cubic feet) than the two-door model. The four-door added 15 inches of rear hip room and eliminated wheelhouse intrusion. It had two bucket seats in front and a folding rear bench for a total seating capacity of five. A front bench was an option. The four-door's drivetrain options were the same as the two-door. Three available trim levels included the Standard, Tahoe, and Sport. This is the 1991 S-10 four-door 4WD Blazer Tahoe. *AAMA*

Chevrolet's original and exclusive W/T1500 Work Truck proved to be popular with working men and others looking for a rock-bottom price for a big 1/2-ton pickup. The W/T was offered only as a regular cab 1/2-ton with a long cargo box with either 2WD or 4WD. In order to hold its price down, it had fewer features than the standard C/K models. Its standard powerplant was the 4.3-liter Vortec V-6 with EFI, linked to a five-speed manual transmission with overdrive. The W/T1500 had a maximum payload rating of 1,870 pounds. This is a 1991 Chevrolet W/T1500 pickup. The W/T featured power steering, power front disc/rear drum brakes, a rear-wheel ABS, and all-season steel-belted radial tires. Notice that the truck displays a "W/T 1500" decal on the bottom right side of its tailgate and does not show a bit of bright metal anywhere. The Chevrolet bow tie trademark is located between the W/T and the 1500. *AAMA*

The Chevrolet Cheyenne pickup was the standard pickup model and a step above the W/T1500. Unlike the WT1500, the Cheyenne was available in 1/2-, 3/4-, and 1-ton versions. The standard cab Cheyenne was built on a 131.5-inch-wheelbase chassis and was available as either a 2WD or 4WD. Buyers could dress up their Cheyenne with a whole host of appearance, convenience, and performance options. This 1991 Chevrolet 3/4-ton K2500 4WD pickup has chrome bumpers, grille, and full wheel covers. The Cheyenne included the same list of standard equipment features as did the W/T. The K2500 3/4-ton pickup carried a maximum GVW rating of 7,200 pounds. Its standard engine was the 160-horsepower 4.3-liter V-6 or 6.2-liter diesel V-8. The 175-horsepower 5.0-liter and the 210-horsepower 5.7-liter V-8s were optional at extra cost. The standard transmission was the five-speed manual with overdrive for gas engines and a four-speed manual with the diesel; its two-speed transfer case was the NP 241. *AAMA*

Chevrolet's 454 SS C1500 regular cab, shortbox pickup was a big hit in its first year, which encouraged management to bring it back for another year. This year it featured even more power than before. Its 7.4-liter (454-ci) V-8 put out 155 net horsepower at 4,000 rpm, and 405 foot-pounds net torque at 2,400 rpm. It had a new four-speed automatic overdrive transmission. Other performance enhancing equipment included a handling package, locking rear differential with 4.10 axle ratio, and Bilstein gas shocks. The 454 SS was only available in Onyx Black. It rode on special B. F. Goodrich T/A P275/60R-15 blackwall tires. Other features included halogen composite headlamps, tinted glass, top-of-the-line Silverado trim with blackout effects, a new H.D. four-speed electronic automatic transmission, dual exhausts, and a 4.10:1 rear-axle ratio. *AAMA*

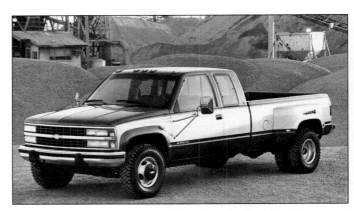

The top of Chevrolet's standard pickup line (the crew cab was still based on the former body style) was the huge K3500 1-ton Extended Cab Big Dooley pickup. The Big Dooley was rated for a maximum payload capacity of 5,038 pounds and maximum GVW of 10,000 pounds. These are impressive numbers. But even bigger was its maximum GCW rating of 19,000 pounds. On top of all that, the Big Dooley Extended-Cab could seat up to six people. All of this towing power came from either a 230-horsepower L19 7.4-liter V-8 or a LL4 150-horsepower 6.2-liter diesel V-8. For either engine, its standard transmission was the four-speed manual and its transfer case was the NP 241. Its 8-foot box was carried on a 155.5-inch-wheelbase chassis. *AAMA*

This is a 1991 Chevrolet standard cab K3500 straight-rail chassis cab with landscaper's body. This heavy-duty 4WD K3500 was rated for a maximum GVW of 12,000 pounds. Its engine choices included only the 5.7-liter gas V-8 and the 6.2-liter diesel V-8. It rode on 16x6.0-inch wheels with LT225/75R16D tires. It was only offered with a four-speed manual transmission. In 1991, Chevrolet introduced a new Class 4 C3500 HD (heavy-duty) chassis cab. It featured straight frame rails for easy mounting of special bodies. It used the same cab, grille, and bumpers as in the C/K pickup line. The 5.7-liter V-8 was standard and the 7.4-liter was optional. Buyers had a choice of four-speed automatic or five-speed manual transmissions. The new 2WD model featured dual rear wheels with low-profile tires and four-wheel disc brakes and a 5,000-pound capacity I-beam front axle with leaf springs. *AAMA*

Chevrolet and Ford ran an exciting race for first place in calendar year pickup sales. Through April 30, Chevrolet C/K pickups sold 226,819 units, while Ford's F series pickups sold 223,094. The model year ended on June 30. Chevrolet had several advantages over Ford in 1991. Chevrolet's popular Sportside truck sold well and Ford didn't have a similar model until later in the calendar year. Chevrolet also had better availability of manual transmissions and short-box extended cab pickups than did Ford. Because of their availability, Chevrolet sold 3 percent more manual-transmission–equipped pickups in 1991 than in 1990. At the very end of the calendar year, Chevrolet got another lift when it began to sell its new extended-cab Sportside C/K models. Chevrolet built short-box extended cab models in 1/2- and 3/4-quarter-ton C/K pickups. This is a 1991 Chevrolet Extended-Cab short-box K2500 pickup. *AAMA*

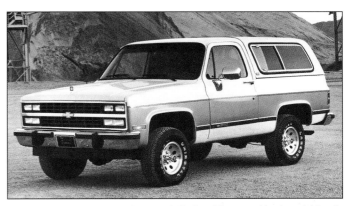

This was the last year for the full-size Blazer with the old body style. Chevrolet's popular full-size truck-based Blazer continued to be America's favorite SUV. The powerful 210-horsepower 5.7-liter gasoline V-8 engine with EFI powered it. A diesel V-8 engine was an option. Transmission choices included the standard four-speed manual and optional four-speed automatic with overdrive (the four-speed automatic overdrive was only for the diesel). The standard Blazer featured power brakes with rear-wheel ABS and power steering. The Blazer's standard trim level was the Scottsdale model. The luxurious upmarket trim model was the Silverado. It included high-back reclining front bucket seats, a center console with storage and beverage pockets, color-keyed carpeting, black rubber floor mats, and an auxiliary lighting package. On the outside, Silverado Blazer featured a chrome grille, dual quad halogen headlamps, bumper guards and rub strips, chrome wheel-opening moldings and wheel covers. The Blazer's GVW ratings were 6,100 pounds for the gas model and 6,250 pounds for the diesel model. *AAMA*

The 1991 Chevrolet trucks again proved to be very popular with the nation's firefighters. The Phoenix, Arizona, Fire Department owned this 1991 Chevrolet C3500 chassis cab with special vent fan body. A local body builder built its vent fan. The regular cab C3500 chassis cab delivered excellent performance from either its 230-horsepower 7.4-liter V-8 or the 6.2-liter diesel V-8. One transmission was offered—the four-speed manual. The 1-ton chassis cab was available on 131.5-, 135.5-, and 159.5-inch wheelbases. Three trim levels included the standard Cheyenne, mid-level Scottsdale, and upscale Silverado. *Greenberg*

All Chevrolet medium-duty conventional cab trucks were Kodiaks. Four models made up the medium-duty Kodiak series— C50-C60-C70 and C70 tandem. The Avondale, Arizona, Fire Department owned this 1991 Chevrolet C60 Kodiak chassis cab with firefighting body. Truck No. U171's service body contained lights and an air compressor. Its maximum GVW rating was 25,000 pounds. Its standard engine was the 210-horsepower 6.0-liter EFI (366-ci) V-8. It produced 325 foot-pounds torque at 2,400 rpm. The 7.0-liter V-8 and 6.6-liter Caterpillar 3116 diesels were options. A five-speed Fuller transmission was standard. Kodiak offered two trim levels. The Scottsdale was base and the Silverado was the top-of-the-line interior. *Greenberg*

The biggest single-axle 1991 Chevrolet Kodiak medium-duty truck was the 37,600 pound maximum GVW rated C70 chassis cab with tank body. Truck No. WT10 was owned by the Riverside County, California, Fire Department. The 235-horsepower 7.0-liter (427-ci) V-8 engine that developed 385 foot-pounds torque at 2,400 rpm powered it. A 14-inch single-plate cerame-tallic clutch was standard with this engine. Both big block gasoline engines for 1991 had new oil sealing, new valve covers with screw-in oil fill caps, structural revisions to their cylinder case, and a one-piece inlet manifold. The oil cooler adapter was dropped. The 1991 Kodiaks also had a new 12,000-pound front axle and an optional 14,600-pound front axle. A new raised roof option for the construction and utility industries was available. The standard wheel for the C70 was a cast steel spoke, the 10-stud disc wheels pictured were an extra cost option. *Chuck Madderom*

Chevrolet's biggest 1991 medium-duty Kodiak was the C70 tandem chassis cab. This firefighting body carried a maximum GVW rating of 54,600 pounds. Full Rockwell "Q" series air brakes and power steering were standard equipment. The Lowell, Indiana, Fire Department owned this truck. Its tank body had a 4,000-gallon capacity, and was made by Kovatch Mobile Equipment Co. The 6.6-liter (403-ci) Caterpillar 3116 inline six-cylinder diesel engine powered it. It was turbocharged and air-to-air aftercooled to deliver maximum efficiency. Only 215 and 250 horsepower versions were offered for the C70 tandem. The tandem featured 34,000-pound Hendrickson rear suspension as standard; also available were 40,000 pound and 44,000 pound Hendrickson suspensions. *Garry E. Kadzielawski*

Chevrolet's complete 1991 commercial chassis cab line consisted of the C/K 2500 and 3500 Regular-Cab and Extended-Cabs, C3500 HD Regular-Cab and C/K Bonus/Crew Cabs. This is a 1991 Chevrolet C3500 Regular-Cab chassis cab with stake body. Chevrolet engineers designed this model with parallel flat-top frame rails and 34-inch rail spacing. Buyers could choose standard 84.5-inch or optional 92.1-inch rear-axle widths. Dual rear wheels were standard on all models. The maximum GVW rating of this truck was a sizable 11,000 pounds. It was powered by the 210-horsepower 5.7-liter V-8; its transmission was the basic four-speed manual. Buyers could choose from either a 135.5- or 159.5-inch wheelbase. LT225/75R16C front and 16D rear tires were mounted on 16x6.0-inch wheels. *Iten Chevrolet*

An optional Sport Appearance Package was available on C/K1500 pickups with Scottsdale or Silverado trim. The packages were designed specifically for the short-box Chevrolet Fleetside pickups to set them apart from the herd. Sport Truck trim items for the 2WD, shown here, included a black grille, side and rear "Sport" graphics, chrome-plated wheels, halogen composite headlamps, body-color front and rear bumpers (rear bumper had rub strip and step pad), special body-side moldings with red accents, and black outside rearview mirrors. An additional option for 2WD models, the Sport Handling Package, had special springs and Bilstein gas shocks and required B.F. Goodrich T/A P275/60R-15 blackwall tires. Pictured is a 1991 Chevrolet C1500 Fleetside with Sport Appearance Package.

Suburbans in 1991 continued with the old body style. This huge, no-nonsense 1991 V2500 Suburban has an aftermarket front push-bumper constructed of heavy channel steel and a heavy-duty electric winch. It was powered by Chevrolet's largest gas engine the 230-horsepower 7.4-liter V-8, which developed an impressive 385 foot-pounds torque. The only transmission for Suburbans was the four-speed automatic with overdrive. Its transfer case was the New Process 241, and it rode on big LT235/85R-16E tires. V2500 was rated for a maximum GVW of 8,600 pounds and a maximum GCW rating of 16,000 pounds when equipped with the 4.10 rear-axle ratio and the 7.4-liter engine. A weight-distributing platform hitch receiver was required when towing trailers over 2,000 pounds. Two trim levels for Suburban included the base Scottsdale shown and the upscale Silverado.

Chevrolet's old standby steel body Step-Van continued to soldier on into 1991. It was still America's most popular forward-control delivery van. The P30 Series Step-Van was offered on four wheelbases: 125, 133, 157, and 178 inches. Body lengths ranged from 10 to 18 feet. This is a 1991 P30 Step-Van with an 18-foot body. The Step-Van's standard engines were the 4.3-liter V-6 and the 6.2-liter diesel V-8; optional engines included the 5.7-liter and 7.4-liter V-8s. Buyers could choose from two transmissions: the four-speed manual and the four-speed automatic with overdrive. Maximum payload and GVW ratings ranged from 878 to 8,363 pounds and 7,600 to 14,100 pounds, respectively. The standard front suspension was independent with coil springs; I-beam front axles were optional at the higher GVWs.

The small end of Chevrolet's high-volume vans were the popular G-30 Hi-Cube Vans with either steel or aluminum bodies. Other standard features included single or dual rear wheels, 125- and 146-inch wheelbases; standard GVW ratings began at 8,600 pounds and went up to 10,500 pounds with 10- or 12-foot bodies. Maximum GVW ratings ranged from 2,758 to 5,753 pounds. Pictured here is a 1991 Chevrolet G30 Hi-Cube Commercial Van with dual rear wheels. Standard engines included the 5.7-liter gas-powered V-8 and the 6.2-liter diesel V-8. The powerful 7.4-liter gas V-8 was optional. A four-speed automatic with overdrive was the only available transmission. Front suspension was independent with coil springs. *Harold Chevrolet*

This 1991 S-10 short bed may appear to be one of Chevrolet's most affordable and popular four-cylinder EL models, but it is actually equipped with the robust 160-horsepower, 230 foot-pounds torque 4.3-liter Vortec V-6. Other than that, it doesn't have many other options, as can be seen. It is a surprisingly quick little truck, capable of embarrassing many larger pickups. Amerigo Furlan of Los Angeles owns it. *Bob Bray*

Chevrolet's conventional commercial van lineup included the minivan Lumina APV, mid-range Astro Cargo Van and full-size G10, G20, and G30 Chevy Van Series. These large vans were available on three wheelbase lengths: 110, 125, and 146 inches. This is a 1991 G20 3/4-ton 125-inch wheelbase Chevy Van in Frost White. For the real big jobs, Chevrolet offered the monster Extended-Body G30 Chevy Van with a 146-inch wheelbase, which was ideal for applications requiring extra load space and high GVW ratings. It had a cargo volume of 306 cubic feet, a 12.3-foot load floor length (without the optional front passenger seat), and a 8,600-pound maximum GVW rating. Standard powerplants for G-Series vans included the 4.3-liter gas V-6 and the 6.2-liter diesel V-8. Optional engines included the 5.0-, 5.7-, and 7.4-liter gas V-8s. The only transmission offered was the four-speed automatic with overdrive.

1992

Detroit enjoyed a recovery year in 1992, with production surging 10.4 percent to 9,731,001 cars and trucks versus 8,811,806 in 1991. Trucks pulled the total production figure up, rising 20.5 percent to 4,064,100, the best year for trucks since 1988. Cars increased by only 4.2 percent. In the truck industry, light-duty models led the way with an increase in production of 20.6 percent, to 3,830,927 units.

As had been true for years, consumers' preference for pickups, vans, and SUVs came at the expense of autos. The insatiable demand by consumers for light-duty trucks worked for the good of the Big Three. It kept them from losing more market share to imported cars, in particular to the so-called transplants, those foreign cars built in the United States. The Big Three continued to own 81 percent of the total industry's production.

While Ford and Chrysler increased their output of both cars and trucks, GM's passenger car output dropped slightly (0.3 percent). GM's light truck total was 1,325,497, up 10.7 percent from 1991. GM truck's total sales rose 10 percent, but underperformed the industry's total sales increase of 12.4 percent.

GMC recognized its 90th year in the truck business with a 19.2 percent sales increase. GMC's light-duties increased 18.8 percent compared with only an 8 percent rise for Chevrolet. GMC's medium-duties were up 18.4 percent compared with Chevrolet's meager 4.2 percent medium-duty increase.

Chevrolet's total calendar year truck sales reached 1,152,346, compared to 1,066,541 in 1991. Chevrolet's light-duty market share dropped to 24.76 percent from 1991's 25.79 percent. Medium-duty's total was 11,022 versus 10,574 in 1991.

An important market segment, which cost Chevrolet heavily, was compact SUVs. A report in midyear 1992 showed that the S-10 Blazer's sales actually declined by 1.2 percent while the Jeep Cherokee and Wrangler and Ford's Explorer were smoking in the sales column. Chevrolet's bright spot in SUV sales was in its full-size (and expensive) models: the Suburban and Blazer posted impressive increases over 1991. Both of these models and the Crew Cab changed over to the full-size pickup styling. Their model designations went from the former R/V to the familiar C/K. The Suburban and Blazer also got four-wheel ABS. The Suburban's K2500 model had an optional 7.4-liter V-8. New for C/K pickups was the Sportside Extended-Cab model.

A second important light-duty truck market segment in which Chevrolet did not compete well was minivans, both passenger and commercial. In 1992, Chevrolet marketed two minivan series: the Astro, with rear-wheel drive, and the newer Lumina front-wheel drive. Yet Chevrolet still fell 311,000 units short of market leader Chrysler.

Chevrolet added muscle to its 4.3-liter V-6 in an attempt to grow sales of its compact trucks. It increased the horsepower of its performance version to 200 at 4,500 rpm and 260 foot-pounds torque at 3,600 rpm. This engine was optional in the Astro van, S-10 Blazer, and S-10 pickups. The idea behind the performance version of the 4.3-L V-6 was to provide the towing and hauling capacity and the smoothness of a V-8, with the fuel economy of a V-6.

Chevrolet engineers first looked at offering a V-8 in compact trucks, but the compacts lacked underhood space for an engine bigger than a V-6. Additionally, a V-8 would have increased retail prices and would have adversely impacted corporate average fuel economy.

Chevrolet engineers hot-rodded the V-6 with a new intake manifold, a new "central-port" fuel-injection system, higher-flow cylinder heads, and a higher-performance camshaft with roller-type cam followers. The net result was a 25 percent increase in peak horsepower and an 11.5 percent increase in peak torque.

The second new engine offering in 1992 was the large V-8 diesel for the heavy-duty 2WD and 4WD pickups. The 6.5-liter turbodiesel provided 190 horsepower at 3,400 rpm and 380 foot-pounds torque at 1,700 rpm.

The new Suburban was completely redesigned, from the wheels up. Compared with the 1991 Suburban, the new model was 2 inches longer and 2.6 inches narrower. Four-wheel ABS brakes were standard. New features inside included a new interior; instrument panel; better seats; and an upgraded heater, ventilation, and airconditioning system. Seating configurations offered from five- to nine-passenger capacity.

The new Blazer's wheelbase was stretched 5 inches, and the overall length grew 3 inches. An all-steel roof replaced the fiberglass roof. Engineers also installed the shift-on-the-fly transfer case that allowed 2WD or 4WD selection while moving.

Chevrolet was the place for vans in 1992. Chevrolet dealers retailed Astros, Lumina APVs, regular-body Sportvans, and extended-body Sportvans plus cargo and conversion versions of all of the above except Luminas. With the arrival of the Lumina APV, Chevrolet began referring to the Astro as a "mid-size" van. The Astro was offered in Regular-Body or Extended-Body versions in 2WD or high-traction AWD. Both rode on a 111.0-inch-wheelbase chassis. The additional length of the Extended-Body was accomplished by adding 10 inches to the length of the body behind the rear wheels. Maximum GVW ratings ranged from a low of 5,700 pounds for the Regular-Body 2WD to 6,100 pounds for the Extended-Body AWD. Then there was the Astro Sport, which was sold as a "custom van" without a custom price. The Sport package included special exterior trim items and special sport suspension items such as front and rear gas-charged shock absorbers and a rear stabilizer bar, Rally Wheels with fat P245/60R-15 white-outlined lettered tires. Astro Sport was not available with AWD but with either body length. The Astro did have the new optional 4.3-liter high-performance V-6 engine and a new rear-door option. The optional new door featured a one-piece lift-glass body-wide door at the top and two individual half-doors that could be opened when the lift-glass was in the up position. This is a 1992 Chevrolet Extended-Body Astro van with AWD equipped with the standard rear panel doors. *AAMA*

Chevrolet's best-selling 1992 S-10 pickups were 2WD regular cab low-line versions with short or long boxes. Generally, the short-box trucks were bought for personal transportation and the long-box trucks for commercial uses. Pictured is a 1992 Chevrolet S-10 2WD long-box pickup. For this market, Chevrolet offered an S-10 EL short-box regular-cab model. It had fewer amenities and options than a standard S-10 and was priced lower. It was offered in either 2WD or 4WD configurations in regular cab or Maxi-Cab. In other words, the S-10 EL was a downsized version of W/T1500 except for a few differences. The EL's standard drivetrain included the 4.3-liter V-6 and a five-speed manual transmission with overdrive. This year the sales of all light trucks increased, with the exception of compact pickups. For the first six months compact truck sales were flat. Prices for 1992 S-10 pickups ranged from $9,192 to $15,394. *AAMA*

Chevrolet's top-of-the-line 1992 compact S-10 pickup was this Maxi-Cab short-box 4WD. It has the optional top-level Tahoe trim. The Maxi-Cab gave the buyer a choice of reclining high-back bucket seats with center console. Soft leather upholstery was an option; the folding rear jump seats were done in vinyl. Other features of the Tahoe included wall-to-wall carpeting, a full-length fabric headliner, extra insulation, and sound-deadening materials. The 160-horsepower 4.3-liter V-6 was standard; the new high-performance 4.3 was optional. The five-speed manual with overdrive was standard and its two-speed transfer case was the New Process 231. The Maxi-Cab had a 122.9-inch wheelbase, a 6-foot box, a maximum payload rating of 1,741 pounds, and a maximum GVW rating of 5,150 pounds. *AAMA*

Chevrolet built both two-door and four-door and 2WD and 4WD S-10 Blazers in 1992. This is a 1992 S-10 two-door 2WD Blazer. Four-wheel ABS was standard on 2WD models. The standard engine for all S-10 Blazers was the 160-horsepower 4.3-liter V-6. The new high-performance 200-horsepower 4.3-liter V-6 was an option. The idea behind the high-performance engine was to provide power for towing and hauling such as was possible with a V-8 engine, but with a V-6's economy. A V-8 was not possible because the small trucks lacked the underhood space for an engine larger than a V-6. Also, the V-8 would be too costly and would adversely affect the corporate average fuel economy. GM engineers found the answer to these problems was to hot-rod the 4.3-liter V-6 with a new variable-geometry intake manifold, a new type of "central-port" fuel-injection system, higher-flow cylinder heads and a higher-performance camshaft with roller-type cam followers. These new features provided a 25 percent gain in peak horsepower and an 11.5 percent increase in peak torque. The new injection system was called "Central-Port Fuel Injection. The new 4.3 was used in Astros, S-10 pickups, and S-10 Blazers as an extra cost option. *AAMA*

Chevrolet's 1992 commercial van series was the Chevy Van. It was available in four gas-powered series and two diesel-powered series. Gas series included the G10, G20, G30, and G30 HD; diesel series included G20 and G30 HD. This 1992 Chevrolet G20 3/4-ton Chevy Van was rated for a maximum GVW rating of 6,600 pounds. Its standard engine was the 150-horsepower 4.3-liter V-6; the standard and only transmission was the four-speed automatic with overdrive. The G20 Chevy Van was available with 110- and 125-inch wheelbases. G30 was only offered with the 125-inch wheelbase. The G30 Extended-Body Chevy Van was offered with a 146-inch wheelbase. This van pictured was ideal for RV conversion for plumbers, carpet installers, and other vocations where a big load space was a necessity. *AAMA*

The Chevy Van was in effect two trucks in one. It was sold as a standard commercial van for any number of applications to conduct America's business. The Chevy Van was also an important vehicle to GM and to America's families as a conversion van for basic transportation. Many families found them the ideal vehicle for trips, vacations, and everyday use. They offered multiple seating and could be specified with the features of most value to the buyer. This is a 1992 Chevy Van G20 125-inch wheelbase conversion. Conversion van specifications were the same as for the standard Chevy Van.

Sportside pickups were available in the 1500 Series as either a 2WD or 4WD short-box model. An Extended-Cab Sportside was added for 1992. The Sportside was the modern version of Chevrolet's famous Stepside pickup. Sportside retained the classic Stepside's flavor, with attractive modern styling. Important features of the regular-cab Sportside short box included: 1/2-ton C/Ks with seating for three, 117.5-inch wheelbase, 6 1/2-foot cargo box, maximum 2WD payload of 1,867 pounds, maximum 4WD payload of 1,976 pounds, maximum GVWs—5,600 and 6,100 pounds for C/K, respectively. Silverado trim was an option. *AAMA*

One of the better-selling workhorse pickups in Chevrolet's 1992 line was the C/K2500 3/4-ton standard cab. The Batavia, Illinois, Fire Department owned this 1992 Chevrolet K2500 standard cab pickup with firefighting equipment. The specialized brush firefighting equipment in its cargo box was by Alex's and it featured a 250-gallon water tank and a 250-gpm pump. K2500's 8-foot cargo box rode on a 131.5-inch-wheelbase chassis. Its maximum GVW rating was 7,200 pounds. The 160-horsepower 4.3-liter V-6 engine was standard. Optional engines included the 175-horsepower 5.0-liter V-8, the 210-horsepower 5.7-liter V-8, the 230-horsepower 7.4-liter V-8, and the 140-horsepower 6.2-liter V-8 diesel. The new 6.5-liter V-8 diesel was not an option for K2500 trucks. The five-speed manual overdrive transmission and NP 241 two-speed transfer case were standard. *Garry E. Kadzielawski*

Another Chevrolet workhorse K2500 pickup in 1992 was the Extended-Cab. Many workers preferred the Extended-Cab model because they could safely store expensive tools and personal items in a lockable closed area. When photographed in April 1993, this truck from Connecticut was in Clearwater Beach, Florida, where its owner was part of a crew working on storm drains. As you can see, the truck has mounting equipment up front for a snowplow—a device not normally required in Florida. The full-size pickup's market share increased from 8 percent in 1991 to 8.5 percent in 1992. Light trucks took a 2.2 percent bigger share of the entire U.S. light vehicle market in 1992 versus 1991—35.2 from 33.0. *Elliott Kahn*

An all-new 1992 Chevrolet model was the C/K3500 Crew Cab pickup with optional dual rear wheels. The Crew Cab offered standard six-passenger seating, including a front bench seat and forward-facing rear bench seat. Chevrolet did not offer the Bonus Cab option with the new series Crew Cab. The Bonus cab in the past was a four-door pickup with one bench seat and an enclosed cargo area behind the seat. Before the days of an Extended-Cab model, the Bonus Cab was Chevrolet's way of competing with the competition's extended-cab pickups. The new Crew Cab was offered in both Cheyenne and Silverado trim. The 210-horsepower 5.7-liter V-8 engine was standard and the 230-horsepower 7.4-liter gas V-8 was an option. Its maximum GVW rating was 10,000 pounds; maximum GCW rating was 19,000 pounds. Required equipment for this rating included the 7.4-liter engine and either a 4.56 or 5.13:1 rear-axle ratio. The Crew Cab's standard transmission was a five-speed manual with overdrive. *AAMA*

Chevrolet provided two chassis cab models for 1992 that had straight, parallel flattop frame rails with 24-inch spacing. These chassis cab trucks were ready for installation of van, dump, stake, utility, and other commercial bodies. The K3500 chassis cab carried a maximum GVW rating of 10,000 pounds. This is a 1992 Chevrolet C3500 H.D. chassis cab with straight, flattop frame rails, carrying a firefighting body. It had a maximum GVW rating of 15,000 pounds, a solid I-beam front axle with a 5,000 pound capacity, and leaf springs. New for 1992 was a standard heavy-duty five-speed transmission with deep low and overdrive and a standard rear-wheel ABS. The new optional 6.5-liter H.D. (400-ci) V-8 turbo-diesel engine was designed and engineered specifically as a turbo-charged engine. It was available in C/K2500-C6P and C/K3500 regular-cab pickups, as well as in C/K2500-C6P, C3500, and C3500 H.D. chassis cabs. It boasted of 190 horsepower and 380 foot-pounds torque. The Colorado DOT used Rescue 1057 for duty at the Eisenhower and Johnson Memorial Tunnels. *Dennis J. Maag*

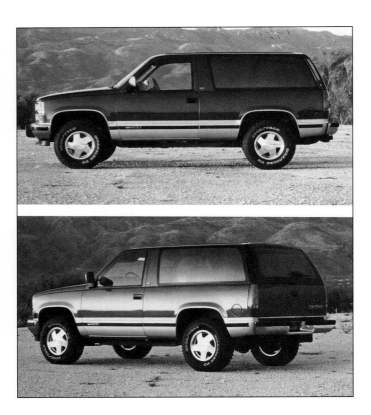

The redesigned 1992 Chevrolet Blazer got a 5-inch longer wheelbase and 3 more inches in overall length. The Blazer was a K1500 model; the former V1500 model designation was dropped. The Blazer benefited from design and engineering upgrades incorporated into the 1988 full-sized pickup design. An all-steel roof replaced the fiberglass roof. Seating capacity increased by one to a total of six. The new Blazer incorporated the same full-frame chassis design as the redesigned full-sized pickup, allowing adaptation of the new 4WD independent system from the pickup. It was powered by the standard 210-horsepower 5.7-liter V-8. Transmission options included the standard five-speed manual or the optional four-speed automatic. The Blazer also received the shift-on-the-fly transfer case, which allowed 2WD or 4WD selection while moving. Towing capacity was bumped up to 7,000 pounds from 6,000. *AAMA*

Chevrolet introduced three major new truck models in 1992—the Suburban, Blazer, and Crew Cab. The Suburban full-sized SUV was completely redesigned for 1992. Its chassis, steering gear, exterior sheet metal, glass, interior, and even the suspension system were new. The new Suburban was 2 inches longer and 2.6 inches narrower. The standard engine was the 210-horsepower 5.7-liter V-8 in the 1500 series and a 190-horsepower heavy-duty version of the same engine in the 2500 series. For heavy-duty hauling or towing, a 230-horsepower 7.4-liter V-8 was optional in the 2500 series. No diesel engine was offered. The fuel tank held 42 gallons. The light-duty engine was mated to the 4L60 four-speed automatic. The two heavy-duty engines were mated to the 4L80E four-speed automatic. A manual was not offered. A new interior, instrument panel, improved seats, an upgraded heater, ventilation, and air conditioning system presented a comfortable environment for passengers. Seating for up to nine persons was provided. Sales of this biggest SUV stayed unusually constant from year to year, always increasing and never having a depressed sales year. *AAMA*

Chevrolet for 1992 again offered an entire range of Tiltmaster COE trucks—W4-W5-W6-W7. Maximum GVW ratings for the four series were as follows: 14,250, 18,000, 22,000, and 30,000 pounds, respectively. This is a 1992 W4 Tiltmaster chassis cab with van body. Payloads up to 9,166 pounds were possible. The W4's engine was a new 135-gross-horsepower 3.9-liter turbo-intercooled four-cylinder diesel with 255 foot-pounds torque for strong low-end power. An engine exhaust brake was standard. The five-speed direct-drive transmission featured synchronized gears for smooth shifting. A four-speed automatic transmission was available. A new Flatlow chassis permitted a body load floor height nearly 6.5-inches lower than a conventional W4 chassis. It also featured a flat floor without wheelhousings for greater cargo volume.

Chevrolet's conventional cab medium-duty truck line for 1992 included models C50-C60-C70 and a C-70 tandem. Maximum GVW ratings ranged from 22,000 to 37,600 pounds for single axles and 54,600 pounds for the tandem-axle C70. This is a 1992 Chevrolet C50 chassis cab with utility body. Chevrolet's medium-duty engine line was short and simple: it consisted of two gas engines and a diesel. Gas engines included the 210-horsepower 6.0-liter (366-ci) V-8 and 235-horsepower 7.0-liter (427-ci) V-8. The diesel was the 6.6-liter (403-ci) inline six turbo-charged and air-to-air aftercooled Caterpillar 3116. Chevrolet offered four versions of the 3116, ranging in horsepower from 170 to 250. The C50's maximum GVW rating was 22,000 pounds. A five-speed Fuller transmission was standard.

The middle-size Chevrolet medium-duty truck was the C60. This chassis cab with a special sign installation body was rated for a maximum GVW of 27,100 pounds and maximum GCW rating of 45,000 pounds. The 210-horsepower 6.0-liter V-8 engine powered this truck. Its SAE net torque rating was 325 foot-pounds at 2,400 rpm. The biggest gas engine, the 7.0-liter V-8, was only available in the C70 tandem. The Cat 3116 diesel was available only in the C60 and C70 Series trucks. The EFI 6.0-liter engine was a truck-only engine, designed and engineered for truck service. In 1991 it was completely redesigned. It featured cast-aluminum pistons with steel struts, heavy-duty bulkheads for crankshaft support, double roller chain and sprocket camshaft drive, stellite exhaust valves, full pressure lubrication, big 26–28-quart cooling system, and an electronic spark control knock sensor.

This is a basic dual-purpose 1992 Chevrolet C1500 regular cab pickup. It's dual-purpose in that this was the pickup most often purchased for a combination of work and personal transportation. Note it has the standard cab and long cargo box. In total, Chevrolet built 10 full-size regular cab pickups—C/K1500 Sportside, C/K1500 regular cab Fleetside short-box and C/K1500, 2500, and 3500 regular cab Fleetside long-box pickups. Standard features of the truck shown included a 131.5-inch wheelbase, an 8-foot box, maximum payload rating of 2,220 pounds and maximum GVW rating of 6,100 pounds, and a choice of Cheyenne, Scottsdale, or Silverado interior and exterior trim. Standard powertrain was the 160-horsepower 4.3-liter V-6 engine and a five-speed overdrive manual transmission.

Chevrolet's P30 Series Step-Van line continued as America's favorite all-purpose high-volume van in 1992. Most often Step-Vans were employed as package delivery-type trucks, but many were used by various businesses and public bodies, including fire departments, for a whole range of specialized applications. Pictured is a 1992 Chevrolet P30 Step-Van with an 18-foot aluminum body. The complete vehicle was sold and delivered by a Chevrolet dealer. Chevrolet also sold the stripped forward-control chassis to the buyer to have his own special body mounted. The Union City Body Co. of Union City, Indiana, manufactured this Step-Van body. In 1998, Chevrolet sold its Step-Van business to Union City Body Co. *Iten Chevrolet*

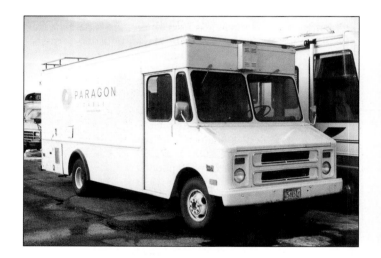

1993

GM announced an ambitious five-year plan for new truck products in 1993. Its plan was to spend $1.2 billion yearly through 1997 on new truck products. This figure was double the amount the company had spent in the previous five years.

At the time, GM was building a new Truck Technology Center on the site of its former Pontiac West plant. This new 1.2-million-square-foot complex would consolidate 4,000 engineering and development people then working in nine separate facilities north of Detroit.

One market development that worked in favor of Chevrolet—and the Big Three in general—was the loss of market share by Japanese light trucks over the previous six years. Japanese brands peaked in 1986 with 20.4 percent of the U.S. light truck market. By 1992, that figure had dropped to 13.5 percent, the same share Japanese brands had had in 1982.

The Japanese penetrated the market originally with the cheapest transportation a buyer could find. That meant low-priced, no-frills mini pickups. Since then, the taste of the American consumer had gone up-market. Customers preferred trucks with the same features they had previously enjoyed in the automobile they had abandoned to buy a truck. When the Japanese tried to follow suit, their trucks sold for more than the American brands. U.S. trade policies and currency exchange rates also operated to the detriment of the imports.

Chevrolet's light-duty truck series and models continued without additions or deletions for 1993. Chevrolet's 1993 truck line improvements included a new four-speed electronic automatic transmission, the 4L60-E. It was GM's first rear-wheel-drive electronic transmission to interface with the cruise control, operating through a powertrain control module, rather than an electronic control module. It was available with the 4.3-liter V-6, the 5.0-liter V-8, the 5.7-liter V-8, and the 6.2-liter diesel V-8. The 4L60E was the older Turbo 700 with new electronic controls, similar to the 4L80E.

This was also the first year the Kodiak offered the new Allison MD "World" transmission. It was a new, electronically controlled five- and six-speed heavy-duty automatic.

Engine modifications were plenty. Chevrolet made available a modified 5.7-liter V-8 for conversion to compressed natural gas, propane, or dual-fuel capability with gasoline. The company increased the horsepower of the 4.3-liter V-6 compact trucks by five, to 165, due to revisions in the cylinder heads, camshaft, intake manifold, and exhaust system. The 6.5-liter turbodiesel was made available on Crew Cab and Extended Cab pickups weighing more than 8,500 pounds GVW. Chevrolet engineers added many other refinements and improvements to make these fine trucks even more dependable and economical.

An important trend in pickups—actually a continuing trend—was the desire for extended-cab models. Chevrolet/GMC was the last of the Big Three to market an extended-cab pickup, which was part of the new series in the 1988 model year. It can safely be assumed that sales figures for GMC pickups were an accurate picture of the industry. In the 1989 model year, GMC sold 17.3 percent of all pickups with extended cabs that were sold that year. In 1990, the percentage jumped to 23 percent, then to 29.8 percent in 1991, and 36.2 percent in 1992.

Changes and improvements in the Astros were mostly confined to engineering advancements. Horsepower of the 4.3-liter V-6 engine was increased by five, to 165, due to revisions in the cylinder heads, camshaft, intake manifold, exhaust gas recirculation system, and exhaust system. The Astro was given the new electronic four-speed automatic transmission, the 4L60-E. It was the first GM rear-wheel-drive electronic transmission to interface with the cruise control, and it operated through a powertrain control module, rather than electronic control module. GM claimed the new Hydra-Matic 4L60-E had the strongest torque-to-mass ratio in its class. Four-wheel anti-lock brakes were made standard on regular and extended cargo vans, as well as wagons. Other improvements included Scotchgarded seats, door and trim panels; a more readable analog instrument cluster; an improved air-conditioning compressor and radiator-fan clutch; new optional brushed aluminum wheels; and improved brake hose material. This is a 1993 Chevrolet AWD extended Astro LT. *AAMA*

Chevrolet's popular compact S-10 pickups received the improved 4.3-liter V-6, electronically controlled automatic-transmission single-rail shifter for the five-speed manual transmission, and Solar-Ray windows. The S-10 offered an entry light under the rearview mirror, a convenience net on extended-cab models, and a new 60/40 reclining front bench seat with center armrest as part of a midyear Tahoe trim package. New 15-inch aluminum wheels were optional for all 2WD S-10 pickups except the EL model. The S-10 pickup was now in its 11th year. Chevrolet dealers had sold millions of these nifty pickups in that time. Pictured here is a top-of-the-line 1993 Chevrolet S-10 Tahoe short box (6-foot) pickup with 2WD.

The 1993 Chevrolet compact S-Blazer received the improved five-speed manual and new smooth-shifting Hydra-Matic 4L60-E electronic four-speed automatic, reclining low-back bucket seats, and Solar-Ray glass. More Scotch protection also highlighted the new models. The tilt steering column was improved with the addition of a new steel sleeve to prevent theft. The S-Blazer's front appearance was updated with an attractive new grille design. The S-10 four-door Blazer had the optional 200-horsepower HP 4.3-liter V-6 engine for greater towing and cruising ability. The four-speed automatic overdrive transmission was required with the 200-horse-power high-performance engine. The 165-horsepower 4.3-liter V-6 was the standard engine for S-10 Blazers. Blazer was available in three trim levels: Standard, Tahoe, and LT. *AAMA*

Improvements and innovations for the full-size 1993 Chevrolet pickups included the new electronic automatic transmission, improved 4.3-liter V-6, modified 5.7-liter V-8 for conversion to gaseous fuel, and expanded availability of the 6.5-liter turbodiesel. Chevrolet's new-for-1993 sport pickup was the flashy Sportside Sport. It was available in the C/K 1500 Series as either a 2WD or 4WD short-box model. It featured cast-aluminum wheels and color-keyed bumpers, grille, and mirrors. This truck stood out in a crowd. Its simple, elegantly styled W/T1500 grille helped the Sportside Sport become a standout. The standard engine for C/K1500 pickups was the 165-horsepower 4.3-liter V-6; options included the 5.0-liter 175-horsepower V-8, the 5.7-liter 210-horse-power V-8, and the 140-horsepower 6.2-liter diesel V-8. *AAMA*

Extended cabs offered additional seating, especially for children. Yet even more important in the minds of buyers was the matter of security, since most pickups had room for only a driver and one passenger. Owners preferred to carry things such as groceries, luggage, pets, tools, and other cargo inside, away from the weather.

Total U.S. truck sales set an all-time record in 1993—5.7 million vehicles. Trucks represented a 15.9 percent sales increase over 1992. SUV and minivan sales increased by a robust 21.7 and 16.5 percent, respectively. Pickup sales, on the other hand, increased 12.7 percent. Despite the industry rise, Chevrolet sales still came in behind Ford, unfortunately.

Medium-duty trucks also fared well in 1993, up 11.4 percent from 1992. Chevrolet's total medium-duty sales reached 11,946 units. Many of Chevrolet's sales were in Class 4 (the 3500HD) at 4,930 units. Chevrolet didn't produce a Class 8 truck in 1993.

As always, Chevrolet's hardest-working pickup was the standard cab C2500 full-size 2WD pickup. There wasn't anything fancy about this truck except that it got the big jobs done for a small price. It carried a full 8-foot Fleetside cargo box on a 131.5-inch-wheelbase chassis. The C2500 was rated for an impressive maximum GVW of 8,600 pounds and a maximum payload rating of 4,178 pounds. If the standard 4.3-liter 165-horsepower V-6 wasn't big enough, either the 175-horsepower 5.0-liter V-8 or 210-horsepower 5.7-liter V-8 gas engines and the 6.2-liter diesel V-8 were options. The rugged five-speed overdrive manual was standard and the four-speed automatic was an option. Standard LT225/75R-16D tires carried a heavy load. *AAMA*

Chevrolet fielded an incredible array of work and play pickups for 1993. Several of them fell into the category of dual-purpose trucks, such as the 1993 Chevrolet C3500 Crew Cab 2WD pickup. Maybe a better term for this Big Dooley would be "tractor." So often it was bought for the express purpose of towing a boat, camper, a commercial trailer, a horse trailer, an enclosed trailer transporting a prize-winning race car, or a valuable collector car. The luxury-level optional Silverado cab trim gave it the same comfort level as an automobile. Due to its long 168.5-inch wheelbase, the Big Dooley rode better than an auto. A chassis cab Crew Cab was an available model for 1993. When equipped with the 7.4-liter gas engine and an approved rear-axle ratio, Crew Cab was rated for a maximum GCW of 19,000 pounds. Maximum GVW rating was 10,000 pounds. The standard engine for Crew Cab was the 5.7-liter 190-horsepower V-8; options included the 230-horsepower 7.4-liter HD V-8 and the 190-horsepower 6.5-liter HD turbodiesel V-8. The standard transmission was the five-speed overdrive manual; the four-speed overdrive automatic was the only option. *AAMA*

The full-size fully restyled and reengineered Blazer returned for its second model year in 1993. Updates included an improved five-speed manual and a new four-speed electronic controlled automatic transmission, recliners in low-back bucket seats and in the passenger side of the split bench seat, Solar-Ray glass, and more Scotchgard seat fabric protection. The Blazer's appeal was that it was an intelligent alternative to an automobile, because it comfortably seated up to six and its big truck's towing ability and excellent 4WD system allowed it to go just about anywhere. Blazer's Insta-Trac 4WD system allowed the driver to shift on the fly from 2WD to 4WD and back at any reasonable speed. The Blazer's only engine was the capable 210-horsepower 5.7-liter V-8. A five-speed overdrive manual transmission was standard, the four-speed overdrive automatic was an option, and the two-speed NP 241 transfer case was standard. Chevrolet only offered Blazer as a 4WD. *AAMA*

The all-new Suburban was in its second model year in 1993. Suburban's updates in 1993 included the new smooth-shifting Hydra-Matic 4L60-E electronically controlled four-speed automatic transmission as standard equipment, a larger radiator with the 7.4-liter V-8, an air cleaner with improved sealing and increased underbody corrosion protection. The tilt steering column was redesigned to improve theft protection. Other features included increased underhood and underbody corrosion protection and additional fabric Scotchgard protection. This low-mileage, like-new 1993 Suburban was photographed in June 1998. It had the optional luxury-level Silverado trim and cast-aluminum wheels. The Suburban could seat up to nine adults in comfort, eight when outfitted with front bucket seats and console. The standard 5.7-liter 210-horsepower V-8 powered the K1500 model. The only transmission was the new automatic; the only available transfer case was the NP 241.

For those living in rural America, particularly horse lovers, an Extended Cab C/K1500 Chevrolet pickup was a necessity. This is a 1993 Chevrolet C1500 short-bed Extended Cab pickup. The Extended Cab short cargo box model was one of Chevrolet's best-selling 1993 models. The available 5.7-liter 210-horsepower V-8 engine provided plenty of towing power, and when mated to the new four-speed overdrive electronically shifted automatic with brake interlock, it was a pleasure to drive. Extended Cab Fleetside short-box pickup was only 218 inches in overall length, that was a full 19 inches shorter than the same truck with the long box. This pickup's towing capacity with the 5.7 and automatic ranged from 10,000 to 15,000 pounds, depending on rear-axle ratios. *Jim Benjaminson*

The Chevrolet Suburban's versatility extended to the nation's fire departments. The Battalion Chief of the Flagstaff, Arizona, Fire Department selected the 1993 K1500 Suburban for his Shift Commander's vehicle. The Suburban looks to be mostly stock except for a rooftop light-bar and its heavy-duty–type front push-bar, which seems to be protecting red lights and horns. The front high-back bucket seats can be seen through the driver window, which means it could seat up to eight. The standard 5.7-liter 190-horsepower HD V-8 with EFI could speed the firefighters quickly to the scene. The electronically shifted four-speed automatic-overdrive transmission with brake interlock was standard. *Greenberg*

This truck, built on the Extended Cab chassis cab, had the 155.5-inch K3500 wheelbase chassis with tapered frame rails. The St. Louis, Missouri, Fire Department owned Truck No. 42, and it was used at Lambert International Airport. Its Fire Combat Skid Unit body was by Toyne. It was equipped with chemical materials for firefighting. The extra space afforded by the cab extension could be used for firefighters or cargo. The K3500 was rated for a maximum GVW of 10,000 pounds. Its standard engine was the 190-horsepower 5.7-liter HD V-8 engine; options included the 230-horsepower 7.4-liter V-8 and the two diesels—6.2-liter and 6.5-liter turbo. The standard transmission was the five-speed manual overdrive; the four-speed overdrive automatic was the only option. *Dennis J. Maag*

Chevrolet offered three types of C/K chassis cabs in 1993. The first was the C/K3500 Series with parallel flattop frame rails and 34-inch spacing for ready installation of van, dump, stake, utility, and other commercial bodies. These trucks were offered on two wheelbase lengths—135.5 and 159.5 inches. Second was a C3500 HD (heavy-duty) straight rail model with dual rear wheels, a solid I-beam front axle with 5,000-pound capacity leaf springs, and a maximum GVW rating of 15,000 pounds. This was Chevrolet's Class 4 truck. These were offered on three wheelbase lengths—135.5, 159.5, and 183.5 inches. Third were the Regular-Cab chassis cab series C/K2500 and C/K3500 Series models that used the tapered frame of the C/K full-size pickup. This series was offered on three wheelbase lengths—131.5, 155.5, and 168.5 inches, the Regular Cab, Extended Cab, and Crew Cab frames. The Union (Franklin County, Missouri) Fire Department owned this 1993 Chevrolet K3500 dual rear wheel, chassis cab with firefighting body on tapered frame rails. It had a 175-gallon water tank and a 200-gpm pump. *Dennis J. Maag*

The 1993 Chevrolet Kodiak offered Caterpillar's 3116 engine with 200 and 275 horsepower ratings and the new Allison MD series electronic transmission designed to match up with the Caterpillar 3116 for ratings up to 250 horsepower. Former 3116 ratings offered for Kodiaks included 170, 185, 215, and 250 horsepower. The MD electronically controlled automatic transmission featured six-speed close ratio and six-speed wide ratio models. A Wabco supplemental exhaust brake was available with the Caterpillar 3116 engine and air brakes. Circuit breakers replaced fuses for 1993. This is a 1993 Kodiak C60 chassis cab with wrecker body. It was powered by the 3116 Cat engine and was mated to a five-speed manual transmission. The C60 was Chevrolet's smallest Kodiak; the Kodiak line consisted of Series C60 and C70 and tandem-axle C70.

Approximately 10 percent of all new full-size pickups sold in 1993 were W/T1500s. That translates to about 50,000 units, which means that management was on to a good thing when it introduced this high-value, low-priced work truck. You didn't have to be a hard hat to buy the W/T. The W/T was an excellent value and it didn't take long for buyers to figure that out. The base price of a W/T was only $14,485. When amenities such as air conditioning, stereo, wheel trim rings, and the PWT2 preferred-equipment package were added, the sticker price rose to $16,761, which was still a very good value. The 4.3-liter Vortec V-6 was standard equipment on the W/T. It put out 165 horsepower at 4,000 rpm and 235 foot-pounds torque at 2,000 rpm and achieved up to 20 miles per gallon fuel economy. Transmission options included the five-speed manual and GM's new electronic control 4L60-E Hydra-Matic automatic. Pictured here is a 1993 C1500 W/T; a K1500 W/T was also offered.

Chevrolet's W-Series tilt-cab chassis ranged from the small W4 to the biggest W7HV; the W5 and W6 were in between. The W4 was available with either gas or diesel power. The gas engine was Chevrolet's own 190-horsepower 5.7-liter V-8 producing 300 foot-pounds maximum torque. The diesel was the Isuzu-built 3.9-liter L4 turbo OHV, intercooled. It developed 135 horsepower and 255 foot-pounds maximum torque. The W4 gas-powered models carried a maximum GVW rating of 11,050 to 13,250 pounds. Diesel-powered models were rated for 11,050 to 14,250 pounds GVW. The gas model offered only GM's Hydra-Matic four-speed automatic with overdrive and lock-up converter, while the diesel model had both a five-speed overdrive manual and an electronic four-speed automatic with lock-up converter and PTO capability. *Iten Chevrolet*

An all-new truck for 1993 was this 3500 HD Van, which provided 10,100 to 14,500 pounds GVW ratings for commercial and recreational vehicles. Called the P-Cutaway Van HD Chassis, it was derived by marrying a chopped G-van cab to a P3500 chassis. Four wheelbase options included 125, 133, 157, and 178 inches. The Series was in two GVW ranges—10,100 to 12,000 pounds and 14,100 pounds. Engine options included the 180-horsepower 5.7-liter HD V-8 and the 230-horsepower 7.4-liter HD V-8; the only transmission was a four-speed HD overdrive automatic, electronically controlled. This is a 1993 Chevrolet P-Cutaway Van HD Chassis with ban body from an independent body builder. *Harold Chevrolet*

Chevrolet's school bus line in 1993 consisted of the B-Series chassis cowl with hydraulic brakes. Hydraulic brake–equipped buses carried a maximum GVW rating of 21,000 pounds on their 189-inch wheelbase chassis. The air brake model was diesel powered only. This model carried a maximum GVW rating of 24,000 pounds. The S-Series was a forward-control chassis only. Two models were offered: The 30,000 pounds GVW-rated chassis had hydraulic brakes and the other 30,000-pound model had air brakes and diesel power only. S-Series buses rode on a 170-inch wheelbase. Pictured here is a 1993 Chevrolet model number B6P042 school bus chassis cowl with diesel power. *Iten Chevrolet*

Have you seen a medium-duty truck with a better appearance than this? Appearance was important. It had been a major consideration of Chevrolet's management since the beginning. But it was only one reason a customer chose a Chevrolet medium. Power was another reason and Chevrolet shone brightly here, too. Chevrolet had the best gas engines in the industry—a 225-horsepower 6.0-liter V-8 and a 255-horsepower 7.0-liter V-8. In addition, Chevrolet had an exclusive agreement with Caterpillar for the Cat 3116 turbocharged air-to-air aftercooled midrange diesel engine. It pumped out from 170 to 275 horsepower and from 420 to 735 foot-pounds of torque and delivered excellent fuel economy. This is a 1993 Chevrolet C60 medium-duty chassis cab with contractor's dump body. *Iten Chevrolet*

Chevrolet's distinctive Lumina APV van was designed and engineered for people moving. With its middle and rear row of seats removed, it became a light-duty delivery truck, and offered 112.6 cubic feet of cargo space. This was by far more than any ordinary station wagon. The Lumina's sliding side door was a big plus for convenience and ease of loading. Its low, bumper-level load floor was another work saver. A front-mounted, FWD 3.1-liter 120-horsepower EFI V-6 engine was standard. A 170-horsepower 3.8-liter V-6 engine was an option. A three-speed automatic was required with the 3.1-liter V-6 engine and a four-speed automatic was required with the 3.8-liter V-6 engine. Wheelbase was 109.8 inches and maximum GVW rating was 5,126 pounds. *Welle's Southtown*

This neat little 1993 Chevrolet S-10 2WD short-box standard cab was a special offer for 1993. Customers could order a 2WD S-10 with manual transmission and Preferred Equipment Group 6 (including Tahoe trim) and they got the 2.8-liter V-6 at no extra cost. Or they could order a 4WD S-10 with standard 4.3-liter V-6, optional four-speed automatic overdrive transmission and they got a set of 15-inch cast-aluminum wheels at no extra cost. The woman who owns this S-10, seated in the truck, was 89 years old when this photo was taken. The pickup had only 30,000 miles registered at that time. Unfortunately, she has since given up driving, but she loved her S-10. *D. E. Short*

Chevrolet's Extended-Cab full-size pickups were winners. People vote with their pocketbooks, and they voted for Extended-Cabs. Chevrolet had three different Extended-Cab configurations: the 1/2-ton and 3/4-ton Fleetside short box; the 1/2-, 3/4-, and 1-ton Fleetside long box; and the 1/2-ton Sportside short box. All three were available as either 2WD or 4WD models. The 3/4-ton Extended-Cab with short box was a favorite with many working people. This truck could haul a heavy load of cargo and/or up to six passengers. Many found it to be the perfect solution for all their transportation needs. The Extended-Cab short box had a wheelbase 14 inches shorter than the Extended-Cab long box. Fourteen inches made a big difference in terms of turning diameters and maneuverability. This is a 1993 Chevrolet K2500 Extended-Cab short box. *Iten Chevrolet*

This is a very unusual truck. The highly desirable special models, especially a low production one like this, are almost always pampered. When photographed early in 1999, this Onyx Black 454 SS was in sad shape. It didn't have body damage, but it had been driven hard and received little or no care. The C1500 454 SS (Super Sport) was a 2WD street machine with selected body blackout effects, a Performance Handling Package, special-production B. F. Goodrich T/A P275/60R-15 blackwall tires, and the largest V-8 engine in any new 1/2-ton pickup. A Custom interior with comfortable high-back bucket seats was standard in the 454 SS. *Iten Chevrolet*

Chevrolet's 1993 van line consisted of the minivan Lumina APV, the mid-size Astro Passenger/Cargo Van, and the full-size Sportvan/Chevy Van passenger and cargo vans, respectively. Chevy Van models included G10, G20, G30, and G30 HD. The most popular model with converters was the 125-inch wheelbase like this G20 Chevy Van conversion. Conversion van's engine options included the base 4.3-liter V-6 and 5.0-, 5.7-, and 7.4-liter gas V-8s and the 6.2-liter diesel V-8. The only transmission available was the four-speed overdrive automatic. *Harold Chevrolet*

The smallest Tiltmaster model Chevrolet marketed in 1993 was the small but powerful W4 chassis cab. The balance of the line consisted of W5, W6, and W7 chassis cab models. Pictured is a W7 standard chassis cab with van body. Two W7 models were offered: W7HV was the standard chassis cab, and the W7T was a chassis cab specifically set up to be a tractor. W7HV was offered on five wheelbases: 142, 154, 181, 197, and 217 inches. Body lengths ranged from 12 to 22 feet. It was powered by a 6.5-liter turbo-intercooled Isuzu inline six-cylinder diesel. It produced 200 horsepower and 410 foot-pounds torque. The only transmission offered was the six-speed manual synchro. Power steering and full air brakes were standard. Tiltmaster's cab tilted up 45 degrees to allow plenty of working room for the mechanic.

Buyers could have their Astro Van in one of three basic ways: passenger, cargo, or conversion. Additionally, the Astro was available with 2WD or AWD and with a Regular- or Extended-Body. This is a 1993 Chevrolet Astro conversion van with AWD and Extended-Body. The Extended-Body added 10 inches behind its rear wheels. The standard engine for AWD Extended-Body Astro was the 200-horsepower 4.3-liter V-6 with CPI (Central-Port Fuel Injection). 2WD models were powered by the 165-horsepower 4.3-liter V-6 with EFI. The only transmission for Astros was the four-speed overdrive automatic. *Harold Chevrolet*

This is a very rare 1993 Chevrolet C2500 Extended-Cab short box. It has the LO5 5.7-liter V-8 and 4L60E automatic transmission, and a trailer towing package. It has Cheyenne trim, but is equipped with two-tone paint and body moldings, items normally seen on Silverado models. Its owner is Warren Egbert of Santa Monica, California. *Bob Bray*

1994

Improvements on the 1994 Astro were minimal, to say the least. They included new graphics on the analog instrument cluster, an optional leather-wrapped steering wheel, Scotchgard-protected carpet was standard as was a driver-side air bag. The Astro line continued to be the van line of "choices." Choices included 2WD and AWD models; Regular-Body and Extended-Body; panel rear doors and Astro Dutch doors; CS, CL, or LT trim; cargo, passenger, or conversion van; seat types, interior colors, exterior colors, and on it goes. Engine choices were limited. The 165-horsepower 4.3-liter V-6 was standard for 2WDs and the 200-horsepower 4.3-liter V-6 was an option. On the other hand, the 200-horsepower 4.3-liter V-6 was standard on AWDs. Pictured here are the 1994 Chevrolet AWD Extended-Body Astro LT (top) and Regular-Body 2WD Astro (bottom). *AAMA*

This was a wonderful year for the automotive industry, especially financially. Overall truck sales expanded from 33 percent of the U.S. market in 1989 to 39 percent in 1993, and were heading for a new record in 1994.

GM was dogged by a variety of start-up problems at the beginning of the model year's production run. In January, sales of light-duty trucks were up 24 percent over January 1993. In the same month, car sales rose by only 8 percent. Manufacturing scrambled to find ways to build more hot-selling pickups, SUVs, and vans. The challenge was how to get more production out of existing plants, rather than investing in new plants, which could become a financial liability if the market slowed down. GM's strategy was to run factories around the clock by adding third shifts at truck and van plants. These steps gave GM up to 200,000 more trucks a year.

GM enjoyed a record profit of $4.9 billion in 1994 compared to its former record of $4.856 billion in 1988. Total 1994 sales reached $155 billion versus $138 billion in 1993. For the first time in five years, GM passed out profit-sharing checks to hourly and salaried workers. Employees received $550 checks—not a great amount, but after five years without any, employees found the check most welcome.

The continuing battle with archrival Ford for market share came out as follows for 1994: Ford took 15.2 percent of the passenger car segment and 29.3 percent of the light-duty truck segment. Chevrolet took 11.2 percent and 23.8 percent, respectively.

For 1995, the CAFE standard for the Big Three was set at 27.5 miles per gallon; GM's overall CAFE was 27.4 miles per gallon.

In December of 1994, GM and the Department of Transportation reached an agreement relating to the 1973 to 1987 C/K pickup trucks with side-mounted fuel tanks, which allegedly were prone to fires during side crashes. GM agreed to pay $51.4 million to support safety programs on which GM and NHTSA would work together. Transportation Secretary Peña had threatened to require a recall of all the 1973 to 1987 pickups still in service.

Chevrolet posted increases in both light- and medium-duty truck sales in 1994, yet lagged behind the overall truck market in both segments: Its market share was down to 23.8 percent and 24.1 percent, respectively, from 1993 market shares of 24.4 percent and 24.6 percent.

Chevrolet's truck sales were held back due to parts shortage, slow start-ups of 1994 models, and production capacity restraints. Chevrolet's bright star was the new S-10 pickup, which actually picked up a .6 point of market share as its volume rose almost 37 percent to more than 67,000 units—193,722 in 1994 versus

167,421 in 1993. Total Chevrolet light-duty truck sales rose to 1,446,966 in 1994, compared to 1,309,879 in 1993. Medium-duty trucks increased from 11,896 in 1993 to 14,809 in 1994. The only models posting sales declines in 1994 were the Astro Wagon, Chevy Van, and Sportvan.

Chevrolet's new S-10 pickup made the transition from a utilitarian carrier to a comfortable passenger carrier. Chevrolet designers broke the mold and designed the new S10 from the inside out, rather than starting with a clay model and worrying about the interior afterwards. This time the customer came first, with a passenger cabin that provided optimum comfort and convenience, even after the rugged truck features were added around it. Leading-edge ergonomic considerations resulted in large, easy-to-reach controls, large gauges, and abundant storage space conveniently situated for both driver and passenger. Chevrolet claimed it had the "best-in-class interior room," and a quietness that rivaled many autos.

The frame was reinforced for greater stiffness, which allowed engineers to tune the suspension for a smoother ride. Buyers could choose between seven "chassis packages," each with different springs, shocks, and tires.

Small pickups provided a platform on which to build even higher-profit SUVs. The new S-10 Blazer built on the new pickup chassis would follow in a year.

Small pickups were also important because they attracted the young buyer, providing a good chance for repeat business. Truck buyers are loyal, and once they find a truck they like, they tend to stick with it.

All full-size C/K pickups, Blazer and Suburban, sported a new look for 1994, with restyled grilles and headlamps.

The Lumina APV was given an optional integral child seat. In addition, the second- and third-row modular seats folded fully upward and forward. Other changes included a restyled instrument panel and switches, an automatic door lock system, and a keyless entry system.

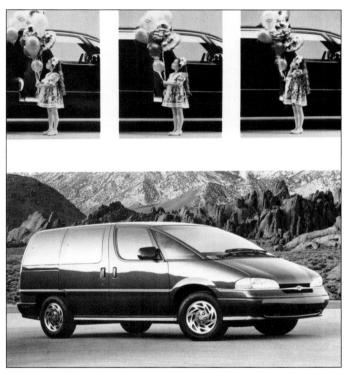

Chevrolet's other small van, the Lumina minivan, had a slightly revised appearance for 1994. Chevrolet designers chopped 2.7 inches off the front to modify the often-criticized "Dust Buster" look. Changes to the front end included a new bumper, hood, and grille. Inside, the Lumina's instrument panel was changed, and a driver-side air bag was added. Chevrolet designers added what they called "layering" of the upper panel cover to cut down on its apparent expanse, a function of the steeply raked windshield. Two built-in child seats were new options for 1994. A driver-side air bag was made standard. The optional power-operated side door was also new. A Lumina cargo minivan for commercial users returned for 1994. It had a maximum payload rating of 1,257 pounds, 115.4 cubic feet of cargo volume, and a maximum GVW of 5,126 pounds. Its powertrain was the same as the passenger Lumina's standard powertrain—3.1-liter 120-horsepower V-6 with EFI and a three-speed automatic transmission. *AAMA*

The S-10 Blazer was scheduled to have a total redesign for 1995. For that reason, changes and improvements for 1994 were held to a minimum. The few changes included the following: a 60/40 split bench seat with cup holders, intermittent wipers, and a longer-life generator were standard equipment. A tilt steering wheel with cruise control was an option. The front-end design, which was new in 1993, carried over without change. The 1994 S-10 Blazer line continued with two- and four-door models and 2WD and 4WD versions for both. Wheelbases were 100.5 and 107 inches for the two- and four-door models, respectively. Two drivetrains for S-10 Blazers included the optional for all Series 200-horsepower 4.3-liter Vortec V-6 with CPI with a four-speed automatic transmission and the standard for all Series 165-horsepower 4.3-liter V-6 with EFI with manual transmission. Pictured is a 1994 Chevrolet S-Blazer Tahoe two-door with 2WD (top) and S-Blazer LT 4WD two-door (bottom). *AAMA*

Chevrolet's completely redesigned S-10 pickup went on sale late in August 1993 as a 1994 model. Chevrolet's small pickup was important to the Division and to GM. Light-duty trucks were key to GM for their absolute volume of sales and for the profit dollars they generated. Chevrolet was GM's number one truck merchandiser. In 1994, Chevrolet sold a total of 1,461,775 trucks and only 1,004,157 cars. Total sales of cars and trucks by Chevrolet represented 49 percent of GM's total unit sales of cars and trucks in 1994. S-10 pickup sales totaled 251,000 for the year. The new S-10 pickup was a winner in every respect. Its interior was roomier, a full 3 inches wider than the former truck, and fractionally taller and longer. The optional reclining seat actually had room to recline. A little more space in these formerly tiny compact truck cabs made a big improvement. New S-10 pickups were (front to back): the off-road ZR2 4WD, an Extended-Cab 4WD, the new Super Sport (SS) 2WD performance option, the 2WD in LS trim with a long box, and the base pickup. *AAMA*

One of Chevrolet's toughest, hardest-working pickups was the K2500 Fleetside Extended-Cab with the 8-foot cargo box. The wheelbase length of this big pickup was a full 155.5 inches. Its maximum GVW rating was 8,600 pounds and its payload rating was an impressive 3,444 pounds. This pickup was owned by the City of Seattle Fire Department. It was an "air mask unit." Its black wheels give it a no-nonsense appearance. Typically, firefighters prefer their trucks well dressed up with chrome and other appearance-enhancing items. Its engine is the 200-horsepower 5.7-liter V-8 with the electronically controlled four-speed overdrive automatic. The New Process 241 two-speed transfer case was standard. *Bill Hattersley*

The best pickup Chevrolet ever built was even better in 1994. Improvements were mostly aesthetic. Chevrolet designers gave the C/K pickups a fresh new front appearance with a new grille and headlamp design. The new look was clean, functional, and refreshing. A prominent chrome bar split the grille horizontally and displayed the famous Chevrolet bow tie trademark in its center. This is a top-selling 1994 Chevrolet K1500 Extended Cab 4WD pickup. Chevrolet offered this truck in either a 1/2-ton, as pictured, or a 3/4-ton, and with 2WD or 4WD. Its wheelbase length was 141.5 inches. Buyers could choose from two GVW ratings—6,200 or 6,800 pounds. Chevrolet split its Power Team Availability into two groups—for trucks with less than 8,600-pound GVWs and trucks with GVWs of 8,600 pounds and above. Engine offerings for the lighter group included the 4.3-, 5.0-, and 5.7-liter gas engines and the 6.5-liter diesel V-8 with and without a turbocharger. Engine offerings for the higher group included the 4.3-, 5.7-, and 7.4-liter gas engines, and the 6.5-liter diesel V-8 with turbocharger. *AAMA*

Chevrolet's Sportside Sport continued to be a good seller. It was a truck for those who wanted to be noticed. On the other hand, it could work, for under its beauty was a tough Chevrolet truck. Sportside, of course, is a reference to its modern fender-side cargo box. The smooth lines of the right rear fender can be clearly seen in the photo of this 1994 Chevrolet K1500 Sportside Sport pickup. This sporty truck was only offered with a short box, but in both 2WD and 4WD configurations. It was offered only in Onyx Black, Teal Green Metallic, or Victory Red exterior colors, with matching bumpers and mirrors, and with its new-design grille. The attractive aluminum wheels were standard equipment. The 2WD model offered an optional Sport Handling Package with special springs and Bilstein gas shocks. The Z71 Off-Road Package was offered with 4WD Sportside Sport. The Z71 package included skid plates, Bilstein high-pressure gas shocks, and "Z71" graphics. *AAMA*

Chevrolet's 1994 commercial truck line featured two cutaways and a chassis-only unit. The biggest seller was the G-Cutaway, a derivative of the G-van series. These units sold well to the camper industry and to outside independent body companies for mounting of hi-cube–type commercial van bodies. This is a 1994 G-cutaway with Passport model camper body from Cobra. Chevrolet supplied only the front section of this unit with a flat platform behind the front section. This vehicle didn't have the usual truck-type parallel frame rails. Chevrolet offered it in two wheelbases: 125 and 146 inches with standard single rear wheels or optional dual rear wheels. They featured big load-carrying capacities with GVWs ranging from 9,200 to 10,500 pounds. The 190-horsepower 5.7-liter gas engine was standard, and the 230-horsepower 7.4-liter gas engine and the 160-horsepower 6.5-liter diesel V-8 were options. *Iten Chevrolet*

Chevrolet's tough mid-size Astro van was popular with America's businessmen for commercial jobs. Chevrolet's entire 1994 commercial van line consisted of this midsize Astro Cargo van, plus the Lumina Cargo minivan and the full-size Chevy Van and Sportvan. The Astro Cargo was available in 2WD and AWD and in Regular-Body or Extended-Body versions. Wheelbase length for both sizes was 111 inches. The 4.3-liter 165-horsepower V-6 was the only engine offered. The only transmission was the four-speed overdrive electronically controlled automatic with brake interlock. Maximum GVW rating was 5,600 pounds; maximum payload rating was 1,922 pounds.

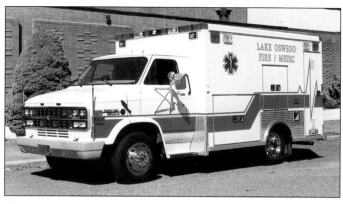

The P-cutaway HD van was a combination of the G30 cab combined with the load-carrying capacities of the forward-control P-chassis with a truck-type parallel ladder-type frame. Wheelbases of 125, 133, 157, and 178 inches were standard offerings, with GVW ratings of 10,100, 11,000, 12,000, 14,100, and 14,500 pounds. The Lake Oswego, Oregon, Fire Department used this 1994 Chevrolet P-30 cutaway HD van with firefighting body. The department's Medic Squad used it. Its body was by Braun NW. The standard 190-horsepower 5.7-liter V-8 engine powered this unit. The standard (and only) transmission offered for P-cutaways was the four-speed, overdrive electronically controlled unit. *Bill Hattersley*

Chevrolet also sold full-size and S-Blazers and Suburbans for commercial use. Suburban was a very popular transportation choice with American companies. One cogent reason for their popularity was due to the Suburban's handsome appearance. A second reason was because Suburbans were the "in" thing. This unique vehicle was a truck, a wagon, and a passenger vehicle. The Suburban did it all. It featured up to 149.5 cubic feet of interior space (with optional rear seat removed and optional center seat folded flat). Up to 10,000 pounds of towing capacity was available. Seating accommodation for up to nine persons was also available. In all Suburban models, the standard engine was the 5.7-liter V-8 with EFI. The only transmission offered in all models was the four-speed, overdrive, electronically controlled automatic. *Iten Chevrolet*

The entire Chevrolet chassis cab line for 1994 was the same as that of 1993. It consisted of the C/K2500 HD 3/4-ton with regular frame and straight frame, C/K 3500 with straight frame, and C3500 HD with straight frame. The 2500 series had a maximum GVW of 8,600 pounds; the C/K3500 had a maximum of 11,000 pounds for the C-models and 12,000 pounds for K-models. The C3500 HD was at 15,000 pounds. The Hualapai Valley Fire Department (Kingman, Arizona) owned this 1994 Chevrolet K3500 chassis cab with regular frame and firefighting body. Brush truck No. 1's body was by Phoenix and it was equipped to fight fires with both water and foam. Its maximum GVW rating of 11,000 pounds was carried on its 131.5-inch-wheelbase frame. The standard drivetrain was the 190-horsepower HD 5.7-liter V-8 and a five-speed heavy-duty overdrive manual transmission. *Garry E. Kadzielawski*

Chevrolet's C3500 HD chassis cab was technically a medium-duty Class 4 truck. Chevrolet counted its production with pickups. A 4WD model was not offered. The C3500 HD had a 15,000-pound maximum GVW rating and a solid I-beam, 5,000-pound capacity front axle/leaf spring front suspension. Frames were all straight rail with dual wheels and parallel, flattop frame rails with 34-inch standard spacing to make mounting bodies quick and inexpensive. These trucks are easily spotted by the filler piece between the grille and bumper, the 19.5x6.0 wheels and 225/70R-19.5F tires. Payload range was from 8,475 to 9,334 pounds. This is a 1994 Chevrolet C3500 HD chassis cab with platform body. The standard drivetrain included the 5.7-liter HD 190-horsepower V-8 engine and five-speed heavy-duty overdrive manual transmission. *Harold Chevrolet*

Chevrolet's medium-duty trucks sold well in 1994, posting a 25 percent increase over 1993. The line continued to consist of Series C60-C70 and C70 tandems. This 1994 Chevrolet C60 chassis cab with platform body was powered by the Caterpillar 3116 (6.6-liter) diesel with turbocharger, air-to-air aftercooled. The various standard models ranged in horsepower outputs from 170 to 275 and from 420 to 735 foot-pounds of torque. Chevrolet had an exclusive deal with Caterpillar for sole rights to use the 3116 engine in a medium-duty truck. Fourteen wheelbase-length chassis cab models were available, eight with the LoPro option. GM also offered two gasoline engines for the medium-duty trucks. One was a 6-liter (366-ci) engine, which delivered 340 foot-pounds torque at 2,800 rpm and 225 horsepower at 4,000 rpm. The other was the 7-liter (427-ci) engine, which delivered 400 foot-pounds torque at 2,800 rpm and 255-horsepower at 3,800 rpm.

This is a 1994 Chevrolet C60 series Kodiak medium-duty chassis cab with a firefighting body. Truck No. 7999 was owned by the McDonnell-Douglas Co. of St. Louis, Missouri, and was used in Fire Service. The Fire-Rescue body was built by EVF. It was designed and equipped to deal with hazardous materials in a confined space. The standard 6.0-liter, 225-horsepower V-8 engine powered this fire truck. Transmission choices included Allison MD automatics and Eaton Fuller manual transmissions. The Eaton Fuller manuals used Eaton Roadranger synthetic lubricants. The first change came at five years or 250,000 miles, reducing off-road maintenance time and life-cycle costs. The industry's premier Bostrom suspension bucket seats were also available. They included a high-back air seat with fabric upholstery, low-back air suspension with fabric upholstery, and Viking II mechanical suspension seat in black vinyl. *Dennis J. Maag*

The front view of this 1994 Chevrolet K30 Crew Cab Fleetside long-box Big Dooley pickup makes it look as long as a football field. That's a bit of an exaggeration, of course, but the reality is that its wheelbase is 14 feet long and its overall length is almost 21 feet! For many owners this was the tow vehicle. In fact, it was hooked up to a good-sized trailer when photographed in the summer of 1998. Its maximum GVW rating was 10,000 pounds and its maximum payload rating was 3,980 pounds. A frame-mounted, weight-distributing hitch and sway bar were recommended. A trailer weighing more than 1,000 pounds loaded must have its own brakes. The 7.4-liter engine produced 230 horsepower and 385 foot-pounds torque.

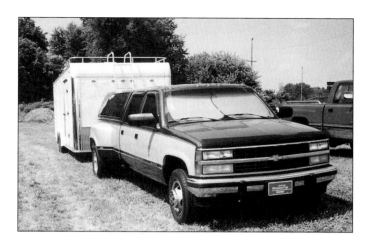

1995

G M enjoyed another good financial year in 1995 with sales topping off at $169 billion and a net income of $6.93 billion. Worldwide, GM sold 8.6 million vehicles and employed 709,000 workers.

Taking a cue from Chrysler and Ford, GM streamlined the way it designed, engineered, and sold cars and trucks. In October, after more than a year of intensive work, the company named 13 Vehicle Line Executives (VLEs) who would lead the new process.

Under the new system, one powerful manufacturing leader took a vehicle from the CAD/CAM (Computer Aided Design/

Computer Aided Manufacturing) terminal through final production. The new process was aimed at reducing infighting between disciplines among GM's seven marketing divisions. The VLEs reported to one of three leaders—mid-size and luxury cars, small cars, and trucks. The truck leader was Clifford J. Vaughan. The VLEs worked closely with a team that included a vehicle chief engineer and a brand manager. The 35 brand managers, approximately one for every model GM makes, established the marketing image of each vehicle and consistently reinforced that image through advertising.

Entering 1995, GM was still strapped for plant capacity for its truck production. GM's management moved to stop building its line of big rear-wheel-drive cars—Cadillac Fleetwood, Chevrolet

Chevrolet's 1995 cargo van offerings included the Lumina Cargo Minivan and progressed up from there. The next step was the midsize Astro Cargo Van. The largest vans were the Chevy Van and Sportvan twins. Chevrolet had more models to choose from than any manufacturer and had a size to fit every job. The Astro Cargo was available in 2WD configuration and in Extended-Body only. In previous years, the Astro Cargo was offered in both Regular and Extended-Body lengths and in 2WD and AWD configurations. This is a 1995 Chevrolet 2WD Extended-Body Astro Cargo. Maximum GVW rating was 5,600 pounds and maximum payload rating was 1,986 pounds. The Astro's standard and only engine was the 190-horsepower 4.3-liter V-6 with CPI. And its only transmission was the four-speed electronically controlled overdrive automatic. The Astro Cargo could carry a full 170.4 cubic feet of cargo and tow up to 5,500 pounds. Its frontal styling was new for 1995. *Iten Chevrolet*

Chevrolet's S-Blazer was all new for 1995. It had been restyled, reengineered, and revitalized into a fresh new vehicle. At last the name confusion between the "small" Blazer and the "big" Blazer was over. The small one was now simply the Blazer. The big one's name was changed to Tahoe. But there was both a two-door and a four-door Tahoe. The Blazer was offered in two-door and four-door and in 2WD and 4WD forms. As with the new S-10 pickup, the Blazer was designed from the inside out, to provide a roomy and useful interior. The Blazer was a key vehicle at Chevrolet. Compact SUVs were hot-selling, profitable vehicles. For the sake of the Division and GM, this new Blazer had to do well. Chevrolet engineers and designers hit a home run with the second-generation compact SUV. Interior design, exterior design, ride, comfort, amenities, quality, options, power—the Blazer had it all. *AAMA*

Chevrolet's interesting and exclusive P-Cutaway Van HD chassis returned for its second year. Four Models constituted the P-Cutaway Van HD series: 125-, 133-, 157-, and 178-inch wheelbases. All models were rated as P30s in two weight classifications—10,100 to 12,000 pounds and 14,100 pounds. This is a 1995 Chevrolet P-Cutaway Van HD chassis with van body from an independent supplier. The standard engine was the 180-horsepower 5.7-liter HD V-8; the 230-horsepower 7.4-liter HD V-8 was optional. The only transmission available was the four-speed heavy-duty overdrive electronically controlled automatic transmission with brake/transmission shift interlock.

Converting Chevy Vans into customized cruisers by changing a plain van into a specialized and personalized recreational vehicle was big business. This was good business for Chevrolet and van converters. No other vehicle priced so low offered the size and comfort of a converted van. Another major benefit of the conversion van was its tremendous towing ability. When equipped with the correct equipment, the G30 van was rated for a maximum GCW of 17,000 pounds (7.4-liter 230-horsepower engine and an electronically controlled four-speed automatic). This is a 1995 Chevrolet G20 Chevy Van converted by an independent supplier. *Harold Chevrolet*

Chevrolet's G-Cutaway Van chassis was a dual-purpose vehicle. The Chevy Van 30 Cutaway consisted of a G30 cab cut away just to the rear of the doors and a flat platform. The back of the cab was open to allow driver access to the body. Chevrolet sold this unit to two industries: motor-home manufacturers and independent body suppliers for special commercial bodies. Two wheelbase lengths were available—125 and 146 inches. Maximum GVW ratings based on the two wheelbase lengths were: 9,200–10,000 pounds for the 125-inch and 9,200–10,500 pounds for the 146-inch. The standard engine was the 180-horsepower 5.7-liter HD V-8, optional were the 230-horsepower HD V-8 and the 160-horsepower 6.5-liter diesel V-8. The only transmission was the four-speed heavy-duty overdrive automatic electronically controlled. Pictured here is a 1995 Chevrolet G30 Cutaway Van chassis with a Jamboree motor home by Searcher. *Iten Chevrolet*

This 1995 Chevrolet C1500 pickup paced the Brickyard 400 Race at the Indianapolis Motor Speedway on August 5, 1995. The 2WD specially prepared pickup had the new Vortec 5.0-liter V-8 with dual exhaust and a 4L60E automatic transmission. This was the first time ever for a Brickyard Pace Truck. It led the NASCAR stock cars around the track at speeds of over 120 miles per hour. A stock L30 Vortec 5000 V-8 engine powered the Pace Truck. The only change from a stock powertrain was the rear axle: a 4.10:1 ratio replaced the stock 3.73:1 ratio. The reason was to give the truck an extra boost when it had to accelerate away from the field. However, the chassis was modified by dropping the center of gravity by 4 inches in the rear and 2 1/2 inches in front. A Bell Tech 33mm stabilizer was installed in front along with Bell Tech one-ton front springs and stock Bilstein shocks. The rear suspension was left stock. *AAMA*

Caprice, and Buick Roadmaster—by the end of 1996 at its Arlington, Texas, plant. This plant was to be converted for pickup and SUV production.

New in April 1995 was the enormously popular Chevrolet Tahoe. This new vehicle gave SUV buyers a four-door choice between the shorter wheelbase two-door Blazer and the huge, long-wheelbase four-door Suburban.

GM's first quarter 1995 was the most profitable in its history, posting a profit of a tidy $1.5 billion. In April, R. L. Zarrella, group executive for North American sales, service, and marketing, outlined his brand management strategy by identifying 35 customer needs. The brand managers would have unprecedented power to decide how to spend advertising money on each vehicle. As an incentive, their compensation was tied to the vehicle's profitability.

GM's earnings in the second quarter set yet another new record of $2.27 billion. During this quarter, Chevrolet began building the two-door Tahoe at its new truck plant in Silao, Mexico, in May. It was in October that GM rolled out its new VLE organization of 13 SVEs, who were to control all facets of vehicle development. There were 35 brand managers in charge of coordinating marketing.

During the same quarter, GM's Chairman John Smale announced in December that he would step down in January 1996. He turned the Chairman's position over to Jack Smith, who had directed GM's resurgence during the past three years as its president and CEO.

The board further promoted Harry Pearce, one of four executive vice presidents, to vice chairman. Pearce also took a seat on the board.

The industry had another good year in 1995 with total sales of cars and trucks topping off at 11,975,000 vehicles, down only 2.2 percent from 1994. Truck output totaled 5,635,000 or nearly even with 1994's total. Trucks captured 47.1 percent of the U.S. production total versus 46.1 percent in 1994. Over the last five years, truck production had grown an average of 2 percent each year. During the five years ending in 1995, SUV production rose an average

Quite possibly the best-selling Chevrolet pickup for personal transportation was the handsome and handy C/K1500 Extended-Cab short-box pickup. It offered seating for up to six or an enclosed, protected, and lockable storage area for important personal or valuable items. New features for 1995 C/K pickups included standard four-wheel ABS, a restyled interior complete with driver-side air bag (on models less than 8,500 pounds GVW ratings), more-comfortable seats, and improved sound systems. Chevrolet designer's instrument panel improvements included standard auxiliary electric power ports, redesigned full-size heater and radio controls with improved ergonomics that could be easily used even when wearing work gloves. The new four-spoke steering wheel housed the driver-side air bag. Pictured is a 1995 K1500 Silverado Extended-Cab short-box pickup with the Z71 option. *Verne Byers*

Chevy Van's line for 1995 consisted of Series G10, G20, G30, G30/6CP, and G30/CPW. The last two series were optional heavy-duty-chassis equipment packages (optional equipment items for increasing GVW and payload ratings). This is a 1995 Chevrolet G30/C6W 146-inch wheelbase Extended Chevy Van. This model was built to contain 306 cubic feet of cargo space and a maximum GVW rating of up to 9,200 pounds. The G30 was also available on a 125-inch wheelbase and the G20 Series was offered with the 125-inch wheelbase and on the 110-inch wheelbase. Some of the standard equipment required for this van's 9,200-pound GVW included 5.7-liter 180-horsepower HD V-8 engine, optional 7.4-liter 230-horsepower HD V-8 engine, and 6.5-liter HD 160-horsepower diesel V-8 engine. There was the standard four-speed heavy-duty overdrive electronically controlled automatic transmission with brake/transmission shift interlock, 4,000-pound front axle and front springs and 6,000-pound rear axle and springs. It had 16.5-inch wheels with LT225/75R-16E all-season radial tires. *Harold Chevrolet*

Chevrolet's sporty pickup offerings had cooled off by 1995 when only one special sport model was a standard offering, the Sportside Sport, a regular Sportside with either a standard cab or an Extended-Cab, which was standard, too. Both versions were only offered with the short box. This is a 1995 C1500 Chevrolet regular cab Sportside short-box pickup. Visually the greatest difference between a Sportside and a Sportside Sport was in its front-end paint scheme—the SS Sport's grille and front bumper were painted body color. The overall paint scheme worked well in giving the Sport a unified, sleek appearance. The Sportside's narrow cargo box with simulated rear fenders captured the classic appearance of Chevrolet's former sporty Stepside models. The Sportside Sport got its get-up-and-go from its optional 5.7-liter V-8 engine. A 4WD version was also available; the Z71 Off-Road Package was an option. The Z71 Off-Road Package contained skid plates and Bilstein high-pressure gas-charged shocks. "Z71" box side graphics were deleted on the Sportside Sport.

This 1995 Chevrolet K3500 standard cab Fleetside pickup is a relatively rare truck. Most 1-ton pickups sold in 1995 left the factory with dual rear wheels. Its electric contractor owner had it rigged out with a rack for ladders and long items plus aluminum utility storage boxes. The standard engine for the K3500 pickup was the 180-horsepower HD 5.7-liter V-8, options included the 230-horsepower 7.4-liter V-8 and the 190-horsepower 6.5-liter HD turbocharged diesel. The standard transmission was the five-speed heavy-duty overdrive manual, and optional was the four-speed overdrive automatic. Its maximum GVW rating was 9,200 pounds. This heavy-duty pickup rode on 16.0x6.5 wheels with LT245/75R-16E all-season radial tires. *Iten Chevrolet*

Another tough, solid, hard-working commercial truck was Chevrolet's K2500 chassis cab with a utility body. Its maximum GVW rating was 8,600 pounds and maximum payload rating was 2,853 pounds. The 131.5-inch wheelbase 3/4-ton chassis cab could accommodate special bodies up to 8 feet. The K2500's standard engine was the 180-horsepower 5.7-liter HD V-8; optional engines included the 230-horsepower HD 7.4-liter V-8 and the 190-horsepower 6.5-liter HD V-8 turbo-diesel. The standard transmission was the five-speed heavy-duty overdrive manual, and optional was the four-speed heavy-duty electronically controlled automatic with brake/transmission shift interlock. Standard transfer case was the two-speed NP 241. *Iten Chevrolet*

After a run of 25 years, one of America's favorite trucks was no more. Actually, it was still around, only its name had changed. Chevrolet's full-size SUV had its first name change since its inception in 1969. Other than the name, the two-door Tahoe was the same wonderful short-wheelbase SUV America first fell in love with in 1969. It seated five in luxury and was as at home on the freeway as it was off-road. Chevrolet only offered it as a 4WD vehicle. The top-of-the-line Tahoe Silverado was downright luxurious. With a 111.5-inch wheelbase, the two-door Tahoe was long enough for comfortable highway cruising and short enough for the dedicated off-roader. *Iten Chevrolet*

The four-door Tahoe was a shortened Suburban. It was 20.4 inches shorter, yet its height and width were the same. Chevrolet's marketing research had disclosed that many Suburban buyers bought because it was their only choice. Subjects in Chevrolet's research group said they wanted seating for up to six and cargo space like the Suburban, but not the Suburban's great length. Specifically what they wanted were four doors, plenty of ground clearance, towing capacity, good visibility, maneuverability, and interior conveniences. They were willing to pay $30,000 for it. Chevrolet designers started with the Tahoe and added 6 inches to the frame to accommodate the second pair of doors, back-seat legroom and cargo space. The four-door Tahoe was built on the full-size short-bed pickup frame and had a 117.5-inch wheelbase and an overall length of 199.1 inches. Cargo space ranged from 70.3 cubic feet behind the second seat to 122.5 cubic feet with the 60/40 split back seat folded. The Tahoe's drivetrain consisted of the 5.7-liter V-8 coupled to a heavy-duty electronically controlled four-speed automatic transmission. *AAMA*

The world's biggest SUV title remained with Chevrolet's Suburban again for 1995. Chevrolet's marketing team preferred the term "Super-Wagon," which fit exactly. An owner could pack in up to 48.5 cubic feet of stuff (with optional rear seat removed and center seat folded), or tow up to 10,000 pounds. Nine passengers could be comfortably accommodated. Since its beginning, the Suburban was a multi-purpose truck. It served well in commerce and for personal transportation. This 1995 Chevrolet C1500 Suburban with special graphics, running boards, and interior modifications was probably not destined for commercial use. GranPrix, a regional converter of vans, pickups, Suburbans, and other SUVs, had modified it. The 1995 Suburban's featured a standard driver-side air bag and four-wheel ABS. Its power came from a 5.7-liter V-8, a 7.4-liter V-8, or the 6.5-liter HD V-8 turbo-diesel.

Chevrolet's 1995 chassis cab line consisted of the C/K regular and Extended-Cab, C3500 HD regular cab only, and C/K Crew-Cab. This 1995 Chevrolet C3500 HD chassis cab with platform is easy to spot because of its 19.5-inch wheels and filler piece between its bumper and standard grille. It was only offered as a 2WD truck. Chevrolet's other Class 4 truck was offered on three standard wheelbase lengths: 135.5, 159.5, and 183.5 inches. The C3500 HD's heavy-duty components included a 5,000-pound front I-beam axle with leaf springs, parallel straight-rail frames with 34-inch spacing and an 11,000-pound-rated rear axle. Standard engine was the 230-horsepower 7.4-liter gas V-8, and optional was the 6.5-liter V-8 turbo-diesel. Maximum GVW rating was 15,000 pounds and maximum payload rating was 9,347 pounds. C3500 HD featured for 1995 a new cab interior, a standard driver-side air bag, and standard four-wheel ABS. *Iten Chevrolet*

A customer shopping for a truck could find the 1995 Chevrolet W4 LCF truck for sale at three dealerships: Isuzu, GMC, and Chevrolet. The 1995 featured a new frame design, easier body mounting, improved durability, and relocation of both the fuel tank and battery box. Its rear wheels featured a 5-inch wider track for greater stability. The W4's also had a more comfortable ride and improved handling due to the use of longer front and rear springs. A new deep-section, straight-channel rail that increased the frame width to 33.5 inches to allow for standardized body installations strengthened the frame. The 10–18 foot bodies had GVW ratings of up to 14,250 pounds. Gas-powered models had the 5.7-liter V-8. Also new was a MXA5D transmission with stronger gears and greater PTO gear torque output and an optional four-speed overdrive automatic with lockup converter for diesel models. *Iten Chevrolet*

Chevrolet's C/K 3500 chassis cab came out of the factory ready for serious work. It featured GVW ratings up to 11,000 pounds (2WD) and 12,000 pounds (4WD), and maximum payload ratings up to 6,588 pounds for the 4WD model. This heavy-duty 1-ton used the HD 5.7-liter 180-horsepower V-8 for standard power and the 7.4-liter HD 230-horsepower V-8 and the 190-horsepower turbo-diesel 6.5-liter V-8 as options. The 7.4 gas and 6.5-liter diesel each offered a stump-pulling maximum 385 foot-pound torque rating. Also available in the chassis cab series was the 2500 3/4-ton in 2WD and 4WD versions and the 3500 1-ton series with straight frame rails in 2WD and 4WD versions. Pictured is a 1995 Chevrolet K3500 standard chassis cab with firefighting body. The Upper Colorado River Interagency Fire Management owned Engine 608. The U.S. Forest Service used it at White River National Forest in Garfield County for brush fire work. *Dennis J. Maag*

The Crew-Cab chassis cab was a truck that could move two loads: a crew of workers and a load in whatever special body the buyer chose. Special bodies ran the gamut including stake, platform, tank, dump, utility, or firefighting. Buyers could choose single or dual rear wheels and 2WD or 4WD models. Maximum GVW rating was 10,000 pounds for both 2WD and 4WD. The maximum payload rating for the 2WD was 4,833, but for 4WD it was only 3,194. The standard engine was the 180-horsepower 5.7-liter HD V-8; options included the 230-horsepower 7.4-liter HD V-8 and the 190-horsepower 6.5-liter HD turbo-diesel V-8. The five-speed manual HD overdrive transmission was standard and the four-speed HD overdrive electronically controlled automatic was the only option. The Boise, Idaho, Airport Fire Department owned Truck No. 7, a 1995 Chevrolet K3500 Crew Cab chassis cab. Its body was a 1988 model Knapheide utility. *Boatwright*

For 1995, Chevrolet's Kodiak Conventionals, when equipped with optional air brakes, came standard with Bendix ABS on all wheels. Chassis changes included an optional Hendrickson 19,000-pound rear air suspension and two Eaton single-drive axles at 26,000 and 30,000 pounds. The Eaton Fuller five- and six-speed transmissions were refined to make shifting easier. Kodiak cab interiors had new fabric and vinyl upholsteries. The optional driver suspension seat was changed from a mechanical design to National's Easy-Aire. This is a 1995 Chevrolet C60 Kodiak chassis cab with van body. Chevrolet continued to offer two gas-fueled medium-duty truck engines: 6.0-liter EFI V-8 and 7.0-liter 427 EFI V-8. Their horsepower ratings were 210 and 235 and torque ratings were 325 and 385 foot-pounds, respectively. *Iten Chevrolet*

of 16 percent annually. Chrysler lost a bit of its minivan volume due to changing over to an all-new generation of minivans. If it wasn't for this fact, the truck industry may well have posted a small increase over 1994 instead of a slight loss. The total for truck sales in 1995 was 5,634,724, versus 5,648,767 in 1994—a mere 14,043-unit shortfall! Chevrolet's total truck sales for 1995 were 1,428,885 versus 1,461,775 in 1994. Medium-duty truck sales topped off at 15,633 compared to 14,809 in 1994.

Chevrolet's major new model introduction for 1995 was the S-Blazer. It was renamed simply the Blazer because the full-size Tahoe was offered as either a two-door or four-door SUV. The new Blazer was built on the S-10 platform, which was new in 1994. It was offered in 2WD and 4WD versions with either two doors or four doors. The Blazer's biggest appeal was its handsome, contemporary, aerodynamic body styling. Other important features included a driver-side air bag, a new dash, and 2 cubic feet more cargo room with the spare tire relocated to under the rear floor area. Sticker price of this vehicle when well equipped was about $26,000.

The standard powertrain consisted of the 4.3-liter CPI L35 V-6 engine and 4L60-E four-speed electronic automatic transmission. Later in the year, the two-door came standard with an NVG 3500 five-speed transmission. NVG stands for the New Venture Gear Co. (formerly the New Process Co.), a transmission and transfer case manufacturer jointly owned by Chrysler and GM.

For 1995, Chevrolet's Kodiak medium-duties, when equipped with optional air brakes, came standard with Bendix anti-lock brakes on all wheels. Chassis changes included a Hendrickson 19,000-pound rear air suspension as an option, and two high-capacity Eaton single-drive axles of 26,000- and 30,000-pound capacities. These options took the Kodiak out of the medium-duty category and put it into the Class 8 heavy-duty range.

Chevrolet's own gasoline 350, 366, 427, and 454-ci V-8 engines had catalytic converters, as did the Cat 3116 diesel.

The C/K trucks were given a redesigned and much improved dash and instrument cluster this year. Also, four-wheel anti-lock brakes were made standard in all full size light-duty trucks.

School bus chassis continued to be a part of Chevrolet's medium-duty truck business in the 1990s as they always had been. Once again, a shortage of product hampered sales is this market. Chevrolet only provided the chassis cowl, but even so, production restraints held school bus production down. Two school bus chassis series were offered. One was the "B" Series 4x2 chassis cowl with gas or diesel power, a 189-inch wheelbase and with either hydraulic or air brakes and 21,000 or 24,000 GVWs. The other was the "S" Series 4x2 forward-control school bus chassis with either gas or diesel power, 30,000 pounds GVW, a 170-inch wheelbase, and either hydraulic or air brakes. This is a 1995 Chevrolet 189-inch wheelbase B-Series school bus chassis cowl with diesel power and air brakes. *Iten Chevrolet*

Sales of medium-duty Chevrolet trucks in 1995 totaled 14,809 units. This represented a 24-percent increase from 1994, but only 1 percent of total Chevrolet truck sales. For only 1 percent of sales was it worth it? Remember that medium-duty truck engineering and manufacturing was the responsibility of the GMC Division, and in turn, Chevrolet was responsible for engineering and manufacturing all light-duty trucks. Medium Chevrolets were badge-engineered GMCs, and light-duty GMCs were badge-engineered light-duty Chevrolets. During the last half of the decade of the 1990s, GM did not have the production capacity to produce all the mediums the market would buy. All mediums were built in the Janesville, Wisconsin, plant. Management was reluctant to expand plant capacity or add shifts. They seemed to be content to live with a one- or two-year waiting period for new trucks. One in four medium-duty trucks coming down the line received a Chevrolet name badge. This 1995 Chevrolet Kodiak chassis cab with a contractor's body was powered by the Caterpillar 3116 diesel. *Iten Chevrolet*

Southern California Gas Company owns this 1995 Chevrolet C2500. It has the LO5 TBI 5.7-liter V-8 and a 4L60I automatic transmission and Cheyenne trim. This truck is the company's standard customer service unit. It is equipped with C-Tech side toolboxes and ladder racks. It also has the KL5 natural-gas engine option, a requirement for engines converted to run on CNG. *Bob Bray*

The newest 1995 Blazer was in reality an old Blazer. The original, compact SUV was a two-door. In 1995, Chevrolet introduced an all-new two-door Blazer. This two-door had some style and pizzazz to it. Note how the sleek roof pillars provide a "coupe" look. It was pleasing to look at and fun to drive. Chevrolet offered two-door Blazer in 2WD or 4WD configurations. It also had the optional Touring Suspension, which was a superb driver-oriented package for making driving fun and hard cornering easy. For those owners who were serious about four-wheeling off-road, the Blazer's firm and rugged 4x4 Off-Road Suspension was mandatory. Standard 4WD drivetrain consisted of the 4.3-liter Vortec V-6 engine and automatic transmission; a manual transmission was offered only in the two-door. *Iten Chevrolet*

This is the engine of the Southern California Gas Company C2500. It is a "bi-fuel" type conversion. It can run on CNG or gasoline. Impco did the conversion. The pressure regulator can be seen between the air cleaner and the master cylinder. The device behind the alternator is the "mass gas flow sensor," which measures the amount of CNG that the engine is using. *Bob Bray*

1996

GM's financial results for 1996 were mixed. That is, sales increased $3.7 billion to $164 billion from $160.3 billion in 1995, but net income slipped from $6.9 billion in 1995 to only $5 billion in 1996, a drop of 28 percent.

GM's good news was its record vehicle sales. Cars and light-duty trucks both set new records. Truck sales in 1996 totaled 1,975,021 versus 1,895,535 in 1995. Car sales increased by 110,000. GM didn't fare as well overseas. Yet it retained its title as the world's top vehicle producer in spite of the fact that GM's total world output dropped 1.4 percent, while the top 10 producers' total output increased by 4.5 percent.

In 1996, GM divested itself of its Electronic Data Systems (EDS) subsidiary. This was the organization GM purchased from H. Ross Perot for $2.5 billion in 1984. Four Delphi interior systems plants were also sold late in the year. Early in 1997, GM sold its Hughes Electronic subsidiary to Raytheon Corp. for $9.5 billion.

A major historic change for GM was the start of the move out of its famous 76-year-old landmark GM Building in Detroit. GM purchased the Renaissance Center complex in Detroit and renamed it the General Motors Global Headquarters at the Renaissance Center. GM expected to relocate most Detroit area employees to the new center over the next several years.

GM's Saturn division began delivering its new EV1 electric vehicles in California and Arizona. These vehicles were offered only on lease. GM delivered 76 electric cars to customers before the end of the year.

This year GM filed a civil lawsuit in Detroit against VW, alleging that VW executives conspired to use secret GM information brought to them by José Lopez, who was the former GM purchasing chief until he defected to VW in 1993.

Chevrolet had another record year of truck sales in 1996. Light-duties increased to 1,481,879 from 1,414,222 in 1995. Medium-duty trucks, on the other hand, declined slightly to 14,745 from 15,633 in 1995. Chevrolet's sales were held down by a lack of light-duty truck production facilities. Chevrolet's pickup sales increased by 2.7 percent versus 1995.

In the hottest segment of the light truck market, the SUVs, Chevrolet fared very well, posting a 23 percent gain. The fact that Chevrolet sold a large quantity of the full-size, high-profit Tahoes and Suburbans boosted GM's profits.

Chevrolet introduced a new name and a new vehicle for 1996, the Chevrolet Express twins—full-size cargo and passenger vans. These were the first new full-size vans from Chevrolet since 1971. The Express had a new heavy-duty, full-ladder-type frame that provided stiffness and improved stability, ride, and handling qualities. In cargo-carrying applications, these full-size vans were subjected to some man-sized loads. Plumbers, electricians, and other tradesmen used them as a storeroom for their tools and equipment. On a daily basis, they loaded up the product and supplies needed for the day's work. The Express van put GM in a stronger competitive position against Ford's Econoline.

The major change in Chevrolet trucks for 1996 concerned engines. Chevrolet engineers boosted power and torque by reengineering the entire line. The new standard engine lineup consisted of the following: Vortec 4300 V-6, Vortec 5000 V-8, Vortec 5700 V-8, and 6.5-liter turbo-diesel V-8. Engines for the heavy models included: Vortec 5700 V-8 HD, Vortec 7400 V-8, and the 6.5-liter turbo-diesel V-8 HD. Increased outputs were achieved by equipping all V-8s with GM's patented Sequential Fuel Injection (SFI). SFI achieved the performance of multiport fuel injection, but with less cost and complexity. The system provided more-accurate fuel delivery and ran smoother than the previous simple throttle-body fuel injection. Other power-boosting changes included a new two-piece intake manifold that breathed into new straight-port, high-compression cylinder heads, and increased compression ratios. New roller valve-lifters cut friction and allowed the use of bolder cam profiles, which helped improve low-end torque. And there were cooling system and exhaust improvements. Another improvement was the addition of OBD II. The Vortec 5700 V-8 engine, now with 250 horsepower and 335 foot-pounds torque, powered this 1996 Chevrolet C1500 Sportside Extended-Cab pickup. This model was only offered as a 1/2-ton, but with 2WD or 4WD. *Harold Chevrolet*

One of Chevrolet's hardest-working pickups was the big K2500 standard cab pickup with an 8-foot cargo box. Chevrolet's 4WD featured independent front suspension (IFS). IFS delivered better ride quality and its rugged construction kept front wheels virtually straight up and down for a stable ride and better steering control. Chevrolet's standard Insta-Trac 4WD system permitted shifting on the fly from 2WD to 4WD High and back at any road speed. The big, rugged K2500 model's maximum GVW rating was 8,600 pounds. With standard cab, the K2500 pickup rode on a 131.5-inch-wheelbase chassis. The standard engine for K2500 was the 220-horsepower 5.0-liter Vortec V-8. This is a 1996 Chevrolet K2500 pickup with street-sanding equipment. *Iten Chevrolet*

Chevrolet offered the Express in two wheelbase lengths, three GVW levels, and an Express Extended version with seating for 15. Chevrolet designers saw to it that the Express looked like a Chevrolet, with its bold C/K pickup-style grille, headlights, and massive front bumper. The Express was designed to give Chevrolet a bigger portion of the commercial van market, and to make a better class "C" motorhome chassis. It used some parts from the C/K pickup line.

Chevrolet truck engines moved into their third evolutionary phase for 1996. In reality, the Vortec engines were such a major improvement that they were considered more revolutionary. First they were the 305, 350, and 454 engines. Second, they became the 5.0-, 5.7-, and 7.4-liter engines. New 1996 designations were the Vortec 5000 (L30), the Vortec 5700 (L31), and the Vortec 7400 (L29) series engines.

The reason for the change in designations was because GM powertrain engineers performed major changes to this time-proven line. Their reference engine was the 4.3-liter Vortec (now 4300 series) V-6, which they had upgraded back in 1992 and placed in the Astro Van and S-10 trucks.

Performance increases were dramatic. For example, the former 305 produced 175 horsepower and 265 foot-pounds of torque. In 1995 output jumped to an impressive 220 horsepower and 285 foot-pounds torque as the Vortec 5000. Similarly, the former 5.7-liter in 1995 produced 200 horsepower and 310 foot-pounds torque, compared to 1996's Vortec 5700 that powered up to 250 and 335 horsepower and foot-pounds torque respectively. The big block 1995 7.4-liter formerly was good for 230 horsepower and 385 foot-pounds torque; as the Vortec 7400 it cranked out 290 horsepower and 410 foot-pounds of torque.

The Vortec system had only one fuel injector with either six or eight nozzles, one for each cylinder. This system lowered the cost, because it was less expensive to manufacture and simpler than the usual one injector per cylinder setup. It was not used, however, on the 454. The Vortec 7400 had only one injector per cylinder design, as the other system could not flow enough fuel for this big engine. The one injector system was often referred to as "CPI" for Central Port Injection.

But that was not all. Other new engine features included high-flow, straight-port cylinder heads. Revised combustion chambers improved airflow with a high-swirl, fast-burn design. The compression ratio for the Vortec 5000 increased from 9.1:1 to 9.4:1. The compression ratio for the Vortec 7400 went from an anemic 7.9:1 to a healthy 9.0:1. All three V-8s also got roller lifters and new steel camshafts that provided for fast-action cam lobes for better idle, faster acceleration, and lower emissions.

The new engines also received GM's OBD-II (onboard diagnostic, second generation) system and more-powerful vehicle control modules. A long-life ignition and single 100,000-mile accessory drive belts were designed to greatly extend major-service intervals.

Late in the year, the new T-Series medium/heavy-duty cabovers were introduced. And the Kodiak was renamed the C-Series (C5500, C6500, C7500, and C8500). Also new was a downward-sloping high visibility hood for gas and low power diesel engine medium-duty trucks.

The overwhelming majority of 1-ton C/K3500 Big Dooley pickups were sold with either an Extended-Cab or a Crew Cab. This standard cab 1996 Chevrolet K3500 Big Dooley was so seldom seen that it looks strange. The extended-arm side-view mirrors show this truck was used for serious towing work: Pulling big loads is what this truck was engineered and powered for. Its standard engine was the 245-horsepower Vortec 5700 V-8 HD. Options included the 290-horsepower Vortec 7400 V-8 and the 6.5-liter 190-horsepower turbo-diesel V-8. At 410 foot-pounds net torque at 3,200 rpm, the Vortec 7400 V-8 was Chevrolet's power champion. Its maximum GVW rating was 10,000 pounds and its maximum payload was 4,019 pounds. With either an automatic or manual transmission, the K3500 Big Dooley was rated for up to 19,000 pounds GCW rating (a 4.56 rear-axle ratio was required). *Harold Chevrolet*

The Extended-Cab short-box C/K1500s continued to be Chevrolet's most popular pickups. New in 1996 was a third door on the driver side. Daytime running lamps became standard. Pictured here is a 1996 Chevrolet K1500 Extended-Cab pickup. Also revised for 1996 was the electronically controlled four-speed automatic transmission. The maximum GVW rating of the K1500 was 6,600 pounds. Base payload was 1,674 pounds. The base engine for K1500 was the 200-horsepower Vortec 4300 V-6, but most buyers preferred the performance delivered by the 250-horsepower Vortec 5700 V-8. *Harold Chevrolet*

Chevrolet was a major player in the commercial truck business. For years, Chevrolet had earned a reputation for producing the most dependable, longest-lasting trucks on the road, and the 1996 models continued the tradition. This is a tough 1996 standard cab K2500 chassis cab with utility body by an independent body builder. Its maximum GVW rating was 8,600 pounds and maximum payload was 4,340 pounds. To shoulder this load, the 245-horsepower Vortec 5700 V-8 HD was its standard engine. All gas engines featured SFI. A five-speed heavy-duty overdrive manual transmission was standard, and the four-speed heavy-duty overdrive electronically controlled automatic was the option. *Harold Chevrolet*

Chevrolet's major players in the commercial chassis cab market for 1996 included the C/K2500, C/K3500, and the C3500 HD. For an unknown reason, Chevrolet identified its C3500 HD Series as a 1-ton truck, even though it was a Class 4. It may have had to do with playing games with total light-duty truck production numbers in its annual race with Ford for top production honors (Ford has its own tricks). A hallmark of Chevrolet chassis cabs had always been, and was true even with the 1-ton 4WD models, their low body-installed height, which facilitated cab entry and exit and loading and unloading. This 4WD crew cab carried a maximum GVW rating of 12,000 pounds. The standard engine was the 245-horsepower Vortec 5700 HD V-8. Options included the 290-horsepower Vortec 7400 V-8 and the 190-horsepower 6.5-liter HD turbo-diesel V-8. Standard transmission was the five-speed HD overdrive manual.

A very popular commercial application for Chevrolet 1-ton standard cab chassis cabs was as a small dump truck for landscapers, construction companies, utilities, and municipalities. Chevrolet built this model in both C/K configurations and with either a 135.5- or a 159.5-inch wheelbase. It, too, carried a maximum GVW rating of 11,000 pounds for C-Series or 12,000 pounds for K-Series. Owners could count on their Chevrolet 1-ton commercial to get the job done. Engine options included the standard 245-horsepower Vortec 5700 HD V-8 and optional 290-horsepower Vortec 7400 V-8 or 190-horsepower 6.5-liter turbo-diesel HD V-8. The Vortec 7400 boasted 410 foot-pounds torque at 3,200 rpm and was Chevrolet's power king. *Harold Chevrolet*

The two standout clues to identifying Chevrolet's Class 4 C3500 HD chassis cab are the filler panel between the grille and bumper, and its 19.5-inch ventilated disc wheels. The rear view of this 1996 Chevrolet C3500 HD chassis cab with stake body gives a view of its 19.5-inch wheels. A third clue, not visible here, are the letters "HD," located low on the cab doors behind the "3500" model number plate. It offered a hefty 15,000-pound GVW rating due to a 5,000-pound capacity I-beam front axle with leaf springs, dual rear wheels, and its large, 19.5-inch wheels and 225/70R-19.5 SF tires. The standard engine was the 290-horsepower Vortec 7400 V-8 and optional was the 190-horsepower 6.5-liter turbo-diesel V-8. The only transmission available was the five-speed HD overdrive manual. *Harold Chevrolet*

Chevrolet's full-size SUVs led the league again in 1996 with three distinct models: two-door Tahoe, four-door Tahoe, and king Suburban. Two-door Tahoe rode on a 111.5-inch wheelbase, the four-door Tahoe on a 117.5-inch wheelbase (same as the standard cab short-box pickup), and Suburban on a 131.5-inch wheelbase (same as the standard cab long-box pickup). This is a 1996 Chevrolet K1500 Suburban. When equipped with the Vortec 7400 engine and other optional equipment, the Suburban was rated for a maximum GCW of 17,000 pounds. The Vortec 5700 V-8 was standard for C/K1500 and C/K2500 Suburbans. The Vortec 7400 V-8 was optional only for C/K2500 Suburbans. The 6.5-liter turbo-diesel was optional for all models. A four-speed electronically controlled automatic with overdrive transmission was standard for C/K1500 with gas engine only and the four-speed heavy-duty electronically controlled automatic overdrive was optional for C/K1500 models with the diesel engine and all C/K2500 Series. *Iten Chevrolet*

Which medium-duty truck would a Caterpillar Equipment Distributor own? Probably the sole medium-duty truck manufacturer installing only Caterpillar diesel engines! This is a C60 Chevrolet Kodiak medium-duty chassis cab with service body owned by Minnesota's Caterpillar distributor. It was powered, of course, by the powerful Caterpillar 3116 (6.6-liter) turbocharged, air-to-air intercooled diesel engine. The standard Eaton Fuller Synchro-6 transmission eliminated the need for a two-speed axle in many medium-duty applications. Chevrolet offered manual transmissions with from 5 to 13 forward speeds. The Allison MD automatic transmission was an option. Buyers had a choice of three frames: the standard 50,000-psi weldable, optional 110,000-psi heat-treated frame, or a fully weldable 80,000-psi. Because it was weldable, the buyer could add toolboxes or steps without compromising integrity. *Ziegler Co.*

Chevrolet's various commercial chassis cabs continued to be very popular with the nation's fire fighters in 1996. The Granbury, Texas, Fire Department owned this 1996 Chevrolet straight frame C3500 HD Class 4 "1-ton" chassis cab with firefighting body. Rescue No. 2's body was by Westex. The extended front bumper contained an electric winch. It could easily carry a heavy load on its 15,000-pound maximum GVW-rated chassis, and its standard 290-horsepower Vortec 7400 V-8 with SFI guaranteed it would arrive in time. Its transmission was the four-speed HD electronically controlled overdrive automatic. *Hansen*

Kodiak offered eight LoPro chassis cab models in 1996, ranging in wheelbase lengths from 143.6 to 260.6 inches with GVW ratings up to 23,900 pounds and accepted body lengths from 9 to 24 feet. This is a 1996 Chevrolet Kodiak LoPro chassis cab with van body. The standard engine for LoPros was the 225-horsepower gasoline 6.0-liter V-8. The 7.0-liter gas V-8 was optional, as were four Cat 3116 diesel engines. Available transmissions included the standard Eaton Fuller five-speed FS-4205B and optional five- and six-speed Eaton Fullers and three models of Allison automatics (AT, MT, and MD), two five-speeds and a six-speed.

Chevrolet launched its all-new full-size vans in the spring of 1996. This was GM large van's first major redesign since 1971. They were a complete frame-up rework of GM's full-size G-van. For the first time, the big vans were built on a full-ladder-type frame. This added considerable stiffness for improved stability, ride, and handling characteristics. The name of the passenger van was changed to the Express models. Express van buyers could choose from two wheelbase lengths (135 or 155 inches), three GVW ratings, and an Express Extended model that could seat up to 15 passengers. The new model numbering system was G1500, G2500, and G3500 for 1/2-, 3/4-, and 1-tons, respectively. A commonality of model numbers between Chevrolet truck types was achieved. GM's redesigned Vortec engine line for 1996 gave these new vans sprightly performance. Pictured here is a 1996 Chevrolet G2500 Express passenger van. *Harold Chevrolet*

The first new Chevrolets with sloped hoods arrived at dealers during the 1996 model year. The basic reason for the change was simply for better visibility. It had a very contemporary appearance, which many buyers found pleasing. For improved forward visibility, especially in congested urban and suburban areas, the sloped hood hit a home run with drivers. Some truck observers believe the sloped hood was designed for gas engines only. That is not true. Diesel engines up to 210 horsepower could be accommodated in the sloped hood. Diesel engines more powerful than 210 horsepower required larger radiators that couldn't be accommodated within the sloped hood. The 1996 Chevrolet medium-duty chassis cab with platform body was America's best-looking medium-duty truck. *Iten Chevrolet*

Caterpillar engineers took the lessons they learned from years of experience with heavy-duty diesel engines and applied them in developing the medium-duty 3116 engine. This engine did an excellent job in medium-duty applications because it developed horsepower and torque over a broad operating range. The 3116 was either mechanically or electronically managed. The electronically managed 3116 featured the leading-edge hydraulically actuated, electronically controlled Unit Injector (HEUI) fuel system. The 3116 HEUI engine electronically communicated (via computer link) with the Allison MD automatic transmission to control shift points. This linkage also enabled the cruise control to work with the automatic transmission. The 3116 was offered with the buyer's choice of either the electronic control (HEUI) or the mechanical control. There were 11 engine ratings with mechanical control—170 to 300 horsepower. There were 7 ratings with the HEUI system—170 to 275 horsepower. This 1996 Chevrolet Kodiak medium-duty chassis cab with contractor's body is powered by the Cat 3116 HEUI. *Iten Chevrolet*

Chevrolet's 1996 two-door Tahoe was rugged, capable, and confident, not to mention good looking. New for 1996 was a 2WD two-door Tahoe. For a tow vehicle the two-door Tahoe was an intelligent choice. Its standard 250-horsepower Vortec 5700 V-8 when linked to a four-speed heavy-duty electronically controlled automatic transmission made a dynamite towing team. An optional engine oil cooler and an auxiliary heavy-duty transmission cooler contributed to the Tahoe's towing powers. When properly equipped the Tahoe was rated for a GCW of 12,000 pounds. The two-door Tahoe was available in Standard, LS, and LT trim levels. Optional high-back bucket seats with center floor console made the miles melt away.

The 1996 Chevrolet S-10 2WD SS (Super Sport or Street Smart) pickup was in its third year. Chevrolet called it a musclecar with a pickup box. Its 180-horsepower Vortec 4300 V-6 was the reason for its name. Chassis modifications included the new ZQ8 Sport Suspension's P235/55R-16 Eagle GA tires on 16-inch-spoke cast-aluminum wheels. The truck pictured here has incorrect tires. Other modifications were de Carbon shocks, special springs, and other suspension enhancements, which gave the SS its fun-to-drive handling. The SS badging and a monotone paint treatment gave the SS a no-nonsense appearance. Note the absence of the usual S-10 rear bumper.

Chevrolet's school bus chassis line remained unchanged in 1996. It consisted of two Series: the B-Series was the chassis cowl models and the S-Series the forward-control chassis. The B-Series contained two basic models. First was the 21,000-pound GVW model with hydraulic brakes and powered by either the 366 gas engine or the Cat 3115 diesel. It rode on a 189-inch-wheelbase chassis. The other B-Series bus was the 24,000-pound GVW chassis cowl with air brakes and the Cat 3116 diesel. It, too, rode on the 189-inch-wheelbase chassis. The S-Series school bus forward-control chassis rode on a 170-inch wheelbase and were rated for a maximum GVW of 30,000 pounds. The S-Series forward-control chassis consisted of four models: two with hydraulic brakes powered by either the 366 gas engine or the Cat 3116 diesel, and two with air brakes powered by the same two engines. This is a 1996 Chevrolet B-Series school bus chassis cowl with a body by Blue Bird. *Iten Chevrolet*

Yes, S-10 pickups were honest commercial trucks. Not every one was used for personal transportation. This 1996 Chevrolet S-10 Fleetside long box with a commercial cover was designed and engineered for hard work. This little Base trim truck rode on a 117.9-inch wheelbase chassis and was rated for a maximum GVW of 4,900 pounds and payload of 1,547 pounds. Powertrain availability included the standard 118-horsepower 2.2-liter L4 with SFI with either a manual overdrive or automatic transmission. Two options included the 170-horsepower or 180-horsepower Vortec 4300 V-6 with SFI and either a manual overdrive or automatic transmission.

The buyers of medium- or heavy-duty trucks "spec it out" to suit the job. Specifying has to do with selecting the right components, the right truck size, gear ratios, capacity, and other features. But it also has to do with choosing components from the right manufacturer. Chevrolet offered buyers components from the industry's finest manufacturers: Caterpillar engines, Eaton Fuller manual transmissions, Valeo clutches, Allison automatic transmissions (the world leader in truck automatics), Eaton drive axles—single and two-speed—Rockwell drive axles and Q-Plus air brakes, Delco generators and batteries, and Michelin tires. That's an unbeatable lineup. The 225-horsepower 366 V-8 engine and an automatic transmission powered this 1996 Chevrolet C60 LoPro chassis cab with contractor's dump body.

Chevrolet had an Extended-Cab model to fit every pickup buyer's needs. This is a K1500 Extended-Cab short-box Fleetside. It was available in 1/2- and 3/4-ton models and with either 2WD or 4WD. This truck was a particular favorite with commercial buyers. Two clues to identify this as a commercial truck are its base steel wheels and an argent-painted molded Duragrille with single rectangular halogen sealed-beam headlamps. An optional "passenger-side easy-access system" (third door) was available. The engine most commercial buyers insisted on was seriously upgraded for 1996. Now called the Vortec 5700 (L31), its horsepower and torque outputs jumped from 200 and 310, respectively, to 250 horsepower and 335 foot-pounds torque. Most of this gain was due to switching from TBI to SFI. *Harold Chevrolet*

Another basic bread-and-butter commercial pickup was Chevrolet's tough K2500 Fleetside regular-cab. Chevrolet engineers were proud of the state-of-the-art safety system built into every Chevrolet pickup. It included a standard driver air bag, standard four-wheel ABS, and crush zones. Its frontal structure was designed to "crush" in a controlled manner during a collision to help absorb crash energy, and the steel side-door beams protected occupants in the event of a side crash. This 1996 Chevrolet K2500 Fleetside long-box pickup with Cheyenne trim is interesting in that it had the optional bright deluxe grille with dual headlamps. It rode on a 131.5-inch wheelbase and was rated for a maximum GVW of 8,600 pounds and a maximum payload of 2,560 pounds. *Harold Chevrolet*

Another interesting 1996 pickup model was the Extended-Cab Fleetside short-box K2500. This truck was typically purchased for personal transportation and towing. The Extended-Cab added versatility not available in a regular-cab: Its lower cushion could be folded up in order to carry cargo items, or with the cushion down it would accommodate passengers. When equipped with the 245-horsepower HD Vortec 5700 V-8 engine, it could tow a trailer with a maximum weight of 7,500 pounds. Accessories for this truck included 16-inch bright steel wheels, running boards, and a husky grille guard. It also has the Silverado deluxe chrome grille.

Chevrolet's lengthy 1996 van lineup consisted of the mini Lumina Cargo, Astro Cargo, Chevy Van, Sportvan, G-Cutaway Van, and P-Cutaway HD Van. The Astro Cargo van was Chevrolet's midsize van. Like the full-size vans, it had a front engine, rear drive layout. Chevrolet engineers designed the Astro in this manner for the express purpose of making it an excellent choice for carrying and towing heavy loads. Its wheelbase length was 111 inches. Only one body length was offered, the long body, formerly called the extended-body. Astro was offered in 2WD and AWD configurations. Maximum GVW rating was 5,850 pounds for the AWD van. The only drivetrain available was the 190-horsepower Vortec 4300 V-6 with the four-speed overdrive automatic. *Harold Chevrolet*

Chevrolet's biggest, longest, hardest-working van with enormous capacity and capability was the G30/C6W. The C6W Series was rated for a maximum GVW of 9,200 pounds and had the optional heavy-duty chassis package. This 1-ton brute had a 146-inch wheelbase and a cargo space of 306 cubic feet. Unlike its competitors, Chevrolet built its longest van with body side panels made of one piece of sheet metal for a fine finished appearance. The standard engine was the 180-horsepower 5.7-liter HD V-8 with EFI. Two optional engines included the 230-horsepower 7.4-liter V-8 with EFI and the 160-horsepower 6.5-liter HD V-8 diesel. The only transmission was the electronically controlled four-speed HD overdrive automatic.

The biggest and strongest Chevrolet van was the P-Cutaway Van HD Chassis with van body from an independent supplier. The strong backbone of the P-Cutaway Van was its heavy-duty ladder frame. P-Cutaway carried a maximum GVW rating of 14,100 pounds. Maximum payload was 8,976 pounds. Its tilt-forward engine cowling opened wide for convenient servicing. Two available wheelbase lengths were 157 and 178 inches and two available engines were the 180-horsepower 5.7-liter HD V-8 with EFI and 230-horsepower 7.4-liter V-8. The only transmission was the four-speed heavy-duty overdrive automatic with electronic control. Front suspension featured a brawny I-beam axle rated for 4,500 pounds and 5,000 pound leaf springs. Standard wheels were 19.5x6.0 inches. *Iten Chevrolet*

One of Chevrolet's hardest-working light-duty trucks was this 1-ton rated G-Cutaway Van. Chevrolet offered G-Cutaways on two wheelbases: 125 and 146 inches (models CG31303 and CG31603, respectively). Either single or dual rear wheels could be ordered on either chassis length. Maximum GVW rating of the 125-inch wheelbase was 10,000 pounds and for the 146-inch wheelbase it was 10,500 pounds. Maximum payload ratings were 5,478 and 5,822 pounds, respectively. Powertrain for both models included the standard 180-horsepower 5.7-liter HD V-8 with EFI and the electronically controlled four-speed HD automatic transmission. Optional engines included the 230-horsepower 7.4-liter V-8 and the 160-horsepower 6.5-liter V-8 diesel.

The other heavy-duty 1996 forward-control chassis was the P-Chassis like this one with a Step-Van body from an independent supplier. This large van featured a strong, big-truck ladder frame. Unlike the P-Cutaway of the same size, P-Chassis featured an independent front suspension with coil springs. P-Chassis was offered in three series: 8,600 pound maximum GVW, 9,000–11,000 pound GVWs, and 12,000–14,100 pound GVWs on five wheelbase lengths: 110, 125, 133, 157, and 178 inches. Three engine choices included the 195-horsepower Vortec 4300 V-6 with SFI and optional 245-horsepower Vortec 5700 HD V-8 with SFI and the 160-horsepower 6.5-liter HD diesel V-8. A five-speed overdrive manual transmission was standard and the four-speed overdrive automatic with electronic control was optional.

Chevrolet's all-new W- and T-Series trucks made their debut late in the 1996 model year as 1997 models. The line consisted of W3500, W4500, and W5500 models and T5500, T6500, T7500, and T8500. Actually, W5500 and T5500 were the same; it's a mystery why they were duplicated. Pictured are a W3500 on the left and a W4500 on the right. The T-Series models shared all mechanicals with the comparable C-Series trucks—engines, transmissions, basic frames, brakes, and axles. W-Series trucks differed from the T-Series trucks. Only the 250-horsepower 5.7-liter V-8 gas engine powered the W3500 and W4500 models. The W5500 was powered by an Isuzu 4.8-liter OHC four-cylinder diesel engine. A GM Hydra-Matic four-speed automatic overdrive was offered for the W3500 and a five-speed manual and four-speed Isuzu automatic for the W4500. *Iten Chevrolet*

An important new 1996 model was the two-door Chevrolet Blazer. Chevrolet designers set out to give the new two-door a fresh, interesting "coupe" look, and they succeeded admirably. Chevrolet offered the new two-door in both 2WD and 4WD configurations. For highway cruising, an optional Touring Suspension was offered. For the sports minded, a rugged and firm 4WD Off-Road Package filled the bill. Two-door Blazer's wheelbase was only 100.5 inches, 6.5 inches shorter than the four-door. Standard drivetrain consisted of the 195-horsepower 4.3-liter Vortec V-6 and the four-speed overdrive automatic.

All minivans including Astro Vans were officially classified as trucks, even though they were designed, engineered, and outfitted for moving people. For 1996, the Astro Van was given a totally new interior for added comfort for up to eight passengers. Rear seats were easily removed to adjust seating and cargo-carrying capacities to suit immediate needs. The Astro's instrument panel was also all new. Driver and front-passenger air bags were standard. The Astro's standard Vortec 4300 V-6 engine was the largest in the industry and delivered sparkling performance. *Harold Chevrolet*

The Southern California Gas Company operates a huge fleet of small and large trucks. This is one of its 1996 Chevrolet C2500 pickups. This truck has the Cheyenne trim and is equipped with the Vortec 5700 engine and the 4L60E automatic transmission. It also has a Gaylord fiberglass bed cover and a Knack tool box. Field supervisors use this truck. *Bob Bray*

1997

The year opened up with a strange twist: cars—not pickups, SUVs, or vans—were the stars of the 1997 Detroit International Automobile Show. Manufacturers showed a total of 40 new car models. GM was at the forefront with 13 new models, including the car everyone was waiting for: the new Corvette.

GM also showed the first-ever production electric car from a major manufacturer. GM's hand-built sporty two-passenger hatchback EV1 was priced at $33,995. It was in actuality only for lease, not for sale. These cars cost GM more than $100,000 each. Their driving range was limited to a maximum of only 90 miles with the battery pack fully charged. EV1 customers were carefully screened to eliminate those for whom the car wasn't suitable in order to protect the car's reputation.

GM's most important new introduction for 1997 was, however, its new line of front-drive vans. GM's previous expensive-to-manufacture, aerodynamic-styled front-drive van was not well accepted by the market. The new van shifted to a mainstream style with a conventional all-steel unibody. GM followed the lead of Chrysler and offered both small and midsize wheelbase lengths with an optional sliding door on the driver side. It was expected that at least 60 to 70 percent of buyers would order the fourth door.

GM's new van was the first global vehicle introduced since the company switched to a VLE development process. Because the new U-van was sold in both North America and Europe, the minivan team was made up of people from GM/Europe and North American Operations. The new team quickly adjusted to the VLE concept and 51 months later, after much work and compromise, the new van was born. Chrysler was the target, of course, and maybe it was good that Chrysler sold minivans in both North America and Europe. The glue that held the diverse group together was simply this, they worked together for "the customer."

Each of the three selling divisions had its own version: Chevrolet Venture (replaced the Lumina APV), Transport for Pontiac, and Silhouette for Oldsmobile. GM also built a model for Opel to sell in Germany.

In 1996, 45 percent of all vehicles sold in the United States were light-duty trucks. These trucks provided all of the North American automotive operating profits of GM, Ford, and Chrysler in 1995 and 1996. The Big Three continued to expand light truck capacity. The big question mark was, would the public taste change and hang the industry out to dry?

GM had its work cut out for itself in 1997. Its market share had fallen to 32.7 percent in 1996, compared with 34.2 percent in 1995. GM claimed it had lost 2 percentage points in 1996 due to a UAW strike, but felt confident it could increase market share to 33 percent in 1997.

The Big Three was strong in trucks but weak in car sales. As of midyear, the Big Three's share of the automobile market was only 60 percent. The Asians and Europeans took 4 out of 10 new car sales.

Chevrolet's major strength in 1997 was trucks: pickups, SUVs, and vans. Therefore, many improvements and changes were made to its most lucrative vehicles.

The S-Series pickup was improved with an optional four-speed automatic, a lighter drive system in 4WD models, and a strengthened and stiffer frame in 2WD versions. S-Series came in six different models in three trim levels. 2WD versions could be optioned with a street-biased SS performance-handling package. The 4WD version could be optioned with the aggressive ZR2 setup. Extended-cab versions could be outfitted with an optional third door.

Full-size Chevrolet C/K pickups could be ordered for personal use or commercial work. New was a standard passenger-side air bag on all models under 8,600 pounds GVW. A natural-gas–powered 5.7-liter/255 horsepower V-8 engine was optional.

The huge four-door Suburban and the shorter wheelbase two- or four-door Tahoe anchored Chevrolet's all-important full-size SUV line. New for 1997 were a passenger-side air bag and improved steering and transmissions, plus a quieter engine-cooling fan. The Suburban could tow up to 10,000 pounds and the Tahoe up to 7,000 pounds. The 7.4-liter V-8 was an option only in the Suburban.

Chevrolet's Express van and wagon, which were new in 1996, were only minimally improved for 1997. The 1-ton G3500 had dual air bags and all models had daytime running

Chevrolet's Sportside short-box pickup was offered in both 2WD and 4WD configurations and with choice of standard or Extended-Cab. This is a 1997 Chevrolet K1500 Sportside with the "Z71" 4WD package. The Sportside short-box was a modern version of Chevrolet's classic Stepside pickup. A new feature for 1997 Chevrolet pickups included a deflatable passenger-side air bag standard on all models under 8,600 pounds GVW. An Electronic Variable Orifice power steering eased low-speed maneuvering. Improvements were also made to transmissions and climate-control systems. Optional was a natural-gas–powered 5.7-liter 255-horsepower V-8. The Z71 4WD package consisted of skid plates and Bilstein high-pressure gas-filled shock absorbers. *Harold Chevrolet*

Chevrolet's middleweight workhorse champion was the C/K2500 standard cab long box. This is a 1997 Chevrolet C2500 standard cab 3/4-ton long box. When employed for serious towing, this truck was powered by one of two optional engines: the 255-horsepower Vortec 5700 V-8 or the 180-horsepower 6.5-liter turbo-diesel. The gas engine produced 330 foot-pounds torque and the diesel 360 foot-pounds torque. Standard transmission was the five-speed overdrive manual; the four-speed overdrive electronically controlled automatic was optional for the gas engine and the four-speed overdrive electronically controlled heavy-duty was optional for the diesel only. The natural gas option was available on the C2500 regular cab pickup with Vortec 5700 V-8 and the optional 8,600-pound GVW rating only.

Chevrolet's hard-working Extended-Cab K2500 pickups were well suited for service as fire trucks. The Phoenix, Arizona, Fire Department owned Truck No. C957. The Hazardous Materials Commander drove it. This truck's drivetrain consisted of the 255-horsepower Vortec 5700 V-8 and the four-speed overdrive electronically controlled automatic, and the two-speed transfer case was the floor-mounted NP 241. An instrument panel-mounted electric shift transfer case was an option. The K2500's maximum GVW rating was 7,200 pounds and its payload rating was 2,755 pounds. *Greenberg*

lights. The new van was well accepted in its inaugural year. The P-Series chassis was given the Vortec engines.

The first Chevrolet S-10 electric pickup truck was delivered on May 20, 1997, to an electric company for use as a service and meter-reading truck. Chevrolet had orders in-house as of August 1997 for 300 of the $33,305 trucks from a number of electric companies across the United States as well as the U.S. Navy and Air Force.

It had a strong frame specially designed to hold 1,300 pounds of lead-acid batteries. This gave the S-10 a weight of 4,200 pounds, about 1,200 pounds more than a gasoline-powered S-10. Yet it could carry a 950 payload. The truck would travel about 50 miles on a charge, which took less than four hours.

Top speed was governed at 70 miles per hour, and 0 to 50 miles per hour was possible in less than 10 seconds. It had FWD, using half the regular S-10's 4WD system to power the front wheels. Much of the powertrain was derived from the EV1, including the 115-horsepower electric motor and regenerative braking system. When the brakes were applied, the motor momentarily turned into a charger, helping to charge up the batteries.

Chevrolet's complete line of 1997 Extended-Cab pickups included S-10 and C/K1500, 2500, and 3500 Series. The biggest of all was the Extended-Cab K3500 Big Dooley 1-ton. Dual rear wheels were standard on C/K3500 Extended-Cab models. This model carried an impressive 10,000 pounds GVW. The Extended-Cab's interior, when equipped with Silverado trim, rivaled that of expensive automobiles. The cab's huge interior offered seating for up to six adults or plenty of storage room for expensive tools, equipment, and personal items. The 250-horsepower Vortec 5700 V-8 HD was standard; the 290-horsepower Vortec 7400 V-8 and the 190-horsepower 6.5-liter HD turbo-diesel V-8 were optional. The Vortec 7400 gas V-8 developed 410 foot-pounds torque versus 385 foot-pounds torque for the turbo-diesel. The five-speed heavy-duty overdrive manual transmission was standard and the four-speed overdrive heavy-duty electronically controlled automatic was an option. *Harold Chevrolet*

The Suburban continued as the biggest and best SUV again in 1997. Changes and improvements consisted of a passenger-side air bag, the second-row outboard shoulder-harness anchors were height adjustable, the Suburban's steering and transmission were improved, and it received a quieter engine-cooling fan than other full-size trucks. The Suburban still led the league in terms of towing power, seating accommodations, luxurious interiors, powerful engines, and convenience options. This is a 1997 Chevrolet K2500 Suburban Battalion Chief's truck shown. Battalion No. 131's Suburban was owned by Farmers Branch, Texas, Fire Department. Its retail list price ranged from $24,500 to $28,500. This Suburban was powered by the 290-horsepower Vortec 7400 V-8 engine, which was mated to a four-speed overdrive electronically controlled automatic transmission. *Hansen*

Chevrolet's full-size chassis cab truck line for 1997 consisted of standard cab and Extended-Cab C/K2500, C/K3500, and C/K3500 with straight frames. This 1997 Chevrolet C2500 standard cab chassis cab is waiting for a special body to be mounted. Chevrolet engineers designed the chassis cabs to handle a variety of special bodies from many independent suppliers. Maximum GVW rating for the C2500 was a remarkable 8,600 pounds and the maximum payload rating for C2500 was also high at 4,269 pounds. To move these big loads, Chevrolet engineers specified the 255-horsepower Vortec 5700 V-8 engine mated to the standard five-speed heavy-duty overdrive manual transmission.

Chevrolet's K3500 Crew Cab chassis cab with single rear wheels presents an odd appearance. The Crew Cab with dual rears carried a maximum GVW rating of 10,000 pounds; with single rears GVW reached only 9,200 pounds. The C/K Crew Cab was standard with single rear wheels, but have you ever seen one in service? Dual rear wheels, or "Big Dooley," was an extra-cost option. The base payload for K3500 Crew Cab was 3,673 pounds. The major attraction of a Crew Cab was simply the fact that it provided comfortable accommodations for up to six big men on two wide, comfortable bench seats. K3500's torsion bar independent front suspension delivered an excellent comfortable but controlled ride. The standard Crew Cab engine was the 255-horsepower Vortec 5700 HD V-8 engine. Options included the 290-horsepower Vortec 7400 V-8 engine and the 190-horsepower 6.5-liter turbo-diesel HD V-8 engines. *Harold Chevrolet*

The bigger and tougher the job, the better Chevrolet's C3500 HD chassis cab performed. Chevrolet advertised C3500 as being "tough enough for any job" and it was. Its maximum GVW rating was a big 15,000 pounds. Maximum payload was equally high at 9,306 pounds. You knew it was big and tough because of its engine lineup: standard power was from the 290-horsepower Vortec 7400 V-8; optional was the 190-horsepower 6.5-liter HD V-8 turbo-diesel. The transmission lineup Chevrolet engineers released for C3500 HD was equally tough: a five-speed heavy-duty overdrive manual was standard and the four-speed heavy-duty overdrive electronically controlled automatic was the only option. *Harold Chevrolet*

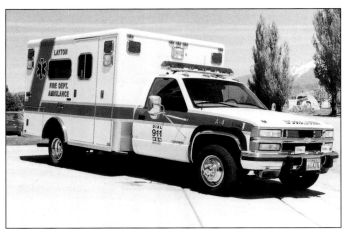

As with every other year, in 1997 the nation's fire departments turned to Chevrolet for quality, dependable, ready-to-go at any time light-duty trucks. This is a 1997 Chevrolet C3500 1-ton chassis cab with ambulance body. The Layton, Utah, Fire Department owned this ambulance. Its body is by Horton. *Boatwright*

The difference between Chevrolet's C3500 HD chassis cab and the regular C3500 chassis cab can be clearly seen in the truck pictured here. The white stripe that outlines the front fender's wheel opening continues under the width of the grille and highlights the C3500 HD chassis cab's additional height. The other obvious difference between this truck and the standard 1-ton is its big 19.5-inch ventilated disc wheels. This truck is a 1997 Chevrolet C3500 HD chassis cab with firefighting body. Brush truck No. Two was owned by the Casa Grande, Arizona, Fire Department. A local firm built its body and it featured a 250-gallon water tank and a 200-gpm pump. *Greenberg*

A tradesman with a big job needs a big van. The answer is the Chevy Van. Chevrolet's advertising said, "Now there's more to work with." Now in its first full model year, it gained in popularity with every passing day. Tradesman went for this big van in a big way. Features they appreciated included rear doors that swung open for a clear opening of 57 inches—enough to accept a standard size pallet, the largest cargo capacity in its class, and choice of two exceptionally long wheelbases—135 and 155 inches. This is a 1997 G2500 Standard Chevy Van in Summit White. Maximum GVW ratings for this model ranged up to 8,600 pounds. Base payload was 2,471 pounds. The optional 220-horsepower Vortec 5000 V-8 engine powered it. Only automatic transmissions were offered, either a four-speed electronically controlled overdrive or a heavy-duty version of same. *Harold Chevrolet*

Chevrolet's G3500 Commercial Cutaway Van program with the new generation 1997 vans consisted of one type only. With the former vans, Chevrolet built two types of Cutaways simply because the former vans did not have a truck-type ladder frame. The first generation mounted a body on the van's flat floor as opposed to a frame. Bodies were now mounted on the rugged ladder frame. This chassis is, of course, much improved in terms of load-carrying capacities. For the past several years Chevrolet built a second Cutaway Van series with a ladder-type frame for the big jobs. Pictured here is a 1997 Chevrolet 177-inch G3500 Cutaway Van. It featured an enormous maximum GVW rating up to 12,000 pounds and a 7,245-pound base payload rating. The base engine for this model was the 245-horsepower Vortec 5700 HD V-8. The only transmission offered was the four-speed heavy-duty overdrive electronically controlled automatic.

Chevrolet introduced a replacement for the Lumina APV called the Venture in the late fall of 1996 as a 1997 model. This was GM's third attempt at competing in the minivan market. Usually it's three strikes and you're out, but in the case of Chevrolet's new minivan, it was three strikes and then hitting a home run. The Venture van's styling was very similar to Chrysler's winning shape, which had also been the model Ford followed for its minivan. The Venture had a leg up on Ford in that it came out of the box with a left-side sliding door. Its 3400 V-6 engine provided plenty of power and worked well with the four-speed automatic. It delivered 180 horsepower and 205 foot-pounds torque. The Venture seated up to seven adults in comfort. Its option list was long and inclusive of all the goodies. It was available in either regular or extended versions, with two trim levels: base and LS. A fully equipped LS listed for about $24,700. *Iten Chevrolet*

Chevrolet fielded two Tahoe models in 1997 named simply the two-door Tahoe and the four-door Tahoe. Of the two, the four-door was the more important. The reality of the marketplace is that consumers prefer the utility and convenience of a four-door. The four-door Tahoe had a unique place in Chevrolet's large SUV lineup. It fit many people's needs even better than the super-size Suburban. The 117.5-inch-wheelbase four-door Tahoe was plenty big. The driver and passengers sat high for excellent visibility. It had the size and power to tow more than most owners would ever need and 4WD was available. It provided comfortable seating for six with more than adequate room for luggage. There was still a significant group of buyers who preferred a two-door full-size SUV like the one pictured here. After all, the original Chevrolet SUV was a two-door truck, so why change a good thing? The 111.5-inch-wheelbase two-door Tahoe also seated six. It carried their luggage and could tow with the best of them. *Harold Chevrolet*

The secret to Chevrolet's popular C-Series medium-duty truck's success was consistency. Chevrolet engineers quietly and consistently improved these trucks little by little, year after year. Take, for instance, the new slope hood on the 1997 Chevrolet C7500 chassis cab. The sloped hood gave the driver a much better view of the road, especially in tight, congested situations, which made his job safer and easier. The sloped hood was standard with gasoline engines and diesel engines up to 210 horsepower. Above this horsepower rating diesel engines required bigger radiators than the sloped hood would accommodate. The high hood was available with gas engines as a no-cost option for buyers who preferred its bigger, huskier appearance. The C7500 model carried maximum GVW ratings from 26,001 to 33,000 pounds. Two gas engines were available: the 366 V-8 and the 427 V-8. *Iten Chevrolet*

Chevrolet's high hood medium-duty truck's appearance was dramatically different from the sloped hood models. In reality this C7500 model could have had the same engine, transmission, axles, springs, and other equipment as another C7500 with a sloped hood, yet still look like a bigger truck. Some buyers simply preferred a huskier appearance. Others preferred the better visibility afforded by the sloped hood. This is a 1997 Chevrolet C7500 chassis cab with diesel power. Caterpillar 3116 diesel engines larger than 210 horsepower required the high hood to accommodate larger radiators for adequate cooling. *Iten Chevrolet*

Chevrolet fielded a complete line of tilt-cab models in 1997. The smaller W-Series consisted of W3500, W4500, and W5500 with maximum GVWs ranging from 11,050 to 19,500 pounds. As their model numbers suggest, these trucks were Class 3, 4, and 5, respectively. The larger T-Series, consisting of models T5500, T6500, T7500, and T8500, had maximum GVWs of 21,000, 26,000, 33,000, and 33,001 pounds. These models were Class 5, 6, 7, and 8 trucks, respectively. A tandem-axle T8500 model was included. The T-Series had gas and diesel power, only the 225-horsepower 6.0-liter V-8 engine, and the Cat 3116 diesel in six power ranges from 170 to 275 horsepower. Pictured here is a 1997 Chevrolet W4500 tilt-cab. *Iten Chevrolet*

Two series constituted Chevrolet's 1997 school bus line. One was the B-Series conventional cowl chassis with hydraulic brakes and either gas or diesel power, and with air brakes and diesel power only. The other was the S-Series forward-control chassis only with hydraulic brakes and a model with air brakes and diesel power only. This 1997 Chevrolet chassis cowl with a Blue Bird school bus body was built on a 189-inch-wheelbase chassis. It had a 24,000-pound GVW rating and was powered by the Cat 3116 diesel engine. The B-Series with hydraulic brakes also rode on a 189-inch chassis but was only rated for 21,000 pounds GVW. *Iten Chevrolet*

Because so many S-10 pickups were purchased for personal transportation, they sometimes aren't thought of as commercial trucks. Yet S-10 pickups were the "right size" for any number of commercial applications. The Extended-Cab pickup, pictured here with a topper, was owned and used by a tradesman in his work, and most likely it doubled for personal transportation. The S-10 offered Chevrolet truck's proven dependability, utility, and power. The 180-horsepower Vortec LF6 4300 V-6 was standard and the L35 Vortec 4300 V-6 developing 190 horsepower was an option. A five-speed overdrive manual was the standard transmission and the four-speed overdrive automatic was optional. *Harold Chevrolet*

Chevrolet's luxurious and comfortable Blazer was highly favored by women. They tended to buy vans and SUVs because these vehicles were engineered and designed to transport people. Chevrolet, of course, was well aware of its markets and purposely targeted the Blazer to women. Part of the sales approach was to sell them on safety. Chevrolet pushed such safety items as air bags, four-wheel ABS, daytime running lamps, a strong steel ladder-type frame, and double-wall doors reinforced with structural steel beams to protect passengers in side collisions. There was the Passlock theft deterrent system and battery-rundown protection that turned off any interior light left on when the vehicle had been turned off for more than 20 minutes. Then there was the peace of mind from Blazer's Insta-Trac 4WD system that let the driver shift on the fly from 2WD to 4WD High and back at any road speed at the push of a button. This is a 1997 four-door 4WD Blazer.

The Astro Cargo was Chevrolet's midsize commercial van. This RWD Cargo compact van rode on a short 111-inch wheelbase and featured a generous 170.4 cubic feet of load space. Two series were offered: RWD and AWD. Maximum GVW ratings for the two series were 5,600 and 5,850 pounds, respectively, and maximum payload ratings were 1,668 pounds for both series. Power was from the standard 190-horsepower Vortec 4300 V-6 with FI; it was mated to a four-speed overdrive automatic with electronic controls. *Rosedale Chevrolet*

Chevrolet's hot-selling 1997 Tahoe line consisted of a two-door and a four-door. The two-door rode on a 111.5-inch-wheelbase chassis and was available in 2WD and 4WD configurations and three trim levels: Base, LS, and LT. Maximum GVW rating for the 2WD model was 6,100 pounds and 6,250 pounds for the 4WD. Engine availability for two-door 4WD Tahoe included the 255-horsepower Vortec 5700 V-8 with SFI and the 180-horsepower 6.5-liter turbo-diesel V-8. The 2WD two-door was only offered with a gas engine. The transmission for all models was the four-speed automatic overdrive. Pictured here is a 1997 Chevrolet two-door 4WD Tahoe. *Iten Chevrolet*

Chevrolet's biggest package delivery-type truck for 1997 was the best-selling vehicle of its type in the United States. This Chevrolet Forward-Control P-Chassis with Step-Van aluminum body from an independent supplier was mainly employed for delivering packages. However, many other customers found it suitably filled a large number of specialized applications. P-Chassis was available in three general series based on GVW ranges: 8,600 pound, 9,400–10,000 pound, and 12,000–14,100 pound. It was available in five models, based on wheelbase lengths: 110, 125, 133, 157, and 178 inches. All P-Chassis models had standard four-wheel ABS. Three engine options included the standard 195-horsepower Vortec 4300 V-6 SFI and optional 235-horsepower Vortec 5700 V-8 SFI HD and 160-horsepower 6.5-liter HD diesel V-8 (395-ci). Transmission options included the standard five-speed manual overdrive and the optional four-speed overdrive automatic with electronic control. *Iten Chevrolet*

The smallest Chevrolet Forward-Control P-Chassis was the 110-inch-wheelbase van. It had a body by Utilimaster Body Co. and was powered by the 195-horsepower Vortec 4300 SFI V-6 engine, using the optional four-speed overdrive automatic transmission. Its maximum GVW rating was 8,600 pounds and its maximum payload rating was 5,093 pounds. Power brakes and steering were standard equipment. Front suspension was independent with coil springs. *Merit Chevrolet*

1998

GM came in for criticism as early as the fall of 1997 for failure to market a replacement for its 10-year-old full-size C/K pickup. GM executives admitted the new truck program was two years behind schedule. Dodge's revolutionary pickup was still a sellout in its fourth year, and Ford's all-new F-150 pickup was doing extremely well. Some insiders at GM had a concern that the new truck was being delayed so long that it was in danger of becoming obsolete before its launch.

Two months later, in an attempt to quell criticism from the motoring press, Chevrolet showed the new truck to a group of auto writers. GM wanted to prove that its styling was not too bland and that the truck had interesting technical features, something the rumor mill conveniently neglected to mention.

GMT800 trucks went into production in midyear 1998. Because the GMT800 was a 1999 product, it will be discussed in section 1999.

Labor relations continued to haunt GM in 1998. The UAW staged a 54-day strike in the summer, closing the company down. It cost GM $2.5 billion and caused its market share to plummet. It was estimated that GM lost $104 pre-tax per vehicle in North America in 1997, while Ford and Chrysler made healthy per-car profits.

GM Chairman Jack Smith took the heat for GM's falling production and profits. His vision was for GM "(T)o be the world leader in transportation products and related services." Smith had been GM's boss since 1992, and could point to a number of accomplishments since taking over. For example, in 1992 it took GM 4.47 workers to build a car; in 1997, it dropped to 3.37. Plant utilization jumped from 68 to 94 percent. Product development time

Chevrolet's 1998 S-10 pickup was a line unto itself, consisting of six distinct models on three wheelbases. Included were the following: Regular Cab Sportside Box; Regular Cab Fleetside Short Box; Regular Cab Fleetside Long Box; LS Extended-Cab Sportside Box; SS Regular Cab Fleetside Short Box or Sportside Box; and ZR2 Regular Cab Fleetside Short Box or Extended-Cab Fleetside Short Box. This is a Chevrolet S-10 Extended-Cab (three doors), Fleetside, 2WD, LS six-foot short box. It was a day rental rig and was equipped with the Vortec 4300 V-6 engine and automatic transmission. The Vortec 4300 had SFI and a high-efficiency ignition system to ensure instant starts. Two Vortec 4300 engines were offered, matched to either a five-speed manual overdrive transmission or an electronically controlled four-speed automatic overdrive transmission. *Robert P. Gunn*

We are so accustomed to seeing the big six-passenger four-door C/K3500 Crew Cab pickup with dual wheels that this truck with single rears looks strange. Actually, single rear wheels were standard. "Big Dooley" dual rear wheels were an extra-cost option. This is a 1998 Chevrolet K3500 Crew Cab pickup with a standard 8-foot box. GranPrix, a van converter, has upgraded this particular truck. It includes special interior items, long running boards, wheels, and special paint. With single rears, Crew Cab was rated for a maximum GVW rating of 9,200 pounds and a maximum payload rating of 3,319 pounds. The standard engine for K3500 was the 255-horsepower Vortec 5700 V-8. The standard transmission was the five-speed overdrive manual and optional was the electronically controlled four-speed overdrive automatic. *Country Chevrolet*

had dropped from 36 months to 24. The six car groups had been consolidated into one, and the two truck groups were made one. A VLE system was established with responsibility for all aspects of a vehicle program, including cost, timing, and profitability. These are a mere sample of productivity and cost-reduction programs initiated since 1992.

Chevrolet's C/K pickup, now in its last year, did not come in for much in terms of technical changes. Even in light of its age, Chevrolet's C/K continued to sell well. It continued to be the second-best-selling vehicle in America. Chevrolet's product planners were counting on the fact that buyers continued to be drawn to its familiar, comfortable look. A well-equipped K1500 extended-cab pickup with leather and the like sold for slightly more than $30,000.

For 1998 the Blazer had a bit more slope to its hood. It continued its legacy of being smooth and steady on the highways, since that's where most Blazers got 95 percent of their use. A well-equipped Blazer listed for just over $30,000.

A report that came out late in 1997 listed the top 10 light trucks as judged on resale value after three years of ownership. Six of the top 10 were SUVs. The Chevrolet Suburban came in second in respect to percentage of value retained—93.09. GMC's Suburban was third at 91.16 percent. Chevrolet's S-10 was sixth at 80.35 percent. Listed in seventh place was "GMC C/K pickups" at 80.28. It's not clear if that meant GMC only or both GMC and Chevrolet's pickups. It is probably safe to assume that it means both, as they are essentially the same truck and C/K means Chevrolet, not GMC.

In November, GM announced plans to spend $1.5 billion to consolidate and modernize its engineering operations in Michigan over the next five years. This was an attempt to reduce the time it takes to get new cars and trucks to market. About $900 million was tagged for upgrading the 42-year-old GM Technical Center in Warren, Michigan, where employees and functions from 14 locations throughout the region were to be consolidated. About 6,000 engineers, scientists, and technicians were to be relocated to Warren from Flint and Lansing. All of GM's North American car engineering

operations eventually would be housed at the tech center.

GM also planned to spend more than $200 million to upgrade its test tracks in Milford, Michigan, and Mesa, Arizona. It planned to spend more than $170 million to complete the consolidation of its engineering operations in Pontiac; and nearly $200 million for powertrain operations in Pontiac, Michigan.

These changes were part of GM's effort to get more control over its product-development process. GM had cut 40 percent off its product-development time in the past three years, but still lagged behind some competitors.

The biggest Extended-Cab pickup Chevrolet built was the K3500 1-ton with 8-foot cargo box. More often than not, this truck was purchased for towing. When properly equipped, this truck was rated for a maximum GCW rating of 19,000 pounds. Its drivetrain consisted of the 290-horsepower Vortec 7400 V-8 and either the five-speed manual overdrive or four-speed overdrive automatic and a 4.56:1 rear axle. It's interesting to note that the 6.5-liter turbo-diesel V-8 developed 430 foot-pounds maximum torque compared to the Vortec 7400's 410 foot-pounds maximum torque. The turbo-diesel was only rated for a maximum GCW rating of 14,500 pounds. Dual rear wheels were also required for the 19,000 pound maximum GCW rating. *Harold Chevrolet*

What made Chevrolet's C/K Extended-Cab pickups so popular was that owners could carry certain items inside where they were kept dry and safe. Many buyers preferred the short box because it was easier to maneuver in city traffic and parking was easier. Chevrolet offered an Extended-Cab in every C/K series. This is a 1998 Chevrolet K1500 Extended-Cab with short box. The top-of-the-line Silverado trim package for Extended-Cabs featured high-back front bucket seats with convenient center console and cabwide three-person rear bench. This truck had the optional "Z71" 4WD off-road package, which included skid plates, Bilstein shock absorbers, and Z71 graphics (replacing 4x4 graphics). Maximum GVW rating was 6,600 pounds. Standard drivetrain was the 230-horsepower Vortec 5000 V-8 and five-speed manual with overdrive. *Harold Chevrolet*

This is the truck for the man who has everything. It's a 1998 Chevrolet C3500 Crew Cab long-box Big Dooley with customization by Cho Cho Customs. Its powertrain consisted of the 6.5-liter turbo-diesel engine and four-speed electronically controlled automatic transmission. The basic truck had a sticker price of $32,000; with the extras added by the conversion, its price rose to about $43,000. The extra money bought the following: special chrome wheels, chrome running boards (they even extended from the back of the rear fenders to the bumper), custom two-tone paint scheme, and a bedliner. It also bought highback leather bucket front seats, huge center console trimmed in wood, two high-back leather bucket rear seats with a small leather seat in between, cut pile carpets, front air dams, a heavy-duty rear bumper with trailer hitch, a high-performance sound system, and other features. *Harold Chevrolet*

Chevrolet's popular Blazer was more than personal transportation, it also found its way into the commercial truck realm. Steve Macke, a Chevrolet medium-duty truck salesman, used this 1998 Chevrolet Blazer four-door. It only makes sense to call on a customer in a vehicle you sell. The real market for Blazer was for personal and family transportation. The Blazer's drivetrain consisted of one engine, the 190-horsepower Vortec 4300 V-6, and standard five-speed manual overdrive transmission. A four-speed overdrive automatic was an option. *Iten Chevrolet*

Chevrolet continued its successful Commercial Cutaway Van Series for 1998. The new van was built on a strong, straight ladder-type frame on three wheelbase lengths—139, 159, and 177 inches. Only G3500 Series vans were offered with maximum GVW ratings up to 12,000 pounds and maximum payload ratings up to 7,300 pounds. Front axles were the independent type. With coil springs, the rear axle was the standard hypoid type with leaf springs. Single rear tires was standard only on the 139-inch wheelbase chassis; dual rears were optional on this model and standard on the two longest wheelbase lengths. Pictured is a 1998 Chevrolet G3500 Commercial Cutaway van on a 159-inch chassis cab with van body by an independent body manufacturer. *Iten Chevrolet*

The Chevy Van came in two sizes: big and bigger. The short wheelbase was 135 inches and the long wheelbase was really long—155 inches. Chevy Van's entire lineup consisted of G1500, G2500, and G3500 standard body lengths and G2500 and G3500 Extended wheelbase models. The Extended wheelbase model offered a maximum interior load space of 176 inches (147 inches to back of the seat). The rear panel doors opened to provide a 56.9-inch opening for loading, the widest in the industry. Maximum GVW ratings ranged up to 9,500 pounds and maximum payload was 4,007 pounds. Available power included the entire Chevrolet Vortec gas engine line: Vortec 4300 V-6 and 5000, 5700, and 7400 V-8s, and the 6.5-liter turbo-diesel V-8. Available transmission options included the four-speed electronically controlled overdrive automatic and the four-speed electronically controlled heavy-duty overdrive automatic. This is a 1998 Chevrolet G3500 Extended wheelbase Chevy Van. *Iten Chevrolet*

Chevrolet's lightest-duty full-size chassis cab was the C/K2500 3/4-ton. It was the lightest, but didn't take a back seat to any truck when it came to work. K2500 chassis was rated for a maximum GVW of 8,600 pounds and maximum payload of 3,815 pounds. This is a 1998 Chevrolet K2500 chassis cab with an Aerotech service body. This body was 103 inches long by 79 inches wide and featured six individual side storage compartments. It also had a pickup-body–type box 100 inches long by 49 inches wide with rear tailgate. Standard power was from the 255-horsepower Vortec 5700 HD V-8 engine. The 290-horsepower Vortec 7400 V-8 and the 195-horsepower 6.5-liter turbo-diesel were options. A five-speed heavy-duty overdrive manual transmission was standard and a four-speed heavy-duty overdrive automatic was the option. *Harold Chevrolet*

Big markets for Chevrolet's C/K3500 Crew Cab chassis cabs were states and municipalities. This 1998 Chevrolet K3500 chassis Crew Cab with dump body is owned by the State of Minnesota's Department of Transportation. The Crew Cab carried a crew of six in comfort as well as materials to and from a work site. This truck had a maximum GVW rating of 10,000 pounds. Its dual rear wheels, "Big Dooleys," were an option; standard equipment was single rears. The Crew Cab rode on an enormous 168.5-inch-wheelbase chassis. Buyers had the choice of three exceptionally powerful engines: the standard 255-horsepower Vortec 5700 V-8, the optional 290-horsepower Vortec 7400 V-8 and the 195-horsepower 6.5-liter turbo-diesel V-8. Transmission options included a five-speed overdrive manual and a four-speed overdrive automatic. *State of Minnesota*

Chevrolet's biggest light-duty chassis cab was the C3500 HD. This was a Class 4 medium-duty truck, but Chevrolet insisted on calling it a light-duty model. It was rated for a maximum GVW of 15,000 pounds, which was in the middle of Class 4's range (14,001 to 16,000 pounds). Class 3's range was from 10,001 to 14,000 pounds. Chevrolet offered the C3500 HD on three wheelbase lengths: 135.5, 159.5, and 183.5 inches. This is a 1998 Chevrolet C3500 HD chassis cab 135.5-inch wheelbase and a dump body from an independent body manufacturer. Only two engine options were offered: the 290-horsepower Vortec 7400 V-8 and the 195-horsepower 6.5-liter turbo-diesel HD V-8. Transmission choices included the five-speed overdrive manual and the four-speed overdrive automatic. *Iten Chevrolet*

By far, Chevrolet's lightest 4WD was the diminutive SUV, Geo Tracker. It was the lightest and lowest priced, too. Its price ranged from $13,000 to $15,000. Nevertheless, it was a tough, rugged, and capable SUV. It was offered as a two-door softtop or a four-door hardtop with either 2WD or 4WD. It was almost identical to the Suzuki Sidekick. Both vehicles were built at the CAMI plant in Ingersoll, Ontario, Canada. New features for 1998 included a standard fold-and-stow rear bench seat on the two-door, enhanced emissions systems, and two new exterior colors. The Tracker's only engine was the 1.6-liter inline four, SOHC, producing 95 horsepower. *Harold Chevrolet*

Chevrolet introduced an all-new W-Series Tilt cab line late in 1997. The new W line consisted of models W3500, W4500, and W5500. Models W3500 and W4500 were available with gas power: the 250-horsepower 330 foot-pounds torque Vortec 5700 V-8. The Isuzu direct-injection 4.8-liter OHC four-cylinder diesel was an option for these models. It was rated for 142 horsepower and 275 foot-pounds torque with a manual transmission and 175 horsepower and 347 foot-pounds torque with an automatic. This W-Series was built in Janesville, Wisconsin; only the cab was imported. Chevrolet used the same chassis and other components as the Conventional medium-duty trucks, except the front spring mounts and steering linkage were unique to the Ws. This 1998 Chevrolet W5500 tilt cab was powered by the same diesel used in the W3500 and W4500 models. Its maximum GVW rating was 19,500 pounds. Manual transmission was a six-speed direct manual only, no options. *Iten Chevrolet*

The Astro Cargo Van was a splendid companion model to complement Chevrolet's spacious new full-size vans. The Astro's 111.2-inch wheelbase and maximum GVW rating of 5,850 pounds (AWD) was a perfect solution for those commercial jobs where the full-size van was just too big. The Astro was rugged, powerful, dependable, and willing to put in a full day's work. It was only available with the extended body and 170.4 cubic feet of cargo space. The Astro's cargo area was large enough to accommodate a 4x8-foot sheet of plywood with the doors closed. Because of the Astro's powerful 190-horsepower Vortec 4300 V-6 engine with SFI, it was rated to tow up to 5,500 pounds. AWD was an extra-cost option. The four-speed overdrive automatic was the only transmission available. *Iten Chevrolet*

Chevrolet's new T-Series tilt cabs ranged all the way up to a huge T8500, and mirrored the C-Series lineup model for models including a tandem axle. The T-Series and C-Series were made on the same assembly line in Janesville, Wisconsin, and shared all components except for cabs. The plant built T-Series models one day per week. T-Series trucks listed for as much as $5,000 more than a comparable sized C-Series model. T-Series trucks shone in city delivery work because of their shorter turning radius and better visibility. Three Allison automatics (four-, five-, and six-speeds) were standard. Manuals included five-, six-, seven-, and nine-speed Eaton Fuller, Spicer, and Isuzu transmissions plus an eight-speed with a two-speed rear axle combination. The only standard gas engine was the Vortec 7400 (454) V-8 in two horsepower ratings: 210 and 270. Maximum GVW ratings ranged from 15,000 to 23,000 pounds for single axle models and 40,000 pounds for the tandem axle truck. This is a 1998 Chevrolet T7500-tilt chassis cab.

Chevrolet offered two medium-duty conventional cab models: The sloping hood (Style No. T40) was standard for gas engines, and for the 175-, 195-, and 210-horsepower rated Caterpillar 3126B diesel engines. The high hood (Style No. T50) conventional cab model was standard for diesel engines developing more than 210 horsepower. The buyer could, however, order a gas engine truck with the high hood or a high hood model with the smaller diesel engine models. The purpose of the sloped hood was simply for better visibility. Some buyers, however, preferred the "big" truck appearance of the high hood model. This is a 1998 Chevrolet C6500 chassis cab with contractor's dump body. Chevrolet's standard gas engines for 1998 included the 225-horsepower 6.0-liter V-8 and the 255-horsepower 7.0-liter V-8. This was the last year for these two faithful old workhorse engines. The reengineered 454 V-8 replaced both engines in 1999. *Iten Chevrolet*

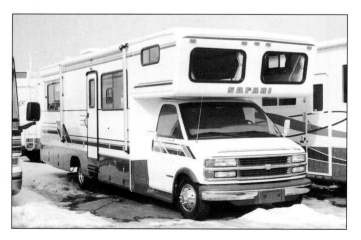

Safari built a Class C motor home on Chevrolet's new 1998 G3500 Commercial Cutaway Van cab chassis. It was built on a 177-inch-wheelbase chassis. Its motor-home body and equipment rivaled that of a Class A motor home in function and opulence (and price). Buyers could choose either the Vortec 5700 HD or Vortec 7400 gas engines or the 6.5-liter turbo-diesel HD V-8. The only available transmission was the four-speed heavy-duty automatic. There was plenty of seating space, legroom, and comfort in Chevrolet's deluxe cab. Getting in and out through the cab's wide doors was easy. *Iten Chevrolet*

The biggest truck Chevrolet built in 1998 was the C8500 conventional tandem. Its maximum GVW rating was 61,000 pounds. This truck has the high hood (No. T50) because it was powered by the biggest available diesel engine: the 300-horsepower Cat 3126B with 860 foot-pounds torque. This engine replaced the Cat 3116 in March 1998. It was slightly larger than the Cat 3116 (7.2 versus 6.6 liter). The Cat's 3126 was a new engine in 1996 and upgraded for 1998 in order to meet tougher emissions standards. These changes were significant enough to require a model number change to 3126B. Changes included moving the jumper tubes internally into the heads, going to three valves per cylinder (two intakes) and a new ECM (Electronic Control Module—Adam 2000). GM no longer had exclusive use to this engine. In fact, it was also a standard offering with Paccar, Freightliner, and Sterling. The 3126B was offered in 11 power ratings from 175 to 300 horsepower and 420 to 860 foot-pounds torque. Chevrolet had the right transmission to match up to every engine rating. Allison four-, five-, and six-speed automatics and five-, six-, seven-, and nine-speed manuals and an eight-speed with a two-speed rear axle made up the broad selection of available transmissions from Eaton Fuller, Spicer, and Isuzu. Allison MD automatics shifted electronically via a computer link between the transmission and the engine's HEUI electronic fuel-injection system. *Iten Chevrolet*

A number of truck converters specialized in meeting the lifestyle demands of discriminating people. These people were involved in horse racing or horse shows and automobile racing. This is a 1998 Chevrolet conventional cab C7500 long wheelbase chassis cab with custom motor-home body and fifth wheel equipment. The trailer could be dropped after arriving at the destination and the truck/motor-home could be used for transportation. The big Cat 3126B diesel engine teamed to an Allison automatic transmission made a comfortable, easy-riding rig for cruising the interstates. Plus, they were an attractive and eye-catching combination. Owners generally lettered and/or decorated these units to suit their tastes. This truck was new and had not been delivered to its owner.

The Chevrolet Venture Cargo minivan was a dependable, versatile worker. The Venture offered excellent versatility due to its four side doors (three side doors were standard) and big back door. Maximum GVW rating on this lightest of all Chevrolet delivery trucks was only 5,357 pounds. Its payload of 1,669 pounds was significant. The Venture's impressive 180-horsepower 3400 V-6 engine with SFI provided power, economy, and efficiency. Its cargo space was big enough to handle a full sheet of 4x8 plywood lying flat on the floor. The only transmission available was the four-speed overdrive automatic with electronic control. Safety features included driver and front-passenger air bags and four-wheel ABS. Venture Cargo could also tow up to 3,500 pounds when properly equipped. *Harold Chevrolet*

Probably Chevrolet's most highly visible special S-10 pickup model was the exciting 4WD ZR2 Off-Road Extended-Cab short-box pickup. Note the ZR2 graphic located at the back of the rear fender. ZR2 Off-Road rode on extra-large 31- x10.5-inch R-15 on/off road tires. These tires were so huge they caused ZR2 to have an extremely high profile, which made it look like a full-size pickup. ZR2 was offered as a regular-cab, too; both had LS trim. It was equipped with the Wide-Stance Sport Performance Package, which provided a firm ride, the kind you want for off-roading, a 190-horsepower Vortec L35 4300 V-6 SFI engine, a reinforced wide-stance chassis with Bilstein gas-charged shock absorbers, and a long list of specific off-road suspension and driveline hardware. *Harold Chevrolet*

What goes around comes around. Never has this old saying been as true as with Chevrolet's relationship with its Japanese partner Isuzu. The proof is seen in the Isuzu "Hombre" pickup. Way back in March 1972, Chevrolet marketed a mini-pickup imported from Isuzu because Chevrolet didn't have a domestic model to compete with the fast-selling Japanese mini-pickups. Now, 26 years later, Isuzu markets a mini-pickup made by Chevrolet because it doesn't have a mini-pickup of its own. Except for the grille, its appearance is the same as an S-10. Isuzu offered it as a Spacecab (extended-cab) or as a standard cab and in both 2WD and 4WD configurations. Two engines included the standard 120-horsepower 2.2-liter inline four and the 175- or 180-horsepower 4.3-liter V-6 (175 for 2WD and 180 for 4WD). Retail prices ranged from about $11,500 for the base model to $24,000 for the Hombre XS Spacecab. Hombres were assembled in the Shreveport, Louisiana, plant. *Walser Isuzu*

Chevrolet's 1998 Forward-Control P-Chassis consisted of five models: CP30542, CP30842, CP31042, CP31442, and CP31842 with wheelbases of 110, 125, 133, 157, and 178 inches, respectively. These models fell into three basic maximum GVW categories: 8,600 pounds, 9,400 to 10,000 pounds, and 12,000 to 14,100 pounds. This is a 1998 Chevrolet Forward-Control model CP31842 178-inch chassis with body from an independent supplier. This model featured a maximum GVW rating of 14,100 pounds. All Forward-Control P-Chassis models featured standard four-wheel ABS. Engines available for P-Chassis included the 195-horsepower Vortec 4300 V-6, 235-horsepower Vortec 5700 HD V-8, and 160-horsepower 6.5-liter HD V-8 diesel. *Harold Chevrolet*

Functionality, practicality, and its load-carrying capacity were the best reasons for choosing the Astro. Available rear Dutch doors added versatility to the Astro Van. When the liftglass was raised and the doors swung wide, one could get close and place heavy items directly inside the van. Standard rear panel doors also opened wide for easy loading. The Astro Van had standard seating for up to eight. The seats were engineered for easy removal and reinstallment as circumstances dictated. The midsize Astro was big on performance; its standard Vortec 4300 V-6 was the most powerful engine in its class. *Harold Chevrolet*

The Southern California Gas Company had just taken delivery on this 1998 Chevrolet C2500 chassis cab with Royal service body when the photo was taken. The Gas Co. ordered it equipped with the Vortec 5700 V-8 engine, 4L80E automatic transmission and Cheyenne trim level. It has a heavy-duty step bumper with a pintle hook and the C6P 8,600 pound maximum GVW package. *Bob Bray*

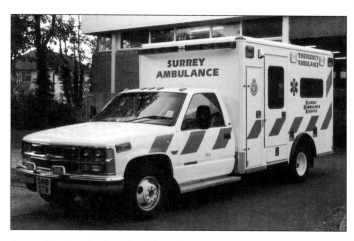

According to *The London Times* issue of January 23, 1999, "Surrey Ambulance Service has eight American-style state-of-the-art ambulances." The article quotes Mr. Richardson, director of operational services, "Ambulance services are facing an increasing number of calls. Last year we responded to 67,087 calls, four percent up on the previous year. This means our vehicles are being pushed to the limit, so we had to find an ambulance to withstand the demand to meet our needs and be safe and comfortable for patients. A working party was established within the service to examine vehicles and this best suited the needs of Surrey Ambulance Service." The service switched to Chevrolet chassis and has found them to be more economical because their larger engines can cope with the increasing demands at no extra cost in terms of miles per gallon. *Photo courtesy of Colin Dunford via the British Ambulance Society and Robert P. Gunn*

1999

This was the "Year of the Silverado." The all-new 1999 Chevrolet pickups were launched in the middle of calendar year 1998. Even though late, their launch was speeded up by the up-front work accomplished at GM's new Truck Validation Center.

The Center gave GM engineers a confidence in the quality of these trucks they had never before experienced. GM's Truck Validation Center is located just down the street from its Pontiac, Michigan–based truck headquarters in a former GM truck plant. The Center is a 750,000-square-foot prototype plant that went online in April 1996. GM invested $110 million in the operation.

The Center is a "mini-factory" using the same carriers, tooling, racking, conveyers, framing stations, and so on as a vehicle assembly plant. The only way in which the Center's assembly line differs from the factory's are the length of the line and a manual-weld body assembly shop. Engineers found the most significant improvement the Center provided over the former "pilot plant" was its real-world line rate so that the operations were set up as they would be done at the plant.

It's interesting that the Validation Center cut its teeth on a truck product, which was the largest program in the history of America's auto industry. Later, the redesigned and reengineered Tahoe/Suburban will complete the same process. Even though model introductions were spaced out over a number of months, all models were designed and engineered at the same time.

The Tracker was redesigned from the ground up for 1999 and became the Chevrolet Tracker. The former Geo name was dropped. Notice the 1999 Chevrolet Tracker sports a new grille design patterned after that of full-size Chevrolet pickups and vans. It was still available as a two-door convertible or a four-door hardtop. Wheelbases were 86.6 and 97.6-inches, respectively. Buyers could choose 2WD or 4WD in either model. A 1.6-liter L4 engine was standard for the two-door and a powerful, lively 2.0-liter, 16-valve DOHC engine was standard for the four-door. Tracker continued to be built in Canada on a ladder-type truck frame, not on a car-type platform like some other small SUVs. *Iten Chevrolet*

For the sport minded and the serious off-roader, Chevrolet presented the 1999 Blazer ZR2 4x4. The special ZR2 was a Wide-Stance Sport Performance Package on a two-door Blazer LS 4WD and included a reinforced, wide-stance chassis with numerous upgrades, 31x10.5 75/R-15 on- and off-road tires, 46mm Bilstein pressurized shock absorbers, and an Underbody Shield Package. The two-door Blazer's wheelbase was only 100.5 inches. Its maximum GVW rating was 4,850 pounds. The only engine available on any Blazer was the SFI 190-horsepower Vortec 4300 V-6. The standard transmission was the four-speed overdrive electronically controlled automatic; on two-door Blazers only, the five-speed overdrive manual was an option. *Iten Chevrolet*

Chevrolet's complete Astro van line for 1999 consisted of a people carrier and a cargo van on one wheelbase (111.2 inches) and in 2WD and AWD configurations. Chevrolet's marketing group made every effort to move Astro upmarket, with luxurious interiors and loads of creature comfort convenience options. The Astro was offered in three trim levels: Base, LS, and LT. An Astro LT offered six high-back reclining seats upholstered in leather and a leather-wrapped steering wheel. Other luxurious features of the upscale Astro included premium sound systems with cassette and CD player; six-way power driver seat; rear-seat audio controls; rear heating and air conditioning; center overhead console with compass, thermometer, etc.; and plenty of cup holders. Powertrain specifications included the 190-horsepower Vortec 4300 V-6 with SFI and a four-speed electronically controlled automatic. *Harold Chevrolet*

Chevrolet's design team was not interested in change for the sake of change, and passed on the temptation to change because it was the thing to do. Changes to the new trucks are so subtle that one has to look twice to notice that it is the new Silverado. In order for these trucks to sell, the buyer has to appreciate the overall important improvements found inside the cab and in nearly every part of the new pickup's mechanical makeup, and forget how its looks stack up to the competition. Chevrolet buyers tend to be conservative and very loyal. That's why the old truck continued to sell well right up to the end. Chevrolet's designers knew this and responded accordingly.

Everything under the new pickup's skin is new as well as its name. For years Chevrolet has used the name Silverado for its top-of-the-line pickup model. It was decided to drop the archaic C/K terminology and adopt Silverado as the new name.

This was the largest new vehicle program in the history of the auto industry. To understand how big the GMT800 truck program is, one has to consider a few figures. Total sales of all the vehicles involved in the program—that is, Chevrolet and GMC full-size pickups, chassis cabs, and SUVs—contributed $25 billion in sales dollars, and accounted for about 1.2 million unit sales in 1997. The new program cost GM about $6 billion. GM expects the new trucks to provide more profit dollars per truck than the old trucks. Its management's plan is for the new trucks to knock Ford out of the number one position in light-truck sales. GM's strategy of marketing GMC and Chevrolet as two distinct and separate trucks (GMC as the up-market model) is because two markets will increase the company's total market potential.

Engineering and manufacturing worked as a team to use as many common parts and processes as possible across the entire spectrum of models, from pickups to Suburbans, to keep cost down.

The Astro cargo van was visually differentiated from the passenger van by its grille and headlight. The center horizontal grille bar on the Astro passenger van continued from one side to the other, whereas in Astro cargo the center grille bar only went from headlight to headlight. However, they were alike in almost every other respect: wheelbase, one body length, and drivetrain. The Astro cargo continued to be very popular with America's businesspeople. For big business as well as small business, it fit a specific niche. At 1,709-pound maximum payload rating Astro was a serious hauler. It made many friends because of initial and operating cost economy. *Iten Chevrolet*

The pickup's most important new features include a super-stiff and strong hydro-formed frame made by using a box-section, hydro-formed front rail mated to a lipped, C-section rear rail on each side. Huge standard disc brakes on all four wheels provide highly effective and reliable stopping power. The wheelbase length on extended-cab models was increased by 2 inches to create a larger and more useful cab interior. Designers retained a 10-inch ground clearance, but the cab floor was lowered an inch to improve the step-in height. The interior design was all new, more efficient, and more comfortable. Chevrolet designers invested a considerable amount of time developing the individual front seats, which are higher and deeper than before. The transmission has an easy towing function that holds gears longer to minimize gear "hunt" in hilly country.

Available engines for Silverado included the L 35 Vortec 4300 V-6; LR4 Vortec 4800 V-8; LM7 Vortec 5300 V-8; LQ4 Vortec 6000 V-8; and L65 6.5-liter HD Turbo Diesel V-8. Horsepower outputs were 200, 255, 270, 300, and 215, respectively. The foot-pound torques developed were 260, 285, 315, 355, and 440, respectively.

The medium-duty line's engine offerings changed considerably for 1999. The venerable 366 and 427 gas engines were dropped and replaced by the Vortec 7400 (454) which has been in the light-duty line since 1996. Its code name is L12. This engine has quite a bit more power than the older throttle-body injected 427, and has been proved to be durable and reliable. The Caterpillar diesels are now the 3126B Series engines, with "HEUI" injection and three valves per cylinder. A new addition is the Duramax 7800 diesel. This is a large Isuzu six-cylinder and is offered in the T-Series cabovers.

Transmissions included the MG5 (NV 3500) five-speed manual for trucks under 8,600 pounds GVW; the heavy-duty five-speed manual for trucks over 8,600 pounds GVW; the M30 four-speed electronic automatic for trucks under 8,600 pounds GVW, and the MT1 heavy-duty four-speed electronic automatic for trucks over 8,600 pounds GVW.

After teasing the public with the Hugger, Xtreme Force, and Xtreme Plus 4 in the three years prior to 1999, Chevrolet relented and gave the public the sport truck it asked for. The production 1999 Chevrolet S-10 Xtreme was a factory-built lowered truck with a total aero package. Additionally, it was equipped with a full manufacturer warranty. Other features included full ground effects, comprising the front and rear fascia, wheel flares, and rocker panels. A monochrome grille and bumpers, along with integrated fog lamps, completed the body changes. The Xtreme rode on 16-inch aluminum wheels.

What set the Xtreme apart from a regular S-10 was the outstanding ZQ8 suspension used in the SS package. This setup lowered the body by 2 inches and included a locking differential and aggressive 3.73:1 rear-axle ratio.

The 2WD only Xtreme offered the standard four- and six-cylinder engine choices, manual or automatic transmissions, regular or extended cab, and Fleetside or Sportside pickup cargo boxes. When equipped with the 4.3-liter 180 horsepower V-6, it would do 0-60 in only 8.6 seconds.

There was also a new heavy-duty class "C" motor home chassis this year. It featured the medium-duty 454 and an Allison automatic transmission.

GM now has Union City Body Co. assemble the motorhome and P-Series chassis.

The smallest and most basic Chevrolet S-10 pickup was the standard cab Fleetside 2WD short box. A truck like this could be driven home for about $12,000. Its wheelbase was small, only 108.3 inches (overall length was 190.1 inches) and its cargo box was 6 feet. The only upscale item on this otherwise base trim-level pickup was its 2WD LS Torqued five-spoke bright aluminum wheels. Its powertrain consisted of a 120-horsepower Vortec 2200 L4 SFI engine and a five-speed manual transmission with overdrive. *Harold Chevrolet*

A more popular S-10 pickup was the Extended-Cab Fleetside with a 6-foot box. This truck offered the driver-side third-door option, the first such option in the compact pickup business. It allowed the driver to easily stow and remove items from behind the front seats. It certainly was a handy option, too, for the owner who had to accommodate more than one passenger. Another reason for an Extended Cab was that it allowed for the maximum amount of leg stretch-out space and room to tilt the seat back to the most comfortable position. The S-10 offered two trim levels: Base and upscale LS. The standard powertrain specs for this 2WD truck included the 175-horsepower Vortec 4300 V-6 and a five-speed overdrive transmission. *Harold Chevrolet*

Chevrolet's marketing efforts for Blazer continued on the track of safety and security with the intention of selling these reliable little 4WDs to women. The Blazer was designed to give driver control over road conditions and thus security and confidence in all types of roads and all weather conditions. The Blazer's new available Autotrac 4WD system gave a big boost to Blazer's security claim. When Autotrac was engaged and Auto 4WD was selected, power was automatically transferred between the front and rear wheels whenever slippage was detected. The sporty little two-door Blazer was available as a 2WD or 4WD and in either base or LS trim and with the optional ZR2 wide-stance sport performance 4x4 package. Standard powertrain included the 190-horsepower Vortec 4300 V-6 engine with SFI and a five-speed manual overdrive transmission; the four-speed overdrive automatic was optional. *Harold Chevrolet*

The commercial Cutaway van from Chevrolet was one of America's most important business vehicles. This was the van that moved huge quantities of all types of goods day in and day out. Chevrolet built it on three wheelbase lengths: 139, 159, and 177 inches with GVWs ranging from 9,500 to 12,000 pounds. This is a 1999 Chevrolet 159-inch-wheelbase chassis cab with side-door van body. Commercial Cutaways built on Chevrolet's new Express vans featured a strong big truck-type ladder frame for maximum loads. The smallest model was available with single rears and the two bigger models with dual rears. There were three engine choices: Vortec 5700 and Vortec 7400 gas V-8s and the 6.5-liter turbo-diesel V-8, and only one transmission: the four-speed heavy-duty overdrive automatic. *Rosedale Chevrolet*

Chevrolet's entire 1999 commercial cargo van line ran the gamut from the little minivan Venture cargo, midsize Astro cargo, the huge Express cargo and passenger vans, and the Express Cutaways with special bodies supplied by various specialized manufacturers. This is a 1999 Chevrolet Express Cargo van. This series was available in three models—G1500, G2500, and G3500—on two wheelbases: 135 inch (Regular-Body) and 155 inch (Extended-Body). Maximum GVWs ranged from 7,100 to 9,500 pounds and payloads ranged from 1,958 to 3,513 pounds. The 245-horsepower Vortec 5700 V-8 engine powered the van pictured here. *Iten Chevrolet*

Chevrolet's biggest delivery vans were the Forward-Control P-Chassis with a Step Van body (steel or aluminum) from an independent supplier. Available chassis lengths included 110, 125, 133, 157, and 178 inches, and maximum GVWs ranged from 8,600 to 14,100 pounds. Overall body lengths (from bumper to bumper) ranged from 16 3/4 to 25 feet. Engines included the Vortec 4300 V-6, Vortec 5700 V-8, and the 6.5-liter naturally aspirated V-8 diesel. GM sold its P-Chassis manufacturing business during the year to its longtime forward-control body builder, Union City Body Co. This is a 1999 Chevrolet 178-inch-wheelbase Forward-Control P-Chassis with a Step Van body. *Harold Chevrolet*

Chevrolet's full-size SUV line for 1999 consisted of the two-door and four-door Tahoes and Suburban. The Suburban continued to rule as the biggest SUV with seating for nine adults in comfort and space for luggage. A massive 149.5 cubic feet of cargo volume with center-row seat folded and third-row seat removed was possible for those times Suburban wore its cargo-moving hat. With the third seat removed, the Suburban provided seating for six and almost 100 cubic feet of cargo space. Buyers could choose from standard rear panel doors or liftglass/dropgate. The Suburban rode on a 131.5-inch wheelbase chassis. The 5.7 was standard in all models; the 7.4 was optional for C/K2500s and the 6.5-liter turbo-diesel was optional for all models. A properly equipped Suburban was rated for a maximum GCW rating of 17,000 pounds—the Vortec 7400 V-8 was required. This is a 1999 Chevrolet K1500 Suburban. *Harold Chevrolet*

Early in the 1999 model year, Chevrolet continued to build the old-style 3/4-ton trucks. This is a 1999 K2500 Extended-Cab short-box pickup. These trucks carried over without change. Beginning in late winter, the new 3/4-ton pickups began to arrive at dealers in limited quantities. Chevrolet's 1999 truck literature showed this truck along with the new Silverado 1/2-tons and advertised the availability of two full-size pickup choices. Old style pickups were available in 2500 and 3500 models with base or LS trim. *Harold Chevrolet*

One of Chevrolet's biggest and best towing machines was the 1999 K3500 4WD Silverado Extended-Cab 1-ton Big Dooley. It featured up to 19,000 pounds GCW rating with dual rears, the 290-horsepower Vortec 7400 SFI V-8 engine, four-speed electronically controlled overdrive automatic transmission, and other equipment. When powered by the 6.5-liter turbo-diesel V-8 K3500's maximum GCW rating was only 14,500 pounds. Chevrolet's only bigger pickup was the six-passenger four-door K3500 Crew Cab. Its cab was bigger, but it wouldn't carry any more cargo or tow a bigger load than the Extended-Cab. *Iten Chevrolet*

The Union Pacific Railroad chose a 1999 Chevrolet C3500 Crew Cab chassis on which to mount a utility body. The Vortec 5700 V-8 engine powered it. It had the four-speed heavy-duty automatic transmission. This truck is in the dealer's lot before being delivered. It had a 168.5-inch wheelbase. This Crew Cab chassis cab, without body, listed for $25,000. *Rosedale Chevrolet*

Chevrolet's C3500 HD commercial chassis cab continued to be a favorite for those in-between jobs, smaller than a medium-duty and larger than a light-duty. Technically, the C3500 HD was a Class 4 with a 15,000 pound maximum GVW rating, which put it at the bottom of the medium-duty classification. Chevrolet built it on three wheelbases: 135.5, 159.5, and 183.5 inches. Pictured here is a 1999 Chevrolet C3500 HD chassis cab with dump body shown on left, parked next to a C3500 chassis cab with a dump body. It is evident in this photo that the C3500 HD is a bigger truck than the C3500. It was powered by the 6.5-liter turbo-diesel V-8 mated to the four-speed heavy-duty overdrive automatic. *Iten Chevrolet*

The 1999 Silverado C/K1500 Extended Cab had a standard third door that featured the widest opening on all 1/2-ton pickups for easy entry and exit. The Silverado's Extended Cab was bigger than either of its two major competitors. The idea was to offer Chevrolet buyers the industry's most comfortable cab. This cab was almost 4 inches longer than the 1998 model. Storage area behind the front seat of Extended Cabs was 22 percent bigger than in the previous model. Front seats had more seat travel than the 1998 pickup. The Silverado offered standard adjustable outboard head restraints for rear seat passengers. This is a 1999 Chevrolet Silverado C/K1500 interior with LT trim. *GM Media Archives*

Chevrolet's 1999 Extended Cab interior with LT trim was the lap of luxury. High-end features included heated outside mirrors, heated six-way power seats, AM/FM stereo with CK and cassette players, electric mirrors, seat lumbar supports, self-dimming rearview mirror, center console, and leather upholstery. Note the standard right-side third door on this 1999 C1500 Silverado Extended Cab short-box pickup. *GM Media Archives*

One has to admit that this is one of the finest styled pickups ever. Pictured here is a 1999 Chevrolet Silverado K1500 Sportside Extended Cab short box. Note how its taillamps fit flush with the wraparound rear fenders. The Sportside's box was made of dent- and corrosion-resistant composite formed by reinforced reaction injection molding (RRIM). It was the largest RRIM production body panel in the light-duty truck industry, and was the first to be compatible with electrocoat zinc primer for holding paint better. The RRIM was also lighter and stronger than the former Sportside's box sides. *GM Media Archives*

Silverado C/K engine lineup for 1999 included the Vortec 4300 V-6 with SFI and Vortec 4800, 5300, and 6000 V-8s with SFI. Horsepower outputs were 200, 255, 270, and 300 and developed foot-pounds torque were 260, 285, 315, and 355, respectively. The Vortec 4800 and 5300 engines had more power and a longer, flatter torque curve than the previous engines. Maximum GCW rating for towing was 8,000 pounds for 1500 pickups and 10,000 pounds for 2500 pickups. This is Chevrolet's top-of-the-line 1999 Vortec 6000 V-8 engine. *GM Media Archives*

The S-10 Xtreme was launched as a 1999 model and begin to arrive at dealerships in February 1999. The basic elements that turned a standard production S-10 into an exciting collector-type pickup included a monotone grille and bumpers; integrated foglamps and name badges; and full ground effects including front and rear fascia, wheel flares, and rocker panels. The Xtreme's sport element came from its thrilling ZQ8 suspension package. This Regular Production Option lowered the body by 2 inches and included a locking differential and an aggressive 3.73:1 rear-axle ratio. The 2WD ZQ8 package contained high-pressure gas-charged 46mm de Carbon shock absorbers, quick-ratio power steering, and P235/55R-16 Eagle GA tires on 16x8-inch unique wheels, all of which gave Xtreme its impressive response in hard braking and quick cornering. There were two engine options for the Xtreme: Vortec 2200 four-cylinder and Vortec 4300 V-6 engine. The Xtreme's three color options included Victory Red, Summit White, and Onyx Black. This truck, powered by the Vortec 2200 engine, was priced at only $18,000. *Harold Chevrolet*

Chevrolet's medium-duty T-Series tilt cabs included T5500, T6500, T7500, and T8500 models. Maximum GVW ratings ranged from 18,000 to 61,000 pounds. The top rating was for a tandem-axle model. Nine wheelbase lengths, from 134 to 248 inches, were available. Powertrain choices included gas and diesel power. Gas power was the Vortec 7400 MD (7.4-liter V-8) producing either 210 or 270 horsepower and 325 or 405 foot-pounds torque. The diesel engine offering was the Isuzu Duamax 7800 (7.8-liter) producing either 200 or 230 horsepower and 441 or 517 foot-pounds torque. Allison automatic transmissions and Eaton 5-, 6-, 9-, and 10-speed manuals and an Isuzu six-speed manual were available. The T-Series was made on the same assembly line as C-Series trucks in Janesville, Wisconsin, using the same frames. The T-Series required a slight modification of the stock frame. The tilt cab's model numbers designated their size classification—Classes 5, 6, 7, and 8. This is a 1999 Chevrolet T7500 tilt cab with van body. *Iten Chevrolet*

The biggest medium-duty truck Chevrolet built in 1999 was the C8500 tandem-axle chassis cab. This giant carried a maximum GVW rating of 61,000 pounds. Its power came from the Cat 3126B's 300 horsepower and 800 foot-pounds torque. Its rear-axle capacity was 45,000 pounds. The high hood was required for this tandem because of the extra-heavy cooling capacity needed by its high-output diesel. The vertical right-hand exhaust stack was an extra-cost option. A Chevrolet T8500 tandem-axle tilt cab of this size was also available. *Iten Chevrolet*

INDEX